Explaining the History of American Foreign Relations

A long-time classic in its first and second editions, *Explaining the History of American Foreign Relations*, 3rd Edition, presents substantially revised and new essays on traditional themes, such as national security, corporatism, borderlands history, and International Relations theory. The book also highlights such innovative conceptual approaches and analytical methods as computational analysis, symbolic borders, modernization and technopolitics, nationalism, non state actors, domestic politics, exceptionalism, legal history, Nation Branding, gender, race, political economy, memory, psychology, emotions, and the senses. Each essay is written by a highly respected scholar in the field, many of whom have risen to prominence since the second edition's publication.

This collection is an indispensable volume for teachers and students in Foreign Relations History, International Relations History, and Political Science. The essays are written in accessible, jargon-free prose, thus making the book appropriate also for general readers seeking an introduction to history and political science.

Frank Costigliola is a professor in the Department of History at the University of Connecticut. His books include *Roosevelt's Lost Alliances*, which won the Society for Historians of American Foreign Relations' Robert H. Ferrell prize for best book. He has received fellowships from the Institute for Advanced Study at Princeton, the National Endowment for the Humanities, the Guggenheim Foundation, the Norwegian Nobel Institute, and the University of Connecticut Humanities Institute.

Michael J. Hogan is Distinguished Professor of History at the University of Illinois, Springfield. He is the author or editor of ten books, including *Origins of the National Security State and the Legacy of Harry S. Truman*, co-edited with Mary Ann Heiss. Hogan is also the recipient of the Beer Prize of the American Historical Association, the Wright Prize of the International Studies Association, and the Society for Historians of American Foreign Relations' Bernath Prize.

Explaining the History of American Foreign Relations

Edited by
FRANK COSTIGLIOLA
University of Connecticut

MICHAEL J. HOGAN
University of Illinois, Springfield

CAMBRIDGE UNIVERSITY PRESS

CAMBRIDGE
UNIVERSITY PRESS

University Printing House, Cambridge CB2 8BS, United Kingdom

One Liberty Plaza, 20th Floor, New York, NY 10006, USA

477 Williamstown Road, Port Melbourne, VIC 3207, Australia

314-321, 3rd Floor, Plot 3, Splendor Forum, Jasola District Centre, New Delhi - 110025, India

79 Anson Road, #06-04/06, Singapore 079906

Cambridge University Press is part of the University of Cambridge.

It furthers the University's mission by disseminating knowledge in the pursuit of education, learning and research at the highest international levels of excellence.

www.cambridge.org
Information on this title: www.cambridge.org/9781107637856

© Cambridge University Press 2016

This publication is in copyright. Subject to statutory exception and to the provisions of relevant collective licensing agreements, no reproduction of any part may take place without the written permission of Cambridge University Press.

First published 2016

A catalogue record for this publication is available from the British Library

ISBN 978-1-107-05418-9 Hardback
ISBN 978-1-107-63785-6 Paperback

Cambridge University Press has no responsibility for the persistence or accuracy of URLs for external or third-party internet websites referred to in this publication, and does not guarantee that any content on such websites is, or will remain, accurate or appropriate.

To our friend and colleague Tom Paterson, who helped to inspire this book, and to George Herring, Mel Leffler, and Andy Rotter, who have been good friends and admired colleagues over many years.

All royalties from this book are being donated to the Society for Historians of American Foreign Relations (SHAFR).

Contents

List of figures		*page* ix
List of contributors		x
	Introduction Frank Costigliola and Michael J. Hogan	1
1	Theories of International Relations Robert Jervis	9
2	National security Melvyn P. Leffler	25
3	Corporatism: from the new era to the age of development Michael J. Hogan	42
4	Explaining political economy Brad Simpson	58
5	Diplomatic history after the big bang: using computational methods to explore the infinite archive David Allen and Matthew Connelly	74
6	Development and technopolitics Nick Cullather	102
7	Nonstate actors Barbara J. Keys	119
8	Legal history as foreign relations history Mary L. Dudziak	135
9	Domestic politics Fredrik Logevall	151
10	The global frontier: comparative history and the frontier-borderlands approach Nathan J. Citino	168

11	Considering borders *Emily S. Rosenberg*	188
12	The privilege of acting upon others: the middle eastern exception to anti-exceptionalist histories of the US and the world *Ussama Makdisi*	203
13	Nationalism as an umbrella ideology *Michael H. Hunt*	217
14	Nation Branding *Jessica C. E. Gienow-Hecht*	232
15	Shades of sovereignty: racialized power, the United States and the world *Paul A. Kramer*	245
16	Gendering American foreign relations *Judy Tzu-Chun Wu*	271
17	The religious turn in diplomatic history *Andrew Preston*	284
18	Memory and the study of US foreign relations *Penny M. Von Eschen*	304
19	The senses *Andrew J. Rotter*	317
20	Psychology *Richard H. Immerman and Lori Helene Gronich*	334
21	Reading for emotion *Frank Costigliola*	356
Index		375

Figures

1 The percentage of cables, sent by American embassies and offices around the world, originally classified secret, 1973–6. *page* 86
2 "Burstiness" graphs showing communications and the fall of Saigon, August 1973–August 1976. 88
3 Topic modeling FRUS. 89
4 Topic modeling of the State Department cables. 91
5 Part of the Declassification Engine's "Sphere of Influence" project. 94

Contributors

David Allen is a doctoral candidate at Columbia University and has published articles in the *Historical Journal* and the *Journal of Cold War Studies*.

Matthew Connelly, a professor at Columbia University, works in international and global history. His publications include *A Diplomatic Revolution: Algeria's Fight for Independence and the Origins of the Post-Cold War Era*, and *Fatal Misconception: The Struggle to Control World Population*.

Nathan J. Citino is associate professor of history at Rice University and the author of *From Arab Nationalism to OPEC*.

Frank Costigliola is professor of history at the University of Connecticut. His most recent books include *Roosevelt's Lost Alliances: How Personal Politics Helped Start the Cold War* and *The Kennan Diaries*. He is a former president of SHAFR.

Nick Cullather is professor of History and International Studies at Indiana University and co-editor of *Diplomatic History*. His latest book is *The Hungry World* (2010).

Mary L. Dudziak, Asa Griggs Candler Professor of Law and History at Emory University, is the author of *Cold War Civil Rights* and *Wartime*.

Jessica C.E. Gienow-Hecht, a professor of history at the Free University of Berlin, is the author of *Transmission Impossible* and *Sound Diplomacy*.

Lori Helene Gronich is a professorial lecturer in International Affairs at George Washington University and a visiting research scholar at Georgetown University.

Michael J. Hogan, a former president of SHAFR, is a professor of history at the University of Illinois, Springfield. He is the author or editor of nine books, including *The Marshall Plan*.

List of contributors

Michael H. Hunt is the Everett H. Emerson Professor Emeritus at the University of North Carolina at Chapel Hill. His recent publications include *The American Ascendancy: How the U.S. Gained and Wielded Global Dominance* (2007) and *Arc of Empire: America's Wars in Asia from the Philippines to Vietnam* (with Steve I. Levine, 2012). He is a former president of SHAFR.

Richard H. Immerman, a former president of SHAFR, is the Edward J. Buthusiem Family Distinguished Faculty in History at Temple University and the Marvin Wachman Director of its Center for the Study of Force and Diplomacy. His most recent book is the *Hidden Hand: A Brief History of the CIA*.

Barbara J. Keys is an associate professor at the University of Melbourne. Her books include *Globalizing Sport* and *Reclaiming American Virtue: The Human Rights Revolution of the 1970s*.

Paul A. Kramer, an associate professor of history at Vanderbilt University, is the author of *The Blood of Government*.

Melvyn P. Leffler is Edward Stettinius Professor of American History at the University of Virginia and Faculty Fellow at UVA's Miller Center. He is the author of *For the Soul of Mankind* (2007), which won the George Louis Beer Prize from the American Historical Association, and *A Preponderance of Power* (1992), which won the Bancroft, Hoover, and Ferrell Prizes. In 2010, he and Odd Arne Westad coedited the three volume *Cambridge History of the Cold War*. He is a former president of SHAFR.

Fredrik Logevall is the Laurence D. Belfer Professor of International Affairs and Professor of History at Harvard University. He is the author or editor of nine books, most recently *Embers of War: The Fall of an Empire and the Making of America's Vietnam*, which won the 2013 Pulitzer Prize for History. He is a former president of SHAFR.

Ussama Makdisi is a professor of history and the first holder of the Arab-American Educational Foundation Chair of Arab Studies at Rice University. He is the author of *The Culture of Sectarianism: Community, History and Violence in Nineteenth-Century Ottoman Lebanon, Artillery of Heaven: American Missionaries and the Failed Conversion of the Middle East*, and *Faith Misplaced: The Broken Promise of U.S.-Arab Relations, 1820–2001*.

Andrew Preston is a professor of American History and a fellow of Clare College at Cambridge University. His most recent books include *Sword of the Spirit, Shield of Faith: Religion in American War and Diplomacy* (2012); *America in the World: A History in Documents from the War with Spain to the War on Terror*, coedited with Jeffrey Engel and Mark Lawrence (2014); and *Faithful Republic: Religion and Politics in the 20th Century United States*, coedited with Bruce Schulman and Julian Zelizer (2015).

Robert Jervis is Adlai E. Stevenson Professor of International Politics at Columbia University. His most recent book is *Why Intelligence Fails: Lessons from the Iranian Revolution and the Iraq War* (2010). He was the president of the American Political Science Association in 2000–01.

Emily S. Rosenberg, emeritus professor and former chair of the History Department at the University of California, Irvine, recently coedited *Body and Nation: The Global Realm of US Body Politics* (2014) and authored *Transnational Currents in a Shrinking World, 1870–1945* (2013), a book published out of her contribution to her edited volume, *A World Connecting: 1870–1945* (2012). She has authored many other books and is a former president of SHAFR.

Andrew J. Rotter, a former president of SHAFR, is the Charles A. Dana Professor of History at Colgate University. He is the author of *Comrades at Odds* and *The World's Bomb*.

Brad Simpson is an associate professor of History and Asian Studies at the University of Connecticut. He is the author of *Economists with Guns: Authoritarian Development and US-Indonesian Relations, 1960–1968*.

Penny M. Von Eschen is the L. Sanford and Jo Mills Reis Professor of the Humanities and Professor of History at Cornell University. She is the author of *Race against Empire* and *Satchmo Blows up the World*.

Judy Tzu-Chun Wu is a professor of Asian American Studies at the University of California, Irvine. She is the author of *Doctor Mom Chung* and *Radicals on the Road*.

Introduction

Frank Costigliola and Michael J. Hogan

Much has changed since the publication of the first edition of *Explaining the History of American Foreign Relations* in 1991. While the Cold War, the focus of most of the scholarship in the field, was winding down, the field of foreign relations history seemed under attack. "We have been told again and again," the very first sentence of the volume noted in an injured tone, that foreign relations history "is a backwater of scholarly inquiry." Critics assailed the field for being ethnocentric, "short on synthesis, and desperately in need of new directions." Editors Michael J. Hogan and Thomas G. Paterson pushed back by bringing together essays demonstrating that foreign relations history was already pursuing new topics and methodologies. The innovations mostly had to do with integrating approaches borrowed from political science, such as bureaucratic politics and world systems analysis. Although the cultural and linguistic turns were already sweeping through other fields of history and other disciplines in the humanities, such post-modern concepts remained largely absent from the first edition, aside from Emily S. Rosenberg's pioneering chapter "Walking the Borders."

By the time the second edition appeared in 2004, foreign relations history had caught up with the changes transforming the larger historical profession. The bottom-up approach of social history popularized in the 1960s–1970s and the emphasis on meaning and representation stressed in the cultural history arising in the 1980s–1990s were reflected in new chapters on how gender, race, memory, culture, and post-modern theory offered useful approaches to foreign relations history. The focus on the Cold War faded somewhat as historians explored other time periods and approached even the 1945–91 era with new questions, such as how did issues develop between North and South, and what commonalities were shared by the modernization projects of Washington and Moscow? The second edition carried forward *Explaining*'s "big-tent," inclusive tradition by featuring ever-important approaches, such as national security, ideology, and political economy.

This third edition demonstrates that the ever more diverse field of foreign relations history (now also called international history or the history of the United States in the world) has surged to the forefront of methodological innovation while retaining its solid grounding in the analysis of political, economic, cultural, and military power in world affairs. In growing more variegated and sophisticated, the field has moved further away from the kind of over-arching synthesis achieved in earlier decades by such nationalist historians as Samuel F. Bemis, by such progressive scholars as Charles A. Beard, and by such supposed realists as George F. Kennan and Hans Morgenthau. Still influential though not hegemonic is William A. Williams' thesis of a persistent drive to secure an Open Door for US trade and investment.

Despite their diverse approaches, the chapters in this volume share, some more explicitly than others, some of the assumptions prevailing among humanist intellectuals in the second decade of the twenty-first century. These ideas, a legacy of the cultural and linguistic turns of previous decades, emphasize the contingency and diversity in human affairs, the subjectivity of belief, and the historicity of tradition. According to these concepts, individuals, groups, and nations tend to construct the meanings of ideas, actions, and developments in line with prevailing cultural norms and practices. Such social construction does not rule out contestations of meaning, outlying actors, and transgressions. Nor does social construction obviate the importance of the physical body, whose thoughts and actions are influenced, though not determined, by cultural milieus. To the degree that such intellectual tenets seem like "commonsense," they are a product of the present era. No doubt a fourth edition of *Explaining* will take a somewhat different perspective.

While the diversity of these chapters makes them difficult to categorize, they do sort themselves, however imperfectly, according to two parameters: whether they focus more on tangible structures or on constructed meanings, and whether they focus more on the institution or on the individual. The word "more" in the preceding sentences is operative: all the chapters address both structures and meanings, though in different ways. Moreover, we cannot explore structures without also understanding the meanings of those structures. Similarly, individuals function within an institutional setting, and institutions are constituted by individuals and groups.

This categorizing becomes clearer when we come down to specifics.

While cognizant of the contingency of meaning, the chapters by Robert Jervis, Melyvn P. Leffler, and Michael J. Hogan focus primarily on traditional concerns about how and why it is that exercising political, economic, and military power in certain ways fosters specific structures of foreign policy and international relations. Although also dealing with tangible structures of power, Brad Simpson, David Allen and Matthew Connelly, Nick Cullather, Barbara Keys, Mary L. Dudziak, and Fredrik Logevall branch off to explore the political and cultural implications of, respectively, the behavior of individual firms, the digital revolution in the archive, the pursuit of modernization and technological advance, the devolving of power onto non governmental organizations, the reliance on legal knowledge to codify or justify foreign policies, and the influence of domestic politics. Nathan J. Citino, Emily S. Rosenberg, and Ussama Makdisi explore the implications of a variety of borders: territorial, conceptual, metaphoric, and disciplinary.

Focusing more on meanings than on structures, Michael H. Hunt and Jessica C. E. Gienow-Hecht investigate the meanings that people attach to the state and nation. While Paul A. Kramer elucidates the structured meanings of race in foreign relations, Judy Tzu-Chun Wu does much the same with respect to gender. Focusing on how people make and are influenced by meanings, the chapters by Andrew Preston on religion, Andrew J. Rotter on the senses, Richard H. Immerman and Lori Helene Gronich on psychology, and Frank Costigliola on emotion explore how the inner lives and thoughts of individuals and groups can shape foreign relations.

Emphasizing the tangible power and interests of the state and taking a global perspective, Robert Jervis compares the three principal models or theoretical structures available to international relations scholars and historians. He details the various iterations of realism, all of which stress the formative influence of the shape of the international system. According to realism, the structure of that system – multipolar, bipolar, or unipolar – has influenced the choices available to nations. The liberal model regards as formative for foreign affairs the economic and political structure of the domestic system. The social constructivist model emphasizes how individuals and states, influenced by the ideals and ideology circulating through society, put together a meaningful conception of what they want to achieve or avoid in foreign affairs. Like Jervis, Melvyn P. Leffler is interested in the tangible power of the state operating in a worldwide system. Striving for a comprehensive synthesis, Leffler uses the concept of national security to integrate Jervis' realist, liberal, and social constructivist models. Leffler goes beyond Jervis, however, in the degree to which he stresses internally generated determinants, particularly the "imperative to protect domestic core values from external threats." The national security approach edges into the realm of meaning, nonstate actors, and the intangible by stressing the importance of "human agency in the construction of core values and the significance of contingency in their implementation."

Michael J. Hogan and Brad Simpson offer complementary introductions to political economy. Hogan's corporatist approach explores the structure of cooperation and competition within which state and nonstate actors shaped America's political economy and interactions with other nations. Corporatism analyzes the inner workings of what Jervis labels the liberal model of national interest. This approach traces the interplay of geopolitical strategy, partisan politics, bureaucratic rivalries, and issues of political culture and identity to show how corporate and labor officials, experts, citizen groups, and public officials thrashed out their differences, especially during the period from the late nineteenth century to the 1950s. For instance, the Truman administration worked with leaders from industry and labor to implement the Marshall Plan through agencies that bridged the public and private sectors. While sharing Hogan's focus on political economy, Simpson's approach emphasizes a later time period when cooperation was less in evidence. Simpson lays out four interrelated dynamics. The first is America's role in a world economy structured along Immanuel Wallerstein's model of a hegemonic core nation or nations, a less developed semi-periphery, and a periphery locked into dependence and poverty. Simpson then expounds on the divergent interests, and hence different foreign strategies, of corporations engaged in various manufacturing and extractive industries. Third is the role of banking and finance in lubricating – or jamming up – the rest of the economy. And fourth is the sphere of state–business–society interaction of Hogan's focus. By addressing some combination of these components, scholars can trace the material factors that shape foreign relations.

The document repository is another kind of structure central to foreign relations historians. That structure is changing fast as the US National Archives digitizes state department documents from the 1970s on and catalogs the growing flood of born-digital documents. David Allen and Matthew Connelly explain how historians can not only cope with these changes but also utilize them to ask new and sharper questions of the past. With digital records and appropriate software, they note, "we can 'read' an entire archive and analyze every available document and withdrawal card at the same time." This could enable some new research protocols, such as measuring the frequency with which policymakers discussed certain issues, tracking the timing and location of "bursts" of interest in a topic, and finding hidden thematic structures in the documents. What, for instance, was the overall shape and focus of US diplomacy in the months before the fall of the Berlin Wall? In the days before the September 11 attacks?

The largely state-oriented, comprehensive structure of foreign affairs conceptualized by Jervis, Leffler, Hogan, and (to a lesser extent) Simpson becomes more complicated when we consider the impact of non-governmental organizations (NGOs), the missionary impulse to modernize supposedly less developed nations, the structure of the law, and the impact of domestic politics. As Barbara Keys emphasizes, NGOs are important not only because they number over 40,000, but also because they underscore the increasingly de-territorialized, transnational nature of an international system in which power flows in complicated ways. NGOs and multinational corporations can influence states, ideas, and individuals. Scholars therefore should not assume that states and individuals are the only players in international relations. As Nick Cullather points out, NGOs and multinational corporations also play a role as lobbyists and as agents of governments interested in promoting development and technological change in other nations. Cullather's approach demonstrates the importance of ideology and constructed meaning, in particular the pervasive belief that the United States could and should act as an agent in advancing the destiny of nations with far different histories and cultures. Faith in development and technology has remained central to US foreign policy since 1949, despite changing circumstances and a record of frequent failure. The persistence of this belief suggests its strong emotional hold. Indeed, Cullather describes how officials romanticized economic development and attached to it their hopes and fears for the future.

The ostensibly rational structure of the law and the often emotional realm of domestic politics offer another approach to foreign relations, as Mary L. Dudziak and Fredrik Logevall demonstrate. Treaties, questions of citizenship, and efforts to legally justify reprehensible practices such as torture are some of the issues that have made law central to governmental, corporate, and individual interactions across national frontiers. Dudziak points out that tracking such legal events as trials and human rights conventions can illuminate underlying debates while yielding an alternate periodization of foreign relations history and a fuller view of state power. Logevall points up what every democratic leader knows: no leader can implement her or his foreign policy unless they win elections or are appointed by someone who has triumphed at the polls. Though domestic politics influences the packaging and often the substance of foreign policy, that constraint is rarely mentioned by leaders not wanting to be seen as risking the nation's blood and treasure for their selfish political purposes. Scholars researching the impact of domestic politics should keep in mind the admission by Anthony Lake, President Bill Clinton's national security adviser: "Nobody talks about it but it's on everybody's mind."

In contrast to the approaches to foreign relations history that focus on the structure of state-to-state relations, borderlands history conceptualizes structures that straddle states, or even questions the centrality of the territorial state. Nathan J. Citino defines a borderland as "a zone of interpenetration between two previously discrete societies." Citino, Emily S. Rosenberg, and Ussama Makdisi challenge scholars to move beyond the US-centric, American exceptionalist view that sees Washington as the primary agent in global affairs and the West as superior to the rest of the world. Citino advises that studying the fringes of states' political and cultural authority can yield insights regarding not just borderland areas and the formation of borders, but also regarding the heartland of a state. Rosenberg views territorial, symbolic, and disciplinary borders as sometimes messy places whose ostensible disorder can invite a creative re-conceptualization of history. She and Makdisi urge scholars to study foreign relations from a non-US perspective, to provincialize the United States while de-provincializing the rest of the world. Makdisi cautions against those who would label themselves as transnational historians while failing to gain language skills and the cultural literacy necessary to understand the history and historiography of regions such as the Middle East or East Asia.

Chapters by Michael H. Hunt and Jessica C. E. Gienow-Hecht return the focus to the nation, although in ways that lean more toward constructed meanings and inner determinants of foreign relations. After defining ideology as a set of convictions that suggest ways for dealing with reality, Hunt goes on to explore the powerful ideology of nationalism. The constitutive elements of nationalism include notions of who is and is not a citizen, who or what appears as a foreign threat, and how the government should defend these conceptions and other core values. Although nationalist currents have always run deep in the United States, this ideology is prominent also in other countries. Nationalism, then, affords opportunity for comparative historical analysis. While nationalism mobilizes the loyalty of inhabitants, Nation Branding, Gienow-Hecht explains, aims to influence the appraisal of outsiders. The approach of Nation Branding examines how states and nonstate actors package cultural events, educational programs, and advertising campaigns to orchestrate approval and respect in influential foreign quarters. This approach offers a means to pursue long-term, comparative analysis that takes into account cultural change over time.

While Nation Branding, nationalism, transnational perspectives, NGOs, borders, borderlands, domestic politics, law, modernization, digital data mining, political economy, corporatism, national security, and international relations all refer in some way to the nation, the approaches of gender, race, religion, memory, the senses, psychology, and emotion refer to the body and mind. This distinction is, of course, relative; human activity and thought create the nation and all things related to it. Nevertheless, since the early 2000s, foreign relations history has joined other scholarly fields in paying increased attention to the physical body, the inner self, personality, thought, sexuality, and to the cultural expression and representation of these aspects of the individual. As Andrew J. Rotter puts it, "relations between people and nations are experiential, embodied." Especially in foreign relations, people encounter each other through what can appear as strange, unpleasant, even disgusting smells, sounds, tastes, touches, and sights. Although such judgments are historically conditioned, cultural interpretations that can be learned and unlearned, they are often assumed to reflect universal values and to "prove" that foreigners are culturally and racially inferior. Much of the US "civilizing" project in the Philippines, Rotter observes, focused on changing how racialized Filipinos looked, smelled, and sounded.

Although Paul A. Kramer also focuses on Americans' self-assumed civilizing mission, he uses a wider lens to trace racist aspects of foreign policy extending into the present. Kramer defines racialized power as combining exception, essence, and domination. He outlines how considerations of race have played key roles in US foreign policy with regard to encounters with Native Americans, diplomacy on behalf of the pre-1861 slave-holding regime, restrictions on migration, formal colonialism, regulating the labor supply, securing corporate profits, pursuing modernization, the "war on terror," and organizing the military. Like race, gender is a constructed category that maps value-laden assumptions about the supposed physical essence of, say, skin color and sexual difference, onto a myriad of social and cultural practices and beliefs. Judy Tzu-Chun Wu explores the insights available to scholars examining gender in terms of both gendered human beings and gender as a signifier of power. Women have played key roles in foreign relations as leaders, migrants, producers, and consumers in the global economy, and workers in the military–sexual complex. Notions about gender are powerful because they map deep beliefs about the "natural" order of the sexes onto other aspects of life, such as relations among nations. US policymakers often dismissed French critiques of American policy as "emotional" or "hysterical" outbursts from a supposedly feminized nation. US officials regarded defeated Japan as a "geisha nation" in need of Washington's masculine protection. An ideology of masculinity prescribed the brash toughness that helped propel the John F. Kennedy and Lyndon B. Johnson administrations into the Vietnam War.

In keeping with the broader revival of interest and faith in the subjective, Andrew Preston and Penny Von Eschen examine religion and memory. Preston advises that "scholarly empathy is as important as scrutiny." Scholars trying to understand a historical actor, whether it is a Woodrow Wilson or a Ronald Reagan, cannot simply dismiss professions of religious faith as hypocrisy. Neither can they accept such declarations at face value; evidence must be interpreted. Religion has often operated as a powerful element in how people interpret their own lives, the interests of the nation, and the world around them. Faith in God, Preston points out, can have an especially powerful impact as it embodies both emotional and rational thought. Probing another aspect of the inner self, Von Eschen explores the creation and impact of memory. Memory is a social process, she writes, especially because memory is intertwined with forgetting. Societal values and hierarchies help determine what materials are saved in archives, which historical events are celebrated, how history is taught in schools, and, not least, what aspects of the past are glorified or denigrated on television and in other media. In the digital age, scholars can perform an intertextual analysis of content on the internet, in books, television, and in other media. Memory is always selective. Scholars can examine the consensus and the contestation over what has been forgotten, memorialized, and made the object of nostalgia.

Focusing on psychology, Richard H. Immerman and Lori Helene Gronich outline how the character traits of an official can influence her or his foreign policy. They point out that many of the concepts and issues of foreign relations history boil down to matters of psychology. Deterrence, brinksmanship, credibility, risk, threat, pride, and respect entail emotionally inflected judgments. Intelligence and counter-intelligence involve high stakes and, often, high emotion. While emphasizing the importance of emotion, Immerman and Gronich see emotion and cognition as linked but separate brain processes. They comment that "preconscious emotional arousal may guide cognitive judgments."

Frank Costigliola, by contrast, views emotion as intrinsic to cognition. He outlines five aspects of looking at history from the inside out. Historians can analyze the impact of emotional thinking on the behavior of individuals and of groups. They can also look at how societal norms for expressing emotions have shifted over time, and how emotions, such as honor and empathy, have themselves changed across time and culture. Finally, scholars can examine how historical actors have sought to defend or attack policies on the basis of their supposed rationality or emotionality. Examining evidence of emotions – and, more generally, recovering the history of subjectivity by looking at psychology, memory, religion, race, and gender – can reveal perceptions, beliefs, motivations, decisions, and actions that might be overlooked if the foreign relations historian did not probe beyond external evidence.

This volume offers twenty-one perspectives on American foreign relations history. Read separately, they demonstrate how the various elements of the field push and pull against each other. Taken as a whole, they offer an overview of the current state of scholarship. These chapters do not systematically review recent literature, detail all topics worthy of inquiry, or summarize all methods and interpretative frameworks. They seek instead to define the state of the field, to outline new analytical models, to show how familiar topics and methods are being rethought, and to reveal the usefulness of questions raised by other disciplines and other fields of US history. These chapters illustrate many of the challenging ways of approaching the study of American foreign relations history and highlight the healthy ferment and rich diversity that mark the field.

I

Theories of International Relations

Robert Jervis

For diplomatic historians to delve into the sub-field of Political Science that studies International Politics or Relations (terms I will use interchangeably) is to enter a world that is both familiar and different. Indeed, it is the similarities that make the differences so jarring. Just as Dean Acheson expressed his bemusement at discovering that International Relations (IR) scholars treated him as an "independent variable," so do many historians find distasteful the notion of variables, especially ones labeled as independent (causes) and dependent (effects), studying historical events as "case studies," seeking generalizations as wide-ranging as possible, valuing "theoretical parsimony," with its emphasis on deploying as few independent variables as possible, and comparing cases that are dissimilar in many ways. But I believe that the very differences between the two fields make interaction potentially fruitful if historians are willing to (temporarily) suspend disbelief.

Obviously, the field of IR is too large to completely cover here, and my survey will be skewed toward international security rather than political economy, international organizations, and transnational trends and flows. In the course of this, I hope to make clear why a chapter on IR theory in some ways fits awkwardly with a book on approaches to the history of American foreign policy.

I will proceed by outlining two related ways of dividing the theoretical approaches to IR: the first between the orientations of Realism, Liberalism, and Social Constructivism, and the second sorting according to whether the main independent variables are located at the level of the individual, the state, or the international system, which lends itself to a discussion of how IR uses comparisons to try to pin down causation. I will concentrate on theories about relations among the most powerful states, which leaves out many important subjects but is most relevant to arguments about American foreign relations.

REALISM

The best known approach to IR is Realism, which comes in several flavors: classical, neoclassical, offensive, defensive, and structural. All share the common starting point that states are usually the main actors in international politics, that considerations of power and security are paramount, that states are (and should be) guided by the national interest as contrasted with sub-national or supra-national interests, and that the world is dangerous both because human nature is malign – or at least has a malign streak in it – and because this realm, unlike domestic society, lacks a higher authority that can protect states and enforce agreements. Any number of aphorisms can be adduced here, and a nice one is by George Washington: "It is a maxim founded on the universal experience of mankind that no nation is to be trusted farther than it is bounded by its interest."[1] Part of the reason for the mistrust and conflict is circular, but the circularity exists in the world rather than in reasoning about it. One source of fear is the knowledge that because others cannot trust the actor's own state, they may preventively move against it, and the understanding of this leads the state to act preventively itself.[2]

Three points of clarification are essential. First, Realists often differ among themselves in the details of how they explain policy and in the prescriptions they offer. Thus, Realists were to be found on both sides of the question of whether the war in Vietnam was necessary. They were united, however, in the way they analyzed the problem, looking at the national interest, the power stakes of the various countries involved, and the likely consequences for national security of various courses of action. They paid little attention to morality, world opinion, international institutions, or economic interests. Second, there is often a tension between Realism as description and explanation and Realism as prescription: Realism has difficulty explaining why states sometimes behave in foolish or self-defeating ways. Third, contrary to what critics often allege, Realism neither urges belligerent policies nor expects them. It fully understands the risks and costs of conflict, especially war, and stresses that the national interest includes a respect for other's interests. Morgenthau's classic *Power Among Nations* stresses the value of conciliation and diplomacy, and E. H. Carr's foundational text *The Twenty Years' Crisis* urged Britain to appease Nazi Germany because it lacked the military and economic power to resist what was seen as limited German expansion. Although it does not speak well for Carr that he excised these paragraphs when the book was reprinted in 1946, his initial stance was fully consistent with Realism. So it is not surprising that the bulk of the Realist community strongly opposed the war in Iraq, arguing that the United States was strong enough to protect itself and its allies against Iraq even if that country developed nuclear weapons, that there would be no conceivable interest that would lead Iraq to provide such weapons to terrorists, and that the post-war reconstruction would be difficult.

Five sub-schools can be located within Realism. Classical Realism starts with Thucydides and extends through Machiavelli, Carr, Morgenthau, and others such as Arnold Wolfers. Not being self-identified social scientists, they were less concerned with rigorous theorizing and the careful separation of variables than are current scholars. Easily derided as "wisdom literature," one can argue that it often, in fact, was wise. By the late 1950s younger scholars were moving away from this form of Realism in the attempt to be more rigorous and systematic, but in recent years the approach has been resurrected in the form of neo-classical Realism.[3] Sharing with the older version an openness to consider a wide range of causal factors, especially domestic politics, it is more modern in seeking analytic rigor and the careful examination of evidence.

More sharply focused are defensive and offensive Realism. Defensive Realists believe that although security concerns are never far from sight, world politics often is fairly benign. But dangers do exist and states must carefully examine the current and likely future international environment to determine whether other powerful states are or are likely to become adversaries. The problem is that others' motives and intentions are hard to discern and, even if they are correctly judged to be presently benign, can change in the future. This does not mean that states do or should make the worst-case assumption and build up their arms and other sources of power as rapidly as possible, however. Not only is this expensive, but it can threaten others who are benign, triggering a security dilemma and leaving the state worse off.[4] Security, not power, is to be maximized. Offensive Realists, on the other hand, believe that the international environment is so uncertain and, at least potentially, hostile that states have no choice but to engage in worst-case planning, to seek regional dominance even if the status quo is satisfactory, and to maximize power. This picture of the world indeed does resemble the stereotype of Realism as expecting and urging belligerence.[5]

Most prominent for the past thirty-five years is Neorealism or Structural Realism, brilliantly developed by Kenneth Waltz in *Theory of International Politics*,[6] a title that is interestingly ambiguous as to whether this is *a* theory or *the* theory. Diverging from classical Realism in putting human nature aside, it is based entirely on an analysis on the international system. Starting from the assumption that its structure is anarchic and reasoning by (perhaps faulty) analogy to markets in the economy, Waltz proceeds deductively in a way that, to use his term, "abstracts from" all other considerations, producing a picture that to those that like it is clear and to those who do not is barren. Waltz would not disagree that his approach is very much a simplification, but he argues that this is the nature of theorizing, and that if his theory explains only a few aspects of international politics, they are central ones. Most importantly, he argues that world politics exists because even adversarial states will join together to stop any one of them from dominating and that, less obviously, bipolar systems are less prone to wars among the great powers than are multipolar ones. The basic reason is that for them security in a multipolar world requires what Waltz calls "external balancing" – that is, relying on allies. This can lead to wars because small allies have sufficient bargaining leverage so that they can drag their partners into war (e.g., a stylized version of World War I) or, conversely, the desire to make allies carry the main burden of resisting the adversary ("buck-passing") can inhibit the formation of a coalition that could block an aggressor, as was the case in the 1930s. Under bipolarity, on the other hand, the superpowers can and indeed must rely on their own resources and engage in what Waltz calls "internal balancing," which avoids the war-inducing complications seen in the earlier part of the twentieth century.

This argument has been severely criticized on both empirical and theoretical grounds. Empirically, the role of institutions and common norms has been stressed, as I will discuss in this chapter. Other scholars, while largely staying within the Realist tradition, argue that the balance of power that Waltz sees as maintaining a system of independent states in fact is not universal but is contingent on domestic and international circumstances.[7] In parallel, Waltz's concept of structure and the role it plays has been called into question, with Alexander Wendt arguing that "anarchy is what states make of it," and Jack Donnelly arguing that Waltz has fundamentally misconceived what structure means in international politics, that the absence of authority above the units does not automatically lead to conflict, and taking seriously the analogy between international politics and oligopoly points in the opposite direction as firms in this situation seek to cooperate.[8]

LIBERALISM

Some of these critiques are rooted in Liberalism, which argues that the national interest comes not from the state and the international system, but from the domestic interests and the way they are aggregated by institutions.[9] Indeed, it is when leaders put the interests of the state rather than the people foremost that wars are most likely to occur. As long as the economic interests that benefit from trade and other forms of economic intercourse can guide state policy, peace is likely to prevail. There are exceptions, of course, but war is usually costly and absent overriding considerations of honor and ethnicity, peace and prosperity are normally joined.[10] World War I is often held up as a counter-example, but the case is far from clear, as many decision-makers thought the war would be short and that economic disruption would be limited, the trading and financial sectors in the state had only limited political power, and the conflict began among the countries that were least economically interdependent.

More generally, Liberals argue that who gains and who loses within a country by greater or lesser exposure to international trade and investment influences domestic alignments and institutions and, through them, foreign policy. Although economic theory indicates that the country as a whole will gain from increased trade, less competitive groups and sectors will not, and this domestic conflict strongly influences the state's foreign economic policy and indeed its security policy as well.[11]

The general argument that foreign policy reflects domestic interests has deep roots in American life. It is no accident that it was an American president who most eloquently argued that democracies are inherently peaceful and that the modern variant of this, Democratic Peace Theory (DPT), has caught on in the United States much more than in other countries. Woodrow Wilson's theory claimed that the foreign policies of democracies had certain characteristics, and so it is labeled monadic by IR theorists; most of the current theories are dyadic in making claims for how pairs or groups of democracies relate to each other (although some problems are created by the fact that upon examination some of the causal mechanisms are actually monadic). DPT exists in many variants, but most trace their roots to Immanuel Kant, resurrected in articles by Michael Doyle that caught the profession's attention.[12] The essence of the subsequent literature is that the interests, institutions, and norms of democracies inhibit armed conflict with each other, and their abilities to appraise their environments and send credible signals serve to avoid many common causes of wars. A central part of the argument goes back to Wilson: the bulk of the costs of a war are borne by the citizens, and in democracies they have great influence over the fate of the leaders. For a leader to enter a losing or costly war is to endanger his or her political future. Norms and common values provide further inhibitions. Democracies are characterized by compromise and avoidance of bloodshed in domestic politics and so are slower to resort to force abroad, especially against countries with similar norms. Democratic institutions produce additional checks on wars because, almost by definition, power is more diffused in them than in authoritarian regimes, and this provides greater opportunities for radical change to be blocked. Furthermore, democracies are more open to information about the world, and while of course this does not guarantee the accuracy of the resulting beliefs, it does mean that these regimes are less likely to suffer the gross distortions of reality that characterized dictatorships such as Hitler's Germany, Stalin's Soviet Union, and Saddam Hussein's Iraq. The other side of this coin is that democracies are relatively transparent, making it harder for them to bluff and making it less likely that their intentions will be misperceived.[13]

The lines of rebuttal are multiple: it may not be democracy but rather aspects of the social or economic system that produces peace; much of the evidence comes from the Cold War era when democracies had obvious realpolitik reasons to stick together; only long-established and mature liberal democracies may exhibit these benign characteristics.[14] Realists, among others, may also be uncomfortable with a theory that seems to be so flattering to the country in which most of the theorists live, and it may be worth remembering that in gaining its independence the United States broke its commitment to the ally whose assistance (given out of self-interest, of course) permitted the revolution to succeed.

One offshoot of DPT is the claim that democracies are particularly likely to live up to their promises and threats because leaders who fail to do so will be punished by their electorates. Labeled the "audience cost theory," this is a variant of Schelling's classic argument that states can prevail in a confrontation by committing their reputations to standing firm.[15] Although alluring, the logic is less than airtight. It assumes that the public is paying attention to the leader's commitments, that it is willing to punish her for not living up to them even if doing so would not be in the national interest, and that other countries accept the argument and believe the commitments to be credible (in which case they will not be challenged and we will never see audience costs actually being incurred). The historical evidence, furthermore, is mixed at best.[16]

Liberal arguments have been extended in another direction as well, toward the role of international institutions in what is known as Neoliberal Institutionalism, which can be traced to Robert Keohane's *After Hegemony*. Although the relatively open economic system in the West in the post-war era would not have been possible without American power, Keohane argued that the institutions that had been established and the interests that grew up around them were able to maintain the system in the face of eroding American power. Contrary to Realist thinking, institutions can facilitate cooperation by establishing regularized channels for communication and problem-solving (lowering the "transactions costs" of establishing and maintaining agreements, to use the language of economists), facilitating trade-offs among different issues, and increasing transparency and the salience of states' reputations by making clear whether they had lived up to their commitments. As institutions develop and serve the needs of the members, the latter delegate more power and autonomy to them, allowing them to become independent actors in their own right instead of, or at least in addition to, being the instruments of state action.

Although the dispute between Neoliberal Institutionalism and Realism has often been put in stark form, the differences, especially with defensive Realism, should not be exaggerated.[17] As Keohane and Lisa Martin have noted, their theorizing starts from the same basic assumptions as Realism and diverges from defensive Realism only when it posits that institutions can develop "a life of their own" and either diverge from or shape the preferences of the leading states.[18] Furthermore, it is not surprising that institutionalism has been applied mainly to the economic sphere, and when it has moved into security it focuses on the institutions that are developed among allies. The ability of institutions to mitigate deep conflicts of interest, and the parallel ability of institutionalism to explain behavior in these situations, is much less clear.

The flourishing of institutions in the economic area not only reflects the basic Liberal argument that as economies develop, important interests will push for the lowering of the barriers to trade and that this can have important political implications, but is also linked to the next school of thought to be discussed,

Social Constructivism, because an open economic system was made possible by a fundamental change in ideas. Liberalism required the replacement of mercantilism, which saw international economic exchange as fundamentally zero-sum, with modern trade theory, which stresses the possibility of mutual gain through comparative advantage, a change that cannot be explained by either Liberalism or Realism.

SOCIAL CONSTRUCTIVISM

Even more than the other approaches, Constructivism is not an it but a they, and so even more than previously I will have to overgeneralize. I will also put aside approaches that are non-positivist in the sense of denying that evidence or events could falsify their views.

We live in a world constructed by men – and for many constructivists, it matters a great deal that it has been males rather than females (whose roles are developed socially rather than being given by biology) who have had most power. Drawing on sociology, seeing beliefs and theories as creating our social world rather than, or at least in addition to, reflecting it, and focusing on the importance of the way people and collectivities think of themselves, this approach was synthesized by Hedley Bull, formulated in a particularly abstract and challenging way by Richard Ashley, and developed in a form that received increasing American attention by Alexander Wendt and Peter Katzenstein.[19] International politics is not created by the imperatives of the international system or the objective economic interests within a country, but is socially constructed through the subjective understandings that are developed and shared through the interactions. Agents and structures do not exist independently, but form, reproduce, and change each other.

Central to these processes are the ideas that permeate society. Contrary to orthodox Marxism and the cynical Realist view of the world, these ideas are not mere superstructure or rationalization for material interests, but are the basis on which individuals and states see their interests. I just noted the crucial role of the rejection of mercantilism in favor of what now seems to be the self-evident truth that trade can be mutually advantageous. Absent this shift, it is hard to imagine significant and lasting cooperation among states. In the late nineteenth century, world politics was also transformed by the salience of the notion that colonialism was morally appropriate, economically advantageous, and a part of what it meant to be a great power. The equally powerful wave of decolonization in the 1950s and 1960s similarly did not merely reflect self-evident material interests. World War II and the Cold War were, to a large extent, rooted in competing ideologies; Realist notions of the national interest or Liberal conceptions of the contest between domestic interests do not take us very far here. Also striking is the fact that in the post-Cold War era almost all countries proclaim their dedication to democracy and human rights.

Ideas about international politics are part of it, not observations from the outside. Realism has been at least in part a self-fulfilling prophecy. States behave according to Realist precepts because that is what their leaders have been taught is the way to behave. For Constructivists, Realist theory is at least part of the cause of conflict and the inability of countries to solve common problems.

Two objections should be noted, however. First, the relationships between ideas and material interests can be reciprocal and complex. It is impossible to summarize the literature here, but I will just note that while the relevant chapter of Wendt's book makes a very strong claim with its title "Ideas all the Way Down," the analysis of changes over time points toward material factors. Second, the Constructivist claim that Realist thinking has led to Realist behavior sits uneasily alongside the claim that Realism cannot account for much of world politics.

Leaders, foreign policy professionals, and members of the interested public learn how the country should behave from formal instruction (although anyone who grades undergraduate papers may doubt how effective this mechanism is), reading the newspaper and related media, and hearing stories about current and past events. To take only the most obvious example, almost everyone in the United States knows the "lessons of Munich," and while the "lessons of Vietnam" are more contested, they have left a powerful imprint. This kind of socialization is vertical, as ideas and understandings are passed on from one generation to the next. Horizontal socialization occurs through the interaction of leaders and countries, as most states conform to the modes of thinking and behavior employed by their peers. Emulation, conscious and unconscious, is common; being out of synch with others can be dangerous. Like individuals, states not only adopt the habits of some others and seek to join desired in-groups, they simultaneously seek to differentiate themselves from those with low status or who they see as different from themselves.

Linked to the processes of socialization is the centrality of identity. National leaders and their countries think of themselves in certain ways that mold their outlooks on the world and how they behave. The United States sees itself as devoted to universal values and willing to make sacrifices for the greater good. Cynics see this as a mere cover for the expansion of American power, but Realists point to the myriad instances, Iraq being only the latest, in which this behavior generates great costs and few benefits. Identities are also linked to discourses that constitute and embody how issues and practices are framed, conceived, and articulated. Thus, a great deal of subsequent American policy followed from seeing and explaining the attacks of September 11, 2001, as an act of war, not a crime, and the appropriate response as a "War on Terror."

Discourses, identities, and many ideas sustained through socialization become so deeply ingrained that they escape awareness. This will be familiar to many historians, who will immediately think of James Joll's argument about the role of unspoken assumptions in bringing about World War I.[20] For Constructivists, a central modern example would be the concept of sovereignty, upon which so much of international politics rests. But Stephen Krasner has shown that sovereignty has actually been quite flexible and that very little about it has been taken for granted.[21] Self-consciousness and manipulation may then play a greater role than Constructivists envision. Related, the stress on socialization entails a troublesome tension. On the one hand, this leads to the expectation that patterns will continue, and for Constructivists it is socialization rather than the anarchic nature of the system or the internal distribution of interests within the state that produces continuity. On the other hand, however, Constructivists stress the possibilities for change and alternative modes of behavior and interaction. If resocialization is fairly easy, however, then socialization must not be terribly powerful.[22]

The ideas important to international politics are normative as well as instrumental. Realists deny the role of conceptions of right and wrong in the international arena; Liberals generally ignore it. For Constructivists, by contrast, normative ideas do not stop at the water's edge. The broad trends of international politics cannot be understood without the moral imperatives felt by individuals and leaders. Can we explain the end of the slave trade and then of slavery otherwise? Colonialism could hardly have taken place had most of European society not believed that it was a moral duty to civilize the rest of the world, and decolonization was similarly produced by more than a cost-benefit analysis. Indeed, the frequent Realist injunctions to statesmen to put aside considerations of morality and what would be best for the world as a whole make sense only if moral impulses are strong.

LEVELS OF ANALYSIS

I want to briefly outline another way of categorizing theories in order to connect with how conflicting arguments can be tested. In his first book, Waltz famously developed what he called three images of the causes of the war.[23] The first focused on human nature, the second on the nature of the state's regime, and the third on the international system. In a review article, J. David Singer noted that these could be extended to more general theories of international politics and labeled them as levels of analysis, a somewhat ill-fitting term that has stuck, and I will use the terms levels and images interchangeably.[24] The second and third levels parallel the historians' notions of *innenpolitik* and *aussenpolitik*.

INDIVIDUALS

In the 1950s, the conception of human nature as embodying the potential for evil was fundamental to thinking about politics, with Reinhold Niebuhr propounding a view based on religion and Hans Morgenthau a secular version. Falling into neglect soon thereafter, human nature returned to the spotlight with the rise of evolutionary psychology, which purported to explain why it was that most violence was committed by young men and also changed the picture by arguing that humans are unique among primates in their propensity to cooperate. Another modern variant borrows from a different part of psychology to look at common cognitive biases that can affect foreign policies.[25] These are constants, however, and so have difficulty explaining the wide variety of policies that states follow. For this, more relevant are arguments about individual differences in values, preferences, beliefs, and images of others.

The fundamental claim here is that leaders vary on these dimensions and that constraints imposed by the other levels of analysis are not so severe as to produce uniformity of behavior. The leader's personality (in a broad sense of the term) matters, something that most lay observers take for granted. This view also underpins notions of democratic accountability for foreign policy, since much of the point of bringing in a new leader is to change the policy. But this does not mean that the argument is correct. To test it – and I am using the term "test" in a loose sense of looking at relevant evidence, not proving or disproving – we need to make comparisons, and the levels of analysis framework is useful because it points us in this direction. Do policies actually change when a leader with different views comes into power? Or, faced with the same circumstances as their predecessors, do they behave quite similarly? At a meeting of the National Security Council in December 1954 Secretary of State John Foster Dulles rejected the call by the Joint Chiefs of Staff for a more aggressive policy toward the Soviet Union by saying that: "he could not help but have some sympathy for [this] general view ..... After all, during the course of the 1952 campaign he had himself called for a more dynamic U.S. policy vis-à-vis Communism. However, experience indicated that it was not easy to go very much beyond the point that this Administration had reached in translating a dynamic policy into courses of action."[26]

THE STATE AND DOMESTIC POLITICS

Waltz's second image was the nature of the state as the source of its foreign policy. For Wilsonians this means whether it is democratic or not, and for Marxists whether it is capitalist or socialist. Obviously, Marxism and Wilsonianism, including the modern versions discussed earlier, are very different in substance but are similar in arguing that neither of the other two images explains most of what is going on. The leaders that rise to the top are socialized into ways of thinking that characterize the kind of state they are in and are constrained by the state's domestic forces. External factors of course matter, but by themselves cannot explain the state's policies, which vary according to the type of state it is. The other side of this coin is that states of the same type will behave similarly, and significant continuities of behavior will characterize states whose regimes remain constant. I will return to this expectation below, and here note that this and the related claims for the domestic level point to the kinds of comparisons we should make to judge their validity.

THE INTERNATIONAL SYSTEM

The third level is the international system and the state's external environment. The system here means anarchy, which is a constant, and polarity, which varies. Waltz's argument for the claim that the major powers are much more prone to go to war under multipolarity than under bipolarity is underpinned not only by the fact that the Cold War did not lead to a superpower war, but also by the decreased power of allies during the Cold War. In 1914, Germany could not afford to see Austria-Hungary weakened or leave the alliance, and Great Britain similarly could not abandon France and Russia. By contrast, in 1956 the United States could bring its two leading allies to heel in the Suez crisis, and it tolerated the later French defection from the military arrangements of NATO with only slight complaints. The argument that internal balancing dwarfed external balancing under bipolarity then points to the relevant historical comparisons that could support or cast doubt on the theory.

The external situation refers to the more detailed aspects of the situation the state is in. Wolfers refers to this as the "billiard ball model" because the argument is that state behavior is essentially a reaction to what others are doing.[27] Discussions of arms races usually endorse this perspective and explain the behavior of each state by what the other is doing, not by the views and characteristics of the leaders or the nature of the state. More broadly, proponents of this view would argue that in many respects the foreign policies of the United States and USSR were strikingly similar during the Cold War.

THE BUSH DOCTRINE AND THE INVASION OF IRAQ AS AN EXAMPLE

It is not too artificial to sort explanations for the invasion of Iraq and the broader Bush doctrine embodied in the 2002 National Security Strategy Doctrine by levels of analysis.[28] Both critics and admirers of the president argue that they bear the stamp of his outlook and personality. For admirers, he and his policies were bold and went to the heart of the problem. To critics, they were superficial, reckless, and misunderstood the problems that the United States was facing and the efficacy of the range of foreign policy instruments that might be deployed. But to both groups, Bush was acting in a highly unusual way. However, these judgments were reached without comparisons, at least explicit ones, and the causal logic that most other leaders would have behaved differently was left untested. Of course, we cannot re-run history with different leadership, but at the very least the implicit counterfactual should be probed, and the only careful attempt to do so makes a good argument that Gore in fact would have behaved very much as Bush did.[29]

Obviously, proof is impossible, but the point is that thinking in terms of counterfactuals and comparisons should make us hesitate before jumping to the conclusion that a first image explanation is correct. Some who question whether so much causal responsibility lies with the identity of the president urge comparisons, not to a hypothetical president, but to American history. John Lewis Gaddis argues that while many were shocked by the idea of a preventive war, they should not have been because the United States has acted preventively throughout its history. Much of the impulse that led to the expansion of the United States from the original thirteen states to its current contours was to prevent foreign threats, and the entrance into both world wars as well as the decisions to fight in Korea and Vietnam were largely preventive.[30] In a similar vein, Stephen Sestanovich has argued that US foreign policy after 1945 has been characterized by reacting to setbacks and challenges by redoubling efforts and taking on larger objectives.[31] More critical observers, often from abroad, comment that Bush's second image view that equated Saddam's horrific domestic regime with an aggressive foreign policy and his counterpart belief that democracy would spring up naturally after the removal of the tyrant were typically American (although to some extent shared by the British).[32] Bush may then have been a reflection of his country's political culture.

Or perhaps of its political economy. Marxists argue that the driving American motive in the Cold War was to keep the world open for American capitalist penetration, and so governments like Mosadeq's in Iran and Arbenz's in Guatemala had to be replaced by ones that were more amenable to the American economic system. Realists generally dismissed these arguments, endorsing the view that security concerns were central to the United States even if some of the fears were exaggerated and the resulting policies were misguided. But the American policy after the Cold War, and especially after September 11, 2001, fits more closely with Marxist than with Realist expectations because despite the drastic decrease in the threat from the external environment there has been significant continuity of behavior, pointing toward internal forces as driving.

Third image arguments, including but not limited to Realism, are not out of the game, however. The problem with the arguments just discussed is that while they fault first image arguments by looking at how the United States has behaved under other circumstances and other presidents, they fail to take the next comparative step of looking at how other great powers behave. The essential claim here is that doing so indicates that this kind of intervention and expansion is typical of great powers that find themselves without adversaries strong enough to check them. States' definitions of their interests tend to expand as their power does, and states in particularly advantageous positions are likely to seek what Wolfers called "milieu goals" that involve spreading their values abroad.[33] Fears grow as well, for reasons that are both objective and subjective. Objectively, the leading power becomes the target for all those who oppose the status quo; subjectively, as old threats disappear ones of lesser magnitude seem to grow in size. For all the claims for American exceptionalism made by critics and defenders of its policies, the United States in fact may be a pretty normal state.

Although not all IR scholars would agree with this argument, for many of them the way to study American foreign relations, or at least the place to start, is with an understanding of how most countries usually behave, not the characteristics of individual leaders or the particulars of the American domestic system. To perhaps overstate the case, there is no separate field of the history of American foreign relations.

A CLOSING NOTE ON CAUSATION AND METHODS

As the previous discussion has shown, IR scholars are deeply concerned with pinning down causation. In closing, I want to note two problems and two cautions. The two problems have similar names, adding to the confusion. The first is the admonition not to select on the dependent variable. All too often social scientists try to explain a phenomenon by looking only at instances in which it occurs. This seems to make sense; what can be learned about the causes of something by looking at instances where it is absent? In fact, a great deal. Without doing so it is impossible to say whether the factors that the scholar believes are playing an important role are also present when the phenomenon of interest does not occur. For example, if we want to know why some crises lead to war, we cannot examine only those that do because what we are interested in are the factors that are not only present in those cases, but absent in cases that end peacefully. At best, searching on the dependent variable can yield necessary conditions, not sufficient ones. (Another problem, of course, is that there can be multiple sufficient causation – i.e., several quite different factors and processes can lead to the same outcome.)

The second problem is selection effects. Here it is the world rather than the scholar that is doing the selecting. To take an example to clarify what this means, in order to show that peacekeeping forces are effective in preventing the resumption of violence in civil wars, it is not enough to demonstrate that peace is likely to be maintained in cases where they are deployed. We also have to undertake the harder task of ruling out the possibility that they are more likely to be dispatched to the less malign conflicts.[34] Strategic interaction and the fact that each side usually tries to anticipate what the other will do, knowing the other is doing likewise, makes causation particularly hard to pin down through standard comparative methods. We are theorizing about actors who have their own ideas about the cause-and-effect relations in the world (and others' beliefs about them, which can be different), and this means that we cannot determine the different impact of two kinds of policy by comparing the outcomes that we see when each is applied because the actor has taken into account the expected results when deciding how to behave.

Two additional factors provide cautionary notes. First, IR scholars usually compare events looking for causal factors, but this loses sight of the possible impact of the passage of time and the possibility that the first event has influenced subsequent ones. Of course, this is exactly what historians focus on. Second, and more broadly, the idea of comparing cases while holding constant all factors except the one of interest does not make sense when we are dealing with an interconnected system.[35] Straightforward notions of causation are called into question here in a way that is more troublesome for political scientists than for historians. The former's quest for precision may be defeated by the nature of the subject matter.

NOTES

1. Edmund Morgan, *The Genius of George Washington* (New York, 1977), p.16.
2. Much of this dynamic goes under the heading of the security dilemma: for excellent surveys, see Ken Booth and Nicholas Wheeler, *The Security Dilemma: Fear, Cooperation and Trust in World Politics* (New York, 2008), and Shiping Tang, *A Theory of Security Strategy for Our Time: Defensive Realism* (New York, 2010).
3. Gideon Rose, "Neoclassical Realism and Theories of Foreign Policy," *World Politics* 51 (October 1998): 144–72; Steven Lobell, Norrin Ripsman, and Jeffrey Taliaferro, *Neoclassical Realism, the State, and Foreign Policy* (New York, 2009).
4. Fareed Zakaria, "Realism and Domestic Politics," *International Security* 17 (Summer, 1992): 177–98; Robert Jervis, "Cooperation Under the Security Dilemma," *World Politics* 30 (January 1978): 167–214; Jack Snyder, *Myths of Empire: Domestic Politics and International Ambition* (Ithaca, 1991); Steven Van Evera, *The Causes of War* (Ithaca, 1999).
5. The exemplar is John Mearsheimer, *The Tragedy of Great Power Politics* (New York, 2001).
6. (Reading, MA, 1979).
7. Stuart Kaufmann, Richard Little, and William Wohlforth eds., *The Balance of Power in World History* (New York, 2007); Victoria Tin-bor Hui, *War and State Formation in Ancient China and Early Modern Europe* (New York, 2005). Also see John Hobson, *The Eurocentric Conception of World Politics: Western International Theory (1760–2010)* (New York, 2012).
8. Alexander Wendt, "Anarchy is What States Make of It," *International Organization* 46 (Spring 1992): 391–425; Jack Donnelly, "The Elements of the Structures of International Systems," *ibid.* 66 (Fall 2012); 609–44.
9. For a good summary of the general position, see Andrew Moravcsik, "Taking Preferences Seriously: A Liberal Theory of International Politics," *International Organization* 51 (Autumn 1997): 513–53.
10. See, for example, Richard Rosecrance, *The Rise of the Trading State* (New York, 1986); Patrick McDonald, *The Invisible Hand of Peace: Capitalism, the War Machine, and International Relations Theory* (New York, 2009).
11. Ronald Rogowski, *Commerce and Coalitions: How Trade Affects Domestic Political Alignments* (Princeton, 1989); Mark Brawley, *Liberal Leadership: Great Powers and Their Challengers in Peace and War* (Ithaca, 1993); Kevin Narizny, *The Political Economy of Grand Strategy* (Ithaca, 2007).
12. Michael Doyle, "Kant, Liberal Legacies, and Foreign Affairs," Parts I and II, *Philosophy and Public Affairs* 12 (Summer and Fall 1983): 205–35, 323–53; for where some of the arguments stand now, see Erik Gartzke and Alex Weisiger, "Permanent Friends?", Michael Mousseau, "The Democratic Peace Unraveled,"

James Lee Ray, "War on Democratic Peace," and Allan Defoe, John Oneal, and Bruce Russett, "The Democratic Peace," all in *International Studies Quarterly* 57 (March 2013): 171–214.

13. See, for example, Kenneth Shultz, *Democracy and Coercive Diplomacy* (New York, 2001); for the arguments that claims for transparency are misplaced, see Bernard Finel and Kristin Lord, eds., *Power and Conflict in the Age of Transparency* (New York, 2000).

14. Erik Gartzke, "The Capitalist Peace," *American Journal of Political Science* 51 (January 2007): 166–91; Joanne Gowa, *Ballots and Bullets: The Elusive Democratic Peace* (Princeton, 1999); Edward Mansfield and Jack Snyder, *Electing to Fight: Why Emerging Democracies go to War* (Cambridge, MA, 2005); Patrick McDonald, "Great Powers, Hierarchy, and Endogenous Regimes: Rethinking the Causes of Peace," *International Organization* 69 (Summer 2015): 557–88.

15. James Fearon, "Domestic Political Audiences and the Escalation of International Disputes," *American Political Science Review* 88 (September 1994): 577–92; Thomas Schelling, *Strategy of Conflict* (Cambridge, MA, 1960).

16. For a summary of the recent arguments, see the articles by Kenneth Schultz, Branislav Slantchev, Jack Levy, Erik Gartzke and Yonatan Lupu, Jonathan Mercer, and Marc Trachtenberg in the symposium in *Security Studies* 21 (July-September, 2012): 369–415, and "Forum on Trachtenberg's 'Audience Costs in 1954?'," *International Security Studies Forum*, No. 1, September 2013, at http://issforum.org/forums/1-trachtenbergaudience-costs-1954.

17. Drawing a stark contrast are John Mearsheimer, "The False Promise of International Institutions," *International Security* 19 (Winter 1994/1995): 5–49, and the replies in ibid., 20 (Summer 1995): 39–93.

18. Robert Keohane and Lisa Martin, "Institutional Theory as a Research Program," in Colin Elman and Miriam Fendius Elman, eds., *Progress in International Relations Theory: Appraising the Field* (Cambridge, MA, 2003), pp. 71–108; Robert Jervis, "Realism and Neoliberal Institutionalism: Understanding the Differences," *International Security* 24 (Summer 1999): 42–63.

19. Hedley Bull, *The Anarchical Society: A Study of Order in World Politics* (New York, 1977); Richard Ashley, "The Poverty of Neorealism," *International Organization* 38 (Spring 1984): 225–86; Alexander Wendt, *Social Theory of International Politics* (New York, 1999); Peter Katzenstein, ed., *The Culture of National Security: Norms and Identity in World Politics* (New York, 1996). European Constructivism tends to be more philosophical and less rooted in evidence and can be tracked by looking at the *European Journal of International Relations*.

20. James Joll, "1914: The Unspoken Assumptions," in H. W. Koch, ed, *The Origins of the First World War* (London, 1972), pp. 307–28.

21. Steven Krasner, *Sovereignty: Organized Hypocrisy* (Princeton, 1999).

22. Dale Copeland, "The Constructivist Challenge to Structural Realism," *International Security* 25 (Autumn 2000): 187–212.

23. Kenneth Waltz, *Man, the State and War* (New York, 1959).

24. J. David Singer, "The International System: Theoretical Essays," *World Politics* 14 (October, 1961): 77–92.

25. For an excellent summary, see Rose McDermott, *Political Psychology in International Relations* (Ann Arbor, 2004).

26. US Department of State, *Foreign Relations of the United States, 1952–1954*, Vol. II, part 1, *National Security Affairs* (Washington, DC, 1984), p. 833. For a further discussion of these issues, see Robert Jervis, "Do Leaders Matter and How Would We Know?" *Security Studies* 22 (April 2013): 153–79.
27. Arnold Wolfers, *Discord and Collaboration* (Baltimore, 1962), p. 19.
28. For further discussion, see Robert Jervis, *American Foreign Policy in a New Era* (New York, 2005), chapter 4.
29. Frank Harvey, *Explaining the Iraq War: Counterfactual Theory, Logic, and Evidence* (New York, 2011).
30. John Lewis Gaddis, *Surprise, Security, and the American Experience* (Cambridge, MA, 2004).
31. Stephen Sestanovich, *Maximalist: America in the World from Truman to Obama* (New York, 2014).
32. For much earlier analysis to this effect, see Wolfers, *Discord and Collaboration*, chapter 15 (co-authored with Laurence Martin).
33. Wolfers, *Discord and Collaboration*, chapter 5.
34. Virginia Page Fortna, *Does Peacekeeping Work?* (Princeton, 2008).
35. Robert Jervis, *System Effects: Complexity in Political and Social Life* (Princeton, 1997); for a parallel discussion by a historian, see John Lewis Gaddis, *The Landscape of History: How Historians Map the Past* (New York, 2002).

2

National security

Melvyn P. Leffler

Since I wrote my initial chapter on national security for this volume more than twenty years ago, the concept's utility for studying American foreign policy has grown. Increasingly linked to the proliferating scholarship on and interest in grand strategy, the attractiveness of the national security paradigm stems from its synthetic qualities; its synthetic qualities arise from the fact that it is not a specific interpretation that focuses on a particular variable as much as a comprehensive framework that relates variables to one another and allows for diverse interpretations in particular periods and contexts.

National security policy encompasses the decisions and actions deemed imperative to protect domestic core values from external threats.[1] This definition is important because it underscores the relation of the international environment to the internal situation in the United States and accentuates the importance of people's ideas and perceptions in constructing the nature of external dangers as well as the meaning of national identity and vital interests. Like grand strategy, the national security paradigm takes cognizance of the fluidity and contingency of events at home and abroad, encourages efforts to identify goals, priorities, and tradeoffs, and focuses on means, resources, and ends.[2]

By encouraging students of American foreign policy to examine both the foreign and the domestic factors shaping policy, by obligating them to look at the structure of the international system as well as the domestic ideas and interests shaping policy, the national security approach seeks to overcome some of the great divides in the study of American diplomatic history. Heretofore, the most influential studies have stressed the moralistic or legalistic or idealistic strains in American foreign policy, or, alternatively, the quest for territorial expansion, commercial empire, and geopolitical influence.[3] Recent accounts tend to reinforce such binaries, pitting America's quest for freedom, democracy, and human rights against its drive for hegemony and empire, although sometimes these divergent interpretive frames are reconciled by discussions of "empire for liberty" or "empire of liberty."[4] Generally, realist historians believe that diplomatic behavior responds (or should respond) to the distribution of power in the international system; most revisionist and corporatist scholars, and most historians who dwell on ideas and ideology, assume that domestic economic requirements, social and cultural forces, and political constituencies are of overwhelming importance. By relating foreign threats to internal core values, the national security model encourages efforts to bridge the gaps between these divergent interpretative approaches, or, more precisely, to see that these variables must be studied in relation to one another and nuanced judgments made about how they bear on one another.

Although the national security approach acknowledges that power plays a role in the functioning of the international system and that interests shape the behavior of nations, it does not reify the salience of power or the centrality of interest in the construction of foreign policy. Barry Buzan, the eminent theorist of international relations, points out that realists who dwell on power and idealists who focus on peaceful norms and liberal institutions often have obscured the meaning of national security, defined as the protection of core values from external threats.[5] "Properly understood," Michael Lind argues, "liberal internationalism and realism are complementary, not antithetical." The national security policy of the United States, Lind emphasizes, has sought to protect "the American way of life by making the world less dangerous with a combination of liberal internationalism in the realm of norms and realism in the realm of power politics."[6]

Like approaches to grand strategy, the national security model explicitly acknowledges that US national security interests are defined in terms of power, economic openness, and the promotion of US ideals.[7] In other words, sophisticated approaches to national security reconceptualize the concept and take explicit cognizance of the impact of culture and identity. National security interests, argues Peter Katzenstein, "are constructed through a process of social interaction"; "security interests are defined by actors who respond to cultural factors." States are social actors operating in social environments. National security and national identity are socially constructed as a result of human agency, and external threats are measured in relation to their perceived impact on core values.[8]

National security, as Arnold Wolfers wrote many years ago, nonetheless remains an ambiguous symbol. Security is used to encompass so many goals that there is no uniform agreement on what it encompasses and hence no universal understanding of the concept. Certainly, it involves more than national survival. But just what is involved is often left vague and indeterminate.[9] Although the ambiguity presents formidable problems to policymakers and contemporary analysts, it should not handicap the work of historians. Indeed, it should explicitly encourage historians to focus attention on matters of central importance: How have policymakers assessed dangerous threats? How have they understood the configuration of power in their own neighborhood, or globally? How have they defined national interests? How have they defined the relationships between interests, the distribution of power, and core values? How have they tried (and sometimes failed) to formulate policies to ensure that their costs do not undermine the core values they are designed to foster? After all, the purpose of American national security strategy, Lind reminds us, "is to defend the American way of life by means that do not endanger the American way of life."[10]

External dangers come in many varieties. The historian of US foreign policy must appraise the intentions and capabilities of the nation's prospective foes. But that step is only the beginning. Views of a potential adversary, after all, are heavily influenced by perceptions of other variables such as one's own strength and cohesion, the appeal of one's own organizing ideology, the lessons of the past, the impact of technological change, and the structural patterns of the international system itself.[11] After independence in 1776, the United States lived in a dangerous neighborhood, surrounded by European adversaries – some strong, some tottering – all eager to contain or crush the infant, vulnerable, faltering young republic. Early American diplomacy evolved in an environment of perceived danger (as well as opportunity). "From the 1780s through the 1820s," writes James Lewis, "the first two generations of policymakers worked to develop policies that would function in harmony to strengthen the bonds between the states, to contain the centrifugal forces within the union, and to lessen the threats from external pressures."[12] After the civil war, perceptions of external danger receded, as the sources of internal division were resolved, a tenuous balance on the European continent persisted, Anglo-American rapprochement began, and US economic strength soared. But that sense of security, which gathered even greater momentum after the defeat of the Central Powers in World War I, was eroded by the faltering of liberal capitalism during the Great Depression, the growth of totalitarianism in the late 1930s, the appeal of fascism and Nazism, and the growth of air power. After World War II, when US policymakers defined the Soviet Union as an inveterate foe, they were influenced by their perception of Stalin as a ruthless, aggressive tyrant and by their inclination to associate Communist Russia with Nazi Germany.[13] But assessments of the international system were also instrumental in shaping the threat perception of American policymakers. Officials imparted dangerous connotations to developments within the international system, such as the proliferation of bilateral trade agreements and exchange controls, the dollar gap, the political instability within European governments, the popularity of leftist and communist parties, and the rise of revolutionary nationalist movements, especially in Asia.[14] Overall, US officials have realized that the preservation of their core values at home requires them to prevent "the domination of the international system by imperial and militarist states and the disruption of the international system by anarchy" and autarky.[15]

In studying the systemic sources of foreign policy behavior, the national security approach demands that analysts distinguish between realities of external danger and the imagined perceptions of threat. This task, as simple as it sounds, is fraught with difficulty because it is often hard for contemporaries and historians alike to agree on what constitutes an actual danger or a perceived threat.[16] Fear drove much of America's early foreign policy, emphasizes Jay Sexton in his recent history of the Monroe Doctrine. "As much as Jefferson and many of his contemporaries waxed lyrical about the virtues of an expanding 'empire of liberty,' their insecurities and perception of threat were just as significant to expansion as was ideology." Yet Sexton also stresses that recognition of their legitimate security concerns, should not obscure the fact that there was often a huge gap between perception and reality. "The Holy Allies were not on the verge of intervening in Spanish America when Monroe delivered his message in 1823," even if the president and his advisers thought they were.[17] Likewise, in the 1840s, Sam W. Haynes acknowledges that "Although their fears were largely unfounded, pro-annexation Democrats viewed alleged British meddling in Texas with genuine alarm ... "[18] Similarly, Nancy Mitchell shows that although German imperial actions in the early 1900s engendered enormous feelings of insecurity and hostility among Americans, German policies were far less threatening than widely perceived. She analyzes how rhetoric, military images, and trade competition conjured up fears and shaped perceptions that were inconsistent with the realities of German behavior.[19] If contemporaries often had trouble discerning reality, historians have found themselves confounded by similar difficulties. For example, the very different interpretations of American diplomacy in the 1920s and 1930s between "realists" on the one hand and "revisionists" or "corporatists" on the other hand rest in part on assessments of the degree of threat to vital US security interests in the interwar years. If there were no real threats before the middle or late 1930s, then contemporary proponents of arms limitation treaties, arbitration agreements, and non-aggression pacts can be viewed as functional pragmatists seeking to create a viable liberal capitalist international order rather than as naïve idealists disregarding the realities of an inherently unstable and ominous balance of power.[20]

Perceptions of events abroad, however, are themselves greatly influenced by the ideas, ideals, and core values of the perceiver. The national security approach demands that as much attention is focused on how the American government determines its core values as on how it perceives external dangers. The term core values is used here rather than vital interests because the latter implies something more material and tangible than is usually the case for a national security imperative. The United States has rarely defined its core values in narrowly economic or territorial terms. Core values usually fuse material self-interest with more fundamental goals like the defense of the state's organizing ideology, such as liberal capitalism, the protection of its political institutions, the championing of its honor and autonomy, and the safeguarding of its physical base or territorial integrity. "The purpose of America is to defend a way of life rather than merely to defend property, homes, or lives," said Dwight D. Eisenhower.[21] Those "who dismiss the idea of 'the American way of life' and focus on 'vital interests' as the basis of U.S. foreign policy," emphasizes Michael Lind, "are guilty of a profound philosophical and political error. For there is no interest more vital in American foreign policy and no ideal more important than the preservation of the 'American way of life'."[22]

To determine core values, historians must identify key groups, agencies, political parties, and individuals, examine their goals and ideas, and analyze how trade-offs are made. Decision-makers, interest groups, legislators, and politicians will have different internal and sometimes conflicting internal and external objectives. Core values are the goals that emerge as priorities after the trade-offs are made; core values are the objectives that merge ideological precepts and cultural symbols such as democracy, self-determination, honor, and race consciousness with concrete interests such as access to markets and raw materials; core values are the interests that are pursued (and sometimes jeopardized) notwithstanding the costs incurred; core values are the goals worth fighting for. In their work on Thomas Jefferson, Robert W. Tucker and David C. Hendrickson illuminate how he converted "questions of interest into matters of right and wrong, which then assumed a kind of independent character and became inseparably annexed to the honor and independence of the country." Likewise, in his work on Woodrow Wilson, N. Gordon Levin, Jr. beautifully describes how the president fused ideological, economic, and geopolitical considerations when faced with unrestricted German submarine warfare. Together, these factors became core values and influenced his decisions for war, for intervention, and for the assumption of political obligations abroad.[23]

Different groups may have different core values or different strategies for pursuing the same core values. Historians argue over whether Jeffersonian Republicans and Hamiltonian Federalists possessed divergent core values or whether they were mostly battling over strategies to achieve the same core values.[24] But there is no questions that southern slaveholders and northern abolitionists possessed a conflicting core value that hugely shaped the foreign policy of the ante bellum era. Republicans, such as Abraham Lincoln, argues Michael Holt, could not allow slavery "any chance to spread... [because it would] betray the legacy of the nation's Founders who dedicated the United States to freedom, not slavery."[25] The struggle between interventionists and isolationists on the eve of World War II illuminates how groups sharing similar core values could disagree about strategies. Interventionists believed aid to the Allies was essential to protect American liberal capitalism and the territorial integrity of the United States; isolationists believed such aid would aggrandize the powers of the chief executive and the federal government, provoke the Axis powers, and thereby endanger not only the nation's physical safety but also its political institutions and ideology – its American way of life.[26] Explaining how core values of interest groups, classes, and voluntary associations are translated into policy requires a careful investigation and a viable theory of the relationship of the state to society.[27]

The effort to show how core values emerge in the policymaking process forces the diplomatic historian to study the importance of foreign policy goals in relation to the officials' other objectives. As they seek to achieve diplomatic aims, officials (and leaders of private organizations) may encounter costs that exceed the value of the goals themselves.[28] For example, much as Republican officials in the 1920s yearned for markets abroad, they were unwilling to forego the protection of the home market; much as they wanted international financial stability, they were reluctant to cancel the war debts or raise taxes; much as they sought good relations with the Japanese, they were unwilling to eliminate the discriminatory provisions in the immigration laws. In these cases the foreign policy benefits did not seem to outweigh the domestic costs. Hence the diplomatic objectives, significant though they were, never became core values.[29] American history is replete with examples demonstrating a quest for territory, markets, and influence and with examples demonstrating restraint. An interpretive framework for the study of American foreign relations should try to explain why the United States did not go to war over Cuba in the 1820s or 1870s, but did so in 1898; why Theodore Roosevelt sent troops to the Caribbean and Central America and why Franklin Roosevelt did not; why Wilson hesitated to intervene in Europe in 1914–16 but chose to do so in 1917; why the United States resisted the role of hegemon in the interwar years yet assumed it after World War II; why the United States eschewed political commitments and strategic obligations in one era while it welcomed them in another.

The protection and pursuit of core values requires the exercise of power. Power is the capacity to achieve intended results. Power may be an end in itself as well as a means toward an end. In the twentieth century, power (including military power) derived primarily from economic capabilities, social cohesion, and political unity. Power stemmed from the scale, vigor, and productivity of one's internal economy and its access to or control over other countries' industrial infrastructure, skilled manpower, and raw materials. Power meant the capacity to inflict harm on adversaries. Power was relative.[30]

But at the outset of the US diplomatic experience, the young nation had little power, considerable disunity, and adversaries on its borders as well as Native American nations within its borders. Individual rights, private property, and open trade as well as territorial integrity and personal safety seemed imperiled by the actions of the British, French, and Spanish as well as by the divisions among the states inflected by sectional, class, and racial strife. The US constitution itself was a peace pact among the states, designed to preserve harmony among themselves as well as to enhance their combined leverage against adversaries abroad.[31] "The greatest fear among American statesmen was the possibility that Old World powers would exploit internal divisions by allying with sections or factions of the union, thus fusing internal and external threats."[32] Fear of their own vulnerability meshed with their recognition that "frequent war and constant apprehension" might produce standing armies and strong central government that could crush the very liberties which the new nation had been created to preserve.[33] The core values of the young republic seemed dependent on a policy of non-entanglement, a balance of power in Europe, and a precarious Union at home.

Open trade, neutral rights, and territorial consolidation and expansion became the foreign policy goals of the new nation, and they were inextricably linked to perceptions of threat abroad coupled with the possibility of disunion at home. Avarice and greed, fear and vulnerability, racism and idealism inspired *and* constrained the drive for markets and territory, for officials were forever aware that the Union was a fragile entity needing to grow yet susceptible to disintegration as a result of its growth. And since the core values of the republic itself – personal security, individual freedom, representative government, private property (life, liberty, and the pursuit of happiness) – were inextricably linked to the preservation of Union, the configuration of power in the American neighborhood and in the Old World always were perceived as crucial to the survival of the physical security, territorial consolidation, and core values of the new nation.[34]

After the American Civil War, external danger receded and US power grew. Although foreign threats were inconsequential in motivating the decision for war in 1898, historians have spent prodigious energy arguing over the mix of ideals, interests, and politics that spurred President William McKinley's decisions to free Cuba from Spain, annex the Philippines, and declare an open-door policy in China. The consequences of the Spanish–American War, along with developments in shipbuilding, naval technology, industry, agricultural productivity, and racial consciousness sparked a growing interest in the configuration of power in East Asia and Europe. Germany was increasingly perceived as a looming danger, a specter that became more ominous during World War I. Woodrow Wilson did not fear an imminent German victory, but he did worry about Germany's ambitions and mounting power. Should Germany win, Wilson worried that "we shall be forced to take such measures of defense here as would be fatal to our form of Government and American ideals." His embrace of a "community of power," to supplant the balance of power, reflected Wilson's deep conviction that he had to reform the international system in order to project America's influence abroad – and its values – and avert "Prussianizing the country and turning it into a garrison state." In other words, America's core values were seen as inextricably linked to the distribution of power in the international arena.[35]

But the perception of threat again receded after the defeat of the Central Powers. This view did not mean that Republican officials turned isolationist. On the contrary, they continued to desire to expand markets, stabilize European affairs, pursue investment opportunities, and gain control over raw materials abroad. Yet those goals did not generate strategic commitments nor become vital interests worth fighting for until changes in the configuration of power in the international system impelled American officials to redefine them as core values.[36] The Axis domination of much of Europe and Asia in 1940 and 1941, for example, endangered markets and investment opportunities.[37] But far more important, Axis aggrandizement enabled prospective adversaries of the United States to mobilize additional resources, coopt other nations' industrial infrastructure, and secure forward bases. Nazi conquests, moreover, raised the possibility that Latin American countries, which had traditionally traded largely with the European continent, would be sucked into the Axis orbit. To deal with autarkic and regimented trade practices abroad and to protect the United States from the growing military capabilities of the adversary, American officials felt they had to mobilize, raise taxes, monitor potential subversives, and prepare to assist or perhaps even take over the export sector of the American economy. Even if the United States had not been attacked and even if the accounts of economic strangulation were exaggerated, core values were at stake. This was not because the Axis powers crushed the self-determination of other nations or jeopardized the world capitalist system, but because foreign threats of such magnitude required a reordering of the domestic political economy, portended additional restrictions on civil liberties and individual rights, and endangered the nation's physical integrity and organizing ideology. The purpose of Roosevelt's partial internationalism, writes John Harper, "was not universal salvation for its own sake but the safeguarding of democracy in the United States." He did not want the United States to become a garrison state. Roosevelt grasped that what happened abroad would affect America's way of life at home.[38]

After World War II, the Soviet presence in Eastern Europe, the vacuums of power in Western Europe and northeast Asia, and the emergence of revolutionary nationalism in the Third World created a similar specter. American core values were perceived to be at risk. The Kremlin might have neither the intention nor the capability to wage war effectively against the United States, but prudence dictated that the United States organize and project its own power to protect its core values. If the country did not do so, if it withdrew to the Western Hemisphere, President Harry S. Truman warned that the American people would have to accept

> a much higher level of mobilization than we have today. It would require a stringent and comprehensive system of allocation and rationing in order to husband our smaller resources. It would require us to become a garrison state, and impose upon ourselves a system of centralized regimentation unlike anything we have ever known. In the end, ... we would face the prospect of bloody battle – and on our own shores. The ultimate costs of such a policy would be incalculable. Its adoption would be a mandate for national suicide.[39]

During the Cold War years, the perception of an external threat to core values inspired US officials to mobilize American power in unprecedented ways. The Marshall Plan and the North Atlantic Treaty Organization (NATO) were two excellent examples. For the first time in American history the US government appropriated billions of dollars for the rehabilitation of European economies and assumed strategic obligations to protect European countries. In the 1920s, Republican policymakers also had been cognizant of the interdependence of the economies of Europe and the United States.[40] Nevertheless, they had eschewed long-term governmental aid and security commitments. How does one account for the willingness of American officials to incur such financial sacrifices and strategic commitments after World War II but not after World War I?

According to the national security approach, the answer rests primarily in the ways American officials perceived external threats to core values. In the mid-1940s, the political and economic vulnerability of Western European governments, the popularity of Communist parties in France, Italy, and Greece, and the economic and social problems beleaguering Germany adumbrated a significant strengthening of the Soviet Union. And if this happened, Truman and his advisers believed, there would be profound repercussions in the way the US government would have to structure its domestic economy and conduct its internal affairs. Because the configuration of power in the international system was profoundly different in the mid-1920s, external developments did not pose as much danger and hence did not justify the allocation of government aid and the assumption of overseas strategic obligations.

But even when the perception of threat was great, the existence of core values placed constraints on the pursuit of foreign policy goals. Aaron Friedberg insightfully shows how "the basic structure of American government institutions, the interests and relative strength of various groups (both within the government itself and in society at large), and the content of prevailing ideas or ideology" circumscribed the growth of a garrison state even during the most scary years of the Cold War. And although these fundamental ideas and institutions did not prevent widespread infringements on personal liberties and individual freedoms during the McCarthy era and did not thwart the growth of executive power and military spending, they nonetheless had a profound impact on the evolution of the Cold War. "By preventing some of the worst, most stifling excesses of statism, these countervailing tendencies made it easier for the United States to preserve its economic vitality and technological dynamism, to maintain domestic political support for a protracted strategic competition and to stay the course in that competition better than its supremely statist rival."[41]

Although occasionally criticized for its disregard of ideological and cultural concepts, the national security approach to the study of American foreign relations should be conceived as perfectly congruent with the new directions of scholarship that dwell on culture, identity, religion, and emotion.[42] Central to the national security approach is the concept of core values. National security is about the protection of core values, that is, the identification of threats and the adoption of policies to protect core values. The new studies on culture, ideology, modernization, religion, and emotion mesh seamlessly with the synthetic qualities of a national security paradigm because they help to illuminate the construction, meaning, and implications of America's core values. The new books on religion, for example, illuminate how religious values, organizations, and symbols inspired the Cold War struggle with communism. Religious leaders and ethnic groups did see their most basic values endangered by an atheistic system that denied the existence of God. They "saw religion," emphasizes Andrew Preston, "as a source of democracy because it protected freedom of conscience, and thus the individual's autonomy from the state. The Soviets, avowedly atheist and materialist, rejected faith completely. Both sides of the Cold War claimed to want peace, progress, and prosperity for the world. But only one side could claim God."[43]

In order to create the conditions for a free society in which individuals could pray, vote, work, and prosper, US officials believed they had to contain state-planning, command economies, and totalitarian regimes seeking hegemony of their own systems and ways of life. The many new books on development and modernization show how non state actors – social scientists, universities, philanthropic organizations, voluntary associations – embraced this struggle to prove the salience of the American way of life to revolutionary nationalist regimes in the Third World. They wanted to use "development aid, technical assistance, foreign investment, and integrated planning," Michael Lathem emphasizes, "to accelerate the passage of traditional societies through a necessary yet destabilizing process in which older values, ideas, and structures gave way to the liberal, capitalist, and democratic ways of life that they recognized most clearly in the United States itself."[44] This did not mean that American NGOs or US policymakers emphasized democracy – indeed they often supported repressive regimes[45] – but they did embrace "development" and "human rights" as part of an American mission to counter the appeal of state-led modernization according to a Soviet model. "Development," writes David Ekbladh, "is crucial to understanding how the United States confronted other ideological systems when they emerged as threats."[46]

The fervor with which the United States waged the Cold War can only be grasped by understanding the role of ideology in the construction of American national identity and national security policy. In his succinct and valuable volume on "manifest destiny," Anders Stephanson reminds us of the puritanical, millenarial, and religious impulses that infused America's approach to the world. Other factors might have influenced the Cold War, he writes, "but the operative framework in which they all fit is the story of American exceptionalism, with its missionary implications."[47] Stephanson's emphasis on American nationalist ideology, sometimes conflated with notions of an American century or a Wilsonian century, pulsates through the literature dealing with modern American foreign relations. "American nationalist ideology," writes John Fousek, "provided the principal underpinning for the broad public consensus that supported Cold War foreign policy."[48]

But when translated into policy, the ideological fervor was always calibrated, sometimes by calculation and sometimes by emotion, sometimes by allies and sometimes by domestic constituencies, sometimes by external danger and sometimes by ideals. In his book on World War II diplomacy and the origins of the Cold War, Frank Costigliola skillfully shows how the emotional sensibilities and personality makeups of Roosevelt and Truman affected their understanding of what could and could not be done in pursuit of America's core values and national security goals. Such accounts remind us of the importance of human agency in the construction of core values and the significance of contingency in their implementation.[49] Likewise, Michael Hogan explains how "the most important constraints on the national security state were built into the country's democratic institutions and political culture." They "channeled American policy and American state making in some directions while damming them up in others. The American people and their leaders, or at least the best of them, would go so far and no further, lest a reckless abandon destroy the very Republic they sought to protect."[50]

As the Cold War ended, Americans celebrated the triumph of their core values. From 11/9/89 to 9/11/2001 – from the demise of the Berlin Wall to the attacks on the Pentagon and the World Trade Center – the United States' physical safety seemed assured and its organizing ideology appeared ascendant. Nonetheless, Saddam Hussein's aggression against Kuwait precipitated the orchestration of an American-led grand coalition to restore the status quo ante. George H. W. Bush believed that a core value was at risk – the territorial integrity and national sovereignty of a small nation in a critically important oil-producing region of the world; a law-abiding international community had to act with the collective use of force. Power, interest, and principle reinforced one another and impelled intervention. After the Persian Gulf War, the president's advisers laid out a national security strategy that comported with the long history of American foreign policy: with the Cold War over, the United States and its allies now had "an unprecedented opportunity to preserve with greater ease a security environment within which our democratic ideals can prosper." Although Bush remained deeply ambivalent about the use of American military power in a post-Cold War environment devoid of threats, he and his advisers planned for "uncertainty" and sought "to shape the future" – a future world order that would be based on America's core values: self-determination, personal freedom, open trade, free enterprise, and private marketplaces. Bill Clinton embraced this same agenda with his strategy of enlargement and engagement, but his foreign policy, like his predecessor's, seemed erratic and episodic.[51] The national security paradigm actually explains this floundering: without any perceived danger to core values, foreign policy was of secondary or tertiary importance to the American people, to legislators, and even to policymakers.

The terrorist attacks on 9/11 shattered this complacency. Fear inspired action. Power enabled action. Hubris justified action. "The great struggles of the twentieth century between liberty and totalitarianism," began George W. Bush's 2002 National Security Strategy Statement, "ended with a decisive victory for the forces of freedom" and demonstrated "a single sustainable model for national success: freedom, democracy, and free enterprise."[52] Officials, legislators, politicians, and pundits could argue over what constituted a real danger and how the war on terror should be conducted, but almost everyone concurred that another terrorist attack had to be prevented. The terrorists, stressed Bush, "kill not merely to end lives ... " They sought to extinguish a "way of life."[53] Bush's advisers feared that terrorism had the capacity to undo the trust on which democratic governance and liberal society were postulated. "Beyond the cost in lives and property," emphasized Under Secretary of Defense Douglas Feith, "the 9/11 attack – *or rather our reaction to it* [my emphasis] – could have far-reaching consequences, especially if it were followed by more such attacks. To protect ourselves physically, we might have to change fundamentally the way we live, sacrificing our society's openness for hoped for safety."[54]

Such motives might evoke skepticism, scorn, or worse. After all, the Bush administration reacted with policies that disregarded international law and individual freedom. For many critics, the national security strategy of the George W. Bush administration actually crushed the very core values that the strategy was supposedly designed to protect.[55]

This paradox actually reminds us of the enduring challenge that has inhered in the national security policies of the United States since its founding. External dangers – sometimes real, sometimes illusory – conjure up perceptions of threat. Officials and observers believe that configurations of power are evolving, or vacuums of power are developing, that will necessitate painful adjustments domestically should they not be thwarted. The Founding Fathers thought this way when they worried about encirclement and violations of America's neutral trade; they feared that they might need to build standing armies or crush internal dissent. Wilson thought this way when he worried about the growth of German power, and so did Franklin Roosevelt. Events abroad could mean endangering core values at home, imperiling the American way of life. Yet, thwarting the trajectory of those developments required actions that also endangered core values. Finding the right balance was (and is) daunting.

National security policy invites wise statecraft. Sometimes we have had it; sometime we have not. As a democratic polity, we possess the ability to debate and correct mistakes; hence the growing interest in grand strategy. It forces us to ponder the meaning of vital interests and core values, the identification of priorities, and the ways to balance means and ends. The challenges are formidable for policymakers – and for historians. The national security paradigm forces us to think more carefully about threats, interests, goals, priorities, and values. We must do so. Our core values are at stake.

NOTES

1. This definition emerges from the writings of P. G. Bock and Morton Berkowitz. See, for example, Bock and Berkowitz, "The Emerging Field of National Security," *World Politics* 19 (October 1966): 122–36.
2. Lawrence Freedman, *Strategy: A History* (New York, 2013): xi, 610–11; Robert J. Art, *America's Grand Strategy and World Politics* (New York, 2009); John L. Gaddis, *Strategies of Containment: A Critical Appraisal of American National Security Policy During the Cold War* (New York, 2005); Hal Brands, *What Good Is Grand Strategy: Power and Purpose in American Statecraft from Harry S. Truman to George W. Bush* (Ithaca, 2014); Charles N. Edel, *Nation Builder: John Quincy Adams and the Grand Strategy of the Republic* (Cambridge, MA, 2014).
3. George Kennan, *American Diplomacy, 1900–1950* (Chicago, 1951); William Appleman Williams, *The Tragedy of American Diplomacy* (Cleveland, 1959).
4. Robert Kagan, *Dangerous Nation* (New York, 2006); Tony Smith, *America's Mission: The United States and the Worldwide Struggle for Democracy in the Twentieth Century* (Princeton, 1994); Michael H. Hunt, *The American Ascendancy: How the United States Gained and Wielded Global Dominance* (Chapel Hill, 2007); Walter L. Hixson, *The Myth of American Diplomacy* (New Haven, 2008); David Reynolds, *America, Empire of Liberty: A New History of the United States* (New York, 2009); Richard H. Immerman, *Empire for Liberty : A History of American Imperialism from Benjamin Franklin to Paul Wolfowitz* (Princeton, 2010); Gordon S. Wood, *Empire of Liberty: A History of the Early American Republic, 1789–1815* (New York, 2009).
5. Barry Buzan, *People, States, and Fear: The National Security Problem in International Relations* (Brighton, UK, 1983), 4–9.
6. Michael Lind, *The American Way of Strategy* (New York, 2006), 23, 38.
7. Christopher Layne, *The Peace of Illusions: American Grand Strategy from 1940 to the Present* (Ithaca, 2006), 8–10.
8. Peter J. Katzenstein, ed., *The Culture of National Security: Norms and Identity in World Politics* (New York, 1996), 1–32, and for the quotations, see p. 2; for a valuable illumination of these matters in the historiography regarding Woodrow Wilson, see Andrew M. Johnston, "The Historiography of American Intervention in the First World War," *Passport* 45(April 2014): 22–9.
9. Arnold Wolfers, "'National Security' as an Ambiguous Symbol," *Political Science Quarterly* 67 (December 1952): 481–502.
10. Lind, *American Way of Strategy*, 22; for an account that stresses how the pursuit of national security has contradicted and undermined America's core values, see William O. Walker III, *National Security and Core Values in American History* (New York, 2009).
11. Kenneth N. Waltz, *Theory of International Politics* (Reading, MA, 1979), 79–101; John J. Mearsheimer, *The Tragedy of Great Power Politics* (New York, 2001), 1–82; Ernest R. May, *"Lessons" of the Past: The Use and Misuse of History in American Foreign Policy* (New York, 1973).
12. James E. Lewis Jr., *The American Union and the Problem of Neighborhood: The United States and the Collapse of the Spanish Empire, 1783–1829* (Chapel Hill, 1998), 10; also see Jay Sexton, *The Monroe Doctrine: Empire and Nation in Nineteenth Century America* (New York, 2011); Edel, *Nation Builder*.

13. John Lewis Gaddis, *We Now Know: Rethinking Cold War History* (New York, 1997), 24–25, 294–96; Wilson D. Miscamble, *From Roosevelt to Truman: Potsdam, Hiroshima, and the Cold War* (New York, 2007); Ralph B. Levering and Verena Botzenenhart-Viehe, "The American Perspective," in *Debating the Origins of the Cold War*, ed. Ralph B. Levering, Vladimir O. Pechatnov, et al. (Lanham, MD, 2001), 1–63; Les K. Adler and Thomas G. Paterson, "Red Fascism: The Merger of Nazi Germany and Soviet Russia in the American Image of Totalitarianism, 1930s–1950s," *American Historical Review* 75 (April 1970): 1046–64.
14. Gabriel Kolko, and Joyce Kolko, *The Limits of Power: The World and United States Foreign Policy, 1945–1954* (New York, 1972); Kevin M. Casey, *Saving International Capitalism during the Early Truman Presidency: The National Advisory Council on International Monetary and Financial Affairs* (New York, 2001); Benjamin O. Fordham, *Building the Cold War Consensus: the Political Economy of U.S. National Security Policy, 1949–1951* (Ann Arbor, MI, 1998); Curt Cardwell, *NSC 68 and the Political Economy of the Cold War* (New York, 2011); Melvyn P. Leffler, "The American Conception of National Security and the Beginnings of the Cold War, 1945–48," *American Historical Review* 89 (April 1984): 356–78.
15. Lind, *American Way of Strategy*, 22.
16. C. Vann Woodward presented the classic argument that US foreign policy was shaped by a long era of "free security," a view that Andrew Preston embraces in his overview of the concept of "National Security." See Andrew Preston, "Monsters Everywhere: a Genealogy of National Security," *Diplomatic History* 38 (June 2014): 477–500.
17. Sexton, *Monroe Doctrine*, 32–3, 10–11.
18. Sam W. Haynes, "Anglophobia and the Annexation of Texas: The Quest for National Security," in *Manifest Destiny and Empire*, ed. Sam W. Haynes and Christopher Morris (College Station, TX, 1997), 117.
19. Nancy Mitchell, *The Danger of Dreams: German and American Imperialism in Latin America* (Chapel Hill, 1999).
20. For reevaluations of the relative strength and efficacy of American military capabilities and foreign policies in the 1920s and early 1930s, see John Braeman, "Power and Diplomacy: The 1920s Reappraised," *Review of Politics* 44 (July 1982): 342–69; also see Melvyn R. Leffler, "Political Isolationism, Economic Expansionism, or Diplomatic Realism: American Policy Toward Western Europe, 1921–1933," *Perspectives in American History* 8 (1974): 413–61; Patrick O. Cohrs, *The Unfinished Peace After World War I: America, Britain and the Stabilization of Europe, 1919–1932* (New York, 2006); Adam Tooze, *The Deluge: The Great War, America and the Remaking of the Global Order, 1916–1931* (New York, 2014).
21. Quoted in Robert R. Bowie and Richard H. Immerman, *Waging Peace: How Eisenhower Shaped an Enduring Cold War Strategy* (New York, 1998), 45.
22. Lind, *American Way of Strategy*, 7. Of course, just what constitutes the "American Way of Life," is open to debate. For example, contrast Lind to William A. Williams, *Empire as a Way of Life* (New York, 1980). Frank Ninkovich links the protection of the American way of life at home to the preservation of "international society" abroad. See Frank Ninkovich, *The Global Republic* (Chicago, 2014).
23. Robert W. Tucker and David C. Hendrickson, *Empire of Liberty: The Statecraft of Thomas Jefferson* (New York, 1990), 179, 72; Levin, *Woodrow Wilson and World*

Politics: America's Response to War and Revolution (New York, 1968); also see Buzan, *People, States, and Fear*, 36–72.
24. For a succinct and incisive analysis, see George Herring, *From Colony to Superpower* (New York, 2008), 64–7ff.
25. Kagan, *Dangerous Nation*, 181–264; Michael F. Holt, *The Fate of Their Country: Politicians, Slavery, Expansion, and the Coming of the Civil War* (New York, 2004), 125–6; William Earl Weeks, *The New Cambridge History of American Foreign Relations, I: Dimensions of the Early American Empire, 1754–1865* (New York, 2013), 210–72.
26. Justus D. Doenecke, *Storm on the Horizon: The Challenge to American Intervention, 1939–1941* (Lanham, MD, 2000); Waldo Heinrichs, *Threshold of War: Franklin D. Roosevelt and American Entry into World War II* (New York, 1988); Lynne Olson, *Those Angry Days: Roosevelt, Lindbergh, and America's Fight Over World War II* (New York, 2013).
27. One can choose from a variety of Marxist or pluralist approaches. One can see the state acting autonomously or as a captive of particular groups or classes. For some stimulating views and essays see Ralph Miliband, *The State in Capitalist Society: An Analysis of the Western System of Power* (New York: Basic Books, 1969); Charles E. Lindblom, *Politics and Markets: The World's Political Economic Systems* (New York: Basic Books, 1977); and Peter J. Katzenstein, ed. *Between Power and Plenty: Foreign Economic Policies of Advanced Industrial States* (Madison, WI: University of Wisconsin Press, 1978); and Charles Bright and Susan Harding, eds., *Statemaking and Social Movements: Essays in History and Theory* (Ann Arbor, MI: University of Michigan Press, 1984).
28. Robert Gilpin, *War and Change in World Politics* (New York: Cambridge University Press, 1981), 50–105.
29. Melvyn P. Leffler, "1921–1932: Expansionist Impulses and Domestic Constraints," in *Economics and World Power: An Assessment of American Diplomacy since 1789*, ed. William H. Becker and Samuel F. Wells, Jr. (New York: Columbia University Press, 1984), 225–75; Cohrs, *Unfinished Peace After World War I*.
30. This definition of power comes from Bertrand Russell and was used by Paul Nitze's Policy Planning Staff in the Department of State in the early 1950s. See Paper Drafted by the Policy Planning Staff, "Basic Issues Raised by Draft NSC 'Reappraisal of US Objectives and Strategy for National Security'," n.d. [July 1952], US Department of State, *Foreign Relations of the United States, 1952– 1954* (Washington, DC, 1984) 2:61 (hereafter FRUS); Freedman, *Strategy*, 162–4; Gilpin, *War and Change*, 67–8; Paul Kennedy, *The Rise and Fall of the Great Powers: Economic Change and Military Conflict from 1500 to 2000* (New York, 1987); and Klaus Knorr, *Power and Wealth: The Political Economy of International Power* (New York, 1973).
31. David C. Hendrickson, *Peace Pact: The Lost World of the American Founding* (Lawrence, KS, 2003); Frederick W. Marks II: *Independence on Trial: Foreign Affairs and the Making of the Constitution* (Wilmington, DE, 1986); Max L. Edling, *A Revolution in Favor of Government: Origins of the U.S. Constitution and the Making of the American State* (New York, 2003).
32. Sexton, *Monroe Doctrine*, 28; Eliga H. Gould, *Among the Powers of the Earth: The American Revolution and the Making of a New World Empire* (Cambridge, MA, 2012).

33. Lind, *American Way of Strategy*, 49.
34. Drew R. McCoy, *The Elusive Republic: Political Economy in Jeffersonian America* (New York: W. W. Norton & Company, 1980); Sexton, *Monroe Doctrine*; Gould, *Among the Powers of the World*; David L. Dykstra, *The Shifting Balance of Power: American-British Diplomacy in North America, 1842–48* (Lanham, MD, 1999).
35. Frank Ninkovich, *Modernity and Power: A History of the Domino Theory in the Twentieth Century* (Chicago, 1994), 52–6; Ross A. Kennedy, *The Will to Believe: Woodrow Wilson, World War I, and America's Strategy for Peace and Security* (Kent, OH, 2008).
36. Cohrs, *Unfinished Peace after World War I*; Melvyn P. Leffler, *The Elusive Quest: America's Pursuit of European Stability and French Security, 1919–1933* (Chapel Hill, 1979).
37. For this view, see Patrick J. Hearden, *Roosevelt Confronts Hitler: America's Entry into World War II* (DeKalb, IL, 1986); Lloyd C. Gardner, *Economic Aspects of New Deal Diplomacy* (Madison, WI, 1964).
38. John Lamberton Harper, *American Visions of Europe: Franklin D. Roosevelt, George F. Kennan, and Dean G. Acheson* (New York, 1994), 64; Ninkovich, *Modernity and Power*, 112–22; David Reynolds, *From Munich to Pearl Harbor: Roosevelt's America and the Origins of the Second World War* (Chicago, 2001); Art, *America's Grand Strategy and World Politics*, 69–110.
39. *Public Papers of the Presidents of the United States: Harry S. Truman, 1952–1953* (Washington, DC, 1966), 189; Melvyn P. Leffler, *A Preponderance of Power: National Security, the Truman Administration and the Cold War* (Stanford, 1992), 1–24, 151–7, 495–8.
40. Leffler, *Elusive Quest*; Michael J. Hogan, *Informal Entente: The Private Structure of Cooperation in Anglo-American Economic Relations, 1918–1928* (Columbia, MO, 1977); Frank Costigliola, *Awkward Dominion: American Political, Economic, and Cultural Relations with Europe, 1919–1933* (Ithaca, 1984); Tooze, *Great Deluge*.
41. Aaron L. Friedberg, *In the Shadow of the Garrison State: America's Anti-Statism and Its Cold War Grand Strategy* (Princeton, 2000), especially pp. 4–5, 60–1; Michael J. Hogan, *A Cross of Iron: Harry S. Truman and the Origins of the National Security State, 1945–1954* (New York, 1998).
42. For critiques, see William O. Walker III, "Melvyn P. Leffler, Ideology, and American Foreign Policy," *Diplomatic History* 20 (Fall 1996): 663–73; Bruce Cumings, "Revising Postrevisionism: or, The Poverty of Theory in Diplomatic History," *ibid.*, 17 (Fall 1993): 563–4ff.
43. Andrew W. Preston, *The Sword of the Spirit, the Shield of Faith: Religion in American War and Diplomacy* (New York, 2012), 412; also see William Inboden, *Religion and American Foreign Policy, 1945–1960: The Soul of Containment* (New York, 2008); Jonathan P. Herzog, *The Spiritual-Industrial Complex: America's Religious Battle Against Communism in the Early Cold War* (New York, 2011); Colleen Doody, *Detroit's Cold War: The Origins of Postwar Conservatism* (Urbana, IL, 2013), 76–92.
44. Michael E. Latham, *The Right Kind of Revolution: Modernization, Development, and U.S. Foreign Policy from the Cold War to the Present* (Ithaca, 2011), 3; also see Nick Cullather, *The Hungry World: America's Cold War Battle against Poverty in Asia* (Cambridge, MA, 2010).

45. See, for example, David Schmitz, *Thank God They're on Our Side: the United States and Right-Wing Dictatorships* (Chapel Hill, 1999); David F. Schmitz, *The United States and Right-Wing Dictatorships* (New York, 2006); Steven G. Rabe, *The Killing Zone: The United States Wages Cold War in Latin America* (New York, 2012).
46. David Ekbladh, *The Great American Mission: Modernization and the Construction of the American World Order* (Princeton, 2010), 2; for human rights, see Sarah Snyder, *Human Rights Activism and the End of the Cold War: a Transnational History of the Helsinki Network* (New York, 2011); Daniel C. Thomas, *The Helsinki Effect: International Norms, Human Rights, and the Demise of Communism* (Princeton, 2001); Barbara, J. Keys, *Reclaiming American Virtue: The Human Rights Revolution of the 1970s* (Cambridge, MA, 2014).
47. Anders Stephanson, *Manifest Destiny: American Expansion and the Empire of Right* (New York, 1995), 124.
48. John Fousek, *To Lead the Free World: American Nationalism and the Cultural Roots of the Cold War* (Chapel Hill, 2000), 2; also see, for example, Frank Ninkovich, *The Wilsonian Century: U.S. Foreign Policy Since 1900* (Chicago, 1999); Smith, *America's Mission*.
49. Frank Costigliola, *Roosevelt's Lost Alliances: How Personal Politics Helped Start the Cold War* (Princeton, 2012); for agency and contingency, also see Immerman, *Empire for Liberty*, 14–15ff.
50. Hogan, *Cross of Iron*, 474–5, 482.
51. The generalizations in this paragraph are based on: Hal Brands, *From Berlin to Baghdad: America's Search for Purpose in the Post-Cold War World* (Lexington, KY, 2008); Derek Chollet and James Goldgeier, *America Between the Wars: From 11/9 to 9/11* (New York, 2008); Melvyn P. Leffler, "Dreams of Freedom: Temptations of Power," in *The Fall of the Berlin Wall: The Revolutionary Legacy of 1989*, ed. Jeffrey A. Engel (New York, 2009), 132–69; Eric S. Edelman, "The Strange Career of the 1992 Defense Planning Guidance," in *In Uncertain Times: American Foreign Policy after the Berlin Wall and 9/11*, ed. Melvyn P. Leffler and Jeffrey Legro (Ithaca, 2011), 63–77. The quotations are from the last iteration of the "Defense Planning Guidance." See Secretary of Defense Dick Cheney, *Defense Strategy for the 1990s: The Regional Defense Strategy* (Washington, DC, 1993), pp. 2ff, available at www.informationclearinghouse.info/pdf/naarpr_Defense.pdf (accessed February 20, 2014).
52. "The National Security Strategy," September 2002, http://georgewbush-whitehouse.archives.gov/nsc/nss/2002/ (accessed February 22, 2014).
53. "Address to a Joint Session of Congress," September 20, 2001, http://georgewbush-whitehouse.archives.gov/news/releases/2001/09/20010920-8.html (accessed February 22, 2014).
54. Douglas J. Feith, *War and Decision: Inside the Pentagon at the Dawn of the War on Terrorism* (New York, 2008), 68–9.
55. See, for example, Jane Mayer, *The Dark Side: The Inside Story of How the War on Terror Turned into a War on American Ideals* (New York, 2008); Lind, *American Way of Strategy*, 125–259; Walker, *National Security and Core Values*, 259–92.

3

Corporatism: from the new era to the age of development

Michael J. Hogan

Scholars have used the term *corporatism* or *associationalism* to describe an economic and political system that is characterized by certain organizational forms, by a certain ideology, and by a certain trend in the development of public policy.[1] Organizationally, corporatism refers to a system that is founded on officially recognized functional groups, such as labor, business, agriculture, and the professions. In such a system, institutional regulating and coordinating mechanisms seek to integrate the groups into an organic whole; elites in the private and public sectors collaborate to guarantee order, stability, and progress; and this collaboration creates a pattern of interpenetration and power sharing that makes it difficult to determine where one sector leaves off and the other begins. Ellis W. Hawley defined corporatism in these terms, his work building on the insights of historians, such as Alfred D. Chandler and Robert H. Wiebe, who identified the organizational revolution and the search for order as major themes in the history of modern industrial society.[2]

Still other scholars delineated the ideology and political culture of the associative state and its champions among progressive political leaders and their counterparts in the private sector. They uncovered a body of liberal thought that celebrated such virtues as voluntarism, managerial expertise, and enlightened self-regulation and cooperation, all in the service of liberal capitalism. They explored the many programs to promote social welfare, tame the business cycle, nurture growth at home, and promote economic development and modernization abroad. They demonstrated how these programs often sought to contain the state by entrusting much of the responsibility for public policy to semi-autonomous agencies, to supposedly nonpartisan experts, and to collaborative systems of economic planning and voluntary regulation. According to most of these studies, those who championed the associative system saw it as a "middle way" between the laissez faire capitalism of a bygone day and the paternalistic statism of an Orwellian nightmare. In this system, partisan politics would supposedly give way to scientific management, public legislatures would yield some of their functions to private forums, and redistributive battles would dissolve in a material abundance in which all could share.[3]

The portrait drawn in this scholarship is fluid rather than static; the relative weight assigned to various components of the associational system, particularly to public versus private power, varies according to historical circumstances, the political power of the groups involved, and the national system under discussion. While corporatism is therefore a useful model for describing modern society at any particular moment, it is best perceived and most fruitfully employed as an analytical device for explaining important, long-term trends in politics, the economy, and public policy over much of the twentieth century. By using it this way, historians have discovered hitherto obscure lines of continuity running throughout the century, and have done so without slighting the significance of new ideas or scientific adaptations and without substituting consensus theory for one that takes account of political struggles. On the contrary, they have focused on efforts to contain group conflict through strategies of growth and through organizational structures that could harmonize differences. They have also talked of competing political coalitions and have sought to integrate important economic and political transformations into the unfolding history of modern corporatism. My own work, for example, describes how the Great Depression of the 1930s combined with changes in the industrial structure to produce the New Deal coalition, an alliance of interests that defeated conservative opponents and elaborated a more state-centered version of the associational design than the one envisioned by Republican leaders a decade earlier.[4]

If corporatism has illuminated important trends in domestic history, it has been no less helpful to a substantial group of diplomatic historians. As these historians realize, political leaders seldom compartmentalize their vision, thinking one way about the domestic system, another about the international system. On the contrary, American policymakers tried to build a world order along lines comparable to the corporatist order that was taking shape at home. Their global design became more elaborate as time passed and circumstances changed, and much of what we know of that design first emerged from scholarship on American foreign policy in the New Era of the 1920s.

Although rejecting the League of Nations and other collective security arrangements, Republican policymakers were heirs to a long tradition of expansionism and dollar diplomacy. They built on this tradition, on the internationalism of the war period, and on a variety of business, financial, and professional institutions that had a growing stake in the global economy. My early work focused on their efforts to reconstruct the international system in the wake of World War I, with similar contributions coming from Carl P. Parrini, Joan Hoff-Wilson, Burton I. Kaufman, Melvyn P. Leffler, Emily S. Rosenberg, and Frank Costigliola.[5]

These studies differed in chronological coverage, topical focus, and point of view, but all shared elements of the corporatist synthesis. The ideology of American leaders, as they elaborated it, echoed the ideology of associational capitalism in the United States. For Republican policymakers, in other words, state trading, national autarky, and unregulated international rivalries posed a threat to global peace and stability comparable to the threat that paternalistic government, class conflict, and the unbridled pursuit of self-interest posed to liberal capitalism and democracy at home. And if the dangers were similar, so were the safeguards. According to these historians, Republican policymakers saw economic growth as a way to eliminate autarky and integrate national economies into a capitalist world order. Growth could be achieved by unleashing private initiative and normal market forces, steps best arranged through most-favored-nation treaties, convertible currencies, the reduction of international indebtedness, and the export of private capital and technical know-how. Government could play a positive role in promoting these initiatives and in organizing the private sector for overseas expansion. But in the international arena, as on the home front, the major emphasis was on scientific, not political, management, and on voluntary self-regulation by cooperating private elites.

Guided by their associational vision, Republican leaders touted a "scientific" settlement of war debts and tariff rates by nonpartisan "experts" and semiautonomous commissions. They joined forces with the financial community to regulate foreign loans, tried to reconcile the differences between private groups with a stake in foreign trade, and sought to bring bankers and manufacturers together in collective programs to expand the world economy. In an era dominated by economic problems, Republican policymakers also fostered an international network of cooperating central banks. They relied on private commissions to modify the reparations settlement imposed on the defeated Germans, and they sanctioned the organization of multinational groups to underwrite development, manage resources, and expand communications. Their goals were peaceful growth and integration without destabilizing competition or excessive intervention by the state. And to achieve these goals, they tried to forge a new order in which market forces and cooperating private groups worked in tandem to regulate the global economy.

While analyzing the New Era vision and the programs that resulted, the historians of interwar corporatism also described the imperfect internationalism that contributed to the collapse of world peace and prosperity after 1929. They noted the failure of Republican leaders to control public opinion, ameliorate group differences, and overcome bureaucratic obstacles. In surveying the complicated negotiations between the United States and other governments, they pointed out the limits inherent in the Republican design as applied to trade and tariff disputes, debt-funding agreements, loan policies, and collective security arrangements. In addition,

Leffler combined his discussion of economic diplomacy with a careful scrutiny of such issues as strategic commitments, neutrality rights, and naval limitations. Costigliola focused attention on the expansion of American technology and mass culture, as well as American business, and Rosenberg did much the same in a volume that traced the evolution of American diplomacy from the late nineteenth century through World War II.[6]

These works put to rest forever what William Appleman Williams once called "the legend of isolationism in the 1920s."[7] They revised substantially the older textbook interpretation of the New Era as a decade of unmitigated reaction, marked by a rigid and ethnocentric diplomacy, and they made it possible to see important connections between the search for order at home and abroad. The best of these works managed to integrate the economic influences identified by revisionist historians into a multidimensional analysis that also took account of geopolitical considerations, not to mention organizational arrangements and bureaucratic determinants. They demonstrated convincingly that a corporatist analysis could be combined with a searching examination of state-to-state relations and the influence exerted by party politics, congressional pressures, and public opinion. Like post-revisionist scholarship, they noted the important role of government elites in shaping foreign policy, but they did not ignore the equally important part played by private experts, international groups, and other non state actors. Indeed, work by Paul W. Drake, Thomas F. O'Brien, and Emily S. Rosenberg has focused particular attention on the influence of multinational corporations and financial missionaries, such as Edwin Kemmerer, especially on their efforts to export American corporate culture and economic values to developing countries.[8]

As evident in this body of scholarship, corporatism also has advantages for those historians who want to move beyond the state in their study of foreign relations or who want to locate American diplomacy in a larger international, comparative, or cultural framework. To be sure, most works in this category do not ignore the state altogether or abandon the nation as a subject of analysis. Nevertheless, they supplement an investigation of government policy with a discussion of private groups and informal diplomacy, just as they explore the connection, noted by Akira Iriye and others, between power and culture in international relations.[9] Indeed, most of the scholars in this group root government policy in American political culture, and some of them, especially Costigliola and Rosenberg, link the pursuit of corporatist policies abroad with the process of cultural expansion and Americanization. Like others in the group, most recently Drake and O'Brien, Costigliola and Rosenberg elaborate the role that non state actors played in the history of American foreign relations, but add social workers, missionaries, filmmakers, and similar carriers of culture to the well-established list of industrialists, bankers, and trade unionists. In addition, Rosenberg's work on financial missionaries combines a traditional account of dollar diplomacy with an analysis that follows the cultural turn of recent scholarship by situating American policy in a context that includes notions of racial superiority, manliness, modernization, and professionalism.

What is more, even though the scholars in this group do not forsake the nation in their analysis, most explore the connection between national policy and various forces, particularly economic forces, at work in the international system. Several also utilize bi-archival or multi-archival research to place national policy in a larger regional or global context, with the most notable example being Charles S. Maier, who used corporatism to compare and describe the political arrangements that took shape between governments, industrialists, trade unionists, landowners, peasants, and other private groups in much of Europe after World War I.[10]

Although corporatist historians first concentrated on the 1920s, virtually all of the works noted above discerned patterns that linked Republican diplomacy to the foreign policy of the Progressive Era and earlier periods in American history. This pattern became even clearer in Gregg Andrews' impressive study of the collaboration between the American government and the American Federation of Labor in shaping US policy toward the Mexican revolution between 1910 and 1924. While Andrews, along with Elizabeth McKillen and others, explored labor's role in foreign policy, including its cooperation with government officials, others remained fascinated by the relationship between government elites and their counterparts in business and banking. This was the case with Linda B. Hall's work on the intertwining of petroleum, banking, and politics in US policy toward Mexico after 1917, and it was also the case with the earlier work of Richard Hume Werking and William H. Becker. These historians described the late nineteenth- and early twentieth-century efforts of American business leaders to establish essentially "quasi-corporative" organizations, such as the US Chamber of Commerce, that could protect their interests at home and abroad. They uncovered the linkages that business groups tried to forge with public policymakers, particularly in the State and Commerce departments, who were devising their own plans to make government more efficient and improve their connections with the private sector. In addition, they described how the search for private gain, including career goals and bureaucratic advantage, often coincided with the promotion of national interests and with the larger themes of professionalism, scientific management, and national efficiency that characterized the progressive period as well as the 1920s.[11]

Other works extended the corporatist analysis from the 1920s to the 1930s, 1940s, and 1950s. Andrew P. N. Erdmann did so for international monetary policy in an article that highlighted a shift in the corporatist balance of power between the private and public sectors from the New Era to the New Deal. David S. Painter did the same for oil diplomacy in a monograph that devoted particular attention to the close collaboration between public policymakers and company officials.[12] Burton Kaufman's study of economic diplomacy in the 1950s added weight to Robert Griffith's important article on the domestic and international aspects of Eisenhower's "Corporate Commonwealth."[13] In her prize-winning book, *The Rich Neighbor Policy*, Elizabeth Cobbs painted a detailed, if benign, picture of American corporate capitalism at work in Brazil under the leadership of Nelson Aldrich Rockefeller and Henry J. Kaiser. A far more malignant picture emerged in Bruce Cuming's brilliant analysis of the Korean War, which stressed in part the connection between US policy, the structure of the American political economy, and the struggle for power between different groups in the United States. Somewhat similar themes emerged in my own work, which analyzed the link between state-making and foreign policy in the first decade of the Cold War and integrated that analysis into a broader study of partisan politics, bureaucratic rivalries, and issues of political culture and national identity. Focusing also on the 1950s, Paul G. Pierpaoli used the corporatist synthesis to present the first systematic history of US economic mobilization during the Korean War, while Federico Romero relied on the corporatist paradigm to examine the collaborative efforts of American government and labor leaders to promote stability and contain communism in Europe.[14]

In addition to these works, Charles S. Maier and I have used corporatism to analyze the evolution of European and American diplomacy from the end of World War I through the early Cold War. My contribution revised conventional interpretations that relied on external factors alone, particularly on the Soviet menace of the early Cold War, to explain the triumph of internationalism in American diplomacy. It saw this triumph as stemming as well from the rise of the New Deal coalition in the United States, a coalition that prevailed against Robert Taft and other conservatives whose anti-Communist strategy ruled out many of the economic and military innovations of the Roosevelt and Truman administrations.[15]

As the preceding discussion points out, the work of corporatist historians describes how internal and external developments (domestic politics and Soviet expansion) led Cold War policymakers to elaborate the associational formulations of the New Era. Through the General Agreement on Tariffs and Trade, as well as the reciprocal trade agreements, they added multilateral ingredients to the Open Door prescriptions of the first postwar period. Through technical assistance schemes they extended Hoover's earlier efforts to export the American way. Through government aid programs, including the Marshall Plan, they enlarged the design for a corporative world order envisioned by their predecessors. And through new alliances and military assistance programs they committed the United States to collective security arrangements that would safeguard their design against potential aggressors. There were organizational innovations, too, including the World Bank and the International Monetary Fund, which tended to formalize the mechanisms of global economic coordination that had taken shape during the Republican ascendancy. As in the 1920s, moreover, Cold War diplomacy was often a by-product of close collaboration between public policymakers and private elites.

At times this collaboration took the form of frequent consultation or the appointment of private leaders to public positions, phenomena described by Painter in his study of oil diplomacy. At times, as my book on the Marshall Plan points out, cooperation was institutionalized in agencies that operated as a bridge between the public and private sectors.[16] Whatever the method, Cold War and corporatism, as I have argued, combined to transform American political culture, the American state, and the way Americans defined themselves.[17]

These works illustrate again how a corporatist analysis can take account of political pressures, bureaucratic rivalries, and geopolitical strategy. Painter integrates these factors in his investigation of oil diplomacy, as does Griffith in his overview of the Eisenhower administration. My book on the Marshall Plan details the bureaucratic wrangling between the administrative agencies involved and outlines the critique of the plan mounted by conservatives in Congress. It also argues that economic aid became a vehicle for reconstructing the elements of a viable balance of power on the Continent, first by reconciling Franco-German differences in the West, then by bringing the participating countries into a unit of sufficient strength and coherence to contain the Soviet bloc in Eastern Europe. Economic policy reinforced geopolitical goals, just as military policy, particularly the North Atlantic Treaty and the military assistance program, sought to reinforce the corporative design for a new European order that inhered in the Marshall Plan.[18]

From works on the late nineteenth century, the Progressive Era, and the interwar period, and from those on the 1940s and 1950s, we now have the rudiments of a corporatist synthesis covering a substantial portion of modern American history. What is more, new work enables us to extend that synthesis from the 1950s through much of the Cold War. Although the Marshall Plan was an effort at economic re-development in Western Europe, a great deal of the thinking that guided American Marshall Planners would be evident as well in subsequent US efforts to foster economic development and modernization in the so-called Third World, from Truman's Point Four program, to Kennedy's Alliance for Progress, and beyond. Indeed, the growing literature on this subject provides perhaps the best example of the corporatist model at work in contemporary scholarship.[19]

David Ekbladh's recent book on modernization and the construction of an American world order is an excellent case in point, as is Matthew Jacobs' equally impressive study of how Americans imagined the Middle East over much of the twentieth century. Both books locate the roots of American postwar development policy in the years prior to World War II, just as I found unexpected continuities between the Marshall Plan and American efforts to rebuild the world economy in the 1920s. Like my own work on the interwar era and the Marshall Plan, Ekbladh and Jacobs also stress many of the key attributes of the associational state that American leaders tried to build at home and abroad. Included here is a reliance on networks of private, sometimes transnational groups, such as religious, business, and philanthropic groups, as well as academic experts, government leaders, and regional or international organizations, all of which played a part in framing the way Americans viewed the world and how this framing shaped their economic and strategic goals. Included as well is an emphasis on public–private cooperation and power-sharing, so typical of American policy in the 1920s, as well as the conviction that difficult domestic or global problems were best handled through scientific management by supposedly non-political experts, whether bankers, labor leaders, agricultural experts, or other specialists, working with each other and with the government.

Jacobs spends some time on the role that oil giant Aramco played in his story, a role foreshadowed by America's resource policy, including its oil policy, in the first postwar decade, when US government leaders worked hard to bring oil, rubber, and other resource producers into collaborative arrangements with each other and with the government in order to eliminate destabilizing competition and advance shared goals. Ekbladh rightly sees the TVA as a model for America's postwar modernization strategies in the Third World. But he also lists other prewar influences, to which I might add such associational initiatives as the Dawes and Young Commissions, the China financial consortium, the Middle East oil consortium, or the arrangements for managing interwar cable and radio communications.[20]

According to Ekbladh, American leaders and their private partners argued strenuously that a program like the Marshall Plan could not be applied with the same positive results in the developing world, where the economic, social, cultural, and political environment was so vastly different. At the same time, however, his analysis shows many important continuities and similarities, including the substantial number of Marshall Planners who subsequently played a part in US economic development programs; Truman's decision to put these programs under the auspices of the Economic Cooperation Administration, which began under the Marshall Plan; and the emphasis, in both Europe and the developing world, on comprehensive planning and on often semi-autonomous regional authorities who were to act much like the Organization for European Economic Cooperation acted under the Marshall Plan.[21]

Many of the themes developed by Ekbladh and Jacobs are also evident elsewhere in the literature on economic development and modernization. Some of this literature focuses on the role of particular groups, such as oil companies, labor organizations, military leaders, philanthropic foundations, international institutions, and government agencies, including the CIA, the Department of Defense, and the State Department. Some of it deals with particular subjects, including efforts to eradicate poverty and control population growth around the world. Some of it concentrates on particular regions, notably Asia, the Middle East, and Latin America, or particular periods, mostly the years after World War II. But running through most of the work in this category are the same themes that can be found in American domestic and foreign policy during the Republican Ascendancy of the 1920s, the New Deal of the 1930s, and the Marshall Plan of the 1940s. These include an emphasis not only on US government policy, but on the role of non state actors and semi-autonomous agencies, the importance of public-private collaboration and power sharing, the stress on scientific management, the reliance on experts, and the search for supposedly non-political and technocratic solutions to pressing international problems. Included as well was the conviction that such strategies would foster growth, promote stability, contain communism, and advance the economic and strategic goals of the United States.[22]

Those writing in this vein generally conclude that American development initiatives failed, sometimes miserably, to clear a path to progressive social change in the developing world. The causes of this failure are too numerous to delineate here. But in part, failure came from the militarization of American aid policies, a change that mirrored the move from the Marshall Plan to the military assistance program in postwar Europe, and in part from the resistance of those who benefited from American aid, a phenomena also noticeable in Europe under the Marshall Plan, which, in the end, was "American made the European way." If the ultimate goal was a new world order cast in the image of American liberal capitalism, what I would call the New Deal version of the associative state, that goal stumbled as well under the weight of a conservative critique that is described by Ekbladh and also by Bradley R. Simpson in his important study of US–Indonesian relations in the 1960s.[23]

This critique is evident, too, in the earlier debates over the Marshall Plan and other postwar foreign policies, not to mention the debates over the national security state that took shape in support of those policies. As noted earlier, my own work tried to tie these debates, indeed the whole national security discourse of the 1940s and early 1950s, to different political coalitions, with the liberal ideology of the associative state tied to the New Deal coalition that emerged in the 1930s. This coalition was led to a great extent by liberal internationalists in the business and banking communities, other organized economic groups, and reformers in the media and elsewhere. It was largely a Democratic Party coalition with particular strength in the North, especially the Northeast, whereas conservative critics found their strength in other regions, in other parts of the economy, and in a growing alliance between the Republican Party and conservative southern Democrats.[24]

Unfortunately, this part of the story remains basically underdeveloped in my own scholarship and in the literature on modernization, including the excellent efforts by Ekbladh and Simpson. Still needed, in other words, is more work that explores the connection between an evolving American economy, domestic political alignments, and both the nature of the American state at home and the state that American modernizers tried to build in other countries.[25] It may be true, for example, that the New Deal coalition gave way to a neo-

Corporatism: from the new era to the age of development

conservative coalition in the 1970s, just as the New Deal version of liberal corporatism gave way to a neo-conservative vision. But does that mean that the age of corporatism is over? Or is the country simply reverting to something akin to Hoover's more conservative associationalism? Does the conservative vision, in other words, simply shift the associational balance of power from some organized groups to others and from government leaders to private actors? Is it still based on the idea of a public–private partnership, does it still assign a role to the state, and does it still stress the importance of scientific management, the rule of experts, and the need for voluntary cooperation and self-regulation? To put it differently, have we come to a point where the associational themes and continuities that link Cold War development strategies back to the interwar period are no longer relevant to historical experience in the last three decades of the twentieth century? I don't think so.

As Philippe C. Schmitter noted several years ago, there are different varieties of corporatism; their central components may remain the same but the relationship between them and their relative weight vary according to national circumstances and the historical period involved.[26] This variety helps to illustrate why corporatism's fuzziness, as some critics see it, may also be its strong suit, namely, its flexibility as an analytical device and its emphasis on historical *process*.[27] These attributes make corporatism particularly useful for explaining change over time and for comparing national systems in an age when different brands of corporatism characterize much of the world. Indeed, one of the most exciting aspects of this concept is the hope it holds for writing what is often termed international history, but which might better be called transnational or comparative national history. As Charles Maier was the first to show in his impressive study of the 1920s, corporatism provides a framework for analyzing how different national systems respond to similar forces, both internal and external, and thus for comparing societies that are usually treated separately.[28] In addition, corporatism may enable us to see the international system as not simply a conglomerate of autonomous institutions, competing states, and rival alliances but as a complex defined by imperatives arising from within the complex itself or projected globally by national corporatisms.

If it is useful to resort to such concepts as revisionism or post-revisionism, then a corporatist approach, as Maier once suggested, "might be described as transrevisionist," in that it "has crossed to new concerns."[29] Corporatism is not for those historians who are content to work with conventional categories of analysis, such as the national interest and the balance of power, or within older interpretative frameworks, such as the realist critique and its subsequent resurgence among post-revisionist scholars. To be sure, a corporatist analysis can take account of strategic and geopolitical notions, which remain important in their own right. But it is far more concerned with the motivating force of liberal capitalism as an ideology; with the economic, political, and social influences on foreign policy in the United States and globally; with the connections between state and society and between national systems and foreign policy; and with the interaction of these systems internationally. In these ways, it shares much with New Left historians and their mentor, William Appleman Williams, though it is far more likely to talk about organized elites, in the tradition of C. Wright Mills, than about ruling classes.[30]

There are so many paradigms now available to students of foreign policy and international relations. This healthy pluralism makes it virtually impossible to think of folding them all together into a single, super paradigm. But I still believe that a corporatist analysis can be part of any effort to synthesize different approaches to the discipline. It is compatible with the approach of international historians who tell their story from the point of view of at least two countries, who use research drawn from both countries, and who are less impressed with American perceptions of the world beyond Washington than with the reality of that world. It is also adaptable to the analytical needs of scholars who are interested in world systems, dependency theory, and the role of non state actors and international institutions. In addition, as my work on the origins of the national security state suggests, it can be used as well by scholars who are interested in state-making and nation-building, or who are interested in discourse analysis and in issues of ideology, political culture, and national identity.[31]

If none of these approaches can absorb the others in a single, coherent paradigm, corporatism can at least bring them together and, in the process, restore some of the connections between diplomatic historians and their colleagues in other fields. But more important is the need for diplomatic historians to reengage the connections between US foreign relations and the nature of the modern state, the process of political alignment and realignment, and the economic, social, and organizational forces at work in national and world economies. Every day brings new, often disturbing, evidence of the importance of these forces in the life around us, at home and abroad. Indeed, they seem to loom larger now than at any time in the last half-century. If the old diplomatic history cut us off from the new work of social and then cultural historians, our current preoccupations tend to isolate us from the political, organizational, and economic aspects of foreign relations, and to forfeit these important topics to experts in other disciplines.

NOTES

1. This chapter updates my contribution to the second edition of this volume. See also, Michael J. Hogan, "Corporatism: A Positive Appraisal," *Diplomatic History* 10 (Fall 1986): 363–72; Thomas J. McCormick, "Drift or Mastery?: A Corporatist Synthesis for American Diplomatic History," *Revisions in American History* 10 (December 1982): 318–30; and Ellis W. Hawley, "The Discovery and Study of a 'Corporate Liberalism,'" *Business History Review* 52 (Autumn 1978): 309–20. McCormick's essay shows how revisionist scholars might adapt corporatism to their own needs and purposes. Hawley's essay enumerates some of the differences,

other than those noted in the text, in the way revisionists and non-revisionists use the concept. For some theoretical background, see Philippe C. Schmitter, "Corporatism is Dead! Long Live Corporatism!" *Government and Opposition* 24 (1989): 54–73; Larry G. Gerber, "Corporatism and State Theory: A Review Essay for Historians," *Social Science History* 19 (Fall 1995): 313–32; Oscar Molina and Martin Rhodes, "Corporatism: The Past, Present, and Future of a Concept," *Annual Reviews in Political Science* 5 (2002): 305–31; Steven Hurst, *Cold War US Foreign Policy: Key Perspectives* (Edinburgh, 2005), 89–109.

2. Hawley, "The Discovery and Study of a 'Corporate Liberalism'"; Wiebe, *The Search for Order, 1877–1920* (New York, 1968); Chandler, *Strategy and Structure: Chapters in the History of the Industrial Enterprise* (Cambridge, MA, 1962); idem, *The Visible Hand: The Managerial Revolution in American Business* (Cambridge, MA, 1977).

3. For a sample of Hawley's work see "Herbert Hoover, the Commerce Secretariat and the Vision of an 'Associative State,' 1921–1928," *Journal of American History* 61 (June 1974): 116–40. See also Joan Hoff-Wilson, *Herbert Hoover: Forgotten Progressive* (Boston 1975); Robert M. Collins, *The Business Response to Keynes, 1929–1964* (New York, 1981); Kim McQuaid, *Big Business and Presidential Power: From FDR to Reagan* (New York, 1982); and Robert Griffith, "Dwight D. Eisenhower and the Corporate Commonwealth," *American Historical Review* 87 (February 1982): 87–122. For a discussion of corporatism, its connections to organizational history and the relevant literature, see Hawley, "The Discovery and Study of a 'Corporate Liberalism.'"

4. Michael J. Hogan, "Revival and Reform: America's Twentieth Century Search for a New Economic Order Abroad," *Diplomatic History* 8 (Fall 1984): 287–310; idem, *The Marshall Plan: America, Britain, and the Reconstruction of Western Europe, 1947–1952* (New York, 1987), 1–25. My argument about the formation of the New Deal coalition borrows from Thomas Ferguson, "From Normalcy to New Deal: Industrial Structure, Party Competition, and the American Public Policy in the Great Depression," *International Organization* 38 (Winter 1984): 41–94.

5. Parrini, *Heir to Empire: United States Economic Diplomacy: 1916–1923* (Pittsburgh, 1969); Hoff-Wilson, *Herbert Hoover*; idem, *American Business and Foreign Policy, 1920–1922* (Lexington, KY, 1971); Kaufman, *Efficiency and Expansion: Foreign Trade Organization in the Wilson Administration, 1913–1921* (Westport, CT, 1974); Michael J. Hogan, *Informal Entente: The Private Structure of Cooperation in Anglo-American Economic Diplomacy, 1918–1928* (Columbia, MO, 1977); Leffler, *The Elusive Quest: America's Pursuit of European Stability and French Security, 1919–1933* (Chapel Hill, 1979); Rosenberg, *Spreading the American Dream: American Economic and Cultural Expansion, 1890–1945* (New York, 1982); Costigliola, *Awkward Dominions: American Political, Economic, and Cultural Relations with Europe, 1919–1933* (Ithaca, NY, 1984). See also Ellis W. Hawley, *The Great War and the Search for a Modern Order: A History of the American People and Their Institutions, 1917–1933* (New York, 1979). For a more recent assessment of Republican foreign policy in Latin America, particularly Hoover's views on economic development and modernization, see William O. Walker III, "Crucible for Peace: Herbert Hoover, Modernization, and Economic Growth in Latin America," *Diplomatic History* Vol. 30, No. 1 (January 2006), 83–117. This list does not

include the contributions by specialists in European international history, especially Charles S. Maier, some of whose articles are cited in subsequent notes.

6. See the citations to Leffler, Costigliola, and Rosenberg in endnote 5.
7. Williams, "The Legend of Isolationism in the 1920s," *Science and Society* 18 (Winter 1954): 1–20.
8. Paul W. Drake, *Money Doctor in the Andes: The Kemmerer Missions, 1923–1933* (Durham, NC, 1989); Thomas F. O'Brien, *The Revolutionary Mission: American Enterprise in Latin America, 1900–1945* (New York, 1996); and Emily S. Rosenberg, *Financial Missionaries to the World: The Politics and Culture of Dollar Diplomacy, 1900–1930* (Cambridge, MA, 1999). See also Cyrus Veeser, *A World Safe for Capitalism: Dollar Diplomacy and America's Rise to Global Power* (New York, 2007).
9. Iriye, *Power and Culture: The Japanese-American War, 1941–1945* (Cambridge, MA, 1981); idem, "Culture and Power: International Relations as Intercultural Relations," *Diplomatic History* 3 (Spring, 1979): 115–28; idem, "War as Peace, Peace as War," in *Experiencing the Twentieth Century*, ed. Nobutoshi Hagihara, Akira Iriye, Georges Nivat, and Philip Windsor (Tokyo, 1985), 31–54.
10. Charles S. Maier, *Recasting Bourgeois Europe: Stabilization in France, Germany, and Italy in the Decade after World War I* (Princeton, 1975).
11. Andrews, *Shoulder to Shoulder? The American Federation of Labor, the United States, and the Mexican Revolution, 1910–1924* (Berkeley, 1991); McKillen, *Chicago Labor and the Quest for a Democratic Diplomacy, 1914–1924* (Ithaca, NY, 1995); Hall, *Oil, Banks, and Politics: The United States and Postrevolutionary Mexico* (Austin, 1995); Werking, *The Master Architects: Building the United States Foreign Service, 1890–1913* (Lexington, KY, 1977); idem, "Bureaucrats, Businessmen, and Foreign Trade: The Origins of the United States Chamber of Commerce," *Business History Review* 52 (Autumn 1978); 321–41; Becker, *The Dynamics of Business-Government Relations: Industry and Exports, 1893–1921* (Chicago, 1982). The phrase "quasi corporative" is taken from Hawley, "The Discovery and Study of a 'Corporate Liberalism.'"
12. Erdmann, "Mining for the Corporatist Synthesis: Gold in American Foreign Economic Policy, 1931–1936," *Diplomatic History* 17 (Spring 1993): 171–200; Painter, *Oil and the American Century: The Political Economy of U.S. Foreign Oil Policy, 1941–1954* (Baltimore, 1986). Painter's is the last of several books on oil diplomacy, all of which provide support to those looking for a corporatist synthesis of American foreign policy. See also the interesting article by Marcelo Bucheli, "Negotiating under the Monroe Doctrine: Weetman Pearson and the Origins of U.S. Control of Colombian Oil," *Business History Review* 82 (Autumn 2008): 529–53. The United Fruit Company and US government officials struck a similar partnership when it came to advancing American interests in Central America. See Jason M. Colby, *The Business of Empire: United Fruit, Race, and U.S. Expansion in Central America* (Ithaca, NY, 2011). For oil policy in a later period, see Dustin Walcher, "Petroleum Pitfalls: The United States, Argentine Nationalism, and the 1963 Oil Crisis," *Diplomatic History* 37 (January 2013): 24–57. Finally, see also, Glenn J. Dorn, "Pushing Tin: U.S. Bolivian Relations and the Coming of the National Revolution," *Diplomatic History* 35 (April 2011): 203–28.

13. Kaufman, *Trade and Aid: Eisenhower's Foreign Economic Policy, 1953–1961* (Baltimore, 1982); Griffith, "Dwight D. Eisenhower and the Corporate Commonwealth."
14. Cobbs, *The Rich Neighbor Policy: Rockefeller and Kaiser in Brazil* (New Haven, 1992); Cumings, *The Origins of the Korean War*. Vol. 2 *The Roaring of the Cataract, 1947–1950* (Princeton, 1990); Pierpaoli, *Truman and Korea: The Political Culture of the Early Cold War* (Columbia, MO, 1999); Romero, *The United States and the European Trade Union Movement, 1944–1951* (Chapel Hill, 1992).
15. Hogan, "Revival and Reform"; idem, *The Marshall Plan*; Maier, "The Politics of Productivity: Foundations of American International Economic Policy after World War II," *International Organizations* 31 (Autumn 1977): 607–33; idem, "The Two Postwar Eras and the Conditions for Stability in Twentieth-Century Western Europe," *American Historical Review* 86 (April 1981): 327–52. See also the very interesting new work by Inderjeet Parmar, *Foundations of the American Century: The Ford, Carnegie, and Rockefeller Foundations in the Rise of American Power* (New York, 2012). Among other things, Parmar describes the important role these powerful foundations, and their collaborators in the corporate sector, played in combating interwar isolationism in favor of the liberal internationalism that came to dominate US foreign policy after World War II.
16. Painter, *Oil and the American Century*; and Hogan, *The Marshall Plan*.
17. Hogan, *A Cross of Iron: Harry S. Truman and the Origins of the National Security State, 1945–1954* (Cambridge, UK, and New York, 1998).
18. Painter, *Oil and the American Century*; Griffith, "Dwight D. Eisenhower and the Corporate Commonwealth"; Hogan, *The Marshall Plan*.
19. I am indebted to Nathan J. Citino for his insights into the literature on economic development and modernization in the Cold War. See Citino, "Modernization and Development," in Artemy M. Kalinovsky and Craig Daigle, (eds.), *The Routledge Handbook of the Cold War* (New York, 2014), 118–30.
20. David Ekbladh, *The Great American Mission: Modernization and the Construction of an American World Order* (Princeton and Oxford, 2010); and Mathew Jacobs, *Imagining the Middle East: The Building of an American Foreign Policy, 1918–1967* (Chapel Hill, 2011). For references to the interwar period and the Marshall Plan, see my own work noted elsewhere.
21. Ekbladh, *The Great American Mission*, 77–188.
22. The literature on development and modernization is both extensive and excellent. The following list is not intended to be comprehensive. Michael E. Latham, *Modernization as Ideology: American Social Science and "Nation Building" in the Kennedy Era* (Chapel Hill, 2000); Nils Gilman, *Mandarins of the Future: Modernization Theory in Cold War America* (Baltimore, 2009); David C. Engerman, *Modernization from the Other Shore: American Intellectuals and the Romance of Russian Development* (Cambridge, MA, 2004); Amy L. S. Staples, *The Birth of Development: How the World Bank, Food and Agricultural Organization, and the World Health Organization Have Changed the World, 1945–1965* (Kent, Ohio, 2006); Greg Brazinsky, *Nation Building in South Korea: Koreans, Americans, and the Making of Democracy* (Chapel Hill, 2007); Matthew Connelly, *Fatal Misconception: The Struggle to Control World Population* (Cambridge, MA, 2008); Bradley R. Simpson, *Economists with Guns: Authoritarian Development*

and *U.S.–Indonesian Relations, 1960–1968* (Stanford, 2008); Michael E. Latham, *The Right Kind of Revolution: Modernization, Development, and U.S. Foreign Policy from the Cold War to the Present* (Ithaca, 2010); Nick Cullather, *The Hungry World: America's Cold War Battle Against Poverty in Asia* (Cambridge, MA, 2010); Mary Brown Bullock, *The Oil Prince's Legacy: Rockefeller Philanthropy in China* (Washington, DC, and Stanford, CA, 2011); and Parmar, *Foundations of the American Century*. For a sampling of relevant articles, see: Daniel Maul, "'Help them Move the ILO Way': The International Labor Organization and the Modernization Discourse in the Era of Decolonization and the Cold War," *Diplomatic History*, Vol. 32, No. 3 (June 2009), 387–404; Erez Manela, "A Pox on Your Narrative: Writing Disease Control into Cold War History," *Diplomatic History*, Vol. 34, No. 2 (April 2010), 299–323; Thomas C. Field Jr., "Ideology as Strategy: Military-Led Modernization and the Origins of the Alliance for Progress in Bolivia," *Diplomatic History*, Vol. 36, No. 1 (January 2010), 147–83. See also, Citino, "Modernization and Development."

23. Ekbladh, *The Great American Mission*, 100–1, 108–9; and Simpson, *Economists with Guns*, 94–5. Simpson, in particular, draws heavily on the earlier work of Bruce Cumings and Thomas Ferguson cited in earlier endnotes.

24. For Ekbladh and Simpson, see the previous note. For the debates regarding the Marshall Plan and the national security state see my books on those subjects, also cited above.

25. There is some very important new work in this area that deserves mention here. See, Bruce Cumings, *Dominion from Sea to Sea: Pacific Ascendancy and American Power* (New Haven, CT, 2010); Mark S. Mizruchi, *The Fracturing of the American Corporate Elite* (Cambridge, MA, 2013); and Elizabeth Tandy Shermer, *Sunbelt Capitalism: Phoenix and the Transformation of American Politics* (Philadelphia, 2013).

26. Schmitter, "Still the Century of Corporatism?" *Review of Politics* 36 (January 1974): 85–131.

27. For the most thoughtful critiques, see John Lewis Gaddis, "The Corporatist Synthesis: A Skeptical View," *Diplomatic History* 10 (Fall 1986): 337–62; idem, "New Conceptual Approaches to the Study of American Foreign Relations: Interdisciplinary Perspectives," *Diplomatic History* 14 (Summer 1990): 405–23; and Leo Panitch, "Recent Theorizations of Corporatism: Reflections on a Growth Industry," *British Journal of Sociology* 31 (June 1980): 159–87. Critics have charged that corporatism is marked by conceptual fuzziness, that it ignores important discontinuities, and that historians have applied the model only to those topics, areas of the world, and periods suited to their purpose. To be sure, the past is prologue in a corporatist analysis, which stresses how historical forces limit the choices available to decision-makers and how change usually comes in evolutionary increments, not in dramatic watersheds. But if used properly, as the discussion of post-World War II diplomacy suggests, corporatism can highlight long-term patterns of policy without ignoring important innovations. Even critics admit that it has proven to be a remarkably fruitful mode of analysis as applied thus far. Further research should enlarge the subjects at its command and expand its chronological horizon.

28. Maier, *Recasting Bourgeois Europe*.

29. Maier, "American Visions and British Interests: Hogan's Marshall Plan," *Reviews in American History* 18 (March 1990): 102.
30. The remarkable influence of Williams' work, beginning with his classic study, *The Tragedy of American Diplomacy* (Cleveland, 1959), is evident in some of the works cited in this chapter, including besides my own work, the books by Michael Latham and Bradley Simpson. See also, among others, Jeremy Kuzmarov, *Modernizing Repression: Police Training and Nation-Building in the American Century* (Amerst, MA, 2012); and Curt Cardwell, *NSC-68 and the Political Economy of the Early Cold War* (New York, 2011). For C. Wright Mills, see his equally classic work, *The Power Elite* (New York, 1956).
31. Hogan, *A Cross of Iron*.

4

Explaining political economy

Brad Simpson

The study of political economy is a seriously neglected area of research and writing in the history of US foreign relations, and international history more generally. Political economy is the study of the relationships among business, state, and society as well as those between economics and international politics. Certain historians, broadly associated with the so-called Wisconsin School, have long focused on the economic dimensions of foreign policy, especially the quest for overseas markets.[1] But most ignore political economy except in the most general of terms – lumping the interests of firms or corporations, banks and the health of the world economy and the global financial system among the "considerations" entertained by policymakers alongside personal, bureaucratic, or geopolitical concerns. Those who have devoted attention to economic concerns largely confine their attention to the views of policymakers, rather than broader social and economic constituencies, or to more abstract conceptions of influence rather than to the economic power of particular actors.[2] In recent years, scholars have turned increasing attention to the role of race, gender, culture, and ideology in shaping the worldviews and policies of US officials, as well as the myriad ordinary Americans engaged with the wider world as non state actors. Yet an understanding of political economy remains essential to any narrative of US power, and to the wider world in which that power is constituted and exercised.

Given space constraints, this chapter will not offer a comprehensive theory of political economy, or suggest that there is a single road map for thinking and writing about it. Rather, we will survey some classic and some more recent works that can suggest how to more productively think, research, and write about the political economy of US foreign relations. Four interrelated dynamics are particularly important to consider: the structure of the world economy and the place of the United States in it; the role of manufacturing and extractive firms; banking and finance; and the relationship between business, state, and society.

THE WORLD ECONOMY

To understand the relationship between economics and US foreign policy, it is important to name the system – the wider field of forces in which US officials, corporations, and other actors operate. This system is a capitalist world system. The essential starting point for understanding its core features and functioning is Karl Polanyi's *The Great Transformation*.[3] In it Polanyi purports to explain the collapse of the nineteenth-century world economy, the rise of fascism and the coming of World War II, but really he is offering a theory of the relationship among states, markets, and what we now recognize as the world system. The nineteenth-century world economy, Polanyi argued, rested on a few key features – the balance of power system, the international gold standard, the self-regulating market, and the liberal state, "itself a creation of the self-regulating market."[4] The state, in Polanyi's view, mediated between domestic society and the world market, both facilitating the outward thrust of goods and capital and regulating or protecting domestic society and the national market from its unwanted consequences. The state can be "strong" or "weak" for either purpose – for example, strong for the purposes of facilitating market access or intervening abroad but weak for the purpose of regulating the domestic market. Polanyi's description is a very good first image for thinking about the state and its relationship to the domestic and world economy, as a site for conflict between contending political and economic forces, as a semi-permeable barrier, and as a set of institutions that both shape and are shaped by the world market.

The historical sociologist Immanuel Wallerstein, building on Polanyi's insights, reminds us that the capitalist world market is also a historical system, with an inherent tendency toward expansion and incorporation.[5] Within that system, which has evolved over the course of the last five centuries, Wallerstein posits a tripartite division of labor in which states, operating according to the principles of comparative advantage, inhabit zones marked by sharply differentiated functions: core (characterized by advanced production in leading sectors), semi-peripheral (commodity production, light manufacturing, labor-intensive industry), or peripheral functions (the hewers of wood and carriers of water). Wallerstein's "world systems theory" functioned as a rebuke to postwar modernization theory, with its developmental teleology of upward mobility converging on a liberal, capitalist future, offering in its place structural analysis of historical capitalism in which mobility was sharply limited. Occasionally, a single country will gain temporary industrial, commercial, financial, political, and military preponderance over its rivals and exercise hegemony. In the last two centuries there have been only two hegemons: Britain in the nineteenth century and the United States since 1945. Some scholars have usefully employed some of the insights of world-systems theory to describe American ascendance in the twentieth century and the liberal order-building quality of US leadership after World War II.[6]

Though the United States emerged from World War II in a position of unrivaled military power, this dominance rested on a preponderant position across the leading commercial, financial, and industrial sectors of the age: most importantly petroleum, but also automobiles, steel, chemicals, aerospace, international banking, pharmaceuticals, and electronics.[7] American hegemony, however, required more than mere structural power: it depended on the agency of policymakers and the many Americans who had begun to envision their own and the country's interests in global terms. Its particular character, moreover – a liberal, American-led economic and political order undergirded by a global system of military containment and intervention – was far from inevitable. Rather, the shape of American hegemony emerged as a result of conflict with an alternative, socialist world system (otherwise known as the Cold War) and the need to police the boundaries of disintegrating European empires and ensure the economic and political integration of newly independent states.[8]

Until its emergence as a global hegemon, however, many American elites viewed US economic and geopolitical interests in regional terms. Most businesses were content to romp around the continental United States – the world's largest domestic market – or aspired after hemispheric dominance, often in competition with European rivals.[9] Scholars of US–Latin American relations, drawing upon a long tradition of critical scholarship dating back to the 1940s, have often deployed dependency theory to explain these patterns of hemispheric dominance. Their structural critique illuminated the long history of Western intervention in the hemisphere, the power of US-based multinational corporations in the region, the unequal terms of trade, which left many countries dependent upon agriculture or the export of raw materials, and the privileged position of local comprador elites whose interests aligned more with their North American counterparts than with local populations.[10]

World systems and dependency theorists were among the first to de-center the Cold War as a lens for thinking about core features of US foreign policy, even as that conflict was shaping the views of generations of historians. Wallerstein, Frank, and others not only moved beyond realpolitik conceptions of US power, but also grounded their analysis of "hegemony" in the history and structure of the capitalist world economy in ways that remain relevant long after the Cold War. Structure, of course, is not explanation, and there remains the task of exploring local or small-scale phenomena in ways that acknowledge and relate to the world economy. We can, as one scholar suggests, "move from the aggregate account to a peasant seizing grain stocks and back again," utilizing theory flexibly and in "a constant dialogue between the evidence and [one's] assumptions and hypotheses."[11]

THINKING ABOUT FIRMS

Having named the system, we can begin to think about some of the actors whose power helps to constitute it: states, firms, non- and intergovernmental organizations, and various transnational flows and processes. Modern firms or corporations are particularly important actors, given their size and influence over both domestic and international politics. Though many foreign relations historians refer indirectly to "corporations" or to "business interests" as actors or influences on policymaking, even the best often fail to ask basic questions about the nature and behavior of firms, the industrial sectors to which they belong, and their policy preferences.[12] These policy preferences often extend beyond simple questions of labor and trade policy to encompass broad questions of national defense, foreign aid, and international order that may seem tangential to firms' narrow economic interests.[13] They may also include efforts to structure the international environment and policies within particular jurisdictions to achieve their own objectives, which – especially in the case of transnational corporations operating in many places at once – may align or conflict with those of the states in which they operate.

To see these processes at work we might start with the archetypal representative of mid-century US hegemony: the multinational oil firm; capital intensive, export oriented, at the leading edge of technology, and seeing the world market as its horizon.[14] One of the oldest accounts remains the best: John Blair's *The Control of Oil*, which expertly traces the emerging structure of the world oil industry in the twentieth century, and the cleavages that have divided firms (national versus international, integrated versus independent, crude long versus crude short) and oil-producing areas (high versus low extraction costs). Blair also illuminates the efforts of the major multinational firms to exercise control over supply and marketing through the exclusion of "outsiders," whose eventual entry into international markets in the 1960s facilitated the wave of nationalizations that followed.[15] When examined in the light of such basic industry features, negotiations over concession arrangements between oil companies and producer states often reveal a fascinating story of intra-sectoral and bureaucratic conflict that might otherwise remain hidden.[16] The desire of some Truman Administration officials to enforce anti-trust laws against Western oil companies operating in the Middle East, for example, was simultaneously an argument against the monopolistic position of the major multinationals and an argument in favor of allowing independents into the region.[17] In short, there was no single national interest with regards to Middle Eastern oil, but rather different visions promoted by national, independent, and multinational firms, each attempting to convince government officials of their respective merits, all couching their efforts in the name of anti-communism.

Firms are not states, and do not look at international politics in the same way as states or other non state actors. While their interests may coincide with states, they may also conflict, especially when there are important sectoral cleavages. It is important, then, to theorize how firms act, form their interests, and relate to state power. Political scientist Gregory Nowell has described a process of "transnational structuring" among early twentieth-century oil firms in which myriad local regulatory battles "constituted a world regulatory struggle, in which the oil companies sought to fit local regulation into the overarching strategy of an international cartel." His research suggests that historians cannot simply look at firm–state relations in one country but must think transnationally, seeking to understand the complex interaction among domestic and international firms and states across national borders.[18] Some scholars have used this "business conflict" model to explore how "international crises divide the business community and ... the resulting business rivalries cause rivalries among states." David Gibbs argues, for example, that intra-sectoral conflict among multinational mining firms shaped the conflicting responses of the United States and its European allies to the Katanga secession crisis that erupted in the Congo following its independence in 1960.[19]

Different industrial sectors, moreover, have different needs and characteristics, and these in turn shape their "foreign policies" and the way they interact with states. Foreign relations historians can take some cues from the vibrant recent literature on commodities and commodity chains – the backwards and forward linkages that connect producers of cotton, sugar, rubber, and other commodities with consumers in other parts of the world.[20] The global apparel and shoe giant Nike, as Walter LaFeber shows, has since its creation functioned as a marketing shell, subcontracting out the assembly of its branded products to local firms in East and Southeast Asia. As a result, Nike became both a participant and the subject of debates about human rights, labor rights, and trade preferences in the Asian nations in which it operated.[21] Service firms or those engaged in cultural production, on the other hand, have different characteristics and needs than those engaged in manufacturing.[22] Industries closely associated with state power, such as weapons and aerospace manufacturing or strategic communications, have their own dual logic – responding to market incentives while subject to the jealous gaze of governments eager to keep disruptive technologies out of the hands of rival states. Kate Epstein's history of the torpedo in the early twentieth century deftly illustrates the shifting landscape of weapons design and manufacturing at a time when states were beginning to rely on private firms to absorb the risk of research and development, creating myriad potential conflicts of interest between them.[23]

Corporations, of course, produce not only goods and services but also labor regimes, which can also fruitfully be examined in a transnational context. Robert Vitalis' pioneering work on the oil company Aramco reveals not only the crucial role of the company in the state-building process in Saudi Arabia but its "importation" of a Jim Crow regime of labor control from mining camps in Mexico and the American Southwest, practices which differed markedly from those of its European rivals.[24] Aramco's operations revealed not only how it pushed for company-friendly policies in both Saudi Arabia and the United States, but how its daily operations helped to constitute regimes of labor, race, and gender relations. Historians have shown how similar processes unfold in the agricultural sector,[25] but have produced few studies on the political economy of mining, timber, and other extractive industries, much less critically analyzed how these extractive sectors and the firms within them shape US foreign relations.[26]

Jefferson Cowie's *Capital Moves*, a history of the electronics firm RCA and its migration from Camden to Memphis and eventually Mexico, integrates all of these levels of analysis, deftly moving back and forth between the global interests of the firm and the local labor relations it produced. Cowie vividly illustrates the rapidly shifting characteristics of the global consumer electronics industry, the ways that technological advances compressed product cycles, RCA's ceaseless search for lower wage labor, and the impact of its operations on workers, gender relations, and local communities in both the United States and Mexico.[27] The hollowing out of old industrial centers in the Northeast and Midwest and the emergence of new nodes of innovation elsewhere, in classic Schumpeterian waves of creative destruction, as well as the proliferation of export-processing zones and other novel means of organizing production, suggests that the nation-state might not be the most fruitful unit of analysis for understanding the workings of the world system. Rather, scholars of political economy should consider the importance of regional differences – core, peripheral, and semi-peripheral zones – within states and not merely those between them.[28]

Researching and writing about firms and foreign policy poses both interpretive and methodological challenges. Firms are not required to keep archives or open them to historians, and the stories companies tell about themselves are usually triumphalist and exceptionalist. Historians must therefore often work around access problems by reading (and reading against the grain) personal papers, company histories, records of business groups, trade publications, and government records concerning the domestic and foreign operations of firms, employing or building theory to explain their significance.[29]

FINANCE AND BANKING

If the capitalist world economy is the structure, and firms among its most important actors, banking and finance are the lubricants that help the system to function. Understanding the political economy of US foreign relations, therefore, means grappling with the structure and operations of the global financial system that the United States has helped to construct, and in which US power is deeply embedded.[30] Unfortunately, international and foreign relations historians have paid inadequate attention to the role of money, banks, bankers, and the global financial system in constituting US power.[31] Researching and writing about bankers and financiers requires looking at the world through their eyes and asking questions of importance to them. How do currency values, interest rates, and inflation affect the relative position of the dollar overseas? What are the most effective mechanisms for insuring the provision of credit abroad and the payment of debt? What role should the government play in mitigating risk or regulating the operations of domestic and international banks? Although historians have produced a handful of studies on government institutions such as the Export-Import Bank and a range of works on the World Bank and International Monetary Fund, *Diplomatic History* has yet to publish a single article on the operations of a private US bank abroad or on the banking career of one of the many officials – such as J.P. Morgan, Averell Harriman, or Douglas Dillon – who played key roles in the formation of twentieth-century US foreign policy.[32] The dearth of studies on these questions surely stems in part from the difficulty of researching them, with scholars forced to rely on personal papers, financial reporting, government records, and, on occasion, the records of international or intergovernmental organizations.

The rise of the United States to global power in the late nineteenth and early twentieth century, however, was inextricably linked to the increasing US need for foreign capital, the overseas operations of US banks, and the growing prominence of the dollar.[33] When American manufacturers began seeking profitable outlets abroad in the late nineteenth century, officials and bankers became increasingly concerned with the role of the dollar in international politics. As Emily Rosenberg and Cyrus Veeser have demonstrated, the advent of dollar diplomacy, a period of forceful US intervention in Central and Latin America, also reflected shifts in the political economy of American overseas investment, as multinational firms committed to a more corporatist vision displaced smaller, more traditional firms, which relied on personal connections and believed in laissez-faire.[34]

The growing prominence of the dollar and US investment capital overseas were closely linked to the gradual unraveling of the gold standard and, by extension, the decline of British sterling, as the reserve currency of global finance. For Polanyi, the gold standard was the lynchpin for the nineteenth-century world economy: lubricating long-distance trade, facilitating currency convertibility, and serving as one of the "powerful moderators of international conflict" before World War I. The United States industrialized in the shadow of the gold standard; its banks alternately cooperating and competing with rival British institutions in the 1920s to manage global finance, going so far as to create the Bank for International Settlements in 1929–30. As Americans seized the mantle of hegemony from Great Britain in the 1940s, US officials, such as Secretary of State Dean Acheson, viewed the British experience with the gold standard as a model for postwar policymaking.[35]

World War I marked a profound shift, as the US emergence as a creditor nation and New York's postwar rise as a global banking and financial center gave American officials, as well as commercial banks with overseas operations and investments, increasing reason to concern themselves with the health of the global financial system and the position of the dollar within it. But this concern, as Charles Kindleberger showed in his classic analysis of the coming of the Great Depression, did not yet extend to a desire to displace Britain as the banker of last resort in times of global financial crisis. When the Roosevelt Administration abandoned the gold standard in 1933, "the snapping of the golden thread was the signal for a world revolution," marking the end of the nineteenth-century world economy without suggesting what might replace it.[36] A dozen years later, US officials took the lead in creating the Bretton Woods system, establishing a modified gold standard and placing the dollar at the center of world trade and finance, a position it has occupied more or less ever since, even after the collapse of Bretton Woods in 1973 and the establishment of the era of free-floating exchange rates.[37]

BUSINESS, THE STATE, POLITICS, AND SOCIETY

Once we understand the system and its key actors we can piece together the whole by connecting firms and sectors to the political system and the process of policy formation. In order, in turn, to link business to policy currents, we must identify the social and economic constituencies for enduring political coalitions. A crucial starting point for such efforts remains the work of Thomas Ferguson, who developed a theory of industrial structure and party competition to explain the emergence of stable party systems in modern American politics. Political parties, he suggested, appeal not primarily to voters but to the investor blocs that fund them and have the financial and informational resources to contest the political process, often focusing on tax, trade, labor, and foreign policy questions unknown to ordinary voters, but of great interest to particular firms and industrial sectors. The New Deal coalition of Franklin Roosevelt, Ferguson demonstrated, rested not only on the mobilization of women, African American, and working-class voters, but also on a "multinational bloc" of high-tech, capital-intensive, multinationally oriented, and globally competitive corporations, banks, and law firms.[38] The "multinational bloc" provided a crucial domestic constituency not only for the New Deal (given that its members could accommodate welfarist labor and social policies) but also for the corporatist foreign policies of the Truman Administration and later, for the trade expansion policies of the Kennedy Administration.[39] It also undergirded the "politics of productivity" and commitment to steady economic growth that Charles Maier has identified as the midpoint around which policymakers oscillated in the postwar period. In other words, changing definitions of those hoariest of chestnuts – the "national interest" and "national security" – reflect not just the pulling and hauling of political parties and bureaucratic factions but the concrete interests of the firms and sectors that help to give them shape.[40]

A political economy perspective offers particular insight into the hegemonic concerns of such US officials of the postwar period as Secretary of State Dean Acheson, who advanced an increasingly global conception of US national security and the reconstruction of an open world economy upon which that security rested. Curt Cardwell suggests that the dramatic expansion of the national security state envisioned by NSC-68 had less to do with the containment of communism abroad than with the maintenance of US domestic prosperity, a nagging "dollar gap," and the health of the world economy.[41] Such concerns also help to explain the reversal of the initially progressive US occupation of Japan and the Truman Administration's decision to seek Japan's re-integration with the raw materials producing areas of Southeast Asia, including Vietnam.[42]

Wartime rearmament and economic mobilization during World War II and the creation of a national security state after 1950 profoundly transformed the domestic political economy. The exponential increase in hydroelectric power, naval and aerospace construction (and later, the computer revolution) rapidly industrialized the American West and Southwest, shifting the center of the nation's gravity and economic dynamism from the East to West coast and creating the domestic constituency for the quadrupling of military spending envisioned in NSC-68.[43] The symbiotic relationship between the emergence of a national security state and private industry, however, did not guarantee the absence of conflict between US officials and agencies and the private corporations who depended upon their largesse. The aerospace industry's efforts to enlarge its global market share, for example, often conflicted with US efforts to preserve close relations with its European allies, a dynamic repeated across other industrial sectors.[44]

The politico-economic coalition for American hegemony remained reasonably stable until the late 1960s, when a series of global political and financial crises and the changing fortunes of US manufacturing reshuffled the calculations of major investor blocs (turning the US auto and steel industries against free trade virtually overnight, among other examples) and with it, the political coalitions of the Republican and Democratic parties.[45] The gradual defection of key sectors of elite public opinion against the Vietnam War in the late 1960s reflected not only disillusionment with the Johnson Administration's rosy predictions of success, but also the inflationary impact of US military spending, which undercut foreign confidence in the dollar and provoked a run on gold in 1968. These setbacks convinced internationalists that the war was threatening the foundations of US global power, and began the gradual unraveling of the Bretton Woods system.[46]

The literature on development and modernization offers one window into this process, as well as a means to explore business–state relations and the political economy of contending developmental visions. Historians have produced a torrent of work on economic development and the politics of modernization, but far less on the political economy of development and of the role and interest of particular firms and industrial sectors in particular visions of development.[47] David Ekbladh, among others, has shown how US officials and businessmen promoted hydroelectric power as a high modernist vision of development.[48] But we know comparatively little about the private firms engaged in the construction of the American century overseas, or about the development policies supported by specific manufacturing, extractive or financial firms.[49] The persistence of public–private partnerships in military contracting, US development assistance, and other core functions of the US state in the twentieth century, and their increasing privatization in the twenty-first, attest to the enduring importance of understanding these dynamics.[50]

The work of Bruce Cumings shows how these complex pieces fit together.[51] His description of the "nationalist" and "internationalist" currents of US foreign policy during the early Cold War, and the social forces that undergirded them, remains the single best scholarly statement we have on the economic constituencies for policymaking. The nationalist and "rollback" policy currents, which enjoyed their brief flowering during the Korean War (and revived unexpectedly after 2001), Cumings shows, represented not only a unilateral vision of US national security interests but also the material interests of discrete firms and industrial sectors, in particular mining, engaged with US policy in East and Southeast Asia.

Cumings has also explored the political economy of West Coast industrialization as a consequence of the rise of the United States as a Pacific power, and the dramatic expansion of that power during World War II.[52] During this period, he notes, the state "took on a central role remaking the industrial and infrastructural face of the United States," creating or underwriting a host of high-technology firms under effective state protection that transformed the region while simultaneously becoming world leaders in their respective sectors: Kaiser, General Motors, Alcoa, Boeing, Douglas, General Electric, and Bechtel, among many others. Cities such as San Diego, Los Angeles, and Seattle industrialized virtually overnight. After the war, the West Coast and Pacific Northwest emerged as the most dynamic region of the United States: socially progressive, economically advanced, dependent upon government spending, and deeply committed to an expansive vision of the American state and US global interests. The region's representatives in Washington, meanwhile, forged an unshakeable, bipartisan consensus in favor of the national security state and the vastly expanded military spending upon which their residents depended for prosperity.[53] A political economy approach here reveals something that might otherwise seem contradictory – why both Democrats and Republicans, liberals and conservatives, remained committed to huge increases in peacetime military spending and vastly expanded government power in foreign affairs, a stance otherwise wholly at odds with American political tradition.

My own work on US–Indonesian relations during the 1960s utilized, on a smaller scale, a political economy approach to explore the novel political and economic coalition that emerged in support of an authoritarian government in Indonesia after 1965. To do so I sought to connect the developmental vision embraced by the Lyndon Johnson administration and the Suharto regime with the particular firms that returned to Indonesia following General Suharto's ascension to power in 1966. Unlike the Kennedy administration, which promoted a comprehensive modernization program for Indonesia, President

Johnson embraced a pared down scheme of military training, technical assistance, and balance of payments credits, channeled through a military–technocratic alliance in Jakarta. But identifying the bureaucratic alliances behind a particular policy is reasonably simple. How does one identify the social and economic constituency for the military-modernizing vision embraced in both Washington and Jakarta after 1965? Working through the commodities and industry files of the US Embassy in Jakarta, I discovered that the US firms that first returned to Indonesia in 1966 and 1967 were small or medium-size companies involved in raw materials extraction and production: mining, timber, independent oil, chemical, and fertilizer companies, and the banks that financed them.[54] These were firms historically tied to the nationalist/expansionist current of US foreign policy and to the right wing of the Republican Party. They can usefully be compared with the internationalist, world competitive firms, which dominated the Indonesian market before 1965: companies such as Stanvac and Caltex; Goodyear; Morrison Knudson; Singer Sewing Machine, Westinghouse, General Motors, and Union Carbide.

At the same time, such small and medium-size firms appealed to political constituencies in Indonesia, especially the armed forces, which sought to build up national industries in the extractive sector through so-called production-sharing agreements balked at by larger companies (such as the multinational oil companies, which had previously dominated the Indonesian market).[55] The support in Washington and Jakarta for a program of military-led modernization reflected not only the pulling and hauling of bureaucratic forces but also the interests of social and economic constituencies with a stake in the outcome. Simply noting that many Indonesians and Americans backed a military dictatorship in Jakarta after 1965, as many historians have done, tells us nothing about why particular firms and actors supported more expansive programs of foreign aid for Indonesia and why others did not; why at certain times and in certain economic sectors and not others.[56] Development, in other words, has its own political economy, and accounts that stress its ideological or political dimensions may do more to obscure than reveal the larger social and economic forces at work.

These thumbnail sketches can do no more than outline a methodological approach that takes political economy seriously. But there is much methodological and interpretive food for thought in the literature cited in this chapter. Collectively, they take the world economy as their starting point, are open to the agency of ordinary people and the contingency of unanticipated events, and excavate the role of both the state and particular firms and sectors in the creation of a novel and dynamic political economy. As William Appleman Williams attempted to do more than fifty years ago in *The Tragedy of American Diplomacy*, this scholarship helps to explain the peculiar nature of American hegemony, and to place the Cold War in its proper perspective. As the Cold War – a conflict that shaped generations of scholarship – recedes into memory, with hundreds of US bases still girdling the globe and no genuine realpolitik threats to American power in sight, such perspectives are more needed than ever. The United States has been a constitutive presence in the modern world economy, helping to shape and in turn being shaped by dynamics that simultaneously enable and constrain the power of the state and social forces within it. Scholars seeking to fully understand the nature of US power in the world must both understand and grapple with these dynamics.

NOTES

1. William Appleman Williams, *The Tragedy of American Diplomacy* (New York, 2009); See also Lloyd C. Gardner, *Economic Aspects of New Deal Diplomacy* (Boston, 1964); Thomas McCormick, *America's Half-Century: United States Foreign Policy in the Cold War and After* (Baltimore, 1995); Joyce and Gabriel Kolko, *The Limits of Power* (New York, 1977); Michael J. Hogan, *Informal Entente: The Private Structure of Cooperation in Anglo-American Economic Diplomacy, 1918–1928* (Columbia, MO, 1977); Emily Rosenberg, *Spreading the American Dream: American Economic and Cultural Expansion, 1890–1945* (New York, 1982).
2. Diane B. Kunz, "When Money Counts and Doesn't: Economic Power and Diplomatic Objectives," *Diplomatic History* 18:4 (1994): 451–62; Volker R. Berghahn, "The Debate on 'Americanization' among Economic and Cultural Historians," *Cold War History* 10:1 (2010): 107–30; Jr, Alfred Eckes and Thomas Zeiler, *Globalization and the American Century* (Cambridge, 2003).
3. Karl Polanyi, *The Great Transformation: The Political and Economic Origins of Our Time* (Boston, 2001).
4. Polanyi, *The Great Transformation*, 24.
5. See Immanuel Wallerstein, *World-Systems Analysis: An Introduction* (Durham, 2004).
6. Michael Hunt, *American Ascendancy* (Chapel Hill, 2008).
7. On the centrality of oil to US industrial structure, see David Painter, "Oil and the American Century," *Journal of American History* 99:1 (June 1, 2012): 24–39.
8. Robert Latham, *The Liberal Moment* (New York, 1997); Herman Schwartz, *States Versus Markets: The Emergence of a Global Economy* (New York, 2010), pp. 177–98.
9. On the nineteenth century see Drew McCoy, *The Elusive Republic: Political Economy in Jeffersonian America* (Chapel Hill, 1996); Thomas Hietala, *Manifest Design: American Exceptionalism and Empire* (Ithaca, 2002); Walter LaFeber, *The New Empire: An Interpretation of American Expansion 1860–1898* (Ithaca, 1998); Thomas Schoonover, *Uncle Sam's War of 1898 and the Origins of Globalization* (Lexington, Kentucky, 2005).
10. The classic statement is Andre Gunder Frank, *Capitalism and Underdevelopment in Latin America: Historical Studies of Chile and Brazil* (New York, 1967); Louis Perez "Dependency," in Michael Hogan and Thomas Paterson (eds.) *Explaining the History of American Foreign Relations* 2nd edn. (Cambridge, 2004), 162–75; Walter LaFeber *Inevitable Revolutions: The United States in Central America* (New York, 1993).

11. Bruce Cumings, *The Origins of the Korean War, Vol. II, The Roaring of the Cataract, 1947–1950* (Princeton, 1991), 10.
12. George Herring's *From Colony to Superpower: U.S. Foreign Relations Since 1776* (New York, 2011), 390, 447, 449.
13. James Kurth, "The Political Consequences of the Product Cycle: Industrial History and Political Outcomes," *International Organization* 33:1 (1979): 1–34; Jeffry Frieden, "The Economics of Intervention: American Overseas Investments and Relations with Underdeveloped Areas, 1890–1950," *Comparative Studies in Society and History* 31:1 (1989): 55–80; Mira Wilkins, *The Maturing of Multinational Enterprise: American Business Abroad from 1914 to 1970* (Cambridge, 1974).
14. David Painter, *Oil and the American Century* (Baltimore, 1986); Simon Bromley, *American Hegemony and World Oil: The Industry, the State System, and the World Economy* (University Park, PA, 1991); Joseph Pratt, "Exxon and the Control of Oil," *Journal of American History* 99:1 (2012): 145–54; Nathan Citino, *From Arab Nationalism to OPEC, Second Edition: Eisenhower, King Sa'ud, and the Making of U.S.-Saudi Relations* (Bloomington, 2010).
15. John Blair, *The Control of Oil* (New York, 1978); see also Edith Penrose, *The Large International Firm in Developing Countries: The International Petroleum Industry* (London, 1968).
16. For an example see Bradley Simpson, *Economists with Guns: Authoritarian Development and US-Indonesian Relations, 1960–1968* (Palo Alto, 2008), 99–109, 233–6.
17. Blair, 77.
18. Gregory Nowell, *Mercantile States and the World Oil Cartel* (Ithaca, 1994), 197–8; Wyatt Wells, *Antitrust and the Formation of the Postwar World* (New York, 2002); for a domestic analogue, see George Gonzalez, *Corporate Power and the Environment: The Political Economy of U.S. Environmental Policy* (Lanham, MD, 2001); Jr, Alfred D. Chandler and Bruce Mazlish, *Leviathans: Multinational Corporations and the New Global History* (Cambridge, 2005), especially pp. 19–45.
19. David Gibbs, *The Political Economy of Third World Intervention: Mines Money and US Policy in the Congo Crisis* (Chicago, 1991), 197.
20. Sidny Mintz, *Sweetness and Power: The Place of Sugar in Modern History* (New York, 1986); Sven Beckert, "Cotton: A Global History," in Jerry H. Bentley et al. (eds.) *Interactions: Transregional Perspectives on World History* (New York, 2005), 48–63; Stephen Topic et al., *From Silver to Cocaine: Latin American Commodity Chains and the Building of the World Economy, 1500–2000* (Durham, 2006).
21. Walter LaFeber, *Michael Jordan and the New Global Capitalism* (New York, 2002).
22. John Trumpbour, *Selling Hollywood to the World: U.S. and European Struggles for Mastery of the Global Film Industry, 1920–1950* (New York, 2002); Jenifer Van Vleck, *Empire of the Air: Aviation and the American Ascendancy* (Cambridge, 2013).
23. Jonathan Reed Winkler, *Nexus: Strategic Communications and American Security in World War I* (Cambridge, 2008); Katherine C. Epstein, *Torpedo: Inventing the*

Explaining political economy

Military-Industrial Complex in the United States and Great Britain (Cambridge, 2013).
24. Robert Vitalis, *America's Kingdom: Mythmaking on the Saudi Oil Frontier* (London, 2009).
25. Bill Winders and James C. Scott, *The Politics of Food Supply: U.S. Agricultural Policy in the World Economy* (New Haven, 2012); Jason Colby, *The Business of Empire: United Fruit, Race, and U.S. Expansion in Central America* (Ithaca, 2013).
26. For partial exceptions, see Glenn Dorn, "Pushing Tin: U.S.–Bolivian Relations and the Coming of the National Revolution," *Diplomatic History* 35:2 (2011): 203–28; Andrew Erdmann, "Mining for the Corporatist Synthesis: Gold in American Foreign Economic Policy, 1931–1936," *Diplomatic History* 17:2 (1993): 171–200; Kevin Danaher, *The Political Economy of U.S. Policy toward South Africa* (Boulder, 1985).
27. Jefferson Cowie, *Capital Moves: RCA's Seventy-Year Quest for Cheap Labor* (New York, 2001); Kari Frederickson performs similar analytical work on the Savannah River Plant scientific and industrial complex. See Frederickson, *Cold War Dixie: Militarization and Modernization in the American South* (Athens, GA, 2013).
28. Daniel S. Margolies, *Henry Watterson and the New South: The Politics of Empire, Free Trade, and Globalization.* (Lexington, 2011); On the importance of regionalism, see Peter Trubowitz, *Defining the National Interest: Conflict and Change in American Foreign Policy* (Chicago, 1998), especially pp. 109–69.
29. Ronald Cox, ed., *Business and The State in International Relations* (Boulder, 1997); Geoffrey Jones and Jonathan Zeitlin, *The Oxford Handbook of Business History* (New York, 2010), 179–319.
30. Schwartz, *States vs. Markets*; Barry Eichengreen, *Globalizing Capital: A History of the International Monetary System*; Sam Gindin and Leo Panitch, *The Making of Global Capitalism: The Political Economy of American Empire* (London, 2013).
31. Journalists have produced some of the few synthetic accounts. See Ron Chernow, *The House of Morgan: An American Banking Dynasty and the Rise of Modern Finance* (New York, 2010); Liaquat Ahamed, *Lords of Finance: The Bankers Who Broke the World* (New York, 2009); Nomi Prins, *All the Presidents' Bankers: The Hidden Alliances That Drive American Power* (New York, 2014); among historians, see Frank Costigliola, *Awkward Dominion: American Political, Economic, and Cultural Relations with Europe, 1919–1933* (Ithaca, 1988); Kathleen Burk, "Finance, Foreign Policy and the Anglo-American Bank: The House of Morgan, 1900–31," *Historical Research* 61:145 (1988): 199–211; H.W. Brands, *The Money Men: Capitalism, Democracy, and the Hundred Years' War Over the American Dollar* (New York, 2007).
32. William Becker and William McClenahan, Jr., *The Market, the State, and the Export-Import Bank of the United States, 1934–2000* (Cambridge, 2003); Michele Alacevich, *The Political Economy of the World Bank: The Early Years* (Palo Alto, 2009); Patrick Sharma, "The United States, the World Bank, and the Challenges of International Development in the 1970s," *Diplomatic History* 37:3 (2013): 572–604; Alan Dobson, "The Export-Import Bank and U.S. Foreign Economic Relations," *Diplomatic History* 29:2 (2005): 375–8.
33. Jay Sexton, *Debtor Diplomacy: Finance and American Foreign Relations in the Civil War Era 1837–1873* (London, 2014).

34. Cyrus Veeser, *A World Safe for Capitalism: Dollar Diplomacy and America's Rise to Global Power* (New York, 2007); Emily S. Rosenberg, *Financial Missionaries to the World: The Politics and Culture of Dollar Diplomacy, 1900–1930* (Durham, 2004).
35. Bryan, Steven, *The Gold Standard at the Turn of the Twentieth Century: Rising Powers, Global Money, and the Age of Empire* (New York, 2010); On the Bank for International Settlements, see Frank Costigliola, "The Other Side of Isolationism: The Establishment of the First World Bank, 1929–1930," *The Journal of American History*, 59 (December 1972): 602–20.
36. Charles P. Kindleberger, J. Bradford DeLong, and Barry Eichengreen, *The World in Depression, 1929–1939* (Berkeley, 2013); Andrew Erdmann, "Mining for the Corporatist Synthesis: Gold in American Foreign Economic Policy, 1931–1936," *Diplomatic History* 17:2 (1993): 171–200; Karl Polanyi, *The Great Transformation*, 26; Block, Fred, *The Origins of International Economic Disorder: A Study of United States International Monetary Policy from World War II to the Present* (Berkeley, 1978), pp. 12–32;
37. Eric Helleiner, *Forgotten Foundations of Bretton Woods: International Development and the Making of the Postwar Order* (Ithaca, 2014); Eric Helleiner, *States and the Reemergence of Global Finance: From Bretton Woods to the 1990s* (Ithaca, 1996); William Glenn Gray, "Floating the System: Germany, the United States, and the Breakdown of Bretton Woods, 1969–1973," *Diplomatic History* 31:2 (2007): 295–323.
38. Thomas Ferguson, "From Normalcy to New Deal: Industrial Structure, Party Competition, and American Public Policy in the Great Depression," *International Organization* 38:1 (1984): 41–94; also important is Jeffry Frieden, "Sectoral Conflict and Foreign Economic Policy, 1914–1940," *International Organization* 42:1 (1988): 59–90.
39. Michael Hogan, *The Marshall Plan: America, Britain and the Reconstruction of Western Europe, 1947–1952* (Cambridge, 1989), 1–26; Robert Latham, *The Liberal Moment: Modernity, Security, and the Making of Postwar International Order* (New York, 1997).
40. Charles Maier, "The Politics of Productivity: Foundations of American International Economic Policy after World War II," *International Organization* 31:4 (1977): 607–33; Charles S. Maier, *In Search of Stability: Explorations in Historical Political Economy* (New York, 1987).
41. Curt Caldwell, *NSC 68 and the Political Economy of the Early Cold War* (New York, 2011); Michael J. Hogan, *A Cross of Iron: Harry S. Truman and the Origins of the National Security State, 1945–1954* (Cambridge, 1998), esp. 69–119, 209–65.
42. William Borden, *The Pacific Alliance: United States Foreign Economic Policy and Japanese Trade Recovery, 1947–1955* (Madison, 1984); Michael Schaller, *The American Occupation of Japan: The Origins of the Cold War in Asia* (New York, 1987); Andrew J. Rotter, *The Path to Vietnam: Origins of the American Commitment to Southeast Asia* (Ithaca, 1989).
43. Ann Markusen, Peter Hall, Scott Campbell, and Sabina Deitrick, *The Rise of the Gunbelt: The Military Remapping of Industrial America* (New York, 1991).
44. Giles Scott-Smith and David J. Snyder, "'A Test of Sentiments': Civil Aviation, Alliance Politics, and the KLM Challenge in Dutch-American Relations,"

Diplomatic History 37:5 (2013): 917–45; Jeffrey Engel, *Cold War at 30,000 Feet: The Anglo-American Fight for Aviation Supremacy* (Cambridge, 2007).

45. Thomas Ferguson, "From Normalcy to New Deal: Industrial Structure, Party Competition, and American Public Policy in the Great Depression," *International Organization* 38:1 (1984): 41–94; Bruce Cumings, "The Origins and Development of the Northeast Asian Political Economy: Industrial Sectors, Product Cycles, and Political Consequences," *International Organization* 38:1 (1984), 1–40.

46. Robert M. Collins, "The Economic Crisis of 1968 and the Waning of the 'American Century'," *The American Historical Review* 101:2 (1996): 396–422; Diane Kunz, "The American Economic Consequences of 1968," in Carole Fink, Philipp Gassert, Detlef Junker, and German Historical Institute, *1968:The World Transformed* (Cambridge, 1998), 83–111; See also Daniel Sargent, "The Cold War and the International Political Economy in the 1970s," *Cold War History* 13:3 (2013): 393–425; David Spiro, *The Hidden Hand of American Hegemony: Petrodollar Recycling and International Markets* (Ithaca, 1999).

47. A notable recent attempt is Guy Laron, *Origins of the Suez Crisis: Postwar Development Diplomacy and the Struggle over Third World Industrialization, 1945–1956* (Baltimore, 2013).

48. Amy Staples, *The Birth of Development: How the World Bank, Food And Agriculture Organization, And World Health Organization Have Changed the World 1945–1965* (Kent, OH, 2006); David Ekbladh, "Mr. TVA: 'Grass Roots' Development, David Lilienthal, and the Rise and Fall of the Tennessee Valley Authority as a Symbol for U.S. Overseas Development, 1933–1973," *Diplomatic History* 26:2 (2002): 335–74.

49. For an important exception see James M. Carter, *Inventing Vietnam: The United States and State Building, 1954–1968* (New York, 2008).

50. Peter Singer, *Corporate Warriors: The Rise of the Privatized Military Industry*, Updated Edition (Ithaca, 2007); Jeremy Scahill, *Blackwater: The Rise of the World's Most Powerful Mercenary Army* (New York, 2008).

51. Bruce Cumings, *The Origins of the Korean War, Vol. II, The Roaring of the Cataract, 1947–1950* (Princeton, 1991), 1–185; Cumings, "Archaeology, Descent, Emergence: Japan in American Hegemony, 1900–1950,"*Parallax Visions: Making Sense of American–East Asian Relations at the End of the Century* (Durham, 1999), 1–33; "'Revising Postrevisionism': Or, The Poverty of Theory in Diplomatic History," *Diplomatic History,* 17:4 (1993), 539–70.

52. Bruce Cumings, *Dominion from Sea to Sea: Pacific Ascendancy and American Power* (New Haven, 2010).

53. Cumings, *Dominion from Sea to Sea*, 300–40.

54. Simpson, *Economists with Guns*, 244.

55. Simpson, *Economists with Guns*, 232.

56. See, for example, H.W. Brands, "The Limits of Manipulation: How the US Didn't Topple Sukarno," *The Journal of American History* 76 (1989): 785–808.

5

Diplomatic history after the big bang: using computational methods to explore the infinite archive

David Allen and Matthew Connelly[*]

When the first edition of *Explaining the History of American Foreign Relations* was published in 1991, it would have been hard to explain to readers why historians would soon find computers indispensable for doing their research.[1] Apple's first laptop, the "PowerBook 100," went on sale that year with a 20MB hard drive, and it cost over $4000 in today's dollars. No digital cameras were available on the consumer market. The World Wide Web was only just emerging, mainly to facilitate communication among scientists. Library catalog terminals were difficult to use, and scholarly article databases still lay far in the future.

Now it is hard to imagine writing a book without word processing software and an internet connection. Whereas the contributors to that first edition a quarter century ago would have had to spend many hours at the library just to find book reviews and check citations, these tasks are done today with a few mouse clicks. Historians now take thousands of photographs in a single archival visit, collecting gigabytes of digitized documents. We are organizing them as text-searchable pdfs in annotated, cloud-based databases, a practice that would have filled previous generations of scholars with wonder.

Remarkable though they are, these are still just technical improvements on time-honored historical tradecraft. The keyboard and screen take the role of the typewriter, databases substitute for filing cabinets and card catalogs, and track changes replace sticky notes. But the advent of digital media and recent advances in information technology portend much more dramatic changes in the very nature of our field, as is already happening in law, journalism, and literary studies. We will soon face an avalanche of electronic records, far too many to cope with using traditional methods.

This chapter describes how scholars might use computational techniques to cope with what William McAllister has called the "Big Bang" in historical source materials. This explosion began with the sudden release of a quarter of a million cables by Wikileaks; a "data dump" now dwarfed by the 2.7 million electronic records available from the State Department's Central Foreign Policy Files (CFPF), spanning the years 1973–8. Even this pales in comparison with what is being created by newer forms of communication, such as the forty million emails generated by Bill Clinton's White House, and the two *billion* emails produced *per year* by Hillary Clinton's State Department.[2]

The digital archive is potentially infinite, as William Turkel notes, but archivists have already had to conduct triage with the relatively small collections of electronic records from the 1970s.[3] They lack the resources to cope with the much greater challenges to come in preservation, declassification, and curation, raising the question of whether archival integrity and proper finding aids will become a thing of the past. Official commissions have repeatedly called for the development of new technology to accelerate the processing of large collections, without resort to crude sampling methods or mass deletion.[4] The federal government has been slow to respond.

The risks in this new era of "big data" are therefore great, but so too are the opportunities. Applying computational methods to vast corpora of electronic records is not only essential to preserve meaningful access to the archival record. It may also begin to provide precise answers to previously intractable historical questions. In turn, it might prompt entirely new kinds of inquiries, once we can start to visualize the flow of information through the diplomatic bureaucracy in novel ways. All this may require fundamental changes in the practice of history. We may have to learn programming languages in addition to foreign languages, make our "data" available to other researchers, and form multi-disciplinary teams to conduct experiments.

Our field is unusually rich in documents, most of them in the public domain and many already available in digital form. Historians of American foreign relations therefore have a unique opportunity to lead the way, developing methods and standards that other scholars will learn from when Facebook and Twitter become the archives of social and cultural history. Reviewing previous attempts to apply computational methods to history reveals many potential pitfalls, whether neglecting older but still important questions and sources, raising false expectations of objectivity, or drawing younger scholars into what may turn out to be methodological dead-ends. Even so, perhaps the greatest risk of all would be not to rethink how we approach archival research when the archive itself is about to explode.

COMPUTATIONAL METHODS 1.0 AND 2.0: FROM CLIOMETRICS TO THE DIGITAL HUMANITIES

Great claims about the potential of statistics and computers in historical research are not new. As long ago as Frederick Jackson Turner there were calls for a quantitative political history, focusing on roll-call voting and election returns, which came of age in the mid-twentieth century in the work of William Aydelotte and others.[5] In the 1950s, social science historians used punch cards and sorters to study urban, demographic, and African-American history. By the 1960s, a growing interest in quantitative and statistical history had spread across the field.[6] Economic historians started to call sources "data" and analyze them with innovative modeling techniques, dubbing themselves cliometricians.[7] Across the Atlantic, *Annales* historians used perforated tape to create data series for commodity prices over the *longue durée*, in what they called "serial history."[8] Articles proliferated in the *Journal of American History* and the *American Historical Review*, announcing the need to train graduate students in statistics and computer programming, lauding what computers would achieve.[9] Books described armies of research assistants and thousands of hours of data input, and came with supplementary volumes full of tables and mathematical formulas. The most zealous members of the movement argued that quantitative methods would eventually take over history, turn it from an art into a science, and rid the profession of ideological cant.[10]

Historians committed to traditional methods reacted in predictable fashion. American Historical Association president Carl Bridenbaugh railed against those who worshipped "at the shrine of that bitch-goddess, QUANTIFICATION."[11] Arthur M. Schlesinger, Jr., told the American Sociological Association that, although he did not deny the value of quantitative tools, nonetheless "almost all important questions are important precisely because they are *not* susceptible to quantitative answers."[12] The debate erupted into public view in 1974, with the publication of *Time on the Cross*, a computational attempt to reinterpret slavery.[13] It was not the first time that the "new" economic history had considered slavery, but Robert Fogel and Stanley Engerman did not just promise a revolution in academic methodology. They insisted that new methods would change public attitudes towards slavery itself, reshaping the contemporary politics of race.[14] Their book garnered unprecedented coverage in *Time* and *Newsweek*, but leading scholars took issue with unrepresentative data, misapplication of formulas and theory, and an agenda that belied the authors' pretensions to ideological neutrality.[15] In the aftermath, Fogel began writing of the limits rather than the promise of quantification, the movement's messianic fervor dissipated, and its adherents either changed tack or moved into other disciplines.[16]

Quantitative methods became dominant in economics and political science, but equations disappeared from mainstream historiography. Yet the cliometricians succeeded in engendering greater reflexiveness about method. As François Furet wrote as early as 1971, the laborious creation of data series made the historian, still male, "aware that he has constructed his own facts," something that Furet called "a revolution in the historiographical consciousness."[17] Looking back nearly three decades later, Joyce Appleby observed that quantitative history had at least made it impossible to deny the structural inequities in American history, even if the statistics had not spoken for themselves. From that insight, she argued, historians realized that deeper analysis required revealing the power relations that had produced the numbers. That research was generally to be qualitative in nature.[18]

Social and cultural history took off, and a zeal for information technology was not reborn until the mid-1990s, with the coming of digital humanities. Then as now, the internet appeared to promise a solution to what was already seen as a crisis in the humanities. Twenty years later, the most important primers still declare that the new field of digital humanities not only revolutionizes the arts, or should, but "upends academic life as we know it."[19] For one of digital history's early trailblazers, Roy Rosenzweig, interactive CD-ROMs and hypertext online publications were guaranteed to bring history to a wider audience, and were thus steps on the "road to Xanadu."[20] For another advocate, Orville Vernon Burton, digital history was to be "a revolution in the history profession that will change the way history is done at every level of scholarship and teaching and throughout the libraries and databases historians use in their everyday work."[21]

Digital humanists have indeed created countless web-based projects, internet forums, and "unconferences." But one of their central preoccupations is whether, and how, all of their blogs, tools, and visualizations add up to a new kind of scholarship that can and should pass peer-review. Digital historians' proudest achievements have not been new discoveries or grand narratives – conspicuous by their absence – but easy-to-use interactive tools and free public platforms like Zotero. So does digital history have to meet the same standard as any other field of history, that is, to demonstrate that it has created new and important knowledge about the past? Or is its main role precisely to expose self-important academic pretensions and "shake things up," as Michael Frisch argues?

An even more fundamental debate concerns how we define and delimit the field. William Thomas suggests that it "is about the medium, not the method," which makes almost any history existing on the web "digital." Many practitioners celebrate collaboration, and point out that not every member of a team needs to have the same skillset. But for Daniel Cohen and William Turkel, only programming historians can do truly advanced research in digital history. All this creates a first mover problem, as Kirsten Sword asks: "Is it wise and fair to launch graduate students into their own, largely unsupported, digital projects when the 'best' work appears in large scale, collaborative ventures, and when scholarly articles and monographs remain our common professional currency?"[22]

One thing seems clear. There is not yet any agreement on how to define either "digital humanities" or "digital history." The debate will likely only be settled when digital historians produce "field-defining" work, the kind of work that commands the respect of the rest of the academy. As the leading scholar Cameron Blevins argues, though, "digital history seems to operate in a perpetual future tense," existing forever in the "sunrise of methodology."[23] By promising a revolution that has not yet come, digital history has aimed to challenge every scholar without challenging anyone in particular. With few publications in leading journals, it is little surprise that discussions about digital history – what it is and what it can do – are happening mainly among self-professed digital historians themselves, rather than historians more generally. In literary studies, an *avant-garde* led by Franco Moretti and Matthew Jockers has already been bold and successful enough to spark a backlash in the core of the discipline.[24] Yet historians in the main evidence little more than mild curiosity about digital techniques, which they are as likely to read about in the arts section of their newspaper as in a scholarly journal.[25] For outsiders, it is all too easy to see digital history as something to teach but not practice, like world history, or even as a harmless form of public outreach.

This is unfortunate, because for historians of American foreign relations a digital turn is coming, whether we like it or not. For literary scholars, the development of huge corpora of digitized books by Google and HathiTrust has made computational analysis possible, but not imperative.[26] The advent of electronic records, on the other hand, has already brought profound changes in the core of our archives. While the growth of digitized and born-digital primary source collections is usually seen as an unmitigated good, the effects are complex, and in some ways deeply worrying.

THE ARCHIVAL EXPLOSION

Historians of the national security state have long been coping with the problem of "big data." What counts as "big," after all, is always relative to what has come before. As long ago as 1961, the advisory committee to the State Department's *Foreign Relations of the United States* (FRUS) series was warning of "the fantastic expansion of materials in the archives," which it called "a crisis of major proportions."[27] Twenty years later, Gerald K. Haines and J. Samuel Walker argued that one of the principal problems faced by historians of the future would be "an almost overwhelming task of sifting and winnowing an enormous amount of documentation."[28] They were right. The foreign policy bureaucracy expanded exponentially over the course of the Cold War, with the growth in size of the State Department and the intelligence community, as well as the addition of new players such as the National Security Council and USAID. The horizons of diplomacy widened too, as decolonization increased not just the number of states but also the burdens of global management, ranging from armed conflict to financial stability, from the eradication of disease to the control of world population growth. Consequently, as William McAllister puts it, our work over the past decades has embraced "more actors, more topics, more interaction, more documents, and more historiographical approaches," adding up "to a vastly larger universe of study."[29]

What is changing now is that more and more of the sources that make up this universe are either being digitized or were "born digital," in the sense that they

Using computational methods 79

were originally created or archived as electronic rather than paper records. Alongside quantitative growth, this is bringing about a qualitative transformation even in the study of the more distant past. The individual researcher can now sift, search, and sort enormous collections with truly unprecedented storage and processing capabilities. The Federalist Papers have long been a test bed for statisticians who seek to perfect techniques in authorship attribution of anonymous documents. Now there is the prospect of applying this and other statistical techniques to much larger corpora, such as the fifteen thousand letters Benjamin Franklin wrote or received during his life, which Stanford's Mapping the Republic of Letters project has begun to quantify and visualize to try to understand Franklin's transnational connections.[30] Over 450 volumes of *FRUS*, dating to 1861, are already available digitally from the State Department Office of the Historian and the University of Wisconsin's Digital Collections, and new volumes are released in a variety of formats, from pdf to xml. Now, like never before, it should be a relatively simple matter to determine, among other things, changes in the relative frequency of references to this or that country or individual across the whole corpus.[31]

These kinds of analysis might be thought simple, except that there are not yet any web applications for the historian to identify anonymous authors, extract and map locations from documents, or conduct frequency analysis of digitized collections. The only tool that is typically offered to users of online archives is the search engine. And when it comes to the electronic reading rooms maintained by every federal department and agency to store documents released under the Freedom of Information Act (FOIA), these search engines can be quite primitive or even non-functional.[32] At the time of writing, the State Department's FOIA reading room alone offers access to over 100,000 records, which someone with modest coding skills can "scrape" (or copy) to create their own database.[33] More challenging to the would-be digital historian are the Remote Archives Capture (RAC) terminals, accessible only at presidential libraries. In an attempt better to manage declassification, the CIA and the National Archives and Records Administration (NARA) have digitized millions of pages of documents, and those digital copies are now starting to be released at libraries from Truman onwards.[34] Moreover, the CIA has declassified some 11 million pages of its own records, but only makes the full collection available at Archives II in College Park, through the CREST system.

These are public sources, and in theory anyone could print out and re-digitize the RAC and CREST materials. Yet much of our public record is already being scanned and sold for profit, as Roy Rosenzweig pointed out many years ago.[35] ProQuest hosts the Digital National Security Archive, home to over 700,000 pages of FOIAed documents.[36] It also owns the History Vault, an agglomeration of documents that includes many of the National Security Files of the Kennedy, Johnson, and Nixon White Houses, plus the archives of all the major American newspapers.[37] Gale/Cengage maintains the Declassified Documents Reference System (DDRS), composed of around 500,000 pages of documents, mainly released through the Mandatory Declassification Review (MDR) requests that scholars have filed at Presidential libraries over the last forty years. DDRS might therefore tell us a great deal not just about history, but also historiographical fashion and declassification policy.[38] But until recently, the only way to explore it and all the aforementioned databases has been by intuiting what terms will yield interesting results from the omnipresent search engine.

Having access to more and more digitized documents has already made it cheaper and easier to conduct primary source research compared to traditional archival expeditions. Considering that some other countries have gone much further than the US in digitizing their national archives, such as Australia, Great Britain, Japan, and Switzerland, it is now possible to do multi-archival international research without ever leaving home. But the advent of "born digital" electronic record collections will again change the nature of our research, beginning with reducing our dependence on scanning and Optical Character Recognition (OCR). OCR, after all, consistently produces some garbled text depending on image quality and software quirks, which is one reason why search engines do not always produce even documents that contain the specified search terms. And scanning does not, by itself, yield metadata, or "data about data," such as the author, recipient, date, and subject of a document. Names and locations embedded in clean text can be extracted through what data scientists call "named-entity recognition." But the process is prone to error, since computers cannot tell whether "Paris Hilton" refers to the celebrity or a place to stay in the French capital.

True electronic records, on the other hand, usually come complete with native metadata, which allow for many more – and more rigorous – forms of analysis. Consider, for instance, the State Department's CFPF, the core collection for the study of American foreign relations in the twentieth century. In the late 1960s, the State Department began to experiment with automatically sorting airgrams. In the middle of 1973 it started to convert all telegrams to machine-readable microfilm. One impetus was a desire to generate internal data about diplomacy, such as through the "Traffic Analysis by Geography and Subject" (TAGS) system. These TAGS are now available to us as one of dozens of different fields of metadata that have been released together with full-text cables through NARA's "Access to Archival Databases" system (AAD).[39] "P-reel," or paper documents that were microfilmed for the record, are currently only obtainable at College Park, but the metadata for each is also available on AAD. Along with "subjects," "concepts," and other information, the metadata provides a history of how each document was declassified. For the hundreds of thousands of documents that remain classified or otherwise unreleased, electronic withdrawal cards are provided, albeit with more limited metadata than the declassified records. Each field adds another layer for potential analysis. And because humans filled each in at the time of record creation, declassification, or archival preservation, their inconsistencies are revealing and interpretable. Simply knowing the sender, recipient, date, and subject makes it possible for the first time to conduct systematic analysis of the overall agenda and volume of American diplomacy. With each new installment, the CFPF will become ever more central in the study of international history since 1973, in digital history, and perhaps even in computer science, since work in the field of natural language processing (NLP) depends on a clean dataset that is rich with metadata.

In assessing what we have and what is yet to come, it is important to realize what we have lost. The CFPF at first glance appears overwhelming both in its size and its seeming completeness. But over one hundred thousand cables were corrupted in the transition to electronic records. For certain periods, most or all of the documentary record has simply been lost. This includes most of the cables from the first half of December 1975, for instance, and 92% of the telegrams from June 1976. Gone are records pertinent to the Indonesian invasion of East Timor, and the American response to the Soweto Uprising. Moreover, a large proportion of what survived intact remains unreleased. Whereas for the 1973 cables, 13% were withheld, for 1976, it was 24%. Withholding often occurs because certain collections are more likely to have national security or personally sensitive information, and NARA has not invested in technology to prioritize documents that require closer scrutiny. All of these records were simply printed out and reviewed page-by-page. And the years in which most of these cables were reviewed coincided with a dramatic decline in appropriations for declassification, from $232 million in 2001 to $48 million in 2004. Spending on declassification has not recovered, such that the inflation-adjusted budget in 2012 was just 15% of what it was in the late 1990s.[40] Consequently, archivists have felt compelled to delete millions of other documents (the exact number is impossible to determine). So large has the archival record become that NARA has lacked the staff to look at more than a small sample before deciding which records have enduring historical significance. Materials that did not make the cut include whole classes of cables concerning scientific research, cultural diplomacy, passports, and visas.[41]

Even in terms of records that survived, research has become more challenging. Paper documents were scanned or inputted into the State Archiving System's "P-reel" in the order in which they were submitted to records managers, not with other documents created concurrently or by the same person. Documents created in 1975 might not have been archived until 1980, and are therefore currently inaccessible without lengthy FOIA delays. Using a keyword search to identify (by metadata only, not full text) a "P-reel" document yields, after consultation with a ring-bound container list, a whole box of random documents that just happened to be scanned at the same time. This loss of archival integrity makes it impossible even to produce a thematic or institutional finding aid, a problem that will become all the more acute when archivists with deep knowledge of these collections retire and their institutional knowledge is lost with them. It is already a disaster for the historian, virtually eliminating any chance of making a serendipitous discovery in neighboring files, or of gaining any greater understanding of the context in which these documents were produced.

The promise of rapid expansion of the virtual archive of American foreign relations can thus distract us from the pitfalls and dark corners awaiting the unwary researcher. So far, historians who wish to explore this archive have only been able to use a search engine. It is not unlike a flashlight, which we shine into the archive if only because we cannot think of what else to use. But computer science is beginning to produce a whole array of new techniques to explore virtual archives, the equivalent of infrared lenses and autonomous drones. It would be foolhardy for historians not at least to try to use them before we stumble much further into the darkness, and before millions more historical records are lost forever.

COMPUTATIONAL METHODS 3.0

So how should we grapple with these digital repositories, once we realize that they are disjunctive and disorganized, and that a large (but to some degree unknown) part of the original documentary record is unavailable because of corrupt files, deletions, and withholding?

Imagine beginning a book on Henry Kissinger's stint as secretary of state, and approaching the source base in the traditional manner taught to graduate students for decades: read everything, and then read around. It would take well over a lifetime for one person to read the cables for those few years, and nearly three years to read just the ones that were sent from Moscow.[42] One would need to add transcripts of Kissinger's telephone conversations, all 15,000 of them, plus the records of his meetings, the State Department papers that were not stored electronically, as well as Defense, Treasury, and intelligence records. Then combine all of that with the personal and non governmental archives that have been mined so profitably over the past decades by historians of American foreign relations. Finally, research in the archives of other countries and international organizations would be essential to correct for the intrinsic bias in a single government's records. Considering that the potential source base for more recent history is much larger, it is clear that new approaches are needed.

What if we made a virtue of necessity, and approached the archive in entirely new ways? Normally, when we go to a large physical archive, we enter with some idea of the key topics, consult the finding aids, learn the scope and content of the collections, and start ordering everything that seems relevant. We then look at the documents one by one, trying to glean insights. Sometimes they give us leads that we follow into other files, until we begin to think that we have some sense of how everything is and was connected. But we never have a very clear picture of the larger whole, since we never see more than a fraction of the full collection. This is the virtue and vice of "close reading."

Using computational methods

Now it is possible to "read" an *entire* archive and analyze *every* available document and withdrawal card at the same time. We can use this power to perform a "first cut," determine the thematic topics that are statistically most prevalent, reveal what kinds of documents are particularly likely to be withheld or redacted, and rank all available documents according to their relevance to our research interests. All this can be done based on the features within the documents themselves, without presuming that we already know what topics are important or sensitive, or what terms might yield documents relevant to our research. We can then alternate from this kind of "distant reading" and other advanced methods to close reading of the usual kind.[43] Only now, we can have more confidence that – if we cannot *actually* see everything – we at least do not have the tunnel vision that results from only reading the results of search queries. So the old and the new are not mutually exclusive, indeed quite the opposite.

For collections such as the CFPF that have irretrievably lost what historians would consider their archival integrity, computational methods may offer the only hope of creating order from the chaos and producing anything like a proper finding aid. Lawyers have already discovered this when faced with huge corpora of documents produced through legal discovery. There is now a multi-billion dollar industry devoted to "e-discovery," albeit one that closely protects its intellectual property. Journalists, who write the first draft of history, were the first to create free public platforms based on machine learning and NLP. These systems automatically cluster documents and organize them in virtual files and folders in ways that resemble textual archives, thus helping the individual researcher to determine where and how to begin reading.[44]

Historians can make excellent use of these systems, but we should also be helping computer scientists to develop new ones better suited to our own work. This requires collaborative research, as the digital humanists argue. Our experience suggests that historians can contribute even if they lack coding skills. Advanced work using NLP and machine learning requires much more knowledge of mathematics and computer science than all but a handful of historians are likely to possess. But as part of a strong, multidisciplinary team, historians play a critical role in defining worthwhile questions to investigate, advising on the tradeoffs of various research protocols, and determining whether the results are valid and interesting or are merely an artifact of a flawed research design. If historians do not start working together with data scientists and developers to create reliable tools for our research, we will not have any say – nor perhaps any understanding – of the compromises and assumptions entailed in putting them together.

Historians and data scientists will also have to work with the professionals who will largely determine what kinds of electronic records we will be able to access in the future. This begins with records managers, who decide whether digital collections will be more (or less) "future-proof." Archivists have been talking about these challenges for much longer than historians, and we should enter their discussions with all due humility.[45] We also have a role to play in helping them determine what records have permanent historical significance. For instance, what in the past seemed like mundane documents on communications procedures and records management may turn out to be the most important of all, since they are an indispensable means of reconstructing how a collection came together. Destroying them is the equivalent of throwing out the owner's manual. If instead archivists keep in mind the potential for data-mining, computer scientists can more easily develop tools to help them process text collections, while historians can better understand the documents themselves. In the meantime, deleting electronic records of any kind has to be a last resort.

In addition to records managers and archivists, librarians play a critical role in helping historians and data scientists negotiate access to collections owned by private vendors. Librarians decide what digital collections to acquire, and as customers they are in the best position to communicate with vendors about the needs of researchers. The greatest need is usually to have the raw data. Vendors are usually open to this idea since they understand that new analytical tools can greatly enhance the value of their collections.

If historians can join forces with data scientists, developers, archivists, and librarians, there is the prospect of creating a vibrant new field of research. Text processing has long depended on a relatively small number of datasets, which are large, machine-readable, public, and rich with metadata, such as the Enron emails and the Internet Movie Database. The State Department cables meet all of these criteria and bear on matters of great and enduring significance. As more and more government communications are released, slowly but still decades sooner than most private or corporate emails, there will be many more such datasets. And because there is a sizable scholarly community devoted to their study both now and stretching into the future (unlike, for instance, the Enron emails), it will be easier to develop and pursue a joint research agenda likely to result in original and important discoveries.[46]

It is still very early days for this kind of computational history, but historians understandably already want to know whether it will sway long-standing debates. Those who expect an algorithm to answer a question like "Who was to blame for the Cold War?" or "Would Kennedy have withdrawn from Vietnam?" will likely be disappointed. Answering these types of questions will always require deep and nuanced reading of key documents. But when we face many millions of electronic records, as we will when trying to reconstruct debates about the Iraq and Afghanistan Wars, even knowing what to read, and what it represents, may require computational methods.

Meanwhile, there are other questions that more easily lend themselves to computational analysis, questions that historians have neglected because, until now, they have been too difficult to answer. For instance, how, without large-scale analysis, could we rank how much attention policymakers devoted to different issues and different areas, considering that every historian tends to claim that it was their subject which was at the "core" or "center" of it all? Similarly, without computational methods, how could we measure the bias in the historical record created by official secrecy, when most historians never mention what they could *not* read because of redactions or withholding?

What follows, unlike the other chapters in this volume, is not a summary of the state of the field. The field barely exists as yet. Instead, it is an introduction to new approaches that should prove particularly useful for historians of American foreign relations. Each technique has the potential to combine the idea of a cold start in a new archive with the sense of fortuitous discovery familiar to all historians. What has changed is that finding patterns and anomalies will increasingly require at least some "distant reading" of thousands or even millions of documents.

FIELDS OF RESEARCH

Counting

Counting is the simplest kind of computation, but it can help to answer some fundamental, neglected questions. In the absence of tools to turn words into data, historians have already resorted to using search engines to tabulate the number of references to this or that historical term.[47] Aside from the problem of corrupted text due to imperfect OCR, this method does not take into account how a corpus changes over time. If newspapers grow in size, for instance, the frequency (if not the proportion) of most terms will also increase. The Google Ngram Viewer would appear to solve this problem, since it displays word frequency relative to other words published in a given year in the Google Books corpus.[48] But it does not allow users to see what part of the corpus is being quantified and graphed. This is a fatal flaw for historians who want to understand the nature of their sources before building arguments on top of them.[49]

These problems can be overcome.[50] When they are, international historians will want to know how the volume of diplomatic activity changed over time, and where it tended to focus. They will likely debate whether the number of telephone conversations or cables transmitted provides a way to measure interest rather than just activity. With metadata, there will be new layers of analysis, and new questions. For instance, which embassies dealt with the most information that was classified secret, and why (Figure 1)? Did that reflect the sensitivity of those communications, or is it an indicator of which embassies tended to overclassify?

Once it becomes easier to turn words into data, new debates will then begin about how to interpret the data. The relative frequency with which diplomats use the term "human rights" in confidential communications, as one example, may or may not indicate whether human rights were a priority in foreign policy, much less whether that was predictive of how the United States would treat a

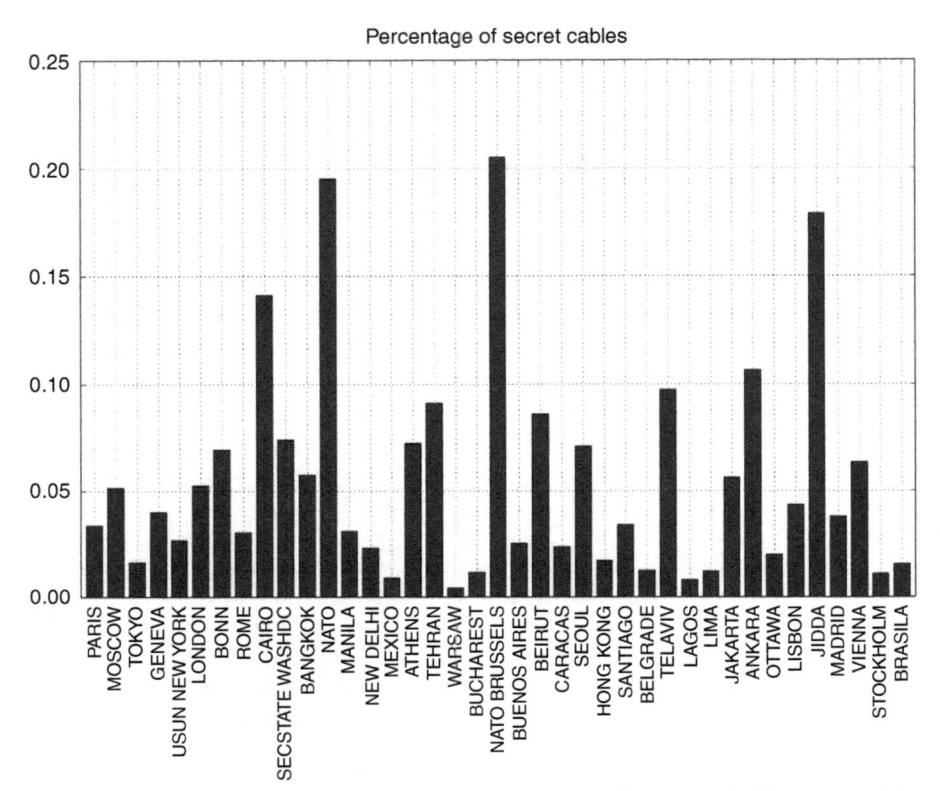

FIGURE I. *The percentage of cables, sent by American embassies and offices around the world, originally classified secret, 1973–6. The embassies, on the x-axis, are arranged in descending order of total volume of communications, from left to right. Source: Cleaned database of fully declassified telegrams, National Archives and Records Administration, Record Group 59, Central Foreign Policy Files, 1973–8, Access to Archival Databases (AAD), aad.archives.gov/aad/series-description.jsp?s=4073&cat=WR43&bc=,sl. We thank Daniel Krasner for the production of this graph.*

friendly dictator. It does show whether, when, and to what extent they believed human rights were worthy of discussion, something human rights scholars fiercely debate.[51] This kind of data is becoming more readily available, so it will become hard to ignore, and standards of evidence may begin to shift.

Traffic analysis

Counting is useful, but some historical phenomena require more sophisticated kinds of quantitative analysis. As William Sewell has written, we have always needed better ways to understand "lumpy, uneven" time, to describe how the pace of history appears to speed up or slow down.[52] The rate of

Using computational methods 87

communications is a seemingly obvious measure of diplomatic activity. But when we plot graphs to reveal these "lumps," do we segment them by year, month, week, day, or hour? No one choice is more objective than another, but too small an increment will reveal many blips, rather than real bursts of activity. Conversely, if the increment is too long, these bursts will become invisible because they average out over time.

One approach that helps to resolve this conundrum is precisely to focus on this quality of "burstiness" in streams of communications.[53] The idea is to segment time into levels of activity as measured by the observed interval between cables. We demarcate the beginning and end of episodes by the escalation or de-escalation of that activity. With this model, we can then identify "bursty" time spans across the entirety of a collection, or between two embassies, and see how they relate to events. This allows us to precisely map the duration of a crisis, and to compare what we find to public assertions of what was going on. For instance, plotting the "burstiness" of communications between Vietnam and Washington between 1974 and 1976 shows how "bursts" track the dates of significant military events and how the final crisis had started long before the Ford administration admitted as much. Only a deeper dive into the documents shows that, in the end, embassy communications were mainly about refugees (Figure 2).

This is an experimental approach, but it already shows that "bursts" of activity can be a function of how the communications flow changes when a secretary of state moves through the network. When he or she goes to a foreign capital, some communications that would ordinarily have been internal to Foggy Bottom become external, leading to heightened cable traffic. How did that shift in communications affect decision-making? It will take more experimentation before this method can reveal unstudied events. We might, for instance, be able to determine whether there are particular types of cables or language within cables that are predictive of bursts of activity, or how particular kinds of metadata interact with the text. We know that intelligence agencies model and measure "chatter" to predict terrorist attacks. We ought to be able to develop our own models for diplomatic communications to model other kinds of events for historical purposes.

Topic modeling

Search engines can be a powerful way to explore document collections, but what if we do not know the exact terms we should be searching for? We may not want to presume that we already know what the "keywords" will be, or the main topics in an archive we have never analyzed before. In probabilistic topic modeling, computer scientists attempt to find the hidden thematic structure in large sets of documents. There are various kinds of models, the most common of which is Latent Dirichlet Allocation (LDA).[54] Topic modeling finds words that are likely to relate to each other statistically, and turns them into strings of

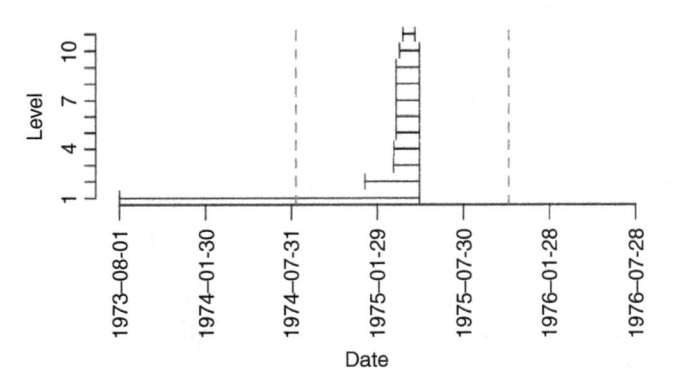

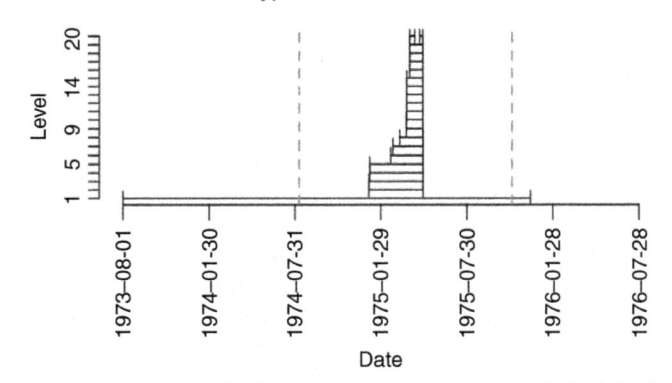

FIGURE 2. *"Burstiness" graphs showing communications and the fall of Saigon, August 1973–August 1976. These two graphs are produced by statistical work that charts traffic analysis. In both cases, a higher "burst" level represents heightened speed of communications, in and out of Vietnam. The upper limit of a "burst" is represented by "k," while "s" is a measure of graphical smoothness. N is calculated by adding the total number of fully declassified cables sent "to" or "from" Vietnam over the period to the number of still-classified cables for which we have the metadata. Dotted lines give dates for the resignation of President Richard Nixon and the firing of Henry Kissinger as secretary of state. Increased "burstiness" tracks important military events as North Vietnamese troops moved south, as well as resulting refugee crises. The precipitous stop occurs on April 30, 1975, with the evacuation of the American embassy in Saigon. Source: Cleaned AAD. We thank Shawn Simpson for the statistical work that produced these graphs.*

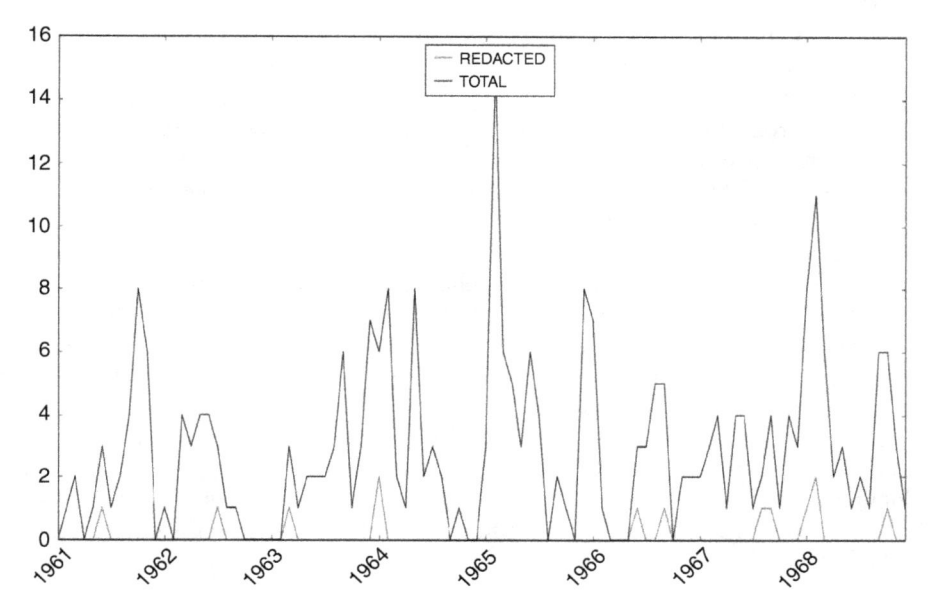

Top words: vietnam, south, communist, north, vietnamese, hanoi, war, communists, asia, saigon

FIGURE 3. *Topic modeling* FRUS. *Topic models find an underlying, hidden structure in text. In this instance, one model of a selection of FRUS volumes relating to the Kennedy and Johnson administrations finds that the words listed below the graph are likely to co-occur with one another, and that the word "Vietnam" is most representative of this topic. The graph shows the prevalence of this topic over time, in terms of number of documents, as well as the number of those documents that remain redacted in published FRUS volumes. Source:* FRUS, *e-pub versions. We thank Thomas Nyberg for the work behind this graph.*

probabilities that make up a theme (Figure 3). To model a corpus, it assumes that a certain number of topics *generated* the documents, which reverses our usual intuition, and that each of the documents in the corpus therefore represents those topics to a greater or lesser extent. It is an "unsupervised" technique, which means that, once the parameters are specified, the algorithm is autonomous, automatically generating the combination of topics that provide the best solution.

Computers cannot actually recognize which topics are meaningful to an historian. Some, for instance, will merely represent words that frequently co-occur, such as conjunctions and modifiers. Here again, these common words, or "stopwords," must be excised with discretion and a broad historical imagination. But once the parameters are defined, one can generate a set of topics that is statistically representative of the underlying themes in a collection. When we recognize the interrelationship of terms our inclination is to label them, something humans can do much better than machines.[55] This "science" is therefore both probabilistic and interpretive all the way down.

Topic modeling is a fairly new and quickly developing field in natural language processing, and the computer scientists doing such research are keen to work with historians to develop better ways of interacting with texts. Models have been developed that take into account historical change, networks of documents, syntax, "burstiness," and even, most interestingly, the influence of particular documents on topic distributions.[56] When used appropriately, topic modeling finds the hidden intellectual structures in our documents. Imagine, for instance, that we wanted to study how the term "national security" has changed meaning over time. Simple searching for the term in various databases will be time-consuming and often frustrating. Topic modeling has the potential not only to identify documents in the archive that are thematically related to national security, whether or not the "keywords" are actually used, but to show how it changed over time. Other applications might include showing how the language of public diplomacy differs from that of private diplomacy, and how certain topics tend to be more highly classified, or take longer to declassify.

Going "off-topic"

This kind of "distant reading" can also be used to find anomalies. Anomalies are one way that we might replicate the accidental archival discovery in the digital era. So, if we take the CFPF from the Kissinger years and apply topic modeling to all the telegrams, we find that individual embassies have specific signatures (Figure 4). The Moscow embassy talks a lot about the USSR, and very rarely about anything else, such that we can accurately predict that a cable originated from Moscow 98% of the time merely from how the words therein represent the typical topic distribution for Moscow. The London embassy, however, serves as a clearinghouse for multiple issues (Europe, NATO, trade policy, and so on), so its signature is much more diverse. If we know that particular embassies have particular signatures, we can see what happens when diplomats go "off" topic, that is, when they use words highly uncharacteristic of the embassy where they are posted.[57]

In a first run of this method, for instance, we found an unusual backchannel communication between the Soviet and American political counselors in Paris, discussing the Arab–Israeli war of 1973.[58] We also found examples of cables sent from unexpected embassies, such as a report on a Kissinger meeting with Willy Brandt sent once the Secretary had landed in Moscow, and a piece of Kremlinology pertaining to Leonid Brezhnev's power in the Politburo, relayed through the Finnish representative to the talks, held in Geneva, that led to the Helsinki Accords.[59] This method could apply not just to space, but also to time. We might, for instance, be able to estimate when a document was written, thereby helping to find documents that represent certain themes in

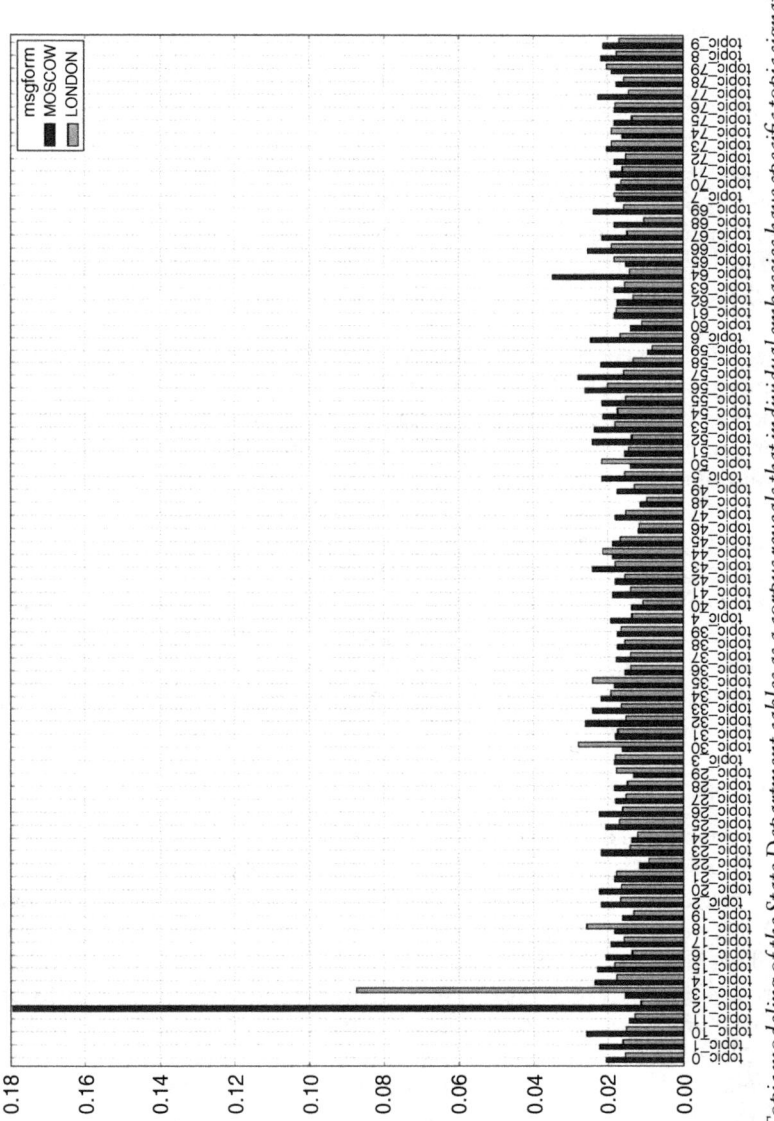

FIGURE 4. *Topic modeling of the State Department cables as a corpus reveals that individual embassies have specific topic signatures. This graph shows, from one model, the proportion of documents sent from Moscow and London that are most associated with a given topic. In this case, eighteen percent of cables sent from Moscow are predominantly about a topic that begins "Soviet, Moscow, October." Nine percent of cables from London are about a topic that begins "London, Bonn, Rome." These signatures can be used to predict from where a given cable "should" have originated. If the text of a cable does not match the usual signature of its sender, a cable is said to be "off" topic, and might be worth close reading. Source: Cleaned AAD. We thank Ian Langmore for the production of this graph.*

foreign policy before or after they become especially common. By trying to predict where a document came from, and when, we can find the unpredictable.

Authorship attribution

If topic modeling is very new, authorship attribution is very old. It dates back to the medieval scholastics, who tried to find ancient authorities for their documents. More recently, common statistical problems have involved verifying Shakespeare plays and the writers of individual Federalist papers. In their famous 1963 article on the latter, Frederick Mosteller and David L. Wallace used the frequency of words like "to," "from," and "upon" to assign contested articles to Alexander Hamilton or James Madison.[60] Since then, computers have made authorship attribution more rapid, powerful, and accurate.[61]

What we might expect from this kind of research depends on the nature of the problem. A solution will be easier if there is a small pool of potential authors, such as a presidential speech or an embassy telegram sent under an ambassador's name. Or we might have a much larger number of candidates, such as an anonymous memorandum that might have been written by one of thousands of different foreign service officers. With National Security Council or Policy Planning Staff memoranda, we might want to determine who wrote specific sections of a given document. In all of these cases, we would need authenticated examples of the writing of all of the candidates. But even if we have no idea who wrote a given text, authorship attribution techniques are reasonably accurate in determining their age and gender. All of these questions are ongoing fields of research in statistics that can help to solve longstanding questions about our sources.

Network analysis

Another well-developed field in statistics and computer science is social network analysis. The idea here is to analyze large collections of texts through the social network that is evoked in them, in ways that build on economic and sociological theory.[62] A network is a collection of people ("nodes") connected by links ("edges"). The most pertinent examples for historians of American foreign relations are the bureaucrats in government departments, and the networks of informants that embassies use to gain intelligence about the country on which they report. Network analysis provides us with ways to view structures like this across a corpus, and to see how the actions of one node have consequences for the rest of the system. Once we have extracted the network in historically representative ways, we can then begin to model it in a way that helps us to read the documents anew.

Franco Moretti has already demonstrated the power of network analysis in analyzing individual plays, using his models to question traditional concepts in the study of literature. What happens, he asks, when you take Hamlet or Claudius out of *Hamlet*?[63] How might literary scholars define the "centrality" of a character?[64] Once historians of American foreign relations have large corpora of documents, we can imagine new approaches to classic questions, beginning with the role of particular agents within larger structures. How, for instance, did networks reflect and affect the flow of ideas and information through a bureaucracy? How did the relative connectedness or isolation of individuals and institutions help determine policy outcomes? We might study how networks developed in ways that would not be expected by the organizational charts of the State Department or the federal government, such as informal networks that formed around particular issues and pushed specific policies. We could investigate how networks of local informants to a diplomatic mission changed before and after a change of government. Modeling would not provide definitive answers, of course, but it should prompt useful questions that might not otherwise occur to us.

Mapping

Of all the digital techniques outlined here, the most established in history is that of mapping. Geographical Information Systems (GIS) have been a key part of historical geography for many years.[65] Its application has been part of a "spatial turn" in certain strands of historiography, especially environmental history.[66] For instance, GIS was used in Geoff Cunfer's innovative history of the Great Plains, in tools like the *Digital Atlas of Roman and Medieval Civilizations* and *A Vision of Britain through Time*, and in an early digital history project led by William Thomas and Edward Ayers, "The Differences Slavery Made."[67] Now, with the pioneering work of Stanford's Spatial History Lab, what Richard White calls "spatial history" seems ripe for takeoff.[68] The historiography of American foreign relations has not quite taken a "spatial turn" in the sense of adopting, as White and others have, the ideas of Henri Lefebvre and other geographers.[69] But international historians have always been interested in space in one way or another.

GIS allows for the mapping of any data point that has a corresponding location, as so many of our sources do. Once we have that kind of data, all kinds of maps can be placed on top of one another, adjusted to show change over time, and so on. Mapping brings the prospect of visualizing some of the most basic aspects of international history. One of our first efforts, as part of our "Declassification Engine" project at Columbia University, has been to begin mapping cable traffic month by month (Figure 5).[70] From there, one can imagine overlaying material capabilities with military potential and alliance structure, for instance, or comparing those capabilities with the amount of bureaucratic attention paid to the countries in question. Classic questions of international history will suddenly become, quite literally, visible.

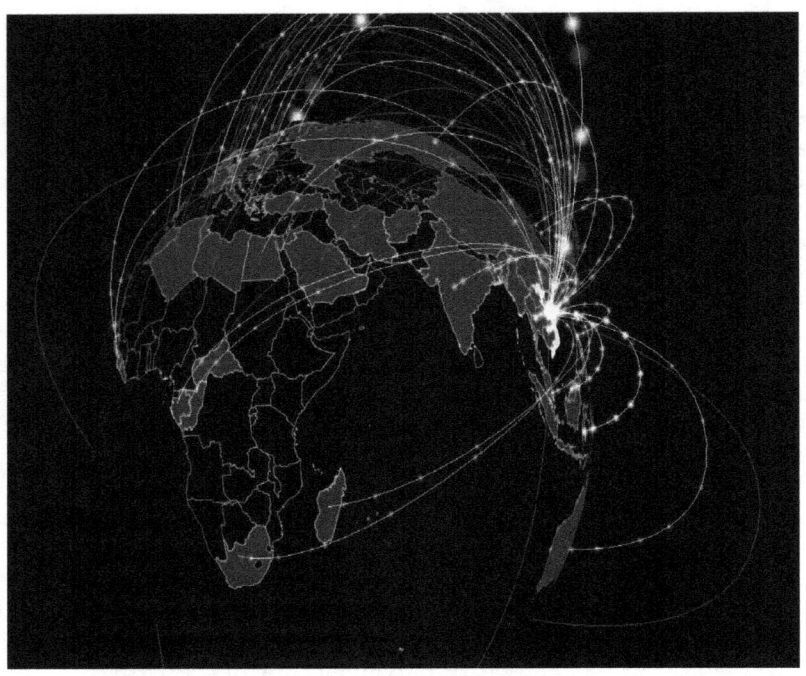

FIGURE 5. *Part of the Declassification Engine's "Sphere of Influence" project, this map shows the countries with which the American embassy in South Vietnam was communicating just before the fall of Saigon. Source: Cleaned AAD. We thank Kalev Leetaru and Dainis Kiusals for creating this map. For more, see* declassification-engine.org/index.py?section=sphere#.

CONCLUSION

Historians might understandably be nervous about the idea of having to learn an entirely new set of methods to explore contemporary diplomatic archives. In fact, at least some of the aforementioned approaches can and will produce tools that anyone will be able to use. But it could take some time. Meanwhile, there are tremendous opportunities for new discoveries to be made by historians who are willing to work collaboratively. To improve certain methods, such as network extraction and topic modeling, computer scientists need to consult with historians and others with deep knowledge of the documents. This research tends to be an iterative process, in which methods are continually refined to produce results that are both valid and significant. While computer scientists necessarily focus on making new discoveries in their own field – and are not usually eager merely to apply known techniques – many look to other disciplines to demonstrate that their work really does help us better to understand real-world phenomena. As computer scientist David Blei writes,

Using computational methods 95

even if new statistical models "are meant to help interpret and understand texts," the models, and the texts they use, still need to be evaluated. "Using humanist texts to do humanist scholarship," he concludes, "is the job of a humanist."[71]

We as historians can do a better job once we realize, as even anti-cliometricians did four decades ago, that each time we write "most" or "likely" we are making quantitative or probabilistic judgments. At least some of those judgments could now be made more precisely, and in a way that can either be validated or disproven. Unlike a lot of the quantitative data used in social science research, ours will not come from coding by research assistants or self-reporting in surveys. We do not, in other words, have to join the international relations researchers who struggle to rate wars on a scale of one to five, or fall into the fallacy sociologists commit when they equate attitudes recorded in polls with actual behavior. We have the immense advantage of using primary sources, and can now use them in a whole new way. Even if we can never use the whole corpus, we have enough of it to mitigate the selection bias and out-of-sample issues that bedevil other disciplines. We need not become obsessed with running regressions or pursuing statistical significance as an end in itself. Instead we can combine computational methods with our traditional strength in closely reading our sources and attending to their context.

Whenever the next edition of *Explaining the History of American Foreign Relations* is published, much of this chapter will likely seem dated. That, at least, is our hope. Our expectation is that more and more digitized and born-digital documents will become available, more even than we envisage here, especially if historians begin to pool the scans and photographs we take in the course of our research into a virtual archive. We presume too that advances in data science will continue at an even more rapid pace, too rapid for us to imagine all the applications. Above all, we hope that historians of world politics take up these methods, determine which have practical utility, and help to develop new ones. Some will be found wanting, but we cannot be afraid to fail. If we do not at least try to come up with new means to cope with the infinite archive, we will not even realize what we have missed. If we start to work together and work across disciplines, we can begin an exciting new period of experimentation, and perhaps even lead the way in the reinvention of history as a data science.

NOTES

* As this chapter explains, the authors are part of a multidisciplinary team that has been exploring applications for text processing and machine learning in diplomatic history. Much of what we have learned has come from collaboration, especially with David Madigan, Daniel Krasner, Ian Langmore, Sasha Rush, Shawn Simpson, Thomas Nyberg, and Rex Douglass. Their individual contributions are also noted in the discussion of specific research

methodologies. Note that the graphs were produced with historical data but are provided for illustrative purposes only. We would also like to acknowledge the generous support of the Brown Institute for Media Innovation and the John D. and Catherine T. MacArthur Foundation.

1. Michael J. Hogan and Thomas G. Paterson (eds.), *Explaining the History of American Foreign Relations* (New York, 1991).
2. William McAllister, "The Documentary Big Bang, the Digital Records Revolution, and the Future of the Historical Profession," *Passport* 41:2 (September 2010): 12–17.
3. "Interchange: The Promise of Digital History," *Journal of American History* 95 (2008): 455.
4. See, for instance, Public Interest Declassification Board, "Transforming the Security Classification System" (December 2012), archives.gov/declassification/pidb/recommendations/transforming-classification.html.
5. William O. Aydelotte, "Quantification in History," *American Historical Review* 72 (1966): 803–25.
6. Robert P. Swierenga, "Computers and American History: The Impact of the "New" Generation," *Journal of American History* 60 (1974): 1045–70.
7. Robert W. Fogel, "The New Economic History," *Economic History Review* 19 (1966): 642–56; Robert W. Fogel, *Railroads and American Economic Growth: Essays in Econometric History* (Baltimore, 1964); Avner Greif, "Cliometrics After 40 Years," *American Economic Review* 87 (1997): 400–3; Douglass C. North, "Cliometrics—40 Years Later," *American Economic Review* 87 (1997): 412–14.
8. François Furet, "Quantitative History," *Daedalus* 100 (1971): 151–67; Emmanuel Le Roy Ladurie, *The Territory of the Historian* (Chicago, 1979).
9. Swierenga, "Computers and American History"; Jerome M. Clubb and Howard Allen, "Computers and Historical Studies," *Journal of American History* 54 (1967): 599–607; William G. Thomas, III, "Computing and the Historical Imagination," in Susan Schreibman, Ray Siemens, and John Unsworth (eds.), *A Companion to Digital Humanities* (Oxford, 2004), digitalhumanities.org/companion/.
10. See several of the articles in Robert P. Swierenga (ed.), *Quantification in History: Theory and Research* (New York, 1970).
11. Carl Bridenbaugh, "The Great Mutation," *American Historical Review* 68 (1963): 326.
12. Arthur Schlesinger, Jr., "The Humanist Looks at Empirical Social Research," *American Sociological Review* 27 (1962): 770.
13. Robert William Fogel and Stanley L. Engerman, *Time on the Cross: The Economics of American Negro Slavery* (Boston, 1974).
14. Alfred H. Conrad and John R. Meyer, "The Economics of Slavery in the Ante Bellum South," *Journal of Political Economy* 66 (1958): 95–130.
15. Herbert G. Gutman, "The World Two Cliometricians Made: A Review-Essay of F + E = T/C," *Journal of Negro History* 60 (1975): 53–7; C. Vann Woodward, "The Jolly Institution," *New York Review of Books* 21 (May 2, 1974); Eric Foner, "Redefining the Past," *Labor History* 16 (1975): 127–38.
16. Robert William Fogel, "The Limits of Quantitative Methods in History," *American Historical Review* 80 (1975): 329–50; Charlotte Erickson, "Quantitative History," *American Historical Review* 80 (1975): 351–65.
17. Furet, "Quantitative History," 160.

18. Joyce Appleby, "The Power of History," *American Historical Review* 103 (1998): 5–6.
19. Matthew K. Gold, "Introduction: 'The Digital Humanities Moment'," in Matthew K. Gold (ed.), *Debates in the Digital Humanities* (Minneapolis, 2012), ix. See also Anne Burdick, Johanna Drucker, Peter Lunenfeld, Todd Presner, Jeffrey Schnapp, *Digital_Humanities* (Cambridge, MA, 2012), and the collection edited by one of history's few representatives in the digital humanities, Daniel J. Cohen: Daniel J. Cohen and Tom Scheinfeldt (eds.), *Hacking the Academy: New Approaches to Scholarship and Teaching from Digital Humanities* (Ann Arbor, 2013).
20. Roy Rosenzweig, "The Road to Xanadu: Public and Private Pathways on the History Web," *Journal of American History* 88 (2001): 548–579. Rosenzweig was the key figure in earlier moves towards digital history. See Roy Rosenzweig, "'So, What's Next for Clio?' CD-ROM and Historians," *Journal of American History* 81 (1995): 1621–40; Roy Rosenzweig and Michael O'Malley, "Brave New World or Blind Alley? American History on the World Wide Web," *Journal of American History* 84 (1997): 132–55; Roy Rosenzweig, "Scarcity or Abundance? Preserving the Past in a Digital Era," *American Historical Review* 108 (2003): 735–62; Roy Rosenzweig, "Can History Be Open Source? Wikipedia and the Future of the Past," *Journal of American History* 93 (2006): 117–46; Daniel J. Cohen and Roy Rosenzweig, *Digital History: A Guide to Gathering, Preserving, and Presenting the Past on the Web* (Philadelphia, 2006); Roy Rosenzweig, *Clio Wired: The Future of the Past in the Digital Age* (New York, 2010).
21. Orville Vernon Burton, "American Digital History," *Social Science Computer Review* 23 (2005): 206–20.
22. "Interchange: The Promise of Digital History," 488, 442–51, 461, 464.
23. Cameron Blevins, "The Perpetual Sunrise of Methodology," January 5, 2015, cameronblevins.org/posts/perpetual-sunrise-methodology/.
24. Franco Moretti, *Graphs, Maps, Trees: Abstract Models for Literary History* (London, 2007); Franco Moretti, *Distant Reading* (London, 2013); Matthew L. Jockers, *Macroanalysis: Digital Methods and Literary History* (Urbana, 2013); Stephen Ramsay, *Reading Machines: Toward An Algorithmic Criticism* (Urbana, 2011). Moretti and Jockers work with the Stanford Literary Lab, the publications of which can be found at litlab.stanford.edu/pamphlets. For the backlash, see Stephen Marche, "Literature is Not Data: Against Digital Humanities," *Los Angeles Review of Books*, October 28, 2012, lareviewofbooks.org/essay/literature-is-not-data-against-digital-humanities; Scott Selisker and Holger S. Syme, "In Defense of Data: Responses to Stephen Marche's 'Literature is Not Data'," *Los Angeles Review of Books*, November 5, 2012, lareviewofbooks.org/essay/in-defense-of-data-responses-to-stephen-marches-literature-is-not-data.
25. See the "Humanities 2.0" series in the *New York Times*, especially Patricia Cohen, "Digital Keys for Unlocking the Humanities' Riches," *New York Times*, November 16, 2010, nytimes.com/2010/11/17/arts/17digital.html, and Patricia Cohen, "Digital Maps Are Giving Scholars the Historical Lay of the Land," *New York Times*, July 26, 2011, nytimes.com/2011/07/27/arts/geographic-information-systems-help-scholars-see-history.html.
26. Google Books, books.google.com; "Google Books History," google.com/googlebooks/about/history.html; HathiTrust Digital Library, hathitrust.org.

27. "Public Report of the Advisory Committee," 1961, John F. Kennedy Presidential Library, Arthur M. Schlesinger, Jr., Personal Papers, Box WH-12.
28. Gerald K. Haines and J. Samuel Walker, "Some Sources and Problems for Diplomatic Historians in the Next Two Decades," in Gerald K. Haines and J. Samuel Walker (eds.), *American Foreign Relations: A Historiographical Review* (Westport, 1981), 335–6.
29. McAllister, "The Documentary Big Bang," 16.
30. Mapping the Republic of Letters, "Visualizing Benjamin Franklin's Correspondence Network," republicofletters.stanford.edu/casestudies/franklin.html.
31. *Foreign Relations of the United States*, State Department Office of the Historian, history.state.gov/historicaldocuments; *Foreign Relations of the United States*, University of Wisconsin Digital Collections, uwdc.library.wisc.edu/collections/FRUS.
32. See, for instance, Central Intelligence Agency, "Freedom of Information Act Reading Room," foia.cia.gov.
33. Department of State, "Freedom of Information Act," foia.state.gov.
34. National Archives and Records Administration, "The Remote Archives Capture Program (RAC)," archives.gov/presidential-libraries/declassification/rac.html.
35. Rosenzweig, "The Road to Xanadu," esp. 564–77.
36. Digital National Security Archive, nsarchive.gwu.edu/publications/dnsa.html.
37. ProQuest History Vault, hv.conquestsystems.com/historyvault/.
38. Declassified Documents Reference System, galenet.galegroup.com/servlet/DDRS.
39. National Archives and Records Administration, Record Group 59, Central Foreign Policy Files, 1973–8, Access to Archival Databases (AAD), aad.archives.gov/aad/series-list.jsp?cat=WR43.
40. Information Security Oversight Office (ISOO), "Annual Report to the President" (2012), archives.gov/isoo/reports/2012-annual-report.pdf: 26.
41. David Langbart, William Fischer, and Lisa Roberson, "Appraisal of records covered by N1-59-07-3-P," June 4, 2007.
42. Calculations based on a reader working an eight-hour day with no days off.
43. This distinction between "close" and "distant" reading is borrowed from Franco Moretti. See Franco Moretti, "Conjectures on World Literature," *New Left Review* 1 (January/February 2000): 54–68; Moretti, *Distant Reading*. Matthew Jockers prefers to think in terms of "macro-" and "microanalysis," arguing that algorithms are not actually *reading* documents (a human activity if ever there was one), but analyzing them. See Jockers, *Macroanalysis*, 22–31.
44. See, for instance, "DocumentCloud," documentcloud.org/home; "The Overview Project," overview.ap.org.
45. Joshua Sternfeld, "Archival Theory and Digital Historiography: Selection, Search, and Metadata as Archival Processes for Assessing Historical Contextualization," *The American Archivist* 74 (2011): 544–75; Alexandra Chassanoff, "Historians and the Use of Primary Sources in the Digital Age," *The American Archivist* 76 (2013): 458–80.
46. Jessica Leber, "The Immortal Life of the Enron E-mails," *MIT Technology Review*, July 2, 2013, technologyreview.com/news/515801/the-immortal-life-of-the-enron-e-mails/.

47. See, for instance, James Belich, *Replenishing the Earth: The Settler Revolution and the Rise of the Anglo-World, 1783–1939* (New York, 2009), 151–2; Samuel Moyn, *The Last Utopia: Human Rights in History* (Cambridge, MA, 2010), 231.
48. "Google Ngram Viewer," books.google.com/ngrams and books.google.com/ngrams/info; Jean-Baptiste Michel, Yuan Kui Shen, Aviva Presser Aiden, Adrian Veres, Matthew K. Gray, The Google Books Team, Joseph P. Pickett, Dale Hoiberg, Dan Clancy, Peter Norvig, Jon Orwant, Steven Pinker, Martin A. Nowak, and Erez Lieberman Aiden, "Quantitative Analysis of Culture Using Millions of Digitized Books," *Science* 331 (January 14, 2011): 176–82, sciencemag.org/content/331/6014/176.full.html.
49. Some scholars have deployed Ngram graphs to back up their claims without appearing to be aware of this issue, an early warning of what awaits if historians do not take more of an interest in how these kinds of tools are developed. See, for example, Daniel Lord Smail and Andrew Shryock, "History and the 'Pre'," *American Historical Review* 118 (2013): 710–12.
50. For recent efforts, see Cameron Blevins, "Space, Nation, and the Triumph of Region: A View of the World from Houston," *Journal of American History* 101 (2014): 122–47, and Cameron Blevins, "Mining and Mapping the Production of Space," Spatial History Project, Stanford University, web.stanford.edu/group/spatialhistory/cgi-bin/site/pub.php?id=93; Franco Moretti and Dominique Pestre, "Bankspeak: The Language of World Bank Reports," *New Left Review* 92 (March-April 2015): 75–99.
51. See, for instance, the periodization debate present in Moyn, *The Last Utopia*; Sarah B. Snyder, *Human Rights Activism and the End of the Cold War: A Transnational History of the Helsinki Network* (New York, 2011); Elizabeth Borgwardt, *A New Deal for the World: America's Vision for Human Rights* (Cambridge, MA, 2005).
52. William H. Sewell, Jr., *Logics of History: Social Theory and Social Transformation* (Chicago, 2005), 9.
53. For the statistical basis of "burstiness," see Jon Kleinberg, "Bursty and Hierarchical Structure in Streams," *Data Mining and Knowledge Discovery* 7 (2003): 373–97.
54. For summaries of topic modeling, especially Latent Dirichlet Allocation (LDA), see Jockers, *Macroanalysis*, 118–53; David M. Blei, "Topic Modeling and Digital Humanities"; David M. Blei, "Probabilistic Topic Models," *Communications of the ACM* 55 (2012): 77–84. For the original statistical explanations, see David M. Blei, Andrew Y. Ng, Michael I. Jordan, "Latent Dirichlet Allocation," *Journal of Machine Learning Research* 3 (2003): 993–1022; Thomas L. Griffiths and Mark Steyvers, "Finding scientific topics," *Proceedings of the National Academy of Science* 101 (April 6, 2004): 5228–35. For an early historical use of topic modeling, see David J. Newman and Sharon Block, "Probabilistic Topic Decomposition of an Eighteenth-Century American Newspaper," *Journal of the American Society for Information Science and Technology* 57 (2006): 753–67.
55. Jonathan Chang, Jordan Boyd-Graber, Sean Gerrish, Chong Wang, David M. Blei, "Reading Tea Leaves: How Humans Interpret Topic Models," *Neural Information Processing Systems* (2009), cs.princeton.edu/~blei/papers/ChangBoyd-GraberWangGerrishBlei2009a.pdf. For more on the strings of words that topic modeling generates, and the coherence of the strings, see Jey Han Lau, Karl Grieser, David Newman, and Timothy Baldwin, "Automatic Labelling of Topic Models," *Proceedings of the 49th Annual Meeting of the Association for*

Computational Linguistics (June 19–24, 2011): 1536–45; Jey Han Lau, David Newman, Sarvnaz Karimi, and Timothy Baldwin, "Best Topic Word Selection for Topic Labelling," *Proceedings of the 23rd International Conference on Computational Linguistics Posters* (August 23-27, 2010): 605–13; David Newman, Jey Han Lau, Karl Grieser, and Timothy Baldwin, "Automatic Evaluation of Topic Coherence," *Human Language Technologies: The 2010 Annual Conference of the North American Chapter of the ACL* (2010): 100–8.

56. David M. Blei and John D. Lafferty, "Dynamic Topic Models," *Proceedings of the 23rd International Conference on Machine Learning* (2006): 113–20; Jonathan Chang and David M. Blei, "Relational Topic Models for Document Networks," *Proceedings of the 12th International Conference on Artificial Intelligence and Statistics* (2009): 81–8; Jordan Boyd-Graber and David M. Blei, "Syntactic Topic Models," *Neural Information Processing Systems* (2008), cs.princeton.edu/~blei/papers/Boyd-GraberBlei2009.pdf; Thomas L. Griffiths, Mark Steyvers, David M. Blei, and Joshua B. Tenenbaum, "Integrating Topics and Syntax," *Neural Information Processing Systems* 17 (2005), psiexp.ss.uci.edu/research/papers/composite.pdf; Gabriel Doyle and Charles Elkan, "Accounting for Burstiness in Topic Models," *Proceedings of the 26th International Conference on Machine Learning* (2009), cseweb.ucsd.edu/~elkan/TopicBurstiness.pdf; Sean M. Gerrish and David M. Blei, "A Language-based Approach to Measuring Scholarly Impact," *Proceedings of the 26th International Conference on Machine Learning* (2010), cs.princeton.edu/~blei/papers/GerrishBlei2010.pdf.

57. We are greatly indebted to Ian Langmore for this idea, and for the modeling behind this technique.

58. Paris to SecState, "Middle East Situation: Soviet Embassy Approach," October 7, 1973, AAD, 1973PARIS26220.

59. Moscow to State, "SecState's Meetings with Brandt and Scheel," March 25, 1974, AAD, document number 1974MOSCOW04262; Geneva to State and Bonn, "Soviet Leadership Matters Bonn for Secretary's Party," February 15, 1975, AAD, 1975GENEVA01022.

60. Frederick Mosteller and David L. Wallace, "Inference in an Authorship Problem," *Journal of American Statistical Association* 58 (1963): 275–309.

61. For summaries of the various methods from literary scholars, see Jack Grieve, "Quantitative Authorship: And Evaluation of Techniques," *Literary and Linguistic Computing* 22 (2007): 251–70; Matthew L. Jockers and Daniela M. Witten, "A Comparative Study of Machine Learning Methods for Authorship Attribution," *Literary and Linguistic Computing* 25 (2010): 215–23; For technical summaries, see Patrick Juola, "Authorship Attribution," *Foundations and Trends in Information Retrieval* 1 (2006): 233–334; Moshe Koppel, Jonathan Schler, and Shlomo Argamon, "Computational Methods in Authorship Attribution," *Journal of the American Society for Information Science and Technology* 60 (2009): 9–26.

62. For a good summary, see David Easley and Jon Kleinberg, *Networks, Crowds, and Markets: Reasoning about a Highly Connected World* (New York, 2010), cs.cornell.edu/home/kleinber/networks-book/.

63. Franco Moretti, "Network Theory, Plot Analysis," *New Left Review* 68 (March-April 2011), newleftreview.org/II/68/franco-moretti-network-theory-plot-analysis.

64. Franco Moretti, "'Operationalizing': Or, the Function of Measurement in Literary Theory," *New Left Review* 84 (November–December 2013), newleftreview.org/II/84/franco-moretti-operationalizing.
65. Ian N. Gregory and Paul S. Ell, *Historical GIS: Technologies, Methodologies and Scholarship* (New York, 2007).
66. Anne Kelly Knowles (ed.), *Placing History: How Maps, Spatial Data, and GIS Are Changing Historical Scholarship* (Redlands, 2008); David J. Bodenhamer, John Corrigan, and Trevor M. Harris (eds.), *Spatial Humanities: GIS and the Future of Humanities Scholarship* (Bloomington, 2010).
67. Geoff Cunfer, *On the Great Plains: Agriculture and Environment* (College Station, 2005); "Digital Atlas of Roman and Medieval Civilizations," darmc.harvard.edu/icb/icb.do?keyword=k40248&pageid=icb.page188865; "A Vision of Britain through Time," visionofbritain.org.uk; William G. Thomas, III, and Edward L. Ayers, "An Overview: The Differences Slavery Made: A Close Analysis of Two American Communities," *American Historical Review* 108 (2003): 1299–1307; "The Differences Slavery Made," valley.lib.virginia.edu.
68. Richard White, "What is Spatial History?" (February 1, 2010), stanford.edu/group/spatialhistory/cgi-bin/site/pub.php?id=29. For one published example, see Caroline Winterer, "Where is America in the Republic of Letters," *Modern Intellectual History* 9 (2012): 597–623; stanford.edu/group/spatialhistory/cgi-bin/site/projects.php.
69. Henri Lefebvre, *The Production of Space* (Chicago, 1991).
70. Declassification Engine, "The Sphere of Influence," declassification-engine.org/index.py?section=sphere#. We thank Kalev Leetaru and Dainis Kiusals for putting together this project.
71. David M. Blei, "Topic Modeling and Digital Humanities," *Journal of Digital Humanities* 2 (Winter 2012), journalofdigitalhumanities.org/2-1/topic-modeling-and-digital-humanities-by-david-m-blei/.

6

Development and technopolitics

Nick Cullather

In 1900 an official commission landed in Manila to establish a colonial government for the Philippines. It included Ohio judge William Howard Taft and a young attorney, Daniel R. Williams, who kept his thoughts in a diary. "It is an interesting phenomenon, this thing of building a modern commonwealth on a foundation of medievalism – giving to this country at one fell swoop all the innovations and discoveries which have marked centuries of Anglo-Saxon push and energy," he penciled on a damp page in October 1901. "I doubt if in the world's history anything similar has been attempted, that is, the transplanting so rapidly of the ideas and improvements of one civilization upon another."[1] It is a familiar enthusiasm, one that might have been expressed at different times by American missionaries in Hawaii, Peace Corps volunteers in Ghana, or economists in Chile. It is not altogether different from President Barack Obama's pledge to poor countries that "we can deliver historic leaps in development."[2]

The United States conducts foreign relations through diplomacy, trade, and war, but also through humanitarianism and science. Such interventions are called development, but development is also a way of seeing other peoples' ways of life as an incomplete project, and the United States as an agent in fulfilling their ultimate destiny. Williams did not specify the "improvements" in store for Filipinos, nor did Obama say what "historic leaps" he had in mind (they probably defined development in vastly different ways) but their shared assumption that the United States was ahead of other nations and could lead them toward a better future is a persistent and powerful theme.

Foreign aid and technical assistance have been part of the diplomatic toolkit since 1948, but even earlier US foreign relations aimed not just to influence other countries but to modernize them: to push them to break with the past and begin a restless search for change and renewal. For over a century, development has been at the core of the American mission. It has justified the expenditure of billions of aid dollars, the upending of whole societies, and the bulldozing of

Development and technopolitics

landscapes, while inspiring visions of the final eradication of poverty, disease, and war.

It makes sense then for historians of foreign relations to investigate these ideas – to ask how Americans defined development, where their ideas came from, what the politics of international development were, and how the United States fit in. History is about time and context, and these questions can only be answered in ways specific to each period and place. Williams thought he was witnessing something never tried before, but it had been, before and many, many times since, with a wide variety of motives, methods, and results.

WHAT IS DEVELOPMENT?

A simple exercise will illustrate the problem of settling on a conclusive definition: download ten photographs from the web of landscapes – neighborhoods, industrial districts, villages, farms, deserts, and suburbs – a variety from across the world.[3] Ask five friends to rank them in order of modernity, from most developed to the least. Then ask them to explain their choices; what makes some places seem more advanced than others? Several things will become apparent. First, there is little agreement, even among people of the same age or social background, on what "modern" means. But second, your friends will have conflicting but equally valid reasons for justifying their choices. Depending on values and experience, progress looks different to different people.

Noah Webster's 1828 dictionary defined development as "an unfolding" as in a story.[4] Many scholars have tried to explain precisely how the concept applies to economic and social evolution. After setting up his philanthropic foundation, John D. Rockefeller urged his minister, Frederick T. Gates, to "find out as best I might, in what human progress really consists, and in what ways progress is to be promoted."[5] He was not the first. Adam Smith saw the division of labor as the mechanism of growth. Condorcet anticipated the perfection of science and the relegation of all religion to the status of superstition.[6] John Stuart Mill, Karl Marx, and Herbert Hoover each ventured their own versions of the past and future development of human societies.[7] Social scientists spent most of the 1950s and 1960s producing a vast literature on theories of modernization. No researcher can venture into this wilderness and expect to find a way out by the end of the semester.[8] Instead of trying to define development, the historian's goal should be to historicize, to discern how characters in a particular setting understood and acted on their own distinctive conceptions of social change, to explain development, in other words, as a story.

Development narratives come in all varieties, but they nonetheless contain elements that recur in the plans and speeches of people in charge. One of these is the importance of time. Societies are described as backward or advanced, as if they exist as points along a universal timeline. The goal of foreign assistance is to move the clock hands forward, to make what Obama called a "historic leap." David Lilienthal, the American engineer who led the Tennessee Valley Authority and then supervised Iran's development effort, found "a definite sequence in history in the change from primitive or non-industrial conditions to more highly developed, modern industrial conditions." The question was whether "we have enough control over our destinies to short-cut those wasted steps."[9] The United States, as a leading nation, set the goal and pace for others. "You can chart the course of our own progress in school attendance statistics, health records, and agricultural productivity figures," Secretary of State Dean Rusk explained. "Our foreign aid program is designed to help others follow the same path of progress."[10]

Rusk assumed schooling, health, and productivity would all be better in the future than in the past, that time and development move in one direction. This linearity helps us identify development ideas as a product of the industrial and scientific revolutions. The founding fathers had a cyclical notion of time, seeing societies as rotating through four stages, from hunting, through pastoral, agricultural, commercial, and then back again. Moreover, they regarded this movement not as progress but as decay. "Are not a people," George Mason asked, "more miserable and contemptible in the last, than in the early and middle stages of society?"[11] By the late nineteenth century, however, the notion that technology, administration, medicine, and national wealth should improve with time gained wide acceptance. When Lyndon Johnson and Dwight Eisenhower visited India they each felt they were seeing into the past, viewing people as they had lived in biblical times.

Paying attention to this discourse of time can help pinpoint ways in which historical figures understood development. A researcher can ask what practices or technologies developers identified with the past, what they saw as obstacles to advancement, what futures they envisioned. Walt W. Rostow, a development theorist and national security adviser, believed there were stages in the development process that were especially dangerous, and US aid ought to be targeted at countries passing through that moment.[12] The 9/11 Report argued that al-Qaeda-style terrorism took root because Middle Eastern oil states modernized too quickly, creating a "widespread feeling of entitlement without a corresponding sense of social obligations."[13] Clearly, tampering with time is a tricky business, but it is the way development practitioners made sense of their work.

Another characteristic of development narratives was a presumed link between individual lives and the transformation of the larger political or economic order. Agencies valued programs or techniques because they instilled new attitudes or problem-solving skills that could migrate to the marketplace or the voting booth. This made the most ordinary aspects of daily life – childrearing, food, work, reproduction – into targets for intervention. Herbert Hoover believed better diets could save Europe from Bolshevism, and in a similar way Hillary Clinton contends that more

Development and technopolitics

schooling for girls will reduce terrorism.[14] By tracing the sinuous logic of these connections, locating their roots in social theory, culture, and movement politics, historians can reveal the stakes of development projects as their proponents saw them.

Finally, historians can translate development narratives by decoding stock terms practitioners used to explain their strategies. Words such as village, tropical, slum, surplus, and gender have a specific usage and etymology in the context of development theory. In the history of foreign relations, locating where and when new phrases ("containment" or "open door") first appeared is often the key to understanding changes in policy and thought, and the same is true for development. Gilbert Rist notes that the term "underdevelopment," first prominently mentioned in President Harry Truman's Point IV address, created "a new way of conceiving international relations."[15] The year "the economy" was coined, 1937, was another such turning point.[16] Sometimes a hidden conflict is revealed in battles over the meaning of a term. For years in the 1950s and 1960s, social scientists debated the identity of "the peasant," specifically whether the peasant was rational in the economic sense. At stake was whether freedom or individualism had any meaning in rural Vietnam.[17] Using the *Oxford English Dictionary* and full-text book and newspaper databases, it is easier than ever before to trace the evolving meaning of keywords and to decipher the significance those words had in specific historical settings.

So to recapitulate, definitions of development are intrinsically contextual. Historians gain an appreciation for what development meant in the past by probing the structure of stories advocates and practitioners told, the way they understood time, the connections they made between small and large transformations, and the jargon words they used. As we shall see, the experience and politics of development are inseparable from the struggle to define it.

WHERE DID DEVELOPMENT IDEAS COME FROM?

When UCLA anthropologist Akhil Gupta interviewed peasant farmers in western Uttar Pradesh in 1991 he found them, without exception, fluent in discussing hybrid seeds, water tables, and the relative merits of organic and chemical fertilizers.[18] Although of recent coinage, the vocabulary of development is as familiar among Nepali shamans and Yörük nomads as it is at an Oxfam fundraiser. The spread of these concepts and assumptions is an important part of their authority; development has become the language for discussing work and welfare across the globe.

Like authors of superhero comics, scholars of development return to the issue of origins: where do ideas come from, how do they acquire their unusual powers, and how do they evolve over time?[19] Some have argued that modernization expresses a perspective intrinsic to the nation state, and accordingly spread together with the growth of the international system.[20] Enlightenment thinkers, such as John Locke, Voltaire, and Immanuel Kant, introduced concepts of the perfectibility of society through science and reason and sketched out an agenda for future progress in the abolition of slavery and war, the expansion of commerce, and the adoption of universal values and rights. Marshall Berman argues that Goethe's *Faust* (1831) is an early developmental parable: "We begin with Faust intellectually detached from the traditional world he grew up in, but physically still in its grip. Then, through the mediation of Mephisto and his money, he was able to become physically as well as spiritually free."[21] The Enlightenment, however, also produced strains of thought that would scupper arguments for universal humanitarianism for decades to come, including scientific racism and Malthusianism.

Abstract yearnings for progress and altruism coalesced into policy language as a consequence of a series of crises, first in the imperial order, and later in the international system. The first was the legitimacy crisis in Britain's "first empire" engendered by the American Revolution. It became clear that maintaining the allegiance of other settler colonies, such as Australia and Canada, would depend on an altered political accommodation under which London would administer but on behalf of colonists and for their benefit.[22] The transitive sense of "development" – as in something that could be made to happen – appeared first in writings on Australia's political economy.[23] Specialists in ethnography, botany, sanitation, and the new art of statistics superintended this new process of planned growth.[24] By the beginning of the twentieth century, the aim of scientifically developing colonial resources for the welfare of the indigenous peoples was a staple of imperial manifestos. "The Philippines are not ours to exploit," William McKinley insisted, "but to develop, to civilize, to educate."[25] The French *mission civilisatrice* and the Dutch Ethical Policy stressed hygiene, irrigation, education, and public works as the underpinnings of imperial legitimacy.[26]

A second crisis arose from the rhetoric of self-determination surrounding the "Wilsonian moment" at the end of World War I compounded by a noticeable shift in the economic function of colonial territories. Under League of Nations rules, imperial governments served as trustees of overseas lands, whose peoples they were obliged to educate for self-government. Meanwhile, mass-production industries were fueling what Charles Maier calls an "empire of consumption" in which subject peoples' demand for consumer goods was essential to the smooth expansion of the imperial economy.[27] Both trends placed a stronger emphasis on expertise in the service of welfare, poverty reduction, and planning. After 1920, the Rockefeller Foundation became a major funder of programs in medicine, agriculture, and statistics, and a supporter of League efforts to establish global standards of nutrition and labor. Much of the repertoire of development – irrigation schemes, disease control, economic planning, plant breeding, urban renewal – had its origins in this period, as did an international class of professional development experts who staffed the fledgling development community.[28]

A growing fear of nationalist revolt stemming from spiraling dissatisfaction with material conditions, what Adlai Stevenson called a "revolution of rising expectations," linked the anxieties of the late imperial period with those of the early Cold War.[29] Development historians often fuse the decades from 1920 to 1960 into an era of High Modernism characterized by a growing commitment to large-scale, state-led *dirigiste* planning schemes.

For early cold warriors, development was seen as a historic force, separate from the great power struggle but instrumental in the hands of an enemy. In the wake of China's revolution, Dean Acheson surveyed the global battle zones and concluded that "there is in this vast area what we might call a developing Asian consciousness... a revulsion against the acceptance of misery and poverty as the normal conditions of life." "The Communists did not create this revolutionary spirit," he explained, "but they were shrewd and cunning to mount it, to ride this thing into victory and power."[30] It was an image that would recur. Fourteen years later Lyndon Johnson's Peace Corps director, Sargent Shriver, told an audience in Honolulu, "The Communists are like your surf riders here; they're just moving on the crest of a wave."[31] Particularly after the Soviet "aid offensive" of 1956, the United States was determined to prevail in the development race.

Historians have identified the 1950s as a culminating moment when social scientists formulated a powerful developmentalist vision and the United States began systematically applying modernization as an instrument of influence. Interdisciplinary teams sponsored by the Massachusetts Institute of Technology's Center for International Studies (CENIS) and the Social Science Research Council worked out the inventory of interlocking concepts – social overhead capital, transitional personality, takeoff – that defined a new orthodoxy. Unlike the improvers of the age of imperialism, social scientists were optimistic that the backward countries could close the distance between themselves and the advanced societies, and that they could do it quickly, perhaps in a single generation. Designed for policymakers, their theories made the jump from university think tanks to the National Security Council by virtue of their uniquely useful combination of conceptual tools. They provided quantifiable measures of progress and principles for the use of aid.[32] CENIS's leading light, Walt W. Rostow, devised indicators to determine the optimal amounts and timing that would allow US assistance to decisively boost a country into self-sustaining growth. Rostovian theory made economic aid a surgical instrument that could "create an environment in which societies which directly or indirectly menace ours will not evolve."[33] Specialists believed the science of development rendered traditional diplomacy – "pacts, treaties, negotiation and international diplomacy" – obsolete.[34] Governments could be stabilized, revolutions averted, and states realigned through precise interventions in the modernization process.

By the 1960s, John F. Kennedy's "Decade of Development," modernization theory had become, in Michael Latham's words, "a sustained projection of American identity."[35] Its widespread authority and acceptance derived its conformity to resonant themes in American culture. Richard Slotkin has observed how closely images of the modernizing encounter match mythic representations of the frontier in nineteenth-century novels or twentieth-century films. In *The Ugly American*, a 1958 bestseller that popularized the Rostovian worldview, characters familiar from movie Westerns enacted the drama of development.[36] So powerful were these stereotypes that nation builders working in Southeast Asia – such as covert operator Edward G. Lansdale or jungle doctor Thomas Dooley – created public personas to match.[37] Broadway and Hollywood productions such as *The King and I* schooled national and international publics in the fundamentals of development doctrine. In representation and reality, modernization was politics disguised as common sense.[38] "What's wrong with the kind of an urge that gives people libraries, hospitals, baseball diamonds, and movies on a Saturday night?" Humphrey Bogart insists in *Sabrina*.[39] Such expressions did more perhaps than policy statements to build the collective certainty, and to spread development ideas to remote corners of Uttar Pradesh.

With air and water pollution at the top of the national agenda and defeat in Vietnam looming, High Modernism had clearly jumped the shark by the end of the 1960s, but recent scholarship finds a strange resiliency; development ideas quickly adapted to détente, the energy crisis, environmentalism, and a rising neoliberal consensus.[40] The volume of money transfers actually increased after 1970, but in the form of private bank loans rather than state-to-state aid. The agenda changed too. Instead of centrally planned *dirigiste* schemes, USAID and the World Bank pushed for deregulation, privatization of state industries, and export-led growth. Industrial countries forged new alliances, such as the G-7, to forestall demands by the Organization of Petroleum Exporting Countries (OPEC) and the nonaligned movement for a fundamental revision of the terms of global trade, a project called the New International Economic Order (NIEO).[41] Endorsed by the UN General Assembly, the NIEO would ban tariff protections and subsidies and allow national regulation of multinational companies. "Sustainable development," Vijay Prashad argues, was a strategy to shut down this radical project.[42]

As this cursory chronology suggests, development practices and concepts originated and spread not by design but by conflict and accommodation amid a running series of political crises. Americans tried to lay claim to the development idea, but it was never an exclusive property. The vocabulary could be appropriated by anyone who had a use for it; Chinese intellectuals employed the language of modernization in the 1920s, and Indian nationalists articulated rival visions of national development decades before CENIS held its first seminar. Korean intellectuals bent Rostovian concepts to fashion a uniquely Korean path to the future.[43] Histories of development highlight the

Development and technopolitics

wide range of social, political, and economic arrangements within market economies and the variety of ambitions called modern.

ANTI-POLITICS AND TECHNOPOLITICS

Theorists long fostered hopes that development would transcend politics by directly addressing the causes of war and replacing partisan maneuvering with clear-sighted, scientific solutions. Professional contacts and the lure of technology did occasionally allow specialists to work around thorny issues that foiled diplomats, but this never entirely allayed suspicions that vaccinating children, damming rivers, and feeding the hungry were all political acts. "Development is no indifferent abstract concept," warned reporter Ryszard Kapuściński. "It always applies to someone in the name of something."[44]

Nonetheless, development's chief appeal for donor nations and autocrats lay in its ability to fold issues of scarcity, rights, and representation into a technical program. Some have labeled this vanishing act "anti-politics," stressing the exclusion of people with inconvenient claims from supervisory boards and expert consultancies.[45] Other scholars, however, note that such attempts backfire by handing opponents powerful analytical tools and modes of analysis with which to assert their own demands.[46] This exchange, through which techniques or technologies are used strategically to "constitute, enact, or embody political goals," has been called "technopolitics."[47] Politics was built into the way a tool or system was used. Aid officials in the 1960s, for instance, hoped irrigation would force peasants to pay attention to schedules, quantities, and effects, and thus instill a scientific mentality that might have effects on election day. Politics could thus be embedded, almost invisibly, in a machine, a plant, a statistic, or a procedure.

Technopolitics can be distinguished from ordinary politics by the importance of material outcomes. Whether the machinery works, if there are deadly side-effects, if numbers go up or down all affect how much influence a technology will have. Material conditions, such as a looming epidemic or a sudden turn from scarcity to abundance, can amplify the voice of one or another faction in a debate. Nor did the urgency or desirability of a technology detract from its political value. Scientists converged on innovations they knew Asians or Africans would need knowing that these would enhance their, and their government's, influence most.

Three elements – technology, statistics, expertise – provide entry points for researchers. Innovators were often outspoken about the political value of new devices or forms of knowledge. When President Harry Truman launched the Point IV aid program he singled out a proven example of American technical prowess, the Tennessee Valley Authority (TVA). Governments around the world wanted to build large-scale dam systems for irrigation or hydropower, and as David Ekbladh has shown, US officials saw TVA as a "weapon" that would counter Soviet ideology with American technological dynamism. The TVA offered a template for resolving stubborn conflicts through collaboration in a purely technical enterprise, and soon US officials were supporting TVA-style solutions to the Arab–Israel dispute and Indo-Pakistani border wars. While domestic critics attacked the TVA as statism run amok, advocates saw it as a model for a new style of democracy, centrally planned but responsive to individual needs. Ultimately, Arthur E. Morgan, TVA's director, insisted, the aim of a multi-purpose dam project was "developing multi-purpose people."[48] Official visitors from Africa, confronting segregated restaurants and water fountains near Morgan's headquarters in Knoxville, however, may have taken a different measure of the TVA's transformative effect.[49] A single technology could resonate across psychological, strategic, and symbolic registers.

Technologies, small or large, came accompanied by their own guiding myths, visions of a future socioeconomic order, and political constituencies. These seldom allowed the United States to remake other societies in its own image, partly because aid officials rejected means and methods used at home, and partly because the constituencies and assumptions surrounding any project tended to contradict each other. Literacy and compulsory education programs in the Shah of Iran's "White Revolution," for instance, were intended to foster critical, independent citizens but also to encourage loyalty to the dictatorship.[50] Moreover, recipient nations recognized the issues of power and prestige at stake. "Technology matters," according to Jenifer Van Vleck, "because it so profoundly shaped other nations' *responses* to U.S. global power, which ranged from willing consent to selective adaptation to outright resistance."[51]

Additionally, technologies have material properties that produced political effects. Timothy Mitchell has contrasted the democratizing effect of coal, a labor-intensive fuel that allowed miners, haulers, and stokers at each step in the distribution chain to exert collective power through strikes, against the centralizing effect of oil, with a small, usually foreign, labor force possessing little political clout. Moves to develop industry by transitioning from coal to oil, such as when India replaced its coal-fired fertilizer plants in 1966, had ramifications beyond efficiency or cost.[52] Indian and American experts each recognized this technical decision as signifying a shift of power to the center.

The term "technology transfer" has little basis in history. Instead of following a direct path from donor to recipient country, innovations wound through thickets of adaptation, appropriation, testing, and subversion, acquiring distinct meanings and symbolisms along the way. Developmental politics was less bilateral than multilayered. Strategies were backed by transnational constituencies of officials and experts who were opposed by other transnational coalitions with their own pet technologies and goals.

Each technical undertaking embroiled practitioners and subjects in a distinctive politics of problematizing, framing, and display. Technologies of measurement were especially effective in identifying and simplifying problems previously outside the purview of state action, and the rise of development

Development and technopolitics

thinking coincided with a flood of statistical innovation. Standards of living, mortality rates, measures of literacy, nutrition, and health defined progress and set standards for the performance of projects. In 1940, economist Colin Clark published the first comparative ranking of the development of all states, and since then indices have defined progress and given policy an apparently empirical foundation. But there are no neutral indicators; as researchers have discovered, quantification is a particularly effective and subtle means of enforcing a worldview. Sally Engle Merry explains that the principal function of indicators is "responsibilization," the assignment of obligations to individuals, the market, and the state. A high infant mortality figure, for instance, might serve as an indictment of cultural or personal practices thereby producing "a shift of responsibility that masks the underlying power dynamics: the indicator itself does the work of critique, and the governed person seeks to conform to the terms of the government."[53]

Statistics also integrated diverse societies into a unified empire, a global market or free world. Racial or cultural categories melted under the pressure of statistics that showed peoples either to be alike or different in degree rather than type, and more often than not their level of health, or income, or labor efficiency was not innate but the product of mismanagement. Nationalists found the norm-making function of statistics especially useful for holding colonial officials to account.[54] For many measures, however, it was never entirely clear if a trend pointed toward progress or its opposite. Population was one such case. A sudden drop in birth rates, known as the "demographic transition," seemed for a time to mark the empirical threshold of modernity. It set many ghastly sterilization programs in motion, but the consensus was never solid, and many experts maintained that high fertility was essential to economic vitality.[55] Although they often measured conditions objectively, statistics were interpreted subjectively and consequently, politically.

Technopolitics also accounts for the influence of technologists, the specialists who introduce and interpret new modes of knowledge. Their occupational identities, the global networks they built, and their efforts to remake their disciplines as policy sciences all entwined with the politics of development. As Tania Murray Li observes, "the claim to expertise in optimizing the lives of others is a claim to power."[56] Demographers, tropical disease specialists, nutritionists, and urban planners embraced development as an expansion of their professional responsibilities. In some cases, such as for agronomists discredited by the Dust Bowl and the collapse of farm prices in the 1930s, international duties offered an escape from critics at home. A large part of the Rockefeller Foundation's mission in its early years was to midwife cross-border coalitions of experts in the fields of medicine, demography, and nutrition. These conferences encouraged belief in the global comparability of problems and solutions. Disciplines shed particularist tenets that interfered with the international transferability of expertise. Population scientists stripped away racial and eugenic agendas, once the core of the field, and constructed a modern science of demography. Quantitative modeling lent economics the probabilistic certainty of the physical sciences while making its prescriptions universally applicable.

As planners and advisers, economists drew blueprints for integrating new states into the postwar American market empire and provided baseline indicators against which the success or failure of regimes could be gauged. They enjoyed a reputation and personal influence few ambassadors or celebrities could match, unless, as with John F. Kennedy's representative in India, the ambassador was a celebrity economist. And while experts practiced politics, they saw themselves as the opposite of politicians; their recommendations were purportedly impartial and value-free. Economic necessity became a convenient justification for top-down and autocratic decision-making.[57] Technopolitics is rife with paradox, and during the 1950s and 1960s, when academic specialists stood at the height of influence, many modernists saw overspecialization as a threat. Such a quintessential technocrat as David Lilienthal believed the Balkanization of Western thought into disciplinary fiefs might lead to World War III.[58]

By tracing the ways historical actors discursively constructed connections between technology and politics a researcher soon finds the full array of anxieties, interests, and bargaining at play in any transnational relationship. The task of the historian is to recapture these subtle but significant battles over meaning and intent. In Indonesia in the 1960s, for example, Muslim groups, the military, and technocrats all read different agendas into modernization initiatives sponsored by the United States. As Brad Simpson shows, US experts believed aid would create an entrepreneurial class, overcome rural "involution," and undermine communist appeal. Islamic scholars believed the same programs were a cover for efforts to secularize the country. Government economists, many of them trained in the United States, saw them as a way to reduce the influence of the military, while the officer corps perceived designs to make the army the permanent guardian of the economic and social order. Each cherry-picked tenets of the overall doctrine to support their claims to authority and resources.[59] In Indonesia and elsewhere, the politics of development lay in a struggle to control the narrative.

For this reason, historians are reluctant to judge programs as successes or failures. The historian's approach is in this respect inimical to that of the development specialist, who evaluates past schemes to find strategies that can be lifted from one context and applied beneficially in another. The practitioner is interested in generalizable factors, the historian in specifics; the practitioner discards context while the historian rummages through the wastebasket to find it again. The historian can usually be confident that any standard used to judge a program after the fact reflects just one of many ambitions that inspired the project in the first place, and likely not one that was important at the time. To make a judgment of this kind, the specialist must oversimplify the model, overlaying the conflict, bargaining, and multiple perspectives with a single monocausal narrative. This makes for good development analysis, but poor history.

Historians should also be skeptical of critiques that draw too clean a line between technical change (imperial, bad, imposed from outside) and the indigenous (authentic, good, ecologically sound). Indigeneity is an attribute defined in contrast to modernization, as part of the same discourse. When the Rockefeller Foundation introduced new high-yielding wheats in India in 1964, the varieties they replaced, bred by agronomists from Ohio State a few years earlier, were redefined as traditional indigenous varieties. Part of the discursive work of development is to delineate historic baselines against which progress can be measured, so labels such as tradition, custom, or age-old should be held in suspicion until exonerated by research. There were many contending interests – governments, corporations, international banks, landlords, peasants, men, women – but none could claim primal innocence.[60]

HOW DOES THE UNITED STATES FIT IN?

Within these global and local dialogues, a distinctly American voice can be difficult to pin down. Development strategy was a potent distillation of the values and self-image the United States wanted to project overseas, but it could also express idiosyncratic or dissident desires for a fresh start, unencumbered by prevailing conventions. General Douglas MacArthur wanted to remake Japan, according to historian Perry Miller, as a "new Middle West – not, of course, the Middle West as it is, or in fact ever was, but as it perpetually dreams of being."[61] Development was never the exclusive preserve of government; NGOs, oil companies, and foundations advanced their own programs, as did freelancers, sometimes supervising large-scale projects singlehandedly. Theorists who articulated "American" visions of development were often recent immigrants, whose impressions of their new country were refracted through bitter personal experiences of repudiation and exile. Development strategy also responded to a continual need for reinvention. American theory and practice had to be distinguishable from others in the game, particularly the Soviet Union. All of this led to a seething blend of imperatives, but a few dominant flavors stand out. These include the use of development to forestall more radical change, a preference for authoritarian modernization, and a tendency toward utopian or dystopian forecasts.

The first, an impulse to restrain runaway social change, reflects a deeply rooted American aversion to revolution. Writing in 1900, military strategist Alfred Thayer Mahan warned against the precipitous modernization of Asia, with its immense population and confined land mass. "Sustained watchfulness and vigorous effort" would be required, he cautioned, "to insure that nothing unduly sudden or extreme occur – nothing revolutionary; that there shall be gained time, the great element of safety, by the operation of which transformation is retarded into evolution."[62] Kennedy's advisers spoke frankly about "controlled revolutions" and plans to steer demands for change into productive channels. The US-owned oil giant Aramco carefully staged displays of modernization while resisting change that might displease its patrons in the Saudi royal family. For the past fifty years, "civic action" programs have been a central component of counterinsurgency campaigns, based on an implicit assumption that development is an antidote to more radical politics. With rare exceptions, American efforts have been directed less at alleviating destitution or misery than at steering the process.

Bill and Melinda Gates regard Ethiopia, a corrupt one-party state with a bloodcurdling human rights record, as one of their "favorite countries" because of its "concrete leadership" on development.[63] This second tendency, to romanticize authoritarian methods when used in the cause of development, reveals an ambivalence about the efficacy of democracy seldom articulated in other contexts.[64] When asked about the relative prospects of democratic India and communist China, both struggling to pull themselves from poverty in the 1950s, high-ranking US officials were sure China would do better. Faith in the efficacy of dictatorial methods led the Kennedy and Johnson administrations to support Latin American military regimes, thought to have the organizational and technical aptitudes necessary to carry out development successfully.[65] A corollary assumption was that societies not already on a stable growth curve were unready for democracy. This reinforced tendencies to turn a deaf ear to dissident parties or use development as a substitute for deliberative politics, with predictable results. In Iran, Guatemala, and elsewhere, the tensions within a policy that upheld the power of repressive, conservative elites while inspiring hopes for broad social transformation triggered exactly the kind of violent upheavals development was intended to prevent.

Finally, while Marxist theory gave Soviet modernizers some confidence about the direction of progress, American thought veered between utopian and dystopian apprehensions. In Congressional debates on the foreign aid bill or foundation planning documents, the developing world was perpetually on the threshold of immanent abundance or dire peril, usually both at once. President George W. Bush's Freedom Agenda set an "ultimate goal of ending tyranny in the world" in terms similar to President Lyndon Johnson's pledge to end poverty or Kennedy's to "eliminate hunger from the face of the earth."[66] US policy tends to focus on famines instead of malnutrition, epidemics rather than disease, crises instead of the persistent but deadly problems of mass poverty. Neo-Malthusianism, which provided a dystopian subplot to development narratives for much of the twentieth century, had complex effects, lending urgency to modernization efforts in the early decades and dampening ambitions after 1970.[67] Development is narrated in future tense, and despite an abundance of visible, immediate problems to address, discussions invariably turn to speculative tomorrows.

Because of its futurist bias, development policy spurns careful analysis of past experience. The spring of 2011 might have been an occasion for historical reflection. The fiftieth anniversaries of the US Agency for International

Development, The Peace Corps, and Kennedy's Decade of Development speech passed without official ceremonies or commemoration. When the MacArthur Foundation proposed a standardized curriculum for a Master's degree in development practice, backed with $16 million in grants for twenty adopting schools worldwide, it included no history courses or readings.[68] Early modernization theorists, especially Rostow, fancied themselves historians, spinning elaborate historical parallels to justify their models, so that when practitioners and subjects rebelled against established theories in the 1970s they rejected historicism too.[69]

In consequence, policy and public debate draw on a mixture of anecdote and myth, a collective bout of false memory syndrome that makes easy pickings for debunkers. Our challenge as historians, though, should not be to deflate the legends, but to recover the hope and tragedy of development as a vital part of human experience for the United States and the world. No aspect of US foreign relations affected so extensively or intimately the daily lives of so many people; no aspect so thoroughly engaged the imagination and energies of Americans. "These things can be done, and don't let anybody tell you different," Truman told Lilienthal. "When they happen, when millions of people are no longer hungry and pushed and harassed, then the causes of war will be less by that much."[70] If national security was the sum of all fears, a nightmare vision of an American garrison state cowering before a hostile Eurasia, development spoke of dreams: a transparent, modernizing world mastering man and the environment with American technology. The stakes of American foreign relations in the last century must be measured against the grandeur of that vision.

NOTES

1. Daniel R. Williams, *The Odyssey of the Philippine Commission* (Chicago: A. C. McClurg, 1913), p. 320.
2. Barack Obama, "Remarks by the President at the Millennium Development Goals Summit in New York," September 22, 2010, http://goo.gl/cO8qzX.
3. Or simply use the images on this site: www.journalofamericanhistory.org/teaching/2002_09/ex1.html.
4. Noah Webster, An American Dictionary of the English Language (New York: S. Converse, 1828), vol. I.
5. Frederick Taylor Gates, *Chapters in My Life* (New York: Free Press, 1977), p. 206.
6. Condorcet, *Sketch for a Historical Picture of the Progress of the Human Mind* (London: Wiedenfield and Nicolson, 1955).
7. For the evolution of the concept from the Enlightenment, see Amanda Kay McVety, *Enlightened Aid: U.S. Development as Foreign Policy in Ethiopia* (New York: Oxford, 2012), pp. 7–37.
8. "Development has thus become one of those words – like security or democracy – which apparently requires no definition, for everyone knows, instinctively, what it is." Kate Manzo, "Modernist Discourse and the Crisis of Development Theory," *Comparative Studies of International Development* 26 (1991) 2: 20.

9. David Lilienthal, *The Journals of David E. Lilienthal*, vol. 1, *The TVA Years, 1939–1945* (New York: Harper and Row, 1964), p. 510.
10. Dean Rusk, "The Foreign Assistance Program for 1967," *Department of State Bulletin*, 54 (April 18, 1966) 1399: 629.
11. Drew R. McCoy, *The Elusive Republic: Political Economy in Jeffersonian America* (Chapel Hill: University of North Carolina Press, 1980), p. 16.
12. W. W. Rostow, *The Stages of Economic Growth: A Non-Communist Manifesto* (Cambridge: Cambridge University Press, 1960).
13. National Commission on Terrorist Attacks in the United States, *The 9/11 Commission Report* (New York: Norton, 2004), p. 53.
14. Julia Irwin, *Making the World Safe: The American Red Cross and a Nation's Humanitarian Awakening* (New York: Oxford, 2013), p. 175; Gayle Tzemach Lemmon, "The Hillary Doctrine: Women's Rights are a National Security Issue," *The Atlantic*, April 8, 2013, http://goo.gl/OLSpVo.
15. Gilbert Rist, *The History of Development: From Western Origins to Global Faith* (London: Zed, 1999), p. 72.
16. Daniel Speich, "The Use of Global Abstractions: National Income Accounting in the Period of Imperial Decline," *Journal of Global History* 6 (2011) 1: 7–28; Zachary Karabell, *The Leading Indicators: A Short History of the Numbers that Rule Our World* (New York: Simon and Schuster, 2014); Diane Coyle, *GDP: A Brief But Affectionate History* (Princeton, 2014).
17. Pierre Brocheaux, "Moral Economy or Political Economy: The Peasants are Always Rational," *Journal of Asian Studies* 42 (1982) 4: 791–803.
18. Akhil Gupta, *Postcolonial Developments: Agriculture in the Making of Modern India* (Durham: Duke, 1998), p. 7.
19. H. W. Arndt, *Economic Development: The History of an Idea* (Chicago: Univeristy of Chicago Press, 1987); J. B. Bury, *The Idea of Progress, An Inquiry into its Origin and Growth* (New York: Dover, 1932); Robert Nisbet, *History of the Idea of Progress* (New Brunswick: Transaction, 1994).
20. James C. Scott, *Seeing Like a State* (New Haven: Yale, 1998).
21. Marshall Berman, *All That Is Solid Melts Into Air: The Experience of Modernity* (New York: Penguin), 1988, p. 52.
22. M. P. Cowen and R. W. Shenton, *Doctrines of Development* (London: Routledge, 1996), pp. 173–252.
23. Hodge, *Triumph of the Expert*, p. 28.
24. Richard Drayton, *Nature's Government: Science, Imperial Britain, and the Improvement of the World* (New Haven: Yale, 2000).
25. Albert J. Berveridge, "The Annual Address: The Development of a Colonial Policy for the United States," *Annals of the American Academy* 30 (1907): 3.
26. Hodge, *Triumph*, pp. 42–3.
27. Charles Maier, *Among Empires: American Ascendancy and its Predecessors* (Cambridge, MA: Harvard, 2006), pp. 238–84.
28. Amy L. S. Staples, *The Birth of Development: How the World Bank, Food and Agriculture Organization, and World Health Organization Changed the World* (Kent, OH: Kent State University Press, 2006).
29. "Adlai Blasts Cut in Welfare to Catch Reds," *Chicago Tribune*, December 10, 1957, p. 1.

Development and technopolitics

30. Dean Acheson, "Crisis in Asia," *Department of State Bulletin*, January 23, 1950, pp. 112–13.
31. Sargent Shriver, *Point of the Lance* (New York: Harper and Row, 1964), p. 9.
32. Nils Gilman, *Mandarins of the Future: Modernization Theory in Cold War America* (Baltimore: Johns Hopkins, 2003).
33. Max Millikan and Walt W. Rostow, "Notes on Foreign Economic Policy," May 21, 1954, in *Universities and Empire: Money and Politics in the Social Sciences During the Cold war*, ed. Christopher Simpson (New York: 1998), p. 41.
34. Quoted in David C. Engerman, "West Meets East: The Center for International Studies and Indian Economic Development," in *Staging Growth: Modernization, Development, and the Global Cold War*, ed. David Engerman (Amherst, 2003), pp. 199–224.
35. Latham, "Introduction," in Engerman, ed. *Staging Growth*, 1–24.
36. Richard Slotkin, *Gunfighter Nation: The Myth of the Frontier in Twentieth Century America* (New York: HarperPerrennial, 1993), pp. 441–88.
37. Jonathan Nashel, *Edward Lansdale's Cold War* (Amherst: University of Massachusetts Press, 2005); James T. Fisher, *Dr. America: The Lives of Thomas A. Dooley, 1927–1961* (Amherst: University of Massachusetts Press, 1997).
38. Christina Klein, *Cold War Orientalism: Asia in the Middlebrow Imagination, 1945–1961* (Berkeley: University of California Press, 2003).
39. Billy Wilder, *Sabrina*, Paramount, 1954.
40. Colin Leys, *The Rise and Fall of Development Theory* (Bloomington: Indiana University Press, 1996).
41. Stephen Macekura, *Of Limits and Growth: The Rise of Global Sustainable Development in the Twentieth Century* (New York: Cambridge, 2015).
42. Vijay Prashad, *The Poorer Nations: A Possible History of the Global South* (London: Verso, 2012), p. 81.
43. Sun Yat-sen, *The International Development of China* (New York, 1922); Sugata Bose, "Instruments and Idioms of Colonial and National Development: India's Historical Experience in Comparative Perspective," in *International Development and the Social Sciences*, ed. Frederick Cooper and Randall Packard (Berkeley, 1997), 45–63; Gregg A. Brazinsky, *Nation Building in South Korea: Koreans, Americans, and the Making of a Democracy* (Chapel Hill: University of North Carolina, 2007).
44. Ryszard Kapuściński, *Shah of Shahs* (New York: Harcourt Brace, 1985), p. 67.
45. James Ferguson, *The Antipolitics Machine: Development, Depoliticization, and Bureaucratic Power in the Third World* (Cambridge, 1990); David C. Engerman, "The Anti-Politics of Inequality: Reflections on a Special Issue," *Journal of Global History* 6 (2011): 143–51.
46. Frederick Cooper, "Writing the History of Development," *Journal of Modern European History* 8 (2010): 11.
47. Gabrielle Hecht, "Technology, Politics, and National Identity in France," in *Technologies of Power: Essays in Honor of Thomas Parke Hughes* (Cambridge, MA: MIT, 2001), p. 256.
48. David Ekbladh, *The Great American Mission: Modernization and the Construction of an American World Order* (Princeton: Princeton University Press, 2010), pp. 52, 100.

49. Robert Rook, "Race. Water and Foreign Policy: The Tennessee Valley Authority's Global Agenda Meets Jim Crow," *Diplomatic History* 28 (2004) 1: 55–82.
50. Michael E. Latham, *The Right Kind of Revolution: Modernization, Development, and U.S. Foreign Policy From the Cold War to the Present* (Ithaca: Cornell, 2011), pp. 148–9.
51. Jenifer Van Vleck, "An Airline at the Crossroads of the World: Ariana Afghan Airlines, Modernization, and the Global Cold War," *History and Technology* 25 (2009) 1: 7.
52. Timothy N. Mitchell, *Carbon Democracy: Political Power in the Age of Oil* (London: Verso, 2013).
53. Sally Engle Merry, "Measuring the World: Indicators, Human Rights and Global Governance," *Current Anthropology* 52 (2011) S3: S88.
54. Cooper, "Writing the History," p. 11.
55. Matthew Connelly, *Fatal Misconception: The Struggle to Control World Population* (Cambridge, MA: Harvard University Press, 2008).
56. Tania Murray Li, *The Will to Improve: Governmentality, Development, and the Practice of Politics* (Durham, NC: Duke, 2007), p. 5.
57. Alden Young, "Accounting for Decolonization: The Origins of the Sudanese Economy, 1945–1964," PhD dissertation, Princeton University, 2013.
58. Jamie Cohen-Cole, *The Open Mind: Cold War Politics and the Sciences of Human Nature* (Chicago: University of Chicago Press, 2014), pp. 13–14.
59. Brad Simpson, *Economists with Guns Authoritarian Development and U.S.–Indonesian Relations, 1960–1968* (Stanford, 2008), pp. 252–3.
60. Frederick Cooper, "Writing the History," 20.
61. Perry Miller, "Teacher in Japan," *The Atlantic*, August 1953, p. 65.
62. Alfred Thayer Mahan, *The Problem of Asia and its Effect Upon International Politics* (London: Sampson, Low, and Marston, 1900), p. 89.
63. David Rieff, "An American Passion for Tyrants," *New York Review of Books*, June 19, 2014.
64. David C. Engerman, *Modernization From the Other Shore: American Intellectuals and the Romance of Russian Development* (Cambridge, MA: Harvard, 2003).
65. Thomas C. Field, Jr., *From Development to Dictatorship: Bolivia and the Alliance for Progress in the Kennedy Era* (Ithaca: Cornell, 2014).
66. NPR, "President Bush's Second Inaugural Address," January 20, 2005, http://goo.gl/DbLosk; Kennedy, "Statement at the Opening Ceremony of the World Food Congress," June 4, 1963, JFK Office Files, Part 1, 11: 1018 [microfilm].
67. Alison Bashford, *Global Population: History, Geopolitics, and Life on Earth* (New York: Columbia, 2014); Paul Sabin, *The Bet: Paul Ehrlich, Julian Simon, and Our Gamble Over the Earth's Future* (New Haven: Yale, 2013).
68. John D. and Catherine T. MacArthur Foundation, "Master's in Development Practice," March 2011, www.macfound.org/media/article_pdfs/MDP_INFO.pdf.
69. Michael Gubser, "The Presentist Bias: Ahistoricism, Equity, and International Development in the 1970s," *Journal of Development Studies* 48 (2012) 12: 1799–1812.
70. Quoted in Alonzo Hanby, *Liberalism and its Challengers: FDR to Reagan* (New York, 1985), pp. 72–3.

7

Nonstate actors

Barbara J. Keys[1]

"Shortly after I left office," former president Bill Clinton told a group in 2005, "I was shaving and I looked in the mirror and I thought, my God, *I have become an NGO*."[2] The remark neatly captures the ubiquity of NGOs in today's world. Previous ex-presidents had taken up various causes, as Clinton did with HIV/AIDS, but in recent decades activities that might earlier have fallen under other rubrics have been swept up in an NGO revolution. The three-letter designation is now so common that it has congealed into a distinct word, independent of its origins as an acronym for nongovernmental organization. Along with other nonstate actors, NGOs have exploded in numbers and in power and influence. As the terrain of global politics has been reconfigured, a booming scholarship in political science, sociology, and anthropology has arisen, which aims to explain how these newly assertive actors influence national and international politics and local lives. In international history, nonstate actors that once hovered on the periphery are moving to the center of scholarly attention.

Rising interest in the role of nonstate actors in international relations is part of a broader shift in the field away from scholarly preoccupation with state-to-state relations. As summed up by two critics in 1971, students and practitioners of international politics traditionally cared almost exclusively about relationships among states. In this view, "the state, regarded as an actor with purposes and power, is the basic unit of action: its main agents are the diplomat and the soldier."[3] The state-driven models of international relations this description captures have been under challenge at least since the 1970s, as it has become glaringly apparent that state power is but one of the drivers of global affairs. Nonstate actors have at their disposal economic or moral assets that translate into direct and indirect political power; some nonstate actors, such as the Palestine Liberation Organization, have military capabilities. As international relations have been transformed, the study of international relations has shifted to adapt to new realities.

The novelty of the scholarly shift and the innovations nonstate actors are bringing to global affairs can easily be overstated. After all, the British East India Company ran a subcontinent in the seventeenth and eighteenth centuries. People have always moved about the world. Networks of traders, religious proselytizers, artists, and intellectuals spread ideas, practices, and goods across political boundaries. What is said to distinguish the last forty or so years (or, according to some accounts, the last century) is the absolute number of nonstate actors, the types of activities they engage in, and the cumulative level of influence they wield. In both popular and academic understanding, the role of nonstate actors has qualitatively changed international affairs in the last few decades. What remains unclear – and hotly debated – is the extent to which this development threatens to undermine or to overturn an international system based on state sovereignty.

The variety of nonstate actors is dizzying. They span local, national, and international nongovernmental organizations, multinational corporations, philanthropic foundations, international media, religious groups, terrorist and criminal networks, individual actors, migrants, and diasporas. The Mafia, Oxfam, Dennis Rodman, al-Qaeda, expatriate communities, pirates, and the stateless Mehran Karimi Nasseri (who lived in a Paris airport for 17 years): all are nonstate actors.[4] Their uncountable millions vastly outnumber the roughly 200 states in the world today. Their activities penetrate into almost every corner of life. In moral or economic terms, their individual or collective power can exceed that of many states. Google's market value of $400 billion, for example, dwarfs the GDPs of many countries in the world.

This chapter covers key methodological issues in the study of the three major types of nonstate actors: NGOs, intergovernmental organizations (IGOs), and multinational corporations.[5] These categories comprise the main institutionalized manifestations of nonstate power. Because intergovernmental organizations are created and nominally controlled by states, they may seem unlikely candidates for the nonstate rubric. Yet they are often placed in the nonstate category as semi-autonomous entities with interests that can diverge from those of the states that comprise them. Although there are other varieties of nonstate actors, the study of these three major groupings raises similar methodological issues and has provided much of the driving force for the rethinking of global affairs in various disciplines.

A wide range of questions can be posed about these groups, and methods and approaches for studying them are highly varied. Despite the fact that nonstate actors have always existed alongside states and have always played a measurable role in international relations, only in the last few decades have political scientists and sociologists begun to develop distinctive tools for approaching the subject. In international history, the study of nonstate actors, such as missionaries and business groups, was often approached in the framework of intercultural relations or as an adjunct to understanding state power. Only recently have international historians moved forcefully to examine nonstate actors in leading roles as full-fledged diplomatic actors. One aspect of the change is simply terminological: early studies on missionaries and cultural exchange, for example, were studies of nonstate actors *avant la lettre*. But a significant part of the shift is also conceptual, a product of more explicit recognition of the need to grapple with deterritorialized, transnational spaces and highly complicated flows of power.[6]

The term nonstate actor denotes a negative category, defined by what it is not rather than by common characteristics. The category itself suggests the continuing dominance of the concept of the state and the embryonic condition of efforts to conceptualize international affairs without affirming the centrality of the state. Moreover, like all artificial constructions, it can oversimplify and distort. Delineating where the "public" ends and the "private" begins is usually a fluid and imprecise exercise. The British East India Company's 1670 charters granted it the right to mint money, to command troops and fortresses, to make war and peace, and to acquire territory.[7] More recent examples, though less dramatic, underscore the difficulties in matching the real world to the ideal types of state and nonstate. Is former president Jimmy Carter a nonstate actor when he engages in personal diplomacy? Was Halliburton's subsidiary Kellogg, Brown & Root a nonstate actor when the US government paid it billions of dollars to assist in the occupation of Iraq? Where is the line between state and nonstate to be drawn when the government works with internet service providers to gather information on ordinary citizens?

As these questions suggest, much of the study of nonstate actors revolves around understanding their relationship to one another and to state power. Reflecting the assumption that the type of power that "matters" in international relations is the military, diplomatic, economic, and cultural power deployed by states, scholarship on nonstate actors often asks questions about efficacy and influence as measured by nonstate actors' effects on the behavior of states. There is also recognition, however, that nonstate actors can wield power – over the spread of ideas, lifestyle choices, perceptions, and so on – that shapes international affairs regardless of measurable effects on what states do.

Nonstate actors can be studied in order to shed light on national histories. A study of American missionary groups might aim to illuminate the history of religion in the United States or to show how these groups influenced US foreign policy.[8] The more provocative thrust of scholarship on nonstate actors, however, challenges "methodological nationalism," which sets the nation-state as the default scale of analysis. Studying nonstate actors on larger scales than the nation can work to de-privilege the nation as the primary "container" of history. Almost by definition, international nongovernmental organizations occupy a transnational space that spans but does not encompass nations, polities, and cultures.[9] Amnesty International, for example, is headquartered in the UK, has 80 national sections, and works in dozens more. Though its US section can be studied to illuminate American developments and its influence on US foreign policy, studying the international organization necessarily involves a transnational frame of reference.[10] Understanding the workings of this transnational space and its influence on global politics is at the heart of much of the innovation in studying nonstate actors.

NGOS

In 1998, former Canadian foreign minister Lloyd Axworthy lauded NGOs as the "world's new superpower."[11] Their history extends back at least a century, even if the name does not. International associations before World War II were called "semi-private," "private," "voluntary," "informal," or "unofficial" organizations; often, they included "union," "conference," or "council" in their names.[12] The term NGO was effectively created by the United Nations (UN), which in Article 71 of its 1945 Charter gave "nongovernmental organizations" consultative status at the Economic and Social Council and in 1950 codified NGO participation rights.[13] The Council's definition includes any international organization not established by intergovernmental agreement. To obtain consultative status at the UN, NGOs must deal with issues of concern to the UN, have a headquarters and a hierarchical structure, and be international in scope.[14]

As with nonstate actor, the category is not unproblematic. The organizations themselves have often chafed at the label, seeing it as an alienating device. (One activist provocatively suggested calling governments "non-people's organizations"; others have recommended redefining the term as "necessary-to-governance organizations.") Some see NGO, like "non-white," as having pejorative connotations and a framing that signals irrelevance in traditional diplomacy.[15] Though most scholars consider NGOs to be nonprofit groups and hence distinguished from other nonstate actors such as criminal organizations, the category is nevertheless extremely diverse, with numerous subgroups such as "mutant NGOs," "mushroom NGOs," Gongos (government-organized NGOs), and Quangos (quasi-autonomous NGOs).[16] As the last two labels underscore, NGOs are often less "nongovernmental" than the typology indicates. Even NGOs that are not formally organized by governments might receive significant funding from governments or intergovernmental organizations, highlighting the blurriness of the lines between nonstate actors and states.

Internationally active NGOs (INGOs) can be found in almost every sphere of social, cultural, economic, and political life: from sports to law, agriculture to education, religion to health. Many of them are well known, including human rights organizations such as Human Rights Watch and Amnesty International; humanitarian entities such as CARE International and Doctors without Borders; environmental groups such as Greenpeace and the World Wildlife Fund; sports bodies such as the International Olympic Committee and the Fédération Internationale de Football Association; and religious organizations such as the World Council of Churches and the World Muslim Congress.

Others, such as the International Electrotechnical Commission, operate out of the public spotlight and often on very small budgets. Lyman Cromwell White's early study of INGOs dates the beginning of the modern type of organization to the mid-nineteenth century, when travel and communications technology began to spark new forms of association.[17] Current estimates suggest that there are over 40,000 international nongovernmental organizations in the world today, with millions of NGOs operating at a local or national level.[18] Only recently has the heavy geographic concentration of INGO headquarters in Paris, Brussels, London, New York, and Geneva begun to be balanced by organizations based in the non-West.[19]

Because NGOs so often act in concert or in competition with other NGOs, studying their role involves understanding their interactions, formal and informal networks, and lines of influence. NGOs often act in concert, as illustrated by the example of the Climate Action Network, which brings together nearly 900 NGOs working on climate change.[20] As the number of NGOs has mushroomed, however, competitive behavior has also become common. International historian Pierre-Yves Saunier notes that whereas the International Committee of the Red Cross and the Save the Children Fund were the only two humanitarian bodies on the ground during the 1935–6 Italo-Ethiopian War, 120 groups jostled elbows in Rwanda during the genocide of 1994–5, where "logo wars" erupted as groups struggled to plant their organization's symbols before television cameras.[21] As scholars increasingly recognize, NGOs are self-interested, seek to "market" themselves, and sometimes engage in misconduct. In short, they are like other international actors.[22]

A central divide in approaches to the study of NGOs lies in how researchers conceptualize the relationship of these organizations to other forms of power, especially state power. One strand of thinking, now on the wane, views INGOs as vehicles for the expression of interests that encompass humanity as a whole. In this view, INGOs work for global causes, whereas governments, corporations, and citizens pursue their own narrow interests. INGOs therefore exist on a higher moral plane, where they are working in salutary fashion to create a global society that is loosening the grip of the old international order based on sovereign states, which is ill-equipped to manage new trans-border challenges. This perspective was prevalent in the 1990s, when many observers celebrated the birth of a post-Westphalian world order in which well-meaning INGOs would supplant the narrowly self-interested power of states.[23] Countering this view are those who argue that INGOs, far from being benevolent forces acting against the state, are in fact serving the interests of powerful states and, whether they intend to or not, abet imperialistic missions.

Those in the former camp tend to approach the study of NGOs through the lens of global society, a concept defined and developed by social scientists in the last few decades. Other labels include international society, transnational civil society, and the global public.[24] As one study put it, whereas states and corporations are self-interested, transnational civil society is a "third force" that aims to promote shared values and the public good.[25] International historian Akira Iriye, in his seminal 2002 volume on the role of nongovernmental organizations in international relations, calls it "global community." Lamenting that diplomatic historians too often dismissed international organizations as irrelevant to the kinds of diplomatic and military activities that were seen to bear on matters of war and peace, Iriye argues that international organizations offer a means to reconceptualize world affairs not as the clash of nations but as a search for order, cooperation, and interdependence.[26] Limiting his scope to nonprofit, nonreligious, nonmilitary, voluntary INGOs with progressive goals, he claims that these groups build transnational networks "that are based on a global consciousness, the idea that there is a wider world over and above separate states and national societies, and that individuals and groups, no matter where they are, share certain interests and concerns in that wider world."[27] As Saunier has suggested, the narrative of global civil society is a refraction of the self-glorifying myths INGOs propagate about themselves, and its prevalence is a function of the fledgling – and, in his view, naïve – state of historical scholarship on these groups.[28]

Related to the global civil society framework is the study of social movements. This field, and the study of transnational social movements in particular, has generated a rich range of "theories" and approaches in sociology and political science.[29] Though NGOs are sometimes excluded from the definition of social movement, it is more accurate to see them as components of social movements, and social movement studies offer much methodological fodder to the scholar of NGOs.[30] Sociologists and political scientists have produced a large body of work on how social movements emerge and the consequences they have. This work has pointed to the importance of understanding the broader political contexts that structure opportunities for action, including political and economic opportunities and constraints and the vulnerabilities of political targets. How activists organize resources and create networks has also been an intense focus of study, particularly around the relationship of social movements to civil society more broadly and to associational cultures in particular locales. Of particular interest to historians are the ways that social movements "frame" their causes to define issues, mobilize support, and create systems of meaning.[31] These approaches – understanding how movements mobilize resources ("resource mobilization theory"), the larger political arenas in which they operate ("political process theory"), and the roles of emotions, culture, and identity – all have relevance to historians and can be helpful to understanding not only social movements but also other nonstate actors.[32]

The concept of "transnational advocacy networks," developed by political scientists Margaret Keck and Kathryn Sikkink in 1998, has been widely influential among scholars of social movements and NGOs. Positing networks rather than individual NGOs as the unit of analysis and showing that NGOs can act simultaneously in domestic and international settings, Keck and Sikkink emphasize that advocacy networks can exert influence by shaping flows of information and thus constitute "an important part of an explanation for change in world politics." Their analysis partially reinforces the primacy of the state by locating it as the target of most advocacy pressures, but also suggests that new forms of global governance beyond the power of the state have been developing.[33]

While INGOs have been studied intensively for how they frame issues, what causes they adopt, and what impact they have had, the internal structures and functions of these organizations have been neglected. We know little about their financing, staffing, or organizational cultures. Most INGOs are structured along national lines, such as Amnesty International with its national sections. The Women's International League for Peace and Freedom in 1924 imagined a "world section" that would be a "psychological laboratory" for rethinking national identifications, but this experiment was an anomaly, and even today most INGOs continue to reinforce national identities in their internal structures. Counterbalancing a predisposition in earlier work to treat INGOs as cosmopolitan, post-national entities, future scholarship is likely to look closely at the national environments of INGOs, how the location of a group's headquarters shape internal and external perceptions of the organization, and how national contexts matter to the ways that INGOs organize and act.[34]

Whereas many scholars see nongovernmental organizations as counterweights to state power and the power of the market, other observers have suggested that NGOs buttress neoimperialist distributions of power. They can point to evidence such as former US Secretary of State Colin Powell's paean to humanitarian NGOs as a "force multiplier" for the US government.[35] Historian Niall Ferguson, a cheerleader for American empire, has approvingly described the United States as an imperial power whose methods of informal rule "rely heavily on nongovernmental organizations and corporations."[36] Critics of American empire tend to agree that the spread of American influence overseas has been fostered by private and public interests acting in concert. A groundbreaking example of such an approach is historian Emily Rosenberg's work on the role of churches, foundations, and civic organizations in the early twentieth century in spreading an American ideology she calls "liberal developmentalism."[37] In a different vein, Matthew Connelly's work on international population control efforts underscores the driving role played by nonstate actors, such as the International Planned Parenthood Federation, in pushing rich countries to embrace a massive, coercive social engineering project premised on violations of human rights. International and nongovernmental organizations "tried to control the population of the world without having to answer to anyone in particular" – sometimes even without the knowledge or consent of governments, Connelly notes.[38]

As skeptics of the moral superiority of an NGO-dominated global society point out, there is nothing inherent in the nature of these organizations that ensures they represent the public interest. NGOs are typically not democratic and do not operate in transparent ways. Information on their personnel, operations, funding sources, and expenditures is often difficult or impossible to obtain. They are not accountable to the people, governments, and businesses they most affect, and they often consist of people in one place speaking for people, often "victims," somewhere else.[39] Usually constructed around a single raison d'être, they pursue causes that are often narrowly defined, rather than considering the broad interests of society as a whole. Sometimes they act in ways that foster their own organizational interests, sensationalizing or distorting issues to spur donations or gain publicity and membership. The global society concept assumes that a set of shared values is spreading, even in the face of much evidence that values remain deeply contested. The concept of civic networks also downplays major asymmetries, as some "nodes" in the networks may wield vastly disproportionate influence.[40] For all these reasons, attending to questions of moral and political legitimacy and accountability is important for students of INGOs.

Recent approaches often begin with the assumption that NGOs and states do not work in opposition but instead share many similarities and are often deeply intertwined. Far from being autonomous, NGOs depend on the provision of public goods by governments, including a civic sphere that allows free speech. Their work often depends on persuading friendly governments to work with them in IGOs or to act against other governments.[41] They often work as subcontractors for or full partners to governments, who implicitly offer them legitimacy. Development NGOs have become a major partner for both governments and IGOs. This type of partnership extends back to the League of Nations, which worked closely with private groups and individuals interested in disarmament, finance, and welfare.[42] Older approaches that assumed that the growth of NGO power meant a reduction in state power have given way to recognition that NGO power works in multiple directions and often in ways that buttress state power.[43]

INTERGOVERNMENTAL ORGANIZATIONS

The study of IGOs, the second prong of the boom in nonstate actor research, exhibits considerable common ground with the study of NGOs. Indeed the two types of organization often work so closely together that they cannot be studied in isolation. Though many US foreign relations historians might agree with a political scientist's characterization of international organizations as a "big yawn," estimates of their importance in international relations continue to rise.[44] As is the case with NGOs, the numbers of IGOs have grown sharply in the last few decades, and they have effected key changes in the international system as they have assumed more wide-ranging roles. In 1900 there were 36 such organizations; a century later, there were thousands.[45] Some of them, such as the UN and NATO, appear often, though rarely centrally, in the work of scholars of US foreign relations. Other well-known IGOs include the European Central Bank, the International Monetary Fund, and the Organization for Security and Co-operation in Europe.

As with NGOs, scholars have often approached the study of IGOs with a normative bias, viewing these organizations as "good" because they spread cooperation, expert knowledge, and humanitarian goals.[46] Historian Amy Staples sees the "international civil servants" of the World Health Organization as genuinely apolitical, "disinterested citizens of the world."[47] The more biographical approach in Joseph Hodge's work, in contrast, underscores how British imperial administrators and technical advisers after World War II moved into UN agencies as development experts, transferring old colonial practices and assumptions to the new environment.[48]

Understanding how IGOs operate in and shape the international system is central to the study of global governance. A concept popularized in the 1990s, it means not world government but, rather, processes for managing tractable global problems through formal institutions. Because IGOs and NGOs so often work closely together, the study of global governance might be said to comprise the study of the relationship between IGOs and NGOs.[49] The study of IGOs, and especially their international secretariats, involves questions similar to those raised by NGOs: what is the nature of their power, how is it exercised, how do they derive their legitimacy, and why do they succeed and fail?

MULTINATIONAL CORPORATIONS

The definition of multinational corporation limits its scope to recent times (when nations and corporations have existed), but firms that cross borders are as old as the modern nation-state, and they have both influenced and practiced diplomacy, often with very substantial effects.[50] Like NGOs, the power and reach of multinational corporations, also known as transnational corporations and multinational enterprises or firms, have grown dramatically over the last two centuries. In 1970 an observer noted that General Motors, Ford, Standard Oil of New Jersey, Royal/Dutch Shell, General Electric, Chrysler, Unilever, and Mobil Oil ranked among the largest forty entities in the world.[51]

The study of multinational corporations and their nineteenth-century antecedents is a neglected area in US foreign relations history, both little investigated and poorly incorporated into existing narratives. Though the influential revisionist paradigm associated with William Appleman Williams focused on the economic underpinnings of foreign policy, it posited an ideology of economic expansion driven primarily by a search for new markets for goods and capital, without detailed examination of actual economic processes or sustained attention to the role of business.[52] (The role of United Fruit in the 1954 CIA-led coup in Guatemala is an important exception to the common neglect of corporations – as distinct from economic interests – in US foreign relations history.)[53] There are signs, however, that the boom in interest in the history of capitalism provoked by the 2008 financial crisis may be spilling over into diplomatic history.

For a detailed discussion of methods for studying multinational corporations, see the entries in this volume by Brad Simpson on political economy and Michael Hogan on corporatism.[54] A few brief points are warranted here. Whereas many scholars of NGOs approach their subjects with a normative bias in their favor, scholars of multinational corporations rarely take that stance. After all, firms do not usually claim to act for the public good. They are profit-seeking, whereas NGOs often define their goals in moral terms and claim to act for others. But as with NGOs, the question of whose interests are being followed is central. If in the euphoric 1990s, obituaries of state power posited that power was devolving not only from states to NGOs but from states to corporations, recent work suggests that multinational corporations, like INGOs, retain a form of national identification and often buttress state power rather than diminish it.[55] Multinational corporations often participate in defining national interests, identifying their own interest with those of the state. And like NGOs, corporations often have close relationships with IGOs. The special agencies of the League of Nations and the United Nations assisted in the development of a world market, despite many disagreements over monetary policy, trade, and development.[56] Methodologies to interpret organizational behavior – how organizations influence each other, how different governmental "regimes" affect how organizations pursue goals, the organizational forms they take, their strategies for allocating resources, and so on – can also be usefully adapted to the historical study of firms.[57]

CONCLUSION

Writing the history of nonstate actors presents many methodological challenges. Some of the best work aims to trace the complex relationships and networks formed between nonstate and state actors and among different varieties of nonstate actors.[58] The decentered, diffused, complex, and uneven nature of these connections makes them both tricky to document and challenging to describe. On a practical level, simply finding sources can be difficult, as many NGOs and MNCs have inaccessible, nonexistent, or disorganized archives. Even when reasonably complete and organized, the records of headquarters may not convey the viewpoints and activities of local or national nodes, and the records of other organizations and governments need to be mined to illuminate crucial interactions and relationships.[59]

Many nonstate actors inhabit a transnational space that is difficult to conceptualize geographically and whose lines of power and influence are difficult to trace. We are all familiar with maps of the world in which lines and colors are determined by the boundaries of states. A map of the world that rendered countries not according to their territorial land mass but relative to the number of multinational corporation headquarters they contained would look very different, making Denmark, for example, look huge.[60] Nonstate actors sometimes use intersticial spaces, such as the airspace between countries, as arenas for the contestation of power.[61] Standard chronologies are also challenged when nonstate actors are placed on the stage. An oft-cited example is the Cold War, typically studied within the framework of superpower conflict but during which many trends and developments arose or accelerated that operated quite independently of East–West competition.[62]

If state-to-state relations are complex, involving competing interests, bureaucratic rivalries, and inputs from domestic politics, ideology, and other forces, the study of nonstate actors multiplies these complexities by an order of magnitude. Links move horizontally: across governments, international funding agencies, and NGOs; as well as vertically: connecting local, regional, national, and international levels. Along these multiple axes people, money, knowledge, and ideas flow in ways that are often extremely difficult to trace and, once traced, even more difficult to narrate. Typically, the targets of action are geographically dispersed and involve a multitude of actors, making it hard to establish causation and agency.[63] Often, failing to follow one of these axes will elide important relationships. For example, the movement of particular individuals from INGOs to IGOs to governments, carrying with them practices and assumptions, can reveal causal lines of influence that would not be obvious with a purely institutional approach that neglected biography.

The study of groups, organizations, individuals, and networks outside the state is an essential task for international historians. Yet leaping on the nonstate actor bandwagon poses potential risks. Might this category and the closely linked term NGO obscure more than they reveal? It is worth considering what exactly is gained by using this conceptual framework and these labels, and what political choices are embedded in their current prevalence. The second edition of this volume had no entry dedicated to nonstate actors. Will the fourth?

NOTES

1. This chapter was funded by an Australian Research Council Discovery Project Grant (DP110100424, 2011–2014). The author thanks Nathan Kurz and Brad Simpson for excellent suggestions.
2. Bill Clinton, Keynote Speech at RehabCare Suicide Prevention Fundraiser, Dublin, May 23, 2005, at www.rehab.ie/press/ClintonAddress.pdf.
3. Joseph S. Nye, Jr. and Robert O. Keohane, "Transnational Relations and World Politics: An Introduction," *International Organization* 25, no. 3 (1971): 329.
4. Important works on other types of nonstate actors include Christopher Endy, *Cold War Holidays: American Tourism in France* (Chapel Hill, NC, 2004), which sets

out the concept of "consumer diplomacy"; Brian Delay, *War of a Thousand Deserts: Indian Raids and the U.S.–Mexican War* (New Haven, CT, 2008); Donna R. Gabaccia, *Foreign Relations: American Immigration in Global Perspective* (Princeton, NJ, 2012); and Judy Tzu-Chun Wu, *Radicals on the Road: Internationalism, Orientalism, and Feminism during the Vietnam War* (Ithaca, NY, 2013), mostly centered on individual activists, including citizen diplomats.

5. This structure follows the definition of nonstate actor in *The Ashgate Research Companion to Non-State Actors*, ed. Bob Reinalda (Farnham, Surrey, 2011).
6. On this point see also Akira Iriye, *Global and Transnational History: The Past, Present, and Future* (New York, 2013), 14.
7. See Hugh Bowen, *The Business of Empire: The East India Company and Imperial Britain, 1756–1833* (Cambridge, 2008). For a look at the history of chartered companies and mercantilism from the perspective of a global history of capitalism, see David Frieden, *Global Capitalism: Its Fall and Rise in the Twentieth Century* (New York, 2006).
8. I am drawing here on Kenneth Pomeranz's discussion of methodological nationalism and challenges to it: Kenneth Pomeranz, "Histories for a Less National Age," *American Historical Review* (2014): 1–3. For an excellent recent example of the study of nonstate actors in a national context, see Sarah Miller-Davenport, "'Their Blood Shall Not Be Shed in Vain': American Evangelical Missionaries and the Search for God and Country in Post–World War II Asia," *Journal of American History* 99, no. 4 (2013): 1109–32.
9. Pomeranz, "Histories for a Less National Age," 2. On these issues see also "AHR Conversation: On Transnational History," *American Historical Review* 111, no. 5 (December 2006): 1441–64.
10. For an example of the former, see Barbara Keys, *Reclaiming American Virtue: The Human Rights Revolution of the 1970s* (Cambridge, MA, 2014), ch. 8.
11. Lloyd Axworthy, "A Ban of the People: The Landmines Campaign and the New Diplomacy," Cambridge University Conference on Global Governance, May 9, 1998, quoted in Nicola Short, "The Role of NGOs in the Ottawa Process to Ban Landmines," *International Negotiation* 4 (1999): 481.
12. The term non governmental organization was used in the interwar years in labor circles. Pierre-Yves Saunier, "International Non-Governmental Organizations (INGOs)," in Akira Iriye and Pierre-Yves Saunier, comp., *The Palgrave Dictionary of Transnational History* (New York, 2009), 573.
13. Volker Heins, *Nongovernmental Organizations in International Society: Struggles over Recognition* (New York, 2008), 15; Lyman Cromwell White, *International Non-Governmental Organizations: Their Purposes, Methods, and Accomplishments* (New York, 1968), 3. For a survey of the history of NGOs, see Jeremi Suri, "Non-Governmental Organizations and Non-State Actors," in *Palgrave Advances in International History*, ed. Patrick Finney (New York, 2005), 223–45.
14. Elizabeth Bloodgood, "The Yearbook of International Organizations and Quantitative Non-State Actor Research," in *The Ashgate Research Companion to Non-State Actors*, ed. Reinalda, 21–2. The *Yearbook of International Organizations*, published by the Union of International Associations since 1908, defines NGOs as formally organized bodies independent of government representation with permanent headquarters, a governing unit, and projects, funding, and members

Nonstate actors

from at least three countries. For a definition of NGOs as post-traditional civil associations, see Heins, *Nongovernmental Organizations*, 17–19.
15. Quoted in Norbert Götz's thoughtful critique, "Reframing NGOs: The Identity of an International Relations Non-Starter," *European Journal of International Relations* 14 (2008): 245.
16. Heins, *Nongovernmental Organizations*, 25.
17. White, *International Non-Governmental Organizations*.
18. Matthew Sparke, *Introducing Globalization: The Ties that Bind* (Malden, MA, 2013), 264.
19. Saunier, "INGOs," 574.
20. "About Climate Action Network," at www.climatenetwork.org/about/about-can.
21. Ibid., 577.
22. See, for example, Alexander Cooley and James Ron, "The NGO Scramble: Organizational Insecurity and the Political Economy of Transnational Action," *International Security* 27, no. 1 (2002): 5–39.
23. In a well-known exchange, Jessica Tuchman Mathews declared the accumulation of power in the hands of states that had begun with the Peace of Westphalia was "over" and that a "novel distribution of power among states, markets, and civil society" had happened that allowed "NGOs to push around even the largest governments." Mathews, "Power Shift," *Foreign Affairs* 76 (1997): 50–66, quotations at 50, 53. In response, Laurence Jarvik denounced NGOs as a "new class" whose activities served the interests of "terrorists, warlords, and mafia dons" by weakening states – the only entities capable of maintaining order. Jarvik, "NGOs: A 'New Class' in International Relations," *Orbis* 51 (2007): 217–38, quotation at 217.
24. For an excellent discussion from an anthropological standpoint about the need to distinguish between civil society and NGOs, see William F. Fisher, "Doing Good? The Politics and Antipolitics of NGO Practices," *Annual Review of Anthropology* 26 (1997): 439–64. As Margaret Keck and Kathryn Sikkink have noted in regard to the "world polity" approach, the question of where and how global norms originate is left unclear. Keck and Sikkink, *Activists Beyond Borders*, 33.
25. Ann M. Florini, ed., *The Third Force: The Rise of Transnational Civil Society* (Washington, DC, 2000), 7.
26. Akira Iriye, *Global Community: The Role of International Organizations in the Making of the Contemporary World* (Berkeley: University of California Press, 2002). For a similar take on global community as generated by international sports events, see Barbara Keys, *Globalizing Sport: National Rivalry and International Community* (Cambridge, MA, 2006).
27. Iriye, *Global Community*, 2–8, quotation at 8. Sociologists John Boli and George M. Thomas articulated an influential "world polity" perspective with similar characteristics: see Boli and Thomas, eds., *Constructing World Culture: International Nongovernmental Organizations since 1875* (Stanford, 2005).
28. Saunier, "INGOs," 574.
29. A very large sociological literature on social movements exists. For an introduction to the subset of this literature that deals with transnational social movements, see Jackie Smith, "Transnational Processes and Movements," in *The Blackwell Companion to Social Movements*, eds. David A. Snow, Sarah A. Soule, and Hanspeter Kriesi (Malden, MA, 2007).

30. Peter Willetts, "Summary," in "What Is a Non-Governmental Organization?" at http://bit.ly/1lLXozc. Scholars of transnational social movements view them as "outsiders" and see NGOs as more institutionalized "insiders." See Sidney Tarrow, "The Dualities of Transnational Contention: 'Two Activist Solitudes' or a New World Altogether?" *Mobilization: An International Journal* 10, no. 1 (2005): 53–72.
31. See Jackie Smith and Dawn Wiest, *Social Movements in the World-System: The Politics of Crisis and Transformation* (New York, 2012).
32. Bert Klandermans and Suzanne Staggenborg, eds., *Methods of Social Movement Research* (Minneapolis, 2002), x–xi.
33. Margaret E. Keck and Kathryn Sikkink, *Activists Beyond Borders: Advocacy Networks in International Politics* (Ithaca, 1998), quotation at 2.
34. Saunier, "INGOs," 575. On this point see also Matthew Connelly, *Fatal Misconception: The Struggle to Control World Population* (Cambridge, MA, 2008), 8–9. Sarah Stroup's recent study, for example, argues that legal, political, and cultural variation in the nations where INGOs are headquartered creates major differences in the forms of action and organization these groups take. Sarah S. Stroup, *Borders among Activists: International NGOs in the United States, Britain, and France* (Ithaca, 2012).
35. Colin Powell, Remarks to the National Foreign Policy Conference for Leaders of Nongovernmental Organizations, Washington, DC, October 26, 2011, at The Avalon Project, avalon.law.yale.edu/sept11/powell_brief31.asp.
36. Niall Ferguson, *Colossus: The Price of America's Empire* (New York: Penguin Press, 2004), 13; see also his description of the type of empire that "rules mainly through firms and NGOS," 11.
37. Emily Rosenberg, *Spreading the American Dream: American Economic and Cultural Expansion, 1890–1945* (New York, 1982).
38. Connelly, *Fatal Misconception*, 7; idem, "Seeing Beyond the State: Population Control and the Question of Sovereignty," *Past and Present* 193 (1996): 197–233 [202].
39. Florini, *Third Force*, 231–2.
40. Heins, *Nongovernmental Organizations*, 34.
41. See ibid., 38.
42. See Patricia Clavin, "Defining Transnationalism," *Contemporary European History* 14, no. 4 (November 2005): 425.
43. On the study of IGOs as bureaucracies, see Michael Barnett and Martha Finnemore, *Rules for the World: International Organizations in Global Politics* (Ithaca, 2004).
44. Susan Strange, "Why Do International Organizations Never Die?" in Bob Reinalda and Bertjan Verbeek, eds., *Autonomous Policy Making by International Organizations* (London: Routledge, 1998), 220. For a survey of IGOs in the Cold War, see Amy L. Sayward, "International Institutions," in Petra Goedde and Richard Immerman, eds., *Oxford Handbook of the Cold War* (New York, 2012), 377–92.
45. Numbers vary according to definition and how groups are counted. See David Held and Anthony McGrew, *Globalization/Anti-Globalization: Beyond the Great Divide* (Cambridge, 2007), 22.
46. See Michael Barnett and Martha Finnemore, *Rules for the World: International Organizations in World Politics* (Ithaca, 2004), ix.

47. Amy L. S. Staples, *The Birth of Development: How the World Bank, Food and Agriculture Organization, and World Health Organization Have Changed the World, 1945–1965* (Kent, OH, 2006), 146.
48. Joseph Morgan Hodge, *Triumph of the Expert: Agrarian Doctrines of Development and the Legacies of British Colonialism* (Athens, OH, 2007). I thank Brad Simpson for bringing this book to my attention.
49. Recent work that explores the relationship among states, IGOs, and NGOs includes Elizabeth Borgwardt, *A New Deal for the World: America's Vision for Human Rights* (Cambridge, MA, 2005); Carol Anderson, *Eyes off the Prize: The United Nations and the African American Struggle for Human Rights* (Cambridge, 2003); and Matthew Connelly, *A Diplomatic Revolution: Algeria's Fight for Independence and the Origins of the Post-Cold War World* (New York, 2002).
50. On the question of definition, see *Leviathans: Multinational Corporations and the New Global History*, eds. Alfred D. Chandler, Jr. and Bruze Mazlish (New York, 2005), 3.
51. Richard W. Mansbach et al., *The Web of World Politics* (Englewood Cliffs, NJ, 1976), 28.
52. On Williams, a good starting point is the H-Diplo roundtable on the 50th anniversary edition of *The Contours of American History*, at www.h-net.org/~diplo/roundtables/PDF/Roundtable-XV-21.pdf. Important studies of the role of US firms include Emily Rosenberg, *Financial Missionaries to the World: The Politics and Culture of Dollar Diplomacy, 1900–1939* (Cambridge, MA, 1999); Walter LaFeber, *Michael Jordan and The New Global Capitalism*, exp. ed. (New York, 2002); and Victoria de Grazia, *Irresistible Empire: America's Advance through Twentieth-Century Europe* (Cambridge, MA, 2005).
53. Stephen Schlesinger and Stephen Kinzer, *Bitter Fruit: The Untold Story of the American Coup in Guatemala* (Garden City, NY, 1982).
54. Geoffrey Allen Pigman, "The Diplomacy of Global and Transnational Firms," in *The Oxford Handbook of Modern Diplomacy*, eds. Andrew E. Cooper, Jorge Heine, and Ramesh Thakur (New York, 2013), 192–208.
55. Alison Fleig Frank, "The Petroleum War of 1910: Standard Oil, Austria, and the Limits of the Multinational Corporation," *American Historical Review* 114 (2009): 16–41.
56. Reinalda, *Ashgate Companion*, 16.
57. Early and influential treatments of private–public interaction are Rosenberg, *Spreading the American Dream*, and Frank Costigliola, *Awkward Dominion: American Political, Economic, and Cultural Relations with Europe, 1919–1933* (Ithaca, NY, 1984).
58. Erez Manela's work on smallpox eradication, for example, looks at states, NGOs, IGOs, MNCs, and transnational "epistemic communities." Manela, "A Pox on Your Narrative: Writing Disease Control into Cold War History," *Diplomatic History* 34 (2010): 299–323. On epistemic communities, or networks of knowledge-based experts, see Peter Haas, "Introduction: Epistemic Communities and International Policy Coordination," *International Organization* 46, no. 1 (1992): 1–35.
59. On the problem of sources, see also Thomas Richard Davies, "Researching Transnational History: The Example of Peace Activism," in *Ashgate Research Companion*, ed. Reinalda, 44–5.

60. Medard Gabel and Henry Bruner, *Global Inc.: An Atlas of the Multinational Corporation* (New York, 2003). On maps (and more generally for an innovative approach to tracing transnational connections), see Emily S. Rosenberg, "Transnational Currents in a Shrinking World," in Emily S. Rosenberg, ed., *A World Connecting, 1870–1945* (Cambridge, MA, 2012), 816–17.
61. On this point see Paul Thomas Chamberlain, *The Global Offensive: The United States, the Palestine Liberation Organization, and the Making of the Post-Cold War Order* (Oxford, 2012). I thank Brad Simpson for this observation.
62. Akira Iriye, *Global and Transnational History: The Past, Present, and Future* (New York, 2013).
63. Connelly, "Seeing Beyond the State," 202.

8

Legal history as foreign relations history

Mary L. Dudziak

"Why did the law matter?" an eminent diplomatic historian once asked of a legal historian. Wouldn't an episode in US international history have turned out the same way even if law had not been part of the story?

This kind of question has been central to the traditional divide between legal and foreign relations history. Skepticism about law as a causal force is the common justification for not focusing on law. That skepticism is based on methodological assumptions about what drives diplomatic history. But just as legal historians have not always been clear enough about the reasons their subject matters, foreign relations historians have been lax in their justifications for neglecting law, even as the role of law and lawyers in foreign relations history has expanded through the twentieth century and after.

This divide is driven, in part, through limitations in the way historians sometimes view law, and the way lawyers sometimes view history. At times, law is thought to be rather one-dimensional: if the law requires X, and X doesn't happen, then law has not had an impact. As I will explain, this way of thinking about law is too simple. In some contexts, lawyers (though generally not legal historians) approach history in a parallel, oversimplified way. History is reified into a stable and knowable past, as compared to the webs of evidence that historians sift and interpret. In the context of constitutional originalism, for example, if the past is knowable in a finite way, then past understandings can constrain the present, enabling "history" to be an anchor protecting against contemporary judicial activism.[1] Neither law nor history is as stable as these approaches suggest. And even though it can often be argued that law, by itself, did not produce a particular outcome, this can be said of many important variables in the history of foreign relations.

In this chapter, I will show that law is already present in some aspects of foreign relations history. Using human rights as an example, I will explore the way in which periodization of legal histories is tied to assumptions and arguments about causality. I will illustrate the way law has worked as a tool in international affairs, and the way law makes an indelible mark, or acts as a legitimizing force, affecting what historical actors imagine to be possible. Influential work on the methodology of legal history shows the way law can help to constitute the social and political context within which international affairs are conducted. And I will argue that the presence of law and lawyers in the history of US foreign relations can no longer be ignored.

For a scholar without legal training, taking up law-related topics can pose special challenges. This chapter ends with a Legal History Survival Guide that includes advice about how to get started and how to avoid mistakes. Although I focus on law and US foreign relations history, my advice would be the same for taking up legal history related to other subjects and for scholarship on other regions of the world. Also included are bibliographic sources that will be helpful for the approaches to legal history described below.

LAW AS FOREIGN RELATIONS HISTORY

If law is thought to be peripheral to American foreign relations history, it is curious that this history has so many lawyers in it. The two Secretaries of Foreign Affairs under the Continental Congress during the founding era were lawyers: Robert R. Livingston and John Jay. The first secretary of state, Thomas Jefferson, was a member of the Virginia bar.[2] "A list of the secretaries and undersecretaries of state of the twentieth century reads like a hall of fame of attorneys," write Jerry Israel and David L. Anderson. The list includes Elihu Root, Henry L. Stimson, Edward R. Stettinius, Dean Acheson, John Foster Dulles, and many more. Israel and Anderson note that "a number of these men served both at the State and the Justice departments, and the number of secretaries of state who have also been attorney general is significant."[3]

In some ways, law itself has long been a central element of leading works in foreign relations history. Efforts to negotiate and ratify treaties, and political struggles over neutrality laws, immigration laws, and reorganization of the military and federal bureaucracies, are staples in the literature. Sometimes the focus is on legal failures. Perhaps the most famous is the Senate's rejection of the Treaty of Versailles and the League of Nations, thereby "breaking the heart of the world" as well as Woodrow Wilson's presidency. In the context of this history and other important treaty debates – from the 1783 Treaty of Paris to NAFTA – US political leaders ratify or reject a particular vision of the American role in world politics through adoption or rejection of a treaty.[4] Statutes as well as treaties have been occasions for political battles over the nature of US foreign policy. An especially important example is Michael Hogan's masterful treatment of the National Security Act of 1947 in *A Cross of Iron: Harry S. Truman and the Origins of the National Security State, 1945–1954*.[5]

Battles over the Treaty of Versailles and the National Security Act of 1947 do more than showcase the way American political leaders fought over the direction of US foreign policy. Statutes and treaties become the legal architecture of state-building. The National Security Act did more than ratify a vision of American national security. It restructured the military and created new departments. Since then, the Department of Defense has grown to a sprawling bureaucracy. It is the nation's largest employer, and defense spending draws approximately 20% of the federal budget, though this number does not include veterans' benefits.[6] Although the statute itself, and subsequent amendments, created the basic organization of federal bureaucratic power, it also laid the basis for new forms of lawmaking. Much of the law of US foreign relations since 1947 is administrative law generated by federal rulemaking. Because of this, the legal history of American foreign relations is not limited to treaties, statutes, and court rulings. Administrative law is foreign relations law. Diving into this regulatory history would illuminate foreign relations state-building, and the legal side of the bureaucratic history of foreign relations.[7]

PERIODIZATION AND CAUSALITY IN HUMAN RIGHTS HISTORY

One way to compare causal arguments and assumptions about the role of law in foreign relations history is to examine the way histories are periodized. If legal enactments punctuate the history, so that eras might be divided into a "before" and an "after" based on the presence or absence of law, then we might find an explicit or implicit causal argument: that law is having an impact on international relations or the human condition within that historical period. The relationship between periodization and causality is especially apparent in scholarship on human rights.

The turn to human rights has been the most notable turn to law in foreign relations history in recent years, with many panels and conference papers on human rights at scholarly meetings. Indeed, Andrew Preston has written that "human rights history is now one of the leading subjects in all fields of historical inquiry."[8]

The human rights history literature ranges from the celebratory and global approach in Paul Gordon Lauren's *The Evolution of International Human Rights*, to focused accounts of the politics attending ratification (or not) of human rights treaties, to wrenching accounts of human rights violations. Human rights is sometimes evoked as an ephemeral concept, a moral idea, grounded in intellectual or cultural history, but these histories are all tied in some way to a legal story of human rights. Lauren's account traces intellectual traditions around the world that he sees coming together in the Universal Declaration of Human Rights in 1948. National interest and international politics are often at odds with the UDHR's moral vision. Cold War politics interfered with American support for the Declaration, for example. For Lauren, law is both the product of politics and a potential constraint. While he embraces a hopeful vision of its potential, human rights law, in his account, is ultimately subject to the more powerful forces of national interests in global politics.[9]

Lauren's work is consistent with the traditional periodization of human rights history. The story builds to the United Nations Charter in 1945, the focus of chapter 6, and the Universal Declaration of Human Rights in 1948 in chapter 7. Reinforcing the way legal change structures the periodization, chapter 8 is entitled "Transforming Visions into Reality: The First Fifty Years of the Universal Declaration," followed by a chapter on its "continuing evolution." For a work written for the occasion of the fiftieth anniversary of the UDHR, its role in structuring the historical narrative is not surprising. The book nevertheless gives us a distinctly non-realist periodization, for it is intended not only as a narrative of a specific legal document, but also of the role of humanitarian norms in global politics.

In *A New Deal for the World*, Elizabeth Borgwardt focuses on an American human rights vision during World War II and its aftermath, as Franklin D. Roosevelt and his administration brought a vision of social justice based on the New Deal into the Atlantic Charter. Her book is a deeply textured account of the rise of the international institutions, including the UN, charged with safeguarding a humanitarian vision for the world. While Borgwardt shares Lauren's interest in the emergence of human rights instruments and institutions, her deep consideration of a particular era helps to emphasize the historical and political contingency of human rights institution-building in the 1940s.[10]

Samuel Moyn challenges the traditional periodization of human rights in *The Last Utopia: Human Rights in History*, focusing on the rise of human rights as a social movement in the 1970s. He finds a rupture from the past as compared with Lauren's search for historical continuities. He also decenters human rights treaties and institutions in the narrative. The power of human rights, he suggests, is its utopian vision. Other forms of utopianism, such as revolutionary communism and nationalist self-determination, had captured attention in prior years. Human rights as a ubiquitous concept and movement emerged in the wake of their collapse.[11]

That Moyn sees human rights as peripheral in the World War II years and after, while Borgwardt sees a human rights vision as centrally important, shows that these two fine historians do not just differ in their interpretations. They are also studying different things. The rise of a broad international rights discourse and movement is what matters to Moyn. Borgwardt instead tells a compelling story of political leaders, institution builders, and the way the "American vision of human rights" helped push the United States in the direction of supporting multilateral solutions to global problems. The origin of ideas and moral conceptions matter to both Moyn and Lauren. For Lauren they culminate in the UDHR, which then takes on its own life. Moyn focuses on law as part of the field of ideas, and as a tool of a social movement. The mere presence of law is not what is important for him, so the emergence of law, such as the UDHR, does not structure his periodization.

Sarah Snyder also focuses on the 1970s; however, her focus is not on the origins of human rights, but rather on their impact during the late Cold War years. She makes a strong causal argument that human rights norms in the Helsinki Accords, and the political activism they motivated, played an important role in the end of the Cold War.[12] In a roundtable on Snyder's book, Akira Iriye suggested that the new human rights history complicates the periodization of foreign relations history itself. Human rights do not fit in the traditional chronology of international relations, he notes, and this shows that there are, instead, multiple chronologies. For Iriye, Snyder's work will help historians get away from "geopolitical determinism."[13]

Perhaps we might see law playing a more concrete and shaping role in the context of war crimes trials. Robert H. Jackson, Supreme Court justice and American prosecutor at the trial of Nazi leaders after World War II, argued that the Nuremberg tribunal provided the victors with a chance to "stay the hand of vengeance and voluntarily submit their captive enemies to the judgment of the law." This made the trial, for Jackson, "one of the most significant tributes that Power has ever paid to Reason."[14] For some scholars, Nuremberg serves as a pivotal moment, a break in historical time.

The trial has been criticized as victors' justice, and Richard Overy writes that the circumstances of the trial suggest that it was "in effect a 'political act' rather than an exercise in law." Still, he writes, "for all its evident drawbacks, the trial proved to be the foundation of what has now become a permanent feature of modern international justice."[15] In that sense, whatever else it may do, law produces more law. Mark Aarons suggests that more was accomplished, and that the trial was a break from the past, serving as "a warning to would be tyrants and mass-killers: the post-war international community would not tolerate the repetition" of such crimes. Whether or not power had bowed to reason, many hoped this legal process was a path toward a more law-regarding future.[16]

So is Nuremberg an example of law's impact in foreign relations history, or of its futility? The hope that even Nuremberg's prosecuting nations would carry forward humanitarian ideas and practices is belied by many accounts of human rights violations in later years. For example, in *Blood Telegram: Nixon, Kissinger, and a Forgotten Genocide*, Gary Bass writes that when US Consul General Arthur Blood cabled National Security Advisor Henry Kissinger about "genocide" unfolding in East Pakistan, the slaughter of Bengalis by the Pakistani army was ignored. President Richard M. Nixon and Kissinger turned a blind eye because Pakistani military leader Yahya Kahn was playing a central role in Nixon's overtures to China. If there was ever an account of the futility of legal prohibitions on mass atrocity, this must be it.[17]

But Bass himself views law as playing a role in international history, at least in the form of war crimes tribunals, even if human rights are constrained by national interests and domestic politics. Nuremberg and other war crimes tribunals stem from the "legalism" of liberal states, he argues, and this legalism has its basis in the domestic politics of these states. It can lead to "bona fide trials" with the possibility of acquittal, rather than simply "show trials." And Nuremberg was "legalism's greatest moment of glory."[18]

As these approaches to human rights history show, law cuts across methodologies of foreign relations history, illuminating fundamental debates about the role of power, interest, and ideas.

LEGAL SPACES AND IDENTITIES IN FOREIGN RELATIONS HISTORY

There is another way that tribunals have an impact. In Nuremberg, as well as in more recent tribunals such as the International Criminal Court, trials are a site of diplomatic history. Legal institutions are literally a place where foreign relations history happens. And these legal spaces enable interactions foreign to some conventional sites of diplomacy. Slobodan Milosevic, for example, was brought before the International Criminal Tribunal for the Former Yugoslavia. Although he was never formally called to account for the "ethnic cleansing" of Albanians in Kosovo, since he died before his trial could come to a conclusion, tribunals have become places where victims of atrocities can, at least, face their accusers and recount the crimes.[19]

Trials are not the only legal spaces in foreign relations history. Law plays a role in demarcating the very boundaries between nations, and legal regimes have an impact on the status of individuals who cross these borders. We might think of the legal spaces between nations – whether physical or conceptual – as "legal borderlands." Like other kinds of borderlands, legal borderlands are fluid. They are contact zones within which legal and national identities are constructed and contested.[20] For example, Mae Ngai shows the way the concept of "illegal alien" was produced in the context of a longer history of labor migration across the US–Mexico border. Christina Duffy Ponsa explores the constitutional law of American empire in the early twentieth century in *Insular Cases*, which defined Puerto Ricans and others as "foreign in a domestic sense," making them subjects of US power but not citizens. Teemu Ruskola and Eileen Scully detail the management of US–Chinese relations through an American consular court system aimed in part at ensuring that unruly Americans in China did not disrupt trade relations. Daniel Margolies focuses on extradition and extraterritoriality in the context of American expansion in the southwest, arguing that "the United States was built in spaces of law," which were "defined by strict sovereign territoriality and unilateralist control." Legal regulation of individuals in these contexts serves more than a policing function. American identity, US conceptions of other peoples and nations, and the nature of international relations are also in play. Law, in these contexts, is a place where foreign relations are managed.[21]

Law is also an aspect of public diplomacy. During the early Cold War years, for example, American diplomats sought to ensure that peoples in other nations understood the nature and structure of the US Constitution. When the United

States faced criticism about civil rights violations during the 1957–8 Little Rock Crisis over school desegregation, the State Department promoted public diplomacy programming that focused on federalism. If peoples of other nations understood the American federal-state structure, they thought, then they would understand that crises like Little Rock were due to a state government's action, and did not reflect on the federal government's commitment to civil rights reform. Major legal reforms such as the desegregation case *Brown v. Board of Education* (1954) and the Civil Rights Act of 1964 were prominently featured in American public diplomacy publications and programs because they were seen as a way of responding to global criticism, thereby improving US international relations.[22]

Just as law was an element of the national identity promoted by the US government during the Cold War, legal reform has played a role in the efforts of other peoples to protect their status in global politics. The nation of Hawai'i wrote constitutions in the nineteenth century in an effort to demonstrate its status as a "civilized" nation. Leaders hoped that a Hawaiian constitution would show imperial powers that Hawaiians were not a "savage" people, ripe for colonial overthrow. Meanwhile American missionaries in Hawai'i imported legal codes from New England in their effort to contain what they viewed as social and moral disorder, thereby civilizing through law.[23]

If law was thought of as a civilizing force in Hawai'i, legal regimes turned on the "civilized" character of the population in other contexts. During the American occupation of the Philippines, Clara Altman shows, fair legal process through a court system was a way to show Filipinos that Americans would govern justly. The law of war was reserved for fighters thought to be engaged in civilized combat, however. The Philippine resistance movement was seen as "savage" and therefore outside the boundaries of civilized justice, and subject to more harsh penalties.[24]

Law was not an alternative to power politics in the global context, Benjamin Coates argues. Instead law and power expanded together during the age of empire. Law "mediated the relationship between U.S. corporations, U.S. power, and foreign states," and became a tool used by American corporations in Latin America and the US government. In Coates' account, money and power were motivating factors, but resolving conflict required law, so that, "for the United States, law-making and empire-making went hand in hand."[25]

LAW AS WAR

If any aspect of US international affairs is outside the domain of law, war would seem to be the most likely candidate. Because of this, it might be surprising to know how deeply law has permeated the battlefield. John Fabian Witt sets the origins of the American law of war in the context of President Abraham Lincoln's strategic decision to take the Civil War into the fabric of Southern life.[26] Nowadays, many law-related decisions that matter to US military history are buried underneath an architecture of law: the legal regulations that implement the law of armed conflict (also known as humanitarian law). Yearly *Operational Law Handbooks*, prepared for Judge Advocates General, break down the law applicable to military action into a guidebook of nearly 500 packed pages. "Operational law" is then made more specific in the rules of engagement for any particular encounter. In this way, the US military acts in a sea of law, aided by the proliferation of JAG officers.[27]

The underlying idea behind embedding military action in law is to professionalize it and to enable a rule of law to apply at the level of fighter pilots and ground troops. This strategic use of law is a beneficial kind of "lawfare," according to former Air Force General Charles Dunlap, Jr., the person credited with coining the term "lawfare" itself. Dunlap explains in an influential essay that lawfare is simply "the use of law as a weapon of war," or the use of law "to achieve a military objective." For Dunlap, war is not a breakdown of law, or action that proceeds outside the law. Instead law is now part of the battlefield, an aspect of military practice. Lawfare can be used for good or for ill.[28]

We see a broader role for "lawfare" in international law scholar Jack Goldsmith's memoir from his service as Director of the Office of Legal Counsel in the George W. Bush administration. In the aftermath of the September 11, 2001, terrorist attacks, the administration was deeply concerned about the possibility of another terrorist attack, and fear of being blamed for not avoiding it. In this environment, Goldsmith writes that the president could only justify the failure to take protective action if he had a good enough reason. "A lawyer's advice that a policy or action would violate the law, especially a criminal law, was a pretty good excuse." Because of this, "the question, 'What should we do?' ... often collapsed into the question 'What can we lawfully do?'" Law came to serve as the outer limits of policy. This created a context in which there was great "pressure to act to the edges of the law."[29]

The idea of the "edges of the law" might suggest a firm boundary between what is lawful and what is outside the law. If that is the case, then a transgression would be thought of as evidence that law did not work. Revelations of CIA "black sites" and extensive domestic surveillance by the National Security Agency might seem to show that law did not matter at all. But it is better, as Ponsa and Ruskola suggest, to see law's edges as a sort of fluid space occupied by imperial subjects. It is a legal borderland in which legal identities and capacities are constituted, as Ngai's work illustrates.

In the context of the Bush administration's War on Terror policies, the legal "edges" were not absolute. They began at the point where legal adviser John Yoo and others found legal justification for waterboarding, and they shifted under Goldsmith, who found the Yoo memos to transgress legal limits, and withdrew them. Wherever the line was, law and lawyers were in the middle of it. Philip Zelikow, executive director of the 9/11 Commission, thought that the role of lawyers in administration decision-making was problematic because "lawyers look to *legal sources* to find an answer," leaving out considerations of morality and diplomacy.[30]

Goldsmith adds that Bush's lawyers "viewed every encounter outside the innermost core of most trusted advisors as a zero-sum game that if they didn't win they would necessarily lose." In this context, arguments about law were volleys in a struggle for power; they were "strategic lawfare."[31] This negative dimension of law is different from Zelikow's. It is not that law blocks out other forms of reasoning, but that it becomes no more than a weapon used by each side in battles, domestic and international. This does not dissolve law into realism, at least not completely. Legal challenges require a legal defense, and a legal defense only works if it can resonate as "law" among a broader public.

Law plays a legitimating role, and so it can relieve decision-makers of the weightiness of their actions. If something is "lawful," after all, it is thought to be morally justifiable. This very feature can be problematic, however. International law scholar David Kennedy argues that codifying armed conflict deprives decisions about warfare of their moral weightiness, and undermines the vitality of a politics of war. "The most unsettling aspect of war today," he writes, "is the difficulty of locating a moment of responsible political freedom in the whole process by which war is conceived, waged, and remembered. Instead, we find humanitarians, military professionals, and statesmen speaking ... a common vocabulary of justification and excuse." For Kennedy, "to regain the experience of free political decision, we will need to awaken in all those who speak the language of war the human experience of deciding, exercising discretion, and being responsible for the results an unpredictable world serves up."[32]

Whether law is simply a useful tool, or whether, as Kennedy suggests, it has overtaken the imaginations of those making decisions about the use of force, it plays too central a role in warfare for historians to ignore it.

LAW AS A CONSTITUTIVE FORCE

In the context of state-building, the expansion of American empire, the management of American public diplomacy, and the arena of armed conflict, we might see law as simply a tool that accomplishes goals that are ultimately driven by the more fundamental determinants of power and interest. In this sense, perhaps law is simply a means to an end. When useful, law is relied upon to accomplish a goal. Viewed this way, perhaps the answer to the question about what law *does* in diplomatic history is modest, and perhaps skeptics about law are correct that the most important features of the history of foreign relations lay elsewhere.

The impact of law is not limited in this way, however. Law is not simply an immediate tool. It creates and structures future opportunities. Robert Jackson is again helpful, this time in his role as US Supreme Court Justice. He described the impact of law in his dissent in the World War II internment case *Korematsu* v. *United States* (1944). It is one thing for military authorities to take harsh action, he noted. Judicial ratification can have more lasting harm.

> A military order, however unconstitutional, is not apt to last longer than the military emergency .... But once a judicial opinion rationalizes such an order to show that it conforms to the Constitution, or rather rationalizes the Constitution to show that the Constitution sanctions such an order, the Court for all time has validated [it]. The principle then lies about like a loaded weapon, ready for the hand of any authority that can bring forward a plausible claim of an urgent need.[33]

Legal precedent extends a ruling beyond the context that gave rise to it. Jackson continued: "Every repetition imbeds that principle more deeply in our law and thinking and expands it to new purposes .... [I]t has a generative power of its own, and all that it creates will be in its own image."[34]

Leading legal historian Robert Gordon explains the generative power of law in an influential article "Critical Legal Histories." "Law" and "society" have often been thought of as separate domains, with law responding to changes in society. But Gordon argues that the social context is not separate from law. Instead, law helps to create it.

> It is just about impossible to describe any set of 'basic' social practices without describing the legal relations among the people involved – legal relations that don't simply condition how the people relate to each other but to an important extent define the constitutive terms of the relationship, relations such as lord and peasant, master and slave, employer and employee, ratepayer and utility, and taxpayer and municipality.[35]

For example, it would be hard to argue that law was unimportant to a slave society because slavery itself "is a legal relationship: It is precisely the slave's bundle of jural rights (or rather lack of them) and duties vis-a-vis others (he can't leave, he can't inherit, he has restricted rights of ownership, he can't insist on his family being together as a unit, etc.) that makes him a slave." Gordon argues that "understanding the constitutive role of law in social relationships is often crucial not only in characterizing societies but in accounting for major social change."[36]

Lauren Benton describes the dynamic relationship between law and its social context in *A Search for Sovereignty: Law and Geography in European Empires, 1400–1900*. In the context of European colonialism, she writes, "every collection of travelers or settlers operated on the assumption of a legal relationship binding subject and sovereign, and every group recognized a formal division of authority between lower and higher levels of legal authority." Often the "law" that mattered was not the formal legal code found in law books, but the law as remembered or practiced in colonial settings. Law's impact on sojourners and settlers "was grounded in their knowledge about past legal practice as well as suppositions about possible future legal entanglements." Various kinds of "inventive applications of law"

Legal history as foreign relations history

were "a familiar kind of strategic cultural practice." As ship captains and others built law into their communications, law "represented an important epistemological framework for the organization and evaluation of evidence of all kinds." Benton argues that what might have looked like "an empty box of lawlessness, a legal void, was in fact full of law."[37]

In Benton's work, it is law and geography that are tangled together in a "malleable epistemological foundation."[38] What about law and foreign relations? Like the slaves in Gordon's example and the ship captains in Benton's, American diplomats, military officers, political leaders, migrants, and others operate with an understanding of the world, and of their own status, that is shaped in part by law. Law does not follow after American encounters with the world. It is part of the way the world is imagined and understood. The law that matters is not always formal law "on the books." To borrow from Benton, it is also the law that is remembered, "grounded in their knowledge about past legal practice as well as suppositions about possible future legal entanglements." As this chapter has shown, even American national identity itself is generated and understood in part through law.

Perhaps a danger of this formulation is that if law seems to be everywhere, perhaps it is too amorphous to do actual *work* in foreign relations history. But as we have seen in the example of law on the battlefield, the practice of lawfare shows that even armed conflict is mixed up with law. There is no "non-law" component to remove from it. Law is more than a tool, to be used or ignored. It marks the terrain of battle; it crafts the pathway of the bullet.

A LEGAL HISTORY SURVIVAL GUIDE

Building legal history into your foreign relations history research may be important or essential. It can also be fraught with peril. Historians without legal training can make mistakes when unaware of the way different areas of law interconnect, or the way jurisdictional or procedural rules affect a case. But even complex areas of law can be mastered sufficiently. An example is Katherine Epstein's book *Torpedo: Inventing the Military-Industrial Complex in the United States and Great Britain*.[39] Trained in military and diplomatic history, Epstein brought that expertise to the project, as well as an understanding of the technological history. But patent law is important to her story. Getting up to speed on that required her to reach out to legal scholars and legal historians who helped steer her to the literatures she needed and helped her avoid errors.

Here are some steps to help you bring law into your project without making mistakes:

- Audit a law school class in your subject area. Do all the reading and participate in class discussion.
- To develop an overview of an area of law, find a well-regarded treatise.
- Ask a legal historian to be on your dissertation committee.

- Attend meetings of the American Society for Legal History (ASLH).
- Present your work in law settings, including ASLH and Law and Society Association meetings. Find opportunities for legal scholars to read your work and comment on it.
- Attend legal history workshops and programs in your area. Some law schools have a legal history workshop series. They will be delighted to have you.
- Take advantage of legal history programs for graduate students and others hosted by ASLH and other organizations.
- Read the Legal History Blog, where new scholarship is discussed and opportunities are often announced.[40]
- Use the Legal Research Guides on the Law Library of Congress website, and attend their Orientation to Legal Research.[41]

Researchers will find these sources to be helpful:

- Bibliographies and bibliographic essays in these works:
  Lauren Benton, *A Search for Sovereignty: Law and Geography in European Empires, 1400–1900* (Cambridge, 2009)
  Martti Koskenniemi, *The Gentle Civilizer of Nations: The Rise and Fall of International Law, 1870–1960* (Cambridge, 2002)
  Paul Gordon Lauren, The *Evolution of International Human Rights: Visions Seen* (Philadelphia, 2003)
  Samuel Moyn, *The Last Utopia: Human Rights in History* (Cambridge, MA, 2010)
  Stephen C. Neff, *Justice Among Nations: A History of International Law* (Cambridge, MA, 2014)
  Anne Orford, *International Authority and the Responsibility to Protect* (Cambridge, 2011)
  A.W. Brian Simpson, *Human Rights and the End of Empire: Britain and the Genesis of the European Convention* (New York, 2001)
- Extensive and helpful citations in the notes of these works:
  George Athan Billias, *American Constitutionalism Heard Round the World, 1776–1989: A Global Perspective* (New York, 2009)
  Stephen M. Griffin, *Long Wars and the Constitution* (Cambridge, MA, 2013)
  Mariah Zeisberg, *War Powers: The Politics of Constitutional Authority* (Princeton, 2013)
- Helpful reference sources:
  David L. Sloss, Michael D. Ramsey, and William S. Dodge, eds., *International Law in the U.S. Supreme Court: Continuity and Change* (Cambridge: Cambridge University Press 2011)
  David P. Forsythe, ed., *Encyclopedia of Human Rights*, 5 vols. (New York, 2009)

- Excellent and accessible overview of many aspects of the law of US international relations:
  Curtis A. Bradley, *International Law in the U.S. Legal System*, 2nd edn. (New York, 2015)
- Best open-access on line sources for access to documents relating to law and US international history:

  The Avalon Project Documents in Law, History and Diplomacy, http://avalon.law.yale.edu/
  Legal Information Institute, Cornell University Law School, https://www.law.cornell.edu/
  Law Library of Congress, http://www.loc.gov/law/help/

NOTES

For helpful comments on an earlier draft, I am grateful to Gary Bass, Elizabeth Borgwardt, Benjamin Coates, and Sam Moyn. Thanks to Parker Guthrie for research assistance.

1. A classic essay by Justice Antonin Scalia, the nation's most prominent originalist, is "Originalism: The Lesser Evil," *University of Cincinnati Law Review* 57 (1988–9): 849–865. A well-respected scholarly account is Keith E. Whittington, *Constitutional Interpretation: Textual Meaning, Original Intent, and Judicial Review* (Lawrence, 1999); and an important new critique is Heidi Kitrosser, "Interpretive Modesty," *Georgetown Law Journal* (forthcoming 2016) <http://papers.ssrn.com/sol3/papers.cfm?abstract_id=2463366>. Jamal Greene outlines the political history of originalism in "Selling Originalism," *Georgetown Law Journal* 97 (March 2009): 657–721. For an analysis and critique of the use of history in legal interpretation, see Helen Irving, "Constitutional Interpretation, the High Court, and the Discipline of History," *Federal Law Review*, 41(1) (2013): 95–126.
2. Frank W. Brecher, *Securing American Independence: John Jay and the French Alliance* (Westport, CT, 2003); Lawrence S. Kaplan, *Entangling Alliances with None: American Foreign Policy in the Age of Jefferson* (Kent, OH, 1987).
3. Jerry Israel and David L. Anderson, "Department of State," in *Encyclopedia of American Foreign Policy: Studies of the Principal Movements and Ideas*, Alexander DeConde, ed. (New York, 2002), 453.
4. John Milton Cooper, Jr., *Breaking the Heart of the World: Woodrow Wilson and the Fight for the League of Nations* (New York, 2001); Thomas J. Knock, *To End all Wars: Woodrow Wilson and the Quest for a New World Order* (Princeton, 1995).
5. Michael J. Hogan, *A Cross of Iron: Harry S. Truman and the Origins of the National Security State, 1945–1954* (New York, 1998). See also Douglas T. Stuart, *Creating the National Security State: A History of the Law That Transformed America* (Princeton, 2008).
6. "About the Department of Defense," Department of Defense website, www.defense.gov/about/; Brad Plummer, "America's staggering defense budget, in charts," Wonkblog, *Washington Post*, January 17, 2013, www.washingtonpost.com/blogs/wonkblog/wp/2013/01/07/everything-chuck-hagel-needs-to-know-about-the-defense-budget-in-charts/.

7. Regulations pertaining to the Armed Forces appear in Title 10 of the US Code, accessible here: www.law.cornell.edu/uscode/text/10. Bureaucracy and foreign relations are revealed in works such as Samantha Power, *A Problem from Hell: America in the Age of Genocide*, 2nd edn. (New York, 2013), which shows the way the reluctance of American presidents to engage in humanitarian interventions resulted in bureaucratic impasses. See also Stuart, *Creating the National Security State*; Kathryn E. Kovacs, "A History of the Military Authority Exception in the Administrative Procedure Act," *Administrative Law Review* 62 (No. 3, 2010): 673–728, accessible here: http://papers.ssrn.com/sol3/papers.cfm?abstract_id=2142056. On administrative state-building outside the foreign relations context, see Daniel R. Ernst, *Tocqueville's Nightmare: The Administrative State Emerges in America, 1900–1940* (New York, 2014); Joanna L. Grisinger, *The Unwieldy American State: Administrative Politics Since the New Deal* (New York, 2012). While there appears to be little on the intersection of US administrative law and foreign relations, New York University hosts a Global Administrative Law Project based on the idea that there is an emerging "global administrative space" in which "the strict dichotomy between domestic and international law has largely broken down." Nico Krisch and Benedict Kingsbury, "Introduction: Global Governance and Global Administrative Law in the International Legal Order," *The European Journal of International Law* 17, no. 1 (2006): 1–13; Benedict Kingsbury, Nico Krisch, and Richard B. Stewart, "The Emergence of Global Administrative Law," *Law and Contemporary Problems* 68 (Summer/Autumn 2005):15–61.
8. Andrew Preston, H-Diplo Roundtable Review of Sarah B. Snyder, *Human Rights Activism and the End of the Cold War: A Transnational History of the Helsinki Network*, www.h-net.org/~diplo/roundtables/PDF/Roundtable-XIII-32.pdf. On the rise of human rights scholarship, see Akira Iriye and Petra Goedde, "Human Rights as History," in *The Human Rights Revolution: An International History*, Akira Iriye, Petra Goedde, and William I. Hitchcock, eds. (New York, 2012).
9. Paul Gordon Lauren, *The Evolution of International Human Rights: Visions Seen*, 3rd edn. (Philadelphia, 2011). See also Lauren's masterful *Power and Prejudice: The Politics and Diplomacy of Racial Discrimination*, 2nd edn. (Boulder, CO, 1996). Helpful edited collections on human rights history illustrate different arguments and approaches. *The Human Rights Revolution: An International History*, Akira Iriye, Petra Goedde, and William I. Hitchcock, eds. (New York, 2012); *Human Rights and Revolutions*, Jeffrey N. Wasserstrom, Greg Grandin, Lynn Hunt, and Marilyn B. Young, eds., 2nd edn. (Lanham, 2007). Important works on the broader history of international law are Martti Koskenniemi, *The Gentle Civilizer of Nations: The Rise and Fall of International Law, 1870–1960* (Cambridge, 2002); Stephen C. Neff, *Justice among Nations: A History of International Law* (Cambridge, MA, 2014).
10. Elizabeth Borgwardt, *A New Deal for the World: America's Vision for Human Rights* (Cambridge, MA, 2005). For a discussion of the human rights vision of American civil rights leaders in the years after World War II, see Carol Anderson, *Eyes off the Prize: The United Nations and the African American Struggle for Human Rights, 1944–1955* (Cambridge, 2003).
11. Samuel Moyn, *The Last Utopia: Human Rights in History* (Cambridge, MA, 2010).

Legal history as foreign relations history 149

12. Sarah Snyder, *Human Rights Activism and the End of the Cold War: A Transnational History of the Helsinki Network* (Cambridge, 2011). See also Daniel C. Thomas, *The Helsinki Effect: International Norms, Human Rights, and the Demise of Communism* (Princeton, 2001).
13. Akira Iriye, "Introduction," H-Diplo Roundtable Review of Sarah B. Snyder, *Human Rights Activism and the End of the Cold War: A Transnational History of the Helsinki Network*, www.h-net.org/~diplo/roundtables/PDF/Roundtable-XIII-32.pdf.
14. "Nuremberg Trial Proceedings Volume 2: Second Day, Wednesday, 21 November 1945 *Morning Session*," Yale Law School: Avalon Project, <http://avalon.law.yale.edu/imt/11-21-45.asp>. On Robert Jackson, see Eugene C. Gerhart, *America's Advocate: Robert H. Jackson* (Indianapolis, 1958).
15. Richard Overy, "The Nuremberg Trials: International Law in the Making," in *From Nuremberg to The Hague: The Future of International Criminal Justice*, Philippe Sands, ed. (Cambridge, 2003), 2.
16. Mark Aarons, "Justice Betrayed: Post-1945 Responses to Genocide," in *The Legacy of Nuremberg: Civilising Influence or Institutionalised Vengeance?* David A. Blumenthal and Timothy L.H. McCormack, eds. (Leiden, 2008), 70. See also Christian Tomuschat, "The Legacy of Nuremberg," *Journal of International Criminal Justice* 4, no. 4 (2006), 830. See also Elizabeth Borgwardt, "A New Deal for the Nuremberg Trial: The Limits of Law in Generating Human Rights Norms," *Law and History Review* 26(3) (Fall 2008): 679–705.
17. Gary J. Bass, *The Blood Telegram: Nixon, Kissinger, and a Forgotten Genocide* (New York, 2013). See also Power, *A Problem from Hell*.
18. Gary J. Bass, *Stay the Hand of Vengeance: The Politics of War Crimes Tribunals* (Princeton, 2000), 12–19, 203.
19. Judith Armatta, *Twilight of Impunity: The War Crimes Trial of Slobodan Milosevic* (Durham, 2010).
20. Mary L. Dudziak and Leti Volpp, "Introduction," *Legal Borderlands: Law and the Construction of American Borders*, Mary L. Dudziak and Leti Volpp, eds. (Baltimore, 2006). In developing the concept of legal borderlands, Volpp and I draw upon the borderlands literature, beginning with Gloria Anzaldúa, *Borderlands – La Frontera: The New Mestiza*, 2nd edn. (San Francisco, 2009).
21. Mae M. Ngai, *Impossible Subjects: Illegal Aliens and the Making of Modern America* (Princeton, 2005); Christina Duffy Burnett [now Christina Duffy Ponsa], "Contingent Constitutions: Empire and Law in the Americas" (PhD diss., Princeton University, 2010); Eileen P. Scully, *Bargaining with the State from Afar: American Citizenship in Treaty Port China, 1844–1942* (New York, 2001); Teemu Ruskola, *Legal Orientalism: China, the United States, and Modern Law* (Cambridge, MA, 2013); Daniel S. Margolies, *Spaces of Law in American Foreign Relations: Extradition and Extraterritoriality in the Borderlands and Beyond, 1877–1898* (Athens, GA, 2011), 2–3.
22. Mary L. Dudziak, *Cold War Civil Rights: Race and the Image of American Democracy*, 2nd edn. (Princeton, 2011).
23. Sally Engle Merry, *Colonizing Hawai'i: The Cultural Power of Law* (Princeton: Princeton University Press, 1999). See also Lauren Benton, *A Search for Sovereignty: Law and Geography in European Empires, 1400–1900* (Cambridge, 2009).
24. Clara Altman, "Courtroom Colonialism: Philippine Law and U.S. Rule, 1898–1935" (PhD diss., Brandies University, 2014).

25. Benjamin Coates, "Transatlantic Advocates: American International Law and U.S. Foreign Relations, 1898–1919" (PhD diss., Columbia University, 2010); Benjamin Coates, "Securing Hegemony Through Law: Venezuela, the U.S. Asphalt Trust, and the Uses of International Law, 1904–1909," *Journal of American History* 102:2 (2015): 380–405. For a helpful essay on the legal history of empire, see Clara Altman, "The International Context: An Imperial Perspective on American Legal History" in *A Companion to American Legal History*, Alfred Brophy and Sally Hadden, eds. (Hoboken, NJ, 2013).
26. John Fabian Witt, *Lincoln's Code: The Laws of War in American History* (New York, 2012).
27. *Operational Law Handbook 2014*, William Johnson and David Lee, eds., International and Operational Law Department, The Judge Advocate General's Legal Center and School, University of Virginia (2014). Operational Law Handbooks since 2007 are accessible on the Library of Congress website: www.loc.gov/rr/frd/Military_Law/operational-law-handbooks.html.
28. Charles Dunlap, Jr., "Law and Military Interventions: Preserving Humanitarian Values in 21st Century Conflicts," November 29, 2001, https://docs.google.com/file/d/1hNOZudMrb2cY_HznEw_DovfzgNCvPZFE7GsfeIGSt7RGqis2teJs6f5OfIJk/edit?hl=en_US.
29. Jack L. Goldsmith, *The Terror Presidency: Law and Judgment Inside the Bush Administration* (New York, 2007), 131; Mary L. Dudziak, "A Sword and a Shield: The Uses of Law in the Bush Administration," in *The Presidency of George W. Bush: A First Historical Assessment*, Julian E. Zelizer, ed. (Princeton, 2010), 45.
30. Dudziak, "A Sword and a Shield," 42–6.
31. Goldsmith, *Terror Presidency*, 126–8.
32. David Kennedy, *Of War and Law* (Princeton, 2006), 171.
33. *Korematsu v. United States*, 323 U.S. 214, 245–46 (1944), Justice Robert Jackson, dissenting.
34. Ibid.
35. Robert W. Gordon, "Critical Legal Histories," *Stanford Law Review* 36 (January 1984): 57–125. For a retrospective on the impact of Gordon's work, see "Symposium on Gordon's Critical Legal Histories," *Law and Social Inquiry* 37 (Winter 2012): 147–215.
36. Gordon, "Critical Legal Histories," 103, 106.
37. Benton, *A Search for Sovereignty*, 23–33. Thanks to Brian Cuddy for suggesting Benton on this point.
38. Ibid., 28 (quoting María M. Portuondo, *Secret Science: Spanish Cosmography in the Spanish and Portuguese Empires* [Chicago, 2009], 11).
39. Katherine C. Epstein, *Torpedo: Inventing the Military-Industrial Complex in the United States and Great Britain* (Cambridge, MA, 2014).
40. Legal History Blog, http://legalhistoryblog.blogspot.com.
41. Research Guides, Law Library of Congress, http://www.loc.gov/law/help/how-find.php; Orientation to Legal Research, Law Library of Congress, http://www.loc.gov/law/opportunities/seminar-orient.php.

9

Domestic politics

Fredrik Logevall

In an interview in the summer of 1965, McGeorge Bundy, a former Harvard dean who served John F. Kennedy and Lyndon B. Johnson as national security adviser and was an architect of the Americanization of the Vietnam War then underway, was asked what was different in the actual conduct of American diplomatic affairs from how it had seemed to be "from the safety of Harvard Yard." Bundy replied that the first thing that stood out was "the powerful place of domestic politics in the formulation of foreign policies."[1]

It was a revealing comment, but not one that should surprise us (except to the extent officials seldom make this admission on the record). For the relationship between domestic politics and foreign policy has been an intimate one throughout the nation's history. It may be debated whether the connection is a good thing or a bad thing – whether overall it has been beneficial to the nation's record on the world stage – but for the moment it is enough to say that it is there and is important. The key shapers of US foreign policy have been politicians, who understand that developments far from America's shores can deeply influence their prospects at the polls, their careers, and their reputations. So it has been with presidents, the most important makers of foreign policy. So also with secretaries of state and defense, who, though often nonpoliticians, are bound to the president's political positions. So with many of those who have headed diplomatic missions abroad; now, as from the republic's early days, many of these assignments are handled under political patronage. So also with lawmakers on Capitol Hill who devote their energies to world affairs and with other leaders in both major parties, in and out of office.[2]

Being officeholders or career-minded appointees, these individuals could hardly be expected to forget domestic politics when they are weighing foreign policy alternatives. And as a general rule in US history, they have not. Already in 1796, it is well to remember, George Washington publicized his Farewell Address partly in order to assist his vice president, John Adams, in the presidential election against Thomas Jefferson – the Address, justly celebrated by later historians as a powerful articulation of foreign policy principles, also served a nakedly partisan purpose.[3] Surveying the foreign–domestic nexus for the two centuries that followed, historian Melvin Small concluded: "[T]he central role of domestic politics in determining American foreign relations has changed little since Washington's day, and, if anything, has increased in potency and complexity."[4]

No doubt some presidential administrations in the nation's history have obsessed more than others about the domestic political implications of their foreign policy decisions, but all, or virtually all, have operated from the assumption that if they stop thinking of the next election, if they ignore the reaction of the other professional politicians in Congress and in the field, they are not likely to prevail electorally or win support for their programs or secure their future reputations.

Which is not to say it is only about winning elections or burnishing personal historical legacies. Politicians often have had particular and deeply felt ideas about international matters, ideas that their party (or a large segment of their party) have shared or endorsed. Often the candidates of the opposing party have had different ideas. Foreign policy, therefore, is about choosing among real policy choices as well as getting partisan advantage from those choices.[5] Yet it cannot be denied that elections are important in determining why the United States has followed the international course it has. In America, the jockeying for political advantage never stops. Viewed from a president's perspective, the next election (whether mid-term or presidential) will arrive all too soon, and presidents are well aware that voters are capable of giving incumbent parties the boot. Moreover, the overall state of a president's relations with Congress and his standing in public opinion deeply influence his ability to get things done and, in general, to lead effectively. Political campaigns are significant because they indicate which foreign policy issues each candidate believes his opponent is vulnerable on, and which issues each candidate believes are likely to strike a response chord in the voting public.[6]

Moreover, throughout much of US history, leaders have had considerable latitude in defining the national interest, for the simple reason that threats to American security have seldom been existential. Shielded by two oceans that acted as vast moats, and with immediate neighbors that were weak, the United States for much of the nineteenth century did not have to concern itself with the specter of military invasion that tormented its European cousins. Then, during the period of the two world wars, America's wealth and power grew enormously just as the strength of many other large states was declining; in a short period of time, it went from a position of limited engagement to one of informal but recognized hegemony over a large portion of the globe. Both before and after attaining great-power status, therefore, Americans lacked the necessity to negotiate and compromise continually in order to survive and prosper – for their nation's security was seldom directly threatened. This in turn meant that from an early point US leaders had the luxury of obscuring the distinction between policy and politics, so that governing became less about the common welfare and more about achieving partisan and personal objectives. Or, as the international relations theorist Kenneth Waltz put it, "absence of threat permits policy to become capricious."[7]

For many analysts, this condition of "free security" (to use historian C. Vann Woodward's phrase) began to erode in the 1930s, and spectacularly so when Japan attacked the naval base at Pearl Harbor on December 7, 1941. The development of transoceanic military technologies in the interwar years, and the collapse of the balance of power in Europe, signaled to Americans, including President Franklin D. Roosevelt, that the days of easy defense were coming to an end. This conviction strengthened after 1945, as advances in technology continued to make the world smaller and as the two superpowers amassed vast nuclear arsenals. Yet it could be argued – as Campbell Craig and I have done in our book *America's Cold War* – that Pearl Harbor did *not* mark a sharp break, that what had been true for most of the nation's history before World War II was also true subsequently: the United States during much of the Cold War and after was objectively safe from external attack, as safe as any nation could realistically hope to be. Not since the days of the Roman Empire had a great power enjoyed such geopolitical fortune.[8]

To be sure, all leaders in all countries are capable of playing politics with foreign policy, of allowing domestic political considerations to enter decision-making. But such tendencies are less common in nations that are more vulnerable geographically and militarily. The prospect of a hanging, as Samuel Johnson famously put it, concentrates the mind. To take an extreme example, Poland in 1938 did not have the luxury of capriciousness – one wrong move and it might be swallowed up. When, on the other hand, the stakes of a misguided or irresponsible foreign policy are not so grave, domestic politics – especially in a democracy such as the United States – naturally takes on a greater role. Politicians, eager to get reelected, to pursue domestic agendas, and to attract contributions, can advocate foreign policies that have little to do with a careful calculation of national interest, knowing that the geopolitical stakes are not momentous. They can exaggerate a given threat and portray it in the most vivid terms possible, the better to get the attention of a generally parochial public and Congress and to score points against the other party.[9]

The distinctive nature of the US political system is also a factor here. The wide dispersion of power and the relative weakness of American political parties distinguish the US system from the more centralized parliamentary systems of Europe and elsewhere and serve to limit executive control over international affairs. Congress, the courts, the press, and myriad interest groups can pronounce on policy, a reality that, when combined with the frequency and regularity of elections, creates a pluralist tradition in American politics and forces leaders to cultivate popular support for their initiatives.[10]

It would seem obvious, then, that those who analyze American foreign policy decisions should give close consideration to the role of domestic politics in decision-making and in the subsequent developments. Attention must, of course, also be given to geostrategic, military, economic, cultural, idealistic, and other influences. On occasion these influences, rather than practical politics, have been decisive. But almost always the nonpolitical factors have been entwined with political imperatives – real or imagined – which need to be pinpointed and analyzed.[11]

And indeed, over the years scholars and other authors have produced some excellent studies of the interrelationship between politics and diplomacy, as we shall see below. What is striking, though, is how often studies altogether omit mention of domestic politics. Some do so because they focus narrowly on high politics and the exchange of diplomatic documents, showing little inclination to get behind the formal papers. These materials, essential though they are, can mislead – American statesmen have always been allergic to admitting, even to themselves, that their foreign policy decisions could be affected by private political interest. In the memorable formulation of Anthony Lake, national security adviser to President Bill Clinton, the discussion of domestic politics in the formulating of US policy on the Middle East was like the discussion of sex and the Victorians: "Nobody talks about it but it's on everybody's mind."[12] As a result, a reader of the vast American archival record, finding little or no evidence of partisan wrangling or election-year strategizing, could (wrongly) conclude that these must have mattered little in shaping US policy.

Furthermore, historiographical trends among diplomatic historians have unquestionably conspired against a prominent place for domestic politics. Most of the early giants in the field, among them Samuel Flagg Bemis, Dexter Perkins, and Arthur Whitaker, focused on state-to-state interaction (Thomas A. Bailey was a notable exception), on high US officials and their counterparts in the countries with which Washington dealt. The research of these "orthodox" historians was often intelligent and exceptionally valuable, but they tended to frame their questions in a manner that allowed them to avoid inquiring into the domestic political calculations that helped shape policy, or the partisan disputes that often accompanied the implementation of that policy. Perkins' study of the Monroe Doctrine of 1823, for example, takes more or less as a given that national security concerns brought about the doctrine, while Bemis' book on Jay's Treaty concludes before the bitter debate in the Congress in 1795–6 on the treaty's implementation. Herbert Feis, an orthodox historian of the early Cold War, likewise focused exclusively on the White House, the State Department, and state-to-state relations in his effort to assign responsibility for the origins of the Soviet–American confrontation.[13]

This emphasis among orthodox historians on high politics met with a spirited response from a group of "revisionist" scholars who came of age in the late 1950s and 1960s. But although revisionists distinguished themselves by emphasizing the importance of domestic forces in the conduct of US foreign policy, they paid curiously little attention to party politics. No less than the traditionalists, they treated the US government as a monolithic actor, albeit one shaped largely by the economic and ideological interests associated with the US government's capitalist structure. The emphasis was on internal sources of foreign policy, but not on partisan wrangling, election-year maneuvering, or other political concerns. In William Appleman Williams' classic New Left study, *The Tragedy of American Diplomacy*, one gets virtually no sense that partisan concerns have frequently played a central role in shaping US foreign policy. In this and other Williams works, Congressional speeches and campaign pronouncements were generally cited only to show the supposed consensus behind American economic expansion.[14]

The irony is rich: orthodox and revisionist authors that otherwise differ across a whole range of interpretive questions share a tendency to treat the American government as a unitary actor unencumbered by internal dissension. The same was true of many of the so-called postrevisionists who followed them, and of the corporatist school of diplomatic history that emerged in the latter years of the twentieth century. The postrevisionists – a loose collection of scholars who did not fit easily into either the orthodox or revisionist camps, and whose research centered on the Cold War – sought to return the focus to the external determinants of American decision-making.[15] The corporatists, for their part, echoed the revisionists in looking closely at the economic and ideological influences that shape American diplomacy, but went beyond them in also analyzing the organizational dimension of policymaking, in showing that elites in both private and public sectors – in labor, business, agriculture, and government – have often pursued shared interests in world affairs. As with the revisionists, however, the close attention paid by corporatists to the domestic sources of American foreign policy did not extend to in-depth consideration of domestic politics.[16]

More recently, the exhortations for foreign relations historians to be first and foremost international or transnational historians have moved the scholarship still further away from a close attention to domestic politics. Much of this work has been extraordinarily valuable, enriching the field and deepening the internationalist dimension of US foreign relations history in numerous ways. And more such scholarship is on the way, as additional foreign archives open up, as greater numbers of historians develop the linguistic skills to work in them, as more non-US scholars enter the fray, and as the documentary materials made available through the heroic efforts of entities such as the Cold War International History Project and the National Security Archive become more heavily utilized. Yet an international history approach, I have suggested elsewhere, can also introduce limitations of its own; among them is an insufficient attention to the internal sources of a state's external behavior.[17]

What is remarkable about this long and distinguished literature – dating back to Bemis and Perkins almost a century ago – is not that it has tended to rank domestic politics below the top in the hierarchy of causality; given the national-security or New Left or – more recently – transnational perspectives to which many historians over the years have adhered, that is to be expected. Rather, what is striking is that domestic politics appears so far down in that hierarchy, if it even makes it on the list at all. And the argument here is that it almost always deserves to be on the list, sometimes very high up. From the development of the two-party system in the 1790s all the way into the twenty-first century, and at most points in between, American leaders chose among foreign policy options partly with practical political concerns in mind. Sometimes those concerns drove the decision-making; other times they did not. But almost always they mattered.

Foreign policy, it turns out, is always a political matter. It is not always a crass partisan matter – it is well to reiterate that the parties historically have tended to speak for different constellations of values and interests, different constituencies with genuine philosophical differences about America's place in the world, and that these differences have sometimes also been evident within parties – but it is always political. Most foreign relations historians would readily concede as much, of course, yet I believe they have too often suggested, wittingly or not, something very different in their work. Too often they have in effect endorsed the standard refrain from presidents themselves: that they ignore domestic politics when formulating national security strategies. Too often they have missed, that is to say, what Campbell Craig and I call the "intermestic" (international–domestic, in which the two are dynamically linked) dimension of policy.[18]

There are exceptions to this historiographical pattern, to be sure, exceptions that can serve as models for foreign relations historians seeking to give proper due to the potential influence of domestic politics. J. C. A. Stagg's publications on the War of 1812, for example, which grew out of deep research in a wide variety of sources (congressional papers, contemporaneous newspapers, and personal letters, in addition to official documents), show that party politics and electoral strategizing permeated the atmosphere in the lead-up to the war, and help bring on the hostilities. As historians before Stagg had demonstrated, the increasingly bitter partisan struggle over domestic and foreign policy in the early years of the century, made worse by the effects of the war between Britain and France, grew into corrosive mutual distrust. Federalists and Republicans were deeply divided on the best policy vis-à-vis Great Britain, and the vote for war followed partisan lines – 81 percent of Republicans in both houses voted for war (98 to 23), and all Federalists voted nay (39 to 0).

But Stagg's research also showed that President Madison's concerns went deeper than defending against Federalist attacks on his commercial warfare policy; he also had to worry about dissension among fellow Republicans, and the possibility that these "malcontents" – who wanted a tougher line against Britain – might form an anti-Madison ticket in 1812. By the spring of 1811, allies in Congress were warning Madison that he had to do something to unify the party; by mid-summer, the pressures of domestic politics made it very hard for the administration to agree to anything short of Britain's total capitulation to US demands. According to Stagg, for

Madison "there seemed to be only one course of action that would be both honorable and effective. He could regain the initiative at home and abroad by moving toward the positions advocated for so long by his Republican opponents. If he did not do so, there was the possibility that they would coalesce into a formidable anti-administration party, make the issue of war and preparedness wholly their own, and turn them against him in the months to come." Therefore, "the nation's honor, the president's political salvation, and the unity of Republican party required that American policy now be directed toward war." Moreover, the strategy worked: by May 1812 the malcontents had faded and a sufficiently large Republican majority had emerged in both houses to renominate Madison. The declaration of war followed in June.[19]

This is not to suggest that Madison's fears for his domestic political standing alone drove the policymaking that led to war with Great Britain. Monocausal history is seldom persuasive history. The violations of American maritime rights, the impressment of American seamen, British incitement of hostile Native Americans, US designs on Canada and Florida, the depressing effects of British policy on American farm prices – each of these mattered as well, as did the long-standing partisan squabbling between Federalists and Republicans. It is also clear, though, that the president's perceived political needs, especially his concern about possibly losing his party's nomination in 1812, shaped US policy in crucial ways. In particular, understanding why the war happened when it did – in a presidential election year, and with the incumbent in a precarious position at home – requires understanding the high-stakes struggle within the Republican party.

Consider also the Monroe Doctrine of 1823. In a provocative work bearing the prosaic title *The Making of the Monroe Doctrine*, Ernest R. May rejected the claim of Perkins and others that conceptions of national interest and foreign policy were supreme in the origins of the doctrine. Instead, May argued, party politics were decisive. ("[T]he positions of the policy makers were determined less by conviction than by ambition.") In May's view the outcome of the foreign policy debates can only be understood in relation to the struggle for the presidency, for the Monroe Doctrine was "actually a by-product of an election campaign." The threat of intervention by the European powers into the Western Hemisphere was more or less non-existent, and American officials knew it; consequently, they could play politics with the British proposal for a joint policy statement – John Quincy Adams opposed joint action, while his bitter presidential rival John C. Calhoun fervently supported it. Adams' candidacy would have been hurt by consummation of an alliance with London since the British were thoroughly unpopular among the US electorate. As secretary of state, Adams would have been condemned for joining with the British even if he opposed the alliance in private cabinet deliberations. Calhoun pushed for acceptance of the London government's offer knowing Adams would be blamed for it, while President Monroe, anxious to leave the presidency with his reputation intact, gave in to Adams to avoid a fight that might tarnish his record.

It is a compelling argument, based on research in a broad array of American and foreign archival sources and newspapers, as well as on thorough familiarity with the existing secondary literature.[20] Some critics complained that May took the argument too far, that officials could not have been as certain as he claimed that no foreign danger existed.[21] Fair enough. One can embrace May's core claim – that party politics were crucial in the making of the doctrine – and also maintain that the international context mattered a great deal. What is really required, and what May succeeded admirably in doing, is to examine domestic politics alongside other factors.

One virtue of Rosemary Foot's two-volume study of US policymaking in the Korean War is that she did precisely that: she situated American policy in both its international and domestic political environment.[22] In subtitling the second volume "The Politics of Peacemaking at the Korean Armistice Talks," Foot had in mind both external and internal politics, and she argued convincingly that Washington's hardline posture in the negotiations cannot be understood apart from careful consideration of the charged domestic political atmosphere in which that posture was adopted. Thus accounts of the armistice talks that posit an American flexibility toward compromise ignore "the presence of domestic political critics in America who were only too ready to equate compromise with that negative term 'appeasement' and to revive support for General Douglas MacArthur's argument that there was 'no substitute for victory.'"[23] When the presidential election campaign geared up in 1952, Republican leaders, including nominee Dwight D. Eisenhower, asserted that Truman had been misguided to agree to negotiations, and that he was compounding the error by continuing them in the face of clear evidence that the communists were using the time to build up their forces in Korea. Even the apparent economic health of the nation was turned against the White House: the prosperity, GOP spokesmen charged, "had at its foundation the coffins of the Korean war dead," slaughter that as yet appeared to have no end. This partisan pressure contributed to the hardening of the administration's bargaining posture in 1952. In Foot's words, "Sensitivity to public charges, to congressional attacks, and to electoral charges that the Democratic administration had been led into a negotiating trap by its 'cunning' enemies, all reinforced the administration's preference for standing firm rather than compromising." Pleas from the State Department for a flexible posture, especially on the nettlesome issue of repatriating prisoners-of-war, fell on deaf ears.[24]

Even as the Korea negotiations were under way, the United States was becoming steadily more involved in another Asian military struggle, this one in Indochina. For more than a quarter century this US involvement would last, first in support of France's effort to defeat revolutionary nationalist forces in Vietnam under Ho Chi Minh, and then, after French forces were defeated in

1954, in an effort to build up and sustain and defend a non-communist bastion in the southern part of Vietnam.[25] It would be America's longest and bloodiest conflict in the second half of the twentieth century – claiming more than 58,000 American and some three million Vietnamese lives – and it would end in defeat, as North Vietnamese forces overran Saigon in April 1975. More than two decades of research on the war has convinced me that US intervention cannot be understood apart from careful attention to the perceived domestic political imperatives that lay behind the decision-making.

Take, for example, the large-scale US escalation of the war in 1965. The keys to Lyndon Johnson's decision to reject a possible negotiated solution that year in favor of an "Americanization" of the war effort, I deduced early in my research, lay not in Vietnam or in the larger international community, but at home in the United States. This realization did not lessen the importance of my multiarchival research; on the contrary, it was precisely the foreign archival documentation that demonstrated most clearly two essential points: first, that the expansion or resolution of the Indochina conflict in 1963–5 (what I refer to as "The Long 1964") depended to a large extent on decisions made in Washington; and second, that domestic political imperatives mattered a great deal in that decision-making. What US officials almost never dared say, certainly not on paper – that Johnson throughout his first year in office was obsessed with winning election in November 1964, and that both before and after voting day he considered all Vietnam options in light of how they would affect his standing at home – foreign officials remarked with regularity.[26]

Nor was Johnson alone among US presidents in allowing personal political concerns to affect his Vietnam policy. Indeed, a good argument could be made that for all the presidents who dealt with Vietnam from 1950 to 1975 – six in all, from Truman to Ford – the Indochina conflict mattered in large measure because of the potential damage it could do to their domestic political position.

This was certainly true of both Johnson's predecessor and successor. It is clear that John F. Kennedy, though a skeptic on Vietnam from an early point in his political career (already in 1951, on a visit to Indochina during the height of the French war, he questioned whether Western military power would ever be able to beat revolutionary nationalists militarily in this part of the world), worried greatly about the domestic political costs that could come from any move to withdraw US support from the Saigon regime. In 1963, with more than 16,000 US military advisers on the scene in South Vietnam, a disillusioned JFK reportedly told several associates of his desire to get out of the conflict. But it could not happen, he added, until after the 1964 election.

In the same way, Richard Nixon had his eyes very much on the home front in making Vietnam policy, not merely in the lead-up to the 1972 election but from the start of his administration – in vowing to get a "peace with honor," he and his national security adviser Henry Kissinger thought as much about voters in Peoria as about leaders in Moscow and Beijing and Hanoi. Top-level conversations captured on the taping system Nixon had installed in the Oval

Office early in 1971, for example, reveal just how deeply concerns about Nixon's domestic standing permeated Vietnam policy discussions that winter and spring. Later, in the summer of 1972, as a negotiated settlement with Hanoi looked to be within reach, Nixon expressed ambivalence about whether the deal should come before or after the US election that November. On 14 August, Nixon told aides that Kissinger should be discouraged from expressing too much hopefulness regarding the negotiations, as that could raise expectations and be "harmful politically." On August 30, Nixon chief of staff H. R. Haldeman recorded in his diary that Nixon did not want the settlement to come too soon. The president, according to Haldeman "wants to be sure [Army Vice-Chief of Staff Alexander] Haig doesn't let Henry [Kissinger]'s desire for a settlement prevail; that's the one way we can lose the election. We have to stand firm on Vietnam and not get soft."[27]

Skeptical readers will wonder if I'm not making the case here rather too strongly. After all, foreign policy issues seldom decide elections in the United States. Does it not follow that American diplomacy and domestic politics must have only minor influence on each other? Not necessarily. For one thing, what matters most is what candidates *think* the importance of foreign policy in a given election will be or could be, rather than what ex post facto analysis shows it to have been. Moreover, although it is true that American voters tend to give their chief attention to domestic matters, savvy politicians know they can ill afford to ignore foreign policy questions. For although domestic issues may be supreme, foreign policy disputes can still matter a lot in swing districts in critical states, potentially deciding who prevails in a national election, or who controls Congress. Such has always been the politician's interpretation of the politics of US foreign policy – and the interpretation of those in advisory positions behind the scenes.

Consider, for example, the care with which presidential aspirants approach Israeli questions and the related matter of the Jewish vote. Small in national totals, this vote has long been considered important in several states along the eastern seaboard and in the Midwest. Already in 1946, with the fate of Palestine unresolved and with mid-term US elections approaching, Zionist leaders saw an opening to push for Jewish statehood and to bury the Morrison-Grady Plan, which proposed a unitary federal trusteeship in Palestine: Arab and Jewish "provinces" would maintain self-rule under British oversight, while Jerusalem and the Negev would stay under direct British control. President Harry Truman was sympathetic to the plan but suppressed his enthusiasm, mostly on account of Zionist pressure. Anxious to protect the Democratic majorities in the House and Senate in the November vote, Truman knew, according to John Judis, that Jews had "considerable clout in New York – the nation's largest and most important state – and some influence over results in Ohio, Pennsylvania, Illinois, and Maryland. In New York that year, a Senate seat, the governorship, and forty-five House seats were being contested. Ohio had a closely watched Senate race."[28]

Two years later, in 1948, Clark Clifford and other Truman aides had electoral politics partly in mind in urging the president to extend recognition to the new state of Israel. Since 1876, Clifford knew, every winner of a presidential election had carried New York State, and he voiced confidence that extending recognition to Israel would help deliver the state to Truman in November. Recognition could also help the president in other states with sizable Jewish populations. The Emergency Committee on Zionist Affairs, and later the American Zionist Council and the American Israel Public Affairs Committee (AIPAC) – the latter self-described as "the most powerful, best-run, and effective foreign policy interest group in Washington" – proved effective in exploiting the potential power of the Jewish vote to gain continued material and diplomatic backing for Israel.[29]

To be sure, the close US–Israeli relationship after 1948 was the product of many things. Israel had the strongest military force in the Middle East, and there were good geostrategic reasons why Washington leaders should seek to maintain close ties with Israel and work together on matters of common interest. Moreover, the convictions of evangelical Christians, as well as the feelings of other Americans touched by the courage of Israel, meant that a broad cross-section of voters could be counted on to back firm US support for Israel's security. Nevertheless, it would be foolish to deny that electoral imperatives influenced US policy toward the Middle East at all points after the late 1940s.

Likewise, America's Cuban policy after 1959 was deeply affected by the influence of the Cuban-American community in South Florida and the desire of presidential contenders to win Florida's sizable chunk of electoral votes. In October 1976, for example, Cyrus Vance, then a foreign policy adviser to Jimmy Carter's presidential campaign, advised that "the time has come to move away from our past policy of isolation. Our boycott has proved ineffective, and there has been a decline of Cuba's export of revolution in the region." If the United States lifted the long-standing embargo on food and medicine, Vance speculated, the Castro government might reduce its level of support for the leftist Popular Movement for the Liberation of Angola (MPLA) in Angola. Carter was sympathetic, but he acted cautiously in the campaign. "There were no votes to be won, and many to be lost, by indicating friendliness toward Castro," historian Gaddis Smith wrote of Carter's thinking.[30]

This is a key point, perfectly obvious to many observers but seldom much examined in the Cold War literature: "There were no votes to be won." Subsequent presidents would encounter the same dilemma when they contemplated a change in Cuba policy. On the one hand, they and their advisers could see that the embargo policy was counterproductive – far from dislodging the Castro regime, the embargo served mostly to buttress the government, enabling Cuban leaders to present themselves as the victims of hegemonic bullying and giving them an excuse to impose nasty and undemocratic policies on the population. On the other hand, US officials had to weigh an alteration to the embargo policy against the perceived power of the militantly anti-Castro Cuban American National Foundation (CANF) to sway the Florida vote. The outcome was never in doubt: the embargo remained in effect. No administration in Washington wanted to risk being labeled with the "soft on Castro" tag.

Or consider, finally, a more recent example: the Iraq invasion of 2003 and its aftermath. Robert D. Blackwill, a mid-level National Security Council officer who was seconded to the 2004 reelection campaign of President George W. Bush, was startled to learn how the Iraq fighting was treated internally by the Bush campaign team. According to Bob Woodward's account,

> Blackwill was struck that there was never any real time to discuss policy. In between the stops or in the air, whenever Iraq came up, it was always through the prism of the campaign. What had the Democratic nominee, Massachusetts Senator John Kerry, said that day about Iraq? What had happened on the ground in Iraq that might impact the president's bid for reelection? As the NSC coordinator for Iraq, Blackwill probably knew as much about the war as anybody in the White House. He had spent months in Iraq with [Director of the Coalition Provisional Authority L. Paul] Bremer. But he was with the campaign only as part of the politics of reelection. Not once did Bush ask Blackwill what things were like in Iraq, what he had seen, or what should be done. Blackwill was astonished at the round-the-clock, all-consuming focus on winning the election. Nothing else came close.[31]

These kinds of calculations were nothing new in American politics. In the decades following the Civil War, for example, few Americans were deeply absorbed in the intricacies of world affairs. Voter attention centered on such domestic concerns as Southern reconstruction, falling prices, and persistent economic downturns. But this reality did not keep national politicians from working hard on the foreign policy sections of their party platforms, or prevent candidates from maintaining careful tabs on overseas developments. It's easy to see why. The two parties were closely matched, and many presidential and congressional elections were decided by tiny margins. A careless pronouncement or factual misstatement, even on an arcane diplomatic matter, could have a grievous effect at the polls, swinging an election the wrong way.

Nor should it be forgotten that many pressing policy issues blur the line between "domestic" and "foreign." This has been the case with tariffs, immigration, witch-hunts against radicals, and, in recent times, with agricultural prices and production and trade deals such as the North American Free Trade Agreement (NAFTA) of 1994. The relation of these problems to party politics – which is often very close – again pulls foreign affairs into the domestic political arena.

Which brings us back to those two national security advisers, McGeorge Bundy and Anthony Lake. Both men saw the policymaking up close; both helped shape key decisions. And what did they find? That domestic politics, in Bundy's formulation, had a "powerful place" in the formulation of US foreign policy; that, in Lake's assessment, "nobody talks about it, but it's on everybody's mind." The point is incontrovertible, not merely for the Kennedy–Johnson era of Bundy and the Clinton years of Lake, but for all periods of the nation's history; as such, it needs to be reflected in the work that foreign relations historians do, in the interpretive frameworks they adopt. For after all, as historian Thomas Schwartz rightly reminds us, "Professional politicians are ambitious people seeking office for individual recognition, career advancement, and the power to affect their societies. No matter how often they might speak of public service, it is naïve not to recognize the more selfish drives in their nature. Such individuals are not likely to forget domestic politics when they are weighing foreign policy alternatives."[32]

The challenge for the scholar, of course, is the one captured in the Lake appraisal: these same individuals are loath to actually admit, especially on the printed page, that they can be influenced by personal or partisan political interest in their foreign policymaking. They wish at all cost to hide their "selfish drives" in the historical record. Ferreting out the evidence will thus not be easy for the historian. But it can be done, as numerous studies over the years have shown. A common denominator in these works is that their authors do not limit themselves to official government documents, but go beyond them to examine newspapers, magazines, congressional papers, and oral histories. Nor need one stop there. Tape recordings and transcripts, where available, can yield highly important information to the historian, as can the personal papers of senior and mid-level White House aides. Those working on the recent past can profit from interviewing former officials and asking probing questions about how policy decisions were reached. Finally, foreign archival material, as noted above and counterintuitive though it may seem, can be immensely illuminating on the intermestic dimension in US diplomacy – these international observers, including ambassadors and their deputies in Washington, are not always accurate in their analysis of the sources of American policy, but their matter-of-fact assertions concerning the role of domestic politics in decision-making can be as informative as they are bracing.

Best of all, scholars who persist in the endeavor, who give serious attention to domestic politics in addition to other influences, who consult a broad array of sources, will, I believe, come closer to what we in this field all seek: the best possible understanding of America's record in world affairs.

NOTES

1. Henry F. Graff, "How Johnson Makes Foreign Policy," *New York Times Magazine*, July 4, 1965, as quoted in James Rosenau, ed. *Domestic Sources of Foreign Policy* (New York, 1967), 4.

2. Fred Harvey Harrington, "Politics and Foreign Policy," in Alexander DeConde, ed, *Encyclopedia of American Foreign Policy: Studies of the Principal Movements and Ideas* (New York, 1978), 774.
3. Alexander DeConde, "Washington's Farewell Address, the French Alliance, and the Election of 1796," *Mississippi Valley Historical Review* 43, no. 4 (March 1957): 641–58.
4. Melvin Small, *Democracy & Diplomacy: The Impact of Domestic Politics on U.S. Foreign Policy, 1789–1994* (Baltimore, 1996), 167. On the themes developed in the present chapter, see also Thomas Alan Schwartz, "'Henry, ... Winning an Election Is Terribly Important': Partisan Politics in the History of U.S. Foreign Relations," *Diplomatic History* 33 (April 2009), 173–90; Jussi M. Hanhimäki, "Global Visions and Parochial Politics: The Persistent Dilemma of the 'American Century'," *Diplomatic History* 27 (September 2003), 423–47; Fredrik Logevall, "Politics and Foreign Relations," *Journal of American History* 95 (March 2009), 1074–78; and Campbell Craig and Fredrik Logevall, *America's Cold War: The Politics of Insecurity* (Cambridge, MA, 2009).
5. For an excellent study showing the deep philosophical differences among American politicians regarding foreign policy in the aftermath of World War II, see Michael J. Hogan, *A Cross of Iron: Harry S. Truman and the Origins of the National Security State, 1945–1954* (New York, 1998).
6. Writes Ralph Levering: "The interplay between candidates and voters, culminating in the voting first in the primaries and then in the general election in November, thus establishes (a) the winners who will have primary responsibility for shaping US foreign policy, and (b) the broad parameters of acceptable political discourse on foreign policy for the foreseeable future." "Is Domestic Politics Being Slighted as an Interpretive Framework?" *Society for Historians of American Foreign Relations Newsletter* 25 (March 1994): 20–1.
7. Kenneth Waltz, "Structural Realism after the Cold War," in G. John Ikenberry, ed., *America Unrivaled: The Future of the Balance of Power* (Ithaca, NY, 2003), 53.
8. Craig and Logevall, *America's Cold War*. For Woodward's formulation, see his article, "The Age of Reinterpretation," *American Historical Review* 66 (October 1960), 2–8.
9. Craig and Logevall, *America's Cold War*.
10. Classic studies of this phenomenon include Gabriel Almond, *The American People and Foreign Policy* (New York: Harcourt Brace, 1950); and, especially, Stanley Hoffmann, *Gulliver's Troubles: Or, the Setting of American Foreign Policy* (New York, 1968). The argument that the decentralized politicization of foreign policy has ironically undermined the original intention of the founders to avoid war and militarization can be found in Daniel Deudney, *Bounding Power: Republican Security Theory from the Polis to the Global Village* (Princeton, NJ, 2007), chapter 6.
11. Students of the interplay between domestic politics and foreign policy often include within their purview – and properly so – a wide range of potential influences, including public opinion, the media, and ethnic groups and other special interest groups. Though I touch on these elements here, I am concerned primarily with party politics, in particular with the impact of partisan calculations and election-year concerns on presidential decision-making in foreign affairs. For a fine overview that defines "domestic politics" broadly, see Small, *Democracy and Diplomacy*. On the

Domestic politics 165

more recent period, see Craig and Logevall, *America's Cold War*; and Julian E. Zelizer, *Arsenal Of Democracy: The Politics of National Security – From World War II to the War on Terrorism* (New York, 2010). Also useful are Robert A. Divine, *Foreign Policy and U.S. Presidential Elections, 1940–1960* (New York, 1974); Robert David Johnson, *Congress and the Cold War* (New York, 2006); Barry B. Hughes, *The Domestic Context of American Foreign Policy* (New York, 1978); Ralph B. Levering, *The Public and American Foreign Policy* (New York, 1978); John E. Mueller, *War, Presidents, and Public Opinion* (New York, 1973); Melvin Small, ed., *Public Opinion and Historians: Interdisciplinary Perspectives* (Detroit, 1970); Jerel A. Rosati, *The Politics of United States Foreign Policy* (New York, 1993); Jack Snyder, *Myths of Empire: Domestic Politics and International Ambition* (Ithaca, NY, 1991); Paula Stern, *Water's Edge: Domestic Politics and the Making of American Foreign Policy* (Westport, CT, 1979); H. Bradford Westerfield, *Foreign Policy and Party Politics: Pearl Harbor to Korea* (New Haven, 1955). On the role of ethnic groups, two valuable studies are Alexander DeConde, *Ethnicity, Race, and American Foreign Policy: A History* (Boston, 1992); and Tony Smith, *Foreign Attachments: The Power of Ethnic Groups in the Making of American Foreign Policy* (Cambridge, MA, 2000). On the press, studies include Bernard C. Cohen, *The Press and Foreign Policy* (New York, 1963); and Louis Liebovich, *The Press and the Origins of the Cold War, 1944–1947* (New York, 1988).

12. Quoted in Aaron David Miller, *The Much Too Promised Land: America's Elusive Search for Arab–Israeli Peace* (New York, 2008), 77.
13. Dexter Perkins, *The Monroe Doctrine, 1823–1826* (Cambridge, MA, 1927); Samuel Flagg Bemis, *Jay's Treaty, a Study in Commerce and Diplomacy* (New York, 1923); idem, *Pinckney's Treaty: A Study of America's Advantage from Europe's Distress, 1783–1800* (Baltimore, 1926); Arthur Whitaker, *The Mississippi Question: A Study in Trade, Politics, and Diplomacy* (Baltimore, 1934); Herbert Feis, *From Trust to Terror* (New York, 1970). Bailey was unusual among his generation in looking at, among other things, the role of public opinion. See his study, *The Man in the Street: The Impact of American Public Opinion on Foreign Policy* (New York, 1948).
14. William A. Williams, *The Tragedy of American Diplomacy* (New York, 1959). Walter LaFeber's brilliant and highly influential first book, *The New Empire*, which dealt with Gilded Age foreign relations, gave little room to the congressional coalition that time and again thwarted the expansionist initiatives of high officials that are a chief concern of the book. *The New Empire: An Interpretation of American Expansion, 1860–1898* (New York, 1963).
15. John Lewis Gaddis, *We Now Know: Rethinking Cold War History* (New York, 1997); Melvyn P. Leffler, *A Preponderance of Power: National Security, the Truman Administration, and the Cold War* (Stanford, CA, 1992); Marc Trachtenberg, *A Constructed Peace: The Making of the European Settlement, 1945–1963* (Princeton, NJ, 1999). Interestingly, Gaddis' first book had given close attention to the influence of domestic politics; see *The United States and the Origins of the Cold War, 1941–1947* (New York, 1972).
16. Michael J. Hogan, *Informal Entente: The Private Structure of Cooperation in Anglo-American Economic Diplomacy, 1918–1928* (Columbia, MO, 1977); Joan Hoff-Wilson, *American Business and Foreign Policy, 1920–1933* (Lexington, KY, 1971); Emily Rosenberg, *Spreading the American Dream: American Economic and*

Cultural Expansion, 1890–1945 (New York, 1982). See also Hogan, "Corporatism: A Positive Appraisal," *Diplomatic History* 10 (Fall 1986): 363–72; idem, *The Marshall Plan: America, Britain, and the Reconstruction of Western Europe, 1947–1952* (New York, 1987); Thomas J. McCormick, "Drift or Mastery: A Corporatist Synthesis for American Diplomatic History," *Reviews in American History* 10 (December 1982): 318–30.

17. Logevall, "Politics and Foreign Relations"; Robert J. McMahon, "The Study of American Foreign Relations: National History or International History," in Michael J. Hogan and Thomas G. Paterson, eds., *Explaining the History of American Foreign Relations* (New York, 1991). Another potential problem arises from the understandable impulse by some international historians to give more or less equal attention to all of the main players in the international system, to treat the United States and the Soviet Union as just two players among many. See, for example, "From the Editors," *Cold War History* 1 (August 2000): iv. Such an approach runs the risk of being ahistorical, by granting some of the actors more influence than they in fact deserve and the USSR and especially the United States less. For numerous research topics in post-1945 international relations, a certain degree of America-centrism is not merely warranted but essential, in view of Washington's preponderant power.

18. Craig and Logevall, *America's Cold War*.

19. J. C. A. Stagg, "James Madison and the Malcontents: The Politics Origins of the War of 1812," *William and Mary Quarterly* 33 (1976): 583–4. See also Stagg, *Mr. Madison's War: Politics, Diplomacy, and Warfare in the Early American Republic* (Princeton, NJ, 1983).

20. Ernest R. May, *The Making of the Monroe Doctrine* (Cambridge, MA, 1975).

21. See Harry Ammon, "The Monroe Doctrine: Domestic Politics or National Decision?" *Diplomatic History* 5 (1981): 53–70; May, "Response to Harry Ammon," Ibid., 71–3.

22. Rosemary Foot, *The Wrong War: American Policy and the Dimensions of the Korean Conflict, 1950–1953* (Ithaca, NY, 1985); idem, *A Substitute for Victory: The Politics of Peacemaking at the Korean Armistice Talks* (Ithaca, NY, 1990). See also the second volume of Bruce Cumings' monumental study of the coming of the war, *The Origins of the Korean War, Volume 2: The Roaring of the Cataract* (Princeton, NJ, 1990), chapter 3; and Steven Casey, *Selling the Korean War: Propaganda, Politics, and Public Opinion in the United States, 1950–1953* (New York: Oxford University Press, 2008). For another Casey book that likewise explores the foreign–domestic nexus to powerful effect, see his *Cautious Crusade: Franklin D. Roosevelt, American Public Opinion, and the War Against Nazi Germany* (New York, 2001).

23. Foot, *A Substitute for Victory*, x–xi.

24. Ibid., 158.

25. For the early period, covering 1940–60, see Fredrik Logevall, *Embers of War: The Fall of an Empire and the Making of America's Vietnam* (New York, 2012).

26. Fredrik Logevall, *Choosing War: The Lost Chance for Peace and the Escalation of War in Vietnam* (Berkeley, CA, 1999). Other works that also attach importance to domestic political imperatives in America's Vietnam policy include Larry Berman, *Planning a Tragedy: The Americanization of the Vietnam War* (New York, 1982); Leslie Gelb and Richard K. Betts, *The Irony of Vietnam: The System Worked*

(Washington, DC, 1978); Daniel Ellsberg, *Papers on the War* (New York, 1972); and, especially, Andrew L. Johns, *Vietnam's Second Front: Domestic Politics, the Republican Party, and the War* (Lexington, KS, 2010). See also Melvin Small, *At the Water's Edge: American Politics and the Vietnam War* (Chicago, 2005).

27. Jeffrey Kimball, *Nixon's Vietnam War* (Lawrence, KS, 1998), 328; H. R. Haldeman, *The Haldeman Diaries: Inside the Nixon White House* (New York, 1994), 500. See also Schwartz, "'Henry, ... Winning an Election Is Terribly Important,'" 173–5; and Ken Hughes, *Fatal Politics: The Nixon Tapes, the Vietnam War, and the Casualties of Reelection* (Charlottesville, VA, 2015).
28. John Judis, *Genesis: Truman, American Jews, and the Origins of the Arab/Israeli Conflict* (New York: Farrar, Straus, and Giroux, 2014), 241.
29. Small, *Democracy and Diplomacy*, 87–8; Smith, *Foreign Attachments*, 110. See also Peter Hahn, *Caught in the Middle East: U.S. Policy toward the Arab–Israeli Conflict, 1945–1961* (Chapel Hill, NC, 2004); Dan Raviv and Yossi Melman, *Friends in Deed: Inside the U.S.–Israeli Alliance* (New York, 1994); David Schoenbaum, *The United States and the State of Israel* (New York, 1993); Edward Tivnan, *The Lobby: Jewish Political Power and American Foreign Policy* (New York, 1987); John J. Mearsheimer and Stephen M. Walt, *The Israel Lobby and U.S. Foreign Policy* (New York, 2007).
30. Gaddis Smith, *Morality, Reason, and Power: American Diplomacy in the Carter Years* (New York, 1986), 116.
31. Bob Woodward, *State of Denial: Bush at War, Part III* (New York, 2006), 335–6. I am grateful to Andrew Preston for drawing this quote to my attention.
32. Schwartz, "'Henry, ... Winning an Election Is Terribly Important,'" 177.

10

The global frontier: comparative history and the frontier-borderlands approach

Nathan J. Citino

> "This trip into the Amazon would help to understand the real potential of Fordlandia: if it were all just an enormous glass container, a cavity made of precious crystal, into which an eccentric millionaire had poured his eccentric dreams; or if, in fact, it really was a pioneering adventure whose goal was to raise the flag of progress in an unknown territory, as unknown as it was beautiful, never to leave."
>
> "So, don't you think, then, that to tamper with Eden is to destroy it?"

Eduardo Sguiglia's novel *Fordlandia*, the source of these two quotations, is a fictionalized account of the rubber plantation established by Henry Ford in the jungles of Brazil.[1] Ford's errand into the Amazon wilderness served a dual purpose. He sought to establish a source of raw rubber for automobile tires other than British-dominated Malaya, while inculcating "backward" peoples with the work ethic and the faith in material progress that characterized Fordism. Ford regulated life in his self-named company town with a giant clock, whose piercing whistle imposed time discipline over the indigenous workforce, just as he hoped that social dancing and proper hygiene would uplift the natives. But Fordlandia was not the success its sponsor envisioned. A clash between Anglo managers and the diverse workforce of Indians and Afro-Caribbean migrants assembled by the company, as well as a rubber-tree blight, doomed Ford's adventure into the twentieth-century global frontier.

Historians of American foreign relations are better positioned than ever before to offer cutting-edge interpretations of the issues raised by Fordlandia in ways that can match the brilliance of Sguiglia's literary treatment. Successive calls for methodological innovation have prompted scholars to borrow from political science, cultural studies, and other disciplines. They have studied nonstate actors and marginalized groups and introduced race, culture, ideology, postmodernism, literary criticism, and gender into their analyses.[2] But these new approaches to US foreign relations have only begun to provide comparative perspective on the American experience in the world and challenge the exceptionalist assumptions that have long been associated with the field.[3] Recent scholarship on borderlands and frontiers, however, offers historians valuable insight into the nature of cultural encounters and shifting cultural identities, the fringes of states' political authority, and the integration of the human and natural resources of peripheral areas into larger systems of economic exchange. Fordlandia serves as a case-study, in which a US corporation developed a transnational rubber frontier as both a capitalist enterprise and an overseas version of Manifest Destiny. Historian Greg Grandin describes Fordlandia as embodying Ford's nostalgia for nineteenth-century settler America and writes of the "frustrated idealism [that] was built into its conception."[4] The diverse group of scholars who study borderlands and frontiers do not simply offer those in US foreign relations another category of analysis to add to their *repertoire*. These subfields have played a pioneering role in studying the relationship between state power on the one hand and transnational movements of capital, people, commodities, and ideas on the other. They have helped to redefine US foreign relations as America in the World and to reorient the American experience within a global, comparative context.

Defining "frontier" and "borderland" is a daunting challenge to say the least, given the myriad cases to which scholars have applied these two terms. Frederick Jackson Turner, whose well-known thesis is a fixture of diplomatic history lectures, replaced the European concept of frontier as national boundary with his account of the North American frontier as "the meeting point between savagery and civilization." Though criticism of Turner's ethnocentrism has been nearly universal, and some scholars have questioned his portrayal of the frontier as "closed" by 1890, others have retained his emphasis on cultural encounter within a shifting political geography. In their comparison of the US and South Africa, for example, Leonard Thompson and Howard Lamar define a frontier "not as a boundary or line, but as a territory or zone of interpenetration between two previously distinct societies." Jeremy Adelman and Stephen Aron have conceived the North American frontier as "a meeting place of peoples in which geographic and cultural borders were not clearly defined." Such a definition therefore minimizes the importance of the state, whose "sharp edge of sovereignty" had been synonymous with the earlier meaning of "frontier." Adelman and Aron distinguish the frontier from "borderlands," which they regard as "contested boundaries between colonial domains" in North America. The term "borderland" can implicitly reinforce the primacy of the state, either by designating the geographic arena for political rivalry among states, or by referring to land both claimed by a state and adjacent to an acknowledged boundary.[5]

But it is not so easy to label a region by reference to state authority or lack of it. Anthropologists Thomas M. Wilson and Hastings Donnan define frontiers as "territorial zones of varying width which stretch across and away from borders, within which people negotiate a variety of behaviours and meanings associated with their membership in nations and states."[6] In their view, frontiers are features of state borders. Historians of Spain's North American empire have been known to use "borderlands" and "frontier" interchangeably or in conjunction with one another, and, indeed, "borderland" is typically rendered "*la frontera*" in Spanish.[7] One geographer even makes the ahistorical claim that frontiers were "common features of the political landscape centuries ago," but by "the 20th century most remaining frontiers had disappeared" with the establishment of recognized state borders. As Lamar and Thompson have observed, scholars with varied training in different fields do not naturally speak the common language needed for writing comparative studies.[8]

Among the most important developments in recent work on North America is the challenge to a teleological account in which borderlands history culminated in the consolidation of the United States and Mexico – the argument that state formation turned contested territories into "*bordered lands*" in the phrase of Adelman and Aron.[9] Rather than an inevitable process by which international diplomacy replaced fluid power relations and citizenship clarified ambiguous frontier identities, historians Samuel Truett and Pekka Hämäläinen point to the borderlands' "open-ended horizons." Where "older national histories emphasized the rising power of states and capital to control America," they write, "newer borderlands histories have dwelt on the limits of this control."[10] This contingent understanding of state power provides historians of America in the World with an important example. As will be seen, recent borderlands histories examine how transnational movements of labor, goods, and capital helped to define state economies, foreign policies, and political identities, even as governments struggled to impose control over such phenomena. And although these themes were central to the story of American continental and overseas expansion, they were hardly unique to it. Their prevalence across a variety of historical contexts invites comparison and offers a powerful challenge to American exceptionalism.

For those in American foreign relations, it is useful first to consider the origins and evolution of the "frontier" and "borderlands" in US historiography to gain perspective on how scholars working in other subfields have sought to contextualize the American state. Turner has remained the touchstone for the study of the American frontier West even as his thesis has sustained successive waves of revision, a generation ago in the form of a New Western History that challenged his celebratory account of Anglo-American settlement and expanded the types of actors and subjects considered part of Western history.[11] Herbert E. Bolton, Turner's student, applied his mentor's thesis to the parts of northern New Spain incorporated into the territory of the United States, and, in the words of one scholar, "virtually created the Spanish borderlands as a field of professional history."[12] Historians of US foreign relations would do well to build on comparative themes developed by colleagues working in these two fields – to begin exploring the global frontier, as it were, in their own backyard.

As fields focused on the projection of state power across geographic distances, American foreign relations history and US Western history have shared a parallel trajectory. Each discipline, after languishing as something of a historiographical backwater, experienced a renaissance characterized by bold attempts to reconceptualize the field and to expand its scope, as well as by much soul-searching and methodological experimentation. Some of this innovation has sought to transcend perennial, dichotomous debates in both literatures: realism versus idealism, isolationism versus internationalism; frontier history versus Western history, closed frontier versus unbroken past. These similarities are not surprising, given that both fields have been repositories for myths of national greatness first articulated by their respective founders, Samuel Flagg Bemis and Turner himself. By celebrating national development and expansion, both diplomatic and Western historians were vulnerable to criticism from colleagues in social history, who exposed the human costs of that expansion and focused attention on groups such as African Americans, Hispanics, women, and Native Americans, whose experiences lay beyond the pale of the nationalist historiographies established by Bemis and Turner.

But the line between diplomatic and Western history has never been entirely distinct, and recent experimentation in both fields has only increased the zone of disciplinary common ground. Since Bemis penned "The Anglo-American Frontier" as the first chapter of *Jay's Treaty*, diplomatic historians have regarded continental expansion as part of their scholarly turf. William Appleman Williams identified Turner's frontier thesis with Open Door expansion overseas and traced the origins of America's free-trading imperialism to nineteenth-century frontier farmers concerned about the agricultural surplus.[13] Later works by Thomas Hietala on Manifest Destiny, Michael Hunt on ideology, Reginald Horsman on race, and Brian McAllister Linn on the Philippine War have in different ways portrayed western expansion as a dress-rehearsal for the acquisition of overseas empire.[14] Some historians have noted that the careers of such figures as Teddy Roosevelt and Herbert Hoover combined the conquest of the continental frontier with expansion abroad, while others have examined how America's emergence as a great power shaped the development of the West.[15] For their part, Western historians, most notably Walter Prescott Webb, have long placed the story of continental expansion against a global backdrop, a trend that has highlighted comparisons between the United States and other "frontier" societies. Significantly, through their use of comparative history, scholars of America's western frontier have been more successful in overcoming the exceptionalist inheritance of Turnerian history than their counterparts in US foreign relations have been in addressing the similar legacy bequeathed to them by Bemis.

Webb's influential work *The Great Frontier* applied the Turner thesis to world history since 1500 and claimed that European expansion into Africa,

Asia, and the western hemisphere represented a four-hundred-year boom for the European "metropolis." As they helped themselves to the *"vast body of wealth without proprietors"* found in these regions, Europeans used the spoils of empire to build the social and political institutions of Western civilization, whose continued existence was placed in doubt, according to Webb, by the closing of the Great Frontier around 1900.[16] For him, the story of European settlement of North America, American independence and expansion, and the extraction of the material wealth of the continent was only one episode in a much larger global saga. Viewed from this perspective, the frontier was not the unique wellspring of American democracy that Turner claims, and North America was only one of many areas around the globe connected to the metropolis during the centuries-long period of European conquest.

The ways in which Webb's successors have reinterpreted his global perspective have been closely connected to the debate about whether the American West should be studied as a distinct region (the trans-Mississippi West, for instance, or the region of aridity west of 100 degrees longitude), or as part of an ongoing frontier process that recurred in different settings as white settlement spread over North America and other continents.[17] In *The Legacy of Conquest*, Patricia Nelson Limerick advocated study of the West as region, though she later sought "to place Western American history back into global history," by comparing the conquest of the region she studies to "other parts of the planet" transformed by European expansion, and even argued for the usefulness of comparative frontier studies.[18] An emphasis on place, however, while acknowledging the larger global story, tends to stress discrete instances of conquest whose special histories are shaped by local factors. Lamar and Thompson point out how different geographies, cultures, and climates helped to mold the histories of white settlement in North America and Southern Africa. Whereas inhospitable South African soils and aridity limited the numbers of white agricultural settlers in the Cape, more favorable conditions in much of North America supported a larger farming population. Southern Africa was therefore home to only about twenty thousand Europeans in 1800, when the European population of North America exceeded 4 million. Different immigration patterns also made these two frontier societies distinct in terms of their ethnic and racial politics.[19]

For historians interested in the frontier as process, Turner's sequential, regional histories, each of them variations on a theme, offer a theoretical basis for comparison. In the introduction to *Under an Open Sky*, William Cronon, George Miles, and Jay Gitlin identify several stages to the recurring frontier process: species shifting, market making, land taking, boundary setting, state forming, and self-shaping.[20] State-building and identity formation are therefore integral to the frontier experience. While Western historians pioneered comparative frontier studies by analyzing how different locales experienced this process as the line of settlement moved east-to-west, Walter Nugent has broadened the comparative frame of reference to encompass European expansion beyond North America. Using this "wide-angle lens," Nugent argues that European settlers had similar, though far from identical, experiences based on the geographies, climates, and indigenous peoples they encountered. In fact, Nugent offers a basic taxonomy that classifies frontiers according to their economic bases and demographic characteristics. Type I frontiers were based upon farming and settled by the "colorless many" families drawn west by the promise of free land. Type I frontiers were more densely populated than Type II frontiers, which were based on natural-resource extraction, mining, and ranching. Evoking images more in tune with popular imagination, the Type II frontier was home to the "colorful few," including cowboys, gold prospectors, prostitutes, and gun-slingers. Nugent draws careful comparisons between North American frontiers and those in Australia, New Zealand, South Africa, Brazil, and Argentina. To cite one example, he trains his lens on California and the Australian province of Victoria, both sites of mid-nineteenth-century gold rushes and ensuing Type II frontiers. Such comparisons, he argues, reveal "that American history is not incomparable or unique" and offer a corrective to "moral superiority and self-righteous missionizing."[21]

Other historians have invoked the world-systems theory of Immanuel Wallerstein to locate North America within the development of the capitalist world economy. Richard White has shown how incorporation into the world system and European trading networks sapped the economic self-sufficiency of Choctaw, Pawnee, and Navajo peoples. William G. Robbins associates the West's transformation with "the ever-expanding boundaries and the constantly changing parameters of capitalism, especially in its national and international contexts." In an important contribution to the place–process debate, Michael P. Malone argues for a "stereopticon" view that seeks to understand how the long-term process of global economic integration transformed the American West. A resource-producing region on the economic periphery, the West, "has been defined by the dialectical tension of those historical factors that defined it as place with those that dictated its changing role in the world order." Malone even suggests replacing the term "frontier" with "globalization," implicitly raising the possibility of comparing the West to other regions similarly affected by the world economy.[22] While Turner set regional history in a national context and moved the frontier to the center of American life, these historians connect the West to changes in the capitalist world system and highlight the historical passage of the United States from the economic periphery to the core.

Recent work explores the dialogue between the frontier and state power while providing further comparative and global context for Anglo settlement in North America. Paul Mapp studies the implications of Europeans' lack of knowledge about the frontier for imperial rivalries among Britain, France, and Spain. "Competing for empire and coping with geographic ignorance went hand in hand in the early modern Americas," he writes, "the demands of each shaping the conduct of the other." While Europeans were forced to rely on Native Americans' non-Cartesian geographic knowledge, French explorers and missionaries helped to map frontiers in Russia and China, states that were also "adding large stretches of territory and vast numbers of people."[23] As heir and critic of Walter Prescott Webb, James Belich compares Anglo settler societies, exploring not only their demographic "explosions" but also their economic "recolonization" by metropolitan centers of capital such as New York and London.[24] Aims McGuinness' path-breaking *Path of Empire* shows how Panama was transformed economically and demographically as part of the United States "empire of movement" following the 1840s gold rush in California. Instead of "separate stages or competing processes," McGuinness insists that "the making of the United States as a transcontinental nation and U.S. expansion overseas" were "coincident with one another and intertwined."[25]

Changes in the understandings of empire and state power have also corresponded to shifting interpretations of Euro-Indian relations in North America. In *The Middle Ground*, White recreated the "village world" of the seventeenth- and eighteenth-century *pays d'en haut*, where Algonquin and French societies "melted at the edges and merged" as a consequence of Europeans' relative weakness. White argues that the Middle Ground faded with US independence because Americans neither understood the cultural conventions that had governed Euro-Indian relations under the French and British, nor, given the weak position of Native Americans after the American Revolution, had any need of them. The Middle Ground, which had been characterized by intermarriage and cultural hybridization, therefore "yielded to stark choices between assimilation and otherness."[26] Indeed, the distinction that Adelman and Aron draw between the "frontier" and "borderlands" usefully focuses attention on Natives' loss of political leverage wherever lines of state authority were clearly drawn. Newer studies reverse this emphasis, however, by portraying Natives as full-fledged participants alongside states in the struggle over North American territories. Brian DeLay focuses attention on Native conflicts with northern Mexican settlements from the 1830s and the implications for US–Mexican relations.[27] Pekka Hämäläinen argues that a Comanche empire overlapped geographically with American power and facilitated the US conquest of northern Mexico. With a nomadic empire based on horse-breeding and assimilating captives, the "Comanches desired the resources of the land," while "Americans wanted legal titles to it." Native raiding siphoned off the Mexican state's wealth, and the "U.S. takeover of the Southwest was significantly assisted by the fact that Comanches and Apaches had already destabilized Mexico's Far North."[28] Recent scholarship has therefore complicated a zero-sum interpretation of relations between Native agency and state power.

Though drawn to the US–Mexican borderlands by a desire to compare them with Turner's Great Western frontier, Bolton was "far more interested in the impact of Spaniards on the frontier than in the influence of the frontier on the Spaniards." Bolton devoted his career to studying the institutional outposts of the Spanish Empire in North America, the presidio and the mission, and the cultural influence of Spain on lands that became part of the United States. He also called for a comparative colonial history of the western hemisphere, an approach he hoped would overcome the Hispanophobic "Black Legend" and shed light on the differences between the British and Spanish colonial legacies. David J. Weber explains Bolton's focus by observing that, unlike the mythical opportunity represented by the frontier in Turner's thesis, the borderlands have more often been the site of racial discrimination and poverty for Hispanics whose lives were tied to the American economy, whether they lived north or south of the border.[29]

Bolton's successors built upon his comparative study of colonialism by exploring the competing and conjoined state-building enterprises of the United States and Mexico. Late twentieth-century scholarship focused especially on studying state-building "from below" and examined how these ventures appeared from the perspectives of different populations. Andrés Reséndez reinterpreted the history of the borderlands during the Mexican–American War by "paying attention to how the Mexican and the American national projects collided there and how conflicts played out at the local level." Reséndez examines the use of rituals and political symbolism in American and Mexican claims to borderlands territory, and he explains how local groups responded to such appeals on the basis of self-interest. Reséndez uses New Mexico as a case study and shows that while local Spanish-speaking officers and merchants acquiesced in annexation to protect their economic interests, Pueblo Indians resisted out of opposition to further land expropriation by Anglos. Colonel Stephen W. Kearny therefore marched into Santa Fe unopposed in 1846 but before long would face rebellion from Taos Pueblos. Lisabeth Haas's study of California examines the persistence of Native American identities despite conquest by the Spanish in the eighteenth century, the ascendancy of local *Californios* who defied Mexico City and obstructed Indian emancipation during the period of Mexican independence, and conquest again by the Americans in the mid-nineteenth century.[30] These subaltern accounts of the United States and Mexico challenge nationalist historiographies but do not necessarily displace the state as the center of historical change.

Borderlands studies, like US foreign relations, underwent a "cultural turn" at the end of the last century that questioned the coherence and unity of the national state. The border assumed metaphorical value, used by individuals and communities seeking to define their ethnic and gender identities throughout what Américo Paredes called "Greater Mexico." Even popular films such as *Lone Star* (1996) and *Traffic* (2000) depicted the borderlands as a place where personal identities are ambiguous and shifting. Scholars, meanwhile, described the borderlands as a site of cultural conflict and syncretism. Paredes showed how the lyrics of Mexican *corridos*, or border songs, challenged Anglo hegemony. According to José E. Limón, though Anglo-Americans have defined themselves culturally by reference to a Hispanic Other, Anglos have also been subject to countervailing impulses, such as sexual desire and affinity for Hispanic culture, which foster "self-doubt within those who dominate." Gloria Anzaldúa's work, *Borderlands/La Frontera: The New Mestiza*, uses both gender and race to describe the place of borderlands *Mestiza* women who define their identities through resistance to Anglo hegemony, Spanish cultural assimilation, and Hispanic male machismo. Such work refocuses borderlands studies on the evolution of separate personal and group identities, an experience that paradoxically requires intimate cross-cultural contact. Through cultural analyses of the borderlands, scholars came to understand identity as contested within each multicultural society and developed symbolic interpretations of the US–Mexico border appropriate to a postmodern age.[31]

Rather than depict a historical progression of expanding state power, the latest borderlands studies describe an open-ended relationship between state policies and flows of people, capital, and commodities. In such accounts, writes Rachel St. John, the borderlands serve as "models for transnational history."[32] Truett examines the "landscape of extraction" straddling the border, where American mining investments depended upon the movement of workers, equipment, money, and expertise. Studying the copper borderlands, he argues, necessitates "tacking back and forth between national and transnational coordinates."[33] St. John similarly notes that the "boundary line ran right through the middle of an increasingly productive landscape of copper mines, ranches, and irrigated agriculture."[34] These transnational enterprises had to contend with, and often sought to influence, the two states' changing customs, taxation, and immigration policies. Extractive industries assembled diverse workforces whose ethnic divisions enabled companies to combat unionism and pay differential wages. "Companies assumed," writes Thomas Andrews about the "transnational space" of the Colorado coalfields, "that the differences in race, nationality, ethnicity, creed, and skill that separated these migrants would make it impossible for them to get along."[35] For Truett, the separate-and-unequal housing provided by the Phelps Dodge copper mining company for Anglo managers and Mexican workers serves as a "metaphor for the U.S. transnational experience." Far from being an exclusive domain of state power, the border was "patrolled by the paternalism of corporate capital" operating on both sides.[36]

Some studies have analyzed the relationship between national identities and visions of modernization on the one hand and migration, whether voluntary or coerced, on the other. "'Are you an American, or are you not?'" is the question that Katherine Benton-Cohen places at the heart of the Bisbee deportation of July 12, 1917, in the mining camps of Cochise County, Arizona. Allegedly asked by Sheriff Harry Wheeler in the course of rounding up 1186 workers, most of whom were Mexicans and eastern European Slavs, this question indicates how labor politics at the border helped to forge national identities along ethnic lines. In the years following Bisbee, writes Benton-Cohen, "'Mexican' and 'white

American' had become mutually exclusive racial categories."[37] Both the United States and Mexico defined national identity through anti-Chinese immigration policies. As a way of distinguishing *mestizaje*, or mixed Spanish-indigenous heritage, some Mexican revolutionaries disparaged Sonoran Chinese as "parasitic and unfit for modernization." For Grace Peña Delgado, the expulsions of "3,500 Sonoran Chinese" from Mexico and 500,000 Mexicans from the United States during the early 1930s "marked an entrenchment of restrictionist immigration policy as official state practice in both the United States and Mexico."[38] Deborah Cohen describes Mexican Bracero agricultural workers in the United States as "transnational subjects." The US and Mexican governments portrayed the wartime and postwar Bracero program not simply as a source of cheap labor for US growers but as "modernization [that] was built around human transformation through migration." For the United States, the program was meant to convey the supposedly benevolent hegemony previously associated with the Monroe Doctrine and the Good Neighbor Policy. In this case, Washington's hemispheric diplomacy aligned with the interests of American agribusiness. And because Mexico "envisioned citizenship" in gendered terms "as a male right," its government linked Braceros to the "cultural modernization of masculinity." As "transnational subjects," however, Braceros forged identities for themselves irrespective of government policies. Returning from America with new consumer goods and attitudes, they could "claim to be modern in Durango."[39] These newest borderlands studies provide useful examples of how migrations and other transnational phenomena help to constitute states.

By attempting to regulate movements across borders, immigration and trade policies have defined state diplomacy and national identity. Laws restricting immigration, explains Mae M. Ngai, "articulate a desired composition – imagined if not necessarily realized – of the nation." Regardless of legal status, however, immigrants have adhered to "collectivities that are not national but transnational, sited in borderlands or in diaspora." This contradiction created illegal aliens as "impossible subjects" who were members of America's society and participants in its workforce but whose existence was "a legal impossibility." Official policies and transnational migration together contributed to shifting definitions of American identity. Filipinos arrived in North America as unwelcome colonial subjects following the US annexation of the Philippines, while in 1930 the Census Bureau began categorizing Mexicans as a separate race. Only during World War II did the government ease restrictions established by the 1882 Chinese Exclusion Act, and Cold War ideology mitigated racial concerns about migrants from Cuba and Vietnam.[40] Animosity toward non-Anglos led to the bifurcation of the state, between an executive that had once administered immigration as "an adjunct of policies governing foreign trade," and the Congress, which responded to voters' nativism by barring certain groups. Immigration and trade policies became "uncoupled" during early twentieth-century tariff battles, when advocates of freer trade convinced American workers that they had more to fear from foreign peoples than imports. "We must," Congressman Martin Dies (D-Texas) declared in 1934, "ignore the tears of sobbing sentimentalists and internationalists, and we must permanently close, lock, and bar the gates of our country to new immigration waves and then throw the keys away." Thus did a breach between the executive and legislative branches open the door for trade and lock the gates against unwanted foreigners. Not until 1965 would immigrant groups successfully partner with the president to roll back the racially restrictive immigration quotas enacted by Congress four decades earlier.[41]

A frontier-borderlands approach to US foreign relations does not simply offer historians transnational themes with which to contextualize the power of the American state. It also provides them with an opportunity to write the United States into world history by comparing it to other instances in which states were constituted by human migrations, trade, and other exchanges. As David Thelen observed, the US–Mexican border offers a "paradigmatic perspective of borderland studies" that encompasses not only "the division of people into separate spheres and opposing identities," but also "interaction between individuals from many backgrounds, hybridization, creolization, and negotiation."[42] Themes similar to those developed by scholars of the US West and US–Mexican borderlands reappear in very different historical contexts. Middle Eastern history, for instance, offers examples of how frontiers helped to shape the institutions of burgeoning states and how state boundaries affected the identities of particular groups. Hämäläinen compares Comanches to the Mongols, another expanding people on horseback who did "not seek to absorb other polities into a single imperial framework" and "needed viable agricultural societies on their borders to guarantee a secure access to carbohydrates, livestock, and other imports through trade, theft, or tribute."[43] More than a century before European contact with the New World, the North African writer Ibn Khaldun identified in his *Muqaddimah*, or introduction to history, a dialectical process across the frontier between settled and nomadic peoples as the basis for the rise and decline of bureaucratic states. Cemal Kafadar references Ibn Khaldun to show how the Ottoman empire originated in western Anatolia along the Muslim–Byzantine frontier. There, despite cultural syncretism between Muslims and Christians, whose fluid identities sometimes overlapped, a powerful *gazi*, or Islamic holy warrior, ethos emerged that became the ideology of the Ottoman state.[44] Kafadar's book examining the Ottoman empire's origins, *Between Two Worlds*, shares its title with a pair of studies about the US–Mexican borderlands, one written by Américo Paredes and another edited by David G. Gutiérrez.[45] Rashid Khalidi explains that for stateless Palestinians, identity verification at border checkpoints and airports, which often excludes or singles them out, "brings home to them how much they share in common as a people."[46] Such examples illustrate the significance of the frontier in Middle Eastern history, just as Middle Eastern borderlands have also been sites of identity formation.

The American experience with frontier-borderlands replicates major patterns in world history, recurring themes studied by both specialists investigating particular cases and world historians engaged in comparative studies. Scholars working in widely differing fields have seen the dialectic between the political center and the frontier as a fundamental factor in state formation. As Mark Bassin notes in his work on Russia, "there is nothing exclusively American about the 'frontier'."[47] Jane M. Rausch has examined the role of a century of frontier wars on the evolution of state and nationalism in Colombia.[48] For these scholars, and those working in other areas, the struggle to subdue a landed frontier is a basic part of state-building.[49] While central governments might seek to control peripheral territory and bestow political identities on frontier peoples through inclusion or exclusion, ethnic and national identities are just as likely to be formed at the periphery as they are to be imposed from the center outward. Peter Sahlins, for example, argues that French and Spanish national identities had coalesced along the Catalan border by the 1820s, long before the infrastructures of the national states developed. Indeed, behaviors and identities in border regions coincide with policies imposed by the political center only when they accord with the needs of local populations. "No matter how clearly borders are drawn on official maps, how many customs officials are appointed, or how many watchtowers are built," write Michiel Baud and Willem van Schendel, "people will ignore borders whenever it suits them."[50]

Though cross-border migrations occur despite state policy, exchanges along cultural frontiers might actually create powerful, if socially constructed, ethnic identities. Frederik Barth first noted the persistence of constructed ethnic identities despite intimate contact and cultural exchange between groups, and David A. Chappell contends that ethnogenesis often occurs in frontier areas where reference to an "Other" provides the basis for identity formation.[51] Igor Kopytoff has reconfigured Turner's perspective on North American history into an "African frontier thesis" that regards the construction of group identities at the periphery of existing polities as the basis of African ethnogenesis. Kopytoff, like Cronon, Miles, and Gitlin, describes a historical frontier process that involves self-shaping and the building of institutions.[52]

This handful of examples suggests the ubiquity of historical themes considered special to the American case and refutes Turner's claim that the "peculiarity of American institutions is, the fact that they have been compelled to adapt themselves to the changes of an expanding people."[53] Such comparisons even make the argument for an *anti*-Turner thesis: the hypothesis that territorial consolidation and cultural encounter have been the usual bases for state-building and identity formation in modern history. Turner's contribution in revising the European definition of "frontier" to fit a supposedly distinctive North American context simply reflects professional historians' fixation with the nation-state at the time that he was writing.[54] State-centeredness led American historiography to treat national consolidation and overseas expansion as distinct topics handled separately by the subfields founded by Turner and Bemis. But as historians have moved away from focusing exclusively on the state, some have begun to rethink US history in a way that folds continental conquest and global economic expansion into a transnational history of the frontier.

Certain scholars have combined expertise on the American West and non-US areas into a transnational perspective that situates the United States within patterns of global economic integration. While comparing the American West to other frontiers, these historians regard the North American conquest and the extension of US economic hegemony over peripheral regions of the globe as elements of a single historical process. William H. McNeill places the frontier at the center of world history by rehabilitating Webb's Great Frontier concept, though unlike Webb, McNeill addresses the experiences of Native Americans by portraying US history as an "extreme case of contact and collision between societies at different levels of skill." McNeill regards technological disparities between cultures as the "principal drive wheel of historical change," a factor that helps to explain why frontiers are not always the egalitarian settings of Turner's thesis. When cash-cropping or extractive industries are involved, frontiers are more likely to yield a "social hierarchy steeper than anything familiar in Europe."[55] Paul Sabin has identified similarities among oil frontiers in Alaska, Ecuador, and elsewhere not as parallel case-studies, but as sharing a "direct *lineage* between earlier American Wests and later developments" linked by common patterns of corporate expansion, missionary activity, and environmental transformation.[56] Kornel S. Chang describes the US–Canadian borderlands as "a critical intersection of colonialism and the Pacific world, where the American West, the Dominion of Canada, the British Empire and Asia intersected and overlapped." Focusing on how Chinese migrants were incorporated into trans-Pacific trade networks as well as excluded by state immigration policies, Chang's study "re-orients borderlands history to the larger worlds of which it was a part."[57] For these historians, the story of the West is a transnational epic that cannot be contained within political boundaries, just as frontier history cannot properly be the exclusive domain of either Western or diplomatic historians.

As part of their attempts to write the United States into world history, various authors have criticized exceptionalist mythmaking about the American frontier. Louis S. Warren reinterprets the leading popularizer of such myths in global perspective by showing how Buffalo Bill Cody's friendship with Bram Stoker may well have inspired *Dracula*.[58] David Wrobel reminds us that nineteenth-century European travel writers were inclined to see the frontier not as a uniquely American symbol but as "one colonial enterprise, among many around the globe," marked by racial violence.[59] In *America's Kingdom*, Robert Vitalis analyzes the Arabian American Oil Company (Aramco)'s export of frontier mythology to Saudi Arabia. There, America's Manifest Destiny mythology reinforced Saudi claims that their kingdom had "never" been colonized and that oil wealth was an earthly reward from God. Aramco developed the Arabian oil frontier using the same corporate paternalism, separate-and-unequal residential camps, and differential wage system present in the American southwest. "It turns out that all firms in the U.S. mining industry organized the labor process in this way," Vitalis explains, "first, throughout the original American empire – Indian territory, Arizona, 'new' Mexico – and later when the firms moved beyond the Caribbean Basin, or what used to be called 'America's Mesopotamia,' and started to explore for minerals in the real Mesopotamia." Among those who ran Aramco was David Dodge, a scion of the Phelps Dodge dynasty. Aramco's British, Colorado-educated vice president James Terry Duce even hired western author Wallace Stegner to celebrate Aramco's enterprise. The company later gave away copies of Stegner's book *Discovery!* after removing references to Dhahran's racial hierarchy.[60] Speaking to a Dallas audience in the 1950s, Duce criticized Walter Prescott Webb for daring to suggest that the global frontier had closed.[61]

From Bisbee to Fordlandia and the Persian Gulf, frontiers combined the transnational movement of workers, investments, and commodities demanded by global capitalism with states' drive to assert "control of bordered political space."[62] Chang describes it as a clash between the "territorializing processes of state formation and the de-territorializing prerogatives of capital."[63] Rather than study the nation-state system as the basis of modern history, scholars of US foreign relations should take from the frontier-borderlands approach the importance of analyzing exchanges between national and transnational forces. This dialectic has built the maze of open doors and locked gates, of container-ship ports and tall fences, that constitutes globalization.[64] Today's US–Mexico border is a microcosm of this contradiction, where an increasingly militarized campaign to control people and narcotics intersects with the flow of goods under the North American Free Trade Agreement (NAFTA). As Deborah Cohen remarks, despite states' pretensions of exerting control over the borderlands, we "should not assume that the transnational subject is going away."[65] By blazing a trail from US foreign relations to America in the World, frontier-borderlands scholarship promises to put the exceptionalist traditions of Turner and Bemis out to pasture. Joining continental settlement and overseas expansion in a continuous historical narrative makes it possible to compare the United States to other frontier societies and to situate the American past within global history. The most celebrated frontier junction, the ceremony at Promontory Point, Utah, inaugurating the first transcontinental railroad, occurred in 1869, the same year in which the Suez canal opened.[66] That golden spike thus signified not the fulfillment of Americans' Manifest Destiny but the dawn of a more interconnected world.

For the next generation of historians, the global frontier still beckons.

NOTES

1. Eduardo Sguiglia, *Fordlandia*, trans. Patricia J. Duncan (New York, 2000), 46–7, 91.
2. See Charles S. Maier, "Marking Time: The Historiography of International Relations," in *The Past before Us: Contemporary Historical Writing in the United States*, ed. Michael Kammen (Ithaca, 1980), 355–87; John Lewis Gaddis, "New Conceptual Approaches to the Study of American Foreign Relations: Interdisciplinary Perspectives," *Diplomatic History* 14 (Summer 1990): 405–23; and Michael H. Hunt, "The Long Crisis in Diplomatic History: Coming to Closure," *Diplomatic History* 16 (Winter 1992): 115–40. For discussion of new approaches in the field, see Michael J. Hogan, "The 'Next Big Thing': The Future of Diplomatic History in a Global Age," *Diplomatic History* 28 (January 2004): 1–21; and Thomas W. Zeiler, "The Diplomatic History Bandwagon: A State of the Field," *Journal of American History* 95 (March 2009): 1053–73.
3. See Ian Tyrrell, "American Exceptionalism in an Age of International History," *American Historical Review* 96 (October 1991): 1031–55.
4. Greg Grandin, *Fordlandia: The Rise and Fall of Henry Ford's Forgotten Jungle City* (New York: Metropolitan Books, 2009), 15.
5. Frederick Jackson Turner, *The Frontier in American History* (New York, 1920), 3; *The Frontier in History: North America and Southern Africa Compared*, ed. Howard Lamar and Leonard Thompson (New Haven, CT, 1981), 7; Jeremy Adelman and Stephen Aron, "From Borderlands to Borders: Empires, Nation-States, and the Peoples in Between in North American History," *American Historical Review* 104 (June 1999): 815, 816; Walter Prescott Webb, *The Great Frontier* (Boston, 1952), 2.
6. *Border Identities: Nation and State at International Frontiers*, ed. Thomas M. Wilson and Hastings Donnan (Cambridge, 1998), 9. See also *Border Approaches: Anthropological Perspectives on Frontiers*, ed. Hastings Donnan and Thomas M. Wilson (Lanham, MD, 1994).
7. See, David J. Weber, *The Mexican Frontier, 1821–1846: The American Southwest Under Mexico* (Albuquerque, 1982); and John Francis Bannon, *The Spanish Borderlands Frontier, 1513–1821* (Albuquerque, 1963).
8. J.R.V. Prescott, *Political Frontiers and Boundaries* (Boston, 1987), 1; Lamar and Thompson, *Frontier in History*, 6.
9. Adelman and Aron, "From Borderlands to Borders," 816.
10. Samuel Truett and Pekka Hämäläinen, "On Borderlands," *Journal of American History* 98 (September 2011): 338, 360.
11. On the centennial of Turner's thesis, see *A New Significance: Re-Envisioning the History of the American West*, ed. Clyde A. Milner II (New York, 1996).
12. Kerwin Lee Klein, *Frontiers of Historical Imagination: Narrating the European Conquest of Native America, 1890–1990* (Berkeley, 1997), 262.
13. Samuel Flagg Bemis, *Jay's Treaty: A Study in Commerce and Diplomacy* (New Haven, CT, 1962), 1–27; William Appleman Williams, "The Frontier Thesis and American Foreign Policy," in *A William Appleman Williams Reader: Selections from his Major Historical Writings*, ed. Henry W. Berger (Chicago, 1992), 89–104; and *The Roots of the Modern American Empire: A Study of the Growth and Shaping of Social Consciousness in a Marketplace Society* (New York, 1969). See

Comparative history & the frontier-borderlands approach

also Patricia Nelson Limerick, "Dilemmas in Forgiveness: William Appleman Williams and Western American History," *Diplomatic History* 25 (Spring 2001): 293–300. On the diplomacy of continental expansion, see Robert D. Schulzinger, "Foreign Affairs and Expansion," in *American Frontier and Western Issues: A Historiographical Review*, ed. Roger L. Nichols (Westport, CT, 1986), 217–34; and Kinley Brauer, "The Great American Desert Revisited: Recent Literature and Prospects for the Study of American Foreign Relations, 1815–1861," in *Paths to Power: The Historiography of American Foreign Relations to 1941*, ed. Michael J. Hogan (New York, 2000), 44–78.

14. Thomas Hietala, *Manifest Design: Anxious Aggrandizement in Late Jacksonian America* (Ithaca, 1985); Michael H. Hunt, *Ideology and U.S. Foreign Policy* (New Haven, CT, 1987); Reginald Horsman, *Race and Manifest Destiny: The Origins of American Racial Anglo-Saxonism* (Cambridge, MA, 1981); Brian McAllister Linn, *The Philippine War, 1899–1902* (Lawrence, KS, 2000). See also Anders Stephanson, *Manifest Destiny: American Expansionism and the Empire of Right* (New York, 1995); Richard Drinnon, *Facing West: The Metaphysics of Indian-Hating and Empire-Building* (Minneapolis, 1980); and Michael Krenn, ed., *Race and U.S. Foreign Policy from Colonial Times Through the Age of Jackson* (New York, 1998), and *Race and U.S. Foreign Policy in the Ages of Territorial and Market Expansion, 1840 to 1900* (New York, 1998). See also John Whitehead, "Hawai'i: The First and Last Far West?," *Western Historical Quarterly* 23 (May 1992): 153–77.

15. See William G. Robbins, "Laying Siege to Western History: The Emergence of New Paradigms," in *Trails: Toward a New Western History*, ed. Patricia Nelson Limerick, Clyde A. Milner II, and Charles E. Rankin (Lawrence, KS, 1991), 182–214; Thomas Dyer, *Theodore Roosevelt and the Idea of Race* (Baton Rouge, 1980); and Jeremy Mouat and Ian Phimister, "The Engineering of Herbert Hoover," *Pacific Historical Review* 77 (November 2008): 553–84.

On the West, war, and the defense industry, see Roger W. Lotchin, *Fortress California, 1910–1961: From Warfare to Welfare* (New York, 1992); *The Atomic West*, ed. Bruce Hevly and John M. Findlay (Seattle, 1998); Gerald D. Nash, *World War II and the West: Reshaping the Economy* (Lincoln, NE, 1990), and *The West Transformed: The Impact of the Second World War* (Bloomington, 1985); Spencer C. Olin, "Globalization and the Politics of Locality: Orange County, California in the Cold War Era," *Western Historical Quarterly* 22 (May 1991): 143–61; and "California at War," Special Issue, *Pacific Historical Review* 63 (August 1994).

16. Webb, *Great Frontier*, 13.

17. On the place–process debate, see Stephen Aron, "Lessons in Conquest: Towards a Greater Western History," *Pacific Historical Review* 63 (May 1994): 125–47; Michael Steiner, "From Frontier to Region: Frederick Jackson Turner and the New Western History," *Pacific Historical Review* 64 (November 1995): 479–501; and David M. Wrobel, "Beyond the Frontier-Region Dichotomy," *Pacific Historical Review* 65 (August 1996): 401–29.

18. Patricia Nelson Limerick, *Something in the Soil: Legacies and Reckonings in the New West* (New York, 2000), 20. See also *The Legacy of Conquest: The Unbroken Past of the American West* (New York, 1987), and "Going West and Ending Up Global," *Western Historical Quarterly* 32 (Spring 2001): 5–23. See also Donald Worster, *Rivers of Empire: Water, Aridity, and the Growth of the American West*

(New York, 1985); and Richard White, *"It's Your Misfortune and None of My Own": A History of the American West* (Norman, OK, 1991), 3–4.
19. Lamar and Thompson, *Frontier in History*, 16–17.
20. William Cronon, George Miles, and Jay Gitlin, "Becoming West: Toward a New Meaning for Western History," in *Under an Open Sky: Rethinking America's Western Past*, ed. William Cronon et al. (New York, 1992), 3–27.
21. Walter Nugent, "Frontiers and Empires in the Late Nineteenth Century," in *Trails*, 161–81; and "Comparing Wests and Frontiers," in *The Oxford History of the American West*, ed. Clyde A. Milner II, et al. (New York, 1994), 831. For an environmental history of post-gold-rush California and Australia that is comparative and transnational, see Ian Tyrrell, *True Gardens of the Gods: Californian-Australian Environmental Reform, 1860–1930* (Berkeley, 1999). See also "Frontiers – A Global View," Special Issue, *Journal of the West* 34 (October 1995).
22. Richard White, *The Roots of Dependency: Subsistence, Environment, and Social Change among the Choctaws, Pawnees, and Navajos* (Lincoln, NE, 1983); William G. Robbins, *Colony and Empire: The Capitalist Transformation of the American West* (Lawrence, KS, 1994), xi; Michael P. Malone, "Beyond the Last Frontier: Toward a New Approach to Western American History," in *Trails*, 156. See also Klein, *Frontiers of Historical Imagination*, 193–4.
23. Paul W. Mapp, *The Elusive West and the Contest for Empire, 1713–1763* (Chapel Hill, NC, 2011), 5, 189.
24. James Belich, *Replenishing the Earth: The Settler Revolution and the Rise of the Anglo World, 1783–1939* (New York, 2009).
25. Aims McGuinness, *Path of Empire: Panama and the California Gold Rush* (Ithaca, NY, 2008), 12.
26. Richard White, *The Middle Ground: Indians, Empires, and Republics in the Great Lakes Region, 1650–1815* (New York, 1991), 50, 518. See also Gregory Evans Dowd, *A Spirited Resistance: The North American Indian Struggle for Unity, 1745–1815* (Baltimore, 1992).
27. Brian DeLay, *War of a Thousand Deserts: Indian Raids and the U.S.–Mexican War* (New Haven, CT, 2008).
28. Pekka Hämäläinen, *The Comanche Empire* (New Haven, CT, 2008), 142, 233.
29. David J. Weber, "Turner, the Boltonians, and the Borderlands," *American Historical Review* 91 (February 1986): 68. See also *Spanish Borderlands Sourcebooks, Vol. 1, The Idea of Spanish Borderlands*, ed. David J. Weber (New York, 1991); David J. Weber, "John Francis Bannon and the Historiography of the Spanish Borderlands: Retrospect and Prospect," in *Myth and the History of the Hispanic Southwest* (Albuquerque, 1988), 55–88; Russell M. Magnaghi, *Herbert E. Bolton and the Historiography of the Americas* (Westport, CT, 1998); and Albert L. Hurtado, "Bolton and Turner: The Borderlands and American Exceptionalism," *Western Historical Quarterly* 44 (Spring 2013): 4–20.
30. Andrés Reséndez, "National Identity on a Shifting Border: Texas and New Mexico in the Age of Transition, 1821–1848," *Journal of American History* 86 [Rethinking History and the Nation-State: Mexico and the United States as a Case Study: Special Issue] (September 1999): 670; Lisabeth Haas, *Conquests and Historical Identities in California* (Berkeley, 1995). See also James F. Brooks, "Violence, Justice, and State Power in the New Mexican Borderlands, 1780–1880," in *Power and Place in the North American West*, ed. Richard White and John M. Findlay (Seattle, 1999), 23–60.

31. José David Saldívar, "Américo Paredes and Decolonization," in *Cultures of United States Imperialism*, ed. Amy Kaplan and Donald E. Pease (Durham, NC, 1993), 292–311; José E. Limón, *American Encounters: Greater Mexico, the United States, and the Erotics of Culture* (Boston, 1998), 103; and Gloria Anzaldúa, *Borderlands/La Frontera: The New Mestiza* (San Francisco, 1987). See also Michael Kearney, "Borders and Boundaries of State and Self at the End of Empire," *Journal of Historical Sociology* 4 (March 1991): 52–74; Jorge A. Bustamante, "Demystifying the United States–Mexico Border," *Journal of American History* 79 (September 1992): 485–90; David G. Gutiérrez, *Walls and Mirrors : Mexican Americans, Mexican Immigrants, and the Politics of Ethnicity* (Berkeley, 1995); and Klein, *Frontiers of Historical Imagination*, 266–73. See also Carlos Fuentes, *The Crystal Frontier: A Novel in Nine Stories*, trans. Alfred MacAdam (New York, 1997).
32. Rachel St. John, *Line in the Sand: A History of the Western U.S.–Mexico Border* (Princeton, NJ, 2011), 5.
33. Samuel Truett, *Fugitive Landscapes: The Forgotten History of the U.S.–Mexico Borderlands* (New Haven, CT, 2006), 184.
34. St. John, *Line in the Sand*, 83.
35. Thomas Andrews, *Killing for Coal: America's Deadliest Labor War* (Cambridge, MA, 2008), 17, 92.
36. Truett, *Fugitive Landscapes*, 115.
37. Katherine Benton-Cohen, *Borderline Americans: Racial Division and Labor War in the Arizona Borderlands* (Cambridge, MA, 2009), 1, 240.
38. Grace Peña Delgado, *Making the Chinese Mexican: Global Migration, Localism, and Exclusion in the U.S.–Mexico Borderlands* (Stanford, CA, 2012), 189, 192.
39. Deborah Cohen, *Braceros: Migrant Citizens and Transnational Subjects in the Postwar United States and Mexico* (Chapel Hill, NC, 2011), 4, 43, 192.
40. Mae M. Ngai, *Impossible Subjects: Illegal Aliens and the Making of Modern America* (Princeton, NJ, 2004), 3–5, 54, 94–7. See also Bartholomew Sparrow, *The Insular Cases and the Emergence of American Empire* (Lawrence, KS, 2006).
41. Donna R. Gabaccia, *Foreign Relations: American Immigration in Global Perspective* (Princeton, NJ, 2012), 50, 129, 144.
42. David Thelen, "Rethinking History and the Nation-State: Mexico and the United States," *Journal of American History* 86 (September 1999): 441.
43. Hämäläinen, *Comanche Empire*, 352.
44. Cemal Kafadar, *Between Two Worlds: The Construction of the Ottoman State* (Berkeley, 1995).
45. Américo Paredes, *Between Two Worlds* (Houston, 1991); and *Between Two Worlds: Mexican Immigrants in the United States*, ed. David G. Gutiérrez (Wilmington, DE, 1996).
46. Rashid Khalidi, *Palestinian Identity: The Construction of Modern National Consciousness* (New York, 1997), 1.
47. Mark Bassin, "Turner, Solov'ev, and the 'Frontier Hypothesis': The Nationalist Signification of Open Spaces" *Journal of Modern History* 65 (September 1993): 473, and *Imperial Visions: Nationalist Imagination and Geographical Expansion in the Russian Far East, 1840–1865* (Cambridge, 1999). See also Kate Brown, "Gridded Lives: Why Kazakhstan and Montana Are Nearly the Same Place," *American Historical Review* 106 (February 2001): 17–48. On Russia's Arctic

frontier, see Yuri Slezkine, *Arctic Mirrors: Russia and the Small Peoples of the North* (Ithaca, NY, 1994).
48. Jane M. Rausch, *Colombia: Territorial Rule and the Llanos Frontier* (Gainesville, FL, 1999), and *The Llanos Frontier in Colombian History, 1830–1930* (Albuquerque, 1993). See also *Where Cultures Meet: Frontiers in Latin American History*, ed. David J. Weber and Jane M. Rausch (Wilmington, DE, 1994); and Catherine LeGrand, *Frontier Expansion and Peasant Protest in Columbia, 1830–1936* (Albuquerque, 1986).
49. See Thomas J. Barfield, *The Perilous Frontier: Nomadic Empires and China* (Cambridge, MA, 1989); Owen Lattimore, *Inner Asian Frontiers of China* (London, 1940); and *Shifting Frontiers in Late Antiquity*, ed. Ralph W. Mathisen and Hagith S. Sivan (Brookfield, VT, 1996).
50. Peter Sahlins, *Boundaries: The Making of France and Spain in the Pyrenees* (Berkeley, 1989), and "The Nation in the Village: State-Building and Communal Struggles in the Catalan Borderland during the Eighteenth and Nineteenth Centuries," *Journal of Modern History* 60 (June 1988): 234–63; Michiel Baud and Willem van Schendel, "Toward a Comparative History of Borderlands," *Journal of World History* 8 (Fall 1997): 211.
51. See *Ethnic Groups and Boundaries: The Social Organization of Culture Difference*, ed. Frederik Barth (Boston, 1969); and David A. Chappell, "Ethnogenesis and Frontiers," *Journal of World History* 4 (Fall 1993): 267–75.
52. Igor Kopytoff, "The Internal African Frontier: The Making of African Political Culture," in *The African Frontier: The Reproduction of Traditional African Societies*, ed. Igor Kopytoff (Bloomington, IN, 1987), 3–84 [esp. pp. 16–17]. On climatic change and ethnogenesis in West Africa, see James L. A. Webb, Jr., *Desert Frontier: Ecological and Economic Change Along the Western Sahel, 1600–1850* (Madison, WI, 1995).
53. Turner, *The Frontier in American History*, 2.
54. For a discussion of how state-centeredness overtook alternative themes in American historiography, see Ian Tyrrell, "Making Nations/Making States: American Historians in the Context of Empire," *Journal of American History* 86 (December 1999): 1015–44.
55. William H. McNeill, *The Great Frontier: Freedom and Hierarchy in Modern Times* (Princeton, 1983), 9–10, 20. See also Malone, "Beyond the Last Frontier," 151–2.
56. Paul Sabin, "Home and Abroad: The Two 'Wests' of Twentieth-Century United States History," *Pacific Historical Review* 66 (August 1997): 308.
57. Kornel S. Chang, *Pacific Connections: The Making of the U.S.–Canadian Borderlands* (Berkeley, CA, 2012), 3–4.
58. Louis S. Warren, *Buffalo Bill's America: William Cody and the Wild West Show* (New York, 2005), and "Buffalo Bill Meets Dracula: William F. Cody, Bram Stoker, and the Frontiers of Racial Decay," *American Historical Review* 107 (October 2002): 1124–57.
59. David M. Wrobel, "Global West, American Frontier," *Pacific Historical Quarterly* 78 (February 2009): 1.
60. Robert Vitalis, *America's Kingdom: Mythmaking on the Saudi Oil Frontier* (New York: Verso, 2009), x.
61. Speech by Duce to the Dallas Council on World Affairs, January 13, 1953, folder: Duce, James Terry, 1946–60, box 13, Charles Habib Malik Papers, Manuscript Division, Library of Congress, Washington, DC.

62. Charles S. Maier, "Consigning the Twentieth Century to History: Alternative Narratives for the Modern Era," *American Historical Review* 105 (June 2000): 808.
    On extractive and cash-crop frontiers, see Richard P. Tucker, *Insatiable Appetite: The United States and the Ecological Degradation of the Tropical World* (Berkeley, 2000); Paul J. Dosal, *Doing Business with the Dictators: A Political History of United Fruit in Guatemala, 1899–1944* (Wilmington, DE, 1993); Jason M. Colby, *The Business of Empire: United Fruit, Race, and the U.S. Expansion in Central America* (Ithaca, NY, 2011); Douglas Yarrington, *A Coffee Frontier: Land, Society, and Politics in Duaca, Venezuela, 1830–1936* (Pittsburgh, 1997); Michael F. Jiménez, "'From Plantation to Cup': Coffee and Capitalism in the United States, 1830–1930," in *Coffee, Society, and Power in Latin America*, ed. William Roseberry, et al. (Baltimore, 1995), 38–64; Mark Pendergrast, *Uncommon Grounds: The History of Coffee and How It Transformed our World* (New York, 1999); Steven C. Topik, "Coffee Anyone? Recent Research on Latin American Coffee Societies," *Hispanic American Historical Review* 80 (Spring 2000): 225–66; and Daniel Yergin, *The Prize: The Epic Quest for Oil, Money and Power* (New York, 1991).
63. Chang, *Pacific Connections*, 4.
64. See Thomas W. Zeiler, "Just Do It! Globalization for Diplomatic Historians," *Diplomatic History* 25 (Fall 2001): 529–51.
65. Cohen, *Braceros*, 228.
66. On nineteenth-century globalization, see Sven Beckert, "Emancipation and Empire: Reconstructing the Worldwide Web of Cotton Production in the Age of the American Civil War," *American Historical Review* 109 (December 2004): 1405–38.

11

Considering borders

Emily S. Rosenberg

This chapter beckons historians of US international and transnational relations to borders – those spaces at which different systems of meaning and organization intersect.

Borders – both territorial and symbolic – can be messy places. They may produce conflict, demoralization, fear, and oppression. They may generate attraction, hybridization, creativity, and liberation. Borders are not one way or they would not be borders. The Berlin Wall marked a border. The metropolitan area of San Diego and Tijuana straddles a border. The journal *Diplomatic History* has been most controversial, and most successful, when it has pushed the borders of its field of study. All of these provide apt, but different, metaphors of the dangers and opportunities represented at borders. As conflicted zones, borders may be unsettled and postmodern in fostering juxtapositions, and – for that reason – they often raise concerns over control and become sites for oppression and policing as well as for resistance, imagination, and even emancipation.

Writing histories of US foreign relations is involved with – and complicated by – borders. Traditional scholarship in diplomatic history dealt largely with bounded states in a fairly defined international system. More recently, scholarship shifted toward a revised nomenclature called "America and the World" and toward transnational themes in which economic and cultural interactions, especially among nonstate actors, have become more visible. In addition, historians of America and the World now work within a larger universe of scholarly discourse that blurs disciplinary borders and debates the saliency of modernist categories and assumptions about the writing of history. Interrogating the borders of politics and power, of culture and knowledge, has been transformative. This chapter, in encouraging readers to think about borders of all kinds, considers some influential theoretical frames and reflects upon various directions suggested by recent scholarship.

MAKING MEANING ALONG BORDERS: OTHERING AND CONTACT ZONES

The border between "West" and "East," "Occident" and "Orient," is surely one of the most structuring, and also contentious, frameworks in global politics. Edward Said's *Orientalism*, a seminal work that has framed academic conversations for over three decades, is an appropriate place to begin a discussion of border-creation.[1] Although *Orientalism* deals with Western representations of the Middle East, the implications of Said's work – and the debates generated by its many critics – extend far more broadly. Said's book draws together a wide-ranging body of Western material, from policy statements to travel accounts, to literature, and links this "orientalist" knowledge to imperial power. Arguing that "political imperialism governs an entire field of study, imagination, and scholarly institutions," it highlights ways in which representations of cultural differences between East and West became sharpened into opposing, essentialized descriptions of self and Other. By encountering and defining Others, the West shaped its own image; that is, representations of the Orient stressing irrationality, backwardness, and timelessness helped define the West as rational, progressive, and historical. Such "knowledge" worked to contain, discipline, and rule people categorized as Other and to justify Western superiority and its "civilizing" mission.

Over the years, numerous criticisms have been leveled at Said's work. Many critics charge that Said compressed together too many kinds of writing about too many diverse places. Western discourses on the Orient (and Others generally) contain greater multiplicity than Said's work suggests. Moreover, the hegemonic discourse that Said describes seemed to replicate itself over time without much modification. By stressing this changeless, binary character, critics ask, did Said contribute to Orientalism in reverse? In addition, does Said's work, by focusing on Europe, effectively reproduce European hegemonic thought even while critiquing it? Said's subsequent book, *Culture and Imperialism*, addresses his critics by adopting a more dynamic and less Western-centered approach.[2]

Despite the critics, Said's framework for dealing with the creation of "otherness" became widely used as a method for examining the representations of cultural borders in many different geographies and relationships, and it proved useful in explaining the cultural dynamics that buttressed imperial structures. "Othering" became a common shorthand for describing any process that constructs subordinate groups as being essentially different from one's own group. By showing how the construction of "knowledge" of the Other accompanies domination, Said raises epistemological questions about Western social science as well as literature. James Clifford, reflecting the questioning that went on in his own discipline of anthropology, writes that "the key theoretical issue raised by Orientalism concerns the status of all forms of thought and representation for dealing with the alien. Can one ultimately escape procedures of dichotomizing, restructuring and textualizing the making of interpretive statements about foreign cultures and traditions."[3] The challenge to be more critical in examining – and creating – texts that deal with a "foreign" arena has reverberated among historians of America and the World. Orientalism has proved a useful framework, for example, in works such as Christina Klein's *Cold War Orientalisms*, Mark Bradley's *Imagining Vietnam and America*, and David Brody's *Visualizing American Empire*.[4]

Transcending issues related to the constructed boundaries between East and West, *Orientalism* ranks as a seminal work on the epistemology of any interaction marked by cultural difference. Said's approach, especially his emphasis on discourse (connecting power and knowledge together in a Foucaultian manner) reshaped US imperial scholarship, both directly and also indirectly, through the many writers associated with "postcolonial studies."

A huge and diverse scholarship, postcolonial studies is too vast to be adequately summarized here. It emerged from Said's insights about the construction of the Other; from Indian scholars associated with Subaltern Studies, which was then adapted to different parts of the globe; and from other theorists who dissected the interconnecting discourses of nation, race, and gender in an imperial context. Initially associated with literary theory and cultural studies, postcolonial theorists have explored the cultural borders that empire-building both induced and undermined. In the words of Robert J. C. Young, postcolonial scholarship "is about turning the world upside down and looking at it from a different perspective, that is, from the perspective of the disenfranchised people, a majority of whom come from the developing world." It is about "provincializing Europe," asking how "can the subaltern speak," and examining the constructions of race, gender, and sexuality within the "tensions of empire."[5]

Mary Louise Pratt's *Imperial Eyes* provides another related and highly influential frame for what she calls "transculturation." She sees borders as "contact zones," which are "social spaces where disparate cultures meet, clash, and grapple with each other, often in highly asymmetrical relations of domination and subordination." In contact zones, power gets deployed but also negotiated, changing all parties to the interaction. Pratt's analysis certainly does not erase inequality in power relationships; she invokes the term "imperial" even in her title. But she cautions that power never flows only one way and that agency is not one-sided. She is attentive to discrete localized interactions – the confusions and singular mutations that mark "contact zones." Her book echoes Said in asking how travel writing "produced 'the rest of the world'" for European readers and, in so doing, also produced Europe's own conceptions of itself; that is, "how subjects are constituted in and by their relations to each other." She also examines travel writing for its "enactment of race and gender relations." But her concept of "contact zones" breaks with ideas of "imperialist" implantations, as she insists upon "interrupting the totalizing momentum" implied by older critiques of imperialist ideology, critiques that she stresses were often as anchored in the metropolis as was imperialism itself.[6]

The influences of postcolonial theory and "contact zones" reshaped histories of America and the World. In the 1990s, for example, two seminal anthologies helped form the basis for new histories of the American empire. Essays in *Cultures of American Imperialism*, edited by Amy Kaplan and Donald Pease, examine the relationships between US expansion and the cultural consolidation of national identities at "home." Most of the contributors, like the editors, draw upon their backgrounds in literary theory to analyze the often-overlapping discourses of nation, race, and gender that delineate "foreign" groups (whether they reside inside or outside of US borders) and to address practices of resistance and the construction of "transcultural identities." The contributors to *Close Encounters of Empire*, edited by Gilbert Joseph, Catherine C. LeGrand, and Ricardo D. Salvatore, closely scrutinize "contact zones" of the US formal and informal empire, bringing the traditions of international, multiarchival historical research to their analyses of the diverse representational processes of encounter.[7] Gilbert Joseph and Emily Rosenberg inaugurated a new book series on "American Encounters/Global Interactions" that sought to welcome such scholarship. Over the past fifteen years, there has been an explosion of research focusing on contact zones of various kinds.

Such scholarship provides a refreshed history of empire that moves away from a focus on a narrowly political or diplomatic (state-centered) narrative to examine social, cultural, and economic constructions that shaped, and were shaped by, all kinds of interactions in imperial space. The subject matter and methodologies of studies of empire, once the purview of historians largely interested in administrative structures, have been transformed. Works such as those by Louis A. Pérez on Cuba; Mary Renda on Haiti; Paul Kramer, Michael Salman, Alfred McCoy, and Vicente L. Rafael on the Philippines; Michel Gobat on Nicaragua; Michael Donoghue on Panama; Laura Briggs on Puerto Rico; and Noenoe Silva on Hawai'i are only a few among many that analyze the diverse meanings of US imperial processes.[8]

The study of specific contact zones that developed because of the offshoring of US business or military enclaves has generated an especially rich literature. Julie Greene's *The Canal Builders* shows how science, technology, and race structured interactions in the digging of the Panama Canal that had lasting effects on all of the disparate groups that were brought together in that endeavor. Alexander Missal's *Seaway to the Future* augments Greene's predominantly social history by introducing cultural and visual theory into a deconstruction of the Canal's dominant dramatic story. US military bases provide other enclaves in which US economic and strategic interests and cultural penetrations both shape and are shaped by local contexts: Jana Lipman's *Guantanamo* and Adria Imada's *Aloha America* are only two examples among many that demonstrate the ways in which different modalities of gender, race, and class distinction shape cultural interactions at US bases. Robert Vitalis' *America's Kingdom* shows the structuring of labor and social interactions that accompanied Aramco's expansion in Saudi Arabia; Greg Grandin's *Fordlandia* and Seth Garfield's *In Search of the Amazon* complement each other's treatments of the impacts of US rubber settlements in Brazil; while Jason Colby's *The Business of Empire* illuminates how United Fruit's plantations in Central America shaped labor forces, race relations, and national identity. All of these intensely researched localized studies show how the global reach of US economic and strategic positions intersected with the specifics of place. What connects such studies is not necessarily a similarity in their conclusions, as contact zones are messy and highly contingent places. They do not structure a new master narrative about foreign relations in the way that, for example, the New Left's economic interpretation did during the 1960s and 1970s. Rather, they contribute to complementary and comparative perspectives that help to illuminate various hierarchies of power and the disparate effects produced within processes of imperial contact.[9]

Such studies dovetail with examinations of similar contact zones that shaped areas that now seem part of the United States but once lay outside its borders. Imperial contact zones have been part of the story of the continental expansion undertaken by European settlers going back to the time of New World "discovery" by Europeans, and historians have recently become more attuned to the idea that scholarly fields now called "borderlands history" and "America and the World" overlap. Although each of these fields has a distinctive genealogy – borderlands history emerging mostly out of "Western history" and "America and the World" emerging mostly from "diplomatic or foreign relations" – both now share common concerns and a common historiography. Nathan Citino's chapter in this volume develops this theme in greater detail. He shows the importance of scholarship that has developed the concept of a "middle ground," and of historians who have worked to re-envision various contact zones within which empires and cultures mixed and clashed. A new literature on settler colonialism, reflected in Walter Hixson's *American Settler Colonialism*, also merges Western and borderland with America and the World histories.[10]

Moreover, a new historiography that envisions oceans not as barriers to exchange but as connectors of cultures and pathways for economic flows provides another example of overlap between borderlands history and America and the World. Scholarship on US-based actors that circulated in borderlands of the Atlantic Ocean is exemplified in books and articles by Marcus Rediker and, for a more recent period, Brooke Blower. More recently, Gary Okihiro's *Island World*, Matt Matsuda's *Pacific Worlds*, and David Igler's *The Great Ocean* have staked out an emerging field of Pacific Studies that stirs social, economic, intellectual, and political history into a mix that smashes some political and cultural borders while also recognizing the processes by which new registers of difference come into being.[11]

Such studies of encounters with "others" and of the complicated nature of "contact zones" have been influenced not only by the growth of social history but also by the cultural and transnational turns of late-twentieth-century historiography – topics which we now take up.

TRANSCENDING BORDERS: TRANSNATIONAL INTERCONNECTIONS

The late-twentieth-century revolutions in markets, technology, media, and migration, all of which accelerated exchanges among citizens and cultures, prompted another kind of thinking about borders. Did not the connectivity and circulation of the modern (or postmodern) era point toward tangled networks of both "international" and "transnational" relationships that fit poorly within the spoke-and-wheel pattern implied in the term "American foreign relations"? The phenomenon called "globalization," a word suddenly seen everywhere as a descriptor of the post-Cold War 1990s, offered new terms and paradigms for conceptualizing complex state and nonstate networks in earlier eras as well.

The more US historians pondered the processes of transnationalism and globalization, the more they recognized that those phenomena had always been a feature of US life. Every era, after all, had formal and informal networks forged through migration, travel, media, religion, trade, investment, advertising, and cultural interactions. This global focus prompted new projects to broaden the study of US history and to mount a frontal assault on US exceptionalism by seeing America within, and intricately connected to, the rest of the world. In the 1990s David P. Thelen, as editor of the *Journal of American History*, reached out to historians throughout the world by sponsoring a number of international initiatives and bringing scholars from outside the United States into an advisory role. In 2000 a group headed by Thomas Bender – in a collaboration between New York University and the Organization of American Historians – produced a report that called on historians to transcend "the nation as the container of American history" and to link the US experience to transnational and global developments. Bender's group advocated recasting US history within global historical trajectories and suggested organizing themes related to, for example, poverty, disease, environmental issues, resources, demography, consumerism, communications networks, and human rights. Akira Iriye's many books, especially *Global Community* (2002), exemplified the burgeoning interest in transnational connections. Iriye and many others urged US historians to become more involved in globalization studies and world history. Ian Tyrrell's *Transnational Nation* followed up this agenda by placing the United States within global interactions that diminished the importance of national borders rather than assuming their preeminence.[12]

The focus on transnational connections – America in the world and the world in America – has opened new arenas for scholarship dealing with a wide variety of nonstate, border-crossing actors who had often been fairly peripheral in US diplomatic or foreign relations histories. It would be impractical to try to build a list of all the recent books on all the different kinds of transnational flows, some of which stood completely apart from states and state policies and some of which ran parallel to or in dialogue with foreign policy goals. But here is a sampling, and the array of topics shown in these works suggests that we are entering a kind of golden age for transnational histories. Books by Christopher Endy, Dennis Merrill, and Kristen Hoganson examine international travelers – armchair and otherwise. David Engerman, Daniel Rodgers, and Matthew Connolly deal with the transnational activities of social scientific and technical experts. Books by Brad Simpson, Michael Latham, David Ekbladh, Nick Cullalther, and Emily Rosenberg center on the transnational engagements of economic professionals. Legal and business expertise-on-the-go is shown in work by Mary Dudziak, Yves Dezalay and Bryant G. Garth, and Brooke Blower. Educators who take their ideas and models abroad are highlighted by Andrew Zimmerman, while networks of transnational radicals – often casting themselves as educators of another kind – are exemplified in studies by Judy Wu and Martin Klimke. Warwick Anderson and John McNeil are among those who examine global networks of disease.[13]

Missionaries and moral reformers as transnational cultural brokers have long been the subject of rich histories, upon which newer studies by Ian Tyrrell and Ussama Makdisi have built. The role of religion in shaping US transnational connections more generally, not specifically through missionaries, has been emphasized in the work of Seth Jacobs, Andrew Preston, and Susan Harris. Sports proves an important nexus both for the construction of ideologies of nationalism and for transnational exchange, as exemplified in studies by Barbara J. Keys, Thomas W. Zeiler, Robert Elias, and Sayuri Guthrie-Shimizu.[14] The surge of studies dealing with the global circulation of commodities and consumerism is far too large to be encompassed or even represented within a few citations in this chapter, but the ways in which specific products may reveal intersections between material and cultural realms make them rich sites for transnational analysis.[15]

Topics associated with cross-border migration have also come into an appropriately closer relationship with histories of America and the World. Books by Madeline Hsu, Donna Gabbacia, Catherine Choy, Erika Lee, and Anita Casavantes Bradford, in addition to the many studies of the porous US–Mexican border cited in Citino's article on borderlands, provide apt illustrations. Historians who deal with the transnational circulations of ideas and people in relationship to race include Gerald Horne, Brenda Gayle Plummer, Thomas Borstelmann, Carole Anderson, Mary Dudziak, Kevin Gaines, James Meriwether, and Nico Slate. Histories of migration, race, empire, labor, and international policies – all once virtually separated into different fields – merge together when considering transnational flows and networks.[16]

The kinds of exemplary works mentioned above deal with a vast array of topics and present few consistencies in methodology or style, but they do, mostly, have a common message: the ambitions of dominant American groups to foster United States-led transformation in lands and peoples are challenged, interrupted, and often appropriated in diverse and surprising ways. Transnational connections – of people, goods, and ideas – do not foster some teleological story of greater understanding, much less of Americanization. As transnational actors bring the world together, they also splinter it apart in new configurations. The processes by which common global influences interact with diverse local situations to produce a wide variety of outcomes is a process that I have, in a recent work, described as one marked by "differentiated commonalities."[17]

Most of the studies of transnational actors do not ignore the realms of politics and diplomacy, but they have reinvigorated the scholarship in these more traditional fields. Overall, the "transnational turn" has broadened the scope of historical investigation, fostered interdisciplinarity, and contributed to innovative methodologies and forms of history-writing.

CROSSING DISCIPLINARY BORDERS IN THE CULTURAL TURN: ISSUES OF RECEPTION AND MULTIVOCALITY

The "cultural turn" in scholarship during the 1980s and 1990s brought yet other kinds of border crossings. In one sense "culture" had always been at the heart of scholarship on American foreign relations. The most influential historians in the field, after all, had long included cultural frames and ideologies within their broader analyses. George Kennan's *American Diplomacy*, a classic of "realist" literature, is primarily a critique of the culture of legalism-moralism that allegedly suffused US policy. William A. Williams' classic *Tragedy of American Diplomacy*, long associated with economic interpretation, involves an exploration of the culture of the "open door," as does my *Spreading the American Dream*.[18] Melvyn Leffler's influential work rests on the concept of animating "core values." Other significant works, mentioned above, have highlighted cultural themes related to assumptions about modernization, science, gender, race, and geography. Indeed, one can scarcely find a work on American foreign relations, present or past, that does not, at some level, advance a cultural interpretation. And for good reason. It is absurd to imagine that the domain of foreign relations might exist outside of the domain of culture.

But if historians of US foreign relations had long recognized cultural context, the cultural turn brought more complicated theoretical and methodological concerns. That turn connoted something far different than invoking cultural assumptions as explanations or context for policy. It challenged historians to grapple with the epistemological problems presented by cultural theory and the debates prevalent in the disciplines that studied culture most intensely: anthropology, literary criticism, and cultural studies. The cultural turn beckoned historians of America and the World to cross borders of disciplines.

Anthropologists for several decades have challenged ideas of cultural "authenticity," the coherence of particular cultures, and their knowability in any unmediated way. Rather than reifying the idea of culture, James Clifford and others stress the "predicament" of culture and its contested, unsettled characteristics. Culture, for anthropologists, is not an explanatory thing but a site of contestation over meaning and knowledge – and ultimately over the power to label and designate truth. Culture encompasses a process of engagement by which meanings are negotiated and renegotiated. Clearly this cultural turn is closely related to the views of literary scholars who shaped postmodern analysis and to the postcolonial theory discussed above. This view of culture has significant implications for histories of international and transnational relationships because the *process* of culture often falls into clearest relief along borders, where meaning-making can be up for grabs.

Media studies and cultural studies contributed insightful scholarship that analyzed the meanings of cultural products. "Response theory," for example, emphasized that meanings lie less in the intent of producers and the structures of production than in their negotiations and mediations with diverse interpretive communities. Stanley Fish became notorious for (among other provocative statements) telling students that there was no text in his class. He did not mean, of course, that he had assigned no books but that textual meanings arose from the reading, not simply from the writing, and thus could be neither stable nor singular.[19] A keener awareness of the politics and variability of cultural reception transformed the ways in which historians began to analyze transnational cultural exchange.

An older tradition of scholarship had often assumed that the expansion of American cultural products acted as a kind of magic bullet to produce predictable Americanizing effects. The classic of this genre from the Marxist left was Ariel Dorfman and Armand Mattelart's *How to Read Donald Duck*, a book that moved assumptions about economic imperialism into the cultural realm and helped spread the term "cultural imperialism," which became prevalent in the 1970s and 1980s.[20] Ironically, the very US informational offensives in the Cold War that Dorfman and Mattelart opposed were also based on magic bullet assumptions. Cost-conscious presidents and congresses, after all, would hardly have funded cultural (what came to be called "public") diplomacy without believing that it would be directly effective in spreading the American Way. Indeed, most twentieth-century governments have, in the name of national security, operated on the premise that informational and entertainment media could be successfully enlisted to promote specific social and ideological goals.[21]

Scholars working in the traditions of the cultural turn and response theory, however, have revealed complexity and multivocality in cultural exchanges.

Excellent studies assessing the impact of specific US Cold War informational programs have confirmed that the established goals of such programs often had ambiguous cultural effects. Penny von Eschen, for example, examines African American "jazz ambassadors," whom the United States Information Agency sent around the world to counter Soviet propaganda campaigns highlighting American practices of racial segregation. These musicians, however, were no mere apologists for America, she writes, and they often used their international prestige to critique the practices of racial injustice that they were sent to belie. The "jazz ambassador" program, it turned out, had many meanings. Hugh Wilford's many outstanding studies provide a similarly complex picture of the dynamics of US cultural diplomacy. Secretly (often invisibly) financing individuals and groups to spread messages, Wilford shows, can easily backfire. What happens when those groups go off-message or, mostly, press messages of their own; if the cover comes off and prompts a backlash; if supported groups clash with each other and each demands backing? So many things can go wrong in the negotiation of meaning. Cultural agencies are seldom the puppet-masters they envision themselves to be; indeed, they can find that they are the ones dangling on strings. Many provocative studies of cultural policies in post-World War II occupied nations show how messages that are intended are not always the messages that prevail: Reinhold Wagnleitner on Austria, Jessica C. E. Gienow-Hecht on Germany, and Hiroshi Kitimura on Japan.[22]

In cases of cultural diplomacy, messages are at least *intended* to be controlled. The multivocality of cultural meanings and issues of reception become even more magnified, however, when various non state messengers, especially diverse media, cross borders. In each new setting, varieties of adaptation, hybridity, and redeployment appear. Within the scholarship on global mass culture that includes advertising, mass-marketed print media, and film, the instability of cultural exchange forms the dominant theme. Victoria de Grazia's *Irresistible Empire* shows how, even as America's "market empire" increasingly drew Europeans into its field of influence, local adaptations generally prevailed. *The Modern Girl around the World*, the product of collective research by scholars of many different cultural areas, examines the local manifestations of the "modern girl," whose image seemed to emerge globally in the early twentieth century.[23] And a special kind of study of cultural boundary-crossing is exemplified in Max Paul Friedman's book, clearly indebted to cultural theory, that examines the various manifestations of the trope of "anti-Americanism."[24]

Rob Kroes' Lego metaphor often seems appropriate. Kroes thinks of the exportation of cultural products as sending forth little Legos that can be continually shaped and reshaped in new forms. Although countries, such as the United States, can send forth lots of figurative Legos, what diverse international consumers make with them can be quite varied and unpredictable.[25] Emphasis on cultural adaptability and redeployment, of course, should not hide discussions of power imbalances; "floating signifiers" do not simply just "float" any more than flows of capital and commodities simply "flow." But the challenge here is to think of culture as complex, interactive, and locally diverse, rather than as single, one-way, and headed toward homogeneity.

The many historians of US international relations who have worked across disciplinary (as well as national) borders, borrowing especially from literary theory, anthropology, and cultural studies, brought insights (as well as controversies) from the "cultural turn" into their field. Academic border-crossing and hybridity has enlarged possibilities and complicated frameworks.

* * * * *

This chapter has highlighted how, in considering borders, recent historical scholarship has theorized changing constructions of "self" and "other" in the "contact zones" where boundaries are often created and challenged; redefined the meanings of boundaries by addressing borderlands and transnational connections; and drawn on interdisciplinary work to reveal how working at the borders of disciplines can have transformative effects. In the past few decades, new methodologies, redefined geographies, and a more robust repertoire of disciplinary practices have brought fresh excitement to a dynamic field that has moved from a principal concentration on "diplomatic history" to a broader consideration of "foreign relations" to a capacious examination of "America and the World."

NOTES

1. Edward W. Said, *Orientalism: Western Conceptions of the Orient* (London, 1979). An influential and justifiably controversial reworking of an East/West divide is Samuel P. Huntington, *Clash of Civilizations and the Remaking of World Order* (New York, 1996).
2. Two summaries of major lines of critique may be found in Ulrike Freitag, "The Critique of Orientalism," in Michael Bentley, ed., *Companion to Historiography* (London, 1997), 620–38, and Andrew J. Rotter, "Saidism without Said: Orientalism in U.S. Diplomatic History," *American Historical Review* 105 (October 2000): 1205–17. Edward W. Said, *Culture and Imperialism* (New York, 1993).
3. James Clifford, "Orientalism," *History and Theory* 19 (February 1980): 204–23.
4. Christina Klein, *Cold War Orientalism: Asia in the Middlebrow Imagination, 1945–1961* (Berkeley, 2003); Mark Bradley, *Imagining Vietnam and America: The Making of Postcolonial Vietnam, 1919–1950* (Chapel Hill, 2000); David Brody, *Visualizing American Empire: Orientalism and Imperialism in the Philippines* (Chicago, 2010).
5. Robert J.C. Young, *Postcolonialism: A Very Short Introduction* (New York, 2003), and *Postcolonialism: An Historical Introduction* (Maldon, MA, 2001); Dipesh Chakrabarty, *Provincializing Europe* (Princeton, 2000), pp. 11–16, introduces the multiauthored and multiedited ten-volume project called *Subaltern Studies: Studies in Indian Society and History* (Delhi, 1983–93); Gayatri Chakravorty Spivak, *A Critique*

of Postcolonial Reason: Toward a History of the Vanishing Present (Cambridge, MA, 1999). Anne McClintock, *Imperial Leather: Race, Gender, and Sexuality in the Colonial Conquest* (New York, 1995), writes in the tradition of postcolonial studies but also provides a critique of the term (pp. 9–17). Ann Laura Stoler, "Tense and Tender Ties: The Politics of Comparison in North American History and (Post) Colonial Studies," *The Journal of American History* 88 (December, 2001): 829–65, expanded in Ann Laura Stoler, ed., *Haunted by Empire: Geographies of Intimacy in North American History* (Durham, 2006), bring the sensibility of postcolonial studies into US history.

6. Mary Louise Pratt, *Imperial Eyes: Travel Writing and Transculturation* (New York., 1992), quotes from pages 4, 7, 5 respectively.
7. Amy Kaplan and Donald Pease, eds., *Cultures of American Imperialism* (Durham, 1993); Gilbert M. Joseph, Catherine C. LeGrand, and Ricardo D. Salvatore, eds., *Close Encounters of Empire: Writing the Cultural History of U.S.–Latin American Relations* (Durham, 1998). Another important collection of is Alfred W. McCoy and Francisco A. Scarano, *The Colonial Crucible: Empire in the Making of the Modern American State* (Madison, 2009).
8. Louis A. Pérez, *On Becoming Cuban: Identity, Nationality, and Culture* (Chapel Hill, 1999), on Cuba; Mary A. Renda, *Taking Haiti: Military Occupation and the Culture of U.S. Imperialism, 1915–1940* (Chapel Hill, 2001), on Haiti; Paul A. Kramer, *The Blood of Government: Race, Empire, the United States, & the Philippines* (Chapel Hill, 2006), Michael Salman, *The Embarrassment of Slavery: Controversies Over Bondage and Nationalism in the American Colonial Philippines* (Berkeley, 2001), Alfred W. McCoy, *Policing America's Empire: The United States, the Philippines, and the Rise of the Surveillance State* (Madison, 2009), Julian Go, *American Empire and the Politics of Meaning: Elite Political Cultures in the Philippines and Puerto Rico during U.S. Colonialism* (Durham, 2008), and Vicente L. Rafael, *White Love: And Other Events in Filipino History* (Durham, 2000), on the Philippines; Michel Gobat, *Confronting the American Dream: Nicaragua Under U.S. Imperial Rule* (Durham, 2005), on Nicaragua; Michael E. Donoghue, *Borderland on the Isthmus: Race, Culture, and the Struggle for the Canal Zone* (Durham, 2014), on Panama; Laura Briggs, *Reproducing Empire: Race, Sex, Science, and U.S. Imperialism in Puerto Rico* (Berkeley: University of California Press, 2002), on Puerto Rico; and Noenoe Silva, *Aloha Betrayed: Native Hawaiian Resistance to American Colonialism* (Durham, 2004), on Hawai'i.
9. Julie Greene, *The Canal Builders: Making America's Empire at the Panama Canal* (New York, 2009); Alexander Missal, *Seaway to the Future: American Social Visions and the Construction of the Panama Canal* (Madison, WI, 2008); Jana K. Lipman, *Guantanamo : A Working-class History between Empire and Revolution* (Berkeley, 2009); Adria L. Imada, *Aloha America: Hula Circuits Through the U.S. Empire* (Durham, 2012); Robert Vitalis. *America's Kingdom: Mythmaking on the Saudi Oil Frontier* (London, 2009); Greg Grandin, *Fordlandia: The Rise and Fall of Henry Ford's Forgotten Jungle City* (New York, 2009); Seth Garfield, *In Search of the Amazon: Brazil, the United States, and the Nature of a Region* (Durham, 2013); Jason M. Colby, *The Business of Empire: United Fruit, Race, and U.S. Expansion in Central America* (Ithaca, 2011).
10. See Nathan Citino's chapter in this volume. Borderland history has been particularly preoccupied with the American Southwest. See, especially, books such

as Pekka Hämäläinen, *The Comanche Empire* (New Haven, 2008); Brian DeLay, *War of a Thousand Deserts: Indian Raids and the U.S.–Mexican War*, (New Haven, 2008); Ned Blackhawk, *Violence Over the Land: Indians and Empires in the Early American West* (Cambridge, MA, 2006); Amy S. Greenberg, *A Wicked War: Polk, Clay, Lincoln, and the 1846 U.S. Invasion of Mexico* (New York, 2012); Walter L. Hixson, *American Settler Colonialism: A History* (New York, 2013).

11. Marcus Rediker, *Villains of All Nations: Atlantic Pirates in the Golden Age* (Boston, 2005), and many of his other books and articles; Brooke L. Blower, "New York City's Spanish Shipping Agents and the Practice of State Power in the Atlantic Borderlands of World War II," *The American Historical Review* 119 (2014): 111–41. Gary Y. Okihiro, *Island World: A History of Hawai'i and the United States* (Berkeley, 2008); Matt K. Matsuda, *Pacific Worlds: A History of Seas, Peoples, and Cultures* (New York, 2012); David Igler, *The Great Ocean: Pacific Worlds from Captain Cook to the Gold Rush* (New York, 2013).

12. Thomas Bender, ed., *Rethinking American History in a Global Age* (Berkeley, 2002); Akira Iriye, *Global Community: The Role of International Organizations in the Making of the Contemporary World* (Berkeley, 2002); Ian R. Tyrrell, *Transnational Nation: United States History in Global Perspective Since 1789* (Basingstoke, 2007).

13. Christopher Endy, *Cold War Holidays: American Tourism in France* (Chapel Hill, 2004); Dennis Merrill, *Negotiating Paradise: U.S. Tourism and Empire in Twentieth-Century Latin America* (Chapel Hill, 2009); Kristin L. Hoganson, *Consumers' Imperium: The Global Production of American Domesticity, 1865–1920* (Chapel Hill, 2007). David C. Engerman, *Modernization from the Other Shore: American Intellectuals and the Romance of Russian Development* (Cambridge, MA, 2003); Daniel T. Rodgers, *Atlantic Crossings: Social Politics in a Progressive Age* (Cambridge, MA, 1998); Matthew J. Connolly, *Fatal Misconception: The Struggle to Control World Population* (Cambridge, MA, 2008). Bradley R. Simpson, *Economists with Guns: Authoritarian Development and U.S.–Indonesian Relations, 1960–1968* (Palo Alto, 2008); Michael E. Latham, *Modernization as Ideology: American Social Science and "Nation Building" in the Kennedy Era* (Chapel Hill, 2000), and *The Right Kind of Revolution: Modernization, Development, and U.S. Foreign Policy from the Cold War to the Present* (Ithaca, 2011); David Ekbladh, *The Great American Mission: Modernization and the Construction of an American World Order* (Princeton, 2010); Nick Cullather, *The Hungry World: America's Cold War Battle against Poverty in Asia* (Cambridge, MA, 2010); Emily S. Rosenberg, *Financial Missionaries to the World: The Politics and Culture of Dollar Diplomacy, 1900–1930* (Durham, 2003). Mary L. Dudziak, *Cold War Civil Rights: Race and the Image of American Democracy* (Princeton, 2000); Yves Dezalay and Bryant G. Garth, *Asian Legal Revivals: Lawyers in the Shadow of Empire* (Chicago, 2010); Brook L. Blower, *Becoming Americans in Paris: Transatlantic Politics and Culture between the World Wars* (New York, 2011). Andrew Zimmerman, *Alabama in Africa: Booker T. Washington, the German Empire, and the Globalization of the New South* (Princeton, 2010); Judy Tzu-Chun Wu, *Radicals on the Road: Internationalism, Orientalism, and Feminism During the Vietnam Era* (Ithaca, 2013); Martin Klimke, *The Other Alliance: Student Protest in West Germany and the United States in the Global Sixties* (Princeton, 2010). Warwick Anderson, *Colonial Pathologies: American Tropical Medicine, Race, and*

Hygiene in the Philippines (Durham, 2006); John R. McNeill, *Mosquito Empires: Ecology and War in the Greater Caribbean, 1620–1914* (New York, 2010).

14. Ian R. Tyrrell, *Woman's World/Woman's Empire: The Woman's Christian Temperance Union in International Perspective, 1880–1930* (Chapel Hill, 1991), and *Reforming the World: The Creation of America's Moral Empire* (Princeton, 2010); Ussama S. Makdisi, *Artillery of Heaven: American Missionaries and the Failed Conversion of the Middle East* (Ithaca, 2008); Barbara Reeves-Ellington, Kathryn Kish Sklar, and Connie A. Shemo, eds., *Competing Kingdoms: Women, Mission, Nation, and the American Protestant Empire, 1812–1960* (Durham, 2010), Seth Jacobs, *America's Miracle Man in Vietnam: Ngo Dinh Diem, Religion, Race, and U.S. Intervention in Southeast Asia, 1950–1957* (Durham, 2004); Andrew Preston, *Sword of the Spirit, Shield of Faith: Religion in American War and Diplomacy* (New York, 2012); and Susan K. Harris, *God's Arbiters: Americans and the Philippines, 1898–1902* (New York, 2011). Barbara J. Keys, *Globalizing Sport: National Rivalry and International Community in the 1930s* (Cambridge, MA, 2006); Thomas W. Zeiler, *Ambassadors in Pinstripes: The Spalding World Baseball Tour and the Birth of the American Empire* (Lanham, MD, 2006); Sayuri Guthrie-Shimizu, *Transpacific Field of Dreams: How Baseball Linked the United States and Japan in Peace and War* (Chapel Hill, 2012); Robert Elias, *The Empire Strikes Out: How Baseball Sold U.S. Foreign Policy and Promoted the American Way Abroad* (New York: 2010).

15. On the growth of this scholarship see Emily S. Rosenberg, "U.S. Mass Consumerism in Transnational Perspective," in Frank Costigliola and Michael J. Hogan, eds., *America in the World: The Historiography of American Foreign Relations since 1941* (New York, 2014), 307–37.

16. Madeline Hsu, *Dreaming of Gold, Dreaming of Home: Transnationalism and Migration between the United States and South China, 1882–1943* (Palo Alto, 2000); Donna R. Gabaccia, *Foreign Relations: American Immigration in Global Perspective* (Princeton, 2012); Catherine C. Choy, *Empire of Care: Nursing and Migration in Filipino American History* (Durham, 2003); Erika Lee, *At America's Gates: Chinese Immigration during the Exclusion Era, 1882–1943* (Chapel Hill, 2003); Anita Casavantes Bradford, *The Revolution Is for the Children: The Politics of Childhood in Havana and Miami, 1959–1962* (Chapel Hill, 2014). Gerald Horne, *Black and Red: W.E.B. Du Bois and the Afro-American Response to the Cold War, 1944–1963* (Albany, 1986), and many subsequent books and articles; Brenda Gayle Plummer, *Rising Wind: Black Americans and U.S. Foreign Affairs* (Chapel Hill, 1996), and Plummer, ed., *Window on Freedom: Race, Civil Rights, and Foreign Affairs, 1945–1988* (Chapel Hill, 2003); Thomas Borstelmann, *Apartheid's Reluctant Uncle: The United States and Southern Africa in the Early Cold War* (New York, 1993), and *The Cold War and the Color Line: American Race Relations in the Global Arena* (Cambridge, 2001); Carol Anderson, *Eyes Off the Prize: The United Nations and the African American Struggle for Human Rights, 1944–1955* (New York, 2003); Mary L. Dudziak, *Cold War Civil Rights: Race and the Image of American Democracy* (Princeton, 2000); Kevin Kelly Gaines, *American Africans in Ghana: Black Expatriates and the Civil Rights Era* (Chapel Hill, 2006); James Meriwether, *Proudly We Can Be Africans: Black Americans and Africa, 1935–1961* (Chapel Hill, 2002); Nico Slate, *Colored Cosmopolitanism: The Shared Struggle for Freedom in the United States and India* (Cambridge, 2012).

17. Emily S. Rosenberg, *Transnational Currents in a Shrinking World* (Cambridge, MA: 2014).
18. George Kennan, *American Diplomacy* (Chicago, 1951); William A. Williams, *Tragedy of American Diplomacy* (New York, 1962); Emily S. Rosenberg, *Spreading the American Dream* (New York, 1982).
19. Stanley Fish, *Is There a Text in This Class? The Authority of Interpretive Communities* (Cambridge, MA, 1980).
20. Ariel Dorfman and Armand Mattelart, *How to Read Donald Duck: Imperialism Ideology in the Disney Comic*, David Kunzle, trans. (New York, 1975), and Dorfman, *The Empire's Old Clothes: What the Lone Ranger, Babar, and Other Innocent Heroes Do to Our Minds* (New York, 1983). John Tomlinson, *Cultural Imperialism: A Critical Introduction* (Baltimore, 1991), provides a thorough critique of the discourse of cultural imperialism.
21. On informational offensives see especially Walter Hixson, *Parting the Curtain: Propaganda, Culture, and the Cold War, 1945–61* (New York, 1997); Kenneth A. Osgood, *Total Cold War: Eisenhower's Secret Propaganda Battle at Home and Abroad* (Lawrence, 2006); Laura A. Belmonte, *Selling the American Way: U.S. Propaganda and the Cold War* (Philadelphia, 2008).
22. Penny M. Von Eschen, *Satchmo Blows Up the World: Jazz Ambassadors Play the Cold War* (Cambridge, MA, 2004); Hugh Wilford, *The CIA, the British Left, and the Cold War: Calling the Tune?* (London, 2003), *The Mighty Wurlitzer: How the CIA Played America* (Cambridge, MA, 2008), *America's Great Game: The CIA's Secret Arabists and the Shaping of the Modern Middle East* (New York, 2013). Reinhold Wagnleitner, *Coca-Colonization and the Cold War: The Cultural Mission of the United States in Austria after the Second World War* (Chapel Hill, 1994), on Austria; Jessica C.E. Gienow-Hecht, *Transmission Impossible American Journalism As Cultural Diplomacy in Post-War Germany* (Baton Rouge, 1999), on Germany; and Hiroshi Kitimura, *Screening Enlightenment: Hollywood and the Cultural Reconstruction of Defeated Japan* (Ithaca, 2010).
23. Victoria de Grazia, *Irresistible Empire: America's Advance through Twentieth Century Europe* (Cambridge, MA, 2006); Alys Eve Weinbaum, et al., eds., *The Modern Girl Around the World: Consumption, Modernity, and Globalization* (Durham, 2008). For other works that caution against simplistic theoretical frameworks about culture in an international setting, see Heide Fehrenbach and Uta G. Poiger, eds., *Transactions, Transgressions, Tranformations: American Culture in Western Europe and Japan* (New York, 2000).
24. Max Paul Friedman, *Rethinking Anti-Americanism: The History of an Exceptional Concept in American Foreign Relations* (Cambridge, MA, 2012). My own effort to examine the multivocality, metaphorical forms, and political uses of foreign policy tropes appears in Emily S. Rosenberg, *A Date Which Will Live: Pearl Harbor in American Memory* (Durham, 2003).
25. Rob Kroes, *If You've Seen One You've Seen the Mall: Europeans and American Mass Culture* (Urbana, 1996).

12

The privilege of acting upon others: the middle eastern exception to anti-exceptionalist histories of the US and the world

Ussama Makdisi

The name of the adolescent field of transnational inquiry "US and the World" suggests its own contradiction.[1] The dyad of the United States and the world hints at a parity, and a distance, between the two terms. And yet the object of pairing the terms is to encourage an anti-exceptionalist historiography that presumably rejects the nationalist myths that remain central to how the United States officially represents itself: as a "leader" of the "free world," as "democratic," as not imperialist, and finally, as vastly superior to and different from every other political culture in the world. Who, then, is best positioned to understand the histories that have been made and unmade by American crossings and encroachments across the world, and the counter-crossings of the peoples, networks, and ideologies that have made their impact felt on America? The self-identified and professionally certified US historian, or historians of the rest of the world upon which and in which the United States has so massively been implicated? This chapter suggests that a deep historiographical imbalance remains between what has largely been accomplished in the transnational turn within US historiography, namely *recognizing* America's place in the world, and what has not been sufficiently done, namely *connecting* with, and thus *delving* into, the complex histories of this world on their own robust, and linguistically and historiographically varied, terrain.

    The transnational and ostensibly anti-exceptionalist imperatives that have driven "US and the World" have already been much debated and discussed among US historians and indeed among scholars in the related field of American Studies. They have intersected quite readily with imperial and postcolonial historiography. They have built on a legacy of the critical study of US imperialism bequeathed to them by New Left scholarship that laid bare an imperialist capitalist American hegemony over the world, or what William Appleman Williams famously described as the "tragedy" of American diplomacy that made interventions across the world "a way of life."[2] Asking neglected historiographic questions (of culture and race in foreign policy studies, for example, or about the international circuits and networks in which Americans were routinely enmeshed), giving voice to the hitherto and historically marginalized groups (African Americans, Native Americans, Central and South Americans, Filipinos, immigrants including Asian-Americans, non-Americans, and so on), and pointing out the economic and political costs of empire have all been important parts of this frontal challenge on American historiographical nationalism.

In the 1990s, a seminal essay by Ian Tyrrell "American Exceptionalism in an Age of International History" and an edited volume *Cultures of United States Imperialism* edited by Donald Pease and Amy Kaplan criticized the insularity of US historiography. Tyrrell indicated very clearly the need for US historians to approach American engagement in the world on several different levels, or what he identified as the local, national, and transnational scales.[3] Kaplan, in turn, called for the need to expose three "salient absences" in American history: "the absence of culture from the history of U.S. imperialism; the absence of empire from the study of American culture; and the absence of the United States from the postcolonial study of imperialism."[4] Daniel Rodgers' *Atlantic Crossings*, Thomas Bender's *A Nation among Nations*, Ann Laura Stoler's intervention on gender and empire in the *Journal of American History*, and Paul Kramer's *The Blood of Government* have all further emphasized the need to think more broadly and transnationally about US history.[5]

In different ways, Tyrrell, Rodgers, Bender, Stoler, Kramer, and many others have substantially broadened what is the proper field of US history. Cognizant of the potentially unsettling implications of transnational history (including the study of empire) for some American historians, Bender reassured his American readers that his project was not about overturning a national frame of history-writing but making it more "enriched." Yet Bender also urged the US historian to become "a cosmopolitan," to be more willing to engage with the unfamiliar, and, in short, to take historiographical risks.[6] His book *A Nation Among Nations* juxtaposed the story of American history – beginning with Columbus' arrival in the New World, to the British colonial age, to the establishment of the United States, the Antebellum era, the Civil War, the Progressive Age, and so on – with parallel experiences and examples from across the world, from China and Japan to the Ottoman Empire and Spain. The irony of Bender's work, however, is that the world appeared to conform to, and thus confirm, America's conventional historiography. Bender sought to internationalize the history of the United States. But the structure of his work appeared less to push US historians out of their comfort zone as to shoehorn diverse histories of the world into a quite familiar American national narrative.

Paul Kramer's history of race and empire in the American conquest of the Philippines engaged directly with Spanish-language accounts and, to an extent, with Filipino historiography. It was more attuned to the need to understand what

Kramer described as the "densely interactive field" between the domestic national and imperial dimensions that made possible American racial formations.[7] The non-American world (in Kramer's case, the Philippines) was not simply a foreign location to demonstrate or expose or reveal fully formed domestic American racial discourses. As Kramer put it in a later essay, acknowledging the "imperial" was essential to expose the contingences of the making of history. "Pulling back from the illusory association of empire with absolute power," Kramer points out, "will allow historians to approach empires as complex circuits of agency in which bottom up and mid-range claims-making was no less typical (if always less welcome) than top-down command. Empire-builders' hesitance to acknowledge that their regimes were, in fact, polities – delicate, unstable balances of force and consent – did not make them otherwise."[8]

That most of these scholars were not specialists in foreign relations pointed to the fact that the hitherto staid field of diplomatic history, which invariably focused on the affairs of state and often identified with its leading figures such as the ubiquitous Henry Kissinger, was a late-comer to this burgeoning field of transnational inquiry.[9] And yet this late arrival has not diminished the enthusiasm with which erstwhile diplomatic and Cold War historians have reinvented themselves as international historians following the transnational turn. *The Wilsonian Moment* by Erez Manela, *A Diplomatic Revolution* by Matthew Connelly, and on a larger scale, Odd Arne Westad's landmark *Global Cold War* and Akira Iriye's edited volume *Global Interdependence* have all made the case that transnational history is not merely an extension of US history, but international history in its own right.[10]

Nevertheless, as an increasing number of US diplomatic historians and graduate students jump on the transnational bandwagon, the presumptive archival and historiographical hegemony of the American component of "US and the World" becomes increasingly apparent. To what extent can or should transnational history be truly delinked from a nationalist subjectivity – from a sense of primary identification with America that is so often assumed, if not always stated overtly in the study of the twentieth-century world dominated by the United States? What happens if and when the temporal frame is shifted backwards into the nineteenth century or forwards into the twenty-first when US power was (or is no longer) as omnipotent as it appeared during the height of the Cold War, or when US or English-language sources cannot dominate the telling of history?[11] At what point does an obsessive fixation with American actors, American machinations, American figures, American historiography, and American representations overwhelm the initial impetus of the field of "US and the World" to reject US exceptionalism? Finally, at what point is the fetish of "transnational" history in danger of becoming, for all its genuinely critical underpinnings, yet another exercise in the American privilege of acting upon and writing about others?

* * *

The study of the United States and the Middle East is one obvious site to interrogate the strengths and limitations of this transnational approach to American history. Nowhere else in the world are the power, stakes and nature of US empire today more obvious than in the Middle East. Nowhere else is US military deployment as aggressively manifest. Precisely because of the massive ideological, economic, political, and military investments made by the United States in the region, and because of the extraordinary pervasiveness of orientalist stereotypes across American culture and media, and because of violent "anti-American" resistance that emanates from the region, the study of the relationship between the United States and the Middle East remains an area that constantly tests the ability of American historians to think outside of a nationalist frame. It is one thing to discuss empire in the abstract; it is quite another thing to do so at a time of seemingly unending war. Leaving aside the open-ended "war on terror" that has seen the United States bomb Iraq, Syria, Yemen, Pakistan, and Somalia in the past decade, the US invasions of Afghanistan and Iraq have precipitated the longest-running wars in America's history.[12]

The study of both the Arab–Israeli conflict and so-called "political Islam," in turn, raise difficult and discomforting questions for anti-exceptionalist (if this is the proper term) historians because they are conflicts that also rage, often violently, in the present. They therefore often demand ethical, moral, and political positions that are not easy to reconcile with the notion of academic neutrality. Giving voice, for instance, to Osama Bin Laden is not nearly as uncontroversial as giving voice *today* to Geronimo. Indeed, US Special Forces who assassinated Bin Laden allegedly used the code name "Geronimo" to describe their target, and entered Pakistani airspace using "Black Hawk" helicopters. Such a symbolic association between two (very different) non-white figures pursued by the US military over a century apart emphasizes a continuous history of empire that has long counted on US historians to be its "camp followers," to borrow from the anthropologist Inga Clendinnen's description of the historiography of the conquest of the Aztecs.[13] Arguably in no other subfield than US–Middle Eastern history has the persistent conventionality of American foreign relations been more obvious – and thus the ramifications for the transnational turn among diplomatic historians as potentially significant.

That the languages, cultures, and histories of the Middle East, Islam, Iran, and the Ottoman Empire are accessible, but far from familiar, to most US historians, increases the challenge of making the transnational turn a substantial one. Arab-Americans, moreover, hardly represent as significant a domestic constituency as do Latino Americans and African Americans, and work on them lacks the same historiographic depth evident in similar work on other immigrant communities.[14] Indeed, there is no other group that have been as openly and persistently vilified in the United States as Arabs and Muslims in the post-1948 period – no other group that have been cast as negatively as the civilizational antithesis to the West.[15] All this makes the case of the Middle East arguably more demanding for historians willing to embrace transnationalism, with its underlying demand for a non-nationalist and "post-exceptionalist" perspective, as a way of scholarship.[16]

A review of the transnational turn of the academic study of US–Middle East relations suggests that there is still some way to go before the cosmopolitanism that Bender called for, or the "imperial" approach that Kramer suggested in 2011 (although, remarkably, his essay had almost nothing to say about the Middle East despite the massive and ongoing US wars in the region), or the anti-exceptionalist promise inherent in the field of transnational history can come to fruition. Indeed, the evidence thus far is that those who were not formally trained in American Studies or US foreign relations have been far more adept at mining the promise of transnational history than bona fide US-centric historians, not simply because they are more likely to work with foreign languages and archives but because they bring into an academic conversation non-American themes, historiographies, and perspectives without which US-dominated transnational history remains, in Erez Manela's apt description, akin "to listen for the sound of one-hand clapping."[17]

* * *

There are three main strands of transnational scholarship in the United States and the Middle East, one represented by scholars of American literature and studies who have explored how Americans represented the Orient and America through their encounters and conflicts in the Middle East. The second consists of historians who would have once been described as diplomatic historians and who have attempted with varying degrees of success to expand the purview of what constitutes the field of US foreign relations. The third strand comprises scholars, trained mostly but not exclusively outside of US history, who have sought to convey richer, and presumably non-orientalist, understandings of American encounters and policies with the Middle East.

The first of these strands has far and away been the most evident. Inspired by Edward Said's landmark 1978 *Orientalism* and by the 1993 Pease and Kaplan volume on the *Cultures of United States Imperialism*, these works fundamentally revolutionized the study of America's cultural relationship with the Middle East. Almost all subsequent works dealt in one manner or another with either the themes that Said had raised about the relationship between representation and power. In art history, geography, or American Studies, works by John Davis, Burke Long, Malini Schueller, Hilton Obenzinger, Timothy Marr, Brian Edwards, and Melani McAlister took their cue from Said directly.[18] In different ways, these authors sought to deconstruct the politics and aesthetics of American visual and literary representations of Palestine, Islam, the Middle East, and North Africa. These books function to nuance Said's argument, and to point out the domestic cultural work that these representations accomplished. Yet almost all of them repeat the basic stance of

Said's argument in *Orientalism* regarding the "brute reality" of the lives, cultures, customs, and histories of the Middle East that Said acknowledged were "obviously greater" than what was said about them in the West. "About that fact this study of Orientalism has very little to contribute, except to acknowledge it tacitly."[19]

American Studies scholars have thus taken the lead in exploring how facets of American identity have been shaped by cultural opposition to, but also engagement with, Islam and the Middle East. The work Marr does for the nineteenth-century American views of Islam complements McAlister and Edwards' work for post-1945 American views of the Middle East and the Maghreb. Collectively, their works are clearly valuable in reminding scholars of how little we should take for granted constructions of national identity and national interests, and how often the metaphorical and actual experiences of the foreign worlds – in this case the Middle East – need to be analyzed as a dynamic, complex, and contested process rather than simply a reflection of a will to power and domination.

Perhaps even more important, these works on transnational networks that linked the people, histories, economies, and representations of the Middle East to North America remind us of the degree to which being transnational in the sense of spatially expanding the arena of American action in and of itself neither necessarily denies nor challenges US empire or American exceptionalism. Accounts by Alex Lubin and Penny Von Eschen underscore how some African American groups and individuals struggled against white supremacy, while others within the African American community subscribed to orientalist views of the Middle East or came to embrace US nationalism and its Cold War outlook.[20] They desired to be incorporated into the center of power politics – to gain, in a sense, the privilege of acting upon others. Marginalized or oppressed groups in an American domestic context often implicate themselves, and are implicated, in the structures of US imperialism in the Middle East.[21]

Yet as important as this strand of transnational scholarship has been to debunk claims of American exceptionalism by exploring the extraordinary history of omission, silence, and violence (whether to African Americans or Muslims for instance) in representations of an exceptional American nation, they nevertheless overwhelmingly do not give form or voice to Muslims and Arabs. To be sure, there is no single way of studying the complex phenomenon of American engagement with and interventions in the Middle East. Palestinian, Iranian, or Iraqi perspectives, for example, do not always necessarily or evenly affect how Americans represent themselves or others. Yet, by the same token, surely in many instances such non-American perspectives have a considerable impact on how Americans acted, thought, and represented themselves. The fact that so much of American Studies work brackets the cultures, histories, and historiographies of the Middle East underscores a significant lacuna in much of current transnational American academic work. It is "transnational" in a

Anti-exceptionalist histories

limited sense – how Americans acted and understood their encounter with the foreign, in which the foreign remains analytically unimportant, a stage upon which an essentially American story can be told.[22] It is difficult to imagine that a missionary who struggled to learn foreign languages, lived in foreign cultures, and represented herself or himself as well as the "native" culture that she or he sought to convert was not deeply aware of being immersed in a history that was by no means purely American or even legible in ubiquitous American historiographical terms, such as race. The very foreignness of the encounters defined her or his representations. The dialectic between the foreign and the familiar, therefore, cannot be captured within a transnational paradigm that analyzes only one side with depth or nuance.

* * *

Scholars of US foreign relations have belatedly taken up the transnational mantle of American historiography. Erez Manela's *The Wilsonian Moment: Self-Determination and the International Origins of Anticolonial Nationalism* is perhaps the most prominent in this regard. The Wilsonian moment, in Manela's account, becomes not simply a reading in American history, but a world event to be understood most comprehensively by incorporating various foreign archives and contexts that make up the historical substance of American involvement with the world. A series of other books also claim a transnational, international, or "global" perspective in order to shed new light on stories that would have once been described as "diplomatic history." Matthew Connelly's multi-archival *A Diplomatic Revolution*, for instance, posited a transnational system of international relations emerging from the conjoined moments of Cold War and decolonization that implicated Americans, French, and Algerians together in an uneven modernity. Matthew Jacobs' account *Imagining the Middle East* depicts the construction and then collapse of a network of "transnational" scholars and officials who interpreted the Middle East through various (and often overlapping) Orientalist, Cold War, and Modernization Theory perspectives.[23] Paul Chamberlin's *The Global Offensive* situates the bitter relationship between the US government and the Palestine Liberation Organization in a global perspective that included Vietnamese communists. His work points to the tremendous possibilities of rethinking how to read standard US diplomatic materials within regional and global perspectives simultaneously, for Chamberlin recognizes that the "Third World" actors were just as engaged in a "global field" as were Americans.[24]

Yet what many of these so-called transnational or global histories do is to suggest rather than immerse themselves in a global perspective. This limitation is especially glaring with regard to the Middle East, where the academic study of Arabic and a serious immersion in Middle Eastern historiography by US historians appears to lag far behind the academic study of Spanish or engagement with Latin American historiography, or for that matter the historiography of American wars in Southeast Asia.[25] Chamberlin's account, for instance, mines US documentation, but is relatively thin on Arabic sources. Equally important, however, is the unfortunate circumstance within US academe: critically studying Zionism and US militarism in the Middle East remains far more controversial than is the study of African American transnationalism, borderlands histories, the US empire-building of 1898, or the transpacific region. This imbalance speaks directly to a crucial limit of anti-exceptionalist histories when they should be most challenging.[26] The obvious trepidation with which many US scholars approach the question of the ethnic cleansing of Palestinians in 1948, for example, contrasts strongly with a modern Arab political subjectivity for which the *Nakba* of 1948 was a seminal event.

The point, to be sure, is not that scholars must agree or adopt an Arab perspective, but the degree to which so-called global or transnational or postnational histories insulate themselves from strongly expressed Arab views. Chamberlain, startlingly, begins his book with a set of confessions in order to emphasize his objective scholarly credentials. He writes that he recognizes "Israel's right to exist" at the same time as he supports the right of the Palestinians to have a "sovereign state" in the West Bank and Gaza, that he does not condone "bloodshed" and that he does not mean to imply any judgment about the "moral balance between the two sides"[27] – statements that, on their own, may well be so idiosyncratic as to defy analysis. Yet precisely because one would be hard-pressed to find such an awkward apologia in global or transnational histories of US policy in Vietnam or Latin America, these confessions reinforce, in their own way, the tremendous otherness of Arab history and humanity, as well as, of course, the current political orthodoxies within the United States.

One must not, of course, police every text and call for archival balance – there is, after all, an extraordinary power and archival imbalance between the United States and Arab governments (think Wikileaks). The task of deconstructing interpretations, assumptions, and representations of American officials and policymakers is clearly valuable in its own right.[28] The task of sifting through declassified State Department papers and other government or agency archives will also remain vital, especially given the fact that modern Arab states have generally refused to allow access to their own archives.[29] Neither must one call for any sort of new methodological or historiographical orthodoxy. After all, several of the most critical discussions of US imperialism and exceptionalism, beginning with William Appleman Williams' *Tragedy* and continuing with Timothy Mitchell's *Carbon Democracy*,[30] are rooted not in self-declared transnational or anti-exceptionalist analysis but rather in interpretations of political economy. Nor must one say that the only way to record an Arab perspective is through Arabic documentation (for that would render much of colonial history in many parts of the world all but inaccessible). But one must insist on more humility in the branding of what is a US-centric history of foreign relations as either transnational or global. Historians need to encourage a new sensibility that can engage in more than one historiographic conversation, and that can historicize non-American perspectives as deeply as it does American ones.[31] After all, the works of many "Third World" writers and scholars who have published in English and French, and who, in many instances, have been in exile, have studied in or migrated to the West, routinely contend with multiple historiographies. Few of these writers, tellingly, could take for granted their country's national power, and almost all of them have had to relate particular experiences of the non-Western world to metropolitan histories and theories.[32] The transnational turn in American foreign relations, until it is accompanied by a more robust training in the languages, cultures, *and* historiographies of other parts of the world, often becomes, inevitably, an exercise in privilege: the privilege of writing about others.

Manela's *The Wilsonian Moment*, for instance, although much celebrated by US historians, was severely criticized for its "eurocentrism" by the historian of China Rebecca Karl because the book projects a Wilsonian paradigm of liberal self-determination as the primary inspiration to Third World nationalists, and ignores the deep and rich genealogies of revolutionary thought and action in the Third World.[33] As important as Manela's insights into Wilson's racist understanding of self-determination are, Karl's criticisms are not isolated ones. Historian Fredrik Logevall has aptly described an "America-centric international history," and Mario Del Pero has lamented what he calls the "insularism" and "historiographical unilateralism" that underlies the recent internationalization of US diplomatic history.[34] Ian Tyrrell, in fact, noted over two decades ago that the interpretative problem has not been an absence of comparative or international perspectives in US history but the "failure of comparative history to transcend the boundaries of nationalist historiography."[35]

How, then, must US historians of foreign relations be robustly transnational or global? The quick and convenient answer, of course, is to abandon the claim of being global or transnational but such a historiographical retreat hardly addresses the problems inherent in an American-based historiography that claims the world as its legitimate field. The more difficult answer is one, I feel, that is perhaps presently unfeasible, for it surely lies, in part, in a need to overcome the self-imposed historiographical and linguistic boundaries that segregate the training of US historians from those of other areas of the world – indeed perhaps even a rethinking of the basic assumption that US foreign relations is something that can and ought to be studied apart from an immersion in the relevant area studies. In other words, "US and the World" historians must aspire to be more than simply rebadged historians of US foreign relations. They must undergo at the very least a dual training, if not an actual dual degree, in both US history and in the relevant area study. The new scholarship of Nathan Citino on Arab and American twentieth-century modernization schemes suggests that this is an eminently feasible path to pursue in the case of the United States and the Middle East in the twentieth century.[36] This duality of perspective does not simply de-exceptionalize US history, but also de-exceptionalizes the relevant part of the world under study.

* * *

It is this duality of perspective and historiography that leads to the third area where the study of the United States and the Middle East is being revitalized by scholars not formally trained in US foreign relations, but rather coming at the problem of transnational history from the vantage point of the Middle East. This is arguably most evident in the work on missionary encounters that brought together American and Arab missionaries, converts, and other protagonists. A new wave of transnational scholarship has demonstrated the substantive benefits of a methodological approach that takes in, and grapples with, both American and Middle Eastern historiographies simultaneously.[37] In the older, hagiographical or exceptional versions of American missionary history told with only one dramatic set of actors, American benevolence was considered a reflection of innate and exceptional American values. These values were, it was assumed, exported to the world; they allegedly inspired a liberal awakening in a dormant Middle East. As we have seen, critical American Studies challenged the idea of benevolence, but often rendered non-American voices and perspectives irrelevant, if not illegible. In the new transnational historiography of American missions, however, American benevolence takes on several contingent meanings and implications in radically different contexts. The genealogy of liberal thought emerging out of missionary encounters is thus recast as a result of highly contested encounters between Americans, Europeans, Arabs, and (until their demise) Ottomans. Americans, in short, do not gift liberalism to the region as the traditional accounts assumed. Rather, a transnational process in which Americans are intimately involved does, such that by the end of the missionary heyday – by the mid-twentieth century – there is both an unprecedented ecumenism among *some* American missionaries who are able to think about Islam as part of modern spirituality, and an unprecedented willingness among *some* Arabs to elaborate a secular and inclusive cultural and national identity. Instead of Samuel Huntington's spurious "clash of civilizations" thesis, the latest wave of historiography deciphers the meaning and implications of often intense and violent cultural clashes that implicate and involve different groups of American and Arabs, not "Islam" and the "West."

The point of a more encompassing historiographical approach, of course, is not to deny or minimize unequal relations of power and the racial, economic, and political hierarchies that have shaped American and Arab relations. Rather, it is to insist that by focusing only on one side of the equation, scholars can miss, quite profoundly at times, the full nature of the object of their critique: whether this be American exceptionalism or orientalism or imperialism in the Middle East. Thus, in a totally different aspect of US–Middle East relations that has to do with state development and the petroleum order rather than Bibles, both Robert Vitalis and Toby Jones illustrate how American involvement in the Middle East has always had Middle Eastern intermediaries, agents and dimensions – and that to understand this involvement, to narrate it, and to appreciate its complexity one has to address these non-American dimensions.[38] *Some* Arabs and others have invested in the idea of American difference at particular points in time – whether because of missionary institutions in the nineteenth century, in Saudi Arabia in the mid-twentieth century, or in Iraq today – and these investments mattered to a greater or smaller degree in understanding what America means, and how Americans have interacted with and represented themselves in the world.

If one admits that the discourse of American exceptionalism often has non-American foundations, it follows that to deconstruct American exceptionalism one has to trace and decipher its global ramifications, intermediaries, and stakeholders. Before we assume the hubris of the "global" – after so long cherishing an exceptionalist "American" vantage point – let us first appreciate that the world is made up of a number of regions and histories and peoples that have consistently defied being lumped together within a single perspective. Thomas Bender was surely right when he challenged US historians "to restore some sense of strangeness" to the writing and appreciation of history involving Americans and the United States.[39]

What is needed is an appreciation of the uneven and unequal dialectic that has long bound Americans and the peoples of the rest of the world together, and an exposition of the layers of historical and historiographical entanglement that have always gone along with it. There is no single method, no single prescription, no single correct way of getting at these myriad encounters, relationships, and dependencies. Nevertheless, there has to be, at the very least, an appreciation of the constitutive qualities of these entanglements that goes beyond a perfunctory acknowledgement of the world in US relations with the world, and then on to empire as usual that, in effect, continues to segregate the United States from the world. The story of American relations with the world ought not to be a story prepared for only American historians, nor should it be narrated only or primarily as an aspect of American history.

NOTES

1. This chapter draws on and revises a longer work that appeared in *Diplomatic History* 38 (2014): 657–84, entitled "After Said: The Limits and Possibilities of a Critical Scholarship of U.S.–Arab Relations." I also thank the students in HIST 594 from the Spring 2013 Semester, Rice University, in particular Nate George, as well as Nathan Citino and Sayuri Guthrie-Shimuzu for their comments on an earlier draft.
2. William Appleman Williams, *The Tragedy of American Diplomacy* (New York, 1972 [1959]), 304. See also, William Appleman Williams, *Empire as a Way of Life:*

An Essay on the Causes and Character of America's Present Predicament Along with a Few Thoughts about an Alternative (New York, 1980).
3. Ian Tyrrell, "American Exceptionalism in an Age of International History," *American Historical Review* 96 (1991): 1031–5.
4. Amy Kaplan, "Left Alone with America," in Amy Kaplan and Donald E. Pease, eds., *The Cultures of United States Imperialism* (Durham, NC, 1993), 11.
5. Daniel T. Rodgers, *Atlantic Crossings: Social Politics in a Progressive Age*, (Cambridge, MA, 1998), Thomas Bender, *A Nation among Nations: America's Place in World History* (New York, 2006), Paul A. Kramer, *Blood of Government: Race, Empire, the United States, and the Philippines* (Chapel Hill, 2006), and Ann Laura Stoler, "Tense and Tender Ties: The Politics of Comparison in North American History and (Post) Colonial Studies," *Journal of American History* 88 (2001): 263–84.
6. Thomas Bender, "Introduction: Historians, the Nation and the Plenitude of Narratives," in Thomas Bender, ed. *Rethinking American History in a Global Age* (Berkeley, 2002), 19, 11.
7. Kramer, *Blood of Government*, 3.
8. Paul Kramer, "Power and Connection: Imperial Histories of the United States in the World," *American Historical Review* 116 (2011): 1383.
9. Erez Manela, "The United States in the World," in Eric Foner and Lisa McGerr, eds., *American History Now* (Philadelphia, 2011), 201–20.
10. Matthew Connelly, *A Diplomatic Revolution: Algeria's Fight for Independence and the Origin of the Post-Cold War Era* (New York, 2002), Erez Manela, *The Wilsonian Moment: Self-Determination and the International Origins of Anticolonial Nationalism* (New York, 2007), Odd Arne Westad, *The Global Cold War: Third World Interventions and the Making of Our Times* (Cambridge, UK, 2005), Akira Iriye, ed. *Global Interdependence: The World After 1945* (Cambridge, MA, 2013).
11. We already have some answers to this in works set during the Cold War that treat the regional dimensions seriously and robustly such as Piero Gleijeses, *Conflicting Missions: Havana, Washington and Africa, 1959–1976* (Chapel Hill, 2002), and Bruce Cumings major two-volume *The Origins of the Korean War* (Princeton, 1981/1990). I thank Nate George for the Gleijeses reference.
12. Barack Obama declared the "war on terror" over in 2013 but nevertheless expanded drone strikes in the Arab world, Afghanistan, and Pakistan. See http://www.usnews.com/news/articles/2013/05/23/obama-global-war-on-terror-is-over. Accessed 9/15/2015.
13. See Inga Clendinnen, "Fierce and Unnatural Cruelty": Cortés and the Conquest of Mexico," in Stephen Greenblatt, ed., *New World Encounters* (Berkeley, 1993), 18.
14. For this reason, the historiography of Arab-Americans has only recently moved from standard assimilation paradigm to a more interesting transnational and comparative analysis. See, in particular, Akram Khater, *Inventing Home: Emigration, Gender and the Middle Class in Lebanon, 1870–1920* (Berkeley, 2001), and Sarah Gaultieri, *Between Arab and White: Race and Ethnicity in the in the Early Syrian American Diaspora* (Berkeley, 2009).
15. Edward W. Said, *Orientalism* (New York, 2003 [1978]), and Melani McAlister, *Epic Encounters: Culture, Media and U.S. Interests in the Middle East since 1945* (Berkeley, 2005 [2001]). See also Amaney Jamal and Nadine Naber eds., *Race and*

Arab-Americans before & after 9/11: From Invisible Citizens to Visible Subjects (Syracuse, 2008).
16. For "post-exceptionalist" see Daniel T. Rodgers, "American Exceptionalism Revisited," *Raritan* 24 (2004): 21–47.
17. Erez Manela, "The United States in the World," 209.
18. John Davis, *The Landscape of Belief: Encountering the Holy Land in Nineteenth-Century American Art and Culture* (Princeton, 1996); Burke O. Long, *Imagining the Holy Land: Maps, Models, and Fantasy Travels* (Bloomington, 2003); Malini Johar Schueller, *U.S. Orientalisms: Race, Nation, and Gender in Literature, 1790–1890* (Ann Arbor, 1998). See also, Obenzinger, *American Palestine*. There are, to be sure, many other authors directly influenced by Said that one could cite. See Alexander Lyon Macfie, ed., *Orientalism: A Reader* (Edinburgh, 2000), esp. 273–345.
19. Said, *Orientalism*, 5.
20. Alex Lubin, *Geographies of Liberation: The Making of an Afro-Arab Political Imaginary* (Chapel Hill, 2014), and Penny Von Eschen, *Race against Empire: Black Americans and Anticolonialism, 1937–1957* (Ithaca, 1997). For a similar criticism of how context changes the implications of radicalism, see Judy Tzu-Chun Wu, *Radicals on the Road: Internationalism, Orientalism and Feminism during the Vietnam Era* (Ithaca, 2013).
21. McAlister, *Epic Encounters*, has an apt concluding chapter named "Military Multiculturalism in the Gulf War and After, 1990–1999" in which she explores the tensions of such implication. This is also a point made by Lubin, *Geographies of Liberation*, 20.
22. For a criticism of transnationalism within American studies, see Bryce Traister, "The Object of Study, or, Are We Being Transnational Yet?" *Journal of Transnational American Studies*, 2(1), Article 14 (2010), available online at http://escholarship.org/uc/item/864843hs.
23. Matthew Jacobs, *Imagining the Middle East: The Building of an American Foreign Policy, 1918–1967* (Chapel Hill, 2011).
24. Connelly, *A Diplomatic Revolution*; Paul Thomas Chamberlin, *The Global Offensive: The United States, the Palestine Liberation Organization, and the Making of the Post-Cold War Order* (Oxford, 2012), 3.
25. Then again, a critical historiography among scholars of US Foreign Relations appears to be far more robust in the case of US–Asian and US–Latin American relations than US–Middle East. See, for instance, Greg Grandin, *The Last Colonial Massacre: Latin America in the Cold War* (Chicago, 2011 [2004]), and Gleijeses, *Conflicting Missions and his Visions of Freedom: Havana, Washington, Pretoria and the Struggle for Southern Africa 1976–1991* (Chapel Hill, 2013). For East Asia, see John W. Dower's *War Without Mercy: Race and Power in the Pacific War* (New York, 1987), and *Embracing Defeat: Japan in the Wake of World War II* (New York, 1999). See also Bruce Cumings, *The Korean War: A History* (New York, 2010), and Lien-Hang T. Nguyen, *Hanoi's War: An International History of the War for Peace in Vietnam* (Chapel Hill, 2012).
26. This is a point I take up in much greater depth in "After Said."
27. Chamberlin, *The Global Offensive*, 10.
28. To wit, one of the most updated volumes that covers US Middle Eastern policy is edited by David W. Lesch. See David W. Lesch and Mark L. Haas, eds., *The Middle*

East and the United States: History, Politics and Ideologies (Westview Press, 2011), now in its 5th edition.

29. Excellent examples of this well-established tradition include Irene L. Gendzier's *Notes from the Minefield: United States Intervention in Lebanon, 1945–1958* (New York, 2006 [1997]), which was reissued in 2006, and the National Security Archive at George Washington University, which was founded in 1985. See www.gwu.edu/~nsarchiv/index.html.
30. Timothy Mitchell, *Carbon Democracy: Political Power in the Age of Oil* (London, 2011).
31. For a similar perspective on internationalizing American history, see Akira Iriye, "Internationalizing International History," in Bender, ed., *Rethinking American History*, 49.
32. I am thinking here in particular of Dipesh Chakrabarty, *Provincializing Europe: Postcolonial Thought and Historical Difference* (Princeton, 2007 [2000]), and Edward W. Said's notion of "contrapuntal" reading in *Culture and Imperialism* (New York, 1994 [1993]). We could explore many possible connections made *across* the Global South along the lines suggested by Vijay Prashad's idea of the Third World as a "project" and not simply a "place," *The Darker Nations: A People's History of the Third World* (New York, 2007).
33. See Rebecca Karl's review of his book in the *American Historical Review* 113 (2008): 1474–6. See also Vijay Prashad's review of the book in the *Journal of Global History* 6 (2011): 153–5.
34. Fredrik Logevall, "Politics and Foreign Relations," *Journal of American History*, 95 (2009): 1076. Mario Del Pero, "On the Limits of Thomas Zeiler's Historiographical Triumphalism," *Journal of American History* 95 (2009): 1080–1.
35. Tyrrell, "American Exceptionalism in an Age of International History," 1033.
36. Nathan J. Citino's forthcoming *Envisioning the Arab Future: Modernization in U.S.–Arab Relations, 1945–1967*.
37. Beth Baron, *The Orphan Scandal: Christian Missionaries and the Rise of the Muslim Brotherhood* (Palo Alto, 2014), Ussama Makdisi, *Artillery of Heaven: American Missionaries and the Failed Conversion of the Middle East* (Ithaca, 2008), and Heather J. Sharkey, *American Evangelicals in Egypt: Missionary Encounters in an Age of Empire* (Princeton, 2008).
38. Robert Vitalis, *America's Kingdom: Mythmaking on the Saudi Oil Frontier* (London, 2009), and Toby Jones, *Desert Kingdom: How Oil and Water Forged Modern Saudi Arabia* (Cambridge, MA, 2010).
39. Bender, ed. *Rethinking American History in a Global Age*, 11.

13

Nationalism as an umbrella ideology

Michael H. Hunt

Ideology is the proper concern of all historians of US foreign relations. Its relevance rests on one simple insight of fundamental importance. To move in a world of infinite complexity, individuals and societies need to reduce it to finite terms. Only then can they pretend an understanding of their environment and have the confidence to talk about it and the courage to act on it. All activities, whether individual or collective, require that simplifying clarity. Policymakers, or for that matter anyone confronting the world, get their keys to "reality" in the same ways that others in their culture do. A process of socialization begins in childhood and continues even as experience confirms or reshapes outlooks and influences behavior. Thus every foreign relations historian, like it or not, constantly comes in contact with the problem of ideology.

Of the many possible definitions, I favor one that identifies ideology as "an interrelated set of convictions or assumptions that reduces the complexities of a particular slice of reality to easily comprehensible terms and suggests appropriate ways of dealing with that reality."[1] Ideologies relevant to foreign affairs are in this sense sets of beliefs and values, sometimes only poorly and partially articulated, that make the world intelligible and interaction with it possible. This broad notion launches historians on a quest for ideas that give structure and meaning to the way policymakers and their people see the world and their country's place in it. This definition does not embody some ultimate truth. It is rather one plausible approach to understanding particular historical moments and personalities that deserves testing against other definitions of ideology.

Arriving at a definition is by itself an important step, which immediately alters the frame of reference. For those studying policymakers, the question becomes "not whether they have an ideology but to what ideology they subscribe; not whether ideology makes a difference but what kind of difference it makes for the shaping of their intentions, policies, and behavior."[2] But the question applies with no less force to the policy establishment, the media, public intellectuals, interest groups, and the public in general. The basic premise that ideology matters and that it is neither simple nor rigid suggests the importance of identifying fundamental notions (for example, about human nature, the constituents of power, and national mission) that policymakers and the public carry in their heads. The search for an answer can go in a variety of directions. It can lead us to look at the mindsets of individuals or collectives. Biographical studies dealing with formative, early years are invaluable for the former, while prosopographical techniques are indispensable for the latter, especially as we attempt to identify commonalities or divergences within or between groups, even generations. It can alert us to the need for greater sensitivity to language and especially to the meaning embedded in "key words" such as "progressive change," "terrorism," or "free world" in our reading of conventional diplomatic documentation and personal correspondence. It asks us to examine rhetoric in a more sophisticated way and to extend our scrutiny to symbols and ceremonies that can reveal much about the form and content of ideology that conventional sources usually do not make explicit.

The notion that ideology is a helpful interpretive key is now generally taken for granted by historians of US foreign relations. This wide acceptance has in turn given rise to something of a problem: the proliferation of ideological constructs germane both to US policy and more broadly to American interaction with the world. Whereas diplomatic historians once limited themselves to contending "realism" and "idealism," we now have scholarship that develops the role of ideas from a great variety of perspectives, including for example under the heading of gender, race, and religion and extending to such notions as economic developmentalism and orientalism. Ideology now appears in such varied form in the interpretive arsenal that the very notion has become baggy.[3]

But problems can also be opportunities to rethink an approach. Of all the kinds of foreign relations "ideologies" now on offer, is there one that occupies a central position? Nationalism is arguably the answer. Let me stress that my suggestion is not meant as a repudiation of the utility of ideology as a general analytic or interpretive category or a skepticism about the various expressions of ideology historians have identified. The latter in particular provide fine-grained ways of making sense of particular situations in a way that nationalism with its broad sweep may not.[4]

Rather, this chapter seeks to suggest the importance of nationalism in four respects. It first of all can, as an interpretive device, play an umbrella, integrative role. Nationalism is the most powerful single influence on American worldviews and thus on policy decisions and on broader, non-policy engagement with the world. Precisely because of its centrality as a general force field, nationalism tends to subsume the other expressions of ideology noted above and to draw attention to the interrelationship among the scattered ideological pieces thus pulled together. Beyond that, nationalism offers an opportunity to think of the US role in the world comparatively. It provides a constant reminder that the United States is one country amidst others also animated by strong or shifting identities. Third in our list of importance, nationalist constructs offer an interpretive bridge to social, economic, and technological forces playing out on a global scale. This connection between nationalism and other, non-ideological facets of foreign relations widens our angle of vision and offers a reminder that trade, travel, communications, immigration, mass production, and modern warfare have not only reshaped the world but also inspired nationalist responses and challenged nationalist constructs with enormously important consequences for policy and foreign relations. Finally, nationalism is an abiding presence through US history and thus provides a sturdy strand for tracing change and continuity and critically considering broad generalizations about national character and experience that are often casually thrown about, sometimes as expressions of the prevailing nationalist-inflected common wisdom.

A couple of key developments have helped raise nationalism's scholarly profile and make the present a particularly favorable moment for highlighting its utility to the US foreign relations field. Several decades of innovative and wide-ranging theoretical literature laid the groundwork for seeing nationalism as a critical, pervasive force. Between the late 1970s and the early 1990s, students of culture, society, and politics rediscovered nationalism as a general concept. Much of the most influential theoretical work now available appeared during that time, and some contributions now rank as classics.[5]

This outpouring of highly regarded and widely read theoretical literature began during the 1990s to leave its mark in the US history field. We now have a substantial and richly monographic body of work. Some items have implications for foreign relations history that need drawing out, while others make the link explicit. If anything, foreign relations historians have been bolder than others in the US field in tackling the question of nationalism in a broadly synthetic fashion.[6]

Those in the ivory tower convinced of the pertinence of US nationalism got dramatic confirmation in the wake of the September 11, 2001, attacks. Its strong grip was strikingly evident in both popular outpourings of grief and anger and in policy declarations rallying the country. In subsequent years, however, national sentiment turned toward the introspective. The failure of armed interventions in the Middle East, the perceptible decline in US international clout and reputation, and domestic political and cultural divisions occasioned widespread soul searching. The shift from self-confidence to self-doubt was reflected in presidential rhetoric. George W. Bush tapped nationalist tropes with apparent ease. By contrast, Barack Obama expressed qualified doubt on the idea of American exceptionalism while claiming US leadership of the "Western world" and US guardianship of universally applicable progressive values in language that seemed not only clichéd but also mechanical. The spectacle of

US nationalism in disarray raised the supremely historical questions of when did the transition begin, what elements were in play, and have there been other times of transition in American history?

For nationalism, as with any sweeping theoretical concept, the devil for the historian is in the details. It is not only the obvious matter of relating the big idea to the evidence. There is the prior problem of deciding from among the possible theoretical formulations which are clear and simple enough to apply but also fresh enough to provide insight. In formulating some working definition that will serve as our basic conception, let us avoid a stark choice between particular approaches in the nationalist literature, often formulated in constructivist and ethno-historical terms. The former puts a stress on the fluidity as nationalists respond to changing circumstances and perspectives. The latter looks for continuity rooted in a people's awareness of place and connection to the past. Let us assume that both approaches offer potentially important insights and that historians can draw from each promiscuously to suit the historical moment or situation under examination.

Whatever the relative appeal of a conception biased toward change or continuity, the historian needs to decide on a rough working definition. An invocation of nationalism resting on some vague or casual formulation is likely to give rise to counterproductive confusion or ungrounded debate. My own reading leads me to think of nationalism in broadest terms as a cultural movement that includes prominently a political program whose goal is a sovereign state giving expression to core collective values. The success of a nationalist project depends on reaching the popular imagination and thus developing the capacity to mobilize consent and support. This critical task of invention and popularization is primarily the business of public intellectuals and political activists addressing a wide range of identity-defining issues extending well beyond conventional politics. Their formulations speak to issues as diverse as family life and gender relations, school curricula, and religious values. While nationalism is in this sense imagined, it does not develop in a vacuum. It is, as the ethno-nationalists insist, dependent on and to a degree limited by the pool of ideas handed down from earlier periods and by prevailing ethnic or geographical circumstances. Depending on the intellectual reservoir and the physical environment, some ways of imagining the national collective are easier to conceive and easier to convey than others, just as bricks are more easily made with straw or fire than without.

From this definition emerges two major propositions that historians should find especially helpful. The first is that nationalism bears recurrent features that define its contours. These features can help us recognize an expression of nationalism when we see it. Suggesting a concrete, systematic way of thinking about these foundational matters may point a fruitful way forward for some and at least provoke others to develop an alternative approach better suited to their interpretive needs and understanding of the theoretical literature.

One of those features proposed here relates to citizenship measured in terms not just of voting but of full participation and opportunity within the life of the nation. Prevailing nationalist notions define who deserves a place in the body politic and how restricted that place may be. Assigned racial characteristics, ethnic ties, class standing, religious or political affiliation, or sexual orientation can serve as the basis for entirely excluding some categories of people and allowing only limited rights to others. These exclusions and qualifications, regardless of whether imposed formally or de facto, give shape to the national community for whom policymakers claim to speak and which interacts in all manner of ways with the broader world.

The best example of how important and dynamic understanding of citizenship can be comes from the twentieth-century United States, which began as an adult white male republic and in a dramatic transformation (without precedent in earlier US history) gave way to a distinctly multi-racial and multi-ethnic understanding of national membership. Women and Native Americans won a place within the charmed circle of citizenship, followed by the whitening of recent immigrant groups (Italians, Jews, and Asians), and finally after much contention the admission of African Americans to the national fold. This shift playing out over five decades can be explained in large measure by the mounting contradiction weighing on those at the helm of the American state. By mid-century, Washington was in a bind. US leaders could not comfortably embrace a policy of international engagement, justified at home no less than overseas, in terms of individual liberty and democratic rights, and at the same time uphold a narrowly defined citizenship so glaringly at odds with those principles.[7]

A second defining features is captured by the term "dangerous other." Nearly a cliché in the theoretical literature, this term highlights the importance of external threats to core common values, which can in turn galvanize an anxious nation and create pressure for conformity and unity. A historian whose main interest is the United States has summed up the multifaceted role an external enemy can play: "Nationalism demands that boundaries against outsiders be drawn, that a dominant culture be created or reinvigorated, and that internal and external opponents of the national project be subdued, nationalized, vanquished, and even excluded or expelled."[8] In other words, a foreign danger can highlight what the nation is about, put the spotlight on deviant groups or norms, and generate solidarity and violence in defense of the collective. The notion of "the dangerous other" underlines how nationalism can be as much about who we are *not* and who we *want* to be as who we in fact *are*.

Perhaps at no time was "the other" more prominent in American thinking and more consequential than during the earliest phase of nationalist formation between the 1770s and 1810s. National identity then embodied a potent preoccupation with threats immediately at hand (natives, Europeans, and enslaved Africans). The British transplants to North America, like their counterparts in other settlement societies, generated ideologies of conquest and domination that had a lasting impact. In particular, views about other peoples that equated physical features with profound, fixed cultural traits commingled to create what a leading historian of US racial attitudes has described as a long-lived "American color line." The resulting worldview, woven into American nationalism from its inception, took "race as a supposed fact of nature that endowed groups distinguishable on the basis of skin color or nonwhite ancestry with differing degrees of intelligence, character, and capability."[9]

The "threatening other" again figured strikingly in the twentieth-century phase of US nationalism. From the late 1890s to the 1950s American nationalists grappled with a rapid succession of menacing forces marked by apparently similar ideological deformities. The anxieties spawned by German imperialism, international Bolshevism, Japanese empire-building, German Nazism, and a communist monolith that split into a Soviet and Chinese threat assumed a prominent place in the national imagination. Each of these perceived threats served to unite and mobilize a country recurrently at war or preparing for war and in turn helped to sharpen and consolidate the reigning state-centered nationalism.[10]

A final feature can be summed up in terms of the state as the agent and advocate of a nationalist vision. No nationalist program is complete until it has a government structure and staff that reflect its values and can defend and promote those values. Nationalism thus deserves to be seen as both an impetus to the rise of the modern state and at the same time intimately entangled with it, providing continuing legitimization and influencing its multifaceted operations. Those engaged in the national project have repeatedly looked to state power as the ultimate embodiment, promoter, and protector of the ideals, assumptions, narratives, and practices that define their cause. The absence of a state leaves nationalist aspirations just that – dreams without means to fully realize them. Conversely, as state capacity grows, so too can the ambitions of nationalists expand. In practice the nation-making and nation-sustaining tasks of the state include clarifying and enforcing the lines of citizenship, surveilling the population, providing a civic education not just in schools but also in other popular sites such as commemorative ceremonies and monuments, sanctioning some views and marginalizing or delegitimizing others, identifying and mobilizing against enemies within and without, and making claims on community resources (both human and material).

The period from the Civil War to the early twentieth century was seminal in the rise of a state that embodied, promoted, and exploited nationalism. The Civil War was more than a victory over an alternative sectional vision of the nation.[11] It also fed state capacity, confirming Randolph Bourne's observation that "war is essentially the health of the State."[12] The central government secured the power to tax the population directly, to draft men for military service, to suspend individual rights (notably the writ of habeas corpus), to paint critics as traitors, to take property, and to compel states to stay within a union once widely considered voluntary and contingent. Federal forces went on to govern and attempt the reshaping of a prostrate South. Washington promised veterans pensions and freedmen support. The Fourteenth Amendment of 1868 shifted the emphasis in protection of individual rights to the federal level and extended the reach of federal courts. The Republican Party put in place a national currency and a national banking structure. It imposed a high tariff to ensure domestic industry a continental market. It promoted public education (notably by supporting land grant state universities), provided incentives for westward settlement, and helped underwrite the construction of transcontinental railroads. In 1891, the federal bureaucracy got into the business of overseeing immigration, taking over from the states the handling of arriving Chinese. Expanding responsibilities translated into a growing federal work force. Unsettled by the rise of powerful states in Europe and in Japan, by the race for colonies, and by the technological possibilities for mobilizing and projecting power, US leaders began shaping a more robust international agenda. They embarked on a naval buildup in the 1880s and developed a strong interest in overseas bases, an isthmian canal, cable and telegraph systems, and a more professional diplomatic corps to defend far-flung interests.

By the beginning of the twentieth century, the government in Washington could exercise social control, command ideological assent, and pursue a far-reaching international agenda. In the process this modern state fundamentally altered how Americans conceived themselves and directed their resources. Warfare continued to play a pivotal role in the process of state-building. A string of wars running from the Spanish–American War to two world wars, Korea, and Vietnam not to mention interventions in China, in Central America and the Caribbean, and along the Cold War containment line engendered an ever larger bureaucracy, a powerful military, an imperial president, and a growing claim on national resources.[13]

These three defining features of virtually all nationalist movements – more or less clearly drawn lines of citizenship, some galvanizing outside specter, and an active state sponsor – give our discussion of the US case a sorely needed historical and comparative grounding. By concentrating on these three features, we can move beyond the swirling set of stock notions that Americans have used to think about themselves and that politicians employ to make their case, especially at election time. We all know the phrases: "the last best hope," "the city on the hill," "the land of opportunity," "the beacon of democracy," "the land of the free." This historically thin, stereotyped past conforms to the universal assumption of nationalists that their faith arises from some abiding, primordial spirit attached to a particular people or place. This historical construct in the minds of American nationalists may be even thinner than most in keeping with their emphatic preoccupation with the future, with its promise of the ultimate global triumph of the American way – to the time (as one historian has suggested) "when progressive, cumulative, irreversible processes of change would have worn away the variety in human experience." (This perspective is supposed to have prompted Richard Hofstadter to quip that America alone of all nations began with perfection and aspired to progress.)[14]

Theoretical work on nationalism suggests a second proposition closely tied to the first one on defining features: that no nationalist construct is fixed. US nationalism has evolved as the three constituent elements have shifted in their individual composition and in their relationship to each other. Those attached to a conventional view of US identity may find this suggestion of flux disturbing and prefer to cling to the more conventional, comfortable idea of a stable, unchanging core to US nationalism. They may point to the persistence of the ideas of liberty, democracy, and free enterprise, and they can imagine those notions not only elevating the United States to an exceptional global position but also enjoying the sanction of some higher, transcendent source such as Providence or Progress. But anyone searching for durable essences will find scant support in the recent nationalism literature. In the United States over its two hundred plus years of history, no less than elsewhere, nationalism is a work always in progress, its defining preoccupations shifting from era to era and combining in significantly different ways. The course of any nationalism is marked (as Lloyd Kramer has put it) by "constant cultural reconstruction as each generation extends, debates, and redefines the meaning of the nation."[15]

Hardly an incidental feature or a mere annoyance, debate and disputation constitute the lifeblood of nationalism, giving it meaning and maintaining its vitality. Out of all the swirling, conflicting dreams about the nation, some will win followers, eclipse established ways of thinking, and perhaps manage to become the new orthodoxy. No nationalism can be fixed because it operates within a context of shifting social patterns, new systems of production and consumption, fresh political ideas, and altered international conditions. They combine in diverse ways to undermine the very foundation on which every dominant nationalist formation sits, and they give rise to new ones. For historians of US foreign relations, seeing nationalism as a work in constant progress has the additional virtue of countering the tendency within the field to privilege the post-1945 period or view it in splendid isolation. A stress on nationalism highlights the degree to which more recent developments have variously built on, transformed, and were limited by earlier nationalist phases. Consider, for example, the relationship of policy to nationalism. Methodologically the link cuts two ways: we understand policy better if we grasp the nationalist construct in ascendancy at the time. But we can also use policy, and especially policy statements and debates, to gauge how strong the nationalist hold is at a particular moment and what elements seem to have the most potent appeal.

What might a sketch of US nationalism look like that follows the two propositions laid out above? What insights might it offer historians of foreign relations? A large, recent, and richly detailed literature offers the basis for a picture in which American nationalism evolves from the 1780s to the 1970s through three distinct phases of construction and contestation as preoccupations with citizenship, dangerous outsiders, and state-building have shifted. Each phase prevailed for about seven or eight decades. And each corresponded to and was heavily influenced by global forces, which created problems, opportunities, and constraints and thus forced nationalists to defend their faith, rethink it, or modify it in particulars. The sketch that follows, far from either exhaustive or definitive, aims to demonstrate that a well-grounded notion of nationalism can do serious interpretive work by refracting what case studies have to say through the prism of the theoretical literature as I understand it.

The story of US nationalism begins with its settler foundations during the late eighteenth and early nineteenth century. It developed as a facet and under the influence of the first age of European empire. Like settler communities elsewhere around the world, those that would come to constitute the United States confronted indigenous peoples along a fluid cultural borderland before demographically overwhelming them. Land was the ultimate prize, intercultural accommodation possible but force was the ultimate arbiter, and ideological justifications for conquest were powerful and enduring.[16]

No less important in defining settler identity was the internal contest over how closely the new nation should follow the British model. This contest helped define the early boundaries of citizenship, led to diminished popular deference to elites, and laid down limits on state power. These fundamentally nationalist concerns together with the drive against indigenous peoples were prominently in play in all the major foreign relations developments of the early national period: the sharp debates over Hamilton's promotion of federal power; the social and political upheaval occasioned by the Jay Treaty and the French Revolution; the Anglophobia that repeatedly roiled politics and policy; the relentless drive to gain control of Native American land; and the political accommodation to slavery as indispensable to the US export economy.

US nationalism underwent a distinct shift during its continental phase, which spanned much of the nineteenth century and which developed in tandem with accelerating globalization and technological innovation. Thanks to the steam engine, expanding railroad networks, and the electric telegraph and underwater cables, goods and information moved at a greatly accelerated pace, integrating the continental market and making dramatically more accessible foreign markets. Out of this technological revolution emerged a corporate order in which production, marketing, and finance flourished on a new scale. GDP growth rates reached historically unprecedented levels, made possible by large-scale capital investments and waves of trans atlantic as well as trans pacific migrants carried by increasingly fast, convenient, and cheap maritime transport. By the end of the century what had been a small, peripheral agrarian economy had far surpassed the leading European powers in output.

Greater confidence and strength marked an end to the embattled nationalism of the earlier period haunted by an array of foreign perils. Americans had proven themselves irresistible on the continent – a point driven home to native peoples not yet reconciled to subordination, to foreign powers foolish enough to cling to ambitions on the continent, and to neighbors who failed to keep a firm grip on their territory.[17] Citizenship as the second defining feature of the continental phase was relatively little changed. The United States remained a white man's republic. As noted above, the state's role was the most in flux during this continental phase.

The third phase of an evolving US nationalism might be described as state-centered. It had begun to take shape at the beginning of the twentieth century, spurred as earlier by the cumulative effects of technological breakthroughs on commerce, travel, immigration, investment, and warfare. The result throughout the Atlantic world and in East Asia was a vortex of trans national activity dominated by self-aggrandizing modern states. European as well as Russian, Japanese, and Chinese elites exploited new possibilities for expanding the sphere of state capacity and action. Government bureaucracies grew in size and specialization, providing political leaders with the means to monitor their people's lives, direct economic activity, deliver social services, mobilize political support, build professional and technologically advanced armed forces, levy mass armies, possess colonies, pursue overseas markets, and command a growing share of expanding national output essential to pay for all these activities. Nationalists everywhere served up a florid vision of unity, power, and purpose that justified state activity on a scale previously unimagined. And once that vision became entrenched, the state had the capacity to perpetuate it. As a classic work on state–society relations put it: "To maintain and transmit a value system, human beings are punched, bullied, sent to jail, thrown into concentration camps, cajoled, bribed, made into heroes, encouraged to read newspapers, stood up against a wall and shot, and sometimes even taught sociology."[18]

This particular three-stage scenario raises questions germane to foreign relations historians grappling with interpretively treacherous recent developments. While state-centered nationalism has proven durable, it has arguably since the 1970s shown mounting signs of vulnerability, with the result that Americans are more and more a nation in disarray. The fundamental disagreements are the perennials: the role of the state (how big and what priorities); the circle of citizenship (how broad and how meaningful); and the nature of international threats (where and how to respond). Each bears critical implications for the US relationship to the world, including notably how to deal with the pressures of globalization working their way through the US economy and society and with regional powers at odds with US claims to predominance. A nationalist lens also helps bring into focus the challenges building against the ascendant state-centered notion of the nation, whether rooted in a consumer republic ideal, an enthusiasm for an untrammeled free market, or a Tea Party fear of cultural change and erosion of individual liberty and local autonomy.

The claims made in this chapter challenge proponents of US exceptionalism who see nationalism as a pejorative. How can, they ask, Americans possibly imagine their own country under the spell of such a dangerous and destructive ideology? The United States has played so benign a role in the world that its animating spirit deserves another name – patriotism. This semantic sleight of hand conveniently sets American values apart from the unsavory, morally tainted passions of other peoples. But patriotism offers no real escape from the net of nationalism. If the two terms are understood to be interchangeable, then the objection to nationalism rests on a distinction without a difference. In that case why not accept nationalism as simply a synonym for patriotism? Alternatively, if the preference for patriotism rests on solid theoretical grounds, where is the literature that traces it across a range of cases in a generally illuminating fashion?

On the positive side, the attention given nationalism here reinforces a familiar methodological point about the importance of taking the power of ideas seriously. Nationalist outlooks and assumptions supply the indispensable frame in which policy debates play out, politicians operate, decisions are made, and the public mobilized. So engrained are nationalist ideas that they can exert their force tacitly, constraining policymakers, sowing discord, narrowing the range of policy options, and even policing the views of those wanting a place in the foreign policy establishment. Make no mistake, wherever policy goes, nationalist ideas of one sort or another are in attendance. No policymaker can put behind a lifetime of socialization into the reigning nationalist paradigm conveyed by civics lessons, political rhetoric, popular celebrations, advertising, songs, and movies. Even those who want to escape the nationalist cage must still deploy nationalist language to win support in the short term and sustain it over the long haul.

But nationalism as an interpretive tool, it is worth stressing, offers more. It provides a way of placing the United States in a global comparative perspective. It invites us to think well beyond the conventional policy domain of diplomatic historians – in terms of the broad global forces that shape nations and the outlook of their people. Nationalism thus helps us draw a connection between US conduct in the world and the social, economic, and technological forces at play shaping that world.

NOTES

1. Michael H. Hunt, *Ideology and U.S. Foreign Policy*, 2nd edn. (New Haven, CT, 2009; originally published in 1987), xi.
2. Serewyn Bialer, "Ideology and Soviet Foreign Policy," in *Ideology and Foreign Policy: A Global Perspective*, ed. George Schwab (New York, 1978), 86.
3. A good example of this proliferation are works highlighting the ways that the American state and its foreign policy in particular has functioned as a heavily gendered enterprise. See, for example, from the last two decades Michelle Mart,

"Tough Guys and American Cold War Policy: Images of Israel, 1948–1960," *Diplomatic History* 20 (Summer 1996): 357–80; Frank Costigliola, "Unceasing Pressure for Penetration": Gender, Pathology, and Emotion in George Kennan's Formation of the Cold War," *Journal of American History* [hereafter JAH] 83 (March 1997): 1309–39; Kristin L. Hoganson, *Fighting for American Manhood: How Gender Politics Provoked the Spanish–American and Philippine–American Wars* (New Haven, CT, 1998); Robert D. Dean, *Imperial Brotherhood: Gender and the Making of Cold War Foreign Policy* (Amherst, MA, 2001); K. A. Cuordileone, *Manhood and American Political Culture in the Cold War* (New York, 2005); Naoko Shibusawa, *America's Geisha Ally: Reimagining the Japanese Enemy* (Cambridge, MA, 2006); and "Special Forum: Gender and Sexuality in American Foreign Relations," *Diplomatic History* 36 (September 2012): 695–772.

4. For my own evolving position, see my contribution to a roundtable in JAH 77 (June 1990): 108–15, a revised and extended version of that contribution appearing in the second edition of *Explaining the History of American Foreign Relations* (New York, 2004), particularly 229–40, and the new afterword in the second edition of *Ideology and U.S. Foreign Policy*, 199–218. I am grateful to Michaela Hoenicke Moore and Paul Quigley for sharing insights from their work on nationalism and to Klaus Larres for the chance for me to try out my ideas on US nationalism in his Krasno lecture series (video available at www.youtube.com/watch?v=fyfGhPXTBfw).

5. For an excellent, up-to-date general introduction, see Lloyd S. Kramer, *Nationalism in Europe and America: Politics, Cultures, and Identities since 1775* (Chapel Hill, NC, 2011), which revises and extends his "Historical Narrative and the Meaning of Nationalism," *Journal of the History of Ideas* 58 (July 1997): 525–6; and his *Nationalism: Political Culture in Europe and America* (New York, 1998). See also Paul Lawrence, *Nationalism: History and Theory* (Harlow, UK, 2005), which surveys changing approaches over the last century and a half. Major works in the 1980s scholarly revival include Benedict Anderson, *Imagined Communities: Reflections on the Origin and Spread of Nationalism*, 2nd ed. (London, 1991; originally published 1983); Ernest Gellner, *Nations and Nationalism*, 2nd edn. (Ithaca, NY, 2008; originally published 1983); Anthony D. Smith, *The Ethnic Origins of Nations* (Oxford, UK, 1986); and E. J. Hobsbawm, *Nations and Nationalism since 1780: Programme, Myth, Reality*, 2nd edn. (Cambridge, UK, 1992; originally published 1990). For a sampling from the literature, see Geoff Eley and Ronald Grigor Suny, eds., *Becoming National: A Reader* (New York, 1996); and John Hutchinson and Anthony D. Smith, eds., *Nationalism: Critical Concepts in Political Science* (5 vols.; London, 2000).

6. For a brief, suggestive survey of changing approaches to nationalism in US history scholarship, see David Waldstreicher, *In the Midst of Perpetual Fetes: The Making of American Nationalism, 1776–1820* (Chapel Hill, NC, 1997), 3–8. For general treatments of US nationalism, see Anatol Lieven, *America Right or Wrong: An Anatomy of American Nationalism* (New York, 2004), which uses a comparative perspective to explore the conflict between an enlightenment creed influential at the founding of the country and a variety of later ethnoreligious impulses; and Patrice L. R. Higonnet, *Attendant Cruelties: Nation and Nationalism in American History* (New York, 2007), which sees alternating cycles of aggressive exclusionary nationalism and a less bellicose inclusionary outlook.

Accounts emphasizing the nationalist sources of US foreign relations include Anders Stephanson, *Manifest Destiny: American Expansion and the Empire of Right* (New York, 1995), which follows the rise and decline of a particularly influential, multi-stranded concept; Trevor B. McCrisken, *American Exceptionalism and the Legacy of Vietnam: US Foreign Policy since 1974* (Basingstoke, Hampshire, UK, 2003); which examines recent policy through the prism of a national sense of exceptionalism; Walter L. Hixson, *The Myth of American Diplomacy: National Identity and U.S. Foreign Policy* (New Haven, CT, 2008), which argues for a persistent sense of special destiny that has spawned a pronounced militarism; Adam Quinn, *US Foreign Policy in Context: National Ideology from the Founders to the Bush Doctrine* (London, 2010), which traces the long-term evolution of basic policy outlooks with each new stage drawing on and being constrained by the previous one; and William O. Walker, *National Security and Core Values in American History* (New York, 2009), which emphasizes the twentieth-century eclipse of republican values by an authoritarian security ethos.

7. Gary Gerstle, *American Crucible: Race and Nation in the Twentieth Century* (Princeton, NJ, 2001); and David R. Roediger, *Working toward Whiteness: How America's Immigrants Became White* (New York, 2005), are excellent starting points on changing conceptions of citizenship.

8. Quote from Gary Gerstle, "Liberty, Coercion, and the Making of Americans," JAH 84 (September 1997): 555.

9. Quote from George M. Fredrickson, "America's Diversity in Comparative Perspective," JAH 85 (December 1998): 871. The Anglo-American construction of "dangerous others" rooted in race has been a subject of longstanding historical interest. The foundational works are Winthrop D. Jordan, *White over Black: American Attitudes towards the Negro, 1550–1812* (Chapel Hill, NC, 1968), condensed as *The White Man's Burden: Historical Origins of Racism in the United States* (New York, 1974) and reissued in 2012 with new introductions; Robert K. Berkhofer, Jr., *The White Man's Indian: Images of the American Indian from Columbus to the Present* (New York, 1978); and Richard Drinnon, *Facing West: the Metaphysics of Indian-hating and Empire Building* (Minneapolis, 1980). For a more recent general treatment, see Audrey Smedley, *Race in North America: Origin and Evolution of a Worldview*, 2nd edn. (Boulder, CO, 1999).

10. This merry-go-round of dangerous others has spawned a large literature. See for example John W. Dower, *War Without Mercy: Race and Power in the Pacific War* (New York, 1986); Michaela Hoenicke Moore, *Know Your Enemy: The American Debate on Nazism, 1933–1945* (Cambridge, UK, 2010); Les K. Adler and Thomas G. Paterson, "Red Fascism: The Merger of Nazi Germany and Soviet Russia in the American Image of Totalitarianism," *American Historical Review* [here after AHR] 75 (April 1970): 1046–64; Abbott Gleason, *Totalitarianism: The Inner History of the Cold War* (New York, 1995); Scott Lucas, *Freedom's War: The American Crusade against the Soviet Union* (New York, 1999); John Fousek, *To Lead the Free World: American Nationalism and the Cultural Roots of the Cold War* (Chapel Hill, NC, 2000).

11. The profound North–South nationalist rupture is the subject of a spurt of recent scholarship: Susan-Mary Grant, *North over South: Northern Nationalism and American Identity in the Antebellum Era* (Lawrence, KS, 2000); Melinda Lawson, *Patriot Fires: Forging a New American Nationalism in the Civil War North*

(Lawrence, KS, 2002); Andre M. Fleche, *The Revolution of 1861: The American Civil War in the Age of Nationalist Conflict* (Chapel Hill, NC, 2012); and Paul Quigley, *Shifting Grounds: Nationalism and the American South, 1848–1865* (New York, 2012).

12. Randolph S. Bourne, "The State" at fair-use.org/randolph-bourne/the-state/ (accessed May 16, 2012).
13. On the first stirrings of the modern US state, see Brian Balogh, *A Government Out of Sight: The Mystery of National Authority in Nineteenth-century America* (New York, 2009); David C. Hendrickson, *Union, Nation, or Empire: The American Debate over International Relations, 1789–1941* (Lawrence, KS, 2009); and Richard Franklin Bensel, *Yankee Leviathan: The Origins of Central State Authority in America, 1859–1877* (New York, 1990). The most helpful general works on later developments are Stephen Skowronek, *Building a New American State: The Expansion of National Administrative Capacities, 1877–1920* (Cambridge, UK, 1982); Lewis L. Gould, *The Modern American Presidency*, 2nd ed. (Lawrence, KS, 2009); and Michael J. Hogan, *A Cross of Iron: Harry S. Truman and the Origins of the National Security State, 1945–1954* (Cambridge, UK, 1998). For a recent exchange over how to conceptualize the American state, see William J. Novak, "The Myth of the 'Weak' American State," AHR 113 (June 2008): 752–72, and the responses by John Fabian Witt, Gary Gerstle, and Julia Adams in AHR 115 (June 2010): 768–800. Brian Balogh, "The State of the State among Historians," *Social Science History* 27 (Fall 2003): 455–63, provides a brief overview of the scholarship relevant to the US case. The literature highlighting the links between state activism overseas and US nationalism is enormous. Recent broad treatments include Paul T. McCartney, *Power and Progress: American National Identity, the War of 1898, and the Rise of American Imperialism* (Baton Rouge, LA, 2006); Frank Ninkovich, *The Wilsonian Century: U.S. Foreign Policy since 1900* (Chicago, 1999); and Susan A. Brewer, *Why America Fights: Patriotism and War Propaganda from the Philippines to Iraq* (New York, 2009).
14. Joyce Appleby, "Recovering America's Historic Diversity: Beyond Exceptionalism," JAH 79 (September 1992): 430 (quote on processes of change), 424 (Hofstadter paraphrase). For an extended assault on the exceptionalist conceit, see Godfrey Hodgson, *The Myth of American Exceptionalism* (New Haven, CT, 2009).
15. Kramer, *Nationalism in Europe and America*, 16.
16. For conceptual grounding on settler colonialism, see Michiel Baud and Willem Van Schendel, "Toward a Comparative History of Borderlands," *Journal of World History* 8 (Fall 1997): 211–42; and Philip D. Curtin, *The World and the West: The European Challenge and the Overseas Response in the Age of Empire* (New York, 2000), 1–17, which distinguishes the settler colony from other imperial forms. For broadly cast works fitting the United States into the settler pattern, see Alan Taylor, *American Colonies* (New York, 2001); and James Belich, *Replenishing the Earth: The Settler Revolution and the Rise of the Anglo-world, 1783–1939* (New York, 2009). See also Jeremy Adelman and Stephen Aron, "From Borderlands to Borders: Empires, Nation-States, and the Peoples in Between in North American History," AHR 104 (June 1999): 814–41, which develops the concept of borderlands as zones of conflict based on three instructive cases; Alison Games, *Migration and the Origins of the English Atlantic World* (Cambridge, MA, 1999), which traces migration patterns from Britain and among its settlements; François

Furstenberg, "The Significance of the Trans-Appalachian Frontier in Atlantic History," AHR 113 (June 2008): 647–77, which emphasizes the impact of imperialism and global warfare; Jack P. Green, "The American Revolution," AHR 105 (February 2000): 93–102, which draws out the political significance of the settler process; Nathan J. Citino, "The Global Frontier: Comparative History and the Frontier-Borderlands Approach," in *Explaining the History of American Foreign Relations*, 2nd edn., ed. Michael J. Hogan and Thomas G. Paterson (New York, 2004), 194–211, which relates borderlands to identity formation; and two fine case studies highlighting the native role in borderland accommodation and conflict, Richard White, *The Middle Ground: Indians, Empires, and Republics in the Great Lakes Region, 1650–1815* (Cambridge, UK, 1991), and Gregory Evans Dowd, *A Spirited Resistance: The North American Indian Struggle for Unity, 1745–1815* (Baltimore, 1992).

17. For authoritative reviews of early nineteenth-century expansion, see Sam W. Haynes and Christopher Morris, eds., *Manifest Destiny and Empire: American Antebellum Expansionism* (College Station, TX, 1997), especially the essays by leading authorities Robert W. Johannsen, Thomas R. Hietala, and Sam W. Haynes.

18. Barrington Moore's observation in his *Social Origins of Dictatorship and Democracy: Lord and Peasant in the Making of the Modern World* (Boston, 1966), 486. See on the broad international trends relevant to US state-building: Raymond Grew, "The Nineteenth-Century European State," in *Statemaking and Social Movements*, ed. Charles Bright and Susan Harding (Ann Arbor, MI, 1984), 83–120; and Christopher Pierson, *The Modern State*, 3rd edn. (London, 2011), a helpful primer.

14

Nation Branding

Jessica C. E. Gienow-Hecht[1]

The central subject of international history is the analysis of relationships among people and states. Although power has traditionally constituted a central category in the study of international relations, culture represents a more recent trend, and since the 1980s there has been a significant movement among historians of foreign relations to integrate the study of culture into the history of international relations. While enriching historical research, this trend has also compartmentalized the study of international relations into those who study "real power" and those who study what is often called "soft power."

This chapter will outline the research on cultural relations as it has developed in the study of international history and discuss the challenges that have arisen due to a paucity of theoretical engagement. The chapter will then develop the concept of Nation Branding as a way to meet these challenges, and also show how it can be applied to the study of the past.

In the lingo of political history, power (political, military, economic) is the ability to make others do what one wants them to do. Culture, in turn, defines what a person or a people want, for others and for themselves.[2] Culture, that is, has a direct impact on the form, the function, and the content of power.

At the same time, culture and power are neither inextricably nor hierarchically intertwined but can exist independently of and oppose each other. Nations may be politically weak but culturally very powerful, and vice versa. For example, Greek culture is known and admired worldwide but the country's political power in the international arena is rather limited. Canada is a diplomatic key player but few people can tell what constitutes Canadian culture. Cultural relations may even have a way of improving while political relations go sour. In the 1930s, thanks to Japan's vigorous cultural diplomacy offensive, US appreciation of Japanese civilization intensified while political relations worsened because of conflicts over China.[3] While Iran's cultural diplomacy, focusing on the treasures of Persian civilization, meets with acclaim abroad, international concern remains regarding the country's nuclear program.

Hegemonic power remains incomplete unless cultural and political power converge and reinforce each other. For this reason, definitions of power often include notions of "influence" (a form of indirect power) and "recognition" – not just as a sovereign political entity but also as an international key player. Nations often bolster their cultural power in an effort to realize aspirations of non-violent political power that have not yet been achieved. Power, in short, does *not* merely encompass the ability to tell others what to do. There is also power in being respected and listened to by virtue of one's political and cultural influence regardless of the nation's military or economic might.

This is why scholars of international relations have recently expanded the analysis of power to include "representation." To borrow the discourse of drama studies, representation is the theatrical display of power.[4] It mobilizes people, visual images, and sounds, all deployed to demonstrate power, as in a military victory parade, the architecture of an embassy, or a ceremony such as a presidential inauguration.[5] All of these reflect the desire for power: either for power that has not yet been achieved or for the solidification of existing power. Recognition requires representation or, in the words of drama studies, theatrical display. As on a stage, power has to be visible, accessible, perceptible, tangible, and, ultimately, convincing in order to exist and continuously assert itself. Power and sensuality, historians Sönke Kunkel and Andrew Rotter have argued, are inextricably linked to each other.[6]

All of this is to say that we can never talk about power as a given. Rather, we need to ask: who is projecting what kind of power and who else wants power by exerting what means? Nation Branding can help us grasp the complexity in the exercise of, and longing for, influence as well as in the organization and marketing of power and power aspirations.[7]

Since the 1990s, terrorism, racism, gender studies, ideology, milieu, diseases, medical innovations, human rights, tourism, and the role of non governmental organizations have developed into standard themes in the study of the history of international relations. These topics all rest on the assumption that the state is only one of many actors, and policy is only one of many forms of liaison and interaction. Much of this historiography has developed in North America. From the deans of culture and international history, including Frank Ninkovich and Akira Iriye, as well as their many colleagues, we have learned a great deal about the significance and role played by tourists, transnational groups, environmentalists, painters, bankers, entrepreneurs, doctors, and journalists in the forging of national identity abroad.[8]

But the new international history has also presented us with a new problem: what to do with the analysis of power? Hegemonic power and the imbalance of power used to be at the center of diplomacy as well as diplomatic history.[9] The new international history, however, has revised and complicated the investigation of power in the sense that power is not always foregrounded.

No field reveals this change as obviously as the research on culture in foreign relations.[10] Since the 1990s, the "cultural turn" has focused on the analysis of culture as an essential condition in the relations between two or more countries, either as the milieu, the instrument, or the motivation for action. Much research has been dedicated to the analysis of cultural foreign relations, which is termed "cultural diplomacy" and "cultural transfer."[11]

Four different themes can be distinguished in the historiography of international cultural relations: First, is the nature and function of actors who implemented the agendas of the superpowers by crafting programs to win over foreign audiences. This theme focuses on decision-making processes and the specific "making" of cultural policy within individual organizations. For example, in her analysis of the United States Information Agency (USIA), Laura Belmonte has pointed to the significance of internal intrigues and tugs-of-war within the US government over the future direction of cultural diplomacy during the early part of the Cold War. Likewise, Nicholas Cull has emphasized the ongoing struggle between members of the USIA and its outlets, such as Voice of America, to adhere to "the truth" in the face of heated internal criticism.[12]

A second theme concerns the function of cultural diplomacy as an alternative to foreign policy. Much of this research focuses on client states, such as the Netherlands and Poland, as well as the role of neutral states, such as Finland and Austria. In Hungary, French historian Anikó Macher observes, government officials worked hard to renew prewar ties to the West by autonomously bolstering cultural contacts, despite the country's political affiliation with the Soviet Union. In Denmark, the local population, liberated by the British, not the US army, for years failed to recognize the United States as a great power and identified with British culture. Such works show that client as well as neutral states often re-accentuated or challenged democratic superpower programs abroad and developed a dynamic on their own, especially when official diplomatic ties were severed or truncated.[13]

A third research theme focuses on informal cross-border relations, especially those of private individual actors and organizations. Studies on transnational networks in the field of medicine, music, and human rights, for example, demonstrate that actors on both sides of the Iron Curtain realized the continuous need for cultural interaction, information sharing, and other informal exchanges in spite of the tense and confrontational climate of the Cold War. Thus, Erez Manela's analysis of East–West medical cooperation in the battle against smallpox testifies to the osmosis of the Iron Curtain when health imperatives so demanded. Likewise, musicologist Peter Schmelz's analysis of the unpublished correspondence between Ukrainian conductor Igor Blazhkov and West German music writer Fred K. Prieberg in the 1960s introduces historians to the idea of an "intimate diplomacy" – an informal exchange between artists at a time when the East–West barrier seemed impermeable.[14]

Finally, the fourth and most recent theme focuses on the role of cultural relations before and after the Cold War. Much of this research has taken its cue from actor-network theory, global history, or both, and it typically implies cultural paradigms, such as exchange, understanding, transmission, imitation, and performativity. These studies imply that such actors as tourists, marriage brokers, conductors, painters, journalists, writers, and bankers may form an international relation sui generis, either in the absence of the state or beside and beyond the government. Thus, Justin Hart explains how cultural diplomacy not only helped contain communism but actually originated prior to the Cold War and reflected an effort to establish the United States as a postcolonial empire.[15] Frank Ninkovich has shown how educated nineteenth-century Americans were far more aware of the world beyond their borders (and not just Europe!) than was previously known, reading about politics in Turkistan or sociopolitical quarrels in the Far East and forging a culture of internationalism long before the United States became internationalist.[16]

These four themes investigate the question of power and influence in very different ways. While the quest for influence (and manipulation) clearly plays a role in the first two approaches, the analysis of action milieus from the perspective of cultural history dominates investigations focusing on simultaneous scenarios of conflict and cooperation.

This side of cultural contacts – that is, culture as power – has received little attention beyond the debate over "US cultural imperialism," a concept coined during the Cold War.[17] "Cultural imperialism" investigated the hegemonic influence of American (or Western) products and ideas. Originally begun as a postwar "public" debate among politicians, journalists, and scholars, the discussion focused on the political advantage of cultural diplomacy and actually called for more information on the United States and cultural artifacts abroad. Indeed, many "cold warriors" lamented the absence of an aggressive cultural foreign policy among US officials and pointed to the Soviet Union as an unwelcome "role model." Consequently, in the years following VE-Day, the US government created a number of proselytizing organizations and programs, such as the United States Information Agency and the Fulbright exchange program, that aspired to export American culture, including literature, music, and art, abroad.

In the 1960s and 1970s, the topic of cultural transfer merged with the emerging discussion over US imperialism. Emphasizing the economic and psychological implications of culture, many scholars seemed to imply that there was too much American culture abroad. A new generation of observers, the "critics of cultural imperialism," interpreted the export of American culture as thinly veiled global economic exploitation. One of the most sensational and path-breaking accounts came from Armand Mattelart, professor of mass communications and ideology at the University of Chile, and Ariel Dorfman, a literary critic and novelist. Both believed that in an effort to protect US economic interests in Chile, the CIA funded and fostered an arsenal of psychological warfare devices to influence the minds of the Chilean people. In their book, *Para leer al pato Donald (How to Read Donald Duck)*, Dorfman and Mattelart berated Hollywood's manipulated version of reality and cautioned Latin Americans against US cultural manipulation.[18]

In the late 1980s, counter critics disputed the concept of cultural imperialism. Rather than seeing the spread of American and Western culture as "imperialism," they interpreted the phenomenon as a multifaceted process of negotiation among ethnic, regional, and national groups. Scholars focusing on local case studies found that foreign audiences did not submissively accept the products of Western culture. Instead, they often displayed mixtures of active and passive resistance to imported commodities and culture.[19] Inspired by visions of globalization, a second group of scholars rejected notions of agency in the study of cultural imperialism altogether. As Frederick Buell phrased it, for almost every academic discipline cultural hybridity was becoming the norm.[20] After about 2000, looking at culture as an expression of hegemonic influence passed from favor among scholars studying cultural transfer.

Scholars of the "cultural turn" thus face two basic challenges. The first is to link their work to traditional and still important issues of power in international relationships. Too frequently, adherents of the traditional and cultural approaches view each other as antagonistic or as irrelevant. The second challenge is to think about a horizon for interpretation. What is, in essence, the concern of international history after the cultural turn and what do we do with the question of power?

Modern psychology emphasizes that power has a social and an interpersonal or intergroup component. Power has to be made sensually accessible by performance (on the display side) and by reception or impression (on the receiving end).[21] In addition to power, whose actuality is evidenced by display and recognition, there is power as an object of desire – power that does not yet exist. The question is: What kind of mechanisms, strategies, information, and agents do we consistently find when considering different epochs, regions, and people? How do we grasp this complexity and not lose sight of the relevance of power in international relations? The concept of Nation Branding offers a way to grapple with these questions.

Nation Branding has become a central term for political decision-makers, cultural diplomats, bureaucrats, and marketing and advertising experts who are concerned with cultural policy. The Center for Public Diplomacy at the University of Southern California has reported a steady interest in Nation Branding since 2005, so much so that the Council of Foreign Relations felt the need to investigate the phenomenon and its significance for foreign policy, in 2007.[22] Think tanks, such publications as *Competitive Identity*, *Brand America*, *Marketing Places*, *DestiNation Branding*, *Trading Identities*, and such journals as *Place Branding and Public Diplomacy* examine how countries as diverse as Iraq and Zimbabwe view themselves, how they wish to be seen, who is in control of the image and which role decision-makers seek to achieve in the international arena.

What does Nation Branding do? Branding, in general, is supposed to create a positive image of the product, be that a drink or a hotel chain, and stimulate a "desire" to own or consume it. At its best, branding helps market – and ultimately sell – not just the product it promotes but a way of life. The product, that is, becomes the key to that life. Like products, different national brands project different lifestyles and values, and like products, these images change over time.

Nation Branding starts with the assumption that there is a close link between the geographical setting of a nation and its image (such as its viewpoints, customs, culinary specialties, specific sounds, landscapes, and agricultural or technological products). Nation Branding also assumes that both aspects influence each other and can be used to promote each other.

Nation Branding experts, like diplomats, believe that the political and economic success of any given country depends on that country's reputation and credibility. They pick specific tools from the advertising industry, then develop strategies focusing on marketing techniques, including the continuous repetition of specific peculiarities of the product/state and the creation of a distinctive "corporate identity."

This roster determines the framework of questions relating to Nation Branding: Which characteristics do image campaigns repeatedly stress? How do they relate to the reality of the state? Who are the target groups, how can they be reached and how can the state be marketed among those groups? Who could best serve as agents and actors of marketing?

Nation Branding assumes a direct link between self-representation and the desire for influence. It does not distinguish between a presumably "democratic" or "positive" cultural diplomacy designed to create "mutual understanding" and "manipulative," "negative" propaganda. Likewise, it is irrelevant whether a state is pre-modern or modern, democratic or authoritarian. Nation Branding, in other words, is a matter of timeless aspiration.

The Nation Branding approach illuminates five different aspects across time, space, and ideology. First, it shows how a given state seeks to create a marketable image that may help to achieve goals that, for whatever reasons, cannot or should not be reached by other means, such as violence or economic sanctions. Second, Nation Branding's focus on concept and structure allows us to compare case studies from different eras and regions that, in the past, used to be distinct (e.g. early modern Spain and contemporary United States). Third, Nation Branding does not prioritize either state or nonstate actors but allows for a fluid interaction between the two. Fourth, Nation Branding considers how imagery is constructed by focusing on three factors: perception, communication, and action/actors. Finally, the concept operates with an open definition of the term "nation." Places and nations derive their existence by intentional external self-representation beyond and within the borders of a state.[23]

As a concept, Nation Branding can best be applied to the history of modernity. Both its terminology and its orientation toward marketing techniques link it to the modern national state. During the transition from the early modern to the modern period, European and North American understandings of nation and power increasingly shifted from individual ("the king") to abstract notions of rule ("the government"). This change included a qualitative, epic change that was central for the modern development of Nation Branding. Abstract state power – rather than personal power – attributed vague points of identification and distinction to the nation, emphasized its significance for people inside and outside of the nation, and, thus, made it more marketable at the same time.

Historians have stressed how this constellation intensified latent international conflicts; they have argued how revised visions of the nation triggered much of the dramatic treaty policy and secret diplomacy of the late nineteenth century. France, Great Britain, and Germany, in particular, sought to increase existing alliances by way of cultural liaison or evoke affinity by cultural display. Informal actors played a central role in this scenario: non-governmental associations, people, entrepreneurs, academics, clerics, aristocrats, intellectuals, writers, and language teachers.

For example, German exchange scholars abroad saw themselves as representatives of the "German *Reich*," more so than representatives of the German Kaiser (even though they owed their travel tickets to the latter). Philosopher Eugen Kühnemann, a renowned expert on Kant and Schiller, traveled to the United States in 1905 to tip public sympathy toward Germany and to lecture local students, faculty, and the community of German-Americans on the "global empire of German thought" ("*Weltreich deutschen Geistes*").[24]

None of the nineteenth-century traveling private actors had a state mandate for cultural contact and exchange. Nevertheless, their activities had a profound diplomatic effect: they addressed the discrepancy between foreign and self-perceptions of the Germans, the French, the British, the Italians, the Americans, the Russians, and the Japanese in the world. These people were the leading cultural diplomats of the nineteenth century. Their goals were heterogeneous, ranging from the French "*mission civilisatrice*" in the colonies to Japan's self-induced modernization programs inspired by foreign voyage. But no matter what their intentions, all of them acted willy-nilly on behalf of and in the interest of the state.

Here we can see how the concept of Nation Branding can help us to grasp various forms of state marketing in history. Nation Branding seeks to promote the popularity or attractiveness of a country in the world. Formal or informal actors resort to communication and advertising strategies, notably brand management, to promote the portrayal and perception of an attractive actor for future cooperation, such as economic exports, foreign investments, political trust, and tourism. Nation Branding considers existing impressions as a point of departure. From that starting point, the current geographical, political, economic, legal, and cultural structures of a state and its society can be mobilized to improve a national image.

This approach facilitates an analysis of the many patriotic individuals and organizations of the late nineteenth century. Many of those were deeply nationalist and dedicated to the goal of exporting a positive image of the homeland. In England, for example, Cecil Rhodes established a prestigious exchange program for students, hoping to consolidate British rule in the world.[25]

These nonstate activities quickly developed an internal self-dynamism that governments both appreciated and disliked. On the positive side, nonstate actors and activities did not incur any administrative or financial costs. In contrast, they promised many international contacts, prestige, and, in the long run, economic advantages. On the downside, these actors and organizations quickly developed ambitions and a vision of their own. Policymakers and administrators in Paris, London, and Berlin began to fear that private actions could be more harmful than useful to the interests of the state. Most of all, they worried about the independence and radicalism on the part of nonstate organizations.

This tense relationship between the public and the private is key to understanding the diffusion of power in the struggle for representation. Various groups of public and private actors battled over which images of the nation should be marketed, who would do the marketing, and how it would be accomplished. Individual perceptions, interests, and policies within a country often contradicted and clashed with one another as well as with various foreign perceptions. Private actors sometimes threatened to turn marginal diplomatic conflicts into a deadly confrontation in which they were privileged to make their letters, pamphlets, and articles sing to save the honor of the nation. Officials concluded there was little they could do about such nongovernmental activities.[26]

Thus, nonstate actors could prove both useful and harmful to the state. Their actions ran the risk of contradicting state policy; first because the discourse and the vision they established rarely overlapped with state interest, and, second, because the state had little control over the actions of private individuals abroad. A lack of state engagement always implied a lack of state control. Even if cultural relations and cultural diplomacy did not constitute a central field of action, even if the state officially declared that cultural relations were the responsibility of nonstate actors, the state had to cope with the consequences, including international tensions and possibly even war.

State administrators changed their view profoundly after World War I, when representation of the nation became a principal task of governments. Germany, Great Britain, the United States, and others created divisions endowed with the job of managing cultural relations and promoting a positive image in the world. The German cultural division in the Foreign Office, the British Council, as well as the US Office for Coordination of Commercial and Cultural Relations between the American Republics all testified to an increased interest in national image management on the part of state officials. In the 1930s, authoritarian states likewise tapped into branding mechanisms – most evidently "corporate identity" – featuring gigantic billboard posters, jingles, and mass advertisements.

Many of the cultural and information programs devised during the Cold War were not new, but the actors and the structure of these endeavors changed fundamentally after 1918. After World War I, the state increasingly sought to control and connect various channels of international cultural communications. Why did governments engage in Nation Branding if they had not done so before? First, during World War I administrators believed that their laissez-faire attitude in the field of culture had perhaps created more antagonism than friendly cultural exchange. As a result, in the 1920s and 1930s policymakers changed their views on the relationship between culture and the state quite profoundly, depending on their country's ideological preference. This change came with the realization that the nation's brand had a direct impact not only on the diplomatic process but on the constitution of power itself.

Second, policymakers became convinced that governmentally appointed bureaucrats were better equipped than private individuals to harmonize foreign and self-perceptions to the advantage of the latter. In many ways, state-run cultural diplomacy did not merely reflect the desire to "correct" negative images abroad but also to counter negative images created by domestic private actors abroad. This realization constituted a revolutionary change in the structure of cultural relations in Europe and the Americas: the state became the advertising agency for the nation.

In the foregoing review of the literature on "cultural imperialism," we can clearly see how the Cold War further expanded the state's involvement in Nation Branding by establishing sizeable information and propaganda programs, exchange venues, and permanent cultural relations in the name of the security state. Both American and Soviet administrators grasped that cultural identity and cultural attractiveness were key to winning prospective client states to their side.[27] Cultural programs, in other words, were designed to win the hearts and minds of people around the world as clients of one or the other power. Cultural productions mutated into powerful instruments of exchange and geostrategy, but also of informal encounters in the form of exhibitions, stipends, plays, and travel programs.

Although students of US cultural diplomacy during the Cold War are familiar with these advertising campaigns, they tend to downplay three things that assume special significance when put into historical context. First, US efforts at Nation Branding represented the continuation of a historical development, in which the United States formed the tail, rather than the head, of self-representation. Second, cultural diplomacy only constituted a small portion of US Nation Branding. For one thing, a multitude of often contradictory aspirations, contested domestic notions of US power, and internal struggles over identity complemented and frequently challenged governmental programs and actions. Many of the ideas hatched by the private–public Cold War consensus never saw the light of day.[28] For another, venues of cultural diplomacy came increasingly under attack as a result of the above-mentioned charges of "US cultural imperialism." Much of US cultural diplomacy as well the domestic criticism it faced, that is, constituted an imitation of what other nations had done and experienced before.

Third, and most importantly, much of what was said and propagated during the Cold War had less to do with that conflict than with the ways in which US interest groups wished to be perceived in a world of growing threats and looming wars. In doing so, they did not differ much from previous actors in Europe. The discussion among these interest groups reflected a defining debate over American identity and consumer capitalism in an international context that preceded the Cold War, and continued thereafter. Programs echoed the desire to inform people at home and abroad what was special and important about US identity and what legitimized America's rise to the top.

The concept of Nation Branding enables scholars to weave together and make sense of these different topics and case studies. Cold War propaganda developed in the context of a continuum spanning centuries. It had less to do with the Cold War proper than with the development of the modern nation-state and its desire to display power in an iconic and marketable fashion. And as the number of government officials charged with the crafting of an international image grew, they encountered increasing resistance and protests associated with democratic societies.

Cultural conflict at home hastened the collapse of state structures that were losing their purpose as the Cold War ended. Marketing strategies and agencies were changing: the branding of the nation became increasingly a task outsourced to nonstate professionals – professionals from the corporate sector with an expertise in branding and marketing. Corporate funding for governmentally organized tours of artists and intellectuals had already existed during the Cold War. But in much of the Western world around the millennium, states resorted to positions not unlike the scenario of great power politics before World War I. States again turned to the private sector by asking nonstate actors to run the brand management of the nation abroad. For instance, the US State Department contacted such foundations as the Brookings Institution, universities such as Princeton, and enterprises such as GM in an effort to win their support for the promotion of cultural relations.

In the twenty-first century, international advertising agencies compete not only to brand consumer products but also entire countries, both old and new. While Scholz and Friends in Berlin, for example, have sought to strengthen Germany's international reputation with the slogan "Land of Ideas," Saatchi and Saatchi in New York devised the "Young Europeans" campaign designed to put Kosovo on the map. The advantages of putting cultural self-representation into the hands of private actors echo nineteenth-century politics: private actors are presumably cheaper, smarter, more professional and self-sufficient. In case of a glitch, they cannot be held politically responsible.

This trajectory cannot be explained by approaches such as state-run cultural diplomacy or public diplomacy. Least of all does the degree of state agency provide a consistent element. Nation Branding allows us to grasp these common features while, at the same time, allowing for the flexibility of other factors, including ideological intention or the absence/presence of government actors. Nation Branding also enables us to see the commonalities among self-representations and cultural relations across various époques.

Nation Branding reflects a turn in our perception of state self-representation, cultural relations, and cultural diplomacy. Since at least the nineteenth century, the nation has developed into a brand product, making its claim to legitimacy by means of imagery, ideas, and sound. Over time, there may have been many forms of national self-representation and interaction. Often they competed with each other, pursuing vastly different goals. In this context, power as a category does not simply encompass one state's ability to make another state do what it wants. Next to it, there is power as a source over visions of self-representation and power as an object of desire.

Students interested in cultural display, transfer, and relations need to make sense of international cultural relations and self-representation in the context of power and imagery. The model of Nation Branding allows us to do so in four different ways: First, it helps us pursue the analysis of the longue durée in international cultural relations. Second, Nation Branding offers a much more nuanced understanding of the historicity of cultural exchange and self-representation as well as the patterns, risks, and challenges of state and nonstate cultural diplomacy. Third, it enables us to analyze past and present forms of national orchestrations of power and attraction beyond time, space, specific actor groups, and cultural divides. Fourth, Nation Branding offers an open and comparative handling of the term "nation" in the context of international history that may benefit both the now dormant debate on nationalism and clarify what we mean when we talk about an "inter-national relation."

In sum, Nation Branding can help us to access and analyze practices of international cultural relations over time and space and to understand the interplay among nation, power, culture, actors, and perceptions. Similar to other recent concepts introduced for the analysis of power relations delineated in this book, Nation Branding can be projected backward to help us analyze the history of international cultural relations and transfer across time and space.

NOTES

1. My heartfelt gratitude goes to the editors of the present volume, Michael Hogan and Frank Costigliola, whose comments and criticism went far beyond the call of duty. Thank you also to Michael Krenn and Justin Hart for earlier readings of a much longer draft of this chapter.

2. Akira Iriye, "Culture and Power: International Relations as Intercultural Relations," *Diplomatic History* 3, 2 (2007): 115–128.
3. John Gripentrog, "The Diplomacy of Art: Japan's Cultural Offensive in the United States, 1933–1937," *Pacific Historical Review*, 84, 4 (November, 2015), 478–516, November 2015.
4. Andreas Kotte, *Theaterwissenschaft: Eine Einführung* [Drama Studies: An Introduction] (Cologne, 2005). On performance studies, see Richard Schechner, *Performance Theory* (London/New York 2003); W.B. Worthen, *Drama. Between Poetry and Performance* (Chichester, 2010).
5. Sebastian Jobs, *Welcome Home, Boys! Military Victory Parades in New York City, 1899–1946* (Frankfurt am Main, 2012).
6. Sönke Kunkel, "Iconic Empire: The United States and the Rise of the Visual Age, 1961–1974," Dissertation, Jacobs University Bremen, 2011; Andrew Rotter, "Empire of the Senses: How Seeing, Hearing, Smelling, Tasting, and Touching Shaped Imperial Encounters," *Diplomatic History* 35, 1 (January 2011), 3–19. For more on the relevance of drama studies, notably the stage concept in international history, see Jessica Gienow-Hecht, "The World Is Ready To Listen: Symphony Orchestras and the Global Performance of America," *Diplomatic History* 36, 1 (January, 2012): 17–28.
7. Nation Branding is not to be confused with nation-building, the outside effort to create new states in fact. Francis Fukuyama, *Nation-building: Beyond Afghanistan and Iraq* (Baltimore, 2006).
8. Akira Iriye, "Culture and International History," *Explaining the History of American Foreign Relations*, ed. Michael Hogan and Thomas Paterson (Cambridge, 2004), 241–56; Frank Ninkovich, *Global Dawn: The Cultural Foundation of American Internationalism* (Cambridge 2009); Christopher Endy, *Cold War Holidays: American Tourism in France* (Chapel Hill 2004); Barbara Keys, *Globalizing Sports: National Rivalry and International Community in the 1930s* (Cambridge, 2006); Thorsten Schulz, *Anfänge globaler Umweltpolitik: Umweltsicherheit in der internationalen Politik (1969–1975)* [The Origins of Global Environmental Policy: Environmental Security in International Politics (1969–1975)] (Munich, 2013).
9. See, for example, Jon Jacobson, "Is There a New International History of the 1920s?" *American Historical Review* 88 (June 1983): 617–45.
10. Frank Ninkovich, *The Diplomacy of Ideas: U.S. Foreign Policy and Cultural Relations, 1938–1950* (New York, 1981).
11. Kenneth Osgood and Brian Etheridge (eds.), *The United States and Public Diplomacy: New Directions in Cultural and International History* (Leiden 2010); Manuela Aguilar, *Cultural Diplomacy and Foreign Policy: German–American Relations, 1955–1968* (New York, 1996); Jessica Gienow-Hecht, *Searching for a Cultural Diplomacy* (Oxford/New York, 2010); Gienow-Hecht and Schumacher, *Culture and International History* (New York, 2003).
12. Laura Belmonte, *Selling America: U.S. Propaganda and the Cold War* (Philadelphia 2009); Nick Cull, *The Cold War and the United States Information Agency: American Propaganda and Public Diplomacy, 1945–1989* (Cambridge, 2009); Jonathan Rosenberg, *How Far the Promised Land? World Affairs and the American Civil Rights Movement from the First World War to Vietnam* (Princeton, 2006); Gienow-Hecht, "Cultural Transfer," *Explaining the History of American Foreign Relations* (Cambridge, 2004), 257–78.

13. Anikó Macher, "Cultural Diplomacy in Hungary from 1957 to 1963 – Echoes of Western Cultural Activity in a Communist Country," in Gienow-Hecht and Donfried, *Searching for a Cultural Diplomacy* (New York and Oxford, 2010), 75–108; Niels Arne Sorensen and Klaus Petersen, "Ameri-Danes and Pro-American Anti-Americans: Cultural Americanization and Anti-Americanism in Denmark after 1945," in *The Americanization of Europe: Culture, Diplomacy, and Anti-Americanism after 1945*, ed. Alexander Stephan (New York, 2007), 115–46.
14. Erez Manela, "A Pox on Your Narrative: Writing Disease Control into Cold War History," *Diplomatic History* 34:2 (April 2010): 299–323; Peter Schmelz, "Intimate Histories of the Musical Cold War: Igor Blazhkov's Unofficial Diplomacy," in *Music and International History*, ed. Jessica Gienow-Hecht (New York and Oxford, 2015), 189–225.
15. Justin Hart, *Empire of Ideas: The Origins of Public Diplomacy and the Transformation of U.S. Foreign Policy* (Oxford, 2013).
16. Ninkovich, *Global Dawn*; Cooper, *Informal Ambassadors*; Kristin Hoganson, *Consumers' Imperium: The Global Production of American Domesticity, 1865–1920* (Chapel Hill, 2007).
17. For a review, see Jessica C. E. Gienow-Hecht, "Shame on US: Academics, Cultural Transfer, and the Cold War: A Critical Review," *Diplomatic History* 24, 3 (Summer 2000): 465–494.
18. Armand Mattelart and Ariel Dorfman, *Para leer al pato Donald* (La Habana, 1971) [translated edition: *How To Read Donald Duck: Imperialist Ideology in Disney Comic* (New York, 1975)].
19. Bassam Tibi, "Culture and Knowledge: The Politics of Islamization of Knowledge as a Postmodern Project? The Fundamentalist Claim to De-Westernization," *Theory, Culture & Society* 12 (1995): 1–24.
20. Frederick Buell, *National Culture and the New Global System* (Baltimore, 1994), 6–7.
21. Ana Guinote and Theresa K. Vescio (eds.), *The Social Psychology of Power* (New York, 2010).
22. L. H. Teslik, "Nation Branding Explained," Diplomacy and Statecraft / Council on Foreign Relations (November 9, 2007), www.cfr.org/diplomacy-and-statecraft/nation-branding-explained/p14776 (accessed March 12, 2014).
23. Benedict Anderson, *Imagined Communities: Reflections on the Origin and Spread of Nationalism* (London, New York, 1983).
24. Thomas Löwer, *Deutsche Professoren in den USA während des Ersten Weltkrieges. Eugen Kühnemann, Hugo Münsterberg und Kuno Francke und ihr Werben für die Deutsche Sache* [German Professors in the U.S. during World War One: Eugen Kühnemann, Hugo Münsterberg and Kuno Francke and their Advertising of the German Cause](Norderstedt, 2003).
25. Thomas J. Schaeper and Kathleen Schaeper, *Cowboys into Gentlemen: Rhodes Scholars, Oxford, and the Creation of an American Elite* (New York, 1998).
26. Jessica Gienow-Hecht, "Cultural Diplomacy and Civil Society Since 1850 or the Anomaly of the Cold War," in Osgood and Etheridge, *Washington and Beyond*, 29–56.
27. David Caute, *The Dancer Defects: The Struggle for Cultural Diplomacy during the Cold War* (Oxford, New York, 2003).
28. Kenneth Osgood, *Total Cold War: Eisenhower's Secret Propaganda Battle at Home and Abroad* (Lawrence, 2006).

15

Shades of sovereignty: racialized power, the United States and the world

Paul A. Kramer

The segregated diners along Maryland's Route 40 were always somebody's problem – mothers packing sandwiches for a daytrip to the nation's capital, Jim Crow on their minds – but they were not always John F. Kennedy's problem. That changed in the early 1960s, when African diplomats began arriving to the United States to present their credentials to the United Nations and the White House. Between the high-modernist universalism of the former and the neo-classical, republican universalism of the latter, at just about the place where ambassadors got hungry, lay a scattering of gaudy, ramshackle restaurants straddling an otherwise bleak stretch of highway. As the motoring diplomats discovered to their shock, the diners excluded black people in ways that turned out to be global: whatever their importance to US foreign policy, African economic ministers and cultural attaches received no diplomatic immunity.[1]

The incoming Kennedy administration soon confronted an international scandal, as the officials filed formal complaints and US and overseas editors ran with the story. "Human faces, black-skinned and white, angry words and a humdrum reach of U. S. highway," read an article in *Life*, "these are the raw stuff of a conflict that reached far out from America in to the world." Kennedy, reluctant to engage the black freedom struggle except where it intersected with Cold War concerns, established an Office of the Special Protocol Service to mediate: its staff caught flak, spoke to newspapers, and sat down with Route 40's restaurateurs, diner by diner, making the case that serving black people was in the United States' global interests. High-level officials argued for the desegregating of Maryland's public accommodations for both visiting dignitaries and African Americans. "Let me say with a Georgia accent," stated Secretary of State Dean Rusk, "that we cannot solve this problem if it requires a diplomatic passport to claim the rights of an American citizen."[2] In the context of Cold War rivalry and African decolonization, Route 40's petty apartheid was no longer just its own. Racialized power had a geopolitics; one that had suddenly brought the President to within two degrees of separation from the owners of the Double-T Diner.[3]

This chapter explores intersections between the politics of racialized difference and the United States' geopolitical histories, and the rich varieties of ways that historians have mapped them.[4] The assertion that the United States' place in the world had something – perhaps everything – to do with race would have been uncontroversial for those who dominated the nation's early political, economic, and social life: slave-based capitalist empire, the displacement and elimination of Native peoples, and a sense of America's Anglo-Saxon roots and destinies were widely understood to be foundational to and defining of the United States itself.[5] Nor would this statement have surprised Native and enslaved peoples who a paid high price for US national-imperial expansion. From the mid-nineteenth century forward, it was the activism and scholarship of the critics of racialized supremacy, both those who suffered under it directly and their allies, who inaugurated the hard work – still unfinished – of shifting race from essentialized, ontological reality and moral norm to social construction and political problem. A rising, critical consciousness developed of the ways that racial systems in the United States formed an integral part of what W. E. B. Du Bois called a global belt of white supremacies, sparked by transnational abolitionism, and intensifying in particular where the expansion of a black public sphere and African Americans' increasingly worldly horizons challenged exploitative, aggressively hierarchical European and US colonialisms at the turn of the twentieth century.[6] By the early Cold War, a sense that the most egregious, visible, and terroristic faces of the US racial state – if not racialized social inequality generally – were, in an interconnected world, an international public relations problem in need of technocratic management, had shifted from outsider politics to establishment circles, including presidential administrations.

But this awareness – vibrant in activist networks, intellectual circles and the black academy – was, for an extremely long time, segregated from the fortified precincts of US diplomatic history. This was not so surprising. With its Eurocentric, Atlanticist orientation, elite-centered methodologies, and aspirational ties to the State Department (an agency with its own deep history of exclusivity, including racial line-drawing), early diplomatic history embarked from confident assumptions about global hierarchy that were inhospitable, where they were not actively hostile, to critical accounts of that hierarchy, including of its racialized dimensions.[7] This said, there were early works that, in recounting the history of US–Japan relations and the centrality of struggles over migration to those relations, necessarily emphasized the politics of racialized exclusion at their center; while important foundations, these works did not establish race as an analytic category more widely.[8]

By contrast, mid-to-late twentieth-century scholarship in the history of US foreign relations witnessed a variety of dramatic openings when it came to the role of race.[9] They were ushered in, first and foremost, by activists and intellectuals during the Vietnam War era that linked anti-racism and anti-imperialism, and critiques of American power to anti-colonial struggles throughout the world.[10] In the long wake of these struggles, late twentieth-century historians of the United States' role in the world began stressing the role of "nonstate" actors (including anti-racist activists); the social-historical experiences of groups that had, up to then, been marginalized within diplomatic historiography, especially African Americans, Latinos and Asian-Americans; and culturalist methods that, in their late twentieth-century modes, foregrounded questions of meaning, identity, and power. Given the centrality of the Cold War to US foreign relations historiography, and African Americans to the study of race in the United States, it made sense that the foundational works connecting race and diplomatic history established the fact of Jim Crow as an international embarrassment in the post-1945 period, and black and anti-racist activists' varied uses of this reality, revelations that were bold and of enduring impact. Especially since historians' discovery of this "Cold War civil rights" nexus, race has (against long odds) emerged as a major analytic category in US foreign relations historiography, figuring both in works that foreground it and, just as importantly, in scholarship with fundamental concerns that lie elsewhere.[11]

Specifically, this chapter will discuss eight domains of scholarship, among many possible others: histories treating the racializing of sovereignty; policymakers' approaches to race; race in cultural histories of American perceptions of the world; the making of transnational racial solidarities; transfers of racial and anti-racial practices; the racial politics of migration and border control; intersections of race and capitalism; and race in US militarization, war-making, and occupation. This chapter's title has two intended implications. First, "shades" suggests the ways that the racialized politics of social differentiation were and are, to important degrees, reflections of – shadows cast by – conflicts over geopolitical questions: who legitimately governed whom, by what means, in the name of what principles, and toward what ends; about the meanings of nationhood and statehood in a globalizing world; and about definitions of and boundaries between legitimate and illegitimate violence. While conventional historiographic approaches have plausibly prioritized the causal power of race in shaping American geopolitics – particularly as the impetus, template or ready-made rationale for imperial projects – my approach here takes seriously the equally plausible but less explored proposition that struggles over the United States' presence and power in the world, unfolding in transnational, imperial, and global contexts, played decisive roles in shaping Americans' notions of racialized difference and its political meanings.

Second, "shades" is meant to evoke degrees, gradations, and variations, as an explicit challenge to stark, counter-productive dichotomies that characterize literatures on both race (white/non-white, racism/anti-racism, racial/civic, exclusion/inclusion) and US foreign relations history (realism/idealism, culture/power, domestic/foreign, empire/democracy). The most generative literature in this field, I'll suggest, exposes the limits of these binaries by looking at the varied, evolving, and conflicting ways that Americans have made sense of their transnational encounters, including in racialized ways; the wide array of US geopolitical projects Americans have engaged in, and the complex, multidirectional ways these histories inform each other.

To begin, the chapter attends to some necessary definitional work. Both despite and because of decades of struggle, race remains hard to pin down.[12] Discussions of race have long been characterized by imprecise, essentializing definitions and intense, moral-political charge – themselves related – as well as identitarian criteria for participation, but more than anything else, by the overwhelming ideological need to cast race as liberalism's other, whatever else it may be: in the case of the United States, at least, a language of "dilemmas" and "contradictions" has long rendered antithetical things that are not, in fact, opposites. In these classic, liberal formulations, race is contrary or external to the ordinary operations of capitalist social relations and national civic membership, and will wither with the advance of their universalizing logics. This fundamental role as negation may be precisely what has given race its expansive, indefinite character; other categories – class and empire come to mind – play similar roles as liberalism's fraught but defining outer limits. It does not help race's clarity that essentializing meanings of the term (as natural, hierarchical typology) and deconstructing ones (as socio-political construct) share the same word, unlike the generative distinction between "gender" and "sex," for example. When invoked without specificity in the context of terminological confusion and conflictual politics, the term "race" can essentialize the very people and situations it is meant to account for (similar to the way early twentieth-century Americans used the adjective "race" to modify only those things pertaining to African Americans).

Equally unhelpful is the unselfconscious hegemony of US-based, Anglophone framings. Due to the relative power and resources of the US academy and publishing in a more and more Anglophone world, and the decisive, transnational impact of the African American freedom struggles during and after the Cold War (itself inseparable from the United States' status as hegemon), American ways of theorizing US-centered racialized systems have become powerful templates for "race" in many other scholarly and political settings. In ways that remain to be fully explored – intended, unintended, ironic, tragic, and productive – post-1945 American theorizations of race, essentialist and anti-essentialist, hegemonic and liberatory, may be one of the United States' most important American Century intellectual-political exports.[13] These conceptualizations, for better and worse, tend to take as their conscious and unconscious object the American subjection of black people – often, more narrowly, Jim Crow – physical criteria of racialized difference, and one-drop rule delineations as defining not only of race in parts of the United States, or the United States, but of "race" generally. While not without its benefits for both scholarly inquiry and emancipation politics, this dynamic – running parallel to Americans' other conflations of nation and globe – expresses its own kind of imperial provinciality. With these contending frameworks in play, it is worth building a fresh historical account on an original conceptual foundation.

For my purposes, racialized power combines exception, descent, and domination. This succinct definition requires unpacking. Race appears here as a verb – something actors past and present do to each other – rather than a noun; as noted above, race in the nominative form hovers uneasily between essentialist and deconstructive tasks. That race modifies power here signals its irreducibly political character: that it is forged and challenged in historical and present-day struggles over power, whatever its proponents' pretensions to primordial history, scientific authority, divine will, or identitarian authenticity. By exception, it refers not only to exceptionalism in an ideological sense (the notion that certain "races" may be positively or negatively exceptional *vis-à-vis* a norm, for example) but to extraordinary exercises of dominating power and the absence or suspension of rights; these political exceptions are neither separable nor derivable from exceptionalist ideologies. Unlike conventional US-centric definitions that foreground physical criteria – often explicitly scientized – the definition presented here emphasizes distinctions of descent, definable through myriad authority systems (religious, historical, kinship-based, scientific) but tied ultimately to questions of reproduction, lineage, and historical continuity, and their relationship to socio-political membership.[14] It is for this reason, among others, that racialized power and gendered power are inseparable: policing and preserving lines of descent requires disciplining gender definitions and sexual behaviors in ways that secure only sanctioned forms of biological and social reproduction. While cultures of bodily differentiation were at the core of slavery and its aftermaths in the Atlantic world, racialized power has been built upon equally compelling distinctions of language, religion, region, occupation, space, technology, and material culture. Finally, race as defined here involves relations of asymmetrical power, power that was limited, among other factors, by the resistance of those subjected to it. Where conventional definitions tend toward a sharp typological distinction between race and its others (as in the long-running debate about when race first emerged), one of the important features of this definition is that, by employing race as a verb, it also renders it both a process and a spectrum: something becomes racialized only to the extent that the separable gears of exception, descent, and domination grind together.

I have built this definition in part to counter one of the most influential, durable and misleading presumptions about "race" in scholarship and public life: that it is reducible to ideational activity, "prejudice," "ideology," and "racism" (understood as a coherent body of beliefs) being three of the most common formulations. The notion that race is simply a matter of (bad) thinking is an old one, dating back at least to the 1920s, and became dominant during the post-1945 period for complex reasons, among them the rise of culturalist thought and survey metrics of "attitude" in the social and human sciences, and the driven, Cold War pursuit of anti-materialist, anti-socialist theories that could displace what for many were compelling accounts of race's profound, structural ties to capitalism. What might be called the mentalizing of race requires a deeper history than is possible here.[15] What is most relevant for present purposes is that in part because of this association with "ideas," race entered the historiography of US foreign relations understood to be a subset of "culturalist" approaches. While this fact promoted a rich literature on the role of racialized ideology in US foreign relations, it reinforced a misunderstanding of race as primarily or exclusively a matter of mind, rather than a mode of power with material, behavioral, social-structural, institutional, and spatial dimensions, alongside ideological ones.[16] It also made race-focused scholarship subject to some traditional diplomatic historians' periodic, revanchist longings to return to the time when their subjects' meaning-making and racialized enterprises could go uninvestigated. As they did with "culture" or "ideas," these historians asked whether race "mattered" by holding it to what they took to be the stern test of "power," defined narrowly: did race affect "policy"?

While late twentieth-century historians of US foreign relations would broaden the field's animating questions beyond "policy," they would also provide a sharp reply to this dismissive inquiry, one sharp enough to constitute a rebuke. When it came to US foreign policy, they demonstrated, race had, indeed, mattered a great deal. From US policymakers' pursuit of the removal and elimination of Native Americans, to fears of a British abolitionist presence in the United States' slave-based empire, to long refusals to recognize independent Haiti and Liberia, to the Anglo-Saxonism that framed and rationalized continental and extra-continental empire-building, to Yellow Peril fears of Japan's empire and Pacific Coast migration in the early 20th century, to resistance to multilateral institutions on the grounds of possible interference with "domestic" institutions such as Jim Crow and immigration restriction, to racialized wars of empire in Asia, from the Philippines to the Pacific Islands and Japan to Vietnam, Laos and Cambodia, to the sense that Soviet and Chinese communisms were sinister in part because of their "Asiatic" roots, to concerns that extreme "domestic" expressions of racial hierarchy would alienate a decolonizing world, to the exceptionalizing of Islam as possessing inherent affinities with terrorist technique: in different ways, at different moments, and with different degrees of intensity, racialized distinction played a critical role in shaping US policymakers' calculus of interest, alliance, enmity, tactics, and strategy.[17]

The definition advanced here intends to move beyond the question of whether a given historical phenomenon or process "was" race or not, toward the question of how precisely it came to be racialized and/or deracialized.[18] How did the politics of exception operate? Against what norm was exception constructed? Was it that the dominant were exceptional, and subordinates made the homogenized norm, or the other way around? What practical, institutional, and policy expressions did exception take? How did the excepted challenge their condition? What, if any, universals did they invoke and organize around? What kinds of descent-lines mattered, and how did they make themselves known? To what extent were inherited characteritics understood to be malleable or fixed? By what mechanisms were they understood to be transmitted across time? How and why did the racialized embrace, transform, or reject these attributions? What kinds of asymmetrical power did the workings of exception and descent authorize and organize? How were subjects' constructed peculiarities forged into arguments for domination, and vice versa? How did those subjected to these regimes negotiate, internalize, and resist them?

Most important for historians and most amenable to their expertise is the question of change over time: how did projects in exception, descent and domination shift, both separately and in their intersection? How did those promoting and challenging them advance their cause, and with what success? While often taken to be historically fixed (a possible conceptual spillover from the notion of race as a form of fixed status), race was profoundly protean, seizing upon socially and historically available distinctions and, in turn, intensifying those distinctions by enlisting them for political purposes. Under changing historical conditions – especially in the face of challenge – constellations of exception, descent, and domination slid, snakelike, out of their particular skins, living to strike another day.

In making sense of race's historical multiplicities, it is useful to map specific phenomena on a spectrum from what I will call absolutizing to civilizing modes of power and differentiation. Both of these represent ideal types, unable to fully capture the idiosyncracies of actual historical processes, but they are nonetheless analytically useful. Absolutizing power spoke in a language of fixity: individuals were assigned to single, all-encompassing social categories defined by unchangeable features; social groups were seen as unable to alter their fundamental characteristics; salient difference was grounded in transcendence, especially in God or natural order. Political life was understood to consist of irreconcilable, zero-sum conflict between something approximating species. Absolutizing power's defining dilemma was category disruption, whether through transgressive sexuality and reproduction, socializing, mobility, or political resistance. It was recognizable in metaphors of walls, barricades, and fortifications – between bodies, categories, and spaces – and of the floods, swarms, and invasions that imperiled them. In US foreign relations history, advocates for the containment of both Asian migrants and globalizing communism, for example, drew on absolutist tropes of menacing flows and beleaguered ramparts.

By contrast, civilizing power was grounded in process: individuals and groups were assessed precisely in terms of their position and potential with respect to advancement in hierarchical, evolutionary time. Standards of civilization were necessarily ones along which subjects could move: bodily comportment, labor discipline, political rationality, material/technological sophistication, education and literacy, capital accumulation, consumption, urbanity. Identity with or proximity to Europe – understood biologically, religio-culturally, or historically – was a core if contested feature. If civilizing power had two defining metrics, they were moralized, patriarchal, heterosexual order – especially, the containing of women's sexuality within male-dominated households – and the capacity of individuals and groups to inculcate civilizing disciplines in what were understood to be peripheries: downward across the social scale, and outward toward the state's geographic fringes. Political life consisted of the use of disciplining standards to gauge degrees of socio-political incorporation, rights, and power. Historical expressions of civilizing power would include Anglo-American Protestant missionary endeavors of the late nineteenth and early twentieth centuries, and Cold War-era programs in international student migration to the United States, both of which sought the global diffusion of civilized and civilizing forms.[19] One clearly recognizable index of civilizing power was the presence of a logic of bipolarity – heathen/convert, bad Muslim/good Muslim – across which progress was possible, desired and required.[20]

For complex political and intellectual-historical reasons, race is often confused with only its absolutizing variant. Indeed, what I am calling civilizing power was (and is) commonly posed as the opposite of "race"; according to conventional (and problematic) definitions of race – as bodily, totalizing, and immutable – civilizing power is not racial. Precisely for this reason, it is important to ask what exactly was exceptionalizing, descent-making, and dominating – racial, in my terms – about civilizing formations? There was the question of how the uncivilized might progress: theoretically capable of universal advance and the rights that came with it, they were simultaneously held back by unique obstacles, particularly by deep, intractable (but not necessarily immutable) traits based especially in culture, social structure, family, and behavior. Only the summoning of extraordinary disciplinary power – surveillance, evaluation, policing, and violence – might advance the uncivilized and gauge their always contingent prospects for socio-political membership. In civilizing formations, absolutist imagery of the other served as the metric of progress, the "base" from which the would-be civilized must seek to climb. Finally, there were the ways that civilizing power's universalizing pretentions required symbolisms of diversity that, in turn, required the fixing of individual and group particularities, emptied of meanings that undermined universalist claims. The formerly uncivilized could only convey civilization's universality if they also, always, represented their uncivilized pasts. By the late twentieth century, imperial diversity – civilized multitudes posing no threat to capital's remorseless, universalizing advance – became one of the defining faces of a globalized market fundamentalism underwritten by US state power.

One of the reasons for civilizing power's misrecognition as anti-racial was its use as a weapon by historical actors in their campaigns against absolutizing power: for them, the capacity of individuals within subordinated groups (at least, some of them), to conform to civilization's strict, legitimate dictates successfully undermined illegitimate, "racial" assertions of wholesale, permanent inferiority. But if, as done here, race is defined in terms of exception, descent, and domination, civilizing power was a key expression of racializing power, arguably one of its most resilient, elusive, and invisible forms. By the early twenty-first century, scholars had begun to capture it with terms such as racial liberalism, color-blindness, flexible racism, inclusionary racism, cultural racism, and liberal accommodation, each concept shedding some light and some darkness.[21] Civilization and its cognates, closely associated with the nineteenth and early twentieth centuries, can seem an awkward rhetorical fit for later periods. But their utility resides in precisely this strangeness: it may point historians' attention to hidden continuities that undermine comforting accounts of rupture – of race's rise and fall – requiring them to ask to what extent the ancestors of modernization theory, neoliberal globalization, and multiculturalism wore Victorian pith helmets.[22]

In large part because of the mistaken identification of race with only its absolutizing variants, US foreign relations historians (among many others) have constructed an overarching narrative that tracks race's high tide in the late nineteenth century and early twentieth century and its mid-century downfall under the combined pressures of anti-fascism, anti-communism, decolonization, and black freedom politics. When writing about periods after about 1975, with so many of race's conventional markers behind them – Jim Crow, race war in Vietnam, the racialized exclusion of immigrants – these historians have found race far harder to identify, with the key exception of the politics of South African apartheid; to the extent that US foreign relations historians factored in race at all, it was relatively easy for them to consign it to the past, whatever recurrent, painful evidence to the contrary.

With race reconceptualized along the lines I've suggested – as the compounding of exception, descent, and domination, with more absolutizing and more civilizing variants – the story of the twentieth century shifts profoundly, from the "fall" of race, to the relative decline of absolutizing formations and the relative triumph of civilizing ones, beginning at the turn of the twentieth century, rather than its midpoint. The relative nature of this shift is critically important. Absolutizing power obviously survived its mid-twentieth-century crises, and the transition toward the hegemony of civilizing modes was partial, fragmented, and embattled, far more evident in some socio-political contexts than others. At the same time, absolutizing and civilizing efforts could and did commingle in a single setting, institution, or project, easily and uneasily. But a transition toward civilizing modes of power and differentiation was nonetheless unmistakable. It was measurable, for example, in political-cultural shifts in American public life from the legitimate political invocation of the Black Beast, the Lazy Native, and the Yellow Peril, absolutizing power's defining others, to the conjuring of the criminal, the terrorist, and the illegal, civilizing power's constitutive enemies. The plausible deniability of these modes of differentiation as "race" when it came to the mid-twentieth-century absolutizing standard – in theory and practice, criminals, terrorists, and illegals can be white – only enhanced their power to conceive, institutionalize, and legitimate relations of exception, descent, and domination.

Despite dogged denials of race's relevance to US foreign relations history and historiography, what strikes even the casual reader is, to the contrary, the rich constellation of literatures in which racialized power features as a theme in the history of United States' relations with the wider world. First, and overarchingly, is a literature that deals with the constitution of sovereignty in the emergent international politico-legal order of the nineteenth century. As Euro-American imperial powers extended their geographic reach, they constituted themselves as sovereigns through a globalizing politics of recognition that set the boundary between statehood and its others at "civilization," subordinating or liquidating polities that failed to meet its Eurocentric "standards," particularly when it came to legal order and the protection of Euro-American migrants and their property.[23] By the early twentieth century, the global map of subordinating sovereignties – binding large parts of Asia, Africa, and the Middle East to Euro-American powers – played a profound role in generating both affirmative and critical senses of "race" itself.

One of the defining features of this civilizationist order was what might be called its particularist universalism: while anchored geographically in Europe and Christianity, it was also necessarily capable of indefinite expansion, at least theoretically. The admission of Japan and the Ottoman Empire into the "society" of recognized states reinforced these claims to universality vis-à-vis exceptions of "race" and religion. Indeed, some scholars have embraced the logic of civilizing internationalism as their own, celebrating non-Western elites' pursuit of international recognition and narrating their gradual triumph over "race," culminating in the rise of the generalized norm of national states in the post-1945 period. In doing so, they have underplayed the ways that civilizationist order encoded exception, descent, and domination in post-absolutist ways.[24] Civilizing internationalism was a system of membership that was also a system of discipline, discipline felt most heavily at aspirant states' social margins (nomads, the poor, women, minoritized groups), as would-be states civilized themselves "internally" in search of international recognition.

The best work in this field explores sovereignty as an idiom of difference, in which the crucial boundary-line was ultimately between those who could be subjected to Euro-American powers, and those that could not; it also critically historicizes civilizing modes rather than analytically and normatively embracing them.[25] In the world of imperial internationalism, racialized difference was often measured in the capacity for self-rule, with certain "races" understood to possess these capacities, while others were lacking them, and thus in need of Euro-American supervision, discipline, and, sometimes, assimilative training. The US national government's repeated violation of treaties with Native Americans, for example, forcefully enacted the non-recognition and strategic recognition of native polities, drawing upon and reinforcing the sense that native peoples remained in a prior, inferior stage of political evolution. When it came to the question of whether differences were absolute or capable of civilizing mitigation, imperial states varied not only between themselves, but internally, their choices dependent on setting, timing, and the peculiarities of local–foreign political relationships. Where "natives" were granted limited degrees of sovereignty, the perceived character of their rule was tapped as a rich font of colonial ideology – apparent irrationality, corruption, superstition, and conflict were carefully extracted from the colonial condition and made to register the intractable barbarism of the colonized and the inherence of "good government" in the racialized geography of the West.[26] While the racializing of sovereignty and the sovereigntizing of race could stabilize colonial rule, they also generated racially aversive anti-colonialisms, particularly where states lacked the required tools for insulating their politics fully from the agency of those subjected to their sovereignty. In the United States and elsewhere, the fear that migrating or enfranchised colonial subjects might compromise metropolitan self-government haunted the dreams of many an anti-colonialist.[27]

Closest to traditional diplomatic-historical methods have been state-centered works that focus on the ways that US state actors – diplomats, executives, legislators, and policymakers – and adjunct civil society elites approached questions of racialized domination based inside the United States (such as Jim Crow) or outside it (such as South African apartheid); this literature has paid particular attention to the conjunctures of Cold War and decolonization politics in delegitimating absolutizing racial power. Some of this literature has focused on the ways officials' ideas about racialized difference shaped their policy approaches toward European colonialism and anti-colonial struggle, particularly when it came to assessing the progressive or regressive character of European domination, and the "maturity" and "stability" of anti-colonial forces.[28] Other scholarship has focused on the ways policymakers came to see absolutist systems – especially those identified with the US South – as a diplomatic impediment, even as they failed to view these systems as problematic in their own right. Once associated with modern statehood itself, the politics of aggressive Euro-American supremacy increasingly came to be seen as dangerously unaligned with the desires of those decolonizers whose allegiance US policymakers anxiously sought. As this scholarship shows, anti-racist and anti-colonialist activists operating both inside and outside the United States – and often moving between these spaces – played a catalytic role in channeling Cold War fears toward anti-segregation, and generating the belated, begrudging official sense that it was not worth losing the world over Whites Only signs.[29] The United States' abiding support for the apartheid regime in South Africa nonetheless made clear the ways that violent, absolutist domination was fully compatible with Cold War notions of anti-communist "freedom."[30]

Race has also figured prominently in scholarship located at the intersection of cultural history and US foreign relations history, which foregrounds questions of rhetoric, symbolism, and imagery – "discourse" – to explore the ideological architecture of Americans' perceptions of the world; much of this literature has centered on the foundational role of racialized and gendered difference in the symbolic constitution of the US national "self" and its many and varied "others." Some scholarship, carried out by foreign relations historians moving toward "culture" and arguing against Cold War claims that Americans were somehow immune to "ideology," identified race as one of a number of belief systems Americans employed to make sense of the world; while this work participated in the broader mentalizing of race, it nonetheless played a decisive role in legitimating race as an object of inquiry for US diplomatic historians.[31] Other work, carried out by American Studies scholars moving toward "the world," and often employing versions of a Saidian analysis of Orientalism, applied cultural studies techniques of deconstructive reading primarily to the work of US cultural producers.[32] This scholarship emphasized continuities in Americans' racialized and gendered perceptions: the ways that recognizable, prior formations were "exported" to make sense of newly encountered situations and populations. While provincial in its questions and methods – particularly to the extent that it labeled itself "transnational" – this literature powerfully demonstrated the ways that Americans have shaped and imagined imperial power relations in racialized and gendered ways.[33] Other scholarship, characterized by transnationalized questions and methods and sources, asked how Americans' visions of the other were forged in specific, historically changing contexts of encounter, and shaped by the agency, cultures, and histories of those they sought to apprehend. Aligned with other histories seeking to challenge national frames of analysis, this work demonstrated that Americans' racialized practices were not strictly derivable from any one national history, but emerged dynamically, contingently, and unpredictably from confluences and collisions between multiple histories.[34]

Emerging at the crossroads of ethnic studies, African American studies, social movement history, and US foreign relations history is research that explores the formation of cross-national solidarities informed by racialized distinction, across sometimes vast geographic space. Some of these works examine varieties of emancipatory politics – especially the connective recognition of common problems and common struggles among those subjected to racialized exception. Especially central to this literature has been the development of a self-consciously transnational politics among African Americans, from the redemptionist, civilizing visions of Africa in the nineteenth century, to the more assertively anti-colonialist politics of the interwar years, allied with Indian, Ethiopian, and Haitian struggles, to the more globalized anti-colonialisms of the post-1945 period, anti-colonialisms that took on rival pro-communist and anti-communist forms. This work has centered on dynamics of intercultural solidarity: the question of how those subjected to racialized power built convergences between themselves and often distant others, how they constructed and maintained long-distance ties, and how they sought to leverage transnational connections into "boomerang" effects on national instruments of power.[35]

While much of this literature celebrates transnational, anti-racist solidarities as such, some works also flag troubling questions of solidarity's misfires, as in some African Americans' support for Japan's colonial conquests in East Asia, understood as the triumph of a vanguardist "colored" empire that would displace and delegitimate white supremacist colonialisms (even as it brought its force against Asian subjects in Korea and China).[36] Other scholarship has examined shared, transnational senses of racialized privilege and power among the globally dominant. Solidarity was not just for subalterns: even as national-imperial states jockeyed with each other for colonies, resources, and markets, their politicians, officials, and intellectuals built compelling inter-imperial narratives of shared mission, danger, and sacrifice. These narratives – grounded in the different idioms of whiteness, Anglo-Saxonism, and the West – crystallized upon, and underwrote, projects in inter-imperial cooperation and alliance.[37] They were often built around long-distance senses of common predicament, especially when it came to the maintenance of racially subordinating labor systems and the restriction of undesired migration, and they helped empire-builders explain their dominance to themselves and others, while embedding nationalist ideologies and pursuits in the transcendent forces of nature.[38]

Allied with solidarity scholarship are histories of the transfer of techniques of racialized domination and resistance: of historical actors' selective borrowing and adaptation of technologies of racialized labor control, migrant exclusion, and socio-political subordination from other societies, on the one hand, and the strategies of organizing, confrontation, and resistance, on the other. The transnational itineraries of segregation, the literacy test, eugenic knowledge and policy, and nonviolent resistance are among the best explored of these trajectories.[39] So, too, have historians painted vivid pictures of efforts to impose segregated spatial and social arrangements by US officials in occupied towns during and after World War II and in the Panama Canal Zone, and by US companies in oil enclaves in the Middle East.[40] These transfers were both enabled by and indexical of broader connections, especially the transport and communication grids that allowed historical actors to move beyond their ordinary frames of reference, finding and inventing solutions that had previously eluded them among what they perceive to be successful outsiders, or extending adapted variants of pre-existing formulas they had the power to execute. This still-small literature seldom links up to scholarship on "transfer" self-consciously, but it nonetheless shares many of its core features, especially accounts of mobile experts, technocrats, and intellectuals: professional comparers and learners who often joined a sense of domestic blockage to optimistic faith (sometimes naïve or utopian faith) in foreign solutions. Borne by steamship, railroad, and airplane, webbed together by conferences, lecture circuits, and journals, these experts grappled with the myriad challenges of remaking parts of their societies with pieces they drew from others.[41] In mapping out this world of transfers, historians face the occupational hazard of homology – of turning perceived similarities of cultures, practices, or institutions in discrete settings into evidence of connection – but this danger does not diminish the prospects for illuminating accounts of the ways racialized systems informed and influenced each other.

Scholarship on the centrality of race to the politics of migration, naturalization, and US boundary control is only recently beginning to intersect with US foreign relations history in earnest. Early work on US–Japan relations necessarily treated the international politics of migration, including its racialized dimensions, but otherwise, US immigration policy history and foreign relations history remained largely separate, a gap that is being rapidly and richly filled as historians reconstruct the complex ways in which US boundaries were shaped by transnational and global processes.[42] This said, race has unavoidably figured prominently in US immigration historiography, given its centrality to US migration and naturalization policy itself. From the 1790 naturalization act, with its exclusionary invitation to "free white persons of good character," to anti-Chinese legislation, to civilizing distinctions among Japanese, Chinese, Indian, and South and Eastern Europeans, to the confidently absolutizing national origins quota system, with its preferences for Northern and Western Europeans, to the post-9/11 targeting of Muslims, Arabs, and South Asians, racialized distinction has played a foundational role in policy and popular determinations of who constituted "desirable" denizens and citizens of the United States and who represented threats.[43]

The racialized dimensions of US immigration policy were also among their most fiercely contested features, as migrants, their communities and states of origin all protested stigmatizing exceptions in law, policy, and enforcement, as well as the essentializing visions they embodied and promoted. Intersecting with the Cold War politicizing of Jim Crow as a global embarrassment was the view that the rigidly absolutist national origins quota system was both a logistical headache (the anti-communist escapees that US policymakers hoped to relocate inconveniently clustered in the tightly restricted regions of Eastern Europe and East Asia) and sent out insulting and inaccurate messages about the United States' friends and enemies.[44] This argument that US immigration policy needed not only to protect "domestic" space from corrupting influences, but to help project US power transnationally and globally rose in influence during the Cold War and its aftermath: the 1965 Hart-Celler Act, for example, best known for dismantling the last vestiges of national origins, was, less familiarly, a tool for attracting the technical experts required for military-industrial competition, facilitating the escape of refugees from communist states, and sending signals about the exceptional capacity of capitalist societies to diversify. While immigration scholarship has tended to thematize and problematize restriction, one of the distinct contributions of an immigration–foreign relations nexus may be to bring critical attention to the geopolitics of opening.[45]

Similarly emerging on the scene are works that interweave questions of race, capitalism, and US foreign relations. Race was relatively marginal to the earliest diplomatic historians who problematized capitalism in US foreign relations, the Wisconsin School; similarly, dynamics of commodification, labor exploitation, capital accumulation, and class power were not emphasized in many of the early histories of US foreign relations that took race seriously. The reasons for this disjuncture are complex. Especially important are both direct and internalized Cold War pressures not to place capitalism in a critical spotlight, and an intractable, polarized rivalry between totalized "race" and "class" critiques. Critical breakthroughs occurred earliest not among foreign relations historians, but among critical intellectuals during the Vietnam War era, especially intellectuals of color, who began to combine critiques of racial domination, colonialism, and capitalism; Martin Luther King, Jr.'s April 4, 1967, "Beyond Vietnam" address is one of the many eloquent expressions of this position.[46] Equally important were histories that connected racial slavery and industrial capitalism; once seen as the pre-modern, feudal precursor to capitalist modernity, slavery was recast as capitalism's foundationally modern laboratory and engine.[47]

With the fading of Cold War polarities, the rise of a critical politics of globalization, and crises of capitalism in the early twenty-first century, new and vital spaces opened up for a scholarship capable of making critical, combined sense of race and capital in the United States' transnational histories. Entering and widening this space is scholarship that explores racialized dimensions of imperial labor regimes: elites' deliberate use of divide-and-rule tactics to split potentially rebellious workers along lines of color, language, and nationality; the ranking of workers along essentializing grids with respect to their propensities for labor, compliance, and rebellion; the vulnerability of race-dominant workers when it came to racializing, nationalizing appeals, and their complicity in promoting, democratizing, and inflicting them on others.[48] As this work shows, there were horrific convergences between racialized exception and the capitalist hyper-exploitation of labor, affinities that were only amplified in exceptionalized, anything-goes spaces of empire. There is also scholarship on racialized dimensions of the economic projects of US government agencies and US-based banks in their transnational operations: the exceptionalizing regimes of economic discipline imposed on some societies but not others; the relentless, essentializing calculus of which peoples were capable of capitalist rationality – self-interest, accumulation, profit maximization, and the exploitation of others, for example – a virtue understood by many to be characteristically white and Western.[49] This literature's main challenge will be to resist the longstanding temptation to reduce race to capitalism's mandates, or capitalism to the logics of race-making; it will succeed only to the extent that it cultivates and sustains a dynamic, dialectical interplay between the politics of exploitation and marginality, capital and exception.

Finally, race figures in complex and varied ways in the historiographies of militarization, war-making, and occupation in the United States. From colonial militias to the late twentieth-century all-volunteer military, racialized distinction has powerfully shaped the building and organization of US military forces, for example. The impulse to exclude non-white men from military service, or to subordinate them within it, derived in part from the perceived dangers of arming and training people subjected to racialized domination. It also owed much to the martial dimensions of American republicanism: to the extent that military sacrifice provided access to US civic belonging, political rights, and veterans' benefits (at least in theory), racially subordinated soldiers and veterans, and their wives, widows, and families, might leverage martial patriotism against race in ways that could undermine supremacist power relations. Pressures to employ and integrate non-white soldiers into US military forces included voracious demands for military labor, political activism by racially subjected groups, and the logistical tangles involved in maintaining segregated forces and facilities.

Until the formal integration of the US military during the early Cold War, the dominant approach to the problem of extracting military labor without conceding troubling rights was subordinated inclusion: segregated units and facilities, the disproportionate assignment of non-white soldiers to stigmatized "labor" duty, highly restrictive policies toward non-white officers (especially when it came to the command of white soldiers), lower military pay, and harassment by soldiers and civilians, all underwritten by imagery that racialized capacities for martial virtue and discipline by casting non-white soldiers as cowardly, lazy, barbaric, insubordinate, and disloyal. As white supremacists feared, racially subordinated soldiers, their families and communities did advance claims for inclusion on the grounds of martial participation: claims that proved especially compelling where the United States' enemies promoted racial ideologies possessing uncomfortable similarities to the United States' own.[50] Furthermore, racially oppressed soldiers' novel, inter-cultural encounters during overseas military deployments could prove politically transformative, especially where these soldiers encountered relative acceptance, recognition, and even celebration, or developed new, critical solidarities.[51] To paraphrase the World War I-era jazz hit, after they'd seen "Paree" – or anywhere else they were less exposed to racist brutality – black soldiers proved harder to keep down on the farm, metaphorically and literally.

At the same time, assertions of rights on the grounds of martial patriotism and sacrifice, and their far less frequent realization, gave non-white people a stake in the US national-imperial state, and the politics of racial inclusion would become increasingly militarized during and after the Cold War: as non-white soldiers came to enjoy the fruits of US global power and segregated military and civilian structures gave way, imperial expansion and racial integration became

Racialized power

powerfully intertwined.[52] While it indexed the racialized character of the US class structure, for example, the "diversity" of the all-volunteer military and the prominence of non-white people in leadership roles was mobilized as a sign of its meritocracy and color-blindness: increasingly detached from the rest of American society, the US military came to represent the inclusionary vanguard of the stratified society for which it fought.

From long before the United States' founding, war proved a crucible in which racialized division was forged, expressed, and contested. In contexts of war-making, existing distinctions of friend and enemy were seized upon and deepened, but also uprooted and transformed, as participants reframed their notions of self, community, state, and opponent amid the exigencies of combat and the broader geopolitics in which it was embedded. Given the importance of racialized supremacy to Anglo-American settler-colonial polities and the US national state at its founding, it is unsurprising that racial hierarchy often played a role in defining the ends of US warfare: from the conquest and removal of indigenous people in the interests of a continental "empire of liberty," to the transnational diffusion of Anglo-Saxon civilization to the world's darker corners, to the modernizing terrors of American counterinsurgency in the decolonizing world, particularly in Southeast Asia, to the civilizing globalism of the "war on terror." In varying ways, American proponents of these wars, and many of the American soldiers who fought in them, justified these campaigns by exceptionalizing and essentializing themselves as protagonists and their opponents as inferiors, rooting these claims in transcendent notions of nature, history, and the sacred.

Race also played a recurrent role in the way Americans approached the means of war: the question of which tactics, strategies, and targets were legitimate and illegitimate. Here the bounding and unbounding of violence was often tied to perceptions of the enemy: their rationale for fighting, their willingness to surrender, and the ease or difficulty of distinguishing combatants from civilians, for example. Racial superiority was keyed to a hierarchy of fighting styles: civilized people – Europe and its offshoots – ostensibly fought legalized, rights-protecting, civilized campaigns, while barbarians fought irregular ones rooted in brutality, concealment, and deception and terrorism. Across the decolonizing world, the racializing of combat and militarizing of racial distinction allowed rebels' guerrilla struggles in contexts of asymmetric warfare to be enlisted as arguments for both the civilizing mission and the abandonment of civilized warfare by dominant powers. It was not, then, simply that Americans waged particular kinds of wars against states and peoples they racialized in particular ways; war-making and race-making were dynamically interwoven processes, with sinister elective affinities between the exceptionalizing of the enemy and their subjection to exceptional forms of violence. Where these dynamics spiraled together most intensely, the result could be racial exterminism, the legitimation of violence against all members of a "race" during war's duration as a matter of tactics and strategy, and genocide, in which the physical elimination of an "enemy race" was war's ultimate goal.[53] This race/war dynamic unfolded not only in battle zones, but in more expansive war zones that included "home fronts": when, for example, people of Japanese descent, including many US citizens, were presumed inherently loyal to Japan during World War II, their already-fragile hold on American civic membership was devastated by what might be called the hard hand of war essentialism.[54] Racially subordinated soldiers and civilians would have complex encounters with racialized US wars, in some cases seeing participation in the campaigns as an opportunity to blunt oppressions directed against them by proving their loyalty and manhood, in other cases losing faith with the US war effort on racial and other grounds, and even forging sympathies and solidarities with the racialized adversary.[55]

Finally, race and war crossed when it came to the politics of legitimation, particularly where the United States confronted states whose national identities were grounded in racist narratives (as in the case of Nazi Germany), or "anti-racist" ones (as in the case of Imperial Japan and the Soviet Union). In such cases, Americans often found their exceptionalist pretensions to democracy and freedom challenged on uncomfortably global terrain, particularly where the propaganda engines of enemy states capitalized upon and amplified US racial domination, exclusion, and violence. As early as the turn of the twentieth century, some Americans had anxiously observed a crisis of white supremacy, evidenced in restive colonial populations and, especially, by the military-imperial rise of Japan.[56] Over the course of the century, anti-racial activists would take advantage of, and deepen, these vulnerabilities. During World War II, for example, they would – within the stringent constraints of wartime loyalty politics – construct critical equivalences between Jim Crow and European fascism through a "Double Victory" campaign against racial terrorisms far and near. Despite the common historical claim that the war against the Nazis and Americans' encounters with the Holocaust delegitimated racism in the United States, fighting extremely racist enemies also managed, to the contrary, to persuade many white Americans that their own racial problematics were comparatively negligible and benign.

Where the United States faced off against powers like Japan and the Soviet Union, which ferociously criticized Euro-American racism and colonialism (while rationalizing away their own), anti-racial activists, as well as many powerful policymakers, argued that the United States must reform itself (at least when it came to Jim Crow and the national origins quota system) to render itself less vulnerable to these charges, particularly before the skeptical eyes of the decolonizing world.[57] Self-reform would also, importantly, free Americans to stigmatize rival states' "domestic" oppressions, as in the case of Soviet anti-Semitism. Such calls to dismantle absolutist systems in wartime were muted by actual and potential charges of disloyalty – particularly where Americans' criticisms of the United States echoed the enemy's – and deflected by increasingly subtle image-making efforts that detached state symbolism from substantive change. While often registered as a factor in the triumph of anti-Jim Crow politics, the Cold War civil rights intersection needs to be explored more fully as one moment in the much longer history of the United States' pursuit of hegemonic legitimacy in a decolonizing world. The defining down of race to merely its absolutist modes, discussed above, is not separable from this history and may, in fact, be one of its most enduring artifacts.

To the extent that US foreign relations historians traditionally followed the analytic lead of the policymakers they studied, there was a certain irony in their reluctance to take race seriously as an analytic category: in their ambivalence, and even hostility, to these inquiries, they were breaking with historical actors, for whom race was often a critical, shape-shifting factor in considerations of the United States' engagements with the wider world. For some, race was ontological reality, nature's gift and burden to statecraft, with the preservation of white supremacy in and among the United States' other state interests. For others, it constituted a managerial concern as the United States – born in settler colonialism and slavery-based capitalism – fought rearguard struggles to achieve hegemonic legitimacy in a world its racial systems defined as largely non-white. For still others, especially anti-racial and anti-colonial campaigners, race was a socio-political problem: one of the core elements of a hierarchical, Eurocentric world order that must be uprooted in the pursuit of social justice both within and between societies. Regardless of their position on its precise meaning, historical actors might have been surprised to hear assertions that race ought to be, at most, a minor consideration in US foreign relations history.

The impulse to take race seriously in histories of the US in the world arose in the wake of mid-twentieth-century social movements that disrupted and problematized naturalized hierarchies of racial exception at national and international scales. As this chapter has attempted to show, the result has been extremely generative in historiographic terms, bringing hitherto understudied dynamics to light and neglected actors to the fore. Among the most important benefits of this literature is its capacity to move forward the de-insulation of US foreign relations historiography itself. Race is one of a number of analytic categories and methodologies – gender and cultural history also come to mind – that have long been central to US historiography and history-writing in general, and can therefore be seen as bridges across the still formidable divides between "domestic" US and "international" histories. To the extent that these analytic categories advance, US foreign relations historians may find it more and more difficult – and, perhaps, less and less desirable – to isolate and exceptionalize themselves *vis-à-vis* other historians of the United States, as well as international and global historians more generally.

In this process, though, historians of racialized power – whether working within national or transnationalized frames – would do well to recognize the ways in which the very meanings of "race" largely derive from mid-to-late twentieth-century intellectual-political framings, forged in the long (and unfinished) struggle against absolutist racial power in the United States: as bodily, color-coded, and mental, scientized and segregating, fixed and fixing. Even as these definitions have enabled both historical analysis and critical politics, they have rendered the operations of civilizing power less visible, in part because of the very ways they have been enlisted in anti-absolutist struggle. Historians of race can and should do more than problematize expressions of racialized power with which John F. Kennedy himself was frustrated, and this task, in turn, requires not only empirical reconstruction, but creative reconceptualization. Shedding critical light on structures of exception, descent, and domination – in their absolutist expressions, and their more subtle and sinuous ones – remains a necessary and urgent task.

NOTES

My thanks to Dirk Bönker, Nathan Connolly, Andrew Friedman, Kevin Kim, Matthew Lassiter, Adriane Lentz-Smith, Noam Maggov, Daniel Margolies, Andrew Rotter, Michael Thompson, Andrew Zimmerman, and the Vanderbilt Americanist workshop for their comments and critiques, and to Frank Costigliola and Michael Hogan for their support.

1. Renee Romano, "No Diplomatic Immunity: African Diplomats, the State Department, and Civil Rights," *Journal of American History*, Vol. 87, No. 2 (2000), 546–79.
2. Quotations from "Big Step Ahead on a High Road," *Life Magazine*, December 8, 1961, 32–9.
3. On Kennedy and African decolonization, see Philip E. Muehlenbeck, *Betting on the Africans: John F. Kennedy's Courting of African Nationalist Leaders* (New York, 2012); James H. Meriwether, "'Worth a Lot of Negro Votes': Black Voters, Africa, and the 1960 Presidential Campaign," *Journal of American History*, Vol. 95, No. 3 (December 2008), 737–63.
4. For helpful historiographic assessments of race and US foreign relations history, see Gerald Horne, "Race to Insight: The U.S. and the World, White Supremacy and Foreign Affairs," in Michael J. Hogan and Thomas G. Paterson, eds. *Explaining the History of American Foreign Relations*, 2nd edition (New York, 2004), 323–35; Ryan M. Irwin, "Mapping Race: Historicizing the History of the Color-Line," *History Compass*, Vol. 8, No. 9 (September 2010), 984–99.
5. Reginald Horsman, *Race and Manifest Destiny: The Origins of American Racial Anglo-Saxonism* (Cambridge, MA, 1981).
6. W. E. B. Du Bois, "The Present Outlook for the Darker Races of Mankind," *A. M. E. Church Review*, Vol. 17 (October 1900), 95–110.
7. On the State Department and racial exclusion, see Michael Krenn, *Black Diplomacy: African Americans and the State Department, 1945–1969* (Armonk, NY, 1999). Also important was the normative imperialism of early international relations scholarship. See Robert Vitalis, *White World Order, Black Power Politics: The Birth of American International Relations* (Ithaca: Cornell University Press, 2015).

Racialized power 265

8. Thomas Bailey, *Theodore Roosevelt and the Japanese–American Crises: An Account of the International Complications Arising from the Race Problem on the Pacific Coast* (Stanford University Press, 1934); Akira Iriye, *Pacific Estrangement: Japanese and American Expansion, 1897–1911* (Cambridge, MA, 1972); Roger Daniels, *The Politics of Prejudice: The Anti-Japanese Movement in California and the Struggle for Japanese Exclusion* (New York, 1969).
9. For a useful collection of essays on race and US foreign policy, see Michael Krenn, ed., *The Impact of Race on U. S. Foreign Policy: A Reader* (Routledge, 1999). See also Krenn's synthesis, *The Color of Empire: Race and American Foreign Relations* (Sterling, VA, 2006).
10. See, for example, the writings of Jack O'Dell: *Climbin' Jacob's Ladder: The Black Freedom Movement Writings of Jack O'Dell* (Berkeley, 2010).
11. Mary Dudziak, *Cold War Civil Rights: Race and the Image of American Democracy* (Princeton, NJ, 2000); Azza Salama Layton, *International Politics and Civil Rights Policies in the United States, 1941–1960* (New York, 2000).
12. For a powerful account of changing theorization of race in the United States, see Thomas Holt, "Explaining Racism in American History," in Anthony Molho, ed., *Imagined Histories: American Historians Interpret the Past* (Princeton, NJ, 1998), 107–19. For an influential theorization of race, see Michael Omi and Howard Winant, *Racial Formation in the United States: from the 1960s to the 1990s* (New York, 1994). For a collection of theoretical works, see Les Back and John Solomos, eds., *Theories of Race and Racism: A Reader* (New York, 2000).
13. For a charged debate on whether or not US-based conceptualizations of race constitute an imperial export, see Pierre Bourdieu and Loic Wacquant, "On the Cunning of Imperial Reason," *Theory, Culture, and Society*, Vol. 16, No. 1 (1999), 41–58; Michael Hanchard, "Acts of Misrecognition: Transnational Black Politics, Anti-Imperialism and the Ethnocentrisms of Pierre Bourdieu and Loic Wacquant," *Theory, Culture and Society*, Vol. 20, No. 4 (2003), 5–29.
14. The more conventional criteria here would be essence, fixity, or immutability. Ideologies and institutionalizations of descent were and are enlisted for essentializing purposes, but I suggest here that making essence the litmus test for race is one element in the broader confusion of absolutizing formations with racialized formations more generally, in the mid-to-late 20th-century mode. In other words, descent is the overarching feature – involved on both ends of the abolutizing/civilizing spectrum – with essentialist understandings of descent present more strongly in instances of absolutizing power.
15. For a powerful account of the related category of "racial individualism," see Leah Gordon, *From Power to Prejudice: The Rise of Racial Individualism in Midcentury America* (Chicago, 2015).
16. Race is, for example, one of the dimensions of Americans' foreign relations ideology in Michael Hunt's foundational work, *Ideology and U.S. Foreign Policy* (New Haven, 1987).
17. It merits stating that the United States was not exceptional in the role that race played in its foreign policy. For a collection that explores the role of race in other states' Cold War politics, for example, see Philip E. Muehlenbeck, ed., *Race, Ethnicity, and the Cold War: A Global Perspective* (Nashville, 2012).

18. For a compelling discussion of "race-making," see Thomas C. Holt, "Marking: Race, Race-making, and the Writing of History," *American Historical Review*, Vol. 100, No. 1 (February 1995), 1–20.
19. Paul A. Kramer, "Is the World Our Campus? International Students and US Global Power in the Long Twentieth Century," *Diplomatic History*, Vol. 33, No. 3 (November 2009), 775–806.
20. For recent instances, see Mahmood Mamdani, *Good Muslim, Bad Muslim: America, the Cold War, and the Roots of Terror* (New York, 2005); Evelyn Asultany, *Arabs and Muslims in the Media: Race and Representation after 9/11* (New York, 2012).
21. The terms racial liberalism, color-blindness, and cultural racism are widely used by scholars. On flexible racism, see Mona Domosh, *American Commodities in an Age of Empire* (New York, 2006). On inclusionary racism, see Kramer, *The Blood of Government: Race, Empire, the United States and the Philippines* (Chapel Hill, 2006). On liberal accommodationism, see George Fredrickson, *The Black Image in the White Mind: The Debate on Afro-American Character and Destiny* (New York, 1971). The politics of respectability can also be seen as a variant of civilizing power. See, for example, Kevin Gaines, *Uplifting the Race: Black Leadership, Politics, and Culture in the Twentieth Century* (Chapel Hill, 1996); Evelyn Brooks Higginbotham, *Righteous Discontent: The Women's Movement in the Black Baptist Church, 1880–1920* (Cambridge, 1994).
22. For linkages along these lines, see Michael E. Latham, *The Right Kind of Revolution: Modernization, Development, and U.S. Foreign Policy from the Cold War to the Present* (Ithaca, 2011); Jon Davidann: "'Colossal Illusions': U.S.-Japanese Relations in the Institute of Pacific Relations, 1919–1938," *Journal of World History*, Vol. 12, No. 1 (Spring 2001), 155–82.
23. Jorg Fisch, "International Civilization by Dissolving International Society: The Status of Non-European Territories in 19th Century International Law," in Martin Geyer and Johannes Paulmann, eds., *The Mechanics of Internationalism: Culture, Society, and Politics from the 1840s to the First World War* (New York, 2001), 235–58; Anthony Anghie, *Imperialism, Sovereignty and the Making of International Law* (New York, 2007).
24. Gerrit W. Gong, *The Standard of "Civilization" in International Society* (Oxford, UK, 1984); Cemil Aydin, *The Politics of Anti-Westernism in Asia: Visions of World Order in Pan-Islamism and Pan-Asian Thought* (New York, 2007).
25. See, for example, Thongchai Winichakul, *Siam Mapped: A History of the Geo-Body of a Nation* (Honolulu, 1994).
26. See, for example, Laura Briggs, *Reproducing Empire: Race, Sex, Science, and U.S. Imperialism in Puerto Rico* (Berkeley, 2002); Kelvin Santiago-Valles, *"Subject People" and Colonial Discourses: Economic Transformation and Social Disorder in Puerto Rico* (New York); Mary Renda, *Taking Haiti: Military Occupation and the Culture of U.S. Imperialism, 1915–1940* (Chapel Hill, 2001); Lanny Thompson, *Imperial Archipelago: Representation and Rule in the Insular Territories under U.S. Dominion after 1898* (Honolulu, 2010); Vicente Rafael, *White Love and Other Events in Filipino History* (Durham, NC, 2000); Warwick Anderson, *Colonial Pathologies: American Tropical Medicine, Race, and Hygiene in the Philippines* (Durham, NC, 2006); Michael Salman, *The Embarrassment of Slavery: Controversies over Bondage and Nationalism in the American Colonial Philippines*

(Berkeley, 2001); Alfred McCoy and Francisco Scarano, eds., *Colonial Crucible: Empire in the Making of the Modern American State* (Madison, 2009); Kramer, *Blood of Government*.
27. Christopher Lasch, "The Anti-Imperialists, the Philippines, and the Inequality of Man," *Journal of Southern History*, Vol. 24 (August 1958): 319–31; Eric Love, *Race over Empire: Racism and U.S. Imperialism, 1865–1900* (Chapel Hill, 2004).
28. Thomas Borstelmann, *The Cold War and the Color Line: American Race Relations in the Global Arena* (Cambridge, MA, 2001); Jason C. Parker, *Brother's Keeper: The United States, Race, and Empire in the British Caribbean, 1937–1962* (New York, 2008); Cary Fraser, *Ambivalent Anti-colonialism: The United States and the Genesis of West Indian, 1940–1964* (Westport, CT, 1994); Mark Bradley, *Imagining Vietnam and America: The Making of Postcolonial Vietnam, 1919–1950* (Chapel Hill, 2003); George White, Jr., *Holding the Line: Race, Racism, and American Foreign Policy toward Africa, 1953–1961* (Guilford, CT, 2005); Andrew Rotter, *Comrades at Odds: The United States and India, 1947–1964* (Ithaca, 2000).
29. Dudziak, *Cold War Civil Rights*; Layton, *International Politics and Civil Rights Policies in the United States*; Brenda Gayle Plummer, ed., *Window on Freedom: Race, Civil Rights and Foreign Affairs, 1945–1988* (Chapel Hill, 2003).
30. Thomas Borstelmann, *Apartheid's Reluctant Uncle: The United States and Southern Africa in the Early Cold War* (New York, 1993); Thomas J. Noer, *Cold War and Black Liberation: The United States and White Rule in Africa, 1948–1968* (Columbia, MO, 1985); Ryan Irwin, *Gordian Knot: Apartheid and the Unmaking of the Liberal World Order* (New York, 2012).
31. Hunt, *Ideology and U.S. Foreign Policy*. On US foreign relations historians' approaches to Edward Said's *Orientalism* and broader questions of ideology, see Andrew Rotter, "Saidism without Said: Orientalism and U. S. Diplomatic History," *The American Historical Review*, Vol. 105, No. 4 (Oct. 2000), 1205–17.
32. The key volume that initiated this approach was Amy Kaplan and Donald Pease, eds., *Cultures of United States Imperialism* (Durham, 1993).
33. For a critique of this "export" model of race, see Paul A. Kramer, "Transits of Race: Empire and Difference in Philippine-American History," in Manfred Berg and Simon Wendt, eds., *Racism in the Modern World: Historical Perspectives on Cultural Transfer and Adaptation* (New York, 2011), 163–91.
34. See, for example, Andrew Zimmerman, *Alabama in Africa: Booker T. Washington, the German Empire, and the Globalization of the New South* (Princeton, 2012); Marilyn Lake and Henry Reynolds, *Drawing the Global Colour Line: White Men's Countries and the International Challenge of Racial Equality* (Cambridge, 2008); Kramer, *The Blood of Government*.
35. The literature on transnational black politics in the nineteenth and twentieth centuries is rich and growing. Key works include Richard J. M. Blackett, *Building an Antislavery Wall: Black Americans in the Atlantic Abolitionist Movement, 1830–1860* (Baton Rouge, 2002); Brenda Gayle-Plummer, *Rising Wind: Black Americans and U.S. Foreign Affairs, 1935–1960* (Chapel Hill, 1996); Brenda Gayle-Plummer, *In Search of Power: African Americans in the Era of Decolonization, 1954–1974* (New York, 2013); Carol Anderson, *Eyes off the Prize: African-Americans, the United Nations, and the Struggle for Human Rights, 1944–1955* (New York, 2003); Carol Anderson, *Bourgeois Radicals: The NAACP and the Struggle for Colonial Liberation, 1941–1960* (New York, 2014);

Penny Von Eschen, *Race Against Empire: Black Americans and Anticolonialism, 1937–1957* (Ithaca, 1997); Kevin Gaines, *American Africans in Ghana: Black Expatriates and the Civil Rights Era* (Chapel Hill, 2006); Nikhil Pal Singh, *Black is a Country: Race and the Unfinished Struggle for Democracy* (Cambridge, MA, 2004); James H. Meriwether, *Proudly We Can Be Africans: Black Americans and Africa, 1935–1961* (Chapel Hill, 2002); Nico Slate, *Colored Cosmopolitanism: The Shared Struggle for Freedom in the United States and India* (Cambridge, MA, 2012); Nico Slate, ed., *Black Power Beyond Borders: The Global Dimensions of the Black Power Movement* (New York, 2012); Frank Guridy, *Forging Diaspora: Afro-Cubans and African Americans in a World of Empire and Jim Crow* (Chapel Hill, 2010); Adam Ewing, *The Age of Garvey: How a Jamaican Activist Created a Mass Movement and Changed Global Black Politics* (Princeton, 2014); Jonathan Seth Rosenberg, *How Far the Promised Land? World Affairs and the American Civil Rights Movement from the First World War to Vietnam* (Princeton, 2005); Robeson Taj Frazier, *The East is Black: Cold War China in the Black Radical Imagination* (Durham, 2014); Minkah Makalani, *In the Cause of Freedom: Radical Black Internationalism from Harlem to London, 1917–1939* (Chapel Hill, 2014); Lawrence S. Little, *Disciples of Liberty: The African Methodist Episcopal Church in the Age of Imperialism, 1884–1916* (Knoxville, 2000); William R. Scott, *The Sons of Sheba's Race: African-Americans and the Italo-Ethiopian War, 1935–1941* (Bloomington, 1993); Sudarshan Kapur, *Raising Up a Prophet: The African-American Encounter with Gandhi* (Boston, 1992); Robert Vinson, *The Americans are Coming!: Dreams of African American Liberation in Segregationist South Africa* (Athens, OH, 2012); Jason C. Parker, "'Made-in-America Revolutions?': The 'Black University' and the American Role in the Decolonization of the Black Atlantic," *Journal of American History*, Vol. 93, No. 3 (2009), 727–50.

36. Mark Gallicchio, *The African American Encounters with Japan and China: Black Internationalism in Asia, 1895–1945* (Chapel Hill, 2000). On "radical Orientalism" among antiwar activists, see Judy Tzu-Chun Wu in *Radicals on the Road: Internationalism, Orientalism, and Feminism during the Vietnam Era* (Ithaca, 2013).

37. Paul A. Kramer, "Empires, Exceptions and Anglo-Saxons: Race and Rule between the British and United States Empires, 1880–1910," *Journal of American History*, Vol. 88, No. 4 (2002): 1315–53; Emily Conroy-Krutz, *Christian Imperialism: Converting the World in the Early American Republic* (Ithaca, 2015)

38. Marilyn Lake and Henry Reynolds, *Drawing the Global Colour Line: White Men's Countries and the International Challenge of Racial Equality* (Cambridge, UK, 2008); Kornel S. Chang, *Pacific Connections: The Making of the Western U.S.-Canadian Borderlands* (Berkeley, 2012); Travis J. Hardy, "Race as an Aspect of the U.S.-Australian Alliance in World War II," *Diplomatic History*, Vol. 38, No. 3 (June 2014), 549–68; David Atkinson, "The Burdens of Whiteness: Asian Immigration Restriction and White Supremacy in the British Empire and the United States, 1897–1924," (PhD dissertation, Boston University, 2010).

39. On the literacy test, see Marilyn Lake, "From Mississippi to Melbourne via Natal: The Invention of the Literacy Test as a Technology of Racial Exclusion," in Ann Curthoys and Marilyn Lake, eds., *Connected Worlds: History in Transnational Perspective* (ANU Press, 2005), 215–22.; on eugenics, see Stefan Kuhl, *The Nazi*

Connection: Eugenics, American Racism, and German National Socialism (New York, 2002); on segregation, see Carl Nightingale, *Segregation: A Global History of Divided Cities* (Chicago, 2012); on racialized labor control, see Andrew Zimmerman, *Alabama in Africa: Booker T. Washington, the German Empire, and the Globalization of the New South* (Princeton, 2012).

40. On the racialized and gendered politics of US military basing, see Maria Hohn and Seungsook Moon, eds., *Over There: Living with the U.S. Military Empire from World War Two to the Present* (Durham, 2010). On race and the US overseas military presence during and after World War II, see Harvey R. Neptune, *Caliban and the Yankees: Trinidad and the United States Occupation* (Chapel Hill, 2007); Graham Smith, *When Jim Crow Met John Bull: Black American Soldiers in World War II Britain* (New York, 1988); Maria Hohn, *GIs and Frauleins: The German-American Encounter in 1950s West Germany* (Chapel Hill, 2002); John Dower, *Embracing Defeat: Japan in the Wake of World War II* (New York, 2000); Yukiko Koshiro, *Trans-Pacific Racisms and the U.S. Occupation of Japan* (New York, 1999); Beth L. Bailey and David Farber, *The First Strange Place: Race and Sex in World War II Hawaii* (Baltimore, 1994). On the Canal Zone, see Michael E. Donoghue, *Borderland on the Isthmus: Race, Culture, and the Struggle for the Canal Zone* (Durham, 2014). On oil enclaves, see Robert Vitalis, *America's Kingdom: Mythmaking on the Saudi Oil Frontier* (Palo Alto, 2006).

41. For an exemplary work of transfer history, see Daniel T. Rodgers, *Atlantic Crossings: Social Politics in a Progressive Age* (Cambridge, MA, 1998).

42. Donna Gabaccia calls on historians to link immigration and US foreign relations histories in *Foreign Relations: American Immigration in Global Perspective* (Princeton, 2012). Gordon Chang argues for the necessity of linking Asian-American histories and US foreign relations histories in "Asian Immigrants and American Foreign Relations," in Warren Cohen, *Pacific Passages: The Study of American–East Asian Relations on the Eve of the 21st Century* (New York, 1996).

43. Mae M. Ngai, *Impossible Subjects: Illegal Aliens and the Making of Modern America* (Princeton, 2004); Moon-ho Jung, "Seditious Subjects: Race, State Violence, and the U.S. Empire," *Journal of Asian American Studies* 14 (June 2011), 221–47.

44. Carl Bon Tempo, *Americans at the Gate: The United States and Refugees during the Cold War* (Princeton, 2008); Madeline Y. Hsu, *The Good Immigrants: How the Yellow Peril became the Model Minority* (Princeton, 2015).

45. Paul A. Kramer, "Imperial Openings: Civilization, Exemption, and the Geopolitics of Mobility in the History of Chinese Exclusion, 1868–1910," *Journal of the Gilded Age and Progressive Era*, Vol. 14 (2015), pp. 317–47.

46. Martin Luther King, Jr., "Beyond Vietnam: A Time to Break Silence," reprinted in Martin Luther King., Jr., and Lewis V. Baldwin, eds., *"In a Single Garment of Destiny": A Global Vision of Justice* (Boston Press, 2014).

47. For the roots of this linkage see, especially, W. E. B. DuBois, *Black Reconstruction: An Essay Toward a History of the Part which Black Folk Played in the Attempt to Reconstruct Democracy in America, 1860–1880* (New York, 1935); C. L. R. James, *The Black Jacobins: Toussaint L'Ouverture and the San Domingo Revolution* (New York, 1963 [1938]); Eric Williams, *Capitalism and Slavery* (Chapel Hill, 1944). For recent works taking up the analysis of slavery-based capitalism, see Walter Johnson, *River of Dark Dreams: Slavery and Empire in the Cotton Kingdom* (Cambridge,

MA, 2013); Edward Baptist, *The Half Has Never Been Told: Slavery and the Making of American Capitalism* (New York, 2014); Sven Beckert, *Empire of Cotton: A Global History* (New York, 2014).

48. David Roediger and Elizabeth Esch, *The Production of Difference: Race and the Management of Labor in U.S. History* (New York, 2012); Julie Greene, *The Canal Builders: Making America's Empire at the Panama Canal* (New York, 2009); Jason Colby, *The Business of Empire: United Fruit, Race, and U.S. Expansion in Central America* (Ithaca, 2011); Jana Lipman, *Guantánamo: A Working-Class History between Empire and Revolution* (Berkeley, 2008); Daniel E. Bender and Jana K. Lipman, eds., *Making the Empire Work: Labor and United States Imperialism* (New York, 2015).

49. Emily Rosenberg, *Financial Missionaries to the World: The Politics and Culture of Dollar Diplomacy, 1900–1930* (Cambridge, MA, 1999).

50. On African Americans in the US military from World War I into the Cold War, see, for example, Adriane Lentz-Smith, *Freedom Struggles: African Americans and World War I* (Cambridge, MA, 2009); Kimberley L. Philips, *War! What is it Good for?: Black Freedom Struggles and the U.S. Military from World War II to Iraq* (Chapel Hill, 2012).

51. See, for example, Maria Hohn and Martin Klimke, *A Breath of Freedom: The Civil Rights Struggle, African American GIs, and Germany* (New York, 2010).

52. Mike Green, *Black Yanks in the Pacific: Race in the Making of American Military Empire after World War II* (Ithaca, 2010).

53. For the classic account of "race war" in the Pacific during World War II, see John Dower, *War without Mercy: Race and Power in the Pacific War* (New York, 1986). On the racialization of enmity during the Philippine–American War, see Kramer, *The Blood of Government*, ch. 2.

54. Greg Robinson, *A Tragedy of Democracy: Japanese Confinement in North America* (New York, 2009); Brian Masaru Hayashi, *Democratizing the Enemy: The Japanese American Internment* (Princeton, 2008); Roger Daniels, *Prisoners without Trial: Japanese Americans in World War II* (New York, 2004). On postwar shifts in American perception, see Naoko Shibusawa, *America's Geisha Ally: Reimagining the Japanese Enemy* (Cambridge, MA, 2006).

55. See, for example, black soldiers in the Spanish–Cuban–American War and Philippine–American War: Willard Gatewood, *Black Americans and the White Man's Burden, 1898–1903* (Champaign, 1975).

56. Gerald Horne, "Race from Power: U.S. Foreign Policy and the General Crisis of 'White Supremacy,'" *Diplomatic History*, Vol. 23, No. 3 (Summer 1999), 437–61; Frank Furedi, *The Silent War: Imperialism and the Changing Perception of Race* (London, 1998).

57. Dudziak, *Cold War Civil Rights*. On the early Soviet indictment of American racism, see Meredith L. Roman, *Opposing Jim Crow: African Americans and the Soviet Indictment of U.S. Racism, 1928–1937* (Lincoln, 2012).

16
Gendering American foreign relations

Judy Tzu-Chun Wu

What is gender analysis and how does it change the way we think about American foreign relations? The term "gender" has multiple meanings and intellectual usages. Gender generally refers to the socially constructed nature of sex roles. The concept of gender challenges biologically essentialist understandings of maleness and femaleness, asserting instead that normative notions of masculinity and femininity are socially defined ideas projected onto biological differences.[1] In addition, the interpretation of gender as a form of performativity argues that there are no stable categories of sex differences.[2] Instead, gender is enacted through repeated and oftentimes unconscious patterns of behaviors or gender scripts that create a fiction of a cohesive and pre-existing identity of manhood or womanhood. Furthermore, scholars of gender note that physiological differences do not necessarily divide neatly into two sexes, as some individuals are intersexed. Similarly, some societies recognize more than two genders, and some individuals are transgendered, that is, they identify with a gender that is not normatively associated with their physical sex.[3] Finally, scholars of gender and sexuality have conceptually delineated these categories. Individuals who transgress gender norms are frequently perceived as transgressing sexual norms in their desires, behaviors, and identifications. However, gender and sexuality do not necessarily align in expected ways with one another.

Scholars have utilized the concepts of gender (and sexuality) for various purposes. Feminist scholars have foregrounded gender in order to challenge naturalized and hierarchical differences between men and women. In some of these studies, gender is interchangeable with the category of woman. That is, some works on gender primarily focus on women. However, other studies have used gender to analyze masculinity as a social construction and to examine how masculinity and femininity are relationally defined. In addition, some scholars argue that gender hierarchies exemplify and justify broader forms of social inequality. As Joan Scott explained, "gender is a primary way of signifying relationships of power."[4] This chapter explicates how these conceptions of gender (and sexuality) can be useful methodological approaches to analyzing US foreign relations.[5] Scholars have broadened and enriched the field of US foreign relations history by focusing on women, masculinity, and on gender as a signifier of power.

WHERE ARE THE WOMEN?

The study of American foreign relations is closely connected to the fields of diplomatic and military history, as well as to political science and international relations. These fields have traditionally focused on elite white men who are in positions of power to broker international relationships. How might focusing on women's roles in international relations change the way we think about US foreign relations?

In a 1990 *Journal of American History* article, Emily Rosenberg identified four approaches to integrating women into the study of foreign relations.[6] First, one might foreground "exceptional" and "elite" women who played important but under-recognized historical roles in foreign relations. Second, historians might look beyond elite actors to analyze how women shaped international relations through sex-segregated and frequently nonstate actor roles, such as nursing, missionary work, and peace movements. Third, scholars need to understand how gendered imaginaries shape broader social and global inequalities. And, finally, the "women in development" scholarship focuses on how women, particularly those in "Third World" contexts are affected by modernization and globalization processes.

Kristin Hoganson expands on Rosenberg's insights in a 2004 essay that was published in the 2nd edition of *Explaining the History of American Foreign Relations*. Posing the question, "What's Gender Got to Do With It?," Hoganson answers that the historical attention to women, gender, and sexuality has helped to transform the field of foreign/international relations history by foregrounding social and cultural history. In other words, focusing on gender encourages historians to look beyond elite state-actors and to understand the cultural values, practices, and worldviews that shape the actions and decisions of these individuals. Hoganson argues that the gender infusion and transformation of the study of foreign relations have been fueled by feminist international relations scholarship, postcolonial studies, and the internationalization of US history.[7]

Building on the important insights of these essays, I will highlight three concepts/methodological approaches that demonstrate how a focus on women gives us new insights into American foreign relations. Each of these approaches incorporates an intersectional analysis. Coined by legal scholar Kimberlé Crenshaw, intersectionality posits that categories of social difference, such as gender, race, class, sexuality, dis/ability, and citizenship, intersect and mutually define one another.[8] In other words, there is no universal conception or experience of womanhood (or manhood). Instead, the lives and gendered expectations of women vary depending on their class status, racial identity, sexuality, able-bodiedness, nationality, and so on. Consequently, scholars of American foreign relations who seek to incorporate "women" in their studies also need to analyze how other categories of social difference intersect with gender.

One way to foreground the historical significance of women in foreign relations is to analyze what Joane Nagel has described as the "military-sexual complex."[9] The phrase "military-industrial complex" highlights the political collusion between American military and political leaders with heads of private industries since the onset of the Cold War. Similarly, the military-sexual complex foregrounds how the institutional culture of the military fosters particular sexual practices. These include the promotion of prostitution, the formation of red light districts, acts of sexual violence, surveillance of same-sex sexuality, and international as well as inter-racial sexual, marital, and parental relationships. These day-to-day intimate interactions deeply shape American foreign policies. Sexualized encounters with US military personnel influence how "locals" and their governments perceive the United States. For example, acts of sexual violence committed by US soldiers in Japan, most notably the rape of a 12-year-old Okinawan girl in 1995, caused a national uproar. Incidents such as these have led the Japanese government to prosecute US military personnel. In light of these military–civilian sexualized encounters, US political and military leaders expend time and energy managing and monitoring these relationships both abroad and at home.[10]

A second approach highlighting how women shaped foreign relations focuses on gender and the global economy. Women have played a central role in the production of global goods, such as textiles, electronics, and agricultural products. These products and the sites of production have historically been subjected to local, national, international, and extraterritorial regulations. To protest working conditions and wages, women have organized across national boundaries for labor rights.[11] Women also have been consumers of cosmopolitan products. By purchasing teas, spices, divans, ottomans, fabrics, and other personal and household decorations, women have brought the global, or at least market fantasies of the global, directly into American homes.[12]

Both producer and consumer roles are connected to and sometimes in conflict with expectations that women serve as biological and social reproducers of their families, communities, and nations. Women work for pay in order to help support themselves, their families, and sometimes their nations.[13] And, gender segregation in the workplace allocates certain jobs and certain pay scales to women based on assumptions regarding their skills and capabilities as well as their economically dependent status. Some women also consume global goods based on their socially assigned responsibilities as caretakers of the home. Finally, some women work for pay as social reproducers by taking care of children, the elderly, and households. These women are "transnational," because they tend to travel across national boundaries to provide these services.[14] Women's roles as producers, reproducers, and consumers are central to the functioning of a global economy.

A third approach to studying women in foreign relations is to examine how female migration shaped the formation of national borders and international relations. Donna Gabaccia argues that immigration should be studied by diplomatic historians. She proposes the concept of "immigrant foreign relations" to highlight how a bottom-up approach to studying life experiences could be coupled with a top-down approach to analyzing international politics.[15] After all, immigration tends to correlate with the economic, political, and military penetration of the US into other countries. American and other Western forms of expansion create the necessary transportation infrastructure, the cultural exposure to the US, and often the motivation to migrate due to worsening economic and political circumstances. For example, Catherine Ceniza Choy traces the migration of professional Filipinas to the US back to the US–Philippine War and the American colonization of the Philippines. The introduction of a US educational system, the spread of American popular culture, and the presence of the US military during and after occupation created a culture of migration, one that fostered Filipino relocation to the metropole.[16]

Migration into and out of the United States has rarely occurred in gender-balanced ways. Until the mid-twentieth century, women, with some exceptions, tended to be in the minority among migrants. However, they often performed important political roles through their migration. In the prize-winning book, *Peace Came in the Form of a Woman: Indians and Spaniards in the Texas Borderlands*, Juliana Barr argues that indigenous women were diplomats. They crossed multiple cultural and national borders, sometimes as captives, and utilized their in-between position to negotiate conflicting political interests among indigenous nations and the Spanish empire.

Women who cross national borders also become subjects of immigration policies as well as international agreements. Scholars such as Martha Gardner and Eithne Luibheid point out the gendered logic of the US state, which has tended to deter women from migrating unless they were "white," middle class, and members of heterosexual family units.[17] During the era of Asian exclusion from the late nineteenth through the middle of the twentieth century, Asian women were not only monitored in immigration stations in the United States. In some cases, the US border extended outward through the pre-screening of potential migrants on their native lands.[18] And in the late twentieth century, national and state governments as well as the popular media targeted undocumented women due to fears about their productive as well as reproductive capacities. Women who crossed national borders were perceived to be drains on the shrinking welfare state.[19]

The military-sexual complex, gender and the global economy, and the international politics of female migration are three approaches that illuminate how a focus on women can expand our understanding of American foreign relations. Studying women as leaders and activists in international politics and international organizations is of course necessary as well.[20] And, framing "domestic" issues, such as suffrage, in an international and imperial context is also important.[21] In addition, examining women in militarized settings and the global economy as well as through migration foregrounds a wider array of female experiences and how they are shaped by and in turn shape foreign relations.

MEN HAVE GENDER IDENTITIES, TOO

The term gender is often used synonymously with the category of women. This approach leaves the category of men as the norm, seemingly unmarked by gender. However, scholars are increasingly interested in analyzing how men are gendered as well and how masculinity matters in international relations. This section will analyze three examples of how to examine masculinity and foreign politics. The first emphasizes the significance of cultural history, the second highlights the importance of emotion, and the third foregrounds how institutions foster particular forms of masculinity.

Kristin Hoganson's 1998 book *Fighting for American Manhood: How Gender Politics Provoked the Spanish–American and Philippine–American Wars* highlights the importance of analyzing masculinity as part of the political culture of the late nineteenth and early twentieth century.[22] Hoganson argues that historians need to make sense of the cultural context, or "the cultural roots," that led political and military leaders as well as everyday Americans to go to war. As she states:

It is tempting to overlook the cultural frameworks that shaped contemporaries' outlooks and instead to focus on precipitating incidents, political and diplomatic wranglings, closed-doors meetings, and the like. But to focus exclusively on immediate causes is to skim the surface of the past, to assume that earlier generations understood their world as we understand ours. To fully understand the descent into war, we need to understand how contemporaries viewed the precipitating incidents, what seemed to be at stake in their diplomatic and political wranglings, and what assumptions they brought to their high-level meetings – and to do that, we need to understand something of their culture.[23]

For Hoganson, understanding the culture of the late nineteenth- and early twentieth-century United States means foregrounding the significance of gender. She argues that "gender convictions – meaning the ideas about appropriate male and female roles – ... did so much to define the contours of late-nineteenth-century U.S. political culture."[24] Dominant gender beliefs at that time defined the realm of politics and economics as a masculine, particularly white male, domain. However, some women were challenging this prerogative through campaigns for suffrage. In addition, the 1890s was a period of economic and political turmoil. Hoganson analyzes the gendered political language of this time period, noting how arguments for war emphasized that it "would bolster American manhood."[25] She notes that gender functioned in two ways in this context:

On the one hand, gender served as a cultural motive that easily lent itself to economic, strategic, and other justifications for war. On the other, gender served as a coalition-building political method, one that helped jingoes forge their disparate arguments for war into a simpler, more visceral rationale that had a broad appeal. As both motive and method, gender helped men from different regions, parties, and walks of life to come together to form a powerful political movement.[26]

Hoganson's work highlights how gender roles, particularly masculinity, culturally shaped how Americans understood their identities and obligations.

While Hoganson's work focuses on gender to explain national culture, Frank Costigliola's book *Roosevelt's Lost Alliances: How Personal Politics Helped Start the Cold War* analyzes masculinity and masculine friendship to highlight the importance of the individual and the emotional for explaining American foreign relations. Costigliola focuses on the relationships among Franklin D. Roosevelt, Winston Churchill, and Joseph Stalin. He argues that each man "had to live with a gender identity more complex than the conventional norms of masculinity."[27] In many ways, moreover, their gender non-conformity forged bonds among the three men.

Costigliola's study analyzes international foreign relations by focusing on the personal identities and interactions of elite leaders. He takes us behind the scene to what Hoganson refers to as closed-door wranglings. However, Costigliola's elite state actors are not always rational-choice actors. Instead, he argues for the need to understand "emotional belief ... [which] entail[s] arranging the evidence to support a conviction that goes *beyond* that evidence."[28] Understanding the masculinity of world leaders such as FDR, Stalin, and Churchill provides insight into how their relationships with one another as men shaped the emotional beliefs that they held about each other, the policies that they proposed, and their respective countries.

While Costigliola focuses on the personal/emotional and Hoganson foregrounds the importance of masculinity on national political culture, Robert D. Dean in his book *Imperial Brotherhood: Gender and the Making of Cold War Foreign Policy* emphasizes how institutions inculcate a particular elite form of masculinity among political leaders.[29] Dean explores the question, "how did highly educated men, who prided themselves on their hard-headed pragmatism, men who shunned 'fuzzy-minded' idealism, lead the United States into a prolonged, futile, and destructive war in Vietnam and Southeast Asia?"[30] Combining both cultural and emotional historical approaches, Dean posits that "the process of foreign policy decision does not and cannot exist in an abstract realm of reasoned calculation of 'national interest.' Instead, it assumes that the men who make the decisions are complex, socially constructed beings, who act from a repertoire of possibilities that are a product of their experience."[31] In other words, foreign policy is "culturally constructed and reproduced";

understanding these policies, according to Dean, requires "an account of the formative patterns of class and gender among the policymakers."[32]

Dean proposes the phrase "imperial brotherhood" to describe the "ideology of masculinity" that was inculcated among US political leaders.[33] This ideology, as Dean explains, "refers to the cultural system of prescription and proscription that organizes the 'performance' of an individual's role in society, that draws boundaries around the social category of manhood, and that can be used to legitimate power and privilege."[34] These ideologies of masculinity were constructed and policed through institutions as well as historical events. Dean emphasizes the importance of particular male-only establishments in inculcating an imperial brotherhood. Institutions, such as "boarding schools, Ivy League fraternities and secret societies, elite military service, metropolitan men's clubs ... [were] where imperial traditions of 'service' and 'sacrifice' were invented and bequeathed to those that followed."[35] Furthermore, historical events, such as the McCarthy era, launched red- and pink-baiting witch hunts; communists and homosexuals both became political targets. Their persecutions prescribed normative masculinity for political leaders who wanted to remain in power. These ideologies of masculinity, nurtured through institutional culture and reinforced through historical events, in turn shaped how US leaders understood military and political challenges to American global power.

Studying masculinity expands historical endeavors by foregrounding cultural, emotional, and institutional history. One approach analyzes national cultural values, another explores personal relationships among elite men, and a third foregrounds how male-only institutions created the culture of masculinity among US leaders. These methodologies posit that scholars need to understand how past historical subjects understood their identities, social roles, and political values in order to explain their decisions and actions. Masculinity scholars argue that gender was and is central in shaping how people make sense of themselves and their societies.

GLOBAL GENDERED IMAGINARIES

In addition to focusing on women and masculinity, scholars of gender and foreign relations also analyze how gender is a signifier of power and hierarchy among nations. That is, countries themselves have gendered national identities. At times, these identities are self-defined. At other times, outsiders may project a particular gender identity onto another country. Scholars have noted how the feminization and, in some instances, the infantilization of particular countries justify masculine and parental domination by other nations, often in the name of protection. In these gendered global imaginaries or worldviews, femininity usually symbolizes weakness and subservience. However, alternative gender imaginaries also existed, ones in which womanhood sometimes served as a model of resistance and strength. This section will analyze how these global gendered imaginaries shaped US relations with the Global South as well as the Global North.

Naoko Shibusawa's *America's Geisha Ally: Reimagining the Japanese Enemy* provides an example of how a global gender and racial imaginary influenced US foreign policy. In her study of US post-World War II relations with Japan, Shibusawa asks how Japan was rehabilitated from being a despised and racialized enemy during World War II to the United States' closest Cold War ally in Asia. She argues that the feminization and infantilization of Japan by American political and cultural discourse encouraged the US public to accept this new alliance. As Shibusawa argues:

The post-war public discourse assumed two "natural" or universally recognized hierarchical relationships – man over woman and adult over child – and compared them to the relationship between the United States, a "white" nation, and Japan, a "nonwhite" nation. Portraying Japan as a woman made its political subjugation appear as natural as a geisha's subservience to a male client, while picturing Japan as a child emphasized its potential to "grow up" into a democracy.[36]

Gender and parental hierarchies, which appear as "natural," help explain acceptance of unequal power relations and obligations between the United States and Japan.

The tropes of the United States as a white, male protector and other nations as racial other, female, childlike, sexually non-normative, and in need of tutelage are echoed in various historical studies of US foreign relations. These gendered imaginaries were central to cultural and political discourse during the US–Spanish and US–Philippine Wars, the US campaigns in Asia during the Cold War, and the US War on Terror.[37] The constructs that posit Asian people as the gender opposite of the United States builds upon an American tradition of orientalism, a Western worldview that regards East and West as unequal opposites that nevertheless mutually define one another.[38]

The US global imaginary did not just focus on countries of the Global South. The United States also feminized and sought to dominate Western nations. In the book *GIs and Germans: Culture, Gender, and Foreign Relations, 1945–1949* Petra Goedde asks how Germany transformed from a World War II enemy into a "client state" of the United States relatively soon after the end of the war. She argues for the importance of informal relations, particularly between American soldiers and the German populace, many of whom were women in the aftermath of the war. In addition to focusing on social history, Goedde also argues for the importance of cultural history, in particular, the gendered global imaginary of the United States and Germany. The cross-cultural gendered relationships between US soldiers and German women and children shaped American understandings of Germany and German understandings of the United States. Goedde argues that "American power over Germans became infused with gendered meaning, creating the perception among both those who held the power and those who submitted to it, that the asymmetry between them was a natural phenomenon."[39]

Frank Costigliola makes a similar argument about the power of gender to naturalize power hierarchies among Western nations. In a 1997 *Journal of American History* article on George F. Kennan, Costigliola points out how gendered and emotional language permeated his famous 1946 telegram arguing for containment of the Soviet Union. Kennan portrayed the Soviet leadership as pathological and "as a masculine rapist." In contrast, he represented Russian people as feminized and in need of Western protection from "the monstrous hypermasculinity of the Soviet Union."[40] Costigliola traces these gendered tropes to Kennan's experience as a foreign officer during the interwar years, when the overwhelmingly male US foreign service bonded over sexual escapades with Russian women. Kennan's gender anxieties also reflected his concerns about developments in US domestic society, namely fears of "gender inversion: men being feminized, women being masculinized, traditional gender roles being destabilized."[41] The gendered and emotive language in the "Long Telegram" had an important policy impact, helping "the Truman administration arrive at a reductive but clear picture of Soviet policy."[42] As Costigliola argues, "gendering works to emotionalize and polarize issues."[43]

Costigliola makes a similar argument about the importance of gender and emotion in his *Diplomatic History* article about inter-country relations in NATO and in his book on US–France relations during the post-World War II era.[44] He cites a NATO official who explained that "metaphors of sex and of the family 'were shorthand; they make it easier to conceptualize complex, nuanced relationships.'"[45] Costigliola points out that these complex, nuanced relationships were also hierarchical and that employing "tropes explicitly or implicitly associated with gender" and sexuality serve "to naturalize relationships of unequal power."[46]

The global gender hierarchies discussed previously tend to assume the inferiority of women and the superiority of men. However, alternative gender imaginaries also existed. Heather Stur's study of gender in the Vietnam War argues that the "dragon lady" image, fostered in US popular culture through much of the twentieth century, helped American soldiers make sense of what they understood as female treachery. The women labeled as "dragon ladies" did not need protection but instead represented a threat to the US military.[47]

Similarly, part of my book *Radicals on the Road: Internationalism, Orientalism, and Feminism during the Vietnam Era* examines the Vietnamese woman warrior image that circulated among American anti-war activists.[48] My study explores the international travels of American antiwar activists and their political dialogues with Asian political leaders. I focus in particular on individuals, mostly non-white and/or female, who largely have been overlooked by the existing historiography. I also introduce the concept of *radical orientalism* to explain how American radicals who wanted to critique

US imperialism sometimes reinforced the binary between East and West. However, they also flipped the hierarchy between the two. Rather than the East being subservient and backwards, decolonizing Asia could provide political inspiration for activists in the West. In fact, Vietnamese peasant women, commonly depicted as meek and weak, could – in the eyes of American activists – become important political mentors. Their underdog status and determination to fight against the most powerful military power in the world inspired activists in the West. The gendered representations of the Vietnamese, particularly Vietnamese women, served as political role models for many US antiwar activists.

These examples of global gender imaginaries reveal how representations and understandings about maleness and femaleness can be mobilized for international political purposes. Inequalities between nations can be "naturalized" through gendered and familial metaphors. And, challenges to global inequalities also might mobilize gendered symbols for purposes of social liberation. Gender, in both these instances, is a symbol of power that could help generate consent or inspire challenges to social inequalities.

CONCLUSION

This chapter highlights three approaches to gendering American foreign relations. Focusing on women expands the definition of political actors and international relations. Women in state as well as nonstate capacities played significant roles in shaping US relations with other countries through the military-sexual complex, the global economy, migration, and in various arenas of politics. Analyzing masculinity can foreground cultural, emotional, and institutional history. Doing so encourages scholars of foreign relations to understand that gender was significant for how their historical subjects understood themselves as well as their obligations to society. Finally, recognizing that gender is a signifier of power leads us to pay attention to gendered language and representations. These cultural and political discourses about masculinity and femininity served as tools to foster hierarchies, obligations, and resistance between nations.

The questions that gender history raises are central to the discipline of history. Gender methodologies encourage us to ask: Who are historical actors? Why did people do what they did? What was the broader context that shaped their worldviews and actions? And, how did people justify relationships of inequality to themselves, to their public, and to the people who are being subjugated? These questions need to be answered to more fully comprehend and analyze the past.

And, for all of these questions, gender historians ask, how did the individual or the society's understanding of maleness, femaleness, or alternative gender formations matter? Did women and men experience and/or enact historical events differently? How did individuals understand their gender identity and did gender influence their politics and actions? How do societies mobilize gendered responsibilities and expectations to support particular international policies or causes? In sum, gender historians ask how and why gender matters.

NOTES

1. Kathleen Canning, *Gender History in Practice: Historical Perspectives on Bodies, Class and Citizenship* (Ithaca, NY, 2006); Donna R. Gabaccia and Mary Joe Maynes, *Gender History Across Epistemologies* (Chichester, West Sussex, 2013); Alice Kessler-Harris, *Gendering Labor History* (Urbana, IL, 2007); Susan Kingsley Kent, *Gender and History* (Basingstoke, Hampshire, 2012); Sonya O. Rose, *What is Gender History?* (Cambridge, UK, 2010); Joan Wallach Scott, *Gender and the Politics of History* (New York, 1999); Peter N. Stearns, *Gender in World History* (London, UK, 2000); Mary E. Wiesner, *Gender in History* (Malden, MA, 2001)
2. Judith Butler, *Gender Trouble: Feminism and the Subversion of Identity* (New York, 1990).
3. Joanne Meyerowitz, *How Sex Changed: A History of Transexuality in the United States* (Cambridge, MA, 2004) and Susan Stryker, *Transgender History* (Berkeley, CA, 2009).
4. Joan W. Scott, "Gender: A Useful Category of Historical Analysis," *American Historical Review* 91:5 (December 1986), p. 1067.
5. Also see Laura McEnaney, Emily S. Rosenberg, Elaine Tyler May, Geoffrey S. Smith, Susan Jeffords, Amy Kaplan, Anders Stephanson, and Bruce Kuklick, "Culture, Gender, and Foreign Policy: A Symposium," *Diplomatic History* 18:1 (1994): 47–124.
6. Emily Rosenberg, "Gender," *Journal of American History* (June 1990): 16–24.
7. Kristin Hoganson, "What's Gender Got to Do with It?: Gender History as Foreign Relations History," *Explaining the History of American Foreign Relations*, edited by Michael J. Hogan and Thomas G. Patterson (New York, 2004), pp. 304–22.
8. Kimberlé Crenshaw, "Demarginalizing the Intersection of Race and Sex: A Black Feminist Critique of Antidiscrimination Doctrine, Feminist Theory and Antiracist Politics," *University of Chicago Legal Forum* (1989): 139–67; and Crenshaw, "Mapping the Margins: Intersectionality, Identity Politics, and Violence Against Women of Color," *Stanford Law Review* 43 (July 1991): 1241–99.
9. Joane Nagel, *Race, Ethnicity, and Sexuality: Intimate Intersections, Forbidden Frontiers* (New York, 2003).
10. Donna Alvah, *Unofficial Ambassadors: American Military Families Overseas and the Cold War* (New York, 2007); Petra Goedde, *GIs and Germans: Culture, Gender, and Foreign Relations, 1945–1949* (New Haven, CT, 2003); Michael Cullen Green, *Black Yanks in the Pacific: Race in the Making of American Military Empire after World War II* (Ithaca, NY, 2010); Maria Höhn and Seungsook Moon, eds., *Over There: Living with the U.S. Military Empire from World War Two to the Present* (Durham, NC, 2010); Elaine Tyler May, *Homeward Bound: American Families during the Cold War* (New York, 1988); Ji-Yeon Yuh, *Beyond the Shadow of Camptown: Korean Military Brides in America* (New York, 2002); Susan Zeiger, *Entangling Alliances: Foreign War Brides and American Soldiers in the Twentieth Century* (New York, 2010).

11. Dorothy Sue Cobble, "A Higher 'Standard of Life' for the World: U.S. Labor Women's Reform Internationalism and the Legacies of 1919," *Journal of American History* 100:4 (March 2014): 1052–85.
12. Kristin Hoganson, *Consumers' Imperium: The Global Production of American Domesticity, 1865–1920* (Chapel Hill, NC, 2007); Mary Yoshihara, *Embracing the East: White Women and American Orientalism* (New York, 2003).
13. Rhacel Salazar Parreñas, *Servants of Globalization: Women, Migration, and Domestic Work* (Stanford, CA, 2001).
14. Eileen Boris and Rhacel Salazar Parreñas, *Intimate Labors: Cultures, Technologies, and the Politics of Care* (Stanford, CA, 2010); Barbara Ehrenreich and Arlie Russell Hochschild, *Global Woman: Nannies, Maids, and Sex Workers in the New Economy* (New York, 2003).
15. Donna R. Gabaccia, *Foreign Relations: American Immigration in Global Perspective* (Princeton, NJ, 2012).
16. Catherine Ceniza Choy, *Empire of Care: Nursing and Migration in Filipino American History* (Durham, NC, 2003).
17. Martha Gardner, *The Qualities of a Citizen: Women, Immigration, and Citizenship, 1870–1965* (Princeton, NJ, 2009), and Eithne Leuibheid, *Entry Denied: Controlling Sexuality at the Border* (Minneapolis, MN, 2002).
18. Sucheng Chan, "The Exclusion of Chinese Women, 1870–1943," in *Entry Denied: Exclusion and the Chinese Community in America, 1882–1943*, ed. by Sucheng Chan (Philadelphia, 1994).
19. Grace Chang, *Disposable Domestics: Immigrant Women Workers in the Global Economy* (Boston, 2000); Lisa Sun-Hee Park, *Entitled to Nothing: The Struggle for Immigrant Health Care in the Age of Welfare Reform* (New York, 2011).
20. Leila J. Rupp, *Worlds of Women: The Making of an International Women's Movement* (Princeton, NJ, 1997); Francisa de Haan, "Continuing Cold War Paradigms in Western Historiography of Transnational Women's Organizations: The Case of the Women's International Democratic Federation (WIDF)," *Women's History Review* 19:4 (September 2010): 547–74; Francisca de Haan, "Eugenie Cotton, Park Chong-ae, and Claudia Jones: Rethinking Transnational Feminism and International Politics," *Journal of Women's History* 25:4 (Winter 2013): 174–89; Katherine Marino, "La Vanguardia Feminista: Pan-American Feminism and the Rise of International Women's Rights, 1915–1946," PhD Dissertation, Stanford University, 2013; Judy Tzu-Chun Wu, "U.S. Feminisms and Their Global Connections," *Oxford Handbook of American Women's and Gender History*, ed. Ellen Harigan-O'Connor and Lisa Materson (Oxford University Press, forthcoming).
21. Allison L. Sneider, *Suffragists in an Imperial Age: U.S. Expansion and the Woman Question, 1870–1929* (New York, 2008).
22. Kristin L. Hoganson, *Fighting for American Manhood: How Gender Politics Provoked the Spanish–American and Philippine–American Wars* (New Haven, CT, 1998).
23. Ibid., p. 3.
24. Ibid.
25. Ibid., p. 8.
26. Ibid., pp. 8–9.

27. Frank Costigliola, *Roosevelt's Lost Alliances: How Personal Politics Helped Start the Cold War* (Princeton, NJ, 2012), p. 3.
28. Ibid., pp. 12–13.
29. Robert D. Dean, *Imperial Brotherhood: Gender and the Making of Cold War Foreign Policy* (Amherst, MA, 2001).
30. Ibid., p. 1.
31. Ibid., p. 3.
32. Ibid.
33. Ibid., p. 5.
34. Ibid.
35. Ibid., p. 4.
36. Naoko Shibusawa, *America's Geisha Ally: Reimagining the Japanese Enemy* (Cambridge, MA, 2006), pp. 4–5.
37. Kristin Hoganson, *Fighting for American Manhood*; Christina Klein, *Cold War Orientalism: Asia in the Middlebrow Imagination, 1945–1961* (Berkeley, CA, 2003); Melani McAlister, *Epic Encounters: Culture, Media, and U.S. Interests in the Middle East, 1945–2000* (Berkeley, CA, 2001); Jasbir Puar, *Terrorist Assemblages: Homonationalism in Queer Times* (Durham, NC, 2007); Andrew J. Rotter, "Gender Relations, Foreign Relations: The United States and South Asia, 1947–1964," *Journal of American History* 81:2 (September 1994): 518–42.
38. Karen J. Leong, *The China Mystique: Pearl S. Buck, Anna May Wong, Mayling Soong, and the Transformation of American Orientalism* (Berkeley, 2005); Douglas Little, *American Orientalism: The United States and the Middle East since 1945* (Chapel Hill, NC, 2002); Zachary Lockman, *Contending Visions of the Middle East: The History and Politics of Orientalism* (New York, 2004); Bill V. Mullen, *Afro-Orientalism* (Minneapolis, MN, 2004); John Tchen, *New York before Chinatown: Orientalism and the Shaping of American Culture, 1776–1882* (Baltimore, MD, 1999); Edward W. Said, *Orientalism* (New York, 1978).
39. Goedde, *G.I.s and Germans*, p. xxi.
40. Frank Costigliola, "'Unceasing Pressure for Penetration': Gender, Pathology, and Emotion in George Kennan's Formation of the Cold War," *Journal of American History* 83:4 (March 1997): 1333.
41. Ibid., p. 1325.
42. Ibid., p. 1313.
43. Ibid., p. 1328.
44. Frank Costigliola, *France and the United States: The Cold Alliance since World War II* (New York, 1992).
45. Frank Costigliola, "The Nuclear Family: Tropes of Gender and Pathology in the Western Alliance," *Diplomatic History* 21:2 (Spring 1997): 163.
46. Ibid.
47. Heather Marie Stur, *Beyond Combat: Women and Gender in the Vietnam War Era* (New York, 2011).
48. Judy Tzu-Chun Wu, *Radicals on the Road: Internationalism, Orientalism, and Feminism during the Vietnam Era* (Ithaca, NY, 2013).

17

The religious turn in diplomatic history

Andrew Preston

Few aspects of the human condition are as complicated as religion. Universal and yet impossible to define because no single definition can capture its diversity and complexity, religion is a source of war and peace, conservatism and liberalism, traditionalism and modernism, nationalism and internationalism, localism and globalism. It is the producer and product of culture, and all that culture entails. Worldwide, in virtually every society, it has provided a basis for the human condition from long before the axial age right through to the present.[1] Yet in the twenty-first century, a digital era of big data, medical miracles, and artificial intelligence, we are more conscious than ever of living in what the philosopher Charles Taylor has called "a secular age."[2]

For diplomatic historians, the problem of religion has been especially acute. Mostly neglected until the last decade or so, religion poses a unique set of methodological and epistemological challenges. This chapter aims to provide a historiographical overview of religion's burgeoning presence in the field; an introduction to the challenges it poses; and a set of guidelines on how it can be used effectively to explain the history of American foreign relations.

Despite its salience to virtually every time period and most topics in American history, until recently the study of religion had been relegated to the margins of historical scholarship. Instead of being considered an integral component of US history writ large, religious history had developed into a specialist subfield, thriving amongst its practitioners but with little appeal and acceptance in the wider historical community. In an influential essay in 2004, Jon Butler observed that modern American historians had a "religion problem": they rarely utilized religious actors or subjects; when they did, it was suddenly and temporarily, with usually superficial results. Butler compared religion to a jack-in-the-box, popping up briefly and unexpectedly before disappearing with little trace.[3] Since then, however, political, social, and cultural historians have worked hard to integrate religion into their broader narratives, so that it now has a central role in topics as diverse as civil rights, ethnicity, citizenship, deindustrialization and the emergence of a services-based economy, mass internal migration, and the rise of the conservative political movement.[4] No longer is the historiographical presence of religion ephemeral, sudden, or brief.

The history of American foreign relations has mirrored this larger trend. Until a decade ago or so, diplomatic historians had their own "religion problem."[5] There were, to be sure, scattered exceptions to this general rule of neglect, particularly those dealing with the formation of American ideology and its role in shaping a distinctive self-conception of the United States as a chosen nation and world redeemer.[6] But for the most part, diplomatic historians either pushed religion to the sidelines or ignored it entirely. Due to cultural and transnational turns, the field of diplomatic history has completely changed, as many of the chapters in this volume illustrate. Taxonomically, it has evolved from "diplomatic history" to "the US and the World" or "US international history," a shift that reflects the change in methodologies and more attention to cultural phenomena and perspectives from the bottom-up. As a category of analysis, however, religion was initially excluded from the initial culturalization of foreign relations history. Studies using race and gender at first led the way; religion lagged behind.

In the late 1990s, Dianne Kirby, an international historian based in the United Kingdom, was one of the first to delve systematically into the religious dimensions of the Cold War, including US foreign policy and how it dealt with communism after World War II.[7] Around the same time, three US-focused studies featured religion in new and innovative ways. In 2000, Andrew Rotter published *Comrades at Odds*, a landmark study of Cold War relations between the United States and India that deployed newer theories of religion, gender, and class (and caste), in addition to more standard topics such as strategy and economics.[8] A year later, Melani McAlister's *Epic Encounters* blended literary criticism and cultural analysis with theories of religion, gender, and race to provide a new interpretation of postwar US relations with the Middle East.[9] And in 2004 Seth Jacobs' book *America's Miracle Man in Vietnam* situated religion alongside race as the determining factor in why and how the Eisenhower administration decided to commit the United States to the survival of South Vietnam.[10]

Yet while the historiographical importance of these works is clear, it is noticeable that all three packaged religion up in a bundle of various other categories of analysis, such as race, gender, and culture. Thus it was not until the publication of William Inboden's groundbreaking *Religion and American Foreign Policy, 1945–1960*, in 2008, that religion stood on its own in the history of American foreign relations in a sustained and consistent fashion.[11] Subtitled *The Soul of Containment*, Inboden's book uses religion not as a primary lens of inquiry, but as its only one. It demonstrates that containment was conceived and directed in part by an ideology grounded in religion. This was a significant milestone in the development of a religious interpretation of diplomatic history. By examining the anti-communist foreign policies of the

Truman and Eisenhower administrations on the basis of an enormous amount of archival research, Inboden conclusively demonstrated two important things: one, that religion was not incidental or peripheral to US foreign policy in the Cold War, but relevant and central; and two, that religion could bear the weight of carrying a heavy causal load.

Since then, there has been a steady flow of books and articles analyzing the history of US foreign relations through the lens of religion. This "religious turn" in diplomatic history, begun by Kirby, Rotter, McAlister, and Jacobs at the beginning of the twenty-first century and entrenched by Inboden a few years later, has enriched the field by providing a much fuller account of the ideological and cultural bases of US foreign policy. Its timing can be partly explained as a collective reaction to the shock of September 11, 2001. Launched by al-Qaeda, a terrorist network espousing an extreme ideology of radical Sunni Islam, the 9/11 attacks forced scholars of international relations, a supposedly secular discipline and subject, to pay attention to religion. 9/11 seemed to vindicate political scientist Samuel Huntington's forecast that the future of world politics would be driven by a "clash of civilizations" in which culture and religion would be more salient than economics or ideology.[12] By "bringing religion into international relations," 9/11 changed the way political scientists and historians approached their subjects.[13]

Nonetheless, works within diplomatic history's post-9/11 religious turn tended to cluster around the usual suspects – that is, topics in which the relevance of religion is demonstrable and to which historians habitually turn for examples of faith-based foreign policies. This applies to Inboden's period of the early Cold War. Between World War II and the early 1960s, the United States not only repositioned itself as a superpower guided by the containment of global communism, it also went through what historians have called another "great awakening" of religious revivals and faith-based politics.[14] As Stephen Whitfield demonstrated in his book *The Culture of the Cold War*, religion, particularly Christianity but also the concept of the United States as a "Judeo-Christian nation," was one of the crucial aspects in the formation of Americans' crusading Cold War mentality.[15] In the past decade, then, the early Cold War has received concentrated attention from historians of foreign relations interested in religion.[16] Correspondingly, historians of domestic US history have recently probed the ways in which the Cold War in turn shaped American religion.[17]

In recent years, clusters of innovative research have formed around other "usual suspects." The statecraft of Woodrow Wilson, for example, has generated a large body of work. Wilson's personal religiosity has always featured in accounts of his politics and foreign policy, and in 1971, Arthur Link, Wilson's most exhaustive biographer, argued that religion was a formative influence on his worldview.[18] Only a few years later, John Mulder followed Link's lead with a painstaking excavation of Wilson's religion and how it shaped his political and diplomatic thought.[19] In the last decade, scholars have drawn even more direct and explicit links between Wilson's religion and Wilsonianism.[20]

Missionaries, another usual suspect, have also received a great deal of attention, from earlier generations of historians as well as in the more recent literature. In the 1960s and 1970s, historians interested in America's imperial turn, both formally in 1898–9 and informally through the imposition of US power overseas during the twentieth century, found rich sources of material in missionary records. As the federal government extended its reach into Hawaii, the Philippines, China, and elsewhere in Asia and the Pacific in the 1890s and the early twentieth century, missionaries seemed to lead the way in entrenching American power.[21] Later, they followed suit in the Middle East.[22] Missionaries were therefore widely perceived, as Walter LaFeber illustrated in his 1963 book *The New Empire*, to be the tip of the imperial spear.[23]

However, recent literature has cast missionaries in a somewhat different light. This shift had two sources. First, historians of the British empire began to portray missionaries as reluctant imperialists who often criticized the United Kingdom's extension of political and military power and aimed to soften its roughest edges.[24] Second, historians of China, Africa, and elsewhere began to invest the recipients of missionary conversion efforts with agency and autonomy; no longer portrayed as helpless victims, Asian Christians became historical actors in their own right.[25] While not denying the relationship between missions and empire, historians are thus recasting missionaries as agents of cultural exchange and transfer; they are, as Ryan Dunch has aptly put it, going "beyond cultural imperialism."[26] It is not difficult to see why. Unlike merchants, missionaries lived among the local population and possessed a grasp of local languages; and unlike diplomats, missionaries lived away from the capital, in the interior, and thus had a more subtle and accurate sense of local politics and culture.[27] They were ideal cultural intermediaries. In this view, missionaries were mostly informal imperialists who, wittingly or not, helped construct a normative American imperium grounded in liberal internationalism and globalization.[28] They were also deeply affected by their cultural encounters with the colonized and non-Western world, and as a result cosmopolitanism and anti-imperialism grew in American missions.[29] In recent decades, moreover, the explosive growth of indigenous Christianity in Asia and Africa has thrown into doubt scholarly assumptions about the amount of coercion needed to spread the gospel.[30] Indeed, a century ago in the Ottoman Empire, China, and Korea, American missionaries spread the empowering and uplifting gospels of national self-determination and individual rights as much as they did the gospel of Christ. From there, missionaries from the liberal, mainline denominations, along with their colleagues in the Protestant ecumenical movement, were integral in building a liberal world order from the Great War to the signing of the United Nations Universal Declaration of Human Rights in 1948.[31]

This broadening out of historical perspectives on missionaries is reflective of a new set of attitudes about the religious influence in American foreign relations. So sharp has the religious turn been that the usual suspects are now not the only topics of choice. Once tied to war and empire, religion is now seen as a much more complex and diverse phenomenon. With this interpretive broadening has come a concomitant expansion of the topics historians are willing to observe through a religious lens. The religious aspects of foreign relations in the interwar period and World War II, for example, have recently been the subject of much greater historical attention.[32] So too has Ronald Reagan, a distinctly un-theological but highly spiritual person who applied religious ideas to the formulation of national security policy – particularly regarding human rights and nuclear disarmament – in clear if idiosyncratic ways.[33]

There has been a significant improvement in the use of religion to explain the history of American foreign relations, yet difficulties persist nonetheless. To start with, what exactly is "religion"? The question is deceptively simple yet fraught with conflict, for there is no single answer that does not preference one worldview over another: the varieties of religious experience in the world are so diverse and complicated that no definition can encompass them all without raising contradictions, exceptions, or inconsistencies.[34] Added to this is the problem, first articulated by Wilfred Cantwell Smith in 1963, that the very concept of "religion" is Western in origin and meaning, and scarcely applies to many of the belief systems found in Africa and Asia.[35] The notion of religion's universality (as opposed to adherents' assumption that their particular faith is or should be universal) was invented during the Reformation, became embedded in European political thought, and then spread through Western imperialism.[36] Later scholars, such as Talal Asad, Daniel Dubuisson, and Tomoko Masuzawa, deepened Smith's insights by exploring the ways in which European state formation and knowledge dissemination entwined to create an artificially cohesive conception of what constituted the phenomenon of religion.[37] As C. A. Bayly points out, in the "long" nineteenth century religion was but one facet of modernity to be codified worldwide along Western/Christian lines.[38] Jonathan Z. Smith's excavation of the historiography of religious history illustrates the ways in which religion is an academic construction, created by European and American scholars for the purposes of classification.[39] For Americanists, a similar challenge is presented by the faiths of slave communities and Native Americans, which do not easily fit the concept of religion, defy easy definition, and have been subject to the homogenizing impulse of Eurocentric models of religious categorization.[40]

"Religion," then, is a problematic term. It endures probably because it is a convenient shorthand for systems of beliefs and practices in a wide variety of cultures and societies. For lack of a better substitute, it is probably unavoidable. Whatever we call it and however we define it, religion continues to prevail throughout the world.

Even if we accept the phenomenon of religion, another problem arises: secularism. For a century, most academics, including historians, believed in secularization theory, which posited that as the world became more modern, it would necessarily become more secular and less religious. Nearly all the prophets of modernity, most notably Karl Marx and Sigmund Freud, believed this to be an iron law of human development. They also perceived it normatively as well as analytically: the decline of religion was a good thing. Intellectuals and academics, particularly sociologists, from Max Weber and the theorists of the Frankfurt School to French post-modernists and American modernization theorists of the Cold War, assumed secularization would proceed alongside modernization. When Daniel Bell famously proclaimed "the end of ideology" in 1960, for example, he included American religion, particularly evangelicalism.[41] Confronted with the endurance of religion in American public life, secularization theorists explained it away by invoking American exceptionalism: the United States was simply different, for a variety of reasons, not only more religious but also unsuited to socialism, and eventually religion would die out even in the United States.[42]

We now know how wrong secularization is as a general theory; there are too many exceptions for it to be sustained as a rule that applies to all societies and all peoples.[43] In fact, beyond Western Europe and pockets of its spinoffs in Australia and North America,[44] it is simply flat wrong. Perhaps it may bear fruit in the next few centuries to come, but as an explanation of the world's past and present it has a poor record. The rise and fall of secularization theory is reflected in the writings of one of the most distinguished religious scholars of the last half-century, Peter Berger. In 1967, Berger's *The Sacred Canopy*, still one of the most influential analyses of religion, provided an explanation for, among other things, the decline of religion. Three decades later, however, when confronted with an overwhelming amount of empirical data showing that religion was not declining in the modern world but growing, Berger acknowledged the limitations of the secularization paradigm.[45] As Berger came to realize, modernity and religion are not antagonistic; indeed, they may even be symbiotic. After all, the most modernizing nations in the world today – China, Turkey, South Korea, and Brazil, to name only a few – are simultaneously experiencing explosive growth in the most pious strains of religion. Globalization and Americanization, both of which are synonymous with relentless modernism, have in fact almost certainly caused the spread of both modernity *and* religion.[46] Recall Daniel Bell, whose timing could not have been worse: his pronouncement of the demise of evangelicalism came right at the dawn of the Religious Right and an era of conservative faith-based politics.

Secularization, it seemed, reflected the desires of its adherents – cosmopolitan intellectuals and scholars for whom religion was indeed declining in significance – rather than the actual world they lived in.[47] For anthropologists and sociologists, this meant they were not fully understanding cultures and societies. For historians, it led to a fundamental misreading of the past.

Following Weber, for example, historians of Europe argued that over time superstition gave way to organized religion, which in turn gave way to science and rationalism.[48] But as Alexandra Walsham has shown, the "disenchantment of the world," to use Weber's term, was never as thorough or complete as historians assumed. Belief in superstition, magic, and religion have all proved to be more enduring than expected, not simply among "primitive cultures" but in the modern West as well.[49]

Methodologically, the prevailing assumptions of secularization theory led historians to assume that people of the past did not mean what they said, at least when they invoked religion to explain themselves. As one scholar admitted, "The sociology of religion is, in fact, the sociology of error.... The problem that activates the sociological machinery is really: how can people possibly believe that?"[50] Witchcraft crazes, for example, could not possibly have arisen from a belief in witches because there is no such thing as a witch. Thus a belief in witches must have been the result of displaced emotional pressures relating to gender, or of macroeconomic forces that were unseen but whose effects were cataclysmic. Similarly, the history of the Crusades and the Inquisition were written as moments in which religion had superficial explanatory power, sitting misleadingly atop the deeper social, economic, and political forces that *really* shaped history. For years, historians argued that when people of the past said they believed in witches, the goals of the Crusades, or the purpose of the Inquisition, what they actually meant was that they felt threatened by social, economic, or cultural changes but could not articulate their fears and so used religion to do it for them.

In American diplomatic history, the best example of this tendency not to take people of the past at face value comes from President William McKinley's famous justification for seizing the Philippines in 1898. Imperialism was controversial, fiercely opposed by many in Congress and a sizeable proportion of the public. McKinley claimed his decision to annex the Philippines was inspired by divine revelation, a claim that diplomatic historians have had a hard time accepting at face value. Akira Iriye's dismissal of McKinley's religious motivations as insincere, and as cover for strategic and economic considerations, reflects a historiographical consensus that religion was peripheral to American imperialism, and perhaps even a distraction.[51] Iriye's thesis has a certain *prima facie* plausibility to it – after all, politicians utter a lot of pious nonsense in order to justify controversial decisions that might be difficult to defend on their actual grounds. Yet historians' dismissal of McKinley's religion is based on assumptions formed in the present rather than the past, without reference to the religious context of late nineteenth-century America. When we examine McKinley's religion, moreover, we discover that he was an intensely devout, evangelical Methodist who prayed to God for guidance and claimed divine inspiration on many issues. Once we uncover McKinley's religious views, his claim seems *the most* plausible explanation. Does this mean that religion was the sole motivating factor in his decision to annex the

Philippines? Of course not. But does it mean that religion can help us unpack McKinley's motivations, and those of many others at the time, and more fully explain the history of American foreign relations? Without a doubt.[52]

In recent decades, historians in other fields have begun to move beyond the academy's secular bias. To take two of our earlier examples, the history of the Crusades and the Inquisition are now explained largely, but not entirely, as having been driven by sincere religious motivation.[53] In a similar fashion, historians of the Enlightenment have reconciled religion with scientific knowledge and uncovered the theological dimensions to what was once considered a thoroughly agnostic age.[54]

This has stemmed from a willingness to take people of the past more at face value. Historians "have not done enough to let our subjects speak in their own voices," argues Richard Wightman Fox, a historian of American religion. "We are too quick to translate their language into ours"; instead, we should "listen carefully" and not jump to decontextualized conclusions.[55] Similarly, Robert A. Orsi stresses that scholarly empathy is as important as scrutiny.[56] Historians must of course retain a critical distance from their subjects and sources; we must not automatically accept what historical actors have handed down to us in books, oral histories, and the archives. Yet we can go too far if we impose our own views on those from the past. Quentin Skinner has rightly warned that it is "nothing less than fatal" for historians to assume that their subjects must have meant something else other than what they wrote and said. "To do so is to assume that, whenever an historian encounters a belief which he or she judges to be false, the explanatory problem must always be that of accounting for a lapse of rationality." As Skinner explains, "this is to equate the holding of rational beliefs with the holding of beliefs that the historian judges to be true. And this is to exclude the obvious possibility that, even in the case of beliefs that nowadays strike us as manifestly false, there may have been good grounds in earlier historical periods for holding them to be true." To take the example of witch-hunting, Skinner points out that it would have been perfectly rational for early-modern Europeans to believe in witches, given the reigning authority of their theology and culture. Indeed, just as it would have been irrational for William McKinley *not* to pray to God for guidance, it would have been irrational for European peasants to deny the existence of witches in the face of the "evidence" presented to them and in light of the religious lens through which they would have interpreted it.[57]

Rational-choice explanations – which have dominated the social sciences, especially economics, political science, and international relations, but have also influenced history – have as their basis the judgment of the analyst (the historian) rather than the agent (the historical actor). They impose an *ex post facto* value judgment (the action was rational/irrational in conception and/or in outcome) that is prone to ahistorical thinking. This might work for the social sciences, which are concerned more with the present and which aim to predict future behavior, but it is not necessarily appropriate to the study of history.[58]

And as intellectual historians have concluded, rationality itself needs to be historicized: as a product of the twentieth century, it says more about scholars' assumptions in the past than it does about how and why their subjects behaved.[59]

Because the field is still for the most part in thrall to rational-choice assumptions and has only recently come to terms with culture, the religion problem remains difficult to resolve for historians of American foreign relations. Until the cultural turn, the field of diplomatic history was methodologically conservative, partly due to the overwhelming availability of archival documents and official records. While historians of the French peasantry or the English working class – to say nothing of preliterate societies in Africa and the Americas – had to be innovative in their quest for primary sources, diplomatic and political historians studied a group of people whose livelihood required them to produce thousands of pages of written documents of carefully articulated reasoning about specific decisions, so there was little need to be innovative. This source bias was coupled with diplomatic history's purpose to investigate the causes, conduct, and consequences of wars and international crises. As a result, scholars of American foreign relations developed a firm belief that historical cause and effect could be isolated, identified, and explained. The cultural turn has gone some way to addressing this problem and broadening out diplomatic history's terms of inquiry, but religion still stands somewhat apart and some historians do not rank it as a structural force on the level of race or gender.[60] Moreover, religious groups have rarely wielded policymaking authority, and those policymakers who have been demonstrably religious – McKinley, for example, or John Foster Dulles – seemingly left little that is religious in the official record.

For this reason, critics of the religious turn have demanded evidence of moments in which "religion trumped the national interest."[61] What is needed, argues another skeptic, is a clear illustration of "what it is specifically about religion that impels diplomats and presidents to do this and not that. We would need, for instance, to hear a president or a chairman of the Senate Foreign Relations Committee say that he has reviewed all the tables, charts, and reports, but cannot come to a final decision until he polls the leaders of American churches, or holds an all-night prayer vigil, or finds a specific direction (or prohibition) in Holy Writ."[62] Yet as Leo Ribuffo, who has written insightfully on religion and foreign relations, points out, "no major diplomatic decision has turned on religious issues alone."[63]

Such criticism sets the bar unreasonably high. For one thing, it ignores the large amount of primary-source material, including at the National Archives in College Park and in various presidential libraries, in which religion does feature explicitly and extensively. For another, it assumes there is such a thing as "the national interest" that is identifiable, objective, and measureable. If that were true, Americans would not argue so bitterly over foreign policy. Was Wilson acting in the national interest when he proposed US membership in the League

The religious turn in diplomatic history 293

of Nations? He certainly thought so, but many Americans and a majority of the Senate did not. Was Reagan acting in the national interest when he pursued arms control with the Soviets? He clearly thought so, but many others – including his own secretary of defense – did not. The fact is, there are thousands of interpretations of what exactly constitutes "the national interest," and all of them are shaped by a person's cultural biases, preconceptions, and ideologies. This is where religion, along with other factors, can help. In the cases of both Wilson and Reagan, religion can have immense interpretive benefit; as historians have shown, religious thought and belief played a large part in why Wilson sought a world organization codified in an international covenant and why Reagan sought the abolition of nuclear weapons.[64]

International relations theorists themselves have complicated realism by recognizing that there is nothing self-evident or fixed about "the national interest" beyond physical survival. Constructivism, which posits that world politics is not mechanical but socially and culturally constructed, is the most influential school of thought.[65] Moreover, securitization theorists within IR, along with a growing number of diplomatic historians, argue that security itself – which one might assume would have an even more fixed and objective basis than the national interest – is also largely a social and cultural construction.[66] And it would be difficult to think of a more salient aspect of society and culture, and the constructions they produce, than religion.

Religion does not pose an unsolvable problem for diplomatic history, yet solving it requires a leap of logical faith that historians are sometimes reluctant to make. Linking religion to diplomatic history requires the forging of plausible connections, grounded in primary-source evidence, between what we know about religion and what we know about foreign policy. Often such connections are clearly evident in the documentary record, but religion can still play a major causal role even when direct connections cannot be found. Policymakers rarely justify their decisions on religious grounds. When they do, it is usually in public with the aim of justifying a decision or outcome, which makes it easy for historians to dismiss as the "mere rhetoric" of political discourse. As Daniel Rodgers has shown, however, "mere rhetoric" can be highly revealing because it casts significant light on the priorities of elites and the extent to which they perceive those priorities are shared by the public. In short, says Rodgers, "Words make mass actions possible."[67]

Linking words to actions is tricky enough; linking religious belief to actions is much more difficult. The simple fact is that religious belief is immeasurable. It belongs to an interior mental world to which only that individual has access (and which even he or she understands imperfectly and subjectively). For this reason, the evangelist Billy Graham preferred to use the term "inquirer" instead of "convert," for who could ever know whether someone had truly converted their faith?[68] Anthropologists and sociologists are similarly reluctant to make claims that a person "believes" something religious. It is, almost by definition, untestable and unverifiable. And if illustrating, corroborating, or measuring belief is difficult in the present, it becomes immensely more difficult when dealing with people of the past.[69] The question of sincerity adds to the problem. Presumably for religion to be a causal agent, the believer would have to believe sincerely; if not, then religion would scarcely have any causal influence at all. But if belief is all but impossible to verify empirically, so too is sincerity.[70]

Fundamentally at issue is the question of motivation: can religion motivate people to do certain things? If the answer is "no," then there is little point in trying to explain the history of American foreign relations (or anything else) by way of religion. This would seem to rule out a large component of what we know about human history, and basic human behavior, and seems wholly implausible. Thus the answer is presumably "yes," which makes it incumbent upon the scholar to provide evidence and theories as to why, how, and when.

Fortunately, the great anthropologist Clifford Geertz provided a compelling framework for the use of religion to analyze the world. Geertz perceived religion as both the product and producer of culture; for adherents, it defines the world as it was, is, and should be (although not necessarily to the exclusion of other factors). "Religion is sociologically interesting not because ... it describes the social order," he wrote, "but because, like environment, political power, wealth, jural obligation, personal affection, and a sense of beauty, it shapes it." From here, the next step to identifying religious motivations for secular actions is not a difficult one. "Religious concepts spread beyond their specifically metaphysical contexts to provide a framework of general ideas in terms of which a wide range of experience – intellectual, emotional, moral – can be given meaningful form." Religious beliefs, Geertz continued, "are also a template. They do not merely interpret social and psychological processes in cosmic terms ... but they shape them." Embedded within religious doctrines are "a recommended attitude toward life, a recurring mood, and a persisting set of motivations."[71] Such motivations could not always be reduced to crude notions of "She did this because she believed that." Instead, religion was one factor, and a very powerful one at that, by which people interpreted their own existence in the world around them. As Geertz explained, "A motivation is a persisting tendency, a chronic inclination to perform certain sorts of acts and experience certain sorts of feeling in certain forms of situations ... Motives are thus neither acts (that is, intentional behaviors) nor feelings, but liabilities to perform particular classes of act or have particular classes of feeling. And when we say that a man is religious, that is, motivated by religion, this is at least part – though only part – of what we mean."[72]

Still, Geertz could not fully solve the riddle of how to measure the immeasurable. How can we identify that which is unobservable, such as religious faith? In his investigations of religious globalization, José Casanova found an answer. To critics who said that a rise in belief around the world cannot be measured because we cannot ever truly know what people believe,

The religious turn in diplomatic history

Casanova replied that he was instead measuring religion's "discursive reality," or what we might call the manifestations of belief.[73] This approach may no longer be satisfactory to scientists and philosophers. Theories of "behaviorism" and "operationism," which measured what people actually did rather than what they thought or believed, provided psychoanalysts and human scientists with a solution to their inaccessibility to inner workings of the brain. With advances in biomedical technology and scientists' ability to map the brain with greater precision, and with the advent of cognitive psychology and other disciplines, that is no longer as much of a problem. And with their positivist overtones, behaviorism and operationism are now widely considered to be philosophically and epistemologically naïve.[74] But for humanists and social scientists who examine religion, including historians, Casanova's "discursive reality" and similar theories retain a high degree of utility. They cannot of course tell us much about why people believe what they do; but they can help us explain how and why their beliefs influence their actions.

People are not robots. They do not simply assess the material world in front of them, make precise calculations in a rigorous cost-benefit analysis, and then act accordingly. They are led as much by emotion as by reason. Indeed, the Enlightenment's distinction between rational and irrational impulses is now widely regarded as artificial and misleading. People are motivated both by emotion and by reason, often in tandem but with emotion often playing the dominant role.[75] Religion is unusual in that it is an aspect of reason and emotion, rationality and irrationality, which testifies to its enormous causal and analytical potential.

Policymakers do of course respond to "exterior" forces – strategic, economic, political. But it is illogical to assume that they do so from a blank slate, with no reference at all to "interior" mental forces such as religious belief (or unbelief). In terms of religion, this means combining Casanova's observable exterior forces with Geertz's analysis of interior worlds.[76] Moreover, there are exterior forces, such as culture or national ideology – or religion – that align with the interior life of individuals. Religion has been and remains an inescapable part of American culture, and that culture helps shape the context in which all forms of politics (including foreign relations) are conceived and unfold. And exploring all these aspects of what motivates human behavior will give us a more complete picture of the history of American foreign relations.

NOTES

1. Robert N. Bellah, *Religion in Human Evolution: From the Paleolithic to the Axial Age* (Cambridge, MA, 2011).
2. Charles Taylor, *A Secular Age* (Cambridge, MA, 2007).
3. Jon Butler, "Jack-in-the-Box Faith: The Religion Problem in Modern American History," *Journal of American History* 90 (March 2004), 1357–78.

4. For representative examples, see: for civil rights, David L. Chappell, *A Stone of Hope: Prophetic Religion and the Death of Jim Crow* (Chapel Hill, 2004); for ethnicity and citizenship, Kevin M. Schultz, *Tri-Faith America: How Catholics and Jews Held Postwar America to Its Protestant Promise* (New York, 2011); for deindustrialization, Bethany Moreton, *To Serve God and Wal-Mart: The Making of Christian Free Enterprise* (Cambridge, MA, 2009); for migration, Darren Dochuk, *From Bible Belt to Sunbelt: Plain-Folk Religion, Grassroots Politics, and the Rise of Evangelical Conservatism* (New York, 2010); and for conservative politics, Daniel K. Williams, *God's Own Party: The Making of the Christian Right* (New York, 2010). For collections with a broad range of approaches and topics linking religion to other aspects of American public life, see Mark A. Noll and Luke E. Harlow, eds., *Religion and American Politics: From the Colonial Period to the Present*, 2nd edn. (New York, 2007); R. Marie Griffith and Melani McAlister, eds., *Religion and Politics in the Contemporary United States* (Baltimore, 2008); and Andrew Preston, Bruce J. Schulman, and Julian E. Zelizer, eds., *Faithful Republic: Religion and Politics in Modern America* (Philadelphia, 2015).
5. Andrew Preston, "Bridging the Gap between Church and State in the History of American Foreign Relations," *Diplomatic History* 30 (November 2006), 783–812.
6. Ernest Lee Tuveson, *Redeemer Nation: The Idea of America's Millennial Role* (Chicago, 1968); William R. Hutchison, *Errand to the World: American Protestant Thought and Foreign Missions* (Chicago, 1987); Anders Stephanson, *Manifest Destiny: American Expansion and the Empire of Right* (New York, 1995). This genre continues to flourish. For more recent examples, see Anatol Lieven, *America Right or Wrong: An Anatomy of American Nationalism* (New York, 2004); Nicholas Guyatt, *Providence and the Invention of the United States, 1607–1876* (New York, 2007); and George McKenna, *The Puritan Origins of American Patriotism* (New Haven, 2007).
7. See Dianne Kirby, "Truman's Holy Alliance: The President, the Pope and the Origins of the Cold War," *Borderlines* 4 (1997), 1–17; Dianne Kirby, "Divinely Sanctioned: The Anglo-American Cold War Alliance and the Defence of Western Civilization and Christianity, 1945–48," *Journal of Contemporary History* 35 (July 2000), 385–412; and Dianne Kirby, ed., *Religion and the Cold War* (New York, 2003).
8. Andrew J. Rotter, *Comrades at Odds: The United States and India, 1947–1964* (Ithaca, 2000).
9. Melani McAlister, *Epic Encounters: Culture, Media, and U.S. Interests in the Middle East, 1945–2000* (Berkeley, 2001; 2005).
10. Seth Jacobs, *America's Miracle Man in Vietnam: Ngo Dinh Diem, Religion, Race, and U.S. Intervention in Southeast Asia, 1950–1957* (Durham, NC, 2004).
11. William Inboden, *Religion and American Foreign Policy, 1945–1960: The Soul of Containment* (New York, 2008).
12. Samuel P. Huntington, *The Clash of Civilizations and the Remaking of World Order* (New York, 1996).
13. Jonathan Fox and Shmuel Sandler, *Bringing Religion into International Relations* (New York, 2004). Within IR, see also Robert O. Keohane, "The Globalization of Informal Violence, Theories of World Politics, and the 'Liberalism of Fear,'" *Dialog-IO* 1 (Spring 2002), 29–43; Fabio Petito and Pavlos Hatzopoulos, eds., *Religion in International Relations* (New York, 2003); Scott M. Thomas, *The*

Global Resurgence of Religion and the Transformation of International Relations: The Struggle for the Soul of the Twenty-first Century (New York, 2005); Monica Duffy Toft, Daniel Philpott, and Timothy Samuel Shah, *God's Century: Resurgent Religion and Global Politics* (New York, 2011); and Timothy Samuel Shah, Alfred Stepan, Monica Duffy Toft, eds., *Rethinking Religion and World Affairs* (New York, 2012). On IR theory's own religion problem, see Jonathan Fox, "Religion as an Overlooked Element of International Relations," *International Studies Review* 3 (Autumn 2001), 53–73. For a provocative disciplinary assessment of religion and IR theory, see Elizabeth Shakman Hurd, *The Politics of Secularism in International Relations* (Princeton, 2008).

14. Leo P. Ribuffo, "Religion in the History of U.S. Foreign Policy," in *The Influence of Faith: Religious Groups and U.S. Foreign Policy*, ed. Elliott Abrams (Lanham, MD, 2001), 14; Jacobs, *America's Miracle Man in Vietnam*, 60–87.
15. Stephen J. Whitfield, *The Culture of the Cold War*, 2nd edn. (Baltimore, 1996), 77–100.
16. See, for example, Kirby, "Divinely Sanctioned"; Dianne Kirby, "Harry Truman's Religious Legacy: The Holy Alliance, Containment, and the Cold War," in Kirby, *Religion and the Cold War*, 77–102; Elizabeth Edwards Spalding, *The First Cold Warrior: Harry Truman, Containment, and the Remaking of Liberal Internationalism* (Lexington, KY, 2006), 199–222; Jonathan P. Herzog, *The Spiritual-Industrial Complex: America's Religious Battle against Communism in the Early Cold War* (New York, 2011); and Philip Muehlenbeck, ed., *Religion and the Cold War: A Global Perspective* (Nashville, 2012).
17. See Angela M. Lahr, *Millennial Dreams and Apocalyptic Nightmares: The Cold War Origins of Political Evangelicalism* (New York, 2007); T. Jeremy Gunn, *Spiritual Weapons: The Cold War and the Forging of an American National Religion* (Westport, CT, 2008); Andrew S. Finstuen, *Original Sin and Everyday Protestants: The Theology of Reinhold Niebuhr, Billy Graham, and Paul Tillich in an Age of Anxiety* (Chapel Hill, 2009); Jason W. Stevens, *God-Fearing and Free: A Spiritual History of America's Cold War* (Cambridge, MA, 2010); Dochuk, *From Bible Belt to Sunbelt*; Williams, *God's Own Party*; Schultz, *Tri-Faith America*; Raymond J. Haberski, Jr., *God and War: American Civil Religion since 1945* (New Brunswick, NJ, 2012); K. Healan Gaston, "The Cold War Romance of Religious Authenticity: Will Herberg, William F. Buckley Jr., and the Rise of the New Right," *Journal of American History* 99 (March 2013), pp. 1133–58; and Matthew Avery Sutton, *American Apocalypse: A History of Modern Evangelicalism* (Cambridge, MA, 2014), 293–366.
18. Arthur S. Link, *The Higher Realism of Woodrow Wilson* (Nashville, 1971), 3–20.
19. John M. Mulder, *Woodrow Wilson: The Years of Preparation* (Princeton, 1978).
20. Malcolm D. Magee, *What the World Should Be: Woodrow Wilson and the Crafting of a Faith-Based Foreign Policy* (Waco, TX, 2008); Mark Benbow, *Leading Them to the Promised Land: Woodrow Wilson, Covenant Theology, and the Mexican Revolution, 1913–1915* (Kent, OH, 2010); Andrew Preston, *Sword of the Spirit, Shield of the Faith: Religion in American War and Diplomacy* (New York, 2012), 233–90; Milan Babik, *Statecraft and Salvation: Wilsonian Liberal Internationalism as Secularized Eschatology* (Waco, TX, 2013); Cara L. Burnidge, "The Business of Church and State: Social Christianity in Woodrow Wilson's White House," *Church History* 82 (September 2013), 659–66; Cara L. Burnidge, *A*

Peaceful Conquest: Woodrow Wilson, the League of Nations, and the Great War of American Protestantism (Chicago, forthcoming). However, not everyone has embraced the religious interpretation of Wilson's politics and foreign policy. For skeptics, see John A. Thompson, *Woodrow Wilson* (London, 2002), 18–20; and John Milton Cooper, Jr., *Woodrow Wilson: A Biography* (New York, 2009), 4–5.

21. Paul A. Varg, *Missionaries, Chinese, and Diplomats: The American Protestant Missionary Movement in China, 1890–1952* (Princeton, 1958), pioneered this interpretive linkage between American missionaries and US imperialism in East and Southeast Asia. For subsequent works in this vein, see Paul A. Cohen, *China and Christianity: The Missionary Movement and the Growth of Chinese Antiforeignism, 1860–1870* (Cambridge, MA, 1963); Marilyn Blatt Young, *The Rhetoric of Empire: American China Policy, 1895–1901* (Cambridge, MA, 1968); John K. Fairbank, ed., *The Missionary Enterprise in China and America* (Cambridge, MA, 1974); Michael H. Hunt, *The Making of a Special Relationship: The United States and China to 1914* (New York, 1983); James Reed, *The Missionary Mind and American East Asia Policy, 1911–1915* (Cambridge, MA, 1983); Jane Hunter, *The Gospel of Gentility: American Women Missionaries in Turn-of-the-Century China* (New Haven, 1984); Kenton J. Clymer, *Protestant Missionaries in the Philippines, 1898–1916* (Urbana, IL, 1986); Yu-ming Shaw, *An American Missionary in China: John Leighton Stuart and Chinese-American Relations* (Cambridge, MA, 1992). More recent examples include Susan K. Harris, *God's Arbiters: Americans and the Philippines, 1898–1902* (New York, 2011); and Sarah Miller-Davenport, "'Their Blood Shall Not Be Shed in Vain': American Evangelical Missionaries and the Search for God and Country in Post-World War II Asia," *Journal of American History* 99 (March 2013), 1109–32.

22. Joseph L. Grabill, *Protestant Diplomacy and the Near East: Missionary Influence on American Policy, 1810–1927* (Minneapolis, 1971); Michael B. Oren, *Power, Faith, and Fantasy: America in the Middle East, 1776 to the Present* (New York, 2007); Ussama Makdisi, *Artillery of Heaven: American Missionaries and the Failed Conversion of the Middle East* (Ithaca, 2008); Heather J. Sharkey, *American Evangelicals in Egypt: Missionary Encounters in an Age of Empire* (Princeton, 2008).

23. Walter LaFeber, *The New Empire: An Interpretation of American Expansion, 1860–1898* (Ithaca, 1963), 72–80, 300–11.

24. Brian Stanley, *The Bible and the Flag: Protestant Missions and British Imperialism in the Nineteenth and Twentieth Centuries* (Leicester, 1990); Andrew Porter, *Religion Versus Empire? British Protestant Missionaries and Overseas Expansion, 1700–1914* (Manchester, 2004). For a comprehensive historiographical overview, see Norman Etherington, ed., *Missions and Empire* (Oxford, 2005).

25. See, for example, Ryan Dunch, *Fuzhou Protestants and the Making of a Modern China, 1857–1927* (New Haven, 2001); and Lian Xi, *Redeemed by Fire: The Rise of Popular Christianity in Modern China* (New Haven, 2010).

26. Ryan Dunch, "Beyond Cultural Imperialism: Cultural Theory, Christian Missions, and Global Modernity," *History and Theory* 41 (October 2002), 301–25.

27. Philip E. Dow, "Romance in a Marriage of Convenience: The Missionary Factor in Early Cold War U.S.–Ethiopian Relations, 1941–1960," *Diplomatic History* 35 (November 2011), 859–95.

28. Ian Tyrrell, *Reforming the World: The Creation of America's Moral Empire* (Princeton, 2010); Preston, *Sword of the Spirit*, 130–34, 175–97.
29. Lian Xi, *The Conversion of Missionaries: Liberalism in American Protestant Missions in China, 1907–1932* (University Park, PA, 1997).
30. On the rapid spread of Christianity in the Global South, see Philip Jenkins, *The Next Christendom: The Coming of Global Christianity* (New York, 2002); Philip Jenkins, *The New Faces of Christianity: Believing the Bible in the Global South* (New York, 2008); John Micklethwait and Adrian Wooldridge, *God Is Back: How the Global Revival of Faith is Changing the World* (New York, 2009); and Mark A. Noll, *The New Shape of World Christianity: How American Experience Reflects Global Faith* (Downers Grove, IL, 2009).
31. John S. Nurser, *For All Peoples and All Nations: The Ecumenical Church and Human Rights* (Washington, DC, 2005); David A. Hollinger, "The Realist-Pacifist Summit Meeting of March 1942 and the Political Reorientation of Ecumenical Protestantism in the United States," *Church History* 79 (September 2010), 654–77; Daniel Gorman, *The Emergence of International Society in the 1920s* (Cambridge, 2012), 213–58; Mark Thomas Edwards, *The Right of the Protestant Left: God's Totalitarianism* (New York, 2012); Preston, *Sword of the Spirit*, 249–51, 275–80, 384–409; Michael Thompson, *For God and Globe: Christian Internationalism in the United States between the Great War and the Cold War* (Ithaca, 2015). There is a burgeoning interest in how religion has helped shape humanitarianism and human rights ideologies and discourses since the mid-nineteenth century. On this historiography, see Abigail Green, "Humanitarianism in Nineteenth-Century Context: Religious, Gendered, National," *The Historical Journal* 57 (December 2014), 1157–75.
32. See, for example, Steven Merritt Miner, *Stalin's Holy War: Religion, Nationalism, and Alliance Politics, 1941–1945* (Chapel Hill, 2003); George J. Hill, "Intimate Relationships: Secret Affairs of Church and State in the United States and Liberia, 1925–1947," *Diplomatic History* 31 (June 2007), 465–503; David Zietsma, "'Sin Has No History': Religion, National Identity, and U.S. Intervention, 1937–1941," *Diplomatic History* 31 (June 2007), 531–65; Michaela Hoenicke Moore, *Know Your Enemy: The American Debate on Nazism, 1933–1945* (New York, 2010); Gorman, *Emergence of International Society in the 1920s*, 213–58; Preston, *Sword of the Spirit*, 291–409; Edwards, *Right of the Protestant Left*; and William C. Inboden, "The Prophetic Conflict: Reinhold Niebuhr, Christian Realism, and World War II," *Diplomatic History* 38 (January 2014), 49–82.
33. Beth A. Fischer, *The Reagan Reversal: Foreign Policy and the End of the Cold War* (Columbia, MO, 1997); Frances FitzGerald, *Way Out There in the Blue: Reagan, Star Wars, and the End of the Cold War* (New York, 2000); Sarah B. Snyder, *Human Rights Activism and the End of the Cold War: A Transnational History of the Helsinki Network* (New York, 2011), 141–6; Preston, *Sword of the Spirit*, 574–600.
34. Religious-studies scholars have created an enormous body of literature investigating the definitional problem, but for a useful overview see Thomas A. Idinopulos and Brian C. Wilson, eds., *What Is Religion? Origins, Definitions, and Explanations* (Leiden, 1998).
35. Wilfred Cantwell Smith, *The Meaning and End of Religion: A New Approach to the Religious Traditions of Mankind* (New York, 1963).

36. Michael D. Bailey, "The Disenchantment of Magic: Spells, Charms, and Superstition in Early European Witchcraft Literature," *American Historical Review* 111 (April 2006), 384. On the concept of "religion" as a product as well as a handmaiden of imperialism, see Kwok Pui-lan, "Empire and the Study of Religion," *Journal of the American Academy of Religion* 80 (June 2012), 285–303; and David Chidester, *Empire of Religion: Imperialism and Comparative Religion* (Chicago, 2014).
37. Talal Asad, *Genealogies of Religion: Discipline and Reasons of Power in Christianity and Islam* (Baltimore, 1993); Daniel Dubuisson, *The Western Construction of Religion: Myths, Knowledge, and Ideology*, trans. William Sayers (Baltimore, 2003); Tomoko Masuzawa, *The Invention of World Religions: Or, How European Universalism Was Preserved in the Language of Pluralism* (Chicago, 2005).
38. C. A. Bayly, *The Birth of the Modern World, 1780–1914: Global Connections and Comparisons* (Malden, MA, 2004), esp. 20, 325–65, 479–81.
39. Jonathan Z. Smith, *Relating Religion: Essays in the Study of Religion* (Chicago, 2004), 160–96.
40. See Albert J. Raboteau, *Slave Religion: The "Invisible Institution" in the Antebellum South* (New York, 1978); Sylvia R. Frey and Betty Wood, *Come Shouting to Zion: African American Protestantism in the American South and British Caribbean to 1830* (Chapel Hill, 1998); and Tisa Wenger, *We Have a Religion: The 1920s Pueblo Indian Dance Controversy and American Religious Freedom* (Chapel Hill, 2009).
41. Daniel Bell, *The End of Ideology* (Glencoe, IL, 1960), 103–4.
42. On secularization theory in the American context, which is both applicable and misleading, excellent places to start are David A. Hollinger, "The 'Secularization' Question and the United States in the Twentieth Century," *Church History* 70 (March 2001), 132–43; Christian Smith, "Introduction: Rethinking the Secularization of American Public Life," in *The Secular Revolution: Power, Interests, and Conflict in the Secularization of American Public Life*, ed. Christian Smith (Berkeley, 2003), 1–96; and Michael O'Brien, "The American Experience of Secularisation," in *Religion and the Political Imagination*, ed. Ira Katznelson and Gareth Stedman Jones (Cambridge, 2010), 132–49.
43. The best assessments of secularization theory and its limitations are Jose Casanova, *Public Religions in the Modern World* (Chicago, 1994); and Talal Asad, *Formations of the Secular: Christianity, Islam, Modernity* (Stanford, 2003). For an unapologetic defense of secularization theory, see Steve Bruce, *God is Dead: Secularization in the West* (Malden, MA, 2002); and Steve Bruce, *Secularization: In Defence of an Unfashionable Theory* (Oxford, 2011). For a thoughtful reassessment in light of the many criticisms of the theory, see Craig Calhoun, Mark Juergensmeyer, and Jonathan VanAntwerpen, eds., *Rethinking Secularism* (New York, 2011).
44. And even when applied to Western Europe, historians now date the advent of secularization to more recent periods than the nineteenth century. See, for example, Callum G. Brown, *The Death of Christian Britain: Understanding Secularisation 1800–2000* (London, 2000), which persuasively argues that Britain did not become a secular society until the 1960s, a full century after earlier historical claims. Moreover, episodes in European history that had been perceived as largely secular, such as World War I, are now interpreted as important thresholds in

European religious history. See Philip Jenkins, *The Great and Holy War: How World War I Became a Religious Crusade* (New York, 2014).
45. See, respectively, Peter L. Berger, *The Sacred Canopy: Elements of a Sociological Theory of Religion* (Garden City, NY, 1967); Peter L. Berger, ed., *The Desecularization of the World: Resurgent Religion and World Politics* (Grand Rapids, MI, 1996).
46. John L. Esposito, Darrell J. Fasching, and Todd Lewis, *Religion and Globalization: World Religions in Historical Perspective* (New York, 2007); Robert Wuthnow, *Boundless Faith: The Global Outreach of American Churches* (Berkeley, 2009); Abigail Green and Vincent Viaene, eds., *Religious Internationals in the Modern World: Globalization and Faith Communities since 1750* (New York, 2012).
47. J. C. D. Clark, "Secularization and Modernization: The Failure of a 'Grand Narrative,'" *The Historical Journal* 55 (March 2012), 161–94.
48. For probably the most influential example of this genre, see Keith Thomas, *Religion and the Decline of Magic: Studies in Popular Beliefs in Sixteenth and Seventeenth Century England* (London, 1971).
49. Alexandra Walsham, "The Reformation and the Disenchantment of the World Reassessed," *The Historical Journal* 51 (May 2008), 497–528; Alexandra Walsham, *The Reformation of the Landscape: Religion, Identity and Memory in Early Modern Britain and Ireland* (Oxford, 2011). See also Michael Saler, "Modernity and Enchantment: A Historiographic Review," *American Historical Review* 111 (June 2006), 692–716. For the American context, see David D. Hall, *Worlds of Wonder, Days of Judgment: Popular Religious Belief in Early New England* (New York, 1989).
50. Ian Hamnett, "Sociology of Religion and Sociology of Error," *Religion* 3 (Spring 1973), 1–2. For a sophisticated example of this secularist assumption at work, see Steven Pinker, *How the Mind Works* (New York, 1997), 554–8.
51. Akira Iriye, "Imperialism and Sincerity," *Reviews in American History* 1 (March 1973), 119–25.
52. I have made this argument about McKinley, the Philippines, and "progressive imperialism" at greater length in Preston, *Sword of the Spirit*, 155–9, 223–32.
53. For the Crusades, see Christopher Tyerman, *Fighting for Christendom: Holy War and the Crusades* (Oxford, 2004); Thomas Asbridge, *The First Crusade: A New History* (London, 2004); Jonathan Phillips, *The Fourth Crusade and the Sack of Constantinople* (London, 2004); and Christopher Tyerman, *God's War: A New History of the Crusades* (London, 2006). For the Inquisition, see Christine Caldwell Ames, *Righteous Persecution: Inquisition, Dominicans, and Christianity in the Middle Ages* (Philadelphia, 2009).
54. Jonathan Sheehan, "Enlightenment, Religion, and the Enigma of Secularization," *American Historical Review* 108 (October 2003), 1061–80; David Sorkin, *The Religious Enlightenment: Protestants, Jews, and Catholics from London to Vienna* (Princeton, 2008).
55. Richard Wightman Fox, *Trials of Intimacy: Love and Loss in the Beecher-Tilton Scandal* (Chicago, 1999), 7, 5.
56. Robert A. Orsi, *Between Heaven and Earth: The Religious Worlds People Make and the Scholars Who Study Them* (Princeton, 2005), esp. 177–204.
57. Quentin Skinner, *Visions of Politics*, vol. 1: *Regarding Method* (Cambridge, 2002), 31–41 (quoted on 31).

58. For an excellent assessment, see Jon Elster, *Explaining Social Behavior* (Cambridge, 2007), esp. 25–8, 191–245.
59. Paul Erickson, et al., *How Reason Almost Lost Its Mind: The Strange Career of Cold War Rationality* (Chicago, 2013).
60. Patricia R. Hill, "Religion as a Category of Diplomatic Analysis," *Diplomatic History* 24 (Fall 2000), 633–40. However, for a corrective that does illustrate how religion can function perfectly well as a category of analysis alongside gender and race, see Maureen C. Miller, "Religion Makes a Difference: Clerical and Lay Cultures in the Courts of Northern Italy, 1000–1300," *American Historical Review* 105 (October 2000), 1095–1130.
61. Richard H. Immerman, Book Review, *San Francisco Chronicle*, March 4, 2012.
62. Allen C. Guelzo, "Faith and Foreign Policy," *National Review*, April 30, 2012.
63. Ribuffo, "Religion in the History of U.S. Foreign Policy," 21.
64. See the citations in Notes 21 and 34 in this chapter.
65. The canonical text is Alexander Wendt, *Social Theory of International Politics* (Cambridge, 1999).
66. For IR, see Barry Buzan, *People, States and Fear: An Agenda for International Security Studies in the Post-Cold War Era* (London, 1991); David Campbell, *Writing Security: United States Foreign Policy and the Politics of Identity* (Minneapolis, 1992); Ole Waever, "Securitization and Desecuritization," in *On Security*, ed. Ronnie D. Lipschutz (New York, 1995), 46–86; David A. Baldwin, "The Concept of Security," *Review of International Studies* 23 (January 1997), 5–26; and Barry Buzan, Ole Waever, and Jaap de Wilde, *Security: A New Framework for Analysis* (Boulder, 1998). For history, see Andrew Preston, "Monsters Everywhere: A Genealogy of National Security," *Diplomatic History* 38 (June 2014), 477–500; and the following essays by John A. Thompson: "The Exaggeration of American Vulnerability: The Anatomy of a Tradition," *Diplomatic History* 16 (January 1992), 23–43; "Another Look at the Downfall of 'Fortress America,'" *Journal of American Studies* 26 (December 1992), 393–408; "Conceptions of National Security and American Entry into World War II," *Diplomacy & Statecraft* 16 (2005), 671–97; and "The Geopolitical Vision: The Myth of an Outmatched USA," in *Uncertain Empire: American History and the Idea of the Cold War*, ed. Joel Isaac and Duncan Bell (New York, 2012), 91–114.
67. Daniel T. Rodgers, *Contested Truths: Keywords in American Politics Since Independence* (New York, 1987), 4.
68. Grant Wacker, *America's Pastor: Billy Graham and the Shaping of a Nation* (Cambridge, MA, 2014), 13.
69. This problem is not unique to the study of religion. For example, David Steigerwald has chided the "subjectivism" of historians of consumerism for making claims about consumer motivation and preference without possessing definitive evidence of what consumers were actually thinking while they shopped. See his "All Hail the Republic of Choice: Consumer History as Contemporary Thought," *Journal of American History* 93 (September 2006), 385–403.
70. It should be said, however, that historians have done an impressive job evaluating the extent to which missionaries were able to convert indigenous societies to Christianity – which of course relies almost exclusively on being able to make confident assertions about sincerity and insincerity. See, for example, David J. Silverman, *Faith and Boundaries: Colonists, Christianity, and Community*

among the *Wampanoag Indians of Martha's Vineyard, 1600–1871* (New York, 2005); and Gabriela Ramos, *Death and Conversion in the Andes: Lima and Cuzco, 1532–1670* (Notre Dame, IN, 2010). This is also evident in a European context: see Christopher M. Clark, *The Politics of Conversion: Missionary Protestantism and the Jews in Prussia, 1728–1941* (Oxford, 1995).

71. Clifford Geertz, *The Interpretation of Cultures* (New York, 1973), 119, 123, 124.
72. Ibid., 96–7.
73. José Casanova, "Rethinking Public Religions," in Shah, Stepan, and Toft, *Rethinking Religion and World Affairs*, 27.
74. Eli Zaretsky, *Secrets of the Soul: A Social and Cultural History of Psychoanalysis* (New York, 2004), 184–88; Joel Isaac, *Working Knowledge: Making the Human Sciences from Parsons to Kuhn* (Cambridge, MA, 2012), 92–124, 227–38. However, scientists, psychologists, and philosophers are increasingly confident they can observe and measure religion's place in the brain and the process of human evolution. See, for example, Pascal Boyer, *The Naturalness of Religious Ideas: A Cognitive Theory of Religion* (Berkeley, 1994); Pascal Boyer, *Religion Explained: The Evolutionary Origins of Religious Thought* (New York, 2002); David Sloan Wilson, *Darwin's Cathedral: Evolution, Religion, and the Nature of Society* (Chicago, 2002); Scott Atran, *In Gods We Trust: The Evolutionary Landscape of Religion* (Oxford, 2002); Daniel C. Dennett, *Breaking the Spell: Religion as a Natural Phenomenon* (New York, 2006); Robert Wright, *The Evolution of God* (Boston, 2009); and Bellah, *Religion in Human Evolution*.
75. For recent arguments along this line, which revive ideas first articulated by the Enlightenment philosopher David Hume, see Jonathan Haidt, *The Righteous Mind: Why Good People Are Divided by Politics and Religion* (New York, 2012); and Joshua Greene, *Moral Tribes: Emotion, Reason, and the Gap Between Us and Them* (New York, 2013). Both Haidt and Greene emphasize the enduring duality of the brain between emotion and reason, Haidt with an analogy to a rider (reason) on an elephant (emotion) and Greene to a multipurpose camera. Both also argue that neither emotion nor reason can properly function without the other. See also Joseph Ledoux, *The Emotional Brain: The Mysterious Underpinnings of Emotional Life* (New York, 1996).
76. For an example, see Francisca Cho and Richard King Squier, "Religion as a Complex and Dynamic System," *Journal of the American Academy of Religion* 81 (June 2013), 357–98.

18

Memory and the study of US foreign relations

Penny M. Von Eschen

> Memory is not reclaimed. It is produced.
>
> Barbara Kirshenblatt-Gimblett

> History is the fruit of power. But power itself is never so transparent that its analysis becomes superfluous. The ultimate mark of power may be its invisibility; the ultimate challenge, the exposure of its roots.
>
> Michel-Rolph Trouillot, *Silencing the Past: Power and the Production of History*

Michel-Rolph Trouillot begins his brilliant analysis of the silences embedded in history in general and the particular erasure of the Haitian Revolution from Western historiography with a tale about how a political act of memory rewrote history. When on March 6, 1836, the Mexican forces led by General Antonio López de Santa Anna broke through the mission turned fort nicknamed "the Alamo," he appeared victorious. But Trouillot argues, when Santa Anna fell prisoner to Sam Houston a week later at San Jacinto, he was doubly defeated. "He lost the battle of the day; but he also lost the battle he had won at the Alamo." When Houston's men punctuated their attacks with shouts of "Remember the Alamo," explains Trouillot, "they doubly made history. As actors, they defeated Santa Anna and neutralized his forces. As narrators, they gave the Alamo story a new meaning."[1] For Trouillot, the inherent ambiguity in the word history entails a slippage between actors and narrators and between agents, actors, and subjects.

Trouillot's account of the Alamo illuminates an insight at the heart of memory studies: history is never unmediated; it is produced. Shifts in meaning-making and perceptions in the present can turn the past as on a pivot, with the ground giving way in what historians call the unstable past, or the unpredictability of the past.[2] The memory of the Alamo, transmuted into an icon for the Republic of Texas, was absorbed into the national identity of the United States. By annexing Texas and going to war with Mexico, the United States forever altered relations with its southern neighbor. And as Trouillot's analysis demonstrates, the inability of Westerners to imagine even the possibility of Africans acting politically distorts Western perceptions of the Haitian Revolution, resulting in similarly momentous foreign policy consequences for the United States and the world.

Among scholars of US foreign relations, Emily Rosenberg has made important interventions in the debates ensuing from the proliferation of memory studies and the often-politicized entanglements in culture wars. Rosenberg's *A Date Which Will Live: Pearl Harbor in American Memory* offers a lucid and insightful synthesis of the literature on memory studies, as she analyzes the shifting and hotly contested history/memory of the December 7, 1941, bombing of Pearl Harbor from its first constructions through its renewed invocations by political actors after the 9/11 terror attacks. For Rosenberg, who emphasizes the multiple mediations in any construction of history, memory is always an act of forgetting and entails complex decisions and practices that determine what is preserved and narrated as history. Therefore, for Rosenberg, it is misleading to speak of history in the traditional sense as a "didactic guide to the future or promising revelation of a 'final truth'." Instead, as a counter to such constructions of history, Rosenberg stresses relational, positional, and unstable meanings, signaled by the constellation "history/memory." Invoking Pierre Nora's *Realms of Memory*, Rosenberg echoes Nora's call for a definition of history that is "less interested in events themselves than in the construction of events over time." Indeed, she argues, "assumptions of stabilized history/memory run counter to the very concept of history/memory." Nora, Rosenberg explains, was less interested in "what actually happened" than in its perpetual reuse, its redeployment under changed social and political circumstances. "Nora, in short," Rosenberg explains, sought to embed history in history.[3]

Scholarly reflection on the relationship between history and memory has coincided with historians' attention to the silences and partial and fragmentary nature of official archives. Such silences and the limits of state archives are critical to understandings the complexities and power relations shaping knowledge production. In her work on the transnational politics of remembrance related to the US war in Vietnam, the anthropologist Christina Schwenkel challenges the binary between official and non-official practice and disputes the notion that history refers to the so-called objective realm of the state and "facts" while memory is constituted by the subjective experiences of individuals.[4] In an acknowledgment of the limitations of official histories, scholars have rejected what Schwenkel has called, the "discursive and epistemological opposition between history and memory," insisting instead on their intersection. Thus, while all historians grapple with the limitations of the historical archive, for scholars of memory, an interrogation of the constructed nature of the archive becomes paramount. To undertake a study of memory is to put such questions front and center.[5]

This is not the place for a comprehensive discussion of this vast literature. Yet, I hope to highlight key themes and methods in memory studies that have relevance for the study of foreign relations and the evolving relationship of the United States in world affairs. Scholars of US foreign policy have employed methodological approaches drawn out of memory studies to productively engage traditional archives. Indeed, insights from memory studies have helped expand our notions of what constitutes appropriate archives, bringing new dimensions to the study of foreign relations. Through individual and collective sleuthing as well as involvement in the State Department's Historical Advisory Committee, historians of foreign relations have expanded the scope of historical topics while enhancing public access to archival sources.

A different set of inquiries, equally fundamental to the development of memory studies, arise from the conviction that history/memory must be investigated as a social/cultural/political process. Scholars have argued that memory is a profoundly social process and cannot be viewed simply in relation to the individual or as a cognitive faculty. Such insights need not diminish the importance of individual experience. Indeed, much of the impetus toward examining memory emerged from scholarship on trauma, particularly among Holocaust survivors; such scholarly reflection on the intersection of individual and culturally constructed memory can inform and enhance biographical and generational approaches to foreign policy actors.[6] Just as remembering is a form of forgetting in the individual psyche, silences are as important as inclusions in historical production.[7] One might add that this complex symbiosis of remembering and forgetting, of material "evidence" and silences, obtains across a wide range of sources. Whether one investigates official state archives, museums, films, or popular cultural practices, such as war re-enactments, all of these engagements with the past represent a process of mixing memory with erasure. To emphasize the key insight that our access to the past is never direct and unmediated and that history and memory are intersecting rather than distinct categories, I will adopt Rosenberg's formulation "history/memory."[8]

Prompting historians to take up the subject of memory has been a trend since the 1970s of rising fascination with public history and memory, particularly in terms of historic preservation, the re-enactment of Revolutionary and Civil War battles, the commemoration of historic sites, and the *American Heritage* magazine.[9] The historian Erica Doss has called this phenomenon America's "memorial mania." This enthusiasm is characterized by the affects of mourning and remembrance as well as the proliferation of public memorials and state-funded historical sites.[10] As historical narratives were produced and consumed in museums, theme parks and through re-enactments, films, and television, our conventional understandings of historical knowledge and individual and collective memory grew increasingly hazy. Indeed, bearing out a key insight of

Trouillot, the academic practice of historical research and writing is rivaled by highly public and increasingly controversial and polarized discussion of the American past. Hence scholars have questioned the distinction made between "the *objective* process of historiography and *affective* commemorative practices."[11]

Indeed, much of the outpouring of work on historical memory has focused on the contested topics of war remembrance and the practices of memorialization.[12] Kirk Savage's *Monument Wars: Washington D.C., the National Mall, and the Transformation of the Memorial Landscape*, and Kristin Ann Hass's *Sacrificing Soldiers on the National Mall* have traced the evolution of the built environment and memorial practices of the National Mall.[13] In addition, Doss and Marita Sturken have examined the contested memorialization of the Oklahoma City bombing and the 9/11 terror attacks.[14] While many have celebrated such public productions of memory as a democratization of history, others have registered alarm at a lack of rigor or disregard for historical truth resulting at worst in populist demagoguery.

Making a case that history is constructed in the interplay of multiple forms of media, texts, cultural performances, and speech acts, Rosenberg has scrutinized debates among historians sparked by public controversies over monuments and the broader obsession with history/memory. She writes, "historians who work in the academy may resist and decry the collapse of distinctions between 'high' and 'low' and between 'rational' history and 'nostalgic' myth, for much of their cultural capital rests on such distinctions." But "in the media nation of post-World War II America – memory, history, and media all reproduce and re-present in *intertextual* relationships among different kinds of cultural material." Especially in this particular media environment, memory and history "are blurred forms of representation whose structure and politics need to be analyzed not as oppositional but as interactive."[15] Similarly, Schwenkel emphasizes that memory moves across space and is produced in the tension between different historical subject positions, media narratives, and cultural practices. Emphasizing the transnational dimensions of remembrance, Schwenkel considers the different subject positions of US and Vietnamese tourists as they encounter representations of the US war in Vietnam and participate in re-enactments of combat at tourist sites constructed in the tunnels of the Chu Chi district in Ho Chi Minh City. Here, "all memory is mediated by other knowledge flows, including that of the mass media," tourist industries, and such practices as re-enactments.[16]

Indeed, the embrace of intertexuality by scholars of memory studies, bringing together political, literary, and mass media representations of the past, has resulted in a broadening of the archive for historians of American foreign relations. Popular culture – not least through representations of the recent or distant past in Hollywood films – has been a fertile site of meaning-making in ways that have influenced public opinion in postwar America. Reading multiple forms of popular culture in relation to the history of international relations has transformed our understanding of foreign policy. Rosenberg's seminal analysis of the 1948 Billy Wilder film *A Foreign Affair* appeared in *Diplomatic History* in 1994. Rosenberg interpreted the film, set in postwar Berlin, as symptomatic of tensions produced by the choices faced by the United States about its role in the postwar world.[17] Over the next decade, Melani McAlister's reading of National Security Council document 68 (NSC 68) in tandem with the 1950s Biblical epics *The Ten Commandments* and *Ben Hur*, and Christina Klein's analysis of post-war US relations with Asia through novels, Broadway musicals, and practices of international adoption, further elaborated the necessity of an intertextual archive for historians of US foreign relations.[18]

Much of the paradigm-shifting scholarship deftly employing intertextual analysis focused on the immediate post-World War II era, and Rosenberg has argued that "the distinction between 'memory' and 'history' is highly contingent upon time, place and project." Yet despite Rosenberg's judicious caution regarding historical specificity, her insights about diverse media flows blurring boundaries between the construction of history and memory has also been critical to pre-twentieth-century studies. The important point here is that innovative memory studies investigating the intersection of media and knowledge flows and the construction of truth claims in unofficial as well as official archives and settings have by no means been focused on late twentieth-century studies. David Blight's study of the politics of memory during the Jim Crow era in the US South shows how the region lost the war, but won the peace in making the memory of the vanquished Confederacy palatable to white Northern audiences. Blight details how three cultural organizations formed during the 1890s – the United Confederate Veterans, the *Confederate Veteran* magazine, and the United Daughters of the Confederacy – "fashioned Confederate memory into a revival crusade and the Old South into a lost racial utopia." This invented past depended on multi-media production, distribution, and consumption that included popular literature and film, along with textbooks and magazines filled with instances of the rare genre of pro-Confederate slave narratives.[19]

In addition to disrupting the binary of "official" versus "non-official" archives, the internationalization of memory studies has fundamentally challenged dominant understandings of twentieth-century "events" fundamental to the field of US foreign relations, including World War II and the Cold War. The 2001 collection, *Perilous Memories: The Asian-Pacific War(s)*, makes a powerful intervention into studies of war memories by arguing that history/memory is truncated by the mainstream perspective that reduces the Pacific theatre of World War II to a 1941–5 US conflict with Japan. The volume enacts a critical recovery of silenced, marginalized, submerged historical memories of a multiplicity of Asian conflicts, brings into relief the mediated and unstable nature of the past, and illustrates how even seemingly basic historical facts, such as periodization, are sites of contestation. From the perspective of the Chinese, for instance, the war would begin with the 1931 Japanese invasion of northeastern China. For Korea, Vietnam, the Philippines, and the Marshallese islands, the war was part of a prolonged struggle for national liberation from colonialism (under Japanese, French, US auspices) beginning long before World War II and continuing long after its conclusion. Here, once again, broadening one's historical frame and archives transforms the fundamental temporal and spatial assumptions of scholars about global war and foreign policy.[20]

In *The Unpredictability of the Past: Memories of the Asian-Pacific War in the U.S.*, editor Marc Gallicchio brilliantly argues that the contemporary disputes over the popular memory and legacy of mid-twentieth-century wars in Asia (which have only increased with the intensifying quarrels over islands involving Korea, Japan, China, and Russia) are significant factors in current affairs. Contending that "memory is a reconstruction of the past, not a reproduction," Gallicchio argues that "attempts to preserve the past inevitably alter it." Significantly, most contributors to the book are historians of international relations, and the volume serves as a powerful example of how memory studies have significantly advanced the field.[21]

Also insisting on the internationalization of memory studies is Daniel Walkowitz and Lisa Maya Knauer's *Memory and the Impact of Political Transformation in Public Space*. Pushing back against US-centric debates in public history, this book illustrates "how historical interpretation of public sites has shifted with the rise and fall of political regimes and changing political currents all over the world." The authors argue for expanding the sphere of public history to include not just museums and monuments as sites of history production and contestation, but also folk songs and un-built monuments. Finding centuries-old precedents and far-flung analogues to what some Americans might have imagined as our unique preoccupation with conflicting memories of the past, the volume's authors suggest a pattern of politicians and politically charged interest groups "with historically specific interests constraining curators, architects, and those with a dissenting view of the past."[22]

Rosenberg's reminder about the contingency of time and place armors us for venturing into the shifting, foreboding terrain of memory studies in the post-Cold War digital world. Whether one studies the America Revolution, the global war of 1914–18, or the US wars in Iraq, whether through the selective digitalization of archives or recent web sources, much, if not the preponderance of history/memory of these events is now refracted through digital media. Rosenberg observes that "internet sites and discussion boards circulate and contest the past in new ways, bringing into sharp relief the fluid and fragmented nature of history/memory. Debates about the past can flower on the Internet and create new hybrid forms of history."[23]

History/memory representations of the Cold War and the War on Terror have been largely constructed in a digital world since the advent of the worldwide web. The first web-browser was launched in 1993, less than two years after the collapse of the Soviet Union. Historians, of course, have debated, at times fiercely, the causes, legacy, scope, and significance of the Cold War before and after 1989.[24] But following the insights and methods of memory studies, an engagement with the history/memory wars outside of the academy located in the circulation of multiple media flows within a digital world, is critical to our understanding of the contested meanings of the Cold War.

Euro-American scholarly discourse occasioned by the end of the Cold War highlighted nostalgia as a major subset of memory studies. While nostalgia is a seventeenth-century medical term, the post-1989 scholarly focus responded to broad popular articulations of nostalgia in the wake of the collapse of Soviet bloc regimes. An investigation of the politicized memory of the Cold War entails a sustained inquiry into expressions of affective popular nostalgia and political and cultural narratives. An intertextual analysis of the post-9/11 production of Cold War history/memory and its mobilization in the war on terror would entail an analysis of content on the internet, television, film, museums, and video games. In the following more limited examples, I offer intertextual readings of Cold War nostalgia and of constructions of history/memory that draw on foreign policy discussions, political speeches, film, and popular culture sites of history/memory production.

Historian Jon Wiener suggests that there is no viable Cold War monument in the United States.[25] But the absence of such a monument has not stopped a litany of Cold War history/memory sites that are as well populated, as they are profitable. At the popular International Spy Museum in Washington DC, visitors exiting the Cold War-era espionage exhibit view a painting of a headless dragon with snakes slithering out from the torso in all directions. In the accompanying description, former CIA director James Woolsey explains the image as a symbol of the foreign policy challenges in a post-Soviet world: "We've slain a large dragon but we now live in a jungle filled with a bewildering variety of poisonous snakes, and in many ways the dragon was easier to keep track of." With the fall of the Berlin Wall and the collapse of the Soviet Union, US politicians and pundits declared victory in the Cold War. Yet celebrations of the West's victory soon betrayed more than a hint of regret for the passing of the Cold War, often viewed in retrospect as an era of relative peace and stability. In this view, both sides had a stake during the Cold War, and the antagonists always knew who and where one's enemies were. By the mid-1990s, the views of many politicians, journalists, and purveyors of popular culture could almost be summed up in the words of a character in a Hollywood film *The Peacemaker*, starring George Clooney and Nicole Kidman: "God, I miss the Cold War."

Scholars have devoted considerable attention to nostalgia within societies of the former Eastern bloc. At the same time, Western expressions of nostalgia abounded, captured in journalism, punditry, and popular culture. Indeed, nostalgia must be understood as a global, as well as a national and regional phenomenon. Quite distinct Western and Eastern expressions of nostalgia emerged amidst a pronounced increase in global economic inequality. Though varying in character and expression, Western nostalgia, like *Ostalgie* in Germany, Yugo-nostalgia, or nostalgia in Hungary and Russia, registered deep anxieties about the ability of market economies to sustain a decent standard of living as populations struggled to come to terms with the disintegration of dreams of the good life for the masses.[26]

Paradoxically, Western nostalgia emerged almost simultaneously with Western triumphalism.[27] What accounts for this dissonant strain amidst celebration? Nostalgic narratives gained traction just as Americans coped with geo-political uncertainty, the decline of living-wage jobs, and diminished social welfare programs. As evidenced in the 1959 "kitchen debates" between Vice-President Richard Nixon and Soviet Premier Nikita Khrushchev, both capitalist and socialist blocs shared a dream of the good life for the masses and competed vigorously over which system could best deliver it. For many on both sides of the former Cold War divide, the post-1991 era – unevenly yet relentlessly – was marked by a loss of collective hope for the good life. Just as critically, the loss of a belief in social progress – for many, the loss of political hope itself – seeped into Western as well as former Eastern bloc sensibilities, and as documented in Charles Piot's *Nostalgia for the Future: West Africa after the Cold War*, into Global South sensibilities as well.[28]

Indeed, nostalgia has worked in multiple registers. Nostalgia was integral to Cold War triumphalism, or what former Soviet Premier Mikhail Gorbachev has called America's "winner complex" – the belief that the West's victory in the Cold War meant that alternatives to liberal capitalist democracy had been forever vanquished.[29] In the construction of this history/memory, nostalgia retrospectively read victory into a past defined by moral rectitude. In this view, the collapse of the Eastern bloc vindicated the US moral imperative to fight the Cold War by any means necessary. Internally contested and failed US policies from Vietnam to Latin America could be justified by America's ultimate victory in the Cold War. Widely promulgated by such academics as Samuel Huntington and Francis Fukuyama, such vindicationist amnesia resounded though the mainstream media.[30]

People across the political spectrum looked back to the Cold War as a time when life seemed more hopeful. The Culture Wars, notably promulgated by Patrick Buchanan at the 1992 Republican National Convention, referenced nostalgia for Ronald Reagan's Cold War when the President had defined the enemy as the "evil empire."[31] With communism defeated, feminists, gays, immigrants, and people of color now supposedly threatened the American way of life. Others saw a social safety net promising dignity in old age and social and economic advancement through education jeopardized by market relations that had been held in check – regulated by government – as long as social democracy had vied with socialism to raise the world's standard of living.

Many Americans vacillated between such explanations as they sought to comprehend the present and fend off a perceived imperiled future.

Viewing the Cold War through a nostalgic lens has shaped how Americans have understood not only the past, but also the present and the future. Indeed, nostalgia worked in multiple registers and continues to do so. Politicians, pundits and others have rehashed assumptions and tropes of the Cold War, selectively mining the past in order to distort contemporary issues. Charges of creeping communism, leveled first at the Clinton health care plan, became rhetorical weapons during both Obama presidential campaigns and attacks on the Affordable Health Care Act by Tea Party activists. The search for a new foreign enemy by policy and media elites in the post-1989 period has been turned inward, resulting in dysfunction in US politics as apocalyptic fears and Cold War-style brinksmanship have led to government shut-downs that brought the United States government to the brink of defaulting on its debt.

Western triumphalism also displaces alternative views about the Cold War and what its ending might entail. The revolutions that brought down Eastern bloc regimes began as movements to reform and humanize socialism, not as pro-capitalist movements.[32] In the United States and Europe, people talked of a "peace dividend" and the hope that a decrease in military spending of the Cold War era might enable spending on education, health care, and the environment. But such expectations were soon replaced by new capitalist economic doctrines of shock therapy for the former Eastern bloc, structural adjustment for the Third World, and deregulation in Western industrial societies.

When Francis Fukuyama proclaimed "the end of history" in 1989, he reflected the George H. W. Bush administration's confidence that capitalist democracy had decisively vanquished all possible alternatives for organizing human society.[33] Accepting the nomination at the 1988 Republican convention, Bush proclaimed US victory in the Cold War. In his version of events, US perseverance and military might, *not* Soviet reforms, diplomacy, and negotiation, had catalyzed the shift in geopolitics: "It's a watershed. It's no accident. It happened when we acted on the ancient knowledge that strength and clarity lead to peace – weakness and ambivalence lead to war. ... I will not allow this country to be made weak again, never."[34] Just as significant as Bush's intent to carry a big stick was his self-serving account of global politics. As a former CIA director who certainly knew that the Soviet Union was not the sole Cold War actor in southern Africa and Afghanistan, Bush remained silent on US support of white minority governments in southern Africa, CIA actions in Afghanistan prior to Soviet intervention, and US officials' support of the anti-Soviet Mujahedeen fighters in Afghanistan.

Like George H. W. Bush's version of the Cold War, the idea that the Cold War era was more stable than what followed it ignores the deaths of millions in Asia, Africa, the Middle East, and Latin America. It further ignores multiple connections between Cold War policies and post-9/11 conflicts including the Soviet and United States arming of Third World dictatorships that enabled later wars of genocide. Narratives that refuse to critically examine the Cold War close their eyes to the proxy wars of the conflict. They ignore Washington's enlistment of Saddam Hussein's Iraq as an ally against Iran after the Shah's overthrow. By erasing the destructive impact of such engagements, the Cold War's major actors are absolved from responsibility for the vexing problems of the present. In this view, post-1991 wars are understood within a frame of a "clash of civilizations" and terrorism is attributed solely to Islamic history and culture. Such views of the past distorted post-1991 foreign policy.

Popular Hollywood films stand in a complex yet critical relationship to Cold War history/memory. *The Peacemaker* ("God I miss the Cold War") was one of many 1990s films imagining the smuggling of nuclear weapons. This scenario complicated rosy narratives about the free movement of people and goods on a global scale. With nuclear arsenals no longer safely controlled by states, they had become a testament to the power of the highest bidder. Indeed, in the film, the stolen bomb is smuggled across the Russian border in an ordinary backpack. *The Peacemaker* exemplifies the dramatization of the chaotic underside of the black market in post-Soviet security, as borders seemed no longer able to contain dangers. The film articulated Western nostalgia by staging the specter of weapons circulating in new and shadowy markets. How is security understood and maintained in a border-shifting globe? How does one measure value in shape-shifting markets with hidden commodities and transactions? With planned economies replaced by new speculation and organized crime, where costs might triple or quadruple overnight, how was one to know what anything was worth? After a truck bomb detonated below the North Tower of New York City World Trade Center on February 26, 1993, the what-if character of films imagining nuclear terrorism echoed press accounts of loose nukes. These films portrayed a world in which violence could suddenly appear in the most mundane, everyday spaces, and sometimes, just as suddenly, disappear.[35]

Most of these films were filled with moral ambiguity. In *The Peacemaker*, the terrorist remains for the most part off stage but in one scene identifies himself as a Yugoslav without a country, not Serbian, Croatian, or Muslim. He seeks revenge for the death of his family and explains his rage toward the West, which stood by, or worse, tried to weaken the Soviet Union by goading nationalist politicians to destroy his home. Yet the dramatic resolution of the film (like others) depends on US special agents to avert nuclear strikes or massive causalities – thus reinforcing the need for Western espionage, agents, and special operations. In evoking both fear and heroism, such films helped produce a structure of feeling that was mobilized in the aftermath of 9/11.

Outside of Hollywood, the emergence of Cold War kitsch circulated in unexpected ways in an increasingly robust market for Cold War-themed goods. As Americans rushed to buy chunks of the Berlin Wall or patronized a Las Vegas "Exclusive" Vodka Vault, to "do shots off Vladimir Lenin's head," a younger generation experienced the Cold War through video games, such as the record-breaking "Call of Duty Black Ops," in which the player's first task is to assassinate Fidel Castro. Opening with a re-enactment of the Bay of Pigs, the game requires players to maneuver through, and hence imagine themselves escaping from a Soviet Gulag camp and journeying through Vietnam's Mekong Delta. Making strong claims to "authenticity," the game is based on real cases with players of Black Ops supposedly experiencing the historical Cold War. Like George W. Bush going after Saddam Hussein, these re-enactments promise to re-write history by indulging players in the visceral fantasy of toppling Castro "this time." As the *New York Times* video games reviewer enthused, "I couldn't wait to go back and try to assassinate Castro and kill Russians." The game reinforces and reflects nostalgia for a bi-polar Cold War world in which Asians, Africans, and Latin Americans are mere backdrops to the "real" fight against the Soviets. The game's celebration of militarism, counter-insurgency, and violence constitutes a fantasy do-over, this time with more firepower.

Popular representations of history from museums to video games and re-enactments rely on claims to authenticity through a "you were there" experience. Such claims reinforce the assumption that individual experience and subjectivity are the sole arbiters of truth. As a counter to these stories, the insistence among scholars of memory studies on the social, cultural, and political context of history/memory is crucial, because it is precisely these contexts that are consistently slighted in the contemporary media environment.

Finally, while it is critical for historians to recognize the constructed nature of "official" as well as "unofficial" archives, this does *not* entail abandoning a rigorous examination of the veracity of truth claims. While the historian must work with an awareness that all archives were shaped by a confluence of human decisions, political projects, cultural assumptions, and bureaucratic practices, all "facts" and all claims are not equal. Densely intertextual studies of history/memory offer the most powerful bulwark against past and present manipulations of history in the service of naïve or cynical political ends. Historians have long critiqued misuses and abuses of history and have issued perennial calls for holding those in positions of power accountable to the past. Such accountability requires attention also to the production of history/memory in a contemporary mass media world defined by a paradoxical condition of oversaturation that itself breeds collective amnesia. This challenge awaits all of us who endeavor to practice the craft of history in the twenty-first century, a moment in which multiple publics have responded to transformations in the global order with a bewildering conflation of historical consciousness, memory, and affect.

NOTES

1. Michel-Rolph Trouillot, *Silencing the Past: Power and the Production of History* (Boston, 1995), 1–2.
2. Marc Gallicchio, ed., *The Unpredictability of the Past: Memories of the Asian-Pacific War in the U.S.* (Durham, 2007).

3. Emily S. Rosenberg, *A Day Which Will Live: Pearl Harbor in American Memory*, (Durham, 2003), 189; Pierre Nora, *Realms of Memory: The Construction of the French Past* (New York, 1996); Paul Ricoeur, *Memory, History, Forgetting*, (Chicago, 2004).
4. Christina Schwenkel, *The American War in Contemporary Vietnam: Transnational Remembrance and Representation* (Bloomington, IN, 2009), 10–11.
5. Certainly, attention to archives, their construction, and their maintenance through institutional and bureaucratic practice has been a longstanding concern, the subject for example of the French philosopher Michel Foucault's 1969 *Archaeology of Knowledge*. Foucault's insights have been central to historians' critiques of the archive over the last decades, including a notable recent work by the historian/anthropologist of European colonialism Ann Laura Stoler. See Stoler, *Along the Archival Grain: Epistemic Anxieties and Colonial Common Sense* (Princeton, 2009).
6. An excellent starting point for this literature is Mieke Bal, Jonathan Crewe, and Leo Spitzer, editors, *Acts of Memory: Cultural Recall in the Present* (Dartmouth, 1998).
7. Rosenberg, *A Day Which Will Live*, 4.
8. Rosenberg, *A Day Which Will Live*, 3. See, also, Andreas Huyssen, *Present Pasts: Urban Palimpsests and the Politics of Memory* (Stanford, 2003).
9. The cultural phenomenon of public memory in the United States inspired such seminal works as Michael Kammen, *Mystic Chords of Memory: The Transformation of Tradition in American Culture* (New York, 1993), and David Blight, *Race and Reunion: The Civil War in American Memory* (Cambridge, MA, 2001).
10. Erica Doss, *Memorial Mania: Public Feeling in America* (Chicago, 2010).
11. Schwenkel, *The American War in Contemporary Vietnam*, 10–11.
12. For an important discussion of this literature, see, Robert D. Schulzinger, "Memory and Understanding in U.S. Foreign Relations," in Michael J. Hogan and Thomas G. Paterson eds., *Explaining the History of American Foreign Relations* (New York, 2004).
13. Kirk Savage, *Monument Wars: Washington D.C., the National Mall, and the Transformation of the Memorial Landscape* (Berkeley, 2009); Kristin Ann Hass, *Sacrificing Soldiers on the National Mall* (Berkeley, 2013).
14. Doss, *Memorial Mania*; Marita Sturken, *Tourists of History: Memory, Kitsch, and Consumerism from Oklahoma City to Ground Zero* (Durham, 2007).
15. Rosenberg, *A Date Which Will Live*, 5.
16. Schwenkel, *The American War in Contemporary Vietnam*, 3.
17. "Foreign Affairs after World War II: Connecting Sexual and International Politics," *Diplomatic History*, Vol. 1. Issue I, 1994, 59–70.
18. Melani McAlister, *Epic Encounters: Culture, Media, and U.S. Interests in the Middle East Since 1945* (Berkeley, 2001); Christina Klein, *Cold War Orientalism: Asia in the Middlebrow Imagination 1945–1961* (Berkeley, 2003).
19. David Blight, *Race and Reunion: The Civil War in American Memory* (Cambridge, MA, 2001).
20. T.T Fijitani, Geoffrey White, and Lisa Yoneyama, *Perilous Memories: The Asian-Pacific War(s)* (Duke University Press, 2001).
21. Marc Gallicchio, editor, *The Unpredictability of the Past: Memories of the Asian-Pacific War in the U.S.* (Duke University Press, 2007).

22. Daniel Walkowitz and Lisa Maya Knauer, eds., *Memory and the Impact of Political Transformation in Public Space* (Durham, 2004), viii. See, also, Jay Winter, *Sites of Memory, Sites of Mourning: The Great War in European Cultural History* (Cambridge, 1995).
23. Rosenberg, *A Date Which Will Live*, 162.
24. Michael J. Hogan, ed., *The End of the Cold War: Its Meaning and Implications* (New York, 1992).
25. Jon Wiener, *How We Forgot the Cold War: A Historical Journey through America* (Berkeley, 2012).
26. For just some of the important scholarship on these multiple and various forms of nostalgia, see Svetlana Boym, *The Future of Nostalgia* (New York, 2002); Charity Scribner, *Requiem for Communism* (Cambridge, MA, 2003); Breda Luthar and Marusa Pusnik, eds., *Remembering Utopia: The Culture of Everyday Life in Socialist Yugoslavia* (Washington, DC, 2010); and Maria Todorova (ed.), *Remembering Communism: Genres of Representation* (New York, 2010).
27. Ellen Schrecker, ed., *Cold War Triumphalism: The Misuse of History after the Fall of Communism* (New York, 2004).
28. Charles Piot, *Nostalgia for the Future: West Africa After the Cold War* (University of Chicago Press, 2010). See, also, James Ferguson, *Global Shadows: Africa in the Neoliberal World* (Durham, 2006).
29. Schrecker, ed., *Cold War Triumphalism*.
30. Mark Hosenball, "Centuries of Boredom in World Without War; An American Theory," Spectrum, *The Times* (London), September 3, 1989, Sunday; Samuel P. Huntington, "Repent! The End is Near," *The Washington Post*, September 24, 1989.
31. Conor O'Clery, "Reagan Lifts Party out of Sleaze: Cold War Memorabilia in Nostalgic Sale at a Political Flea Market," *The Irish Times*, August 19, 1992, CITY EDITION, World News, Houston Letter, p. 4; John F. Harris, "One for the Gipper: Loyalists Toast Reagan Amid Nostalgia for '80s," *The Washington Post*, August 18, 1992.
32. Scribner, Charity, *Requiem for Communism* (Cambridge, 2003); Serotte, Mary, *1989: The Struggle to Create a Post Cold War Europe* (Princeton, 2011).
33. Mark Hosenball, "Centuries of Boredom in World Without War; An American Theory," Spectrum, *The Times* (London), September 3, 1989, Sunday.
34. George H. W. Bush, speech accepting the Republican Party nomination, August 18, 1988. www.presidency.ucsb.edu/ws/?pid=25955.
35. For an analysis of the new geographies of war, see, Derek Gregory, *The Everywhere War The Geographical Journal*, Vol. 177, No. 3, September 2011, pp. 238–50.

19

The senses

Andrew J. Rotter

The so-called "cultural turn" in foreign relations history has produced the revelation, among others, that participants in encounters between people and nations have not just brains but bodies. People do not only think about each other, even in order to dominate them; they meet each other hand to hand, face to face, body to body; they form impressions of others and have feelings about them. Their reactions are not always considered but may be instinctive and visceral. People feel about each other a mix of wonder at the seemingly different, and fear – of bodily penetration, pollution, or infection. The body is a membrane, as Laura Otis has argued, permitting osmosis that may be pleasurable or enlightening but also threatening.[1] In their encounter with the new and strange, people *feel* – delight and alarm, hope and danger, arousal and disgust, exhilaration and terror.

It is through their senses that people apprehend each other and their environments. The senses are to some extent physiological phenomena. Yet it will not do to place the senses entirely in the realm of biology, for sensory perceptions are the products of history and culture. The body registers from its sensory encounters not fixed, universally held impressions, but interpretations of what it apprehends based on its experiences learned over time and according to place. The human "sensorium" has changed through time, as print largely replaced the oral transmission of information in modernizing societies and thus elevated sight over hearing and the other senses. What humans liked as sounds, smells, feeling, and tastes changed too, for reasons that were both sanitary and aesthetic. As Norbert Elias has argued, changes in manners during the European Enlightenment reflected new ways of contrasting the civilized with the primitive, with far-reaching consequences for the senses.[2] What looks attractive, sounds pleasant, smells appealing, feels right, and tastes good varies according to cultural and individual predilection. "So," concludes Robert Jütte, "there can be no such thing as a natural history of the senses, only a social history of human sense perception."[3]

To each sensory stimulus there is an emotional response, or several responses. Encounters with the unfamiliar often inspire the most powerful sensory and emotional reactions; the perceived strangeness of the Other is registered in the strength of the body's response to it. But there is nothing inherent in Otherness. The discomfort people feel when they apprehend difference is learned and can be unlearned. And yet it is a pervasive feature of human interaction to represent as inferior those who offend the senses, who look wrong, sound shrill or too loud, smell strong, whose skin is rough or haptic environment uncomfortable, whose food is literally distasteful. All sensory perceptions are invented things. They are powerful nonetheless.

Senses inspire emotions, create impressions of Others and then prompt behaviors toward them. The examples given here concern the US empire in the Philippines, 1898–1946. They cluster around each of the five senses in sequence, though with the understanding that no sense can stand alone as a category of analysis, since all five senses interact constantly. These are not just anecdotes of sensory impressions. Rather, they illustrate the persistence into the twentieth century of belief in what Elias called the "civilizing process." Americans saw as their mission in the Philippines the civilization of some number of the "natives," the achievement of which was necessary before self-government could possibly be conferred. By "civilization" the Americans meant many things: whiteness (honorary only, for the fairest-skinned Filipinos), Christianity (most Filipinos were Catholics, which was a start), literacy in English, masculinity (men who displayed forthrightness and physical vigor), femininity (women who were domesticated and modest). And civilization meant, said the dictionary, "the state of being refined in manners, from the grossness of savage life, and improved in arts and learning."[4] Civilized people respected the senses. They looked clean and alert; their eyes met yours, they revealed themselves. They spoke with resonant and well-modulated voices, comprehensibly – meaning in English. Their bodies and breath smelled fresh, not stale or sharp. Their skins were refined and smooth, as indicated by the type of clothes they wore, for no civilized skin could bear the feel of coarse garb. And they ate politely, with utensils not fingers, and their food and drink were palatable. Making Filipinos mannerly was one of empire's projects.

Seeing: Most Americans saw the Philippines and the Filipinos for the first time when they arrived in the islands after 1898. The Americans were soldiers, then government officials, civil servants, businessmen, and teachers. They were conquerors, which predicted what and how they saw. They sent to the United States photographs, drawings, and written accounts – word pictures for compatriots to read – of what they witnessed, and the gaze they directed at the land and its inhabitants offered a vision that Americans took for true, accustomed as they were to trusting their eyes. They interpreted the Philippines through the act of viewing it.

They found some of it attractive. Edith Moses, wife of Bernard, one of the first American Commissioners in the Philippines, thought the island of

The senses

Mindanao "a beautiful tropical country ... the jungle of our imagination." The upland "wild tribes" were "picturesque," and the Catholic churches in Manila surprised her with their elegant proportions and lack of ostentation.[5] The bright colors of Filipinos' clothing appealed to many Americans. Women wore in their hair "strings of beads, some of them of beautiful agate."[6]

Yet most Americans thought the Philippines a savage land, uncivilized in appearance and in the ways its inhabitants abused the sense of sight, as they beheld and were beheld by others. The landscape could be striking, but also disorienting in its tropical starkness; "there was a monotony about it all that caused one soon to weary of it: great glaring stretches of white sand."[7] Admiration for the physical presence of Filipinos was overmatched by fear, distaste, or revulsion. Part of the problem for the American military attempting to defeat the Filipinos fighting for independence from 1899 to 1902 was the insistence of the people on concealing themselves. The *insurrectos* hid in the jungle, using guerrilla tactics against the Americans. They deceived American vision through tricks, disguises, even magic. If a group of *insurrectos* encountered an American force, complained Henry Hoyt, they would "vanish in the jungle and 'presto change'" into white coats and pants, and thus "emerge innocent *amigos* clad in white."[8] "Experience taught," wrote Emily Conger, "that the most guileless in looks were the worst desperadoes of all."[9] Filipinos were notorious, claimed the Americans, for masking their feelings and intentions. The racist pejorative "gook" was coined by American troops in the Philippines. The word likely comes from the expression "goo-goo eyes," which suggested feigned innocence concealing bad intentions.[10] "I know that the Filipino is disposed to conceal his true feelings when in opposition to the person whom he is addressing," said the islands' first American Governor William Howard Taft, "and I know that these characteristics are calculated to make the Americans impatient and condemn the race" – though Taft himself counseled forbearance.[11]

If Filipinos hid and deceived, they also, paradoxically, revealed too much, especially through their scandalous habits of dress. The "Igorrotes," wrote the American Episcopal Bishop Charles Henry Brent, were naked, tattooed "savages."[12] On Negritos, the people "go almost naked, with no other clothing than a small clout .... The women use an apron which is somewhat longer than that of the men."[13] Even in the capital visitors could be surprised: "It gives one just arriving from America a bit of a shock," wrote John Bancroft Devins, "as he drives about the streets of Manila, to see children running around clad principally in their brown birthday suits .... The laboring men are in all stages of dress. Some of them have scarcely more than a cloth around their loins."[14]

Nakedness exposed what Americans considered ugliness. Dark skin was unattractive to many whites. Albert Sonnichsen, held captive by Filipino fighters for ten months in 1899, recalled a young lieutenant whose "appearance was far from prepossessing. Being unusually black, he was short of stature, thick-lipped, and pock-marked, a typical full-blooded Filipino."[15] The pockmarks came from smallpox, common in the archipelago until vaccination brought it under control. Worse was the disfigurement of leprosy. Before the Americans arrived, lepers were cared for by their families, and were occasionally allowed into the public square. Americans were horrified at the sight of lepers. William Freer found that "the condition of the people was pitiable; their faces were swollen and blotched, the bridge of the nose was usually sunken and sometimes lacking, arms and legs were withered and deformed and all had raw sores."[16] The wife of Emily Conger's cook had neither smallpox nor leprosy. But Conger found her hideous when she turned up one day. She had "one eye crossed, a harelip," and a "mouth and lips stained blood red with betel juice." Conger "screamed at her to run away."[17]

Instead the woman stayed, and Conger overcame her revulsion and made her a servant – and the women grew close. Here was a way forward, beyond the tricks of vision, the concealment, the disgust of seeing the exposed or ugly. Americans could get used to what they saw; people do. Moreover, they could by their own lights improve matters. Americans mapped the islands, locating the inhabitants and allowing them to "be magnified and easily seen."[18] Early twentieth-century Americans were frequently reformers. They might start with the farthest-flung outpost of their empire and make Filipinos a sight for civilized eyes. They could not make Filipinos white, though they increasingly shared governing with the lightest-skinned of them, (literally) enlightened *illustrados*. They would cure their unsightly diseases, and if they could not, as with leprosy, they would remove the afflicted to a colony on Culion Island, away from their offended gaze. In the schools the Americans built and staffed they would teach Filipino children the importance of clothing. "We cannot disregard clothes," wrote the authors of a textbook on hygiene and personal deportment. "Good clothes can aid in making us attractive, and poorly fitting or dirty clothes can aid in giving others a bad impression of us."[19] A government manual offered this advice: "Anyone who is always considerate of the feelings of others has good manners.... It is most unkind to stare at or comment upon the infirmity of anyone, or call another's attention to it. People who are lame, ugly, cross-eyed, fat, or peculiar in any way, are sure to be over-sensitive; and they do not like to have their peculiarities noticed. Many who are afflicted with birthmarks of some sort are so sensitive that they do not care to go among people; and left by themselves, they live lonely, unhappy lives. We can make such people much happier by helping them to forget that they are not just like the rest of us."[20]

By the early 1920s, as Americans were contemplating a timetable for Philippine independence, there was reassuring news from a government mission: "the Philippine people possess many fine and attractive qualities – dignity and self-respect, as shown by deportment, complete absence of beggars, personal neatness and cleanliness, courtesy and consideration to strangers and guests, boundless hospitality, willingness to do favors for those whom they come in contact ... they are refined in manner, filled with racial pride, light-hearted and inclined to be improvident."[21] A bit more time was needed. But there was hope that any offense earlier given to the civilized gaze would soon be forgotten.

Hearing: Americans who came to the Philippines in the twentieth century disliked noise. Progressives in the United States sought to reduce cacophony. Noise, according to Karin Bijsterveld, meant "conflict and complexity, rudeness, wildness, primitiveness, irrationality, impressive behavior and revenge ... Noise meant chaos, silence meant order, and rhythm meant control within and over societal life."[22] The lower classes, people of color, and recently arrived immigrant groups, were alleged to be especially noisy – a perception that transferred easily to Filipinos.

In the Philippines, noise meant danger to the soldiers who had come to "pacify" the *insurrectos*. Since they could not see their enemies, the Americans knew they were under attack only when bullets from smokeless enemy Mausers whizzed overhead.[23] The heard environment in the Philippines, its "soundscape," played tricks on the soldiers: they heard noises that bore "resemblance ... to firing," complained Dana Merrill. "Thunder for example when distant has a popping roar exactly like a nigger shooting affair .... Then bambo[o] when burned unsplit pops off like a Mauser, and dozens of camp sounds keep one on the qui vive all the time."[24] Information about the enemy was hard to come by, since even *amigos* were "the biggest liers [sic] on the face of the earth."[25]

As the war wound down, American civilians arrived determined to put the soundscape right. They were heartened by a couple of things: the Filipinos were, Americans said, an imitative people who readily absorbed lessons about sound, and they were naturally musical, with innate ability to carry a tune. "They are very fond of music," George Telfer wrote to his wife. "Even the poorer classes have pianos and play well .... Every place we go instruments are brought out and we hear 'After the Ball,' 'Ta ra ra boom de lay,' etc .... Some of them are really fine performers."[26] Even the smallest villages had uniformed bands. The Philippine Constabulary Band, established by Governor Taft in 1902 and under the baton of the African American bandleader Walter Loving, was, according to Taft's wife, "one of the really great bands of the world."[27] The trouble came when enthusiasm outran discipline – something Americans frequently imputed to people they considered more emotional than cerebral. Filipinos played too loud and too fast, or they chose inappropriate songs for the occasion, such as "Hot Time in the Old Town Tonight" during funerals.[28] Or, William Cameron Forbes complained, the "bands often played simultaneously and always different tunes."[29]

Far worse than band music was the general level of noise throughout the archipelago, suggesting not just lack of discipline but something uncivilized. In the Philippines, the day began with the "clatter and chatter" of people engaged more in gossip than in work.[30] The men "loved to orate."[31] Carriages bounced noisily through unpaved streets, traveling by railroad meant hearing the bleating of goats and the cries of roosters being transported, and bells rang constantly and seemingly at random from church spires.[32] Camped near Itogan in May 1902, Edith Moses recorded a series of aural intrusions: "People talk of the vast solitude and the stillness of the night. I never heard so many noises in my life. There was a steady crunch, crunch, and the frequent snort of our horses as they cropped the short grass. A thousand insects filled the air with whizz and whirr, making me re-cover my ears precipitately, only to uncover them at some unusual sound. From far away came the tap of a native drum. A melancholy owl, or night bird, with a hoarse cry, wheeled round and round our mountain top. Now and again a low guttural sound from the Igorrotes caused me to reflect on the tales I had heard of head hunters."[33]

Americans believed it was possible to civilize the soundscape of the Philippines, in ways small and large. Forbes, who served as governor 1908–13, acted on his exasperation about cacophonous Filipino bands. When he visited the town of Morong two bands struck up the "Star-Spangled Banner" simultaneously, but one played it more quickly and, when finished, started in on "insurrection music." Forbes stopped the bands, told their leaders and Morong's mayor (*presidente*) that he would not tolerate disrespect to the anthem, and ordered the bandleaders and the *presidente* to Manila for a further scolding. "I shall permit no lack of courtesy to the American flag nor to the national music," he wrote.[34] Forbes also embarked on a major road-building program, ensuring quieter transport. The American military in the Philippines prohibited cockfighting, prompting villagers in Pandacan to produce Italian operas in the former cockpits.[35]

Most of all, Americans tried to change the soundscape by making English the medium of instruction and then the official language of the islands. Hundreds of American teachers were summoned to set up schools throughout the country. They were to teach children how to speak proper English, so that they would become comprehensible to each other (permitting national unity) and to the Americans (making them more governable). Americans encountered inadequate or nonexistent school buildings and children unprepared for the discipline of the classroom. In Manila, schools lacked light and ventilation, and their windows opened on streets noisy with traffic: "Carromatas [carriages] and carabao [water buffalo] carts rumble past, street hawkers shout their cries, and all the sounds of a quarreling, jostling, idle population burst into the room." Things were hardly better inside, "owing to the habit of studying aloud"; it sounded "like pandemonium let loose; all the pupils studying together, making a deafening, rasping noise."[36] David Barrows, the first American superintendent of education, endorsed "simplified spelling" of English words and the admission into the lexicon of common Tagalog words.[37] Others stressed the use of schools, and English, to teach children civilized behavior. Filipinos would learn manners of speaking and listening:

American educators urged that children restrain their "desire to talk and whisper – in these things gaining self-control day by day. The essence of moral behavior is self-control."[38] Girls should "cultivate a soft, gentle voice," and were told that "no well-bred person will make offensive noises with mouth, nose, finger-joints, or any part of the body."[39]

Some Filipinos doubted the value of learning English, or of being acoustically disciplined by Americans. The writer Teodoro Kalaw feared English would corrupt Filipino girls, who were "chattering in a strange language ..., unconscious victims of modernity."[40] But the Americans thought they were succeeding. In his Eighth Annual Report, Barrows observed that "Filipino students are generally quiet in their seats, obedient, respectful, and lovable." Their "achievement of letters marks the transition from barbarism to civilization."[41] The new soundscape of independence was taking hold. At the birth of the Philippines commonwealth on November 15, 1935, the Filipino band played the "Star-Spangled Banner" and "Hail to the Chief." By contrast, on Philippine Independence Day (July 4, 1946), the band played both the US and Philippine national anthems. The latter, "Lupang Hinirang" ("Chosen Land"), was commissioned by Emilio Aguinaldo in 1898 to accompany the declaration of independence from Spain. The Americans had previously banned its performance.[42]

Smelling: Smell is at once the most evanescent and enduring of the five senses. Dozens of Americans commented briefly on the odors they encountered in the Philippines. Yet their memories of smell surely lingered. "Odors," writes the novelist Patrick Süskind, "have a power of persuasion stronger than that of words, appearances, emotions, or will. The persuasive power of an odor cannot be fended off, it enters into us like breath into our lungs, it fills us up, imbues us totally. There is no remedy for it."[43] Humans distinguish between the civilized and the primitive on the basis of smell, the aesthetic and moral evaluation of which is learned. Those worried about the penetration of their body membranes are most worried about odors, which cannot be anticipated or "fended off"; odors mark "the boundary between self and other." "We" smell good, or not at all, while ethnic, racial, gender, or class Others reek: of their strange foods, of a "hircine" smell attributed by whites to blacks, of reckless sexuality, of the sweat of manual labor.[44]

Americans in the Philippines were disgusted and threatened by strong smells. Progressives who sought quiet also craved odorlessness, or sweet odors. Americans had only recently decided that they (and especially newly arrived immigrants) should wash with deodorizing soap, and that their cities needed underground sewers to carry off wastes that were not just offensive but increasingly understood to produce disease. The advent of the germ theory, which advanced unsteadily during this period, persuaded sanitationists and doctors that stench itself did not cause illness. Yet stench remained associated with disease. The discovery that human waste was the source of cholera joined the pragmatic with the aesthetic: feces must be contained because they were disease-producing *and* disgusting. Those unwilling to control their wastes were thus a threat to public health *and* offensive to civilized order.[45]

In the Philippines, the Americans encountered smells that were sometimes appealing. An American hygiene manual endorsed the Filipina practice of rubbing coconut oil in the hair but cautioned against using too much, because "many oils or pomades have a distinct odor which is most offensive to people with good taste."[46] Other odors were unambiguously awful. Cockroaches stank, as did carabao meat, the ubiquitous goats and pigs, lepers with "their foul-smelling gangrenous ulcers," and even the disinfectants used to combat germs.[47] And, while American health experts demanded that Filipino farmers wear shoes to prevent hookworm, they also acknowledged that, "as shoes do not permit free evaporation of perspiration, the perspiration accumulates on the feet and on the stockings and produces an offensive odor if the stockings are not changed at least once a day."[48]

Worst of all was the smell of excrement, animal but especially human. In 1898 Manila had the Philippines' only underground sewers, but these were inadequate for the capital's size. Most of the city's sewage ran in open ditches to the *esteros* – canals – near the Pasig River, or was dumped in the river by private contractors using open carts.[49] "Calls of nature are attended to wherever (as well as whenever) it is the most convenient – indoors or out of doors," George Telfer wrote his wife. "It is worse among the rich than among the poor for the former confine the deposit to their houses – while the latter go out into the street. Capt. Prescott has been on smelling detail among the monasteries near us. He is a very robust man, but he has to excuse himself from the balance of the party now and then – to vomit."[50] Outside Manila, latrines were unheard of and residents relieved themselves through holes in the floors of their houses or a short distance away. Travelers complained about the smells, and sanitation officials scoured the countryside, urging Filipinos to treat their "evacuated intestinal contents as poison," instructing villagers how to build safe latrines, driving livestock and people away from water sources, and warning about "the dangers of promiscuous defecation."[51]

Smells would improve gradually during the nearly five decades of US occupation. By cajolery and coercion the Americans got more Filipinos to build and use latrines, and sewer systems were built in the cities. Frank Murphy, the US governor in the mid-1930s, noted that Manila's *esteros* now carried "heavy water traffic" and did not mention their smell.[52] By 1934, forty percent of rural dwellers had latrines – still a significant shortfall, but far more than in 1898.[53] A textbook on hygiene instructed students to use their noses "as nature intended .... The sense of smell was given us for protection as well as for pleasure. It is our sense of smell that tells us whether the air is fit to take into the body."[54] Thus armed, the people of the Philippines might aspire finally to a sweet-smelling or odor-free environment, one consistent with civilization and thus their political autonomy.

Touching (and Feeling): Touch and feel – together, hapticity – "lies at the heart of our experience of ourselves and our world," writes Constance Classen.[55] Touching is voluntary, initiated by the curious. Feel is involuntary: what surrounds the skin cannot be controlled, as smell cannot. The temperature of the air, the strength of the wind, or even the touch of another one does not expect, can create haptic delight or discomfort. Recalling how things feel to themselves, people also imagine how contact might feel to others, as when one sees another wearing a garment that one knows to be prickly. (This happened frequently in the Philippines, where residents wore coarse fabrics against their skins.) By the late nineteenth century, Americans believed that skin must be smoothed and softened by bathing. Respectable people covered their skin against exposure to the elements or prying eyes, kept it clean, and free of sore or blemish. Those who allowed their skin to be abused were uncivilized.[56]

As with the other senses, hapticity in the Philippines was not altogether unpleasant for the Americans. Filipinos had a sensitive touch with sewing needles, enabling them to make undergarments of special delicacy.[57] Or their touch could be admirably strong: Henry Hoyt and Ralph Buckland were carried from boats to shore on the backs of small but powerful Filipinos.[58] But most Americans found the islands haptically uncomfortable. It began with the climate. "The sun rose, a great red ball of fire, and we felt its penetrating rays before it had left the horizon," wrote Edith Moses. In mid-July 1900 she lamented: "For a week I have been trying to write a letter but cannot summon energy to do so. I have begun several and then have succumbed to the climate. It is not very hot and there is a breeze through the house all the time, but the atmosphere is damp, warm, and clammy."[59] "The heat this month has been awful," Ernest Tilton wrote to his wife Julia, in April 1900. "We have found it necessary ... to wear wool undershirts which makes it very hard to stand, but it is better than being laid up with the 'mulligrubs,' this, the natives say is the cause with white people as they catch cold in the bowels."[60] Like the British in India, Americans wrapped their abdomens at night with "stomach bands," said to ward off cholera, allegedly carried on the night air.[61]

The land itself was uneven, sticky, impenetrable, its touch as harsh as that of the air. Iron-wheeled carts exaggerated the roughness of the landscape. When the Americans arrived the roads were poorly surfaced. American governors emphasized road building to smooth and speed transport across the islands. The sultry air buzzed with insects, and these, along with the ants and roaches that crawled along the ground, threatened the skin with disgusting or alarming contact. (There were satisfactions to be had through haptic encounters with insects: "At one place ten million young wingless locusts were crossing a river *on the railway bridge.* We made paste of at least five million, and the locomotive could hardly draw the train over the slippery mass. Everyone was in good spirits.")[62]

Americans often regarded bodily contact with the Filipinos as defiling. Filipinos were filthy, in need of lessons in hygiene. "One glance," wrote Emily

Conger, "and there was a wild desire to take those dirty, almost nude creatures in hand and, holding them at arm's length, dip them into some cleansing caldron." They neither changed their clothes nor washed their hands.[63] They spat freely, and their sputum might be infected with the germs of tuberculosis.[64] Rather than isolating the contagiously ill, Filipinos gathered around patients, tightly packed into airless rooms. If the patient died, there followed nine days of mourning and feasting, in which all those who had been exposed to the patient congregated closely together.[65] Lepers offended the senses of sight and smell, but the idea of contact with them was the most terrifying of all. Lepers who had been allowed to "wander around at will" in the Philippines before the Americans came were now confined to Culion Island, out of physical contact with healthier bodies.[66]

The Americans fought against defiling contact as determinedly as they battled *insurrectos*. Shaken by the amount of venereal disease afflicting American soldiers, military officials sent suspected prostitutes to hospitals, where they were charged for treatment.[67] Hygiene experts urged that Filipinos smooth their rough faces with daily massage and ice rubs, and refrain from applying to babies heated coconut shells or leeches, said to prevent convulsions.[68] Authorities urged that tuberculosis patients be isolated or go to hospitals, and a 1908 law prohibited in Manila the depositing of "sputum, saliva, phlegm or mucus upon the floor of any church, schoolhouse, public building or ... sidewalk," and forbade the sick from "working in ... a cigar or cigarette factory" or "dancing in a public dance hall."[69] Against cholera Americans tried to remove Filipinos from contact with infected water; to fight smallpox they used vaccination, penetrating skin with needle.[70]

By the 1920s, Americans believed they had to some extent succeeded in improving the felt environment. Roads got markedly better.[71] Public health improved, suggesting that contact had lessened between the sick and the healthy. And respectable Americans – not just soldiers seeking sex – proved increasingly willing to touch the people they had previously viewed as defiling. At *bailes*, held whenever Americans visited villages, Americans danced with Filipinos. Governor Francis Harrison had reportedly washed his hands with carbolic soap after greeting some Igorots in 1913. Eight years later, Governor Leonard Wood got in some "great handshaking" with residents of Narvacan, and felt no need to wash himself afterward.[72]

Tasting: The encounter with the food and eating habits of another culture can be jarring. "We are apt to call barbarous whatever departs widely from our own taste and apprehension," wrote David Hume.[73] Like smell, taste is an intimate sense, one drawn deep into the body. Eating and drinking are necessary, but they can also be dangerous. The first tendency of those newly arrived in an outpost of empire, especially if it is environmentally distinct from the metropole, is to resist ingesting local food and drink, relying instead on whatever can be brought into the colony from home. Yet it is seldom possible to insulate oneself permanently against local foods; there are temptations that the tongue cannot altogether resist. Tastes change, of necessity and learned preference. The Self and the Other may find common ground in food and drink.

It was so for Americans in the Philippines. Empire was sustained by metaphors of ingestion, so the Americans "devoured" or "swallowed" the Philippines, and Filipino children were told to stay indoors when the soldiers arrived "or the Americans will eat you."[74] American troops carried their rations with them, and they fought sustained by hardtack, beans, "milk toast made with condensed milk, which is nasty," canned meat, canned fruit, and canned butter – "like Vaseline in consistancy [sic]."[75] Americans were suspicious of Filipino food. Aboard a Spanish steamer in 1899, Emily Conger spurned the dinner she was offered: "There was a well prepared chicken with plenty of rice but made so hot with pepper that I threw it into the sea; next, some sort of salad floating in oil and smelling of garlic; it went overboard. Eggs cooked in oil followed the salad; last the 'dulce,' a composition of rice and custard perfumed with anise seed oil, made the menu of the fishes complete." She dined instead on "crackers and cheese, oranges, figs and dates."[76] The alternative seemed to many Americans disgusting and threatening. Philippine bananas were "acid" and "flavorless," guava jelly "gummy," sweet potatoes "watery and stringy," watermelon "like bread soaked in water."[77] Carabao was hard for Americans to digest.[78] Worst were grasshoppers and beetles, boiled then dried and sold in markets for a penny a cup.[79]

It wasn't just what Filipinos ate, but how they prepared food, conducted themselves at the table, and treated eating surfaces that dismayed many Americans. A dinner for Ralph Buckland featured guava jelly. The Filipinos ate first: "The first one took a spoonful of the jelly, licked it off, stuck the spoon back, and passed the tin on up the line, each in turn licking off a spoonful. We did not eat any jelly that meal." After that glasses of water were distributed. The Filipinos drank half the water in their glasses, then gargled noisily with the rest, creating a "sort of hydraulic tooth-brush." The Americans were "pretty well put out," their "delicacy ha[ving] received a severe jolting."[80] A health manual written for school children insisted that people not eat "decayed or dirty food – food that smells and that has been exposed to flies, dust and dirty hands." Tables should be elevated and kept clean. Diners should have their own plates and utensils, and should not eat with fingers from a common dish. "Do not eat your food rapidly and ravenously," the authors advised. "It looks ill-bred and is bad for your health. Take your time and chew your food thoroughly." And: "Exchanging food which has been partially eaten is particularly bad. You should never eat anything which has been in the mouth of someone else or which has been bitten by another person."[81]

Americans rejoiced when they could get a "genuine" American meal, perhaps featuring eggs, bacon, pancakes, and coffee.[82] Yet they acknowledged that the ingredients for meals like these were obtained locally. And they began to express appreciation for the food they found in the Philippines. Markets were filled with fruits and vegetables, and once

Americans got used to Filipino varieties they enjoyed them. Travelers received generous hospitality in Philippine homes, and were often treated to lavish banquets. "Excellent food everywhere," pronounced Leonard Wood in 1921. "We had for dinner the most remarkable fish."[83] William Freer attended a *baile* in Bayombong, and ate well "in Spanish style ... All of the food was well prepared, very palatable and nicely served."[84] Back in Manila, Edith Moses missed the spicy fare she had tasted on a trip south. "Our American menu lacks 'color,'" she lamented.[85]

The longer Americans stayed in the islands, the more they stretched their palates to include local foods, often blending items they could import from the United States with Filipino dishes. Sometimes Americans taught their Filipino cooks to make the foods of home, using ingredients that came to hand. At times they allowed improvisation. On Thanksgiving Day 1901, Walter Cutter and his fellow soldiers had baked potatoes, chicken with stuffing, white bread, onions, cranberry sauce, and pumpkin pie.[86] On a June Thursday thirty-three years later, Governor Frank Murphy hosted, aboard the S.S. *Mayon*, a dinner that featured chow chow, anchovy paste, Spanish omelet, a local fish soup, rice, and bananas – along with prime rib, baked potatoes, and English steamed pudding.[87] Here was a hybrid menu for a hybridizing empire, one made by a people who had tried to convince another to eat other foods and with better eating habits, and had found it more satisfying, in the end, to compromise.

CONCLUSION

Empire provides scope for understanding how the senses worked: it is part of a negotiated hegemony, of the desire of one group to "civilize," by its own lights, another. But do the senses work as a category of analysis for US foreign relations generally, in situations in which the United States lacks the ability or desire to control others, where encounters seem limited to diplomats, and where civilization is not on the agenda? Yes. Foreign policy decision-making in Washington does not occur in a vacuum. A cultural field unites policymakers and their advisers with information generated not only by diplomats but by travelers, writers, reporters, and with their own racial, gendered, and religious predilections. No one comes free of cultural entanglement; ideas, prejudices, and emotions concerning others are part of the policymakers' matrix. Note, too, that by the twentieth century many of those directly responsible for shaping US foreign policy traveled, or had traveled, to the places about which they were making decisions. William Howard Taft had several years' experience in the sensory environment of the Philippines before becoming secretary of war, then president. John and Robert Kennedy visited India in 1951, where both men, suffering from "the usual tummy trouble ... kept pushing pieces of the curry chicken and the papaya underneath the lettuce so they wouldn't have to eat it."[88] President Dwight Eisenhower visited Pakistan in late 1959. Later, he remarked on "the odors he [had] encountered between the airport and the

The senses

city of Karachi."[89] Understanding the power of the senses, their influence on sparking emotion, and the emotional valence of human decision-making, let us assert the importance of the sensorium in shaping US foreign relations.

Readers might agree. But how does a foreign relations historian – or any historian – go about researching the senses? Daniel Wickberg has observed that the "sensibilities are not organized in archives and conveniently visible for research purposes; they are almost never the explicit topics of the primary documents we use," and though "senses" and "sensibilities" are not synonyms the point holds for both.[90] Yet there are ways to explore the role of the senses in international encounters. Several can be inferred from the endnotes of this chapter. Travelers comment on their sensory impressions of a place, so their memoirs and diaries are helpful. (Everyone talks about the weather.) War enhances sensory perception. Women seem more often than men attuned to their senses, or at least more willing to write about them. What people see in other places emerges from their descriptions and photographs of them. One learns about the heard environment by reading accounts of Others' music and noise and of efforts to understand and teach language, often revealed in files concerning education, which frequently include manuals designed to teach mannerly and sanitary behavior. For smells, there are materials about sanitation, disease, and public health, and these offer clues about how places and the people in them felt. Food is a frequent subject of conversation among travelers, and cookbooks can suggest connections between once-distinct cuisines. And, as with all work that falls within the realm of "culturalist" foreign relations, it is necessary to read with care material that previous historians have considered marginal, trivial, personal, or immaterial to the alleged hard logic of diplomacy.

Finally, it is important for historians to play anthropologists and experience fully the places about which they are writing. Too often, one suspects, the researcher working on US foreign relations in another country moves, head down, between hotel and archive and back again. He needs to get out more. She needs to see, hear, smell, feel, and taste the new place, just as visitors or diplomats must have done, and must still do. Like diplomatic postings, research trips are not just intellectual encounters but somatic ones. There is not, of course, an easy relationship between how one senses a place and how someone a hundred years ago would have done it; sense perceptions change over time. The point, merely, is that relations between people and nations are experiential, embodied. That is the alpha and omega of doing sensory and foreign relations history.

NOTES

1. Laura Otis, *Membranes: Metaphors of Invasion in Nineteenth-Century Literature, Science, and Politics* (Baltimore, 1999).
2. Norbert Elias, *The Civilizing Process: Sociogenetic and Psychogenetic Investigations*, trans. Edmund Jephcott. Rev. ed. (Malden, MA, 2000), 50, 111.

3. Robert Jütte, *A History of the Senses from Antiquity to Cyberspace*, trans. James Lynn (Cambridge, UK, 2005), 9.
4. *Webster's Dictionary of the English Language, Corrected and Enlarged* (New Haven, 1841).
5. Edith Moses, *Unofficial Letters of an Official's Wife* (New York, 1908), 100, 147, 163.
6. Charles Henry Brent to Edith [sister], Feb. 13, 1903, Box 63, Charles Henry Brent Papers, Manuscript Division (MD), Library of Congress (LC), Washington, DC.
7. Ralph Kent Buckland, *In the Land of the Filipino* (New York, 1912), 75.
8. Henry F. Hoyt, *A Frontier Doctor* (New York, 1929), 230.
9. Emily Bronson Conger, *An Ohio Woman in the Philippines* (Np, nd), 131.
10. Paul A. Kramer, *The Blood of Government: Race, Empire, the United States, and the Philippines* (Chapel Hill, 2006), 127.
11. W. H. Taft, address at Union Reading College, Manila, Dec. 17, 1903, reprinted in John Bancroft Devins, *An Observer in the Philippines, or, Life in Our New Possessions* (Boston, 1905), 397.
12. Brent to Evelyn, Nov. 26, 1908, Brent Papers, Box 54; Brent to Edith, Feb. 13, 1903, Box 63, both Brent Papers.
13. *Report of the Philippine Commission to the President*, vol. III (Washington, 1901), 389.
14. Devins, *An Observer*, 56.
15. Albert Sonnichsen, *Ten Months a Captive Among Filipinos: Being a Narrative of Adventure and Observation During Imprisonment on the Island of Luzon* (New York, 1901), 127.
16. William B. Freer, *The Philippine Experiences of an American Teacher: A Narrative of Work and Travel in the Philippine Islands* (New York, 1906), 202.
17. Conger, *Ohio Woman*, 72.
18. David Brody, *Visualizing American Empire: Orientalism and Imperialism in the Philippines* (Chicago, 2010), 112.
19. William H. Brown, Paul F. Russell, and Clara Palafox Cariño, *Health Through Knowledge and Habits* (Boston, 1933), 142.
20. Alice M. Fuller, *Housekeeping and Household Arts: A Manual for Work with the Girls in the Elementary Schools of the Philippine Islands* (Manila, 1911), 53.
21. "Report of the Special Mission to the Philippine Islands to the Secretary of War (Wood-Forbes Report)," 1922. RG 350, Bureau of Insular Affairs, General Records Relating to More Than One Island Possession, Confidential File, 1914–1935, Box 9, National Archives II, College Park, MD.
22. Karin Bijsterveld, "The Diabolical Symphony of the Mechanical Age: Technology and Symbolism of Sound in European and North American Noise Abatement Campaigns, 1900–40," in Michael Bull and Les Back, eds. *The Auditory Culture Reader* (Oxford, 2003), 165–89 (182–3).
23. William C. Brown to Helen [sister], Jan. 26, 1901, William C. Brown Papers, Box 2, United States Military History Institute (USMHI), Carlisle, PA.
24. Typescript, "The Personal Journal of Lieutenant Dana True Merrill, Philippine Islands, 1898–1901," Dana True Merrill Papers, Box 1, USMHI.
25. Guy V. Henry to Mother, Mar. 25, 1901, Guy V. Henry Papers, Box 3, USMHI.
26. Sara Bunnett, *Manila Envelopes: Oregon Volunteer George F. Telfer's Spanish-American War Letters* (np, 1987), 29.

27. Mary Talusan, "Music, Race, and Imperialism: The Philippine Constabulary Band at the 1904 St. Louis World's Fair," *Philippine Studies*, 52, 4 (2004), 499–526; Mrs. William Howard Taft, *Recollections of Full Years* (New York, 1914), 221.
28. Conger, *Ohio Woman*, 107, 151; Freer, *Philippine Experiences*, 94; Benjamin E. Neal Diaries, entry for February 28, 1902, Benjamin E. Neal Papers, Box 1, Syracuse University Library, Syracuse, NY.
29. W. C. Forbes Journal, vol. I, December 6, 1904, W. C. Forbes Papers, Houghton Library, Harvard University, Cambridge, MA.
30. Conger, *Ohio Woman*, 70.
31. Katherine Mayo, *The Isles of Fear: The Truth About the Philippines* (New York, 1924), 208.
32. Mary H. Fee, *A Woman's Impression of the Philippines* (Chicago, 1910), 46–50; Devins, *An Observer*, 77–8; Laurence Halstead Memoir, Halstead-Maus Family Papers, Box 1, USMHI.
33. Moses, *Unofficial Letters*, 286–7.
34. Forbes Journal, vol. II, December 1909.
35. *Report of the Philippine Commission to the President*, vol. II, 411.
36. David P. Barrows, "Report Upon the Public Schools of Manila," Dec. 1, 1900, David P. Barrows Papers, Box 6, Bancroft Library, University of California, Berkeley; Conger, *Ohio Woman*, 61.
37. Barrows to Charles P. G. Scott, Sept. 29, 1904, Barrows Papers, Box 1.
38. "Manners and Morals," *The Philippine Teacher*, 2, no. 2 (July 1905), 17.
39. Fuller, *Housekeeping*, 54–5.
40. Stanley Karnow, *In Our Image: America's Empire in the Philippines* (New York, 1989), 201–2.
41. Eighth Annual Report of the Director of Education, July 1, 1907, to June 30, 1908 (Manila, 1908), Barrows Papers, Box 6.
42. Karnow, *In Our Image*, 256, 323.
43. Patrick Süskind, *Perfume: The Story of a Murderer*. Transl. John E. Woods (New York, 1986), 82.
44. Jim Drobnick, "Preface" to Drobnick, *The Smell Culture Reader* (Oxford, 2006), 14–15; Gunnar Myrdal, *An American Dilemma: The Negro Problem and Modern Democracy*, vol. I (New York, 1944), 107; Constance Classen, David Howes, and Anthony Synott, *Aroma* (London and New York, 1994), 161.
45. Alain Corbin, *The Foul and the Fragrant: Odor and the French Social Imagination* (Cambridge, MA, 1986), 227.
46. Brown, Russell, and Cariño, *Health Through Knowledge and Habits*, 147–8.
47. Brown, Russell, and Cariño, *Health Through Knowledge and Habits*, 267; *Report of the Commission*, vol. II, 144; Milton Walter Meyer, *Letters Home: The Meyers and Capiz, 1919–1943* (Claremont, CA, 2003), 90; Victor Heiser, *An American Doctor's Odyssey* (New York, 1936), 239; Moses, *Unofficial Letters*, 222.
48. Department of Public Instruction, Bureau of Education, *Graded Exercises in Sentence Rhythm and Emphasis Through Inflection* (Manila, 1940), 62.
49. Department of the Interior, Bureau of Public Health, *Annual Report of the Commissioner of Public Health*, Sept. 1, 1903–Aug. 31, 1904 (Manila, 1905), 15–16, 76; Victor Heiser, *Annual Report of the Bureau of Health for the Philippine Islands*, July 1, 1908–June 30, 1909 (Manila, 1909), 6; Victor G. Heiser, "Sanitation in the Philippines: With Special Reference to its Effect Upon

Other Tropical Countries," *The Journal of Race Development*, 3, 2 (Oct. 1912), 121–34.
50. Bunnett, *Manila Envelopes*, 110.
51. Ruth H. B. Hunt Travel Diaries, June 9, 1929, Box 1, Special Collections, Syracuse University Library; Warwick Anderson, "Excremental Colonialism: Public Health and the Poetics of Pollution," *Critical Inquiry* 21, 3 (Spring 1995), 640–69; Warwick Anderson, *Colonial Pathologies: American Tropical Medicine, Race, and Hygiene in the Philippines* (Durham, NC, 2006), 27–8, 104–5, 124, 127.
52. "In Manila, I Have Noticed That:," nd [1934], Frank Murphy Papers (microfilm), Reel 98, Bentley Historical Library, University of Michigan, Ann Arbor, MI.
53. Memorandum by G. C. Dunham, Adviser to the Governor-General on Public Health, Sept. 14, 1934, Murphy Papers, Reel 99.
54. Fuller, *Housekeeping*, 201.
55. Constance Classen, *The Deepest Sense: A Cultural History of Touch* (Urbana, IL, 2012), xi.
56. Richard J. Bushman and Claudia I. Bushman, "The Early History of Cleanliness in America," *The Journal of American History* 74, 4 (March 1988), 1213–38.
57. Kristin Hoganson, *Consumers' Imperium: The Global Production of American Domesticity, 1865–1920* (Chapel Hill, 2007), 95–6.
58. Hoyt, *Frontier Doctor*, 248; Buckland, *Land of the Filipino*, 135.
59. Moses, *Unofficial Letters*, 2, 30, 51.
60. Ernest R. Tilton to Julia S. Tilton, Apr. 19, 1900, Rollin N. Tilton Papers, Box 43, USMHI. "Mulligrubs" described intestinal distress.
61. Bunnett, *Manila Envelopes*, 68.
62. Moses, *Unofficial Letters*, 229.
63. Conger, *Ohio Woman*, 51, 70.
64. Brown, Russell, and Cariño, *Health Through Knowledge and Habits*, 37–8.
65. Ken De Bevoise, *Agents of Apocalypse: Epidemic Disease in the Colonial Philippines* (Princeton, 1995), 101.
66. Grace Paulding Memoirs, William and Grace Paulding Papers, Box 1, USMHI; Victor G. Heiser, Address to American Mission to Lepers, Jan. 10, 1927, Victor G. Heiser Papers, Series I, American Philosophical Society, Philadelphia, PA.
67. De Bevoise, *Agents of Apocalypse*, 86–7.
68. Mrs. Samuel Francis Gaches, *Good Cooking and Health in the Tropics* (Manila, 1922), 334; Juan Miciano, Ariston Bautista, Mariano Martin, and Manuel Gomez, "The Care of Infants," *Annual Report of the Commissioner of Public Health*, Sept. 1, 1903-Aug. 31, 1904, 269.
69. Emilia Lantin, "Care of a Tuberculous in the Home," Philippine Islands Antituberculosis Society, Proceedings of the First National Congress on Tuberculosis, Manila, Dec. 13–18, 1926 (Manila, 1927), 573; Fernando Calderon, "Tuberculosis in the Philippine Islands," ibid., 36–7.
70. Victor G. Heiser, Annual Report of the Bureau of Health for the Philippine Islands, July 1, 1908–June 30, 1909 (Manila, 1909), 39–40.
71. Leonard Wood diary, May 5 and 13, 1921, Leonard Wood Papers, Box 19, MD, LC.
72. Peter W. Stanley, *A Nation in the Making: The Philippines and the United States, 1899–1921* (Cambridge, MA, 1974), 202–3; Wood diary, May 26, 1921, Wood Papers, Box 19.

73. David Hume, "Of the Standard of Taste," in Carolyn Korsmeyer, ed., *The Taste Culture Reader: Experiencing Food and Drink* (Oxford, 2005), 197.
74. Kramer, *Blood of Government*, 207; Augusto V. De Viana, ed., *The I Stories: The Events in the Philippine Revolution and the Filipino-American War as told by Its Eyewitnesses and Participants* (Manila, 2006), 116.
75. Hoyt, *Frontier Doctor*, 205; Ernest R. Tilton to Julia S. Tilton, Mar. 16, 1900, Tilton Papers, Box 43; Bunnett, *Manila Envelopes*, 30, 43.
76. Conger, *Ohio Woman*, 56.
77. Fee, *A Woman's Impression*, 50; Conger, *Ohio Woman*, 98; Sonnichsen, *Ten Months a Captive*, 91.
78. Moses, *Unofficial Letters*, 118.
79. Freer, *Philippine Experiences*, 62; Walter L. Cutter, typescript, "Wearing the Khaki," Walter L. Cutter Papers, USMHI.
80. Buckland, *Land of the Filipino*, 65–6.
81. Brown, Russell, and Cariño, *Health Through Knowledge and Habits* 223, 228–31.
82. Buckland, *Land of the Filipino*, 72.
83. Wood Diary, May 18, 1921.
84. Moses, *Unofficial Letters*, 57; Taft, *Recollections*, 165; Freer, *Philippine Experiences*, 29–30.
85. Moses, *Unofficial Letters*, 147.
86. Cutter, "Wearing the Khaki."
87. Menu for Thursday, June 28, 1934, S.S. *Mayon* Murphy Papers, Reel 99.
88. Fraser Wilkins, interview by William W. Moss, Feb. 23, 1971, John F. Kennedy Library, Boston, MA.
89. Memorandum of conversation with the President, Sept. 26, 1960, Dwight Eisenhower Papers, Ann Whitman File, International Series, Box 27, Dwight D. Eisenhower Library, Abilene, KS.
90. Daniel Wickberg, "What Is the History of Sensibilities? On Cultural Histories, Old and New," *The American Historical Review*, 112, 3 (June 2007), 661–84 (669).

20

Psychology

Richard H. Immerman and Lori Helene Gronich

Was Richard M. Nixon mad when he acquired responsibility for US foreign policy? The attention paid to his personality suggests that many people believed him to be so, or close to it. In one context Nixon evidently preferred it that way: Although he possessed no secret plan to fulfill his campaign promise to end the war in Vietnam, he intended to persuade North Vietnam and its allies that Hanoi must either agree to a quick peace or face the consequences of a madman with the power to unleash America's nuclear arsenal. "They'll believe any threat of force Nixon makes because it's Nixon," the president confided to his chief of staff, H. R. "Bob" Haldeman. "I want the North Vietnamese to believe I've reached the point where I might do *anything* to stop the war. We'll just slip the word to them [that we] can't restrain him when he's angry... and Ho Chi Minh himself will be in Paris in two days begging for peace."[1]

Whether Nixon sincerely sought to portray himself as a madman, was mad to think he could, or was just plain mad is difficult to determine, although many have tried.[2] Recollections of conversations often are mistaken. This one, however, is true.[3] Still, even if it was not, the question invites us to consider the complex relationship between psychological approaches and the history of American foreign relations. Personality studies long dominated the field, but new developments in social and cognitive psychology have opened up additional avenues for inquiry and interpretation. It is these new directions, along with more traditional approaches, that reinforce the notion that people, as individuals and as members of policy-relevant groups, can and do influence the course of foreign affairs. Nixon, it turns out, is not alone.

HISTORY'S SLOW EMBRACE OF PSYCHOLOGY

Historians were long skeptical about the utility of applying psychology in an effort to understand American foreign relations. In part this skepticism evolved from the levels-of-analysis question: Are the sources of state conduct to be found at the level of the external environment, domestic circumstances, or the individual policymaker?[4] Diplomatic history, reflecting realist roots that extend back to Thucydides, traditionally favored the systemic (external environment) level. Diplomatic historians, accordingly, portrayed policymakers as rational actors with fixed human natures seeking to advance the national interest through cost–benefit analyses. Because psychology introduces elements beyond situational rationality, it appeared inappropriate – and discomforting.[5]

Early on, in fact, historians greeted those who waded into the murky waters of psychology with open hostility. This was particularly characteristic of studies that took a psychoanalytic or "psychohistory" approach. Historians' resistance to such methodologies is understandable. Untrained to make psychodynamic diagnoses, uneasy about the sources, and unsympathetic to the perspective, they were unwilling to lend credence to this work regardless of the author.

Contributions such as the study of Woodrow Wilson and Colonel Edward House by Alexander and Juliette George, published originally in 1956 and revised in 1964, were emblematic of this concern. George and George argued that Wilson's counterproductive behavior, especially his refusal to compromise over the League of Nations, was explicable primarily, albeit not solely, by his relationship with his father and his consequent compulsive personality. Although exemplary in its methodology due to the lengthy and intense psychoanalytic training of the authors and the years they spent immersed in the available biographical details of Wilson's life, the subsequent publication of the more than sixty volumes of Wilson's papers and the revelations about the declining state of his health indicated there was much more to be done.[6] The George and George book provoked the criticism of the papers' venerable editor and Wilson biographer Arthur Link, who challenged the data as well as the conclusions. Eventually, Link conceded a degree of irrationality to Wilson, but he rejected the Georges' psychoanalytical diagnosis. Joining forces with a physician, Edwin Weinstein, he promoted a physiological and neurological explanation. A war of words ensued, and consensus remains elusive.[7]

The controversy underscores the problem of collecting and assessing evidence of this kind. Few policymakers leave the mountains of papers, especially intimate and introspective letters and diaries, required for this type of study. Further, contemporary policymakers are likely to reveal themselves most candidly in telephone conversations or emails, many of which historians may not ever be able to access, or if they can, they may find it all but impossible to sift through the data.[8]

What is more, as the effort to uncover the hidden histories of "ordinary people" grew in popularity, historians increasingly characterized political history, especially the Rankean tradition of international relations, as pedestrian and conservative. From this perspective, the history of US foreign policy appeared to be top-down history of the worst sort. In another context, historians might have considered the application of psychological theory as a welcome innovation. Yet in the post-Vietnam historiographic climate, it seemed more of the problem than the solution. We would be studying the personalities and cognitions of the elite: leaders and decision-makers who in the majority of instances were white and male. In fact, the emphasis on sociology, cultural anthropology, and *mentalité* left little room for the individual. Unless historians were going to probe the psychology of broad-based groups rather than specific leaders, prudence dictated that they borrow theories and approaches actions and "cross-fertilize" historical perspectives from disciplines other than psychology.[9]

Historians of US foreign relations have progressively overcome these impediments. The subtitle of one of the Society for Historians of American Foreign Relations (SHAFR) most enthusiastically received Stuart Bernath Lectures is "Exploring the Psychological Dimension of Postwar American Diplomacy."[10] Psychological theory also laid the foundation for SHAFR's 2007 presidential address.[11] In sharp contrast to the reception accorded early psychoanalytic work, historians have praised studies of foreign relations that apply psychological theories, particularly those studies that combine impressive archival research with methodological sophistication and rigor.[12] This trend indicates that historians are recognizing that a psychologically informed approach to international affairs is a valuable complement to work emphasizing broader social developments and situational contexts. After all, the history of US foreign policy is the history of specific human choices, and the actions of individuals working alone or as members of policy groups shape, make, and implement these choices.

PERSONALITIES AND POLICY

The literature on political psychology suggests a plausible array of linkages between a policymaker's *observable* personality traits, such as communicative skill and rhetoric, and his or her behavior. Some social scientists have gone so far as to postulate relationships among these traits, producing typologies that generate predictions about styles and policies.[13] This approach borders on the dangerously reductionist, yet identifying finite relationships can prove insightful.[14] The evidence suggests, for example, that individuals confident in their ability to control events tend to take a more activist stance in foreign affairs, and that the norm in the West, at least during the Cold War, was for extroverted leaders to advocate for better relations with communists, whereas introverts did not.[15] Historical analyses of the contrasts between Johnson's and Kennedy's personalities, their respective power needs, and their differing styles of dealing with subordinates reinforce such arguments, and juxtaposed against other variables, they also suggest that had Kennedy lived, the American experience in Vietnam would have been different.[16]

Even if such counterfactuals are dismissed as fruitless, the premise that one's character traits can affect decisions remains compelling. For example, one archivally based examination presented credible evidence that President

Johnson's Vietnam policy reflected his psychological attributes. His propensity for "we–they" thinking, as well as his passionately personal identification with the cause of the United States, prompted a diminished capacity for assessing information and advice.[17]

Dogmatism, mental complexity or flexibility, and similar attributes or traits can likewise affect policy choices and the conduct of state and non state actors. They are foundational elements of an individual's overall personality. The history of American foreign relations is punctuated with fascinating and psychologically compelling people. For example, in the early years, Benjamin Franklin, Thomas Jefferson, John Quincy Adams, and William H. Seward come to mind. Later, Theodore and Franklin D. Roosevelt, George F. Kennan, James V. Forrestal, John Foster Dulles, John F. Kennedy, Lyndon B. Johnson, Henry Kissinger, and Zbigniew Brzezinski stand out. More recently, Andrew Young, Ronald Reagan, Bill Clinton, Madeleine Albright, George W. Bush, and Condoleezza Rice are all notable. Their personal dispositions and that of the many allies and adversaries who surrounded them did not alone determine policy – environmental and situational variables have sometimes been decisive. But predispositions, attributes, motives, and emotions, as well as other elements that constitute personality, including what Fred Greenstein labels "emotional intelligence," that is, the ability to "manage ... emotions and turn them to constructive purposes," also play a role.[18]

That role can only be inferred because history does not repeat itself. Nevertheless, common sense requires and indeed supports such notions, and a few counterfactual excursions illustrate that examples abound. A secretary of state less self-confident, audacious, stubborn, and, we would add, highly principled than John Quincy Adams might have failed to orchestrate the transcontinental treaty of 1819 with Spain, settled for a joint Anglo-American declaration of policy toward the Western Hemisphere instead of the Monroe Doctrine, or refused to sacrifice his life-long ambitions for an American empire because he judged the expansion of slavery intolerable.[19] Imagine the possible impact on history had the 1931 Japanese invasion of Manchuria occurred under the watch of a president with the "character" of Teddy Roosevelt in contrast to that of Herbert Hoover.[20] Had a person less influenced by an Ulster ethnicity than Dean Acheson been secretary of state in 1949, the United States may well have vigorously challenged British objections and supported inviting Ireland to join the North Atlantic Treaty Organization.[21] Negotiations to end America's military engagement in Vietnam and pave the way for Nixon to visit the People's Republic of China surely would have proceeded differently if conducted by someone less secretive and devious than Henry Kissinger.[22] And while we cannot rule out a president other than George W. Bush invading Iraq in 2003, it is hard to imagine that an alternative "decider" surrounded by a different set of advisors would have followed precisely the same course. Doubtless the relationship between the president and his father mattered, but determining just when and how much poses serious challenges.[23]

Barack Obama's biography suggests that he may be the most psychologically compelling president yet. Although it is still too early for the release of archival evidence, when this material becomes accessible it will be fascinating to see how historians account for his administration's policy choices. One can only imagine the salience they will assign to his personality and those of his distinctive advisers, including Hillary Rodham Clinton, Susan Rice, Samantha Power, and John Kerry. How these complicated and strong-willed individuals collectively formulated the American responses to the Arab Spring, or the choice to "lead from behind" in Libya, or the decisions on Syria and Iran will be particularly telling.[24]

GROUP DECISIONS AND POLICY

Linking personality to policy is but one approach. Based on an early model of affect-based decision-making, Irving Janis' well-known "groupthink" hypothesis suggests that small groups at the highest levels of government may unconsciously court foreign policy disasters by striving for unanimity. Terminating deliberations prematurely or promoting overly optimistic expectations, they develop an in-group/out-group mentality and thus engage in a "concurrence-seeking tendency." Janis characterizes the Kennedy administration's Bay of Pigs decisions as an example of a policy fiasco that involved "shared illusions and other symptoms [of groupthink], which helped the members to maintain a sense of group solidarity. Most crucial were the symptoms that contributed to complacent over-confidence in the face of vague uncertainties and explicit warnings that should have alerted the members to the risks of the clandestine military operation."[25]

Although historians today criticize Janis' evidence and the specificity of his claims, the policy community often applies his insights, and it does so in ways that are both reflexive and superficial. The most widely known contemporary public references to this phenomenon are the 9/11 Commission Report on the decision to invade Iraq and the review of that policy's underlying intelligence undertaken by the Senate Select Committee on Intelligence. Each study explicitly applies the groupthink notion, but both neglect to identify the particular high-level "group" they are considering and pay scant attention to alternative and plausible interpretations. They fall short of addressing the influence of available intelligence or pre-existing beliefs and images about al-Qaeda or Saddam Hussein, and they overlook the very real possibility that a rational-choice interpretation of the opponent's behavior might have explained what seemed to be perplexing actions.[26] Guarding against simplistic applications of the "groupthink" hypothesis by addressing each of its nuances and all of its dimensions should be fundamental in future policy and scholarly inquiries.

The multiple-advocacy approach to group decision-making stresses the utility of a vigorous and uninhibited exchange of viewpoints as an antidote to the groupthink tendency.[27] We are persuaded, for example, that studies of the Eisenhower administration's policy deliberations on Indochina would have benefited from such a psychologically informed multiple-advocacy perspective since the president strongly encouraged disciplined debates among experts throughout the government. The dilemmas posed by the successive French regimes did precipitate some policy making procrastination, and even a bit of wishful thinking at times. Nevertheless, as John Foster Dulles indicated in his testimony to Congress on May 11, 1954, four days after the fall of the French fortress at Dienbienphu, the administration had made every effort to keep an open mind about Indochina. "We do not want to operate on what has been referred to as the domino theory," he noted, vividly illustrating the administration's openness to debate rather than a need to mislead the legislature or the public.[28] Similarly, as time passed and the administration confronted the ineffectiveness of their Vietnamese ally, Ngo Dinh Diem, and detected the lack of unity within the Communist bloc, it repeatedly engaged in spirited discussions. Still, it concluded that the Geneva settlement was the best arrangement the United States could achieve.[29]

COGNITIONS, MOTIVATIONS, PERCEPTIONS, AND POLICY

Another stream of psychological work focuses on the cognitive processes that prompt people to interpret their environments in particular ways. Cognitive approaches can help assess the potential for a diplomatic policy initiative to succeed or fail and provide insight about an interpretation of data collected, directly or indirectly, on the threat or promise posed by an adversary or ally. They can also assist in establishing a basis for inferences about the normally and oftentimes deliberately ambiguous, or even deceptive, behavior of others.[30]

It has become almost axiomatic that the assimilation and interpretation of information, the grist for the policymaking mill, does not occur in a contextual vacuum. Decision-makers frequently rely on the "lessons of history," drawing analogies to define a situation or identify a phenomenon.[31] For Jeane Kirkpatrick, failure to support the "contras" in Nicaragua was tantamount to appeasement. "It's not Vietnam that's the appropriate analogy," she argued, "it's Munich."[32] Paul Wolfowitz, an obsessive student of the holocaust, believed that history teaches that humankind must eliminate evil leaders or suffer the consequences. His policy fixation on attacking Saddam Hussein's Iraq reflected this assessment.[33] Students of the crises in Bosnia and Kosovo will need to determine the relationship between Madeleine Albright's complicated family history and her advice on the use of force during the Clinton administration.[34] Psychological theories can help to explain how and why decision-makers act in this manner, and in the process they can provide clues for locating errors in judgment or perception. They can likewise alert us to conditions such as stress and anxiety that can affect deliberations and their outcomes.

The two cognitive perspectives that are probably the most valuable for historians of US foreign relations involve attributions and schemas. Attribution theorists seek to explain behavior by noting that individuals function like "naïve scientists" or "constructive thinkers." They judge the actions of others by looking for and accumulating clues; this is a logical, systematic, and rational process (unless emotions interfere). Schema theorists contend that our ability to assimilate information is limited; as a consequence we are "cognitive misers." We categorize the knowledge we have into schemata, mental or cognitive structures that fit the knowledge into a pattern. In other words, drawn primarily from what we have learned from previous experiences, we develop and retain preconceived notions, including beliefs and other information about how social objects and phenomena relate to one another.

Intimately tied to the concept of schemata is the identification of heuristics. These shortcuts to rationality allow individuals to reduce complicated problem-solving tasks to simple judgments; they are strategies for managing information overload. Typical are the *availability* and *representative* heuristics, by which people evaluate the extent to which the characteristics of a person, country, or political system – any object – are linked to a category of that same object: Using the *availability* heuristic, we draw inferences based on whatever pattern or frame of reference most easily or rapidly comes to mind. A military man, such as General Lucius D. Clay, is predisposed to interpret the 1948 coup in Czechoslovakia as evidence that the Soviets appeared poised to invade Europe with "dramatic suddenness." Depending on one's conceptual or generational background, a policy analyst might employ the *representativeness* heuristic and see Filipinos as American Indians, or Egypt's Gamal Abdel Nasser and Iraq's Saddam Hussein as Adolf Hitler's identical twins. Guatemala's Jacobo Arbenz Guzmán had to be a communist according to 1950s thinking. If it looks like a duck and acts like a duck, it is a duck. Korea is another Manchuria; Khe Sanh, another Dienbienphu.

These perspectives help to explain how people make sense out of the complex world in which they live. They also help to account for important errors of judgment and inference. Attached to each perspective, or explanation for how we perceive and diagnose, are a series of "biases" or common mistakes: We tend, for example, to overestimate the influence of personal dispositions on behavior and to underestimate the influence of situational influences (commonly referred to as the fundamental attribution error). Or we often are influenced more by vivid, concrete data than that which is pallid and abstract; a nonevent (the dog that did not bark in the dark; the Soviet intervention that did not occur) may be overlooked altogether. Or because we believe we know our own motives and intentions, we may assume others know them as well. Or we do not always distinguish between the inferences we draw from the data we receive and the data itself. Or we overlook base rate statistics and overestimate the size of the sample we used to generate a heuristic or category (Hitler was sui generis). There are many other biases, but we have made our point.

Most fundamentally, cognitive psychologists uniformly agree that once we form a belief we only reluctantly discard or even qualify it. We normatively interpret new evidence as conforming to our prior beliefs. If it is consistent with them, we will accept it; if it is inconsistent or ambiguous, we will discredit, distort, or ignore it. This propensity is most pronounced when the belief is deeply felt and deeply held. Our values may be hierarchically ordered, but our beliefs and knowledge are interconnected, forming a system; when incoming information is so discordant that we can no longer ignore it, we will revise our least fundamental notions before even questioning our core assumptions. Our most highly valued beliefs or deepest knowledge systems are thus minimally disconfirmed. By establishing the parameters of an individual's "particular type of 'bounded rationality,'" belief systems and knowledge can serve as sets "of lenses through which information concerning the physical and social environment is received."[35]

Those theories that pertain to our strategies for coping with complexity highlight the influence that beliefs and knowledge have on perceptions and behaviors. A growing body of thought concentrates on the potential interplay between our wants, needs, and fears and the information stored in our schemata. Psychologists who emphasize motivations argue that our judgments are largely a function of emotions as opposed to mental capacities. Perhaps the most prevalent motivation for human error is the need to reduce the anxiety an individual experiences when confronting a severe dilemma. This stress can lead to such tactics as bolstering, in which one chooses one option by extolling its virtues and denigrating all alternatives; defensive avoidance, in which people refuse to acknowledge a threat; or hyper-vigilance, in which one makes an impulsive commitment stemming from panic to the least objectionable alternative.[36]

Because these theories dovetail with many of our experiences, a few well-known examples from the recent past will suffice. No matter how forcefully Mikhail Gorbachev pushed for arms control, he did not alter then-Secretary of Defense Dick Cheney's estimation of the Soviet threat. Cheney could "explain away" Gorbachev's behavior by attributing it to the administration's own "peace through strength" posture, by dismissing it as a tactic to lull the non-communist world into complacency, or by acknowledging that Gorbachev himself was different but would not last. Cheney trusted Boris Yeltsin no more than Gorbachev. He continued to counsel that the United States must keep a watchful eye on Russia and the Soviet Union's other successor states and take the utmost care before agreeing to any arms control or force reduction measures. Cheney's core beliefs and images remained frozen in a Cold War mentality. Judging from his tough response to Russia's 2008 conflict with Georgia, they have yet to thaw.[37]

An early work of Immerman's shows how an awareness of psychological factors can enhance the interpretation of US foreign relations beyond great power dynamics. In his *The CIA in Guatemala,* Immerman argues that

Washington's exaggerated assessment of the communist threat there resulted in the decision to intervene in 1954. Immerman arrived at this interpretation after analyzing what he described as a "Cold War ethos" that had pervaded American society in the post-war period. Had he been familiar at that time with the literature on cognitive psychology and belief systems, he could have strengthened his analysis. Immerman could have clarified what he saw as the Cold War ethos by linking it to schema theory or attribution theory. He could likewise have offered a framework for understanding how Americans perceived or defined the threat in Guatemala and why they interpreted the imposition of local labor codes, agrarian reforms, and other liberal measures as evidence of Soviet influence.[38]

Psychological perspectives could also help to explain why nothing the Guatemalan government did or said seemed to shake Washington's pre-existing beliefs. When the Arbenz regime purchased arms from Czechoslovakia in a last-ditch attempt to defend the revolution against the impending American invasion it predicted, Eisenhower administration officials jumped to the conclusion that the communist threat was spreading and placing Guatemala's neighbors in peril. Indeed, just a few years later, the CIA linked Fidel Castro to Arbenz and applied the same covert operations strategy it had developed for Guatemala to the island of Cuba. This suggests that intelligence analysts were cognitive misers who unconsciously employed the availability heuristic followed by the representative heuristic to address their problem. The availability shortcut would have led them to associate the Castro regime with the Arbenz government, and the representativeness shortcut would then have prompted them to plan the Bay of Pigs effort based on the Guatemala model.[39]

Most of us, at one time or another, have sought to identify the influences on a policy makers' perceptions. And once we have judged a leader's perspective to have been subjective, regardless of the extent, we have concluded that psychological factors warranted consideration. One need not classify Thomas Jefferson's relationship with France as a "long affair" to assess his perceptions of the French as complicated by his emotions, beliefs, values, and/or motives, or to see the American intervention in Iraq as a fiasco in order to assess the inadequacy of post-invasion reconstruction planning as a triumph of "desirability over feasibility."[40] In arguing that there was a very rational, pragmatic, and even human side to Joseph Stalin, President Dwight D. Eisenhower repeatedly recalled conversations that General Dwight D. Eisenhower had held with the Soviet leader. "[D]amn near all he talked about was all the things they needed, the homes, the food, the technical help. He talked to me about 7 people living in a single room in Moscow just as anxiously as you or I'd talk about an American slum problem."[41] Eisenhower's recollection supports the psychological notion that first-hand experiences, particularly those that take place at an earlier time in one's career or are remembered vividly, can powerfully affect subsequent perceptions, images, and actions.[42]

Education and career experience can similarly influence patterns of advice. Dean Rusk and Adlai Stevenson, along with other longtime civilians, fundamentally shaped the most recognized course of the Cuban missile crisis. They proposed diplomatic solutions to President Kennedy while his military men, Admiral George Anderson and Generals Curtis LeMay, Walter Sweeney, Maxwell Taylor, Earle Wheeler, and others advocated the use of force. Similarly, in 1968, Rusk and other civilians in the Johnson administration offered diplomatic overtures for the president to contemplate in order to de-escalate the Vietnam War, while Johnson's career military experts, including Generals Taylor, Wheeler, and William Westmoreland, suggested military options instead. In the Eisenhower administration, Secretary Dulles and other civilians presented the president with diplomatic solutions to the Indochina crises of 1953-4, while Admiral Arthur Radford, General Matthew Ridgway, General Nathan Twining, General Walter Bedell Smith, and other military officers, focused their attention on military solutions.[43]

Psychological evidence also indicates that decisions about what best serves the national interest often depend on how officials frame policy choices. We learn from prospect theory that people are more likely to accept greater risks if they perceive the potential outcome as a loss rather than as a gain. Roosevelt's assessment of domestic and international environments after the Munich Conference, for example, seems to reflect this calculation. He moved away from the status quo and selected the risky option of increasing assistance to the British, potentially incurring the wrath of opponents at home and overseas. Similarly, this psychological perspective may have had a pronounced effect on Jimmy Carter when he chose to approve the risky military mission to rescue the hostages in Iran.[44] Although conclusions based on experiments do not necessarily make for universal certainties or always take into account specific cultural or temporal differences, when the historian looks at the twists and turns of US foreign policy in Vietnam or the postures of both Washington and Moscow during the Cuban missile crisis, the psychological literature on risks and the framing of decisions is illuminating.[45]

Ironically, political psychologists often place cognitive and motivational explanations for policy behavior in opposition to one another despite growing evidence of their interrelationship. New psychological research suggests that preconscious emotional arousal may guide cognitive judgments, and that internal cognitive dynamics may then produce what we call intentional motivations.[46] Such a "dual process" model holds great potential for historians of American foreign relations. Any of us who have ever read a situation report from the State Department or a non governmental organization, an intelligence estimate by a governmental agency, or a memorandum of National Security Council proceedings will profit from understanding the psychological lenses through which we perceive the world and draw inferences. An awareness of our cognitive patterns and sensitivity to the possible influences of emotions and knowledge, perhaps bolstered by recent advances in neuroscience, can help us to explain many foreign policy choices.[47]

DETERRENCE, DIPLOMACY, AND THE SECURITY DILEMMA IN FOREIGN POLICY

The very nature of psychology leads us to associate it with abnormal behavior, distorted perceptions, compromised processes, and other phenomena discussed above. Yet its relationship to international affairs is so pervasive as to be unexceptional. Deterrence, brinkmanship, credibility, commitment, reputation, risk, threat – these and many more conventional entries in the historian's lexicon are essentially psychological concepts. Central to each are perceptions, fears, wants, values, goals, and parallel mental phenomena. The psychological aspects of foreign relations became more pronounced in the atomic age. Leaders frequently manipulated their nuclear capabilities for the purpose of producing diplomatic and political solutions. The resultant control of the destinies of entire populations by a small set of people whose biases, perceptions, emotions, and other human qualities call into question – *pace* Nixon and his madman theory – the rationality of key decisions.[48]

The nuclear revolution and prospect of Armageddon is but one exemplar of the integral and thus unexceptional relationship of psychology to international politics.[49] What analysis of negotiations, for example, can overlook the psychology of the different actors? Success or failure at the bargaining table depends largely on how the hand is played as well as the chips one holds. Outcomes can turn on the ability of one participant to "read" or mislead another, the flexibility or inflexibility of the respective individuals or personalities, comparative risk-taking tendencies, and personal or group attributes, styles, or cognitive dynamics. Actors often adopt negotiating strategies in light of the predicted response they will generate, both at home and abroad. Employing carrots and sticks, or sugar and vinegar, are all psychological ploys.[50]

Likewise, the concept of a security dilemma – often thought of as a mathematical or economic construct – is fundamentally rooted in psychology. The idea that measures intended to increase the security of one nation can generate fears or insecurity in another nation is a key factor in analyzing policy choice. Consider all the historical studies that emphasize the failure of antagonists to distinguish between offensive and defensive weapons and force structures, and that reveal how such spirals of misunderstanding and misperception fed tensions and conflict.[51]

Much of the literature on the origins of the Cold War accents this phenomenon. To quote John Lewis Gaddis' initial study, "It seems likely that Washington policy-makers mistook Stalin's determination to ensure Russian security through spheres of influence for a renewed effort to spread communism outside the borders of the Soviet Union."[52] It seems no less likely that the ominous inferences Kennedy drew from Nikita Khrushchev's War of Liberation speech of January 1961, and the threatening inferences Khrushchev drew from Kennedy's inaugural and State of the Union addresses shortly thereafter, fueled a spiral of misperception that climaxed with the crises of the next year.[53]

What is more, most students of the history of US foreign relations are now comfortable applying the descriptive term "personal diplomacy." No doubt the catalyst was Woodrow Wilson's decision to travel to Versailles and the much-debated consequences. But it was the dynamic that developed between the Grand Alliance's Big Three during the Second World War that confirmed for a broad audience the salience of personality to both the conduct and outcome of negotiations. At Tehran and Yalta especially, personal diplomacy involved more than "just" the interplay of Franklin Roosevelt, Winston Churchill, and Joseph Stalin, three almost larger than life individuals and leaders. What proved most fascinating was evidence that illuminated how each developed strategies to exploit the strengths and the weaknesses of the others, how they each sought to play one off against the other, how critical the notion of "trust" became, and other psychologically driven dimensions. Indeed, assessments of which of the Big Three was most effective – or most culpable – often rested on psychologically based criteria. Historians' evaluations of the negotiations among Roosevelt, Churchill, and Stalin differ dramatically, but virtually all agree that these meetings and their results, to a greater or lesser degree, would have been different were it not for Roosevelt, Churchill, and Stalin. Conversely, as Frank Costigliola argues, the disintegration of the personal relationships among the Big Three influenced the breakdown of the alliance and the onset of the Cold War.[54]

This stress on the personal nature of diplomacy continued as the Cold War ebbed and flowed, reinforced by the concept of "summitry." Nevertheless, it was perhaps the series of encounters that propelled the end of the Cold War that cemented the place of personal diplomacy in the hierarchy of interests among historians of US foreign relations. Without the distinctive contributions that Reagan, Gorbachev, and their advisers made to these summit meetings, first in Geneva, then Reykjavik, then Washington, and then Moscow, it seems inconceivable that the Cold War could have ended when it did, and how it did.[55] Although it seems likely that neither side fully understood the other due to differences in historical experience, ideology, social or cultural backgrounds, geography, and other considerations, one can readily infer from the oral testimony of the "witnesses" to the end of the Cold War that their sustained interactions, coupled with other key influences on perception, allowed the principals to overcome differences in their respective conceptual worlds and achieve enhanced empathy and thus improved understanding and relations.[56]

After the Cold War ended relations between Washington and Moscow became, if anything, more "personalized." Surely the next generation of scholars will seek out evidence about the policy significance of Bill Clinton's decisions to define US interests in Russia as contingent on the viability, reliability, and even sobriety of Boris Yeltsin. Central questions to explore must include the psychological bases of the American president's attachment to "Ol' Boris," a drinker like Clinton's own stepfather, and the extent to which this attachment affected the US response to Russia's behavior in Chechnya or the epidemic of political corruption throughout the Eurasian region.[57] It also appears that George W. Bush may have personalized his relations with Vladimir Putin even more than Clinton did with Boris Yeltsin. It took only one meeting with the Russian leader to convince him that by looking Putin "in the eye" he "was able to get a sense of his soul." That their relationship soured so dramatically prompted Barack Obama's effort to "reset" it later on.[58] Historians cannot recognize the role of "personal chemistry" in diplomacy without first conceding the impact of psychology in the conduct of foreign affairs.

INTELLIGENCE IN FOREIGN POLICY

Intelligence, a fundamental aspect of US foreign relations since Benjamin Tallmadge organized the Culper Ring and Nathan Hale sacrificed his life to serve the cause of American independence, is a specific arena that cannot be analyzed without taking psychology into account. The core mission of the Central Intelligence Agency is the collection and interpretation of information. No activity depends more on perceptions and inferences, the core concerns of cognitive psychology.[59] The legendary head of the CIA's Office of National Estimates, Sherman Kent, focused on this dependence when he explained why the September 1962 Special National Intelligence Estimate on the military build-up in Cuba missed the Soviet deployment of offensive missiles. The answer lay "in man's habits of thought," Kent wrote. The ambiguity of the evidence forced analysts to make judgments. "When we reviewed once again how cautiously the Soviet leadership had threaded its way through other dangerous passages of the Cold War, when we took stock of the sense of outrage and resolve evinced by the American people and government since the establishment of a Communist regime in Cuba, when we estimated that the Soviets must be aware of these American attitudes, and when we then asked ourselves would the Soviets undertake the great risks at the high odds – and in Cuba of all places – the indicator, the pattern of Soviet foreign policy, shouted out its negative." The reason US intelligence analysts "missed the Soviet decision to put the missiles into Cuba," Kent concluded, is that "we could not believe that Khrushchev could make [such] a mistake."[60]

A CIA internal history suggests that the same dynamics drove errors about the likelihood the Soviet Union would invade Afghanistan in 1979.[61] They also contributed to the notorious 2002 National Intelligence Estimate on Weapons of Mass Destruction in Iraq. Yet in this case, the outcome was the opposite of the judgments leading up to the Cuban missile crisis and the Afghanistan invasion. Lacking current details, analysts based their judgments about Iraq's capabilities on their image of Saddam Hussein and what they knew about his past patterns: what they termed "cheat and retreat." They assumed that because Saddam had hidden weapons of mass destruction earlier on and secretly sought to acquire nuclear arms in the 1980s, he had done so again. In addition, because the CIA had failed to detect Saddam's arsenal before and even after the 1991 Gulf War, analysts a decade later were predisposed to exaggerate the likelihood of worst-case scenarios, thus overestimating the reliability of questionable testimony and falling victim to Iraq's "deceptive practices," to quote the CIA's post-mortem.[62]

The CIA, of course, does not confine itself to analyses and estimates; it also engages in covert operations, which can include propaganda campaigns, political action, and paramilitary ventures. These, too, invariably rely heavily on psychology. President Eisenhower went so far as to designate C. D. Jackson his special assistant for psychological warfare, and his administration's strategy for overthrowing the Arbenz government in Guatemala, by the CIA's own admission, was "dependent upon psychological impact rather than actual military strength." Successor administrations may not have believed as avidly in "psywar," but it has remained a staple instrument of American policy.[63] If policymakers recognize the seminal relationship between psychology and foreign affairs, so should scholars.

CHALLENGES AND OPPORTUNITIES

Although our research, and that of many others, shows that psychological perspectives can assist in interpreting evidence, it cannot and must not be used to compensate for a lack of evidence. To illustrate, during the interregnum between Stalin's death and Eisenhower's "Chance for Peace" address, the perceptions of the US president and Secretary of State John Foster Dulles conflicted starkly. Eisenhower was more inclined to explore the possibility that Georgi Malenkov was not a clone of Joseph Stalin and that some kind of détente with the Soviets was possible. Yet by allowing Dulles publicly to denounce the new Kremlin leadership at the same time that he was seeking to extend an olive branch to the Russians, Eisenhower all but assured there would be no chance for peace. A number of psychological theories are candidates for addressing this apparent paradox. But without better data, we are hesitant to apply any of them.[64]

Even when the evidence is available, the historian aiming to use psychology effectively must study it. This means going beyond one or two general textbooks. There is a broad literature to consider, and no one perspective should be employed mechanically.[65] Similarly, scholars must refrain from getting carried away with psychology's explanatory power. The temptation to fit evidence to support a theory is seductive. Understanding an individual or group is necessary but not sufficient to understanding the policy. To assume there is always a direct linkage between beliefs or cognitions, motivations or perceptions, and international relations behavior would be misguided.

Even if the historian has developed adequate expertise in psychology, is judicious in its application, and has the requisite documents available, there remains the problem of practicality. Ideally we should identify everyone involved in the policy process and then examine them each to determine which attributes or judgments appear most related to what behavior, investigate their individual and group contributions, and take into account the psychological influences on the policy process itself. This is an ambitious assignment. In addition to the research involved, it requires one to devise a method of weighing individual and group actions in proportion to their influence on the decision. And even once that is accomplished, it is necessary to factor in domestic and systemic variables that may shape and constrain behavior if we are to complete the analysis. This challenge is as demanding and complex as learning foreign languages or developing any other area of expertise. Yet it is also richly rewarding, and can fully complement new directions in social, cultural, and international history as well as US foreign policy.

From George Washington and Henry Knox to Ronald Reagan and Jeane Kirkpatrick to George H. W. Bush and Colin Powell, to Barak Obama and Hillary Clinton foreign policies are almost always choices. No one figure alone determines the course of foreign affairs; environmental features and situational conditions are always influential. But when policy directions can be shaped by human actions, their contributions are essential. It may take years to reach confident conclusions, but at a minimum, psychological variables are important mediators between the environment and human activity. Behavior is the product of *interactions* between people and the situations in which they find themselves.[66] Psychological theories allow us to gain additional insights about the history of US foreign relations. Applying these perspectives presents great opportunities as well as great challenges. We must remain mindful of both.

NOTES

1. H. R. Haldeman with Joseph DiMona, *The Ends of Power* (New York, 1978), 82–3.
2. The quality varies, but the most obvious examples are Bruce Mazlish, *In Search of Nixon. A Psychohistorical Inquiry* (New York, 1972); Arthur Woodstone, *Inside Nixon's Head* (New York, 1972); Fawn Brodie, *Richard Nixon: The Shaping of His Character* (New York, 1981); James David Barber, *The Presidential Character: Predicting Performance in the White House*, 4th edn. (Englewood Cliffs, NJ, 1992); Vamik D. Volkan, Norman Itzkowitz, and Andrew E. Dod, *Richard Nixon: A Psychobiography* (New York, 1997). In addition, "classics" such as Garry Wills, *Nixon Agonistes: The Crisis of Faith: The Fall of Richard Nixon*

(New York, 1975); Theodore H. White, *Breach of Faith: The Fall of Richard Nixon* (New York, 1975); Stephen E. Ambrose's three-volume *Nixon: The Education of a Politician: 1913–1962; The Triumph of a Politician: 1962–1972; Ruin and Recovery: 1973–1990* (New York, 1987, 1989, 1991); and Joan Hoff, *Nixon Reconsidered* (New York, 1995) remain valuable for providing insights on Nixon's personality. See also Fred I. Greenstein, *The Presidential Difference: Leadership Style from FDR to Obama*, 3rd edn. (Princeton, 2009), esp. 91–110.
3. Jeffrey P. Kimball, "The Vietnam War," in *A Companion to Richard Nixon*, ed. Melvin Small (New York, 2011), 386
4. J. David Singer, "The Level-of-Analysis Problem in International Relations," in *International Politics and Foreign Policy: A Reader in Research and Theory*, ed. James N. Rosenau, rev. edn. (New York, 1969), 20–9.
5. Kristen Renwick Monroe with the assistance of Kristen Hill Maher, "Psychology and Rational Actor Theory," in "Political Economy and Political Psychology," ed. Kristen Renwick Monroe, Special Issue of *Political Psychology* 16 (March 1995): 1–21.
6. Alexander L. George and Juliette George, *Woodrow Wilson and Colonel House: A Personality Study* (New York, 1964); On the Georges' methodology, see Fred I. Greenstein, *Personality and Politics: Problems of Evidence, Inference, and Conceptualization* (Princeton, 1987), 61–96. See also the research note in George and George, *Wilson and House*, 317–22.
7. Illustrative of the polemical exchange is Edwin A. Weinstein, James W. Anderson, and Arthur S. Link, "Woodrow Wilson's Political Personality: A Reappraisal," *Political Science Quarterly* 93 (Winter 1978–79): 585–98; Edwin A. Weinstein, *Woodrow Wilson: A Medical and Psychological Biography* (Princeton, 1981); Alexander L. George and Juliette L. George, "Woodrow Wilson and Colonel House: A Reply to Weinstein, Anderson, and Link," *Political Science Quarterly* 96 (Winter 1981–82): 641–65. On the continuing controversy, see Jerrold M. Post, "Woodrow Wilson Reexamined: The Mind–Body Controversy Redux and Other Dispositions, *Political Psychology* 4 (June 1983): 289–306; Stephen G. Walker, "Psychodynamic Processes and Framing Effects in Foreign Policy Decision-Making: Woodrow Wilson's Operational Code," *Political Psychology* 16 (December 1995): 697–717.
8. Scholars have produced outstanding psychobiographies. See, for example, Vamik D. Volkan and Norman Itzkowitz, *The Immortal Ataturk: A Psychobiography* (Chicago, 1984); Elizabeth Wirth Marvick, *The Young Richelieu: A Psychoanalytic Approach to Leadership* (Chicago, 1983); Robert C. Tucker, *Stalin as Revolutionary,1879–1929: A Study in History and Personality* (New York, 1973); Robert C. Tucker, *Stalin in Power: The Revolution From Above* (New York, 1989). But none are archivally driven. Moreover, in biographies of American leaders the most persuasive use of psychological theory has not been presented by historians. For example, in addition to above cited studies, see Brodie, *Richard Nixon*; Betty Glad, *Jimmy Carter: In Search of the Great White House* (New York, 1980); Volkan, Itzkowitz, and Dod, *Richard Nixon*; Stanley Renshon, *In His Father's Shadow: The Transformations of George W. Bush* (New York, 2004).
9. Robert Dallek did just that when he attempted to explain much of America's international behavior as the product of "displacement." See Dallek, *The American Style of Foreign Policy: Cultural Politics and Foreign Affairs* (New York, 1983).

10. Robert McMahon, "Credibility and World Power: Exploring the Psychological Dimension in Postwar American Diplomacy," *Diplomatic History* 15 (Fall 1991): 455–71.
11. Richard H. Immerman, "Intelligence and Strategy: Historicizing Psychology, Policy, and Politics," *Diplomatic History* 32 (January 2008): 1–23.
12. A good example is Deborah Welch Larson, *Origins of Containment: A Psychological Explanation* (Princeton, 1984). See also Deborah Welch Larson, *Anatomy of Mistrust*; Robert Jervis, *The Meaning of the Nuclear Revolution: Statecraft and the Prospect of Armageddon* (Ithaca, 1989); and Richard Ned Lebow and Janice Gross Stein, *We All Lost the Cold War* (Princeton, 1993). It is revealing that an earlier study, William A. Gamson and Andre Modigliani, *Untangling the Cold War: A Strategy for Testing Rival Theories* (Boston, 1971), was all but ignored.
13. The best-known case is James David Barber, *Presidential Character: Predicting Performance in the White House*, rev. 4th edn. (Upper Saddle River, NJ, 2008). Barber published the first edition in 1972.
14. Fred I. Greenstein, "Personality in Politics," in *Handbook of Political Science*, vol. 2, *Micropolitical Theory*, ed. Fred I. Greenstein and Nelson W. Polsby, 8 vols. (Reading, MA, 1975), 2–3; Paul A. Kowert, "Where Does the Buck Stop?: Assessing the Impact of Presidential Personality," *Political Psychology* 17 (September 1996): 421–52.
15. Margaret G. Hermann, "Leadership Personality and Foreign Policy Behavior," in *Comparing Foreign Policies: Theories, Findings, and Methods*, ed. James N. Rosenau (New York, 1974), 201–34; Margaret G. Hermann, *Handbook for Assessing Personal Characteristics and Foreign Policy Orientations of Political Leaders* (Columbus, 1983); Lloyd S. Etheredge, *A World of Men: The Private Sources of American Foreign Policy* (Cambridge, MA, 1978). Ronald Reagan may be the exception or the rule depending on how one interprets his attitudes, and at what juncture of his presidency one seeks to interpret them.
16. Fred I. Greenstein and Richard H. Immerman, "What Did Eisenhower Tell Kennedy about Indochina? The Politics of Misperception," *The Journal of American History* 79 (September 1992): 568–87. See also Frederik Logevall, *Choosing War: The Lost Chance for Peace and the Escalation of War in Vietnam* (Berkeley, 1999); David Kaiser, *American Tragedy: Kennedy, Johnson, and the Origins of the Vietnam War* (Cambridge, MA, 2000); Robert Dallek, *An Unfinished Life: John F. Kennedy, 1917–1963* (New York, 2003); Randall Wood, *LBJ: Architect of Ambition* (New York, 2006).
17. Fred I. Greenstein and John P. Burke, in collaboration with Larry Berman and Richard H. Immerman, *How Presidents Test Reality: Decisions on Vietnam, 1954 and 1965* (New York, 1989). Less persuasive is the argument that Johnson's behavior in Vietnam, and for that matter Nixon's, was the product of an admixture of humiliation and narcissism that can be traced to early childhood. See Blema Steinberg, *Shame and Humiliation: Presidential Decision Making on Vietnam* (Montreal and Pittsburgh, 1996).
18. Greenstein, *Presidential Difference*, 6.
19. Paul C. Nagel, *John Quincy Adams: A Public Life, A Private Life* (New York, 1997); Richard H. Immerman, *Empire for Liberty: A History of American Imperialism from Benjamin Franklin to Paul Wolfowitz* (Princeton, 2010), 59–97.

Psychology

20. Edmund Morris, *The Rise of Theodore Roosevelt* (New York, 1979), *Theodore Rex* (New York, 2001), and *Colonel Roosevelt* (New York, 2010).
21. John T. McNay, *Acheson and Empire: The British Accent in American Foreign Policy* (Columbia, MO, 2001).
22. Walter Isaacson, *Kissinger: A Biography* (New York, 1992); Jussi M. Hanhimaki, *The Flawed Architect: Henry Kissinger and American Policy* (New York, 2004).
23. Thomas S. Langston, "'The Decider's' Path to War in Iraq and the Importance of Personality," in *The Polarized Presidency of George W. Bush*, ed. George C. Edwards III and Desmond King (New York, 2007), 145–72.
24. Barack Obama, *Dreams of My Father: A Story of Race and Inheritance* (New York, 2007); David Maraniss, *Barack Obama: The Story* (New York: 2012); Carl Bernstein, *A Woman in Charge: The Life of Hillary Rodham Clinton* (New York: 2007); William Chafe, *Bill and Hillary: The Politics of the Personal* (New York, 2012). In his memoir Robert Gates paints many, often unflattering, portraits of Obama and his national security team. Robert Gates, *Duty: Memoirs of a Secretary of War* (New York, 2014).
25. Irving L. Janis, *Groupthink; Psychological Studies of Policy Decisions and Fiascoes*, rev. edn. (Boston, 1982), 47.
26. National Commission on Terrorist Attacks Upon the United States, *The 9/11 Commission Report: The Final Report of the National Commission on Terrorist Attacks* (New York, 2004); US Senate, Select Committee on Intelligence, 108th Congress, *Report on the U.S. Intelligence Community's Prewar Intelligence Assessments on Iraq*, Ordered Reported on July 7, 2004, accessed on October 21, 2012, at web.mit.edu/simsong/www/iraqreport2-textunder.pdf, p.18. For a retrospective and rational-choice perspective on Iraq's curious behavior, see Kenneth M. Pollack, "Spies, Lies, and Weapons: What Went Wrong," *Atlantic Monthly* 293 (January-February 2004): 78–92.
27. Alexander L. George and Erik K. Stern, "Harnessing Conflict in Foreign Policy-Making: From Devil's to Multiple Advocacy," *Presidential Studies Quarterly* 32 (September 2002), 484–505.
28. Quoted in Richard H. Immerman, "Between the Unattainable and the Unacceptable," in *Reevaluating Eisenhower: American Foreign Policy in the Fifties*, ed. Richard A. Melanson and David Mayers (Urbana, 1987), 145.
29. Richard H. Immerman, "The United States and the Geneva Conference of 1954: A New Look," *Diplomatic History* 14 (Winter 1990): 43–66; Jessica M. Chapman, *Cauldron of Resistance: Ngo Dinh Diem, the United States, and 1950s Southern Vietnam* (Ithaca, 2013).
30. For a recent overview based on a series of case studies, see Steven A. Yetiv, *National Security through a Cockeyed Lens: How Cognitive Bias Impacts U.S. Foreign Policy* (Baltimore, 2013).
31. Yueng Foong Khong, *Analogies at War: Korea, Munich, Dien Bien Phu and the Vietnam Decisions of 1965* (Princeton, 1992).
32. Shirley Christian, "Nicaragua Week in Review," *New York Times*, April 19, 1985, accessed on December 27, 2013, at www.nytimes.com/1985/04/19/us/nicaragua-week-in-the-capital.html.
33. Immerman, *Empire for Liberty*, 196–231.
34. See, for example, Michael Dobbs, *Madeleine Albright: A Twentieth Century Odyssey* (New York: 1999); Thomas W. Lippman, *Madeleine Albright and the*

New American Diplomacy (Boulder, 2000); Madeleine Albright with Bill Woodward, *Madam Secretary: A Memoir*. (New York, 2003); Madeline Albright with Bill Woodward, *Prague Winter: A Personal Story of Remembrance and War, 1937–48* (New York, 2012).

35. Alexander L. George, "The Causal Nexus between Cognitive Beliefs and Decision Making Behavior: The "Operational Code' Belief System," in *Psychological Models in International Politics*, ed. Lawrence S. Falkowski (Boulder, 1979), 103; Ole R. Holsti, "The Belief System and National Image: A Case Study," *Journal of Conflict Resolution* 6 (September 1962): 245; Mark Schafer and Scott Crichlow, "Bill Clinton's Operational Code: Assessing Source Material Bias," *Political Psychology* 21 (September 2000): 559–71; Stephen G. Walker and Mark Schafer, "Theodore Roosevelt and Woodrow Wilson as Cultural Icons of U.S. Foreign Policy," *Political Psychology* 28 (December 2007): 747–76. For the concept of "bounded rationality" see Herbert A. Simon, *Administrative Behavior: A Study of Decision-making Processes in Administrative Organization*, 2nd edn. (New York, 1957). The classic treatment of the intersection between beliefs, perceptions, and behavior is Robert Jervis, *Perception and Misperception in International Politics* (Princeton, 1976).

36. Irving L. Janis and Leon Mann, *Decision Making: A Psychological Analysis of Conflict Choice, and Commitment* (New York, 1977), 85–95, 199. For a brief review of additional perspectives and a discussion of their utility in foreign policy decision-making research, see Daniel Kahneman and Jonathan Renshon, "Why Hawks Win," *Foreign Policy* 158 (January/February 2007): 34–8.

37. Don Oberdorfer, *From the Cold War to a New Era: The United States and the Soviet Union, 1983–1991* (Baltimore, 1998), 343; Raymond L. Garthoff, *The Great Transition: American-Soviet Relations and the End of the Cold War* (Washington, DC, 1994), 537.

38. Although Alex Roberto Hybel's *How Leaders Reason: US Intervention in the Caribbean Basin and Latin America* (Oxford, 1990), 49–69, draws heavily on the evidence Richard Immerman presented in the *CIA in Guatemala: The Foreign Policy of Intervention* (Austin, 1982), and he develops an analogical theory of foreign policy making, we believe this approach overlooks important historical developments and nuances, thus limiting its ability to explain the Eisenhower administration's estimate of the communist danger in Guatemala and its decision to employ covert action to eradicate the threat.

39. In addition to Immerman, *CIA in Guatemala*, see Nick Cullather, *Secret History: The CIA's Classified Account of Its Operations in Guatemala, 1952–1954* (Stanford, 1999). For more on the expectation that decision-makers will employ the availability heuristic *before* the representativeness heuristic, see Lori Helene Gronich, "The Cognitive Calculus Theory of Decision: A New Explanation for Policies of War and Peace" (paper presented at the annual meeting of the American Political Science Association, Philadelphia, PA, August 30–September 3, 2006), accessed December 11, 2013 at http://convention2.allacademic.com/one/apsa/apsa06/index.php?click_key=1&PHPSESSID=kjrh617cm8gpakk4nohq3b97, p4.

40. Conor Cruise O'Brien, *The Long Affair: Thomas Jefferson and the French Revolution, 1785–1800* (Chicago, 1998); Aaron Rapport, "The Long and Short of It: Cognitive Constraints on Leaders' Assessments of 'Postwar' Iraq," *International Security* 37 (Winter 2012/2013): 133–71.

41. Robert R. Bowie and Richard H. Immerman, *Waging Peace: How Eisenhower Shaped an Enduring Cold War Strategy* (New York, 1998), 46.
42. Jervis, *Perception and Misperception*, 239–62.
43. For details, see Gronich, "The Cognitive Calculus Theory of Decision;" and Lori Helene Gronich, "Why America Remained at Peace: The Cognitive Calculus Theory, The Cuban Missile Crisis of 1962 and the Indochina Crises of 1953–54" (paper presented at the biennial meeting of the *Journal of Policy History* and the Institute for Policy History, Richmond, VA, June 6–9, 2012), authors' possession.
44. Amos Tversky and Daniel Kahnemann, "Rational Choice and the Framing of Decisions," *Journal of Business* 59 (October 1986): S251–S278; Barbara Farnham, *Avoiding Loss/Taking Risks; Prospect Theory and International Relations* (Ann Arbor, 1995); Barbara Farnham, *Roosevelt and the Munich Crisis: A Study of Political Decision-Making* (Princeton, 1997); Rose McDermott, "Prospect Theory in International Relations: The Iran Hostage Rescue Mission," *Political Psychology* 13 (June 1992): 237–62. For a discussion of the potential as well as the limitations of this perspective, see Jack S. Levy, "Prospect Theory and International Relations: Theoretical Applications and Analytic Problems," *Political Psychology* 13 (June 1992): 283–310.
45. Yaacov Y. I. Vertzberger, *Risk Taking and Decisionmaking: Foreign Military Intervention Decisions* (Stanford, 1998); Mark L. Haas, "Prospect Theory and the Cuban Missile Crisis," *International Studies Quarterly* 45 (June 2001): 241–70.
46. Susan T. Fiske and Shelley E. Taylor, *Social Cognition: From Brains to Culture*, 2nd edn. (Los Angeles, 2013): 31–58. For earlier studies, see Janice Gross Stein, "Building Politics into Psychology: The Misperception of Threat," *Political Psychology* 9 (June 1988): 257; Robert Jervis, "Political Psychology: Some Challenges and Opportunities," *Political Psychology* 10 (September 1989): 487; Stephen G. Walker, "Psychodynamic Processes and Framing Effects in Foreign Policy Decision-Making: Woodrow Wilson's Operational Code," *Political Psychology* 16 (December 1995): 697–717.
47. For a brief review of some promising new techniques in neuroscience, see Fiske and Taylor, *Social Cognition*, 20–5. For an early application of neuroscience approaches to politics, see *Man is By Nature a Political Animal: Evolution, Biology and Politics*, ed. Peter K. Hatemi and Rose McDermott (Chicago, 2011).
48. Richard Ned Lebow, *Between Peace and War: The Nature of International Crisis* (Baltimore, 1981); Alexander L. George and Richard Smoke, *Deterrence in American Foreign Policy: Theory and Practice* (New York, 1974); Robert Jervis, Richard Ned Lebow, and Janice Gross Stein, *Psychology and Deterrence* (Baltimore, 1985); Francis J. Gavin, *Nuclear Statecraft: History and Strategy in America's Atomic Age* (Ithaca, 2012).
49. Jervis, *The Meaning of the Nuclear Revolution*.
50. For psychologically informed examinations of competing negotiation strategies, see Robert Axelrod, *The Evolution of Cooperation* (New York, 1984); Charles E. Osgood, *Alternative to War or Surrender* (Urbana, 1962); Arthur A. Stein, "When Misperception Matters," *World Politics* 34 (July 1982): 505–26. For a case study using psychological theories to explain negotiations, see Deborah Welch Larson, "Crisis Prevention and the Austrian State Treaty," *International Organization* 41 (Winter 1987): 27–60.

51. Glenn H. Snyder, "'Prisoner's Dilemma' and 'Chicken' Models in International Politics," *International Studies Quarterly* 15 (March 1971): 66–103; Robert Jervis, "Cooperation under the Security Dilemma," *World Politics* 30 (January 1978): 167–214. Jervis argues that the distinction between deterrence and the "spiral model" is a function of respective images of an enemy and the related perceptions of intentions. Jervis, *Perception and Misperception*, 58–113.
52. John Lewis Gaddis, *The United States and the Origins of the Cold War, 1941-1947* (New York, 1972), 355. See also Raymond L. Garthoff, *Détente and Confrontation: American-Soviet Relations from Nixon to Reagan* (Washington, DC, 1985); Melvyn P. Leffler, *A Preponderance of Power: National Security, the Truman Administration, and the Cold War* (Stanford, 1992); and Vladislav Zubok and Constantine Pleshakov, *Inside the Kremlin's Cold War: From Stalin to Khrushchev* (Cambridge, 1996).
53. Katherine Lavin, "Kennedy, Khrushchev and the Missile Crisis: The Politics of Cumulative Misperception," *The American Undergraduate Journal of Politics & Government* 1 (Fall 2001): 169–83.
54. Herbert Feis, *Churchill, Roosevelt, Stalin: The War They Waged and the Peace They Sought* (Princeton, 1957); Warren Kimball, *Forged in War: Roosevelt, Churchill, and the Second World War* (New York, 1997); Frank Costigliola, *Roosevelt's Lost Alliances: How Personal Politics Helped Start the Cold War* (Princeton, 2012).
55. See the transcripts of a conference of former Soviet and US decision-makers on the end of the Cold War held at Princeton University, along with scholarly commentary, published in *Witnesses to the End of the Cold War*, ed. William C. Wohlforth (Baltimore, 1997). See also, Vladislav M. Zubok, "Gorbachev and the End of the Cold War: Perspectives on History and Personality," *Cold War History* 2 (January 2002): 62; Jack Matlock, *Reagan and Gorbachev, How the Cold War Ended* (New York, 2004); James Mann, *The Rebellion of Ronald Reagan: A History of the End of the Cold War* (New York, 2009); James Graham Wilson, *The Triumph of Improvisation: Gorbachev's Adaptability, Reagan's Engagement, and the End of the Cold War* (Ithaca, 2014).
56. Robert Jervis, "Perception, Misperception, and the End of the Cold War," in *Witnesses to the End of the Cold War*, ed. Wohlforth, 227–39.
57. Strobe Talbott, *The Russia Hand: A Memoir of Presidential Diplomacy* (New York, 2002). For a bracing look at the ways in which alcohol consumption may have influenced US foreign policy in the Nixon years, see Seymour M. Hersh, *The Price of Power: Kissinger in the Nixon White House* (New York, 1983), 108–10.
58. Caroline Wyatt, "Bush and Putin: Best of Friends," *BBC News*, June 16, 2001, accessed December 15, 2013, at news.bbc.co.uk/2/hi/1392791.stm; Peter Baker, "The Seduction of George W. Bush: How The President of Good and Evil Bromanced Vladimir Putin. And How a Warm Friendship Turned to Ice," *ForeignPolicy.com*, November 7, 2013, accessed December 15, 2013, at www.foreignpolicy.com/articles/2013/11/05/the_seduction_of_george_w_bush_by_vladimir_putin#sthash.Z2EmnMoV.ETMMSpco.dpbs.
59. See Ernest R. May, *Knowing One's Enemies: Intelligence Assessment before the Two World Wars* (Princeton, 1986); John Ferris, "Coming in from the Cold War: The Historiography of American Intelligence, 1945–1990," *Diplomatic History* 19 (Winter 1995): 87–115; Richard H. Immerman, "Intelligence and Strategy."

Psychology

60. Sherman Kent, "A Crucial Estimate Relived," accessed on December 15, 2013, at https://www.cia.gov/library/center-for-the-study-of-intelligence/csi-publications/books-and-monographs/sherman-kent-and-the-board-of-national-estimates-collected-essays/9crucial.html.
61. Douglas MacEachin, *Predicting the Soviet Invasion of Afghanistan: The Intelligence Community's Record*, accessed December 7, 2012 at https://www.cia.gov/library/center-for-the-study-of-intelligence/csi-publications/books-and-monographs/predicting-the-soviet-invasion-of-afghanistan-the-intelligence-communitys-record/predicting-the-soviet-invasion-of-afghanistan-the-intelligence-communitys-record.html.
62. CIA Intelligence Assessment, "Misreading Intentions: Iraq's Reaction to Inspections Created Picture of Deception," January 5, 2006, accessed February 2, 2013, at www.gwu.edu/~nsarchiv/news/20120905/CIA-Iraq.pdf; Robert Jervis, *Why Intelligence Fails: Lessons from the Iranian Revolution and the Iraq War* (Ithaca, 2010).
63. Quoted in Immerman, *The CIA in Guatemala*, 161. See also John Lewis Gaddis, "Intelligence, Espionage, and Cold War Origins," *Diplomatic History* 13 (Spring 1989): 191–212; Gregory F. Treverton, *Covert Action: The Limits of Intervention in the Postwar World* (New York, 1987); and Rhodri Jeffreys-Jones, *The CIA and American Democracy*, 2nd edn. (New Haven, 1998).
64. Bowie and Immerman, *Waging Peace*, 109–22.
65. For the distinction between rote methods of "classification" and informed methods of "diagnosis" see Alexander L. George, "Some Uses of Dynamic Psychology in Political Biography: Case Materials on Woodrow Wilson," in *A Source Book for the Study of Personality and Politics*, ed. Fred I. Greenstein and Michael Lerner (Chicago, 1971), 80.
66. Greenstein, *Personality and Politics*, 7; Robert Jervis, "Political Decision Making: Recent Contributions," *Political Psychology* 1 (Summer 1980): 98, xxii.

21

Reading for emotion

Frank Costigliola

Dean Acheson appeared angry. The former secretary of state fumed at the "foolishness" unleashed by George F. Kennan's radio broadcasts over the BBC in November–December 1957. Kennan, who in 1946–7 had pushed for containing the Soviet Union, was now urging negotiations leading to a US–Soviet military "disengagement" from Central Europe and the establishment of a neutral, reunified Germany. Acheson was proud of having helped create a prosperous West Germany anchored in US-led NATO. Now Kennan was fanning hopes for an easing of East–West tensions and perhaps even an end to the division of Germany. Those changes would undo Acheson's handiwork and undermine America's predominance in Europe. The elder statesman hit back hard, and with a proven strategy. He assailed his opponent's credibility as a rational, sound thinker. In a January 1958 statement published widely in the US and European press, Acheson charged that "Mr. Kennan has never, in my judgment, grasped the realities of power relationships."[1] Here was Kennan, who had made his reputation as a hard-headed "realist," being accused of woolly-minded, emotional thinking. In a lead article in *Foreign Affairs* Acheson went as far as to associate Kennan with the "'unlovely hordes of apes and monkeys'" from mankind's evolutionary past, those "'flighty'" creatures with "so much love for absurd and idle chatter."[2] From his perch as a top Washington journalist, James Reston opined that Acheson's newspaper attack ranked as a "public service," for "next to the Lincoln Memorial in moonlight, the sight of Mr. Dean Acheson blowing his top is without doubt the most impressive sight in the capital."[3]

It is not surprising that such incidents, and foreign relations more generally, entail emotional thinking and reactions. The foreign/transnational/international relations of individuals, groups, and states are often high-stakes, cross-cultural, nail-biting ventures. Despite the "realist" assumption that foreign policy remains the domain of the rational actor appraising objective national interests, emotion has figured prominently in the making of foreign policy. Emotional perceptions have predisposed foreign policymakers to propose or oppose policies, make friends or enemies, pursue peace or war. Without succumbing to emotional determinism, historians can examine how culturally inflected, complex emotional reactions – such as insecure pride, craving for respect, anxiety about change, and fear of appearing fearful – have complicated international relations at all levels.[4] Emotions history enables us to delve deeper into the thoughts, motivations, and behavior of historical actors.[5]

There are at least five potential aspects to looking at human motivation and behavior from the inside out. First, historians can study the impact of emotional thinking on the behavior of individuals. Kennan's passion for Russia helps explain the seeming contradictions in his first advocating containment of the Soviet Union, and then calling for negotiations to reverse that policy.[6] Henry A. Kissinger's authority and self-cultivated reputation as a realistic statesman help obscure the extent to which his judgment was wrenched by his volcanic emotions.[7] Second, scholars can investigate how emotions circulated within groups, such as America First circles opposed to US entry into World War II, the foreign policy establishment in Cold War America, or the frightened and angry public in post-9/11 America. Emotions helped mobilize opinion and instigate action. Third, historians can examine how the societal norms – that is, the often contested "feeling rules" for expressing and repressing emotions – have changed over time, across cultures, and in accord with who wields power.[8] Consider, for instance, the norms prevailing in the United States for displays of anger or unhappiness with domestic affairs, such as race relations, or with foreign policy.[9] For many Americans, those norms shifted from the tighter rules of the early 1950s McCarthy era to the more permissive environment of the 1960s–70s, when emotion-suffused civil rights and anti-Vietnam War demonstrations became commonplace. Of course, the feeling rules remained in dispute: what some Americans defended as legitimate, even patriotic protest, others despised as unpatriotic rioting. Historical actors with greater power – whether it was the United States in the world arena, men in a patriarchal society, or bosses in a workplace – have usually assumed that their displays of anger had greater justification than similar expressions by the less powerful. Indeed, the powerful have often regarded their feelings as largely rational and legitimate while being quick to condemn the lesser folk as dangerously emotional.

Fourth, emotions themselves have a history. How people have conceptualized anger, courage, sentimentalism, depression, and other emotional responses has not remained constant. Emotion-suffused reactions, such as pride or shame in one's country or loyalty to the nation, have also changed over time, across cultures, and among individuals and groups. For instance, the meanings attached to honor have shifted since the nineteenth century, when upper classes in Europe and America regarded a deadly duel as appropriate in avenging an insult. While honor among nations in Europe once loomed as an issue justifying war, that norm was altered by the horrors of fascist nationalism and the world wars.[10] Consider, too, the shifting, often contested, emotions that in the United States have attached to the Fourth of July, to November 11 (which was originally celebrated as World War I Armistice Day), and to V-J Day. Barbara Keys has shown how Americans in the 1970s channeled dismay and guilt over their nation's behavior in the Vietnam War into a self-congratulatory empathy for victims of human rights abuses in other countries. Normative modes for expressing regret, sorrow, and anger over the human and material costs of fighting America's wars modulated from the postwar disillusionment of the 1920s, to the get-the-job-done attitude of the 1940s, to the renewed disenchantment following the Vietnam War and the second war in Iraq.

Finally, there is a history of how societies have tended to conceptualize emotion and its relation to supposedly objective rational thought.[11] On the one hand, most Americans have subscribed to a Western tradition, going back to Aristotle, that polarizes reason and emotion while linking the former with the mind and the latter with the body.[12] The resulting mind/body binary privileges rational, objective thought as normative and masculine. Emotions are correspondingly coded as subjective and as generally feminine.[13] Because this binary was so widely assumed, smearing a person, such as a Kennan, or a foreign policy, such as "cowardly appeasement," as emotional proved a powerful rhetorical strategy.

Venturing into emotions history releases a cascade of questions. Can a history of felt meaning actually discern the emotions of a historical figure such as Acheson? The answer has to be no. Yet although historians cannot actually recover what Acheson was thinking – nor anything else from the past – they can examine his apparent feelings and their cultural and political context. For the historian, the greatest significance lies in why he wanted to display his anger so blatantly and why that expression won such obvious gestures of approval. To what system of values was Acheson appealing when he depicted Kennan as mystical and emotional rather than as realistic and rational? How did Acheson himself, in the atmosphere of Freudian-influenced, Cold War America, view the impact of emotion on public opinion? What was the relationship between the widely held assumptions that rational thinking trumped emotion, and that waging the Cold War was necessary and proper?

Still broader issues arise. What are emotions such as anger? How do they affect thinking? How does emotion relate to reason and to cognition? Can we, as historians or as people, actually separate out emotions from other aspects of thought? How does the recent research by neuroscientists and cognitive scientists bear on these questions? These questions flow from the central challenge addressed by this chapter: How can scholars use emotions as a useful category of historical analysis, and why should they embrace this approach?

What do we mean by "emotions"? Emotions are an elusive concept, and no simple definition can suffice. An important aspect of emotions is that they are thought processes by which we appraise something as important, as having

Reading for emotion

value and meaning to us. They are, in other words, an aspect of cognition, a way of learning about something.[14] Emotions both reflect and influence bodily sensations and sensory perceptions. For instance, visual processing by the brain takes place within a context shaped by signals stemming from the amygdala and other brain regions. Sensory perceptions such as vision are never pure, but rather are always inflected with emotion. Emotional thoughts are also involved in even the most abstract reasoning. While ubiquitous in our thoughts and in our sense of ourselves, emotions also grab our attention. A stranger breaking into one's home, an aggressor invading a neighboring country, a flag rippling in the wind, a beautiful sunset, a cute child, an attractive person, an out-of-control disease, a lost loved one, a victory or a defeat, a poignant memory, inspirational language, or an audacious publicity campaign by a Kennan – such stimuli can spark bodily feelings that are processed by the brain and expressed as thought that is inextricably both emotional and rational.

Cultural as well as biological factors render emotions elusive. While we experience emotions as an aspect of integral thought, we (particularly those of us in the Western world) also tend to conceptualize them in terms of two traditional polarities that go back to Aristotle: body versus mind and nature versus nurture. The body versus mind binary is so entrenched in Western culture, and so handy when trying to discuss emotions, that it keeps slipping in through the back door no matter how much we affirm the unitary nature of thought.

A frontal assault aimed at a single, definitive understanding of emotions is counterproductive. It is more appropriate to our quarry to pursue a variety of lateral approaches, and then triangulate them to arrive at some usable concepts. We might as a practical matter focus more on the adjectival form, emotional, rather than try to pin down precisely what is an emotion. For instance, honor, loyalty, respect, pride, resentment, and other such culturally inflected reactions clearly pertain to emotion – they are emotional – but they do not constitute a discrete emotion. Indeed, even the supposedly "basic emotion" of fear is more complex, composite, and indeterminate than the reductive term "fear" would indicate. As a political scientist puts it, "fear often manifests itself less as 'fear of X' and more as an unsettling anxiety whose opacity permits latitude and flexibility in how 'X' is imagined."[15]

Neither psychologists nor philosophers agree on a definition of emotion. The word itself is problematic. The blanket term *emotion* is a coinage that in English goes back only to the 1800s. More precise is an older usage that distinguishes between the supposedly more selfish and violent passions and appetites, and the supposedly more enlightened sentiments and affections. The change in language reflected broader intellectual developments. While the terminology of "passions," "lusts," and "affections" harked back to the Bible, the word "emotion" connoted a more modern perspective. Shifting to the supposedly more scientific term "emotion" did not, however, resolve what would prove enduring debates regarding, first, how the mind interacts with the body and, second, whether there exist universal, basic emotions that have remained unchanged over time and across cultures.[16]

We might metaphorically represent emotions as border-crossing phenomena. The historian Benno Gammerl suggests that emotions lie at "the thresholds that separate and connect... the individual and society, inside and outside, the actor and her or his communicative partner, nature and culture, subjective and objective dimensions, norms and experiences, performances and discourses, as well as between body and language."[17] As the political scientists Emma Hutchinson and Roland Bleiker put it, "emotions arise from a combination of both conscious and unconscious as well as cognitive and bodily perceptions."[18] Hunches, stemming from that broad gray area straddling rational and emotional thinking, may represent real knowledge that is impossible to access with conscious thought. A metaphor popularized by Daniel Kahneman distinguishes between fast and slow thinking. He argues that as the human brain evolved in an environment that stressed survival, it privileged quick, forceful appraisals that would prepare the body for fight or flight.[19]

As the preceding sentences illustrate, models of emotion and notions about them almost invariably involve the conceptual device of metaphor. By explaining something more abstract in terms of something more concrete, metaphors facilitate our understanding. Yet that understanding is limited by the aptness of the metaphor and by the inevitable gap between the words and that which they are trying to represent. For instance, despite the common metaphor, we do not really "spend" time. Nor do emotions actually "cross" "borders."[20]

Ascertaining the mental state of historical actors is challenging. It can be hard enough figuring out the emotional states of others, or even ourselves, in the present, let alone in the past. There is always a gap between what people felt and what historians can know about those feelings. Added to the interpretive divide between words and feelings is the puzzle of discerning the apparent emotions of illiterate historical actors. (In the latter instance, court documents, paintings, music, and evidence concerning clothing and food can be useful.)

While not easy, the problems entailed in appraising emotions are not radically different from other challenges facing scholars, regardless of their methodology. Scholars cannot avoid some disjuncture between their representations and the events or developments they are trying to represent. Nor can even the most elegant concept fully capture the more elusive reality it is trying to snare. Finally, there is the limitation of all written history: the impossibility of fully recovering anything from the actual past, even historical shards more tangible than how Dean Acheson felt more than a half-century ago.

Acheson, Kennan, and most of their contemporaries believed that emotions are irrational, and that emotions and reason are separate and inherently in opposition. In other words, they subscribed to a tradition going back to Plato, who held that reason should be the master of the passions. The Scottish humanist David Hume argued that, to the contrary, reason was and ought to be the servant of the passions. Thomas Jefferson posited that reason and what he called sentiment were properly co-rulers of the mind. Despite their differences, all these thinkers divided emotions from reason.

In sharp contrast, the current consensus among neuroscientists and humanist scholars holds that emotional and rational thinking are not clearly differentiated mental states; indeed, they are neurologically indistinguishable. Recent brain research has demonstrated the impossibility of neatly separating out rational from emotional thinking.[21] Rational decisions require emotional input. Indeed, brain-damaged individuals who have difficulty feeling also encounter problems making rational decisions. The brain does operate differently, of course, when processing the realization that an intruder is threatening to kill you, and the cognition entailed in adding a list of numbers. After a comprehensive review of the literature on neuroimaging, the neurologist Kristen A. Lindquist and her associates (2012) concluded that categories of emotion, such as fear, as well as emotion in general emerge not from certain, dedicated regions of the brain, but rather from multi-region "assemblies of neurons within distributed networks." They add, "We hypothesize that these networks combine and constrain one another like ingredients in a recipe." The areas of the brain that give rise to emotions "are also involved in constituting other cognitive and perceptual events." In other words, emotions, like other forms of thought, result from an integrative, nearly brain-wide processing of impulses. The causation that results in emotion flows in many directions at once.

The takeaway for historians is that categorizing reason, emotion, belief, intuition, and memory into distinct, separate forms of thought reflects not how the mind works, but rather culturally specific social construction. Prevailing societal and cultural norms also shape how individuals use words, gestures, and actions to express emotions and other aspects of thought. This point about the cultural construction of emotional expression is crucial. While scholars cannot know for sure what historical actors felt, we can find evidence of feeling rules, that is, evidence of what people in the past thought they should feel or show that they were feeling. We can expect to find evidence of how members of society reacted to those who lived up to, and those who violated, prevailing norms for the expression and repression of feelings. As the historian and psychologist Jeremy T. Burman has put it, the scholar has "to reconstruct the context in which a coherent logic of feeling can be read across a grouping of individuals."[22]

Though Barbara Rosenwein's notion of emotional communities was developed for a quite different historical context (Europe in the early Middle Ages), her concept is useful for the history of foreign relations. Emotional communities are social collectivities of varying degrees of cohesion, people who share feeling rules enforced by group pressure. Of course, such rules are often contested and conflicting. Historical actors, with their individual personalities and emotional styles, no doubt moved among a variety of emotional communities as they interacted with neighbors, family, animals, and members of other groupings. The imagined community that constitutes a nation also constitutes an emotional community or a number of overlapping emotional communities. Ritualized meetings of NATO, ANZAC, the Warsaw Pact, the G8, G20, and other groupings exposed participants to emotion-inducing narratives, ceremonies, and other cultural practices that fostered emotional communities with their own norms for emotional display. By looking at the patterns of interaction and expression of such communities, historians can try to uncover structures of feeling. How did such norms for emotional expression and suppression change over time and across cultures?

In contrast to the emotional communities theorized by Rosenwein, the emotional regimes posited by William M. Reddy enforce rules more rigidly in a context of sometimes violent constraining power. Reddy argues that the question of who gets to express which emotions and in what ways underlies and reinforces power relations in domestic society. A political and cultural regime enforces its authority through an "emotional regime" by enforcing the standards for expressing and repressing emotions. Nicole Eustace, a historian of the early American Republic, examines how shifting rules about emotion undermined or reinforced hierarchy and thereby accelerated change. Endorsing Reddy's argument that "emotional control is the real site of the exercise of power," Eustace defines "politics [as] just a process of determining who must repress as illegitimate, who must foreground as valuable, the feelings that come up for them in given contexts and relationships."[23] We can extrapolate these concepts to international relations. For instance, hegemons such as the United States reserve the right to lash out in anger or fear at weaker nations in ways that are not possible or acceptable by most other nations. After 9/11 the United States retained much of its status as a supposedly responsible and moral leader of the world community even after its egregious invasion of Iraq in 2003.

Emotional styles and other aspects of individual personality intersect in various ways with the norms of emotional communities and emotional regimes. While unfailingly deferential toward the austere secretary of state, George C. Marshall (who had rebuffed President Franklin D. Roosevelt's efforts at chumminess), Kennan as director of the State Department Policy Planning Staff demanded respect and brooked little opposition from other staff members. He regarded Acheson, when the latter succeeded Marshall as secretary of state, as really a peer who should follow his (Kennan's) advice. Historians might examine how the emotional culture (resulting from the interplay of emotion rules and the dispositions and personalities of leaders) that permeated the corridors of the state department differed from what Acheson the lawyer had encountered in the courtroom or that which enveloped Kennan and his fellow scholars at the Institute for Advanced Study.

Groups, in constituting emotional communities and regimes, circulate emotions. To be sure, emotions originate in and are felt by individuals. Nevertheless, as the political scientist Jonathan Mercer has argued, "people do not merely associate with groups, they can become those groups through shared culture, interaction, contagion, and common group interests."[24] What Emile Durkheim called "collective effervescence" fosters a shared identity grounded in trust, solidarity, and pride. As Mercer puts it, "who we are is what we feel. Identity and emotion depend on each other." He adds that "feeling shame or pride in one's state is an example of feeling like a state. Although a person can feel like a state, a state cannot feel like a person."[25]

Moods are a dispositional tendency to feel a certain kind of emotion. As compared to emotions, they are more diffuse, global, and less rational. Blending into each other, emotions and moods lie along a spectrum of feeling that is more rational and defined on the end of emotions and less so on the end of moods. While people are generally more aware of why they are experiencing a certain emotion, they may have difficulty explaining a mood. An intense emotion may leave a lingering mood. For instance, fury by officials in the US embassy in Moscow during the 1930s–1940s at the Kremlin's purge of innocent victims, brutality toward the Poles and others, and refusal to permit free contact with Soviet citizens led to a lingering mood of resentment. This mood and flare-ups of emotion predisposed Kennan and his colleagues to negative cognitive appraisals of Soviet actions and policies. The commonplace metaphors "atmosphere of hope" and "climate of fear" refer to such moods. Moods, like an emotional predisposition for or against a certain country, can influence foreign relations.[26]

Americans' understandings of moods, emotions, and other aspects of interiority have been influenced by psychological theories, particularly those of Sigmund Freud. From the time of the psychiatrist's visit to the United States in 1909 to the 1980s, public discourse was awash with Freudian interpretations promising optimistic therapy, relaxed sexual inhibitions, and access to the unconscious.[27] Woodrow Wilson was the subject of two psycho-biographies, the first published in 1956.[28] In December 1957, William L. Langer – a professor of international relations history at Harvard, top official of the Office of Strategic Services (OSS) during World War II, consultant to the CIA, and author of the semi-official diplomatic history *The Challenge to Isolation* – delivered his presidential address to the American Historical Association. Langer proclaimed psychohistory the "next assignment" for historians. Compared to the "scientific" basis of psychoanalytic theory, he argued, "the home-spun, common-sense psychological interpretations" employed by most historians had become "woefully inadequate, not to say naive." He urged graduate students to incorporate into their training work at "psychoanalytic institutes."[29]

It was coincidental, but nevertheless telling in terms of the ideas swirling through mid-century America, that only a few weeks after Langer's address Acheson referred to a Freudian concept in explaining his fear about the impact of Kennan's BBC broadcasts. Acheson worried that by holding out the possibility of an easing of tensions with Moscow, Kennan would undermine the willingness of Americans and Western Europeans to endure "the working and sweating" necessary to bolster the "Free World" against the communists. Acheson had evidently absorbed the Freudian notion of a primal, inescapable struggle pitting the freedom and creativity of Eros against the order and duties of civilization. To the editor of *Foreign Affairs*, he complained that "Kennan has released the libido and all the inhibitions which made a non-communist world organization possible."[30] Proud of his leadership in having shaped US policy in the Cold War, the former secretary of state evidently appreciated both the "inhibitions" required to sustain that conflict and the regimented "organization" facilitated by it. While presuming the primacy of reason, Acheson, like many others, understood the power of emotion.

With this introduction to what emotions are, how they fit with other aspects of integral thought, how their expression is conditioned by the norms of emotional communities and regimes, and how they have been understood, we can first explore some techniques for doing emotions history, and then review some examples. Historians studying the emotions do not need special training in neuroscience or psychology. Rather they need to read texts carefully and take seriously such evidence as discussion of emotion, words signifying emotion, emotion-provoking tropes, gestures, other visual and sensory cues, habitual behaviors, excited behaviors, ironies, silences – and the cultural contexts of these and other expressions.[31] No such evidence, of course, should be taken at face value. Emotion words are sometimes used not to express feelings, but rather to label and judge them. Historical actors may refer to an opponent's emotions as a way to discredit them. Consider, for instance, the connotations of the descriptives "a frenzied audience" and "an angry crowd." A reference to emotion might also express an ironic attitude rather than actual feeling. A display of apparent emotion, even a supposedly revealing facial expression, can actually be intended to deceive the observer. The expression might also reflect conflicting intentions. The historian Ruth Leys, a skeptic of the thesis that basic emotions are universal across time and culture, points out that "facial displays cannot be considered simple readouts of underlying 'basic emotions' because they are intentional communicative signals that aid in the negotiation of social encounters."[32] Metaphors and other tropes can indicate not just the presence of emotion, but also how historical actors conceptualized such feeling. Silences, such as soldiers in battle not referring to fear and danger, can reveal which feelings an emotional community or regime valorized and discussed, and which it tended to repress, at least publicly.[33] Social interactions generally give rise to emotional interactions, and vice versa.

In part, the emotional turn developed as a reaction to postmodernist skepticism about the autonomy or even importance of the individual subject. While keeping in mind the influence of societal emotion rules on individual expression and repression of feelings, scholars can also focus on the individual's self, inner subjectivity, and body. Historical evidence about bodily movements, gestures, pleasure, and pain can suggest emotional reactions. That the former secretary of state was indeed angry with Kennan seems more likely in view of Acheson's recent fall on the ice, which resulted in a broken arm and his suffering exhaustion from having to "sleep sitting up."[34]

Along with promise, emotions history entails challenge. As the previous paragraph suggests, Acheson had reason to feel irritated in early 1958. Observers described him as angry. Nevertheless, historians cannot know for sure whether he was in fact angry when he issued his press statement, when he wrote his scathing article for *Foreign Affairs*, or during the entire public debate. Emotions are slippery in other ways as well. Emotions words such as "anger," "fear," "love," and "jealousy" – and the distinct feelings they endeavor to reference – are socially constructed categories. While such categories are necessary for us to anchor and make sense of our feelings, they are nevertheless imprecise because they reduce the subtleties and complexities of emotional reactions. In expressing a sentiment – such as "I favor this policy"; "Russia's actions threaten us all"; or "I love you" – we are simplifying what was, originally, a more inchoate and probably more ambiguous set of brain processes. Moreover, the very enunciation of an appraisal through speech or writing reinforces that judgment, renders it more concrete, and reduces its complexity. As Reddy puts it: "Emotions are at once managerial and exploratory. An emotional expression is an attempt to call up the emotion that is expressed; it is an attempt to feel what one says one feels."[35]

Such complications notwithstanding, examining emotions history can deepen our understanding of the behaviors, motivations, impulses, and beliefs of historical figures as well as the societal and cultural contexts in which those actors operated. In the case of Acheson, the observations of contemporaries constitute evidence that they thought he was angry and, more importantly, that he had a right to feel angry and that he should feel that way.

Of greater historical significance than Acheson's actual emotional state was his desire to be perceived as angry. A display of anger was key to his strategy against Kennan. Furthermore, this expression of feeling was deemed appropriate, even applauded, by his fellow members of the foreign policy establishment, the group that would determine whether Kennan's proposal for disengagement from the Cold War would get any traction. With apparent pride Acheson boasted to his son-in-law, William Bundy, that in a face-to-face confrontation with Kennan, "there was blood flowing out from under the door."[36] Reston, though joking, was also making a point by describing Acheson's anger as a spectacle so "impressive" that only the moonlit Lincoln Memorial could rival it. If Reston had wanted to criticize the harsh reaction to Kennan's proposal, he could have depicted the former secretary of state as a blustering has-been who was emotionally overreacting himself even as he criticized Kennan's "mystical" thinking. Like Reston, Hamilton Fish Armstrong, editor of the Establishment organ *Foreign Affairs*, signaled high-powered approval when he responded to Acheson's attack by asking him to write an article, giving it pride of place as the lead essay in the very next issue, and not penciling out the language that compared Kennan to a chattering ape. Even Acheson's habitual critics, such as Secretary of State John Foster Dulles and Vice-President Richard M. Nixon, congratulated him for his supposedly clear-headed articulation of the issues. In sum, Acheson's display of anger garnered implicit or explicit praise from powerful figures while Kennan's arguments for disengagement were attacked as unrealistic and emotional.

How Acheson displayed his apparent anger and how Reston and others reacted to that expression of emotion reflected how they had internalized societal norms. Although individuals or groups may challenge these norms, they generally cannot avoid explicit or implicit reference to them. Emotional power works discursively: The approbation of Acheson's apparent anger by powerful leaders reflected and reinforced the convention that outrage and slashing attack were appropriate in beating back any questioning of Cold War orthodoxy.

Expressions of anger and reactions to such displays are often evidence relations of unequal power. "Since Antiquity," the historian of emotions Ute Frevert observes, "rage had been seen as a prerogative of the powerful."[37] With the advent of Western industrial society, however, self-control became a marker of the expected behavior of adult white males, especially those of the upper classes.[38] An exception was in war, when venting righteous anger in fighting for the cause seemed fitting for the courageous patriot. This norm has carried over to the Cold War and the post-9/11 "global war on terror." As the historian of emotions Peter N. Stearns notes, the goal was "controlled use so that properly socialized adults would be masters of a fund of anger, with the experience to target it appropriately."[39] The endorsement of Acheson's anger demonstrated how displays of "noble rage" by elite white males – especially when they were fuming over the danger of compromise with enemies or over the need for greater military effort – was perceived as tough-minded, hard-headed, realist thinking.[40]

As the descriptors in the previous sentence indicate, such attitudes are associated with conventional notions of masculinity. Of course, women can assume the masculine position by also adopting a "hard-headed" stance. A negative valence has generally attached to anger expressed by people of either gender opposing "tough," supposedly realistic policies. For the most part, those who enforce social conventions interpret as dangerous and inappropriate displays of anger by those less powerful: women, African Americans, other racial minorities, the poor, and the young. Those with less power also encounter difficulty in being perceived as responsible, sound thinkers. Whether in the classroom, the corporate board room, or the international conference room, a male in authority raising a voice in anger and a female acting in the same way are usually perceived differently. Displays of anger by a student, a corporate underling, or a representative of a non-Western nation usually seem transgressive, unlike such expressions by those with greater authority. Although there are exceptions to the rule, in general the greater one's power, the greater one's freedom to express emotions, particularly those that signal force. Just as emotions are always expressed or repressed within a context of power, so, too, are relations of power always to some extent emotional. Historians, then, can track expressions of anger and of other vehement feelings – and the responses to such expressions – as calibrators of power relationships.[41]

Politicians have used anger and other emotions to push the public in certain directions regarding foreign relations. The George W. Bush administration leveraged the anger and fear arising from the September 11, 2001, attacks to mobilize public support for war in Afghanistan and then in Iraq. Those wars were not inevitable.

Historians might parse the emotional aspects of the response to 9/11. Since emotions are integral to thought, feelings seep into judgments – even those judgments that policymakers believe are wholly rational. It might be the case that Bush and his top advisers were spurred to decide for war not only by anger and guilt over the terrorist attacks, but also by prideful confidence in the efficacy of military force, post-Cold War triumphalism, yearning for purpose and prerogatives, and desire to remake the Middle East. Such an emotional disposition may have helped Bush officials convince themselves, despite some contrary evidence, that the dictator Saddam Hussein did indeed possess weapons of mass destruction, and that a war to remove that danger and transform the region would prove easy and profitable. The president may also have felt a desire to finally one-up his more cautious father. While these suppositions are speculative, they could help guide research when adequate primary source documentation becomes available. Historians could also analyze the degree to which such emotional factors weighed in the decision of the Bush administration not to interpret 9/11 as an attack of war but rather as a horrific crime mandating going after only Osama bin Laden and al-Qaeda. It was not foreordained that the United States would also remove the Taliban government in Afghanistan and then plan a war against Iraq. Indeed, it would take the Bush administration more than a year of fanning worries about supposed weapons of mass destruction before it could persuade Congress and the public that war with Saddam Hussein was necessary.

What the Bush administration did was not wholly unprecedented. Since at least the 1840s, presidents have tried to harness the anger and fears of the public to get the wars they wanted – whether it was James K. Polk insisting that Mexicans had attacked Americans along the disputed border with Texas, William McKinley exploiting sensational reports of Spanish atrocities in Cuba, Woodrow Wilson dramatizing the deaths of Americans aboard Allied ships sunk by German submarines, Franklin D. Roosevelt playing on fear and dislike of the Nazis to proclaim a pre-Pearl Harbor naval war with Germany, Harry S. Truman using Cold War tensions to justify intervention in Korea, Lyndon B. Johnson exploiting anxieties about the yellow peril of Asian communism, or George H. W. Bush warning about Iraq's aggression and impending control of Middle East oil. Of course, the emotions entailed in the various lead-ups to war were more complex than this list would suggest. Leaders and their advisers may have subscribed only to a degree, or not at all, to the emotions they were trying to evoke in others.

Emotions influence public affairs in other ways as well. How did officials and the public evaluate and respond to the anger displayed against Japanese-Americans after Pearl Harbor? How did various officials, the media, and intellectuals react to public and private expressions of emotion during the Cuban missile crisis? While the origins of the Cold War might seem like an exhausted topic, the modulations in mood, perspective, and belief among Americans, Germans, Russians, and others have not been studied in depth. Of key importance at the end of World War II was people's confusion about what they were feeling and should be feeling. In early 1946, emotionally evocative, simplifying manifestos – such as Kennan's "long telegram," Churchill's "Iron Curtain" speech, and Stalin's so-called election address – mobilized that confusion and anxiety in the formation of Cold War ideology. Historians might also re-examine incidents in international and in transnational relations for evidence of shifting emotional norms regarding such issues as war, human rights, and migration. Despite our inability to access precisely what historical actors were feeling, we can analyze the cultural norms with which people expressed their feelings, the cultural lens through which their contemporaries interpreted those expressions, and, insofar as we can be self-reflective, the assumptions that blind our own perspectives as historians.

Emotions figure in foreign relations not just in terms of what leaders actually do, but also in regard to what those officials intend and how others interpret their intentions. The political scientist K. M. Fierke has observed that "leaders are not merely the rational carriers of intent but must be sensitive to multiple layers of meaning and emotion over which they have little control and which must be negotiated alongside interstate negotiations."[42]

Conflicting interpretations of intent help explain the gap between diplomatic achievements gained at Yalta and the political controversy afterward. Mindful of what he referred to as the "inferiority complex" of Joseph Stalin, an ailing Franklin D. Roosevelt endured the grueling journey to far-off Yalta intending to parlay this gesture of respect into concrete political advantage.[43] In analyzing the emotional valence and political ramifications of such gestures, historians must keep in mind the potential gap between intent and effect. Intent is not a solely subjective matter but rather an intersubjective one. What a nation or an individual intends with an action and what intention is actually conveyed may be two different things. Similarly, regardless of the emotions one intends to evoke in others, one's actions or demeanor may trigger quite different feelings in the target and among other observers.

To return to Yalta: While the supremely self-confident Roosevelt had little compunction about displaying homage to Stalin, other Americans seethed at the perceived humiliation. The Pentagon's liaison to the Red Army, General John R. Deane, later described what seems like an extraordinary emotional reaction. "No single event of the war irritated me more than seeing the President of the United States lifted from wheel chair, to ship, to shore... in order to go halfway around the world" to meet the Kremlin chief.[44] While FDR's sacrifice offended Deane, the display apparently had the intended effect on the dictator. Observing Stalin at Yalta, secret police chief Lavrenty Beria marveled "how full of consideration he is where Roosevelt is concerned, when, as a rule, he is dreadfully rude." An adviser to FDR remarked that the Kremlin chief "deferred to [Roosevelt] and his whole expression softened when he addressed the President directly."[45] Such "consideration" and "expression" yielded political dividends. Prime Minister Winston S. Churchill and his aides complained that on issue after issue, "Stalin made it plain at once that if this was the President's wish, he would accept it."[46] In terms of diplomacy at Yalta, Roosevelt's intended emotional impact on Stalin had greater consequence than the unintended irritation of Deane. With regard, however, to the politicized postwar charges that Stalin had bullied the supposedly "sick man at Yalta" into giving away Eastern Europe, the outrage typified by Deane would circulate widely and become an emotion-evoking fixture of Cold War orthodoxy. Like most conflicts in foreign/international/transnational relations, the Cold War generated intense feelings and was fueled by them.

The prevailing assumption about the polarity between reason and emotion and the superiority of the former furnishes adversaries with a versatile weapon. Whether foes are themselves appealing more to emotion or to reason while attacking an opponent, they can usually accuse the other side of being irresponsibly emotional and unsound. Armstrong drew attention to *Foreign Affairs* by publishing an emotionally evocative lead article that likened Kennan's recommendations to those of a "chatter[ing] chimpanzee" while disparaging his strategy as a "wishful fantasy" that would doom the West to a "timid and defeatist policy."[47] To ensure that his journal remained at the fulcrum of the debate, the editor urged Kennan to respond in its pages. Armstrong even suggested that Acheson, in "the ferocity of his attack," had rendered himself vulnerable. Armstrong advised Kennan to play that hyper-emotionalism "to advantage" by showing "a restraint and fairness" that the former secretary of state had abandoned.[48] The lesson for historians here is that regardless of whether participants argued for or against disengagement from the Cold War – or took a position on almost any other issue – the claim to reason, the appeal to emotions, and the charge of emotionalism remained potent weapons.

With regard to emotions history, the scholar's task is not simply to point to the presence or the importance of emotions, but rather to discern which blend of emotions was in play; the strength of these feelings; in what ways they were influenced by cultural norms, relations of power, and individual personalities; how they intersected with other aspects of thinking; and how they were perceived by others. Acknowledging the ubiquity of emotions is a first step toward integrating them into the historiography. We should think of emotions as a category of historical analysis, analogous to gender, class, and race. Examining evidence of emotions and, more generally, recovering the history of subjectivity, can reveal perceptions, beliefs, motivations, decisions, and actions that might be overlooked if the historian focuses only on external behavior. In addition to looking at the ways that individuals, such as an Acheson or a Kennan, or groups were influenced by culturally inflected feelings, historians can also examine the cultural context of these thoughts and actions. Last but not least, scholars should aim for awareness of how their own feelings condition their approach to history.

NOTES

I am indebted to Diann Bertucci, Barbara Keys, Michael Hogan, Mel Leffler, and Andy Rotter for their helpful comments on this essay, For an historical approach focused on close reading of language, see Frank Costigliola, "Reading for Meaning," in Michael J. Hogan and Thomas G. Paterson (eds.), *Explaining the History of American Foreign Relations*, 2nd edn. (New York, 2004), 279–303.

1. "Acheson Rebuffs Kennan on Withdrawal of Troops," *New York Times*, January 12, 1958, p. 1.
2. Dean Acheson, "The Illusion of Disengagement," *Foreign Affairs*, 36 (April 1958): 371. Acheson was not the only one to imply that Kennan's apostasy had reduced him to a less-than-human status. William Hard, the editor of *Reader's Digest*, wrote Acheson: "Will you send me George Kennan's skin to hang up on my office wall? You took it off completely." Hard to Acheson, January 14, 1958, box 15, Dean Acheson papers, Sterling Library, Yale University, New Haven, CT.
3. James Reston, "New Proposals for Old Disposals," *New York Times Book Review* (March 2, 1958), p. 26.
4. See, for instance, Frank Costigliola, *Roosevelt's Lost Alliances: How Personal Politics Helped Start the Cold War* (Princeton, 2012).
5. For recent work, see Susan J. Matt and Peter N. Stearns (eds.), *Doing Emotions History* (Urbana, 2014); Cristian Tileaga and Jovan Byford (eds.), *Psychology and History* (New York, 2014); Frank Biess and Daniel M. Gross (eds.), *Science and Emotions after 1945* (Chicago, 2014); Ute Frevert et al. (eds.), *Emotional Lexicons* (Oxford, UK, 2014); William G. Rosenberg, "Reading Soldiers' Moods: Russian Military Censorship and the Configuration of Feeling in World War I," *American Historical Review*, 119 (June 2014), 714–40; Andrew A. G. Ross, *Mixed Emotions* (Chicago, 2014); "Forum on Emotions and World Politics," *International Theory*, 6 (November 2014); "AHR Conversation: The Historical Study of Emotions," *American Historical Review*, 117 (December 2012), 1487–1530; Jan Plamper, "The History of Emotions: An Interview with William Reddy, Barbara Rosenwein, and Peter Stearns," *History and Theory* 49 (May 2010): 237–65; Barbara Keys, "Henry Kissinger: The Emotional Statesman," *Diplomatic History* (2011), 587–609; Jessica C. Gienow Hecht (ed.), *Emotions in American History* (New York, 2010). For a how-to guide, see Barbara H. Rosenwein, "Problems and

Methods in the History of Emotions," *Passions in Context*, No. 1, www.passionsincontext.de/index.php?id=483. For more focused studies, see Joanna Burke, *Fear: A Cultural History* (Emeryville, CA, 2005); Jan Plamper and Benjamin Lazier (eds.), *Fear across the Disciplines* (Pittsburgh, 2012); Michael Laffan and Max Weiss (eds.), *Facing Fear* (Princeton, 2012); William I. Miller, *The Anatomy of Disgust* (Cambridge, MA, 1997); ibid., *Humiliation* (Ithaca, 1993); ibid., *The Mystery of Courage* (Cambridge, MA, 2000); Sianne Ngai, *Ugly Feelings* (Cambridge, MA, 2005); Philip Fisher, *The Vehement Passions* (Princeton, 2002).

6. Frank Costigliola, "'I React Intensely to Everything': Russia and the Frustrated Emotions of George F. Kennan, 1933–58," *Journal of American History* (2016),
7. Barbara Keys, "Henry Kissinger: The Emotional Statesman," *Diplomatic History* (2011), 587–609.
8. Arlie Hochschild, "Emotion Work, Feeling Rules and Social Structure," *American Journal of Sociology*, 85 (1979), 551–75.
9. See, for instance, Antoine J. Banks, *Anger and Racial Politics: The Emotional Foundation of Racial Attitudes in America* (New York, 2014).
10. Ute Frevert, *Emotions in History – Lost and Found* (Budapest: Central European University Press, 2011), 31–85.
11. Paul Erickson and Judy L. Klein, *How Reason Almost Lost Its Mind: The Strange Career of Cold War Rationality* (Chicago, 2013).
12. As William M. Reddy notes, "the anthropological literature has turned up few communities that distinguish between thinking and feeling in the way that is common in Western-influenced contexts." (Reddy, "Humanists and the Experimental Study of Emotion," in Biess and Small (eds.), *Science and Emotions after 1945*, 58.
13. It is common in Western language usage to construct meaning by conceptualizing things in terms of pairs that require one item to be not just dissimilar to, but less valued than the other. In other words, we tend to organize, define, and evaluate things according to what they are not or to what they are opposed. The result is binary oppositions, such as self/other, we/them, healthy/sick, sane/crazy, masculine/feminine, rational/emotional, logical/illogical, moral/corrupt, disciplined/uncontrolled, sound/foolish, civic/selfish, trustworthy/unreliable, good/wicked, active/passive, objective/subjective. The first term in each binary set is more highly valued by Western and other societies, generally by women as well as men. The masculine/feminine polarity refers to conventional assumptions about masculine/feminine, not to the behavior of actual people. Indeed, a woman may act or talk "like a man" and a man may act or talk "like a woman." Because the terms in each of the pairs are mutually exclusive, binaries help accentuate differences, thereby underplaying the possibility of a position intermediate between the opposites. For example, rather than falling into either the rational or emotional category, actual thinking entails both. A further reason that binaries are powerful organizers of thought is the tendency we have to associate together the first terms of each pair (such as healthy people are rational, disciplined, sound, and more likely male) and do so likewise with the second terms (sick people are emotional, uncontrolled, foolish, and more likely female). For a fuller discussion, see Costigliola, "Reading for Meaning."

14. As the psychologist Luiz Pessoa puts it, emotion and cognition are *functionally integrated systems*, namely, they more or less continuously impact each other's operations." "Beyond brain regions: Network perspective of cognition-emotion interactions," *Behavorial and Brain Sciences*, 35 (2012): 159 (emphasis in original).
15. Ross, *Mixed Emotions*, 18.
16. See Thomas Dixon, "'Emotion': The History of a Keyword in Crisis," *Emotion Review*, 4 (October 2012): 338–44.
17. Benno Gammerl, "Emotional Styles – Concepts and Challenges," *Rethinking History*, 16, 2 (June 2012): 162.
18. Emma Hutchinson and Roland Bleiker, "Theorizing emotions in world politics," *International Theory*, 6, 3 (November 2014): 496. See also Rose McDermott, "The Feeling of Rationality: The Meaning of Neuroscientific Advances for Political Science," *Perspectives on Politics*, 2, 4 (December 2004): 692.
19. Daniel Kahneman, *Thinking, Fast and Slow* (New York, 2011). See also Jonathan Haidt, *The Righteous Mind* (New York, 2012).
20. See, for instance, Zoltan Kövecses, *Metaphor and Emotion* (New York, 2000).
21. An irony entailed in emotions history is that the integral nature of expressed thought evacuates the notion of stand-alone, graspable emotions. Is it not a chimera to study emotions if they cannot be isolated from other aspects of thought? To be sure, scholars can try to distinguish between thinking that is relatively more or less emotional, discern which emotions are in play, analyze the norms influencing the expression and suppression of emotion, and trace the impact of emotions on decisions and actions. Nevertheless, a commitment to pursue emotions history, just like a dismissal of its importance, can reflect the individual scholar's personal, perhaps unacknowledged inclinations. Indeed, scholars drawn to this or to any other methodology or thesis should keep in mind that, as the political scientists Janice Bialy Mattern has observed, "the more intensely we are drawn to an idea, the less capable we are of perceiving its logical frailties or rejecting it." (Janice Bialy Mattern, "On Being Convinced: An Emotional Epistemology of International Relations," *International Theory*, (November 2014), 593.
22. Jeremy T. Burman, "Bringing the Brain into History: Behind Hunt's and Smail's Appeals to Neurohistory" in Tileaga and Byford (eds.), *Psychology and History*, 82.
23. Nicole Eustace, *Passion is the Gale: Emotion, Power, and the Coming of the American Revolution* (Chapel Hill: University of North Carolina Press, 2008), 11.
24. Jonathan Mercer, "Feeling like a State: Social Emotion and Identity," *International Theory* (November 2014): 515.
25. Ibid. Durkheim in Ross, *Mixed Emotions*, 33. See also Dawn T. Robinson and Jody Clay-Warner (eds.), *Social Structure & Emotion* (San Diego, 2008).
26. See Matthias Siemer, "Mood Experience: Implications of a Dispositional Theory of Moods," *Emotion Review*, 1, 3 (July 2009): 256–63.
27. Nathan G. Hale, Jr., *The Rise and Crisis of Psychoanalysis in the United States* (New York, 1995), 3–9, 74–101; Eli Zaretsky, *Secrets of the Soul* (New York, 2004), 138–216.
28. Alexander L. George and Juliette L. George's (1956) biography and Sigmund Freud and former ambassador to Moscow and Paris William C. Bullitt's biography written years earlier and published after Bullitt died in 1966.
29. Langer, "Next Assignment," 286–7, 303.

30. Acheson to Hamilton Fish Armstrong, January 23, 1958, box 1, Hamilton Fish Armstrong papers, Mudd Library, Princeton University.
31. For a how-to introduction, see Barbara H. Rosenwein, "Problems and Methods in the History of Emotions," *Passions in Context*, No. 1, www.passionsincontext.de/index.php?id=483.
32. Ruth Leys, "'Both of Us Disgusted in My Insula': Mirror-Neuron Theory and Emotional Empathy" in Biess and Gross (eds.), *Science and Emotion*, 7 6.
33. See, for instance, Rosenberg, "Reading Soldiers' Moods," 714–40.
34. Acheson to Armstrong, January 23, 1958, box 1, Armstrong papers; James Reston, "'Elevate Them Guns a Little Lower,'" *New York Times*, January 18, 1958, p. 10.
35. Jan Plamper, "The History of Emotions: An Interview with William Reddy, Barbara Rosenwein, and Peter Stearns," *History and Theory*, 49 (May 2010): 240.
36. William P. Bundy and Mary A[cheson] Bundy, interview with John Lewis Gaddis, December 6, 1987, box 1, John Lewis Gaddis papers, Mudd library, Princeton University.
37. Frevert, *Emotions in History*, 92. See also Barbara H. Rosenwein (ed.), *Anger's Past* (Ithaca, 1998).
38. Peter N. Stearns, *American Cool: Constructing a 20th Century Emotional Style* (New York, 1994).
39. Ibid., 31.
40. Frevert, *Emotions in History*, 97.
41. See David Redlawsk and G. Robert Boynton (eds.), *Feeling Politics* (New York, 2006).
42. K. M. Fierke, "Emotion and Intentionality," *International Theory* (November 2014): 567.
43. Costigliola, *Roosevelt's Lost Alliances*, 195.
44. John R. Deane, *Strange Alliance* (New York, 1947), 160. Another president who sparked unintended emotions was Barack Obama, who bowed to the emperor of Japan as a sign of respect. Critics erupted in apparent anger at Obama's alleged subservience or even treason.
45. Costigliola, *Roosevelt's Lost Alliances*, 242.
46. Ibid.
47. Acheson, "Illusion of Disengagement," 371, 378, 379.
48. Armstrong to Kennan, January 22, 1958, box 38, Armstrong papers.

Index

1882 Chinese Exclusion Act, 177
2002 National Security Strategy, 19
9/11, 286, 313, 367
  American policy after, 20
  and Bush administration, 36, 367
9/11 Commission Report, 104, 338

Aarons, Mark, 139
Access to Archival Databases system (AAD), 80
accountability, democratic, 18
Acheson, Dean, 9, 65, 107, 136, 337, 356, 360, 370
  and postwar policymaking, 64
Adams, John Quincy, 151, 157, 337
Adelman, Jeremy, 169
Affordable Health Care Act, 312
African diplomats, race in the US, 245
African-American transnationalism, 210
After Hegemony (Keohane), 14
al-Qaeda, 286
  and modernization, 104
Alamo, the, 304
Albright, Madeleine, 339
Allen, David, 2
Alliance for Progress, 48
Aloha America (Imada), 191
Altman, Clara, 141
America and the World, 188
America's Geisha Ally: Reimagining the Japanese Enemy (Shibusawa), 278
America's Kingdom (Vitalis), 180, 192
America's Miracle Man in Vietnam (Jacobs), 285
American Civil War and US power, 31

American diplomacy and digital records, 81
American Diplomacy (Kennan), 195
American Exceptionalism in an Age of International History (Tyrell), 204
American foreign relations
  and psychology, 334–6
  historiography of, 93
history
  psychological approaches, 334–44
  perspectives on, 8
American frontier, 170
American hegemony and socialism, 60
American Heritage magazine, 306
American Historical Association, 76
American Historical Review, 76
American Israel Public Affairs Committee (AIPAC), 161
American Settler Colonialism (Hixson), 192
American Sociological Association, 76
American Zionist Council, the, 161
Amnesty International, 121, 125
analysis, levels of, 18
anarchy, 19
Anderson, Carole, 194
Anderson, David L., 136
Anderson, George, 343
Anderson, Warwick, 194
Andrews, Gregg, 46
Andrews, Thomas, 176
Anglo hegemony, 176
Anglo-American rapprochement, 27
Annales historians, 76
Anomalies and archival discovery, 90
ante bellum era, 204
  foreign policy of the, 29

anti-Castro Cuban American National Foundation (CANF), 162
anti-exceptionalist historiography and US/world relations, 203–13
Anzaldúa, Gloria
  Borderlands/La Frontera: The New Mestiza, 176
Appleby, Joyce, 76
Application Programming Interface (API), 84
Arab Spring, 338
Arab–Israeli dispute/conflict, 90, 110, 206
Aramco, 62, 114, 192
archival integrity, loss of, 81, 83
arguments
  first image, 19
  second image, 20
  third image, 20–1
armed conflict, law of, 142
Aron, Stephen, 169
Asad, Talal, 288
Ashley, Richard, 15
associationalism, 42
associative state, 42
  New Deal version of, 50
Atlantic Crossings (Rodgers), 204
attribution, authorship, 92
audience cost theory, 14
authorship attribution, 92
Axis domination in Europe, 32
Axworthy, Lloyd, 122
Aydelotte, William, 76
Ayers, Edward, 93

balancing
  external, 11–12
    and bipolarity, 19
  internal, 12
    and bipolarity, 19
Bank for International Settlements, 64
banking and finance in the capitalist world economy, 63–5
Barrows, David, 322
Barth, Frederik, 179
Bass, Gary, 139
  Blood Telegram: Nixon, Kissinger, and a Forgotten Genocide, 139
Bassin, Mark, 179
Baud, Michiel, 179
Bay of Pigs, 342
Bayly, C.A., 288

Beard, Charles A., 2
Becker, William H., 46
Belich, James, 174
Bell, Daniel, 289
Bemis, Samuel Flagg, 2, 154, 171, 180, 181
Ben Hur, 308
Bender, Thomas, 193, 204, 207, 213
  A Nation among Nations, 204
Benton, Lauren, 145
  A Search for Sovereignty: Law and Geography in European Empires, 144
Benton-Cohen, Katherine, 176
Berger, Peter
  The Sacred Canopy, 289
Beria, Lavrenty, 369
Berlin Wall, 35, 188, 313
Berman, Marshall, 106
Bernath, Stuart, 336
Between Two Worlds (Kafadar), 178
Big Bang in research material, 74
big data and historians, 78
Bijsterveld, Karin, 321
billiard ball model, 19
bin Laden, Osama, 206, 367
Bisbee deportation, 176
black freedom struggle, 245
Blackwill, Robert D., 162
Blair, John
  The Control of Oil, 61
Blazhkov, Igor, 234
Blight, David, 308
Blood of Government, The (Kramer), 204
Blood Telegram: Nixon, Kissinger, and a Forgotten Genocide (Bass), 139
Blood, Arthur, 139
Blower, Brooke, 192, 194
Bolton, Herbert E., 170
border crossings. *See* borders; borderlands
  and culture, 195–8
borderlands, 170, 194
  legal, 140
Borderlands/La Frontera: The New Mestiza (Anzaldúa), 176
borderlands studies, 175–7
borders
  as contact zones, 190
  between East and West, 189–93
  cross-border relations, 234
  transnational connections and, 193–5
  understanding. *See* borderlands
Borgwardt, Elizabeth, 138

Index

New Deal for the World, 138
born digital electronic record collections, 80
Borstelmann, Thomas, 194
Bourne, Randolph, 222
Bracero program, 177
Bradford, Anita Casavantes, 194
Bradley, Mark
  Imagining Vietnam, 190
Brandt, Willy, 90
Bremer, L. Paul, 162
Brent, Charles Henry, 319
Bretton Woods, 65, 66
Bridenbaugh, Carl, 76
Briggs, Laura, 191
British East India Company, 120
  charter, 121
Brody, David
  Visualizing American Empire, 190
Brown v. Board of Education, 141
Buchanan, Patrick, 311
Buckland, Ralph, 327
Buell, Frederick
  National Culture and the New Global System, 236
Bull, Hedley, 15
Bundy, McGeorge, 151, 162
burstiness, 87
Burton, Orville Vernon, 77
Bush doctrine, 19–21
Bush, George H. W., 35, 312, 368
  and the Cold War, 312
Bush, George W., 36, 162
  and American core values, 36
  and the Iraq War, 19–21
  first image view of, 19
  Freedom Agenda, 114
  Iraq invasion and, 337
  second image view of, 20
Business of Empire, The (Colby), 192
Butler, Jon, 284
Buzan, Barry, 26

cable traffic, mapping of, 93
Calhoun, John C., 157
Canada, 232
Canal Builders, The (Greene), 191
Capital Moves (Cowie), 63
capitalist world system, 59
Carbon Democracy (Mitchell), 210
Cardwell, Curt, 65
Carr, E. H.

The Twenty Years' Crisis, 10
Carter, Jimmy, 121
  views on Cuban relations, 161–2
Casanova, José, 294
causal relations, factors affecting, 21–2
Center for Public Diplomacy, The, 236
Challenge to Isolation, The (Langer), 363
Chamberlin, Paul, 209, 210
  The Global Offensive, 209
Chandler, Alfred D., 42
Chang, Kornel S., 180
Chappell, David A., 179
Choy, Catherine, 194
Choy, Ceniza, 274
Churchill, Winston S., 276, 369
Citino, Nathan J., 3, 192, 194, 211
Civil Rights Act, 141
Civil War, 141, 162, 204
  and nationalism, 222
Clark, Colin, 111
Classen, Constance, 325
Clay, Lucius D., 340
Clendinnen, Inga, 206
Clifford, Clark, 161
Clifford, James, 189, 196
Climate Action Network, 123
Clinton, Bill, 35, 119
Clinton, Hillary Rodham, 104, 338
cliometricians, 76
Clooney, George, 310
Close Encounters of Empire, 191
Coates, Benjamin, 141
Cobbs, Elizabeth
  The Rich Neighbor Policy, 47
Cohen, Daniel, 77
Cohen, Deborah, 177, 181
Colby, Jason
  The Business of Empire, 192
Cold War, 15, 19, 141, 155, 205, 223, 309
  American motive in, 20
  and America's winner complex, 311
  and cultural relations, 235
  and the foreign policies of the US and USSR, 19
  and United States perception of threats, 32
  and world systems theory, 60
  during the McCarthy era, 33
  factors influencing, 34–5
  United States and, 34
Cold War civil rights, 247
Cold War International History Project, 155
colonialism. *See* decolonization

Comanches, 174
Communications, rate of, 86–7
computational techniques
   and the infinite archive, 74–5
computers and research, 74–5
Condorcet, 103
Confederate Veteran magazine, 308
Conger, Emily, 319, 320, 326, 327
Connelly, Matthew, 2, 125, 194, 205, 209
constructivism, 15
consumption, empire of, 106
contact zones, 191–3
Control of Oil, The (Blair), 61
core values and national security, 28–31
corporatism, 42–6
   interwar, 44
Costigliola, Frank, 3, 35, 43, 45, 279
   and elite leaders, 276
   Roosevelt's Lost Alliances: How Personal Politics Helped Start the Cold War, 276
counting as a computational method, 85–6
Cowie, Jefferson
   Capital Moves, 63
Craig, Campbell, 156
Crenshaw, Kimberlé, 272
CREST system, 79
Critical Legal Histories (Gordon), 144
Cronon, William, 172
Cross of Iron: Harry S. Truman and the Origins of the National Security State, 136
cross-border migration, 194
cross-border relations, 234
Cuba
   American policy and, 161–2
   Communist regime in, 346
   presidential elections, 161
   Special National Intelligence Estimate on the military build-up in, 346
Cuban missile crisis, 347
Cull, Nicholas, 234
Cullather, Nick, 2, 194
Culper Ring, 346
cultural conflict, 241
cultural diplomacy, 197, 234, 241
cultural policy- and decision-making, 234
cultural reconstruction, 224
cultural relations. *See* cultural reconstruction
   and international history, 232–42
   and the Cold War, 235
cultural turn, 195–8, 234, 236, 317
Culture and Imperialism (Said), 189, 191
Culture of the Cold War, The (Whitfield), 286

culture wars
   and foreign relations, 305, 311
Cultures of United States Imperialism (Pease & Kaplan), 204, 207
Cumings, Bruce, 67
Cunfer, Geoff, 93
Cutter, Walter, 328

data dump, 74
Date Which Will Live: Pearl Harbor in American Memory, A (Rosenberg), 305
Davis, John, 207
de Grazia, Victoria
   Irresistible Empire, 197
de Santa Anna, Antonio López, 304
Dean, Robert D., 276
   Imperial Brotherhood: Gender and the Making of Cold War Foreign Policy, 276
Deane, John R., 369
Decade of Development, modernization theory of, 108
Declassification Engine, 93
Declassified Documents Reference System (DDRS), 79
decolonization. *See* colonialism
   African, 245
defensive realism, 11, 14
DeLay, Brian, 174
democracies
   avoidance of war and, 13
   foreign policies of, 13
democratic accountability, 18
Democratic Peace Theory (DPT), 13, 14
dependency theorists and the Cold War, 60
development
   definition of, 103, 105
   and dictatorial states, 114
   history of, 105–9
   and technopolitics, 109–13
   understanding what it is, 103–5
   and US foreign relations, 102–3
   US influence and, 113–15
Devins, John Bancroft, 319
Dezalay, Yves, 194
Diem, Ngo Dinh, 339
Dies, Martin, 178
digital archive, the, 75
Digital Atlas of Roman and Medieval Civilizations, 93
digital history, 77
digital humanities, 77–8

Index

Digital National Security Archive, 79
digital repositories, 82–5
digitized books and computational analysis, 78
Dillon, C. Douglas, 64
diplomatic archives researching, 94–5
diplomatic history, 339–44
Diplomatic History (Costigliola), 64, 188, 279
diplomatic policy
 and cognitive approaches, 339–44
Diplomatic Revolution, A (Connelly), 209
Discovery! (Stegner), 181
distant reading, 90
Dodge, David, 181
Dodge, Phelps, 181
dogmatism, and foreign relations decisions, 337–8
dollar diplomacy, 64
domestic politics and foreign relations, 151–63
Donnan, C. Hastings, 169
Donnelly, Jack, 12
Donoghue, Michael, 191
Dorfman, Ariel, 236
Dorfman, Ariel and Armand Mattelart
 How to Read Donald Duck, 196
Doss, Erica, 306
Double-T Diner, 245
Doyle, Michael, 13
DPT. *See* Democratic Peace Theory (DPT)
Drake, Paul W., 45
Du Bois, W. E. B., 246
Dubuisson, Daniel, 288
Duce, James Terry, 181
Dudziak, Mary, 2, 194
Dulles, John Foster, 18, 136, 339, 347, 366
Dunch, Ryan, 287
Dunlap, Charles, 142
Dutch Ethical Policy, 106

East Pakistan, genocide in, 139
East–West medical cooperation, 234
East–West tensions,
 US views on, 356
Economic and Social Council, 122
Economic Cooperation Administration, 49
economic system and peace, 13
e-discovery, 83
Edwards, Brian, 207
Eisenhower, Dwight D., 28, 104, 158, 328
Ekbladh, David, 34, 48, 49, 50, 66, 109, 194
electronic records, issues with transition to, 81
Elias, Norbert, 194, 317

embassies
 and off-topic discussions, 90
 signatures of, 90
Emergency Committee on Zionist Affairs, The, 161
emotional communities, 361
emotional regimes, 362
empire of liberty, 28
Endy, Christopher, 194
Engerman, David, 194
Engerman, Stanley
 Time on the Cross, 76
Epic Encounters (McAlister), 285
Epstein, Katherine
 Torpedo: Inventing the Military-Industrial Complex in the United States and Great Britain, 145
Erdmann, Andrew P. N., 46
ethnic cleansing in Kosovo, 140
ethnogenesis, 179
 African, 179
evolutionary psychology, 17–18
Evolution of International Human Rights, The (Lauren), 137
Explaining the History of American Foreign Relations, 1, 2, 74, 95
external balancing, 11–12
 and bipolarity, 19
external danger and perceptions of threat, 27–9

Facebook, 75
Fascism, 59
Faust (Goethe), 106
Feith, Douglas, 36
Ferguson, Niall, 125
Ferguson, Thomas, 65
Fierke, K. M., 368
Fighting for American Manhood: How Gender Politics Provoked the Spanish–American and Philippine–American Wars (Hoganson), 275
firms, importance to foreign policies, 60–3
first image argument, 19
Fish, Stanley, 196
Fogel, Robert
 Time on the Cross, 76
Foot, Rosemary, 158
 The Politics of Peacemaking at the Korean Armistice Talks, 158
Forbes, William Cameron, 321
Fordlandia (Grandin), 192
Fordlandia (Sguiglia), 168

Foreign Affairs (Kennan), 356
foreign aid, 102
Foreign Affair, A, 308
foreign policies
  and domestic politics, 151–63
  of democracies, 13
  of the US and USSR, 19
foreign policy, 156
  goals of the United States
    early years, 31
  and group decision-making, 338–9
  national security approach to, 10, 25–6
  security fears and, 27–8
foreign relations
  and development, 102–3
  and dogmatism, 337–8
  and gender, 271–2, 277–80
  and its emotional responses, 356–70
  and women, 272–5
  gendering American, 280–1
  psycho, 344–6
foreign relations historian
  and research about the senses, 329
foreign relations history, 1–2
  and legal history, 145–7
  and periodization of law, 137
  the law and, 136–7
Foreign Relations of the United States (FRUS), 78
Fourteenth Amendment, the, 223
Fousek, John, 34
Frank, Alison Fleig, 60
Frankfurt School, 289
Franklin, Benjamin, 79
Freedom Agenda, 114
Freedom of Information Act (FOIA), 79
Freer, William, 320, 328
Frevert, Ute, 366
Friedman, Max Paul, 197
Frisch, Michael, 77
frontier, 169–70
  American, 169
  definition of, 169
  global, 169, 171
Fukuyama, Francis, 311, 312
Furet, François, 76

Gabaccia, Donna, 194, 274
Gaddis, John Lewis, 20, 344
Gaines, Kevin, 194
Gallicchio, Marc, 309
Gardner, Martha, 274
Garth, Bryant G., 194
Gates, Bill, 114
Gates, Frederick T., 103
Gates, Melinda, 114
Geertz, Clifford, 294
gender and men, 275–7
General Agreement on Tariffs and Trade, 47
Geographical Information Systems (GIS), 93
George, Alexander, 335
George, Juliette, 335
German *Reich* and exchange scholars, 238
Germany
  and World War I, 31
Gibbs, David, 62
Gienow-Hecht, Jessica C. E., 3, 197
GIs and Germans: Culture, Gender, and Foreign Relations, 1945–1949 (Goedde), 278
Gitlin, Jay, 172
global civil society framework, 124
global community, 124
Global Community (2002), 193
global frontier, 171
globalization, 193
Global Offensive, The (Chamberlin), 209
Gobat, Michel, 191
GIs and Germans
  GIs and Germans: Culture, Gender, and Foreign Relations, 1945–1949, 278
Goethe
  Faust, 106
gold standard, the decline of, 64–5
Goldsmith, Jack, 142
Good Neighbor Policy, 177
Google Ngram Viewer, 85
Gorbachev, Mikhail, 311
Gordon, Robert, 144
Grandin, Greg, 169
Fordlandia, 192
Great Depression, 27, 43, 64
Great Frontier, The (Webb), 171
Great Ocean, The (Igler), 192
Great Transformation, The (Polanyi), 59
Greene, Julie
  The Canal Builders, 191
Griffith, Robert, 46
Gronich, Lori Helene, 3
group decision-making and foreign policy, 338–9
groupthink hypothesis, 338
Guantanamo (Lipman), 191
Gupta, Akhil, 105
Guthrie-Shimizu, Sayuri, 194

Index

Haas, Lisabeth, 175
Haines, Gerald K., 78
Haitian Revolution, 304, 305
Haldeman, H.R., 160, 334
Hale, Nathan, 346
Hall, Linda B., 46
Hämäläinen, Pekka, 170, 174, 178
Hamilton, Alexander, 92
Hamiltonian Federalists, 29
Harper, John, 32
Harriman, W. Averell, 64
Harris, Susan, 194
Hart, Justin, 235
Hart-Cellar Act, 258
Hass, Kristin Ann
  Sacrificing Soldiers on the National Mall, 307
Hawai'i legal codes, 141
Hawley, Ellis W., 42
Haynes, Sam W., 28
Helsinki Accords, 90
Hendrickson, David C., 29
Hietala, Thomas, 171
High Modernism, 107, 108
Hispanophobic overcoming, 175
historical research
  and computational methods, 304–14
history
  and foreign relations, 304–14
  rewriting, 304
Hixson, Walter
  American Settler Colonialism, 192
Ho Chi Minh, 158, 334
Hodge, Joseph, 127
Hoff-Wilson, Joan, 43
Hogan, Michael J., 1, 2, 35, 128, 136
Hoganson, Kristen, 194, 272
  Fighting for American Manhood, 275
Holt, Michael, 29
Holy Allies, 28
Hoover, Herbert, 103, 104, 171
horizontal socialization, 16
Horne, Gerald, 194
How to Read Donald Duck (Dorfman & Mattelart), 196
Hoyt, Henry, 319
Hsu, Madeline, 194
human nature, 17–18
human rights history, 137–8
  periodization of, 137–40
Hume, David, 326, 361
Hunt, Michael H., 3

Huntington, Samuel, 286, 311
Hussein, Saddam, 347
  and Kuwait, 35

idealism, 218
ideas and material interests
  relationship between, 16
ideology
  and nationalism, 217
  definition of, 217
Igler, David
  The Great Ocean, 192
IGOs, 126–7
Imada, Adria
  Aloha America, 191
image management, national, 240
Imagining the Middle East (Jacobs), 209
Imagining Vietnam and America (Bradley), 190
Immerman, Richard H., 3
immigration and trade policies, 177–8
Imperial Brotherhood: Gender and the Making of Cold War Foreign Policy (Dean), 276
Imperial Eyes (Pratt), 190
Inboden, William
  Religion and American Foreign Policy, 285
Indochina, US intervention in, 64, 158–9
INGOs, 122–3, 125
Institutions and cooperation facilitation, 14–15
intelligence and US foreign relations, 346–7
intergovernmental organizations (IGOs), 126–7
internal balancing, 12
  and bipolarity, 19
International Criminal Tribunal for the Former Yugoslavia, 140
International Electrotechnical Commission, 123
international history
  and cultural relations, 232–42
international nongovernmental organizations
  statistics on, 123
International Planned Parenthood Federation, 125
international relations
  and masculinity, 275–7
International Spy Museum, 310
internationalism
  and American diplomacy, 47
  partial, 32
internationally active NGOs (INGOs), 122–3, 125
Iraq
  invasion of, 19–21, 162, 337

Iraq war
  opposition to, 10
Iriye, Akira, 45, 124, 139, 193, 233, 290
Iron Curtain, and cultural interaction, 234
Irresistible Empire (de Grazia), 197
Island World (Okihiro), 192
isolationism, the legend of, 45
Israel, Jerry, 136
Israeli–Palestinian issue, 160–1
Italo-Ethiopian War
  humanitarian groups and, 123

Jackson, C. D., 347
Jackson, Robert H., 139
Jacobs, Matthew, 48, 49
  Imagining the Middle East, 209
Jacobs, Seth, 194
  America's Miracle Man in Vietnam, 285
Janis, Irving, 338
Japan
  and post-war US relations, 206–13, 278
Jay, John, 136
Jay's Treaty, 154, 171, 225
jazz ambassadors program, 197
Jefferson, Thomas, 28, 29, 136
  and reason and sentiment, 361
Jeffersonian Republicans, 29
Jervis, Robert, 2, 3
Jim Crow, 245, 248
Jockers, Matthew, 78
Johnson, Lyndon B., 67, 104, 159, 367
Johnson, Samuel, 153
Joll, James, 16
Jones, Toby, 213
Joseph, Gilbert, 191
Journal of American History, 76, 193, 204, 272, 279
Judis, John, 160
Jütte, Robert, 317

Kafadar, Cemal, 178
Kahn, Yahya, 139
Kahneman, Daniel, 360
Kaiser, Henry J., 47
Kalaw, Teodoro, 323
Kant, Immanuel, 13, 106
Kaplan, Amy, 191, 204, 207
Kapuściński, Ryszard, 109
Karl, Rebecca, 211
Katzenstein, Peter, 15, 26
Kaufman, Burton I., 43, 46

Kearny, Stephen W., 175
Keck, Margaret, 124
Kennan, George F.
  American Diplomacy, 195
Kennan, George F., 2, 279, 356, 370
Kennedy, John F., 328
  Alliance for Progress, 48
  and the Vietnam War, 159
  race and, 245
Kennedy, Robert F., 328
Keohane, Robert, 14
  After Hegemony, 14
Kerry, John, 162, 338
Keys, Barbara J., 2, 194
Khaldun, Ibn
  Muqaddimah, 178
Khrushchev, Nikita S., 311
  War of Liberation speech, 345
Kidman, Nicole, 310
Kindleberger, Charles, 64
Kirby, Dianne, 285
Kirkpatrick, Jeane, 339
Kissinger, Henry, 82, 139, 357
Klein, Christina, 308
  Cold War Orientalisms, 190
Klimke, Martin, 194
Knauer, Lisa Maya, 309
Kopytoff, Igor, 179
Korean War, 67, 158
Korematsu v. United States, 144
Kramer, Paul A., 3, 6, 191, 204
  Blood of Government, 204
Krasner, Stephen, 17
Kroes, Rob, 197
Kühnemann, Eugen, 238
Kunkel, Sönke, 233

LaFeber, Walter, 62
  The New Empire, 287
Lake, Anthony, 154, 162, 163
Lamar, Howard, 169, 172
Langer, William L.
  The Challenge to Isolation, 363
Lansdale, Edward G., 108
Last Utopia: Human Rights in History, The (Moyn), 138
Latent Dirichlet Allocation (LDA), 87
Latham, Michael, 34, 108, 194
Lauren, Paul Gordon, 138
  human rights and, 17–18
  The Evolution of International Human Rights, 137

Index

law
  as a constitutive force, 143–5
  and foreign relations history, 136–7
  legitimating role of, 143
  operational, 142
  and public diplomacy, 140–1
  and social relationships, 144
  as war, 141–3
lawfare, 142, 145
League of Nations, 136, 293, 335
  rejection of, 43
Lee, Erika, 194
Lefebvre, Henri, 93
Leffler, Melvyn P., 2, 43
Legacy of Conquest, The (Limerick), 172
legal borderlands, 140
legal history, 135–7
legal institutions
  and foreign relations, 140–1, 144
legalism-moralism, 195
LeGrand, Catherine C., 191
LeMay, Curtis, 343
levels of analysis, 17, 18
  doctrine, 19
Levin, N. Gordon, 29
Lewis, James, 27
Li, Tania Murray, 111
liberalism, 12–15
Lilienthal, David, 104, 112
Limerick, Patricia Nelson
  The Legacy of Conquest, 172
Limón, José E., 175
Lincoln, Abraham, 29
  and the Civil War, 141
Lind, Michael, 26, 29
Lindquist, Kristen A., 361
Linn, Brian McAllister, 171
Lipman, Jana
  Guantanomo, 191
Livingston, Robert R., 136
Locke, John, 106
Logevall, Fredrik, 2, 211
Long, Burke, 207
Luibheid, Eithne, 274

MacArthur Foundation, 115
MacArthur, Douglas, 113, 158
Macher Anikó, 234
Madison, James, 92
  concerns of, 156
  war with Great Britain, 157
Mahan, Alfred Thayer, 113

Maier, Charles S., 46, 47, 51, 65
  empire of consumption, 106
Makdisi, Ussama, 3, 194
Making of the Monroe Doctrine, The
  (May), 157
Malenkov, Georgi, 347
Mandatory Declassification Review (MDR), 80
Manela, Erez, 207, 234
  *The Wilsonian Moment: Self-Determination
  and the International Origins
  of Anticolonial Nationalism*, 205,
  209, 211
Manifest Destiny, 169, 171, 181
Mapp, Paul, 173
mapping, 93
Margolies, Daniel, 140
Marr, Timothy, 207
Marshall Plan, 32, 47, 49, 50
Marshall, George C., 362
Martin, Lisa, 14
Marx, Karl, 103
Marxism, 18
Maryland's public accommodations
  desegregating of, 245
Maryland's Route 40, 245
Mason, George, 104
Massachusetts Institute of Technology's Center
  for International Studies (CENIS), 107
Masuzawa, Tomoko, 288
material interests and ideas, relationship
  between, 16
Matsuda, Matt
  Pacific Worlds, 192
Mattelart, Armand, 236
Mattelart, Armand and Ariel Dorfman
  How to Read Donald Duck, 196
May, Ernest R., 157
  The Making of the Monroe Doctrine, 157
  views on the Monroe Doctrine, 157–8
McAlister, Melani, 207, 308
  Epic Encounters, 285
McAllister, William, 74, 78
McCarthy era, 33, 277, 357
McCoy, Alfred, 191
McKillen, Elizabeth, 46
McKinley, William, 31, 106, 290, 367
McNeil, John, 194
McNeill, William H., 180
medical cooperation, East–West, 234
men and gender, 275–7. *See* gender and men
mercantilism, 15
Meriwether, James, 194

Merrill, Dana, 321
Merrill, Dennis, 194
Merry, Sally Engle, 111
metadata, 80
Mexican–American War, 175
Miles, George, 172
milieu goals, 20
militarization
  historiographies of, 260
  race and, 260
military-sexual complex, 273
Mill, John Stuart, 103
Miller, Perry, 113
Mills, C. Wright, 52
Milosevic, Slobodan, 140
Missal, Alexander
  Seaway to the Future, 191
mission civilisatrice, 238
missionaries
  as cultural brokers, 194
Mitchell, Nancy, 28
Mitchell, Timothy, 110
  Carbon Democracy, 210
modeling, 90
Modern Girl around the World, The, 197
modernist universalism, 245
modernization
  and migration, 177
  postwar, 49, 59, 285
  theory, 108, 209
Monroe Doctrine, 28, 157–8, 177, 337
  and threat, 157
Monument Wars: Washington D.C., the National Mall, and the Transformation of the Memorial Landscape (Savage), 307
moral reformers
  as cultural brokers, 194
Moretti, Franco, 78, 92
Morgan, Arthur E., 110
Morgenthau, Hans, 2, 17
  Power Among Nations, 10
Morrison-Grady Plan, 160
Moses, Edith, 318, 325, 328
Mosteller, Frederick, 92
Moyn, Samuel, 138
  The Last Utopia: Human Rights in History, 138
Mulder, John, 286
multinational corporation, 127–9
Muqaddimah (Khaldun), 178
Murphy, Frank, 324, 328

Nagel, Joane, 273
Nakba, 210
Nasseri, Mehran Karimi, 120
Nation among Nations, A (Bender), 204
Nation Branding, 232–42
National Culture and the New Global System (Buell), 236
National Intelligence Estimate on Weapons of Mass Destruction, 346
national security
  definition of, 26
  and social interaction, 26
National Security Act, 136
national security approach
  core values and, 33–4
  criticism of, 33
National Security Archive, 155
National Security Council, 18, 78, 92, 107, 308
national security policy, external threats, 25
National Security Strategy, 19, 36
nationalism, 218–27
  revolutionary, 32
NATO. See North Atlantic Treaty Organization (NATO)
naturalization act, 258
neo-classical realism, 11
neoliberal institutionalism, 14
neo-Malthusianism, 114
neorealism, 11–12
network definition of, 92
network analysis, social, 92–3
New Deal, 49–51, 65
New Deal for the World, A (Borgwardt), 138
New Empire (LaFeber), 287
New Era, 43
New International Economic Order (NIEO), 108
Ngai, Mae M., 177
NGOs, 119, 122–6
  and multinational corporations, 128
  and social movement, 124
  as a global community, 124
  statistics on, 123
  study of, 123–4
  view of Colin Powell, 125
Niebuhr, Reinhold, 17
Ninkovich, Frank, 233, 235
Nixon, Richard, 139, 159, 311, 334, 366
nongovernmental organizations. See NGOs
nonstate actors
  categories of, 122
  methodological challenges of, 128–9

Index

overview of, 119–22
questions for understanding, 120
types of, 120
variety of, 120
Nora, Pierre
   Realms of Memory, 305
North American Free Trade Agreement (NAFTA), 162, 181
North Atlantic Treaty Organization (NATO), 32, 48
   and French defection, 19
Nostalgia for the Future: West Africa after the Cold War (Piot), 311
Nowell, Gregory, 61
Nuremberg trial, 139, 140

O'Brien, Thomas F., 45
Obama, Barack, 102, 104, 219, 338
   and US–Russian relations, 346
Obenzinger, Hilton, 207
off-topic discussions, 90–2
offensive realists, 11
Office of Strategic Services (OSS), 363
Office of the Special Protocol Service, 245
Okihiro, Gary
   Island World, 192
Oklahoma City bombing, 307
Open Door expansion, Turner's, 171
operational law, 142
Operational Law Handbooks, 142
Optical Character Recognition (OCR), 80
Organization for European Economic Cooperation, 49
Organization of American Historians, 193
Organization of Petroleum Exporting Countries (OPEC), 108
Orientalism (Said), 207
Orsi, Robert A., 291
Otis, Laura, 317
Overy, Richard, 139
Oxford English Dictionary, 105

Painter, David S., 46
Palestine Liberation Organization, 119, 209
Panama Canal Zone, 257
paper documents, 81
Paredes, Américo, 175, 178
Parrini, Carl P., 43
Paterson, Thomas G., 1
Peacemaker, The, 310, 313
Pearl Harbor, 153, 305
Pease, Donald, 191, 204, 207

Peña Delgado, Grace, 177
Pentagon, 35
Pérez, Louis A., 191
Perilous Memories: The Asian-Pacific War(s), 308
Perkins, Dexter, 154, 157
Pero, Mario Del, 211
Persian Gulf War, 35
personality traits and foreign relations decisions, 336–8
Philippine War, 171
Philippines official commission in, 102
Philippines and the Filipinos
   and the American civilizing process, 318
   American senses and the, 318–28
Pierpaoli, Paul G., 47
Piot, Charles
   Nostalgia for the Future: West Africa after the Cold War, 311
Plummer, Brenda Gayle, 194
Point IV aid program, 48, 109
Polanyi, Karl, 64
   The Great Transformation, 59
Policy Planning Staff memoranda, 92
political economy, 58
political psychology and observable personality traits, 336–8
politics on domestic and foreign policies, 162
Politics of Peacemaking at the Korean Armistice Talks, The (Foot), 158
Polk, James K., 367
Ponsa, Christina Duffy, 140, 142
Popular Movement for the Liberation of Angola (MPLA), 161
postrevisionists, 155
power, 236
   and core values, 30–1
   racialized, 245–64
Power Among Nations (Morgenthau), 10
Power, Samantha, 338
Prashad, Vijay, 108
Pratt, Mary Louise
   Imperial Eyes, 190
P-reel, 80, 81
Preston, Andrew, 3, 34, 137, 194
Prieberg, Fred K., 234
Progressive Age, 204
Progressive Era, the, 48
ProQuest, 79
psychological perspectives, challenges to reading foreign relations history, 347–8

psychology
    and international affairs, 344–6
    evolutionary, 17–18

quantitative history, 75, 76

racialized power, 245–64
Radford, Arthur, 343
radical orientalism, 279
Radicals on the Road: Internationalism, Orientalism, and Feminism during the Vietnam Era, 279
Rafael, Vicente L., 191
rapprochement, Anglo-American, 27
Rausch, Jane M., 179
Reagan, Ronald, 288
    and the Cold War, 60, 311
realism, 15–16, 218
    defensive, 14
    neo-classical, 11
    schools of, 11–12
    structural, 11–12
Realist theory and Constructivists, 16
realists
    views and the Iraq war, 10
    defensive, offensive, 11
Realms of Memory (Nora), 305
recolonization, economic, 174
record declassification, 79
Reddy, William M., 362
Rediker, Marcus, 192
Reformation, 288
religion
    and the human condition, 137–8
    and US transnational connections, 194
    core values and, 34
Religion and American Foreign Policy, 1945–1960 (Inboden), 285
Remote Archives Capture (RAC) terminals, 79
Renda, Mary, 191
Republic of Texas, and Mexico, 305
Republican
    ascendancy, 47, 50
    policymakers and corporatism, 44
    policymakers and economic growth, 44
Republican Party, 223
research, fields of
    counting, as a method of, 85–6
Reséndez, Andrés, 175
response theory, 196
Reston, James, 356

revolutionary nationalism, 32
Ribuffo, Leo, 292
Rice, Susan, 338
Rich Neighbor Policy, The (Cobbs), 47
Ridgway, Matthew, 343
Rist, Gilbert, 105
Robbins, William G., 173
Rockefeller Foundation, 111
Rockefeller, John D., 103
Rockefeller, Nelson Aldrich, 47
Rodgers, Daniel, 194, 293
    Atlantic Crossings, 204
Roosevelt, Franklin D., 30, 36, 138, 153, 276, 367, 368
    and the New Deal coalition, 65
Roosevelt, Theodore, 30, 171
Roosevelt's Lost Alliances: How Personal Politics Helped Start the Cold War (Costigliola), 276
Rosenberg, Emily S., 1, 3, 43, 45, 64, 125, 191, 194, 272, 305, 307, 308, 309
    A Date Which Will Live: Pearl Harbor in American Memory, 305
    Walking the Borders, 1
Rosenwein, Barbara, 361
Rosenzweig, Roy, 77, 79
Rostovian worldview, 108
Rostow, Walt W., 104, 107
Rotter, Andrew J., 3, 233
Route 40, Maryland's, 245
Rusk, Dean, 104, 245
Ruskola, Teemu, 140, 142
Russia. *See* Soviet Union

Sacred Canopy, The (Berger), 289
Sacrificing Soldiers on the National Mall (Hass), 307
Sahlins, Peter, 179
Said, Edward, 189, 190
    Culture and Imperialism, 189
    Orientalism, 189, 207
Salman, Michael, 191
Salvatore, Ricardo D., 191
Saunier, Pierre-Yves, 123, 124
Savage, Kirk
    Monument Wars: Washington D.C., the National Mall, and the Transformation of the Memorial Landscape, 307
scanning, dependence on, 80
Schendel, Willem van, 179
Schlesinger, Arthur M., Jr., 76
Schmelz, Peter, 234
Schmitter, Philippe C., 51

Index

Schueller, Malini, 207
Schwartz, Thomas, 163
Schwenkel, Christina, 305, 307
Scully, Eileen, 140
search engines, 87
Search for Sovereignty: Law and Geography in European Empires, 1400–1900 (Benton), 144
Seaway to the Future (Missal), 191
second image argument, 20
Second World War, 15. *See* World War II
secularization theory, 289
segregated diners, 245
selection effects, 21
senses
  and emotions, 318
  as products of history and culture, 317–29
Sestanovich, Stephen, 20
Sewell, William, 86
Sexton, Jay, 28
Sguiglia, Eduardo
  Fordlandia, 168
Shibusawa, Naoko
  America's Geisha Ally: Reimagining the Japanese Enemy, 278
Shriver, Sargent, 107
Sikkink, Kathryn, 124
Silva, Noenoe, 191
Simpson, Brad, 2, 50, 112, 128, 194
Singer, J. David, 17
Skinner, Quentin, 291
Slate, Nico, 194
slavery, 144
  and core values, 29
  as a legal relationship, 144
  reinterpretation of, 76
Slotkin, Richard, 108
Small, Melvin, 152
Smith, Adam
  and the division of labor, 103
Smith, Gaddis, 161
Smith, Walter Bedell, 343
Snyder, Sarah, 139
Social Constructivism, 14–17
social network analysis, 92–3
social relationships
  and law, 144
  and national security, 26
Social Science Research Council, 107
social scientists and modernization, 103
social system
  and peace, 13

socialization, 16–17, 217, 227
  horizontal, 16
Society for Historians of American Foreign Relations (SHAFR), 336
Sonnichsen, Albert, 319
Soul of Containment, The, 285
Soviet Union
  and Kennan's broadcast, 356
  and World War II, 27
Spanish–American War, 31
Spatial History Lab, Stanford, 93
Special National Intelligence Estimate on the military build-up
  in Cuba, 346
sports and US transnational connections, 194
St. John, Rachel, 176
Stagg, C. A., 156
Stalin, Joseph, 276
Stanford's Mapping the Republic of Letters project, 79
Staples, Amy, 127
State Department's Central Foreign Policy Files (CFPF), 75
Stearns, Peter N., 366
Stegner, Wallace
  Discovery, 181
Stephanson, Anders, 34
Stettinius, Edward R., 136
Stevenson, Adlai, 107
Stimson, Henry L., 136
Stoler, Ann Laura, 204
structural realism, 11–12
Sturken, Marita, 307
Subaltern Studies, 190
Suez crisis, 19
Süskind, Patrick, 323
Sweeney, Walter, 343
Sword, Kirsten, 77

Taft, William Howard, 102, 319
Tallmadge, Benjamin, 346
Taos Pueblos
  rebellion of, 175
Taylor, Charles, 284
Taylor, Maxwell, 343
technical assistance, 102
technology transfer, 110
technopolitics, 109, 111
Telfer, George, 321, 324
Ten Commandments, The, 308
Tennessee Valley Authority (TVA), 109
Thelen, David P., 109, 178, 193

theories
  audience cost, 14
  categorizing, 17
Theory of International Politics (Waltz), 11
third image arguments, 20–1
Third World, 32, 34
Third World dictatorships, 312
Thomas, William, 77, 93
Thompson, Leonard, 169, 172
Thucydides, 11, 335
Tilton, Ernest, 325
Time on the Cross (Fogel & Engerman), 76
topic modeling, 87–90
Torpedo: Inventing the Military-Industrial Complex in the United States and Great Britain (Epstein), 145
totalitarianism, 27
Traffic Analysis by Geography and Subject" (TAGS) system, 80
Tragedy of American Diplomacy (Williams), 68, 155, 195, 210
Transnational Nation (Tyrrell), 193
transnationalism, 193
  the borderlands and, 176
  transnational advocacy networks, 124
  transnational connections, 193–5
  transnational cultural brokers, 194
Treaty of Paris, 136
Treaty of Versailles, 136
Trouillot, Michel-Rolph, 304, 307
Truett, Samuel, 170, 176
Truman, Harry S., 32, 33, 35, 367
  and the Point IV aid program, 109
  and underdevelopment, 105
  and Zionist pressures, 160–1
  Point IV program, 48
Tucker, Robert W., 29
Turkel, William, 75, 77
Turner, Frederick Jackson, 75, 169, 181
Twenty Years' Crisis, The (Carr), 10
Twining, Nathan, 343
Twitter, 75
Tyrrell, Ian, 194
  American Exceptionalism in an Age of International History, 204
  Transnational Nation, 193

Ugly American, The, 108
Unpredictability of the Past: Memories of the Asian-Pacific War in the U.S, The, 309
US Chamber of Commerce, 46
US Constitution, 30

US Supreme Court Justice, 143
UDHR's moral vision, 137
Under an Open Sky, 172
United Nations Charter, 138
United Nations Universal Declaration of Human Rights, 287
United States
  and preventive war, 20
  core values of and power, 31
  foreign capital and, 64
  foreign policy
    and external dangers, 27
    and world relations, 203–13
  foreign relations
    and emotional responses to, 356
    and intelligence, 346–7
  intervention in Central and Latin America, 64
  and the Israeli–Palestinian issue, 160–1
  and Middle East relations, 206–13
  physical safety of, 35
  political system distinctive features of, 153
  view of itself, 16
  as a white man's republic, 226
  World War II, 27, 30, 60
United States Information Agency (USIA), 234
Universal Declaration of Human Rights, 137
USAID, 78

Van Vleck, Jenifer, 110
Vance, Cyrus, 161
Veeser, Cyrus, 64
video games and Cold War era-themed, 313
Vietnam War, 279
  Americanization of the, 151
  public opinions and, 66
Vision of Britain through Time, A, 93
Visualizing American Empire (Brody), 190
Vitalis, Robert, 62, 181, 213
  America's Kingdom, 180, 192
Voice of America, 234
Voltaire, 106
von Eschen, Penny, 197

Wagnleitner, Reinhold, 197
Walker, J. Samuel, 78
Walkowitz, Daniel and Knauer, Lisa Maya
  Memory and the Impact of Political Transformation in Public Space, 309
Wallace, David L., 92
Wallerstein, Immanuel, 59, 60, 173
  world system theory, 59
Walsham, Alexandra, 290

Index

Waltz, Kenneth, 17, 19, 153
  theories on international politics, 11
war
  and law, 141–3
  causes of, 17
  cost of, 12
War on Terror, 16, 142, 278, 309
Warren, Louis S., 180
Washington, George, 10
  Farewell Address of, 151
Webb, Walter Prescott, 171, 172, 174, 181
  The Geat Frontier, 171
Weber, David J., 175
Weber, Max, 289
Wiener, Jon, 309
Weinstein, Edwin, 335
Wendt, Alexander, 12, 15, 16
Werking, Richard Hume, 46
Wheeler, Earle, 343
Wheeler, Harry, 176
Whitaker, Arthur, 154
White Revolution, Iran's, 110
white supremacies, global belt of, 246
White, Lyman Cromwell, 123
White, Richard, 93, 173
Whitfield, Stephen
  The Culture of the Cold War, 286
Wickberg, Daniel, 329
Wiebe, Robert H., 42
Wikileaks, 74
Wilder, Billy, 308
Wilford, Hugh, 197
Williams, Daniel R., 102
Williams, William Appleman, 2, 45, 52, 68, 127, 171
  The Tragedy of American Diplomacy, 155
Wilson, Thomas M., 169
Wilson, Woodrow, 13, 30, 36, 136, 286, 335, 363
  theory of foreign policy and, 13, 31
Wilsonianism, 18

Wilsonian Moment, The (Manela), 205, 209, 211
Wisconsin School, 58
wisdom literature, 11
Witt, John Fabian, 141
Wolfers, Arnold, 11, 19, 20, 26
Wolfowitz, Paul, 339
women
  and the senses, 329
Women's International League for Peace and Freedom, The, 125
Wood, Leonard, 326, 328
Woodward, Bob, 162
Woolsey, James, 310
world economy
  19th century, 59
  capitalist: finance and banking in, 63–5
World Health Organization, 127
World Trade Center, 35
  bombing, 313
World War I, 12, 16, 64
  and Germany, 31
World War II, 35, 49
  American human rights vision and, 138
  and the United States, 27, 30, 34
  and UN agencies, 127
  the Soviet Union after, 32
World Wide Web, 74
world-systems theory, 173
Wrobel, David, 180
Wu, Judy Tzu-Chun, 3, 194

Yaqub, Salim, 211
Yoo memos, 142
Young Commissions, 49
Young, Robert J. C., 190

Zeiler, Thomas W., 194
Zelikow, Philip, 142
Zimmerman, Andrew, 194